DOOMED
TO
SUCCEED

DOOMED

— TO —

SUCCEED

—————————— ☆ ——————————

THE U.S.–ISRAEL RELATIONSHIP

FROM TRUMAN TO OBAMA

—————————— ✡ ——————————

DENNIS ROSS

FARRAR, STRAUS AND GIROUX   NEW YORK

Farrar, Straus and Giroux
18 West 18th Street, New York 10011

Owing to limitations of space, all acknowledgments for permission to
reprint previously published material appear on pages 473–74.

Library of Congress Cataloging-in-Publication Data
Ross, Dennis.
  Doomed to succeed : the U.S.-Israel relationship from Truman to Obama / Dennis Ross. —
First edition.
    pages   cm
  Includes index.
  ISBN 978-0-374-14146-2 (hardcover) — ISBN 978-0-374-70948-8 (e-book)
  1. United States—Foreign relations—Israel.   2. Israel—Foreign relations—United States.
3. United States—Foreign relations—1945–1989.   4. United States—Foreign relations—1989–
I. Title.

E183.8.I7 R67 2015
327.7305694—dc23

                                                                                2015010959

Designed by Abby Kagan

Our books may be purchased in bulk for promotional, educational, or business use.
Please contact your local bookseller or the Macmillan Corporate and Premium
Sales Department at 1-800-221-7945, extension 5442, or by e-mail at
MacmillanSpecialMarkets@macmillan.com.

www.fsgbooks.com
www.twitter.com/fsgbooks • www.facebook.com/fsgbooks

1   3   5   7   9   10   8   6   4   2

To the memory of Fred Lafer, who was my friend,
a mentor, and a role model

CONTENTS

PREFACE

On March 28, 2011, President Obama was in the Situation Room for a secure video conference with David Cameron, Nicolas Sarkozy, and Angela Merkel. The president periodically held calls with his British, French, and German counterparts on a host of issues. Now, looking ahead to the G-8 summit, to be hosted by President Sarkozy in Deauville, France, they discussed the upheaval in the Arab world and how economic support from the G-8 countries, as well as from the larger circle of the G-20, could help the transformations in Egypt and Tunisia succeed.

As the special assistant to the president on the National Security Council staff responsible for an area that ran from Morocco to India, I was there to provide any support the president needed on this issue, as well as on Libya. Notwithstanding Merkel's presence (Germany had decided not to provide direct military support to the campaign in Libya), Cameron and Sarkozy were bound to raise it. Their ambition to defeat Muammar Qaddafi's forces exceeded their means to sustain air-to-ground missions at the level of intensity needed. Though Cameron and Sarkozy had accepted the president's ground rules for launching the campaign—that the United States would use its unique military assets initially, and for a finite period, to shape an environment in which it would be safe for the British, French, and others to carry out the mission of protecting Libyan civilians—they were now eager for the president to extend the time our forces would assume the lion's share of the burden.

The discussion, however, took an unexpected turn. After discussing Libya, plans for the upcoming G-8 summit, and the multinational means that could be mobilized to support Egypt, the three European leaders shifted their focus, launching into a diatribe against Benjamin "Bibi" Netanyahu, Israel's prime minister. There was a venom seldom heard when leaders talk about other leaders. They took turns excoriating him, describing him as unreliable and a liar, who rendered peacemaking impossible and whose unwillingness to take the necessary steps for peace would help to radicalize the Arab Spring—and thereby threaten all of our interests in the region. They even accused President Obama of "enabling" Netanyahu's obstinacy.

But what was driving the popular uprisings in the Arab world was the profound sense of injustice in the different countries, and not the Palestinian issue, as important as it was. This "awakening" among Arab publics was about their self-determination and their future, not the destiny of the Palestinians. Yet you would not have known that from these leaders' preoccupation with Netanyahu and the consequences of the stalemate on Israeli-Palestinian peace. They did not evidence the slightest recognition that Israel might have needs or that Abu Mazen (Mahmoud Abbas), the Palestinian leader, might bear some of the blame for the absence of movement on peace. The president sought to redirect the discussion and to explain to his European counterparts some of these realities and Netanyahu's predicament. These three leaders were having none of it. They made it clear that if Obama did not present American principles on peace to force Netanyahu's hand, they would do so.

At one level, I was not surprised. Much of my time, and that of other senior officials, was devoted to defending Israel from moves designed to single it out for extensive international criticism. Whether it was trying to head off a move at the Human Rights Council, or a critical political statement from the European Union, or a possible UN resolution condemning Israel, it seemed that this Israeli government was a lightning rod—and in constant need of our help. Like it or not, many of our allies were fixated on Israel's alleged responsibility for the enduring conflict with the Palestinians and how this affected our collective position in the Middle East.

Still, I was struck not only by the vitriol but also by who was conveying it. These leaders prided themselves on being friends of Israel. Sarkozy and Merkel were publicly outspoken in this regard. Sarkozy had consciously dissociated himself from his predecessor, Jacques Chirac, and his demonstrably pro-Arab legacy. And yet here they were seemingly holding Netanyahu solely responsible for the breakdown in the peace process and for what they perceived to be the dire ramifications for the region of the unresolved conflict.

I wondered if this was about Netanyahu or if there was something deeper going on. Were attitudes changing toward Israel, with Netanyahu serving as a convenient pretext? I could also not help thinking about the irony of President Obama—who had been consistently vilified in parts of the American Jewish community for being too critical of Israel—being cast in the role of Israel's defender before our closest allies.

I remained in the Obama administration until the end of 2011. During that time I witnessed—and was often in the middle of—the constant pull and push in our relationship with Israel. There were moments of tension—even anger—between the leaders. Yet the areas of cooperation continued to deepen. Moreover, our support for Israel, even in tough budgetary times, was expanded. True, there was a congressional push for increased support, but it was rarely a case of having to impose it on a reluctant administration.

After leaving the administration, I continued to travel frequently to Israel, meeting both with those in and outside the government, including the prime minister. I saw the rising concern about the delegitimization movement internationally, a movement fed by the Palestinian belief that this was Israel's vulnerability and therefore its own point of leverage. The United States remained the main bulwark against this movement, and although I understood that Israel needed to do much to help itself, I wondered whether we would continue to make the effort to stand with Israel. President Obama often said in my presence that whoever was in the Oval Office would support Israel, but that our influence on others would diminish. He pointed to votes in the UN General Assembly where, along with Micronesia and maybe Canada, the United States and Israel often stood alone.

Was Obama right that we would continue to back Israel regardless of who occupied the Oval Office? I knew that a constituency within his administration was not enthusiastic about doing so. But I also knew that every administration I had served in, starting with the Carter administration, had such a constituency. Indeed, in earlier times, it had been far stronger. With the current efforts to isolate Israel internationally seeming to have more impact with our key European allies, could this constituency emerge stronger and redirect our policy? Was the trajectory of our relationship—which seemed to move in the direction of ever closer collaboration even with presidents who did not have an instinctive attachment to Israel—bound to continue?

The more I have thought about these questions, the more they seemed to require a deeper look, particularly at a time when the Middle East is experiencing such upheaval. I say this even though I recognize that it is not new for Israel to be singled out in the international arena. After all, the UN General Assembly adopted the grotesque "Zionism is Racism" resolution in 1975. Resolution 3379 embodied the effort to reject and delegitimize Israel, led by the Arabs but supported by the so-called Non-Aligned Movement and backed by the Soviet bloc in its competition with the West during the cold war. With the end of the cold war, that era of ostracism and rejection of Israel seemed to be over. The resolution was rescinded. And, with the Madrid Conference in 1991, which brought Israel and its Arab neighbors to the same peace table, and the Oslo Accords in 1993 and 1995, which produced mutual recognition between Israel and the Palestine Liberation Organization, Israel could do business everywhere in the world.

So what changed? Why are we now seeing a new effort to isolate and delegitimize Israel? One reason clearly is that Madrid and Oslo seem today to signify a bygone era. The once-significant promise of peace is gone, and what is left is a constant competition between Israelis and Palestinians to see who can score more points against the other, rather than who can be responsible for resolving differences. Twenty years of peace efforts have not ended the occupation of the Palestinians, and the Palestinians have become far more adept internationally at presenting themselves as victims and Israel as victimizers. By contrast, Israel presents a different face to the world than it once did.

Benjamin Netanyahu, Israel's prime minister, is not Yitzhak Rabin, a leader who took initiatives on peace and commanded respect internationally as a result. Avigdor Lieberman, Israel's foreign minister until 2015, bears little resemblance to Shimon Peres, Rabin's foreign minister. Lieberman often seemed to delight in provoking the international community rather than being a sympathetic or persuasive public spokesman for Israel's cause. The United States cannot be a substitute for what Israel must do for itself. And there will surely be new challenges, given the scope of conflict and the potential for change in the Middle East in the coming decade.

No one predicted the turmoil we are now seeing, least of all the Middle Eastern leaders who have been swept away in its wake or who are now struggling for legitimacy and to define the identity of the region. While humility should be the order of the day in predicting what will unfold in the Middle East, one thing is clear: the U.S.-Israel relationship is going to be buffeted by the transformation that is taking place.

Some, like the European leaders noted above, will see in the Arab Awakening increased costs of association with Israel, particularly given the likelihood that populist attitudes will drive the behaviors of Arab governments.

Others are likely to see in the transformation of Arab countries enormous uncertainty. For them, the one existing verity in the Middle East is that Israel will remain a stable country and will be a solid and reliable friend of the United States. As such, the U.S.-Israel relationship should become more—and not less—important.

As someone who has been at the center of Middle East policy making in four administrations, including with President Obama, and as someone who was an original author of strategic cooperation between the United States and Israel in the Reagan administration, I feel a special obligation to address this subject. I have participated in shaping the U.S.-Israel partnership and seen how far it has come over the last thirty years. I have worked closely with every Israeli prime minister since Yitzhak Shamir in the 1980s on every aspect of policy, including, of course, on the issue of peace. I have been a part of the debates about the relationship and how it affects our other interests in the region. Those debates tend to revolve around the same themes. Some administrations emphasized the costs to us of our association with Israel while others did the opposite, seeing in it the value more than costs. Interestingly, once the taboo on cooperating with Israel on security matters was broken by John F. Kennedy, it was not reversed, even in those succeeding administrations that felt we paid a high price with the Arabs for our ties to Israel.

I certainly have seen how cooperation responded to our respective needs. But I also saw how it was not sufficient to limit periods of tension in the relationship, and why, as a result, I was often called on during these problematic times to help manage ties between our two governments—and (very often) between our two leaders. Because of that experience, I understand the fault lines in the relationship as well as what it will take to keep it on a sound footing during a time of regional transformation.

To be sure, our relationship with Israel cannot be easily separated from our assumptions about the region. From the moment of Israel's founding in 1948, there have been those in the American national security establishment who have felt our interests in the region lie elsewhere; their views have been shaped by a particular analysis of the Middle East and the factors that drive the Arabs. Their views—and our approach to the area as a result— have often missed the mark. Unfortunately, too often our policy makers did not understand the fundamental realities in the region—and seemed unwilling or unable to learn lessons. We not only made basic mistakes, but we repeated these over time. Those past mistakes, and their underlying rationales, continue to echo today.

It is for this reason that it is important to understand how the U.S.-Israel relationship evolved. The United States was not Israel's strongest or most important ally through its formative years. In no small part this was because we feared how the Arabs would respond if we drew too close to Israel. True, the United States recognized Israel within eleven minutes of its declaration of independence, and this had great political meaning for Israel's acceptance internationally, if not in the Middle East. But the United States was not Israel's main supplier of either economic or military assistance through the first two decades of its existence. Only after the 1973 Yom Kippur War and the ensuing Camp David Accords in 1978 did the United States assume this mantle. And only during the 1980s and the Reagan administration was Israel finally considered a strategic asset and treated as an ally and a partner. I want to describe the change in the relationship as the United States and Israel became strategic partners against the Soviet Union in the 1980s, how they became strategic partners on peace in the 1990s and in the Bush administration after 9/11, how the two became strategic partners in the war on terror. The Obama administration has not only continued the security partnership writ large but has actually improved it. And yet at the same time, divergent views on what constituted peace, how to attain it, and how to sustain it highlighted that the basis for the strategic partnership was no longer as clearly defined as it had been previously. Once again, past arguments about the costs of our ties to Israel reemerged.

To my surprise, as I began to review the record prior to my time in shaping and managing the U.S.-Israel relationship, I was struck by the similarity of the arguments. I found them recycled, often (to my amazement) couched in the exact same terms. I saw the same failure to learn from mistakes or to ask what our erroneous assumptions should have taught our policy makers about what actually drove the region. As such, I became even more convinced of the importance of looking at the past to learn more about what we should be doing in the present—and the future.

In the end, this book looks at the policy from Truman through Obama in order to examine not only what it tells us about the U.S.-Israel relationship—and why it has continued to develop despite periodic differences—but also what it tells us about the region and how we ought to be operating in it. What is possible in our relations with the Arabs? How does our relationship with Israel affect our position in the area? Is Israeli-Palestinian peace the sine qua non for transforming our position? Where and how should we operate differently with Israel, and what should we ask the Israelis to do differently with us and others?

My hope is that this book will challenge readers to think hard about these issues.

DOOMED
TO
SUCCEED

1

THE EVOLUTION OF
U.S. POLICY TOWARD ISRAEL

Today, the relationship between the United States and Israel is extolled by American presidents. We take it for granted that presidents will stress their commitment to Israel and to the ties that bind us. But it was not always this way. Harry Truman faced enormous resistance within his administration to his decision to recognize the Jewish state. Similarly, selling or providing arms to Israel was taboo until President Kennedy decided to do so—again, a controversial decision within his national security apparatus. Later, during the first week of the 1973 war, Richard Nixon initially resisted Israeli near-desperate pleas to resupply weaponry, following the major losses of aircraft and tanks the Israelis had suffered. Although Nixon eventually provided a massive resupply of arms to Israel, his decision had more to do with cold war concerns that Soviet weapons could not be seen to defeat American weapons than with any special relationship that existed between our two countries.

From the perspective of history, the relationship has clearly evolved. And to understand where the relationship is today and where it is going, particularly during a period of transition in the Middle East, it is important to understand why the relationship changed. To do so, I will examine the policy and approach of every administration since Israel's birth. I will offer a narrative of the policy and the key developments in each administration, starting with Harry Truman's. I will outline each president's basic instincts or mind-set toward Israel and toward our policy in the region, as well as the basic assumptions that seemed to guide the national security establishment and senior officials about Israel and the region—and whether there was unanimity or division.

What will emerge from the review is remarkable continuity—not of policy, necessarily, but of arguments. Over and over again, we will see recycled concerns that too close a relationship with Israel will harm our ties to the Arabs and damage our position in the region. Until the 1990s, the fear was that we would drive the Arabs into a Soviet embrace. After the fall of the Soviet Union in 1991, the concern was that it would damage our relationship with the Arabs and make us targets of jihadist terrorism. The debates that center on these issues produced a pattern: when an administration is judged by its successors to be too close to Israel, we distance ourselves from the Jewish state. Eisenhower believed that Truman was too supportive of Israel, so he felt an imperative to demonstrate that we were not partial to Israel, that we were in fact willing to seek closer ties to our real friends in the region—the Arabs. President Nixon, likewise, felt that Lyndon Johnson was too pro-Israel. In his first two years, he, too, distanced us from Israel and showed sensitivity to Arab concerns. President George H. W. Bush believed his former boss, Ronald Reagan, suffered from the same impulse of being too close to Israel. He, too, saw virtue in fostering distance. And President Obama, at the outset of his administration, certainly saw George W. Bush as having cost us in the Arab and Muslim world at least in part because he was unwilling to allow any gap to emerge between the United States and Israel.

In none of these instances do we actually gain any benefit to our position in the region. Our influence does not increase; our ties with the conservative Arab monarchies do not materially improve. Neither is there any decline in those relationships during administrations that are putatively seen as being closer to Israel. Our ties with the more radical Arab regimes are not good, but then again—with the possible exceptions of the Kennedy administration's concerted effort to reach out to Gamal Abdel Nasser and the Reagan administration's support for Saddam Hussein in the Iran-Iraq War—they were never good.[1]

Yet arguments that we must distance ourselves from Israel are not discredited when the predicted positive outcomes do not occur. Nor are these arguments discredited when the anticipated terrible consequences of drawing closer to Israel fail to materialize. With regard to the latter, when we recognized Israel in 1948, or later when we sold arms to Israel and the Soviets couldn't replace us in the area, and when the flow of oil from the region was not lost, no one questioned why these devastating outcomes did not happen. No one asked what was wrong in our assumptions about the dynamics of the Middle East. Remarkably, there seem to be few lessons ever learned.

These assumptions are obviously about more than Israel's place in the region and its neighbors' reactions to it. They also involve the perceived forces of change and whether and how we should relate to them. Late in the Eisenhower administration, the president signed a policy directive that effectively called for us to "accommodate" radical Arab nationalism. The assumptions that guided that posture are similar to the arguments in parts of the Obama administration in 2011 and 2012 that argued that the Muslim Brotherhood represented the wave of the future in the region and that our more conservative Arab friends were on the wrong side of history—and our policy needed to reflect that. In the late 1950s and in John Kennedy's first two years in office, the logic of that policy was pursued and failed to deliver. Yet no one asked how or even whether the radical Arab nationalists like President Nasser of Egypt could alter their aims without betraying their very identity. The same may be true today with Islamists. It makes sense to take a hard look at these kinds of assumptions and evaluate them in light of what drove the radical nationalists in the past and what factors may drive the Islamists today.

If there was ever a time to rethink assumptions and gain a better handle on the dynamics that are likely to shape the Middle East, this is surely it. Because the American approach to Israel over time was generally derivative of our broad approach to the region, one way to rethink assumptions is to see which ones took hold, why they endured, where they were off base, and how they need to be changed. That is why I examine every administration from Harry Truman to Barack Obama and how each approached both Israel and the region.

Harry S. Truman: The Struggle to Adopt a Policy

"Struggle" is the right word to describe the policy of the Truman administration toward Palestine and the emergence of the Jewish state of Israel. President Truman had to contend with the reality that none of his senior national security officials saw any strategic benefit in supporting Jewish aims in Palestine. On the contrary, they saw only costs. These attitudes carried over from the Second World War, when concern about alienating the Arabs was prevalent, given the fear that it might trigger a loss of bases in the Middle East and disrupt the resupply from the region to the European theater and Lend-Lease operations into the Soviet Union. With the advent of the cold war, the approach to the Middle East was defined by what was perceived to be necessary to "contain" the Soviet Union. This is the context in which Truman and his national security advisers shaped foreign policy. But that was not the only contextual factor affecting Truman and the approach to Palestine and the Jewish question. He had inherited a legacy as well.

Franklin Delano Roosevelt left President Truman a muddled legacy on Jewish aspirations in regard to Palestine. To Jewish leaders and groups, he promised his sympathy and support for a Jewish state and allowed them to issue statements in his name. However, with the Arabs, he privately assured them that nothing would be done that would be hostile to their interests. Indeed, after authorizing Rabbis Stephen Wise and Abba Hillel Silver to declare, in his name, on March 9, 1944, that the U.S. government had never approved of the White Paper of 1939* and expressing "his conviction that when future decisions are reached, full justice will be done to those who seek a Jewish national home," he had the State Department send reassuring messages to Arab leaders that no decision would be made without "full consultation with both Arabs and Jews."[2] This was his pattern on the issue: he juggled the conflicting attitudes and pressures and basically equivocated, believing there would be time after the war to solve the problem.

But it was not only that he felt he had time. He also had great faith in his own ability to persuade or charm leaders. Roosevelt was certain that he could bring around the king of Saudi Arabia on the Palestine question. He arranged to see Ibn Saud on his return from the Yalta Conference on the navy cruiser USS *Quincy* in the Great Bitter Lake in the Suez Canal. In

---

*The White Paper of 1939 was a major reversal of British policy on Palestine, which since the Balfour Declaration of 1917 had favored the establishment in Palestine of a Jewish national home. Under Arab pressure, and with war looming in Europe, the British government issued the White Paper to place restrictions on Jewish immigration and settlement in Palestine, in contradiction of the League of Nations Mandate on Palestine. Incidentally, the then senator Harry Truman inserted into the *Congressional Record* his denunciation of the White Paper as an act of surrender to the Axis powers, saying, "It has made a scrap of paper out of Lord Balfour's promise to the Jews." (*Congressional Record*, 76th Cong., 1st sess., 1939, vol. 84, pt. 13, appendix, pp. 2231–2232, quoted in Michael J. Cohen, *Truman and Israel* [Berkeley: University of California Press, 1990], p. 45.)

advance of this meeting, he told his new secretary of state, Edward R. Stettin-ius, Jr., that he would "point out to Ibn Saud what an infinitesimal part of the whole area was occupied by Palestine and that he could not see why a portion of Palestine could not be given to the Jews without harming in any way the interests of the Arabs."[3]

Unfortunately, his meeting with Ibn Saud did not go as he envisioned. The king was implacable in his opposition, telling the president the Germans and not the Arabs should pay for what had been done to the Jews in Europe. The Arabs would die "rather than yield their land to the Jews."[4]

It was not the king of Saudi Arabia who was persuaded in the meeting but rather President Roosevelt, who underwent a seeming change of heart. So much so that he reassured the king that he would "do nothing to assist the Jews against the Arabs" and would "make no move hostile to the Arab people."[5] When he reported to the Congress on the Yalta summit, he added to his prepared text the unscripted comment that "of the problems of Arabia, I learned more about that whole problem, the Moslem problem, the Jewish problem, by talking with Ibn Saud for five minutes than I could have learned in [the] exchange of two or three dozen letters."*[6] True to form, Roosevelt sought to reassure Jewish leaders of his intent after his comment to the Congress. Once again, he allowed Rabbis Wise and Silver to publicly reaffirm his strong support for the "Zionist position."[7]

But in truth, his private views seemed to have evolved. After seeing Ibn Saud, he no longer believed he could convince the Arabs to accept a Jewish state. Unlike his wife, Eleanor, who was convinced of the Zionist strength and readiness to "risk a fight with the Arabs" over Palestine, he was concerned that the Arab numbers would "in the long run win out."[8] Just weeks before he died, in April 1945, he met privately with the leaders of the American Jewish Committee, Jacob Blaustein and Joseph Proskauer, who were not Zionists and did not favor the creation of a Jewish state. He told them that in the present conditions a Jewish state in Palestine was impossible to achieve.[9] Perhaps he was only telling them what he thought they wanted to hear, but his words echoed what he had told his wife after the Ibn Saud meeting. Given the strategic concerns that had dominated his thinking about the region during the war, the views of his national security advisers, and his

---

* Thirty-two years later, President Jimmy Carter would use similar words to describe his first meeting with President Hafez al Assad of Syria, reflecting the impact of the discussion on his thinking and producing much the same unease in the Jewish community as Roosevelt had evoked.

concerns about the survivability of a Jewish state, it should come as no surprise that his aide David Niles—who would also serve in a critical role with
President Truman—later said that he had "serious doubts . . . that Israel
would have come into being if Roosevelt had lived."[10]

In short, Truman inherited from Franklin Roosevelt a legacy of contra-
dictory promises to Jewish and Arab leaders, a national security team strongly
opposed to Jewish aspirations or interests in Palestine, and a public political
posture embodied in the 1944 plank of the Democratic Party platform that
gave strong support to the Zionist goals in Palestine.

Truman also inherited something else: the horrific stories emerging about
the concentration camps and the reality of the Holocaust. General Eisenhower toured the camps in mid-April 1945, shortly after Roosevelt's death.
Shocked by what he saw, he invited leading members of the U.S. media to
come and report on the gruesome, barbaric reality so the American public
could see what the Nazis had done. Their reports not only generated great
sympathy for the Zionist cause but also were a reminder that we now had
responsibility for taking care of the survivors in the camps. For President
Truman, the roughly one and a half million "displaced persons" (DPs), a
quarter of a million of whom were Jewish, were now an American responsibility, as we had control over the camps. Understandably, Truman saw both
a practical and a deeply troubling humanitarian problem. For Roosevelt, the
question of Palestine could be deferred. For Truman, the humanitarian
challenge was immediate and real—and required action.

Overview of the Truman Policy and Key Developments

Reports of Jews dying in the camps after liberation by U.S. forces led American Jewish organizations to press for immediate steps to remedy this grim
reality. On June 22, 1945, President Truman appointed Earl G. Harrison, the
dean of the University of Pennsylvania Law School, to go to Europe and investigate the conditions in the camps and recommend a course of action.
The Harrison Report detailed the unsanitary conditions, shortages of food,
and the fact that Holocaust survivors were still wearing the same prison
garb. "As matters stand now," he wrote, "we appear to be treating the Jews as
the Nazis treated them except that we do not exterminate them." The survivors, he said, wanted nothing to do with a Europe that had persecuted them;
they feared coming to America. They wanted only to go to Palestine. Anyone
going to the camps, he added, would find it "nothing short of calamitous to

contemplate that the gates of Palestine should be soon closed." He called for the Jewish DPs to be treated differently from other refugees, and recommended that 100,000 of the Jewish DPs be allowed to go to Palestine immediately, with others permitted to follow—and concluded that "the civilized world owes it to this handful of survivors to provide them with a home where they can again settle down and begin to live as human beings."[11]

Truman was shocked by the report. But the British remained the mandatory power in Palestine, and they determined whether Jewish survivors could come. Against the advice of the State Department, at Potsdam, Truman asked Winston Churchill to lift the 1939 White Paper's restrictions on immigration without delay.[12] But with the Conservative Party losing to the Labour Party in the elections immediately after Potsdam, Churchill was out and Clement Attlee was in.[13] Truman shortly sent Attlee a copy of the Harrison Report under the cover of a personal letter, in which he asked the new prime minister to lift the quota limiting Jewish immigration into Palestine and to permit 100,000 refugees to enter as soon as possible.

Attlee, saying that any such action without prior consultation with the Arabs would "set aflame the whole Middle East," was not willing to accept the Harrison Report's call for Jews to be treated differently from other DPs or Truman's request to permit 100,000 to move quickly to Palestine. Facing the reality that congressional and public pressures were growing on Truman to do something about the Harrison Report recommendations, Attlee initially suggested that the British turn the broader Palestine problem over to the United Nations. However, by mid-October 1945, Attlee had changed his position and proposed instead a joint Anglo-American Committee to study the problem of where Europe's Jews might go. In proposing the committee, he hoped not just to buy time but also to have prominent American and British figures develop a common approach that would not plague our policy toward Palestine and the Middle East.[14]

Truman agreed to the formation of the committee provided the work would be done quickly. He asked that its findings be produced within 120 days, and that it address the plight of the Jews in Europe and the conditions in Palestine for absorbing them. Secretary of State James Byrnes made clear to the British that President Truman was not walking back on his request to have 100,000 Jewish DPs enter Palestine as soon as possible.[15]

Over the next several months, the members of the Anglo-American Committee spent time in the DP camps in Europe. They witnessed Jewish survivors pleading to go to Palestine, and they traveled to Palestine and met extensively with the Jewish and Arab leaders there. Notwithstanding their different attitudes initially, they produced a consensus report that was unveiled on May 1, 1946. Much to the chagrin of Attlee and Foreign Secretary Ernest Bevin, the committee recommended the immediate issuance of 100,000 certificates for Jewish DPs and recommended the lifting of the White Paper's restrictions on land sale and immigration for Jews coming to Palestine. For the longer term, the committee came out against either an Arab or a Jewish state, calling instead for economic development, education, and reconciliation between Arabs and Jews, with neither ascendant over the other.[16]

President Truman embraced the call for the immediate immigration of the 100,000 and the end to the restrictive provisions of the White Paper, but he essentially ignored the longer-term recommendations. Attlee and Bevin initially temporized, saying the recommendation on the 100,000 could be considered only after knowing what financial and military responsibilities the United States would assume in helping to implement the recommendations and how these recommendations might actually be integrated. In all, Bevin raised ten subjects that needed full consideration before anything could be done on the main recommendations of the Anglo-American Committee. By the end of the month, Bevin's ten subjects had become forty-three, all of which had to be fully investigated. In his memoir, Dean Acheson observed that the British were obviously playing a delaying game and imposing demands that Acheson called nonstarters.[17]

In response, Truman wrote Attlee in early June, saying that we would deal with all the issues the British were raising, but he wanted work to begin immediately on addressing the need to move the 100,000. He promised that the United States would assume the responsibility for transporting them and paying for their temporary housing in Palestine. And he added that we would consider additional assistance as needed.

Attlee deflected again, saying that before there could be movement on the DPs, the political and military consequences of acting on the recommendations had to be fully considered and resolved. Truman appointed a cabinet-level committee to work with the British on how to implement the recommendations. Henry F. Grady headed the committee, and Truman instructed him and his American colleagues to work out the differences with the British but to get the 100,000 moved.

With the American team going to London in July 1946, these discussions led to a new proposal, ostensibly about implementing the Anglo-American recommendations but framed as what became known as the Morrison-Grady Plan (Herbert Morrison led the British half of the discussions). The plan finally resolved the issue of the DPs but only as part of a larger resolution of the Palestine question. The plan called for the creation of two autonomous provinces—one Arab and one Jewish—in a new federal arrangement for Palestine in which the British retained centralized control over critical territory, security, foreign affairs, taxation, and immigration. The Jewish province would total fifteen hundred square miles and would be located largely on the coastal plain. While Grady thought they had met their responsibility to fulfill the recommendations of the Anglo-American Committee—and Truman was initially inclined in private to accept the plan—Judge Joseph Hutcheson, the American chair on the committee, declared the Morrison-Grady Plan a "sell out." He said it nullified the committee's recommendations and was inconsistent with the League of Nations Mandate because of its creation of cantons and restriction on Jewish immigration to Palestine.[18]

That the Arabs rejected it was no surprise. They had rejected every previous proposal that did not call for an Arab state in Palestine with an end to Jewish immigration and with the Jews accepting their status as a minority under Arab rule. But Jewish leaders in Palestine and the United States vehemently rejected it as well. While the Jews had reluctantly been willing to accept the Anglo-American Committee recommendations by focusing on its revocation of the White Paper's restrictions, they saw no redeeming elements in the Morrison-Grady Plan. It left immigration in British hands; it created an autonomous Jewish province—not a state—and one with no connection to Jerusalem and on territory significantly smaller than what the British Peel Commission Report had proposed in 1937. The White Paper had supplanted the Peel Commission recommendations for Jewish statehood, as the British sought to curry favor with the Arabs with war looming in 1939—and the Jewish leaders in Palestine and America saw Morrison-Grady as an extension of the White Paper's retreat.

They were not alone. Editorials in leading U.S. newspapers attacked it; congressional leaders denounced it; and Truman, notwithstanding his initial inclination to accept it, after holding a cabinet meeting on the plan, agreed to reject it.[19] Jewish leaders were sufficiently exercised that they asked to see the president before his rejection of it, but he was not keen to see them or congressional delegations that wanted to inveigh against it. He finally relented and agreed to see James G. McDonald, who had been a U.S. member of the Anglo-American Committee. McDonald said that it was not an easy meeting. Truman was unhappy about all the pressure he was under, and McDonald told him that if he accepted the Morrison-Grady Plan just so he could get 100,000 survivors to Palestine, not only would Jewish leaders be outraged but he also would be sacrificing "Jewish interests in Palestine." In response, Truman told McDonald, "Jews aren't going to write the history of the United States, or my history."[20]

But for now he had Acheson convey to the British that he could not accept the Morrison-Grady Plan. At roughly the same time, David Niles called Nahum Goldmann, the leader of the Jewish Agency, and told him the president was fed up with the British and the Zionists, and was close to washing his hands of the whole matter. If Goldmann hoped to prevent such an eventuality, Niles told him, the Jewish Agency needed to come up with a plan to replace Morrison-Grady. Goldmann got the board of the Jewish Agency to agree to a partition plan, calling for a Jewish state in a part of Palestine. According to Allis and Ronald Radosh, Goldmann then got key American Jewish leaders, including Rabbi Silver, to accept their scheme and subsequently presented this plan to Dean Acheson, who after three meetings was prepared to support it.[21] Niles and Acheson presented it to Truman in early August, and Niles, "with tears in his eyes," told Goldmann that Truman had accepted the plan and instructed Acheson to inform the British.[22] Although the British would reject the plan, it appears that this is the first moment Truman became willing to support partition of Palestine into a Jewish state and an Arab state.

Support, of course, is one thing; actual policy is another. But in October 1946, just before Yom Kippur, the holiest day of the year in the Jewish faith, Truman was to make a statement that moved him publicly in the direction of partition. With congressional midterm elections looming, with nothing having been accomplished on moving Jewish survivors to Palestine over the preceding year, and with Truman's likely challenger in 1948, Governor Thomas Dewey, anticipated to adopt a public posture of support for Jewish statehood, Truman decided to issue what became known as the Yom Kippur statement. Acheson describes the statement as being driven at least in part by the British decision to postpone, until mid-December, talks they had planned with Arab and Jewish leaders on what to do in Palestine. For Truman, the delay meant that once again any possible movement on the Jewish refugee issue would be deferred.

Given that, the president chose to reaffirm his interest in the issue and urge that "steps be taken at the earliest possible moment to admit 100,000 Jewish refugees to Palestine." Truman also said that it was his belief that the Jewish Agency's proposal of "a viable Jewish state in control of its own immigration and economic policies in an adequate area of Palestine instead of" its entirety "would command the support of public opinion in the United

States." While the statement was focused more on what the U.S. public could support, it certainly signaled a readiness to accept partition as a solution. Toward the end of his Yom Kippur statement, Truman added that he could not "believe that the gap between the proposals [presumably the Jewish Agency's and Morrison-Grady] which have been put forward is too great to be bridged by men of reason and good will. To such a solution our Government could give its support."[23] In other words, he was not wedded to a particular solution, but partition was an acceptable one.

Needless to say, the British were not pleased with this statement, which he had conveyed to them prior to issuing it. Still, it is not the reason their efforts to broker a solution between the Arab and Jewish leaders failed. There was simply no give in the Arab position. From the time of the Arab Revolt in Palestine of 1936–1939, the Arab position had been a maximalist one. They rejected the Peel Commission Report; they rejected the Anglo-American Committee recommendations; they rejected the Morrison Grady Plan. They would accept only an independent Arab state, with an end to immigration and land sales to Jews. They left no room for a solution. Even the small number of leading Jewish figures in Palestine, such as Judah Magnes, who were open to a binational state found no responsiveness from the other side.[24]

For the British, there was only a dead end. They were facing continuing pressure from Truman on allowing Jewish DPs to go to Palestine and an increasingly costly conflict with the Jewish community and leadership there. As a result, on February 18, 1947, Prime Minister Attlee announced that the United Kingdom was turning the problem of Palestine over to the United Nations to find a solution.

On April 2, 1947, the United Nations General Assembly formally received the request from the British to put the question on its fall agenda. Prior to that discussion, the British also asked that a special session of the UNGA be convened to create a committee to investigate what to do about Palestine. In late April, the UN Special Committee on Palestine (UNSCOP) was formed and subsequently mandated to study the issue and make a recommendation that would then be voted on by the UNGA during its fall session. Although the United Kingdom had asked the UN to take on this challenge, it announced that it would not enforce an outcome that was not accepted by both Jews and Arabs.

In effect, the British were putting the world on notice that they were unloading the problem—unless, of course, the world supported their approach to resolving it. To President Truman, having the UN assume responsibility was appropriate. In his eyes, it reflected what he believed the United Nations had been created to do. But turning the problem over to the UN also meant that he did not have to deal with it.

In early September, UNSCOP issued majority and minority reports. The majority supported partition of Palestine into a Jewish and an Arab state, with a two-year transition period before each state would become independent and a ten-year economic union between the two. The UN would manage the transition period. The majority proposed that Jerusalem be an international city. A minority on the committee favored an ongoing trusteeship arrangement instead of partition. The majority report offered a map that outlined the makeup and boundaries of the two states. Secretary of State George Marshall, in a speech to the UN on September 15, offered a cautious endorsement of the majority report, saying that the United States would give great weight to its recommendations. Given the opposition of most of his senior experts, however, he privately agreed that we should work to modify the UNSCOP territorial recommendations to make them more palatable to the Arabs.

At the United Nations, U.S. officials quietly sought to shift the Negev out of the Jewish sector of the partition plan. For the Arabs, having the Negev in their putative state in Palestine would create territorial contiguity among Egypt, Arab Palestine, and Transjordan. However, the Negev was the majority of the territory assigned to the Jewish state, with access to the Red Sea and the ability to absorb massive numbers of Jewish immigrants. The United States was the only country discreetly trying to redefine the territorial part of UNSCOP's plan. This possibility was aborted after a private meeting between President Truman and Chaim Weizmann, the venerable Zionist leader who would become Israel's first president. Weizmann, a renowned chemist, showed Truman a map, explained all the agricultural advances that were being made by the Jews in Palestine, how they were reclaiming the desert, and outlined the significance of the Negev to the Jewish state's prospects for development. After the meeting, Truman gave the U.S. delegation explicit instructions that UNSCOP's plan should not be changed and the Negev should remain within the Jewish state.[25]

On November 29, 1947, the partition plan was adopted in the General Assembly by a vote of thirty-three to thirteen, with eleven abstentions. However, this did not mean the U.S. government was going to support it. We voted for the plan, but with the British immediately declaring they would not enforce partition and would withdraw their forces from Palestine on May 15, 1948, pressure quickly grew within the State Department and the other national security agencies to reverse our support for partition and in its place favor UN trusteeship. Only that, in the eyes of senior national security officials, could prevent a vacuum and contain the violence.

In December, the administration, ostensibly to limit the scope of violence, embargoed all U.S. arms going to Palestine. This effectively penalized only the Jews, as the British continued to provide weapons to Arab armies and these leaked to Arab forces in Palestine. The internal drumbeat to reverse our posture would influence Truman to the point that he was willing to change our position on partition, provided the UN Security Council decided it was unworkable and voted for an alternative. Although that never happened, Warren Austin, the head of our UN delegation, announced on March 19, 1948, that the United States now favored trusteeship because we did not believe partition could be implemented.

Truman was blindsided by this announcement—by his own appointee, no less. At the time he did not publicly contradict Austin, but he would exact a measure of revenge when, much to the surprise of our delegation at the UN, he recognized the State of Israel on May 15—at a time when our representatives were still making the case for trusteeship. Our de facto recognition had great value symbolically, particularly as it gave immediate credibility and international standing to the new Jewish state. But American support for Israel for the remainder of Truman's term remained more symbolic than material.

We maintained the arms embargo even after Israel was invaded by Egypt, Syria, and Jordan in May 1948, following the declaration of statehood. This stayed in force throughout Truman's tenure. Amid the efforts to stop the fighting, there was again support within the administration for the new State of Israel to surrender the territory of the Negev. Truman opposed this, but he would not countenance any further expansion by Israel of its territory, even in response to aggression against it. Indeed, when Israel repulsed Egypt's invasion and was holding part of the Sinai, Truman threatened that if Israel did not withdraw from the Egyptian territory, the United States would "undertake a substantial review of its attitude toward Israel."[26] Similarly, during the peace talks at the Lausanne Conference in 1949, Truman was frustrated by what he saw as Israel's inflexibility on territorial adjustments and Palestinian refugees, saying at one point that unless the Israelis were "prepared to play the game properly and conform to the rules they were probably going to lose one of their best friends."[27]

Truman was a good friend of Israel. But he faced constraints, and the actual support he provided was limited. To understand why, it is useful to take a closer look at his mind-set, the assumptions of leading officials in the national security apparatus, the context in which they operated, and the overall legacy Truman bequeathed to President Eisenhower.

Truman's Mind-Set and Countervailing Forces

Truman's approach to Palestine was necessarily influenced by the far broader context of the enormous national security challenges he faced. He had to rebuild Europe economically and ensure it would not fall prey to the Soviet Union. He had to manage a new role and place for the United States in the world and, in the process, construct from scratch a new security architecture. Saving Greece and Turkey from collapse with the Marshall Plan, forging the NATO alliance, countering the Berlin blockade with the airlift—all of this at the same time he was trying to deal with the humanitarian trauma of the DPs, which itself was related to the rehabilitation in Europe. A Jewish state in Palestine might be desirable for him, but at this stage it was a distraction from other priorities. In other words, getting Jewish survivors to Palestine is what mattered to him; statehood could wait, and in any case would require working with others.

His own words at the time reveal much about his instinct, mind-set, and priorities. At a press conference after his return from Potsdam in August 1945, when he was asked about the American position on Palestine, he said, "The American view of Palestine is, we want to let as many of the Jews into Palestine as is possible to let into that country. Then the matter will have to be worked out diplomatically with the British and the Arabs so that if a state can be set up there they may be able to set it up on a peaceful basis. I have no desire to send 500,000 American soldiers there to make peace in Palestine."[28]

The humanitarian need was, as he put it, his "primary concern." It was urgent, and the inability to address it frustrated him with the British and Zionists, who both seemed to be more focused on resolving the broader issue of Palestine while the Jewish survivors still languished in the camps.[29] In his opinion, Prime Minister Attlee and Foreign Secretary Bevin's positions lacked "all human and moral considerations."[30] But he also railed against Rabbis Stephen Wise and Abba Hillel Silver for insisting on the establishment of a Jewish state when it "is not in the cards now . . . and would cause a third World War."[31] He was not going to commit American forces to something that he considered neither a priority nor central to American interests. Indeed, he was to repeat on a number of occasions that he would not commit U.S. troops to Palestine. His openness to the Anglo-American Committee recommendations and even the Morrison-Grady Plan reflect his preoccupation with getting the 100,000 Jewish DPs into Palestine and his hope that there could be a peaceful settlement.

It is worth noting that his anger toward the British and Jewish leaders was not limited to what he saw as their misplaced priorities. He also blamed them for the lost opportunity to settle things peacefully. It was the Jewish opposition to the Morrison-Grady Plan that James McDonald first raised with the president—and that Vice President Henry Wallace echoed in the cabinet meeting called to discuss the plan—that triggered Truman's outburst about the Jews: "Jesus Christ couldn't please them when he was here on earth, so how could anyone expect that I would have any luck?"[32]

In the end, Truman's desire to avoid either taking responsibility for Palestine or having to commit U.S. forces to preserve the peace there explains, at least in part, why he supported partition and not trusteeship. He was not prepared to impose an outcome. Partition, he was repeatedly told, meant fighting on behalf of the Jews. However, once it became clear that the Jews had effectively created a state and were imposing it themselves, he was willing to accept that fact and respect it. Moreover, he was in no way prepared to fight the Jews to impose trusteeship.

And that, no doubt, was a function not just of practicality but also his basic sympathy for the Jewish state. In response to Chaim Weizmann's congratulatory note to Truman on winning the 1948 election, the president wrote a highly personal letter dated November 29—the first anniversary of the UN's adoption of the partition plan. Truman noted that the two of them were abandoned by so-called experts who spoke of their "supposedly forlorn lost causes." He went on to observe that Israel's opponents were regrouping their forces after being "shattered" and he recognized Weizmann's "concern to prevent the undermining of [his] well-earned victories." Later in the letter he told Weizmann, "how happy and impressed I have been at the remarkable progress made by the new State of Israel. What you have received at the hands of the world has been far less than was your due. But you have more than made the most of what you have received, and I admire you for it."[33] Clearly, there is a sense of vindication that is personal and also reflective of his attitudes toward the experts who failed to understand him or Israel or the will of the Jewish people to succeed in their state. Israel was now an accomplished fact, and Truman stressed his readiness to help Israel with loans for project assistance and his willingness to encourage the Arabs to negotiate directly.

The tone of the letter was warm, at times even emotional. It was certainly a missive of one friend to another. In many ways, it was in keeping with Truman's personal attitudes, which lent themselves to support for Israel within bounds and within the context of our other interests and priorities. The limits of our support would be seen very shortly. In fact, only a month later, he allowed the State Department to pressure Israel to stop its offensive in the Sinai and withdraw its forces, even threatening to end support for Israel's membership in the UN. Weizmann was so troubled by the U.S. posture that on January 3, 1949—only five weeks after receiving Truman's warm personal letter—he wrote to the president pointing out that the Egyptian army had invaded Israel with the purpose of destroying the Jewish state, and now the United States was threatening to withhold support for Israel's membership in the UN at the very time it was supporting Egypt's membership in the Security Council.[34]

Truman's support for Israel was real, but it was limited. Context mattered. Given his priorities in Europe and the Middle East, he could not risk a fundamental breach with the British, and the last thing he wanted was the British to be fighting the Israelis. Thus, if the British threatened to invoke their treaty with Egypt to stop Israeli forces in the Sinai, pressure needed to be put on the Israelis, not the British.

Moreover, his unhappiness over the Israeli approach to negotiations, particularly their reluctance to allow at least some Arab refugees to return after the 1948 Arab-Israeli War, seemed to reflect not just the limits of his support for Israel but also his sense that Israel needed to respect the humanitarian concerns of others. In a note at the time, Truman wrote, "I am rather disgusted with the manner in which the Jews are approaching the refugee problem."[35]

If nothing else, Truman's attitude and approach suggested that politics was not his major concern. Clark Clifford, who served as White House counsel from 1946 to 1950, took great umbrage at the charge that domestic political pressures caused Truman to support partition and recognize Israel.[36] He decried revisionist historiography and asserted that "the facts totally refute the assumptions of the revisionists."[37] Why did their argument take hold?

To begin with, there is no denying that the pressures were real, and at certain points they may have had an impact. For example, Truman's ultimate decision on the Morrison-Grady Plan—which he initially supported—clearly resulted from intense domestic pressure. Dean Acheson explained to the British that political pressure made it impossible for Truman to accept Morrison-Grady, saying that "in view of the extreme intensity of feeling in centers of Jewish population in this country neither political party would support" it.[38] Nonetheless, in his memoirs, Acheson sounds much like Clifford in asserting that what drove Truman was "a deep conviction." Acheson writes that he did not share the president's views on Palestine but that the British and others who saw him acting out of "domestic political opportunism" were simply wrong.[39]

No doubt George Marshall's opposition to recognition and his emotional outburst in a meeting with Truman on May 12, 1948, helped to foster the perception that Truman was motivated by political considerations. Clifford describes the May 12 meeting in his memoirs, and Marshall's own memorandum summarizing the meeting confirms the basic thrust of what happened. Truman opened the meeting by saying that a Jewish state would become a reality two days later, and he wanted to discuss what the United States should do. Truman asked Marshall to lay out the State Department's position, and Marshall did so, concluding with the recommendation that the United States continue to support UN trusteeship and not make any decisions on recognition. Then the president asked for Clifford's views. Clifford made the case that trusteeship was "unrealistic. Partition into Jewish and Arab sectors has already happened. Jews and Arabs are already fighting each other from territory each side presently controls." Clifford went on to argue that early recognition was consistent with the president's policy from the outset, a Jewish state already existed for all practical purposes, a trusteeship would postpone the promise of actual statehood indefinitely, let down and discriminate against the Jews, and encourage the "Arabs to enlarge the scale of violence."[40] According to Clifford, Marshall became increasingly agitated as he spoke and responded not to Clifford's points but by asking why Clifford was present: "Mr. President, I thought this meeting was called to consider an important and complicated problem in foreign policy. I don't even know why Clifford is here. He is a domestic adviser, and this is a foreign policy matter." Marshall charged that Clifford was "pressing a political consideration with regard to this issue. I don't think politics should play any part in this."[41]

Under Secretary of State Robert Lovett interrupted at this point, leaping in to raise several arguments for opposing recognition: it was questionable under international law to offer recognition before there was a state; the president would harm his prestige by making a transparent attempt to win the Jewish vote; and given our intelligence reports about Soviet infiltration of Jewish Communist agents into Palestine, there was a danger that if the Jewish state came into being it would be a front for the Soviets.[42] Clifford pointed out there was no evidence for the latter and the Jews going to Palestine were fleeing communism. Marshall, still in high dudgeon, blurted out: "If the President were to follow Mr. Clifford's advice and if in the elections I were to vote, I would vote against the President."[43]

Silence followed Marshall's outburst and Truman ended the meeting quickly, telling Marshall, "I understand your position, General, and I am inclined to side with you in this matter." In fact, although he would not declare our recognition before Israel declared itself a state, he recognized it immediately afterward—and that reflected an understanding worked out between Clifford and Lovett, who had been disturbed by the meeting and felt the need to repair the damage done between the president and Marshall.[44]

But the enduring image of Truman "playing politics" was heavily shaped by Marshall's position and the fact that the national security establishment aligned itself solidly against the emergence of a Jewish state in Palestine. Before enumerating their key arguments and broad mind-set, it is worth recalling that on partition, recognition, and support for Israel, Truman, for the most part, acted out of conviction, and not for political reasons. One example in particular stands out in substantiating this point: In the fall of 1948, there was pressure on Truman to go beyond de facto recognition and recognize Israel formally and legally. Chester Bowles, then a Democratic candidate for governor of Connecticut, pleaded with him to do so, saying that if Truman delayed granting full recognition, he risked losing Connecticut in the presidential election in November. Action along these lines, Bowles wrote, "is vital." He went on to say, "I know how important it is in Connecticut; and if we are up against it here, it must be infinitely tougher in New York."[45] Truman certainly needed every bit of help he could get, being a decided underdog to Thomas Dewey, and yet he did not move on granting formal recognition. In the words of Allis and Ronald Radosh, "Truman knew that not granting de jure recognition could harm his presidential bid, [but] he refused to do it."[46]

Still, he would not try to undo the reality that a Jewish state now existed—and he supported it. Imagine how difficult it was for him then to confront the unanimous opposition of his national security advisers, who saw any move to help the Jews or to support a Jewish national homeland as a threat to our vital interests. On the one hand, his instincts impelled him to help the Jewish survivors and get them out of the camps and into Palestine. On the other, his advisers conjured up terrible consequences for acting in any way that alienated the Arabs.

Even Dean Acheson, consistently loyal to Truman, shared that same basic assumption: the effort to transform Palestine into a Jewish state capable of absorbing a million or more immigrants would "imperil . . . all Western interests in the Near East."[47]

What guided these assumptions? Why did all Truman's major foreign policy advisers—Marshall, Lovett, James Forrestal, George F. Kennan, Chip Bohlen, and Acheson—share these assumptions?[48] In no small part, it tended to stem from what those who dealt with the Arabs heard about their unalterable opposition to Jewish immigration and Jewish statehood in Palestine. William Eddy, who was our ambassador to Saudi Arabia during the Roosevelt administration—and served as the translator for FDR during his meeting with Ibn Saud—wrote in preparation for the president's post-Yalta meeting in Potsdam that the king had warned that "if America should choose in favor of the Jews, who are accursed in the Koran as enemies of the Muslims until the end of the world, it will indicate to us that America has repudiated her friendship with us."[49] This fundamental hostility, the impossibility of getting the Arabs ever to accept the Jewish state (or even increased Jewish presence in Palestine), our stake in good relations with the Arabs, and the certainty that there would be dire consequences in alienating them on this issue became deeply ingrained and animated the views of Truman's advisers. State Department officials constantly spoke of an "aroused Arab world"—aroused against us if we were seen as siding with the Jews. This theme became a mantra for them.[50] If there was a core assumption that shaped their mind-set, this was it—and, as we will see, it has endured in the national security establishment even when actual behaviors belied predictions of the consequences of taking steps to aid or support Israel.[51]

Ironically, there is evidence that Ibn Saud's stated views did not in fact reflect his actual position; his views evolved and became more practical. Khayr al-Din al-Zirkili, who worked for the Saudi king, revealed that contrary to what Ibn Saud told both Eddy and President Roosevelt about his immutable opposition to our support for the Jews in Palestine and the impact it would have on our relations, he actually tempered his views in order to guard against the Jews aligning with his archenemies, the Hashemites in Transjordan.[52] But such facts—validated as well by Churchill's meetings with Ibn Saud in which the king made clear that he was advising moderation

to the Arabs of Palestine and he wouldn't join the conflict—did not penetrate the worldview of the "Wise Men" and their subordinates in the Truman administration or afterward.[53]

During Truman's presidency, the mind-set was reflected in a consistent
set of arguments by officials such as Loy Henderson, who headed the Near
East and African Affairs office in the State Department. He had a special role
not only because of his responsibility for the Middle East during this period
but also because he had previously worked on Soviet and Eastern European
affairs and as such brought to bear expertise on the major preoccupation of
Truman-era foreign policy. Henderson, who as the U.S. ambassador to Iraq
heard Iraqi officials express sentiments much like Ibn Saud's, was preoccupied with ensuring that the Soviets did not gain a foothold in the Middle
East. He warned that a Jewish state, by damaging our relations with the
Arab world, would guarantee that eventuality.[54] Henderson brought an almost missionary zeal to his opposition, warning Secretary Marshall in one
memo that "partitioning of Palestine and the setting up of a Jewish State [is
opposed] by practically every member of the Foreign Service and the Department who has been engaged . . . with the Near and Middle East."[55]

For Henderson and George Kennan, the head of the Policy Planning
Staff in the State Department and the author of the containment strategy
toward Russia, the dire consequences we would suffer were, of course, not
limited to opening up the Middle East to the U.S.S.R.: we and our European
allies would lose our access to Arab oil, and this would make the recovery of
Europe impossible. We would have to fight the Arabs to impose partition
because the Jews were weak and would be overwhelmed by the Arabs; we
would lose our bases in the Middle East as a result. And, of course, as Lovett
said in the May 12 meeting, intelligence showed that the Jews coming to
Palestine included many Communist agents, and the Jewish state would be
a Communist client.

The groupthink in the national security establishment was so deep—
and the certainty of the terrible consequences so great—that the inherent
inconsistencies in the arguments were somehow overlooked. How could the
Jewish state be a Soviet client and not cost the Soviets with the Arabs?

But these convictions were deeply embedded in the collective mind-set
of the national security bureaucracy. A CIA analysis issued on the eve of the
UN partition vote asserted that "without substantial outside aid in terms of
manpower and material, they [the Jews] will be able to hold out no longer
than two years." It went on to argue that "in the event partition is imposed
on Palestine, the resulting conflict will seriously disturb the social, eco-

nomic, and political stability of the Arab world, and U.S. commercial and strategic interests will be dangerously jeopardized."[56] In a similar vein, in response to Truman's request for an estimate of how much military assistance the United States could provide Palestine, the Joint Chiefs of Staff (JCS) warned that military intervention would constitute such a "political shock" that it would be the equivalent of a Soviet military conquest of the region— and would limit our access to oil, lower our living standards, and reduce our military strength.[57]

Secretary of Defense James Forrestal was profoundly opposed and, like Loy Henderson, seemed to be on a mission against the Jewish state. For him, Jewish weakness required the United States to rescue the Jews at the expense of our oil interests. As he told Clark Clifford, "You just don't understand. There are four hundred thousand Jews and forty million Arabs. Forty million Arabs are going to push four hundred thousand Jews into the sea. And that's all there is to it. Oil—that is the side we ought to be on."[58] And if we lost access to that oil, in his eyes the certain consequence of being on the side of the Jews, "American motorcar companies [would] have to design a four-cylinder motorcar sometime within the next five years."[59] To Forrestal, that would have been a calamity.

In a joint memo, George Kennan and Loy Henderson cataloged the disastrous consequences for the United States if the partition resolution was implemented—and outlined a strategy for its reversal. They wrote that our support for the partition plan had already "brought about loss of U.S. prestige and disillusionment among the Arabs," and that the UN decision served the "Soviet objectives of sowing dissension and discord in non-communist countries," an argument presumably made to explain why the Soviets had supported it. Worse, the partition plan could succeed only if the United States sent troops to enforce it. The Arabs would see this as a "virtual declaration of war" against them. And to what end? After all, they judged that "it [was] improbable that the Jewish state could survive over any considerable period of time." They concluded by recommending that we reverse the decision and support either a UN trusteeship or something akin to the Morrison-Grady Plan.[60]

No senior national security official dissented. Only Clark Clifford offered a set of systematic arguments against this prevailing view, and he was special counsel to the president—a position, as noted, that Secretary of State

---

* Though it might seem a trifle, there were six hundred thousand Jews in Palestine at the time Forrestal stated this "fact" to Clifford.

Marshall saw as an exclusively domestic, political one. And yet Clifford challenged the "Wise Men" on every one of their arguments not on political but on national security grounds. In a memo to Truman in March 1948, Clifford stated that the arguments against partition were "completely fallacious." The Soviets would exploit our retreat from supporting partition because it would indicate that we were unprepared to stand by our commitments, and this was "as certain as the rising of tomorrow's sun." Similarly, we would not lose our access to oil because: "the Arab states must have oil royalties or go broke," particularly as 90 percent of Saudi governmental revenue came from oil sold to the United States, and the Arab states had no other customer. He added that King Ibn Saud had "publicly and repeatedly refused even to threaten the United States with a cancellation of oil leases, despite his dislike for our partition position." As he put it, the simple truth was that their "need of the United States is greater than our need for them." Finally, unlike those who feared Arab opposition and its consequences for our national security, he concluded that we needed to stand up to the Arabs for the sake of our larger interests and stakes: "The United States appears in the ridiculous role of trembling before threats of a few nomadic desert tribes. This has done us irreparable damage. Why should Russia, or Yugoslavia, or any other nation treat us with anything but contempt in light of our shilly-shallying appeasement of the Arabs?"[61]

In a subsequent memo, in May, Clifford argued that the partition was a fact, and the Jews had effectively created a state. Therefore, the president had a choice: he could recognize a Jewish state or, if he favored a reversal, he would need to use force, sanctions, threats, or persuasion against the Jews—none of which had worked thus far. Recognition would allow the president to regain prestige lost internationally over the previous months and, ironically, help with the Arabs because they respected "reality rather than sentimentality."[62]

Ultimately, the Wise Men's greatest success was Warren Austin's speech, which publicly reversed our position on partition. But this turned out to be a pyrrhic victory. Truman was stunned and embarrassed by it and determined to right what he considered to be a wrong. In his autobiography, he recounts his indignation and his resolve "to make it plain that the President of the United States, and not the second or third echelon in the State Department is responsible for making foreign policy, and, furthermore, that no one in any Department can sabotage the President's policy . . . The civil servant, the general or admiral, the foreign service officer has no authority to make policy."[63]

Still, it would have been remarkable if the unified opposition of his lead-ing national security officials had not affected Truman and his policy. Indeed, consider the context and Truman's priorities in responding to a new world, a cold war with the Soviets, the establishment of a policy of containment—with its main architects and those who were responsible for its implementation all adamantly opposed to the emergence of the Jewish state. That their assessments proved to be wrong did not seem to register with them. Support for partition did not drive the Arabs away from us and into the Soviet embrace. How could it, when the Soviets supported partition and actually criticized the United States when it appeared to back away from it after Austin's speech?

Similarly, this same national security establishment predicted that, at enormous cost to our relations with the Arabs, the United States would have to come to the rescue of the Jews, because otherwise they would be defeated. Of course, the Jews were not defeated by either the Arabs of Pales-tine or their Arab neighbors in the Arab-Israeli War. Just the opposite—and not because we in any way came to Israel's aid. On the contrary, we im-posed an arms embargo both before and after the declaration of state-hood, and once again the argument was that if we provided weapons, it would alienate the Arabs and push them to the Soviets. That prediction proved fallacious as well. When the Soviet proxy, Czechoslovakia, provided arms in April 1948—arms critical to the Yishuv's* military gains in the spring and after statehood was declared—the Arabs were not alienated from the Soviets. What did it tell us about the Arabs that Kennan, Henderson, Lovett, Marshall, Forrestal, and the intelligence community missed? And why was Clifford's argument that the Arabs needed to sell us their oil dis-missed, even when he proved to be right and there was no loss of access for either America or the Europeans? Even when Ibn Saud, whose hostility toward the Jews and Israel was supposedly so fundamental, did not alter his policy toward the United States after we supported partition and then recog-nized Israel, no one seemed to take note. No senior members of the State Department, the Pentagon, or the CIA seemed to perceive that Ibn Saud's need for U.S. support trumped his opposition to Israel. And none of the policy makers asked whether we should rethink some of our assumptions about the region and draw some lessons from seeing that Arab leaders could be opposed to Israel and yet seek to preserve American backing and ties because their own interests required it.

* The Jewish community in Palestine.

Senior officials maintained their hostile posture toward the Jewish state and continued to see only risks associated with U.S. support for it. Arms could not be provided. Assistance of any sort should be limited. Israel should be pressured to pull back from Sinai, to be open to concessions on territory and refugees, and to accept that we would keep our distance. We might try to organize the Middle East Defense Organization (MEDO), but Israel could not be part of it because it would be the kiss of death with the Arabs.

It took courage for Truman to recognize Israel, even if it was, for Clifford, not only morally right but also practically necessary. Truman offered economic loans and some small grant assistance. In general, his posture toward Israel after he offered recognition was largely what his national security advisers wanted. Our support was limited in practice, even as Truman would later take great pride in his support for the emergence of the state.

David Ben-Gurion described his meeting with Truman in May 1961, early in the Kennedy administration, as tinged with emotion. He said he had told Truman he did not know how he would be recorded in American history, "but his helpfulness to us, his constant sympathy with our aims in Israel, his courageous decision to recognize our new state so quickly and his steadfast support since then had given him an immortal place in Jewish history." Truman's eyes, Ben-Gurion observed, filled with tears, and Israel's first prime minister said he had rarely seen "anyone so moved."[64] Clifford later explained this, saying, "These were the tears of a man who had been subjected to calumny and vilification, who had persisted against powerful forces determined to defeat him, who had contended with opposition even from within his own administration. These were the tears of a man who had fought ably and honorably for a humanitarian goal to which he was deeply dedicated."[65]

Clifford may well have been right. Truman was driven by humanitarian concerns and he resented resistance, but his policy was ultimately balanced, and in practice, his support for Israel was limited. Even recognition required accepting what was already a fact. But it was a fact that Marshall and the others were not keen to accept or fully understand. It was their opposition that colored the views of Dwight Eisenhower and his secretary of state, John Foster Dulles. They would prove far less balanced than Truman, and they would lack any of the emotion that he attached to the Jewish state.

2

THE EISENHOWER
ADMINISTRATION AND THE
PURSUIT OF ARAB ALLIES

Dwight Eisenhower and John Foster Dulles shaped America's foreign policy as a team. Their views on the Middle East were heavily influenced by their preoccupation with the need to counter the Soviet Union. Notwithstanding a declared policy of rollback—theoretically undoing and shrinking the Communist bloc as opposed to simply "containing" it—the Eisenhower policy, in practice, was no more offensive than the policy of the Truman administration.* However, unlike Truman, whose focus had been in Europe as his administration forged first the Marshall Plan and then the NATO alliance, and in Asia where the United States fought a grinding war in the Korean peninsula, Eisenhower and Dulles saw the Middle East as the main arena of competition with the Soviets. For them, it was in the Middle East where they needed to close the ring of encirclement and produce new allies to counter the Soviets.[1]

This explains American pursuit of the Baghdad Pact—successor to Truman's effort to create the MEDO. However, given their 1930 treaty relationship with Iraq, it was the British who took the lead, and although the

---

* Other than covertly backing coups, or attempted coups, in order to displace what were perceived as Soviet-leaning regimes—in Iran in 1953, Guatemala in 1954, and Syria in 1957—the Eisenhower administration basically adopted a posture of containment.

United States offered material and moral support, it did not actually join the pact. Indeed, our desire to attract Egypt—and the fear that Britain's colonial taint would stigmatize us—led to the Eisenhower-Dulles decision not to become a formal member of the pact.[2]

Nonetheless, the desire to develop allies in the area as part of our anti-Soviet strategy led Dulles to take an extensive trip to the Middle East in May 1953. The partners that the Eisenhower administration sought in the region were the Arabs, not the Israelis, and Dulles was not subtle in expressing this aim in his meetings. During his trip, he told the Arabs essentially what they wanted to hear. He told Lebanese leaders that the administration would "seek policies which would be more fair and more just than those of the past" and that it was "prepared to consider measures and concert actions to prevent aggression by Israel."[3] Similarly, in Egypt, he suggested to Deputy Prime Minister Gamal Abdel Nasser, the real power in the Revolutionary Command Council (RCC)* that domestic considerations would not limit the assistance the United States would provide his country because "the Republican Administration does not owe the same degree of political debt as did the Democrats to Jewish groups."[4] He would also tell the titular head of the RCC, Prime Minister Muhammad Naguib, that "if arms, and economic help are justified in the case of Egypt, and if Egypt itself desires these things from the US, the US would be prepared to consider making the Egyptian Army a real force in the world."[5]

To be fair, Dulles did not tell the Arabs one thing and the Israelis another. He told Prime Minister David Ben-Gurion that one of the purposes of his trip was to indicate U.S. interest to the Arabs, who felt that the new administration offered them an opportunity to improve relations. Moreover, he was not persuaded by Ben-Gurion's argument that the Arabs would use arms against Israel and not against the Soviet Union, and that the Arabs needed "economic development" and not arms. Dulles countered by saying that the Arabs needed to know their concerns would no longer be ignored by the United States. And, just as he had done with the Arabs, Dulles told Ben-Gurion "that the United States would not carry out a policy partial to Israel and that the United States would not indefinitely finance Israel immigration."[6]

The United States was providing some assistance to Israel, but nothing close to its needs at the time. During the Truman administration, loans from the Export-Import Bank amounted to $100 million in 1949 and $35

---

* The RCC was set up to supervise Egypt and Sudan after the Egyptian Revolution of 1952.

million in 1950. The total of grant assistance was $65 million.[7] In the first years of the Eisenhower administration, the amount of American aid was reduced, and in October 1953, Eisenhower suspended assistance when the Arabs complained that Israel was trying to develop hydroelectric power by diverting the Jordan River. The message was clear: there would be no reluctance to distance ourselves from the Israelis, and even penalize them, as we pursued partnerships with the Arabs.

One way to make it easier for the Arabs to partner with us against the Soviets was to end the conflict with Israel. Settling the conflict, or at least managing it, was an early priority for Eisenhower. In the fall of 1953, the administration launched an effort, led by the president's special representative, Eric Johnston, to try to do so. Johnston decided to use water—a shared need—as a basis for areas of commonality. Since the United States had forced the Israelis not to divert waters from the Jordan River, Johnston's approach was to share the river, with new schemes for irrigation that required cooperation among the Israelis, Jordanians, Palestinian refugees, and Syria. Ultimately, although Israel was prepared to accept his proposals, the Arab League rejected them on the grounds that they would also benefit Israel, not only the Arabs.

Though the Johnston Plan was pursued intermittently over the next few years, Dulles tried a more comprehensive and political approach to forging a settlement.[8] In a speech to the Council on Foreign Relations in August 1955, he called for repatriation of Arab refugees to Israel, water development, border adjustments, and security guarantees. In essence, Dulles hoped to get the Arabs to end the conflict, if not make peace, by addressing their concerns on refugees and territory, borrowing concepts the British had raised during the Truman administration for settling the conflict. These concepts were refined in Project Alpha, a joint Anglo-American effort. Dulles wanted the Israelis to allow seventy-five thousand Arab refugees to return and to concede most of the Negev desert in order to permit territorial contiguity between Jordan and Egypt—which meant Israel would give up a major part of its territory, the same area that Ben-Gurion saw as the key to absorbing massive Jewish immigration. Both were anathema to Israel; nonetheless, at one point, Moshe Sharett, who served as foreign minister and later replaced Ben-Gurion as prime minister for two years, proposed a seven-point peace plan that included territorial and border adjustments, compensation for Palestinian refugees for all the property that they had left behind, free port facilities for Jordan in Haifa, and a road across the Negev to create a Jordanian connection to Egypt.[9]

Late in 1955 and into 1956, Eisenhower and Dulles tried to promote a secret channel between Nasser and Ben-Gurion. They employed Robert Anderson, the former secretary of defense, in this role, using the CIA, under the code name Project Gamma, to manage this secret channel.[10] Interestingly, Nasser's turn to the Soviets for a massive arms deal in late September 1955—a deal nearly ten times the size of what he had been discussing with the Eisenhower administration—seems to have spurred Project Gamma as a way of bringing the Egyptian leader back into the American fold.

For some time, leading CIA operatives including Kermit Roosevelt, Jr., and Miles Copeland, Jr., who had been quietly dealing with Nasser, were convinced he could be brought around to an anti-Soviet posture if we met his needs, including on weapons.[11] Indeed, even prior to the Free Officers coup that ousted King Farouk of Egypt in 1952, Copeland had been in contact with some of the coup plotters. He developed a close relationship with Hassan Tuhami—one of the original Free Officers and trusted by Nasser. Copeland, whose code name was Jones, became part of a small constituency within the CIA that felt we could influence Nasser—and shape Egypt and the Middle East accordingly.[12]

While the size of the arms deal with the Soviets should have set off alarm bells about Nasser's ambitions and determination to defy the West, neither seems to have entered the administration's assessments—much less altered them. On the contrary, Dulles went out of his way to rationalize Nasser's turn to the Soviets for arms, saying, "It is difficult to be critical of countries which, feeling themselves endangered, seek the arms which they sincerely believe they need for defense."[13]

Nasser, in his dealings with Kermit Roosevelt, had said he needed arms in the aftermath of a large-scale Israeli reprisal raid into the Gaza Strip on February 28, 1955. In keeping with its general posture, the administration spokesmen sided with the Egyptians, calling the raid "indefensible," and the U.S. ambassador to the UN, Henry Cabot Lodge, joined the UN condemnation of Israel, saying, "Whatever the provocation might have been in this case, there was no justification for the Israeli military action at Gaza."[14]

It was in this context that we explored providing Nasser an arms package worth $27 million. While Kermit Roosevelt warned Dulles that Nasser might turn to the Russians if he was not satisfied, the scope of the Soviet arms deal was dramatically greater than anyone anticipated and indicated much about Nasser's larger aspirations in the region.

In fact, the arms deal boosted Nasser's stature dramatically in the Middle East. Later, Eisenhower would say that "our attitude toward Soviet penetration naturally hardened" as a result, "but we did not cease our efforts to make Nasser see the benefits of strengthening his ties with the West."[15] The vehicle for doing so was the Anderson mission. Peace would, in the eyes of the administration, lessen Nasser's need for weapons—assuming, as administration officials did, that it was Israel driving his appetite for arms. But by March 1956, even though Anderson had met multiple times separately with Nasser and Ben-Gurion and promised Nasser significant economic assistance if he would move on peace, the efforts had come to naught. Nasser was neither willing to meet with Israelis, nor, as Anderson would cable Dulles, was he prepared to take a leadership role in promoting peace.[16] In his diary, Eisenhower put most of the blame for the failure on Nasser, writing, "Nasser proved to be a complete stumbling block. He is apparently seeking to be acknowledged as the political leader of the Arab world"— which ruled out any deal with Israel.[17] While he put the lion's share of the blame on Nasser, Eisenhower also found fault with Ben-Gurion, observing that Israeli leaders were "anxious to talk with Egypt" but willing to make "no concessions whatsoever in order to obtain a peace," his goal being to gain arms from us, "as a means of ensnaring the U.S. as a protector."[18]

After Nasser's massive arms deal with the Soviets, Ben-Gurion became obsessed with acquiring sufficient weapons to offset what he feared would be a major Egyptian military advantage. In his conversations with Robert Anderson, Ben-Gurion emphasized that with Egypt now capable of threatening Israeli cities with little warning, Nasser would have no motivation for peace with Israel. He pressed for the United States to end the restriction on providing arms to Israel, saying this was necessary if there was to be any chance for Anderson's peace efforts to succeed. Ben-Gurion followed up his conversations with Anderson with letters to Eisenhower—which had an air of desperation. On February 14, 1956, he wrote the president, saying, "Every day that passes without our receiving from your country or her allies planes and tanks . . . brings the danger ever closer and deepens the feeling that we are being abandoned by our closest friends . . . No Arab country is ever likely to make peace with a defenceless Israel."[19]

The Ben-Gurion—Eisenhower correspondence continued through the spring, with Eisenhower asking for restraint even in the face of ongoing guerrilla attacks out of Gaza by fedayeen against Israeli villages. Ben-Gurion's response to an Eisenhower letter on April 10 was not geared to weapons— he was now secretly getting much more support from France—and focused principally on explaining what Israel was facing and that if Eisenhower had been aware of the entire situation with Egypt, he would have done more than "merely expressing . . . hope that we would abstain from military acts."[20] Ben-Gurion's reaction may have been a response to Eisenhower's plea for restraint, but it also reflected his increasing conviction that Israel would have to act militarily against Nasser before his forces posed too great a threat to Israel's well-being. By the spring, France was providing Israel weapons and agreed that military action against Nasser was justified given the threat he posed in the area—and particularly to the insurgency France was facing in Algeria. This was the backdrop to the Suez War of 1956.

At the same time, the Eisenhower administration's approach to Nasser was also hardening—not because of the attacks out of Gaza but because of Nasser's rejection of Anderson's mission. It was at this point that the administration became disinclined to finance the Aswan Dam, which set in motion a train of events that led to Nasser's nationalization of the Suez Canal and a break between Eisenhower and the British, French, and Israelis over Suez.

Aswan, the Suez War, and the Eisenhower Doctrine

The High Dam at Aswan would control the flow of the Nile River and prevent its annual flooding of the delta. Aside from the practical benefits, it would be a huge symbol of development, and the Eisenhower administration believed our willingness to help finance it was a strong incentive we could provide Nasser. Support for financing the dam was offered in December 1955, three months after the initial Soviet arms deal with Nasser, and the project had the backing of the president of the International Bank for Reconstruction and Development, Eugene Black, and those in the CIA who felt that Nasser remained "gettable." With the failure of the Anderson mission, however, both Eisenhower and Dulles soured on Nasser, doubting that he could be dissuaded from his turn to the Soviets. Not surprisingly, their interest in financing Aswan also dissipated. Three developments led the administration to revoke its offer on the dam in July: Nasser's announcement in April that he was considering a Soviet offer to finance the dam, his recognition in May of "Red China," and a major new arms deal with the Soviets concluded in June.[21]

Ironically, at the same moment that the administration decided to walk away from its offer to finance the dam, Nasser decided to accept the original U.S. terms that had been offered in December. His ambassador to the United States came to see Dulles on July 19, 1956, to tell him about Nasser's change of heart, only to find out that the United States was revoking its offer. This was conveyed privately, then released publicly as well, which Nasser saw as an effort to humiliate him. Dulles thought that he would teach Nasser a lesson—but he failed to consider what the Egyptian president might do in response. One week later, on July 26, Nasser surprised the world by announcing the nationalization of the Suez Canal. In his speech, Nasser bitterly attacked the United States and the colonial powers, and justified taking this step by proclaiming that he needed to raise revenues to pay for the dam. The nationalization, like the arms deal with the Soviets, played not only to Egyptian pride but also to the deep-seated impulse in the region to humiliate those on the outside who had humiliated the Arabs for so long.

For the British and French, nationalization was the last straw. The British, whose economy could be crippled if they could not use the canal, saw this as a blow to their position in the Middle East. They communicated immediately to Eisenhower that time was of the essence, that recourse to the UN ran the risk of allowing time for the international community to adjust to this intolerable action, and that the U.K. was already contemplating military action.[22] The French, in Eisenhower's words, had "an even more emotional view than the British" and were ready to join the British in considering joint military action to reoccupy the canal.[23]

Eisenhower urged calm, preferring a diplomatic path to resolve the issue. This effort stretched over several months, with the United States first organizing a conference to try to hammer out an understanding, using the original 1888 Constantinople Convention on the canal, which mandated free passage "without distinction of flag," in peace and war, through this international waterway. Later, Dulles developed the idea of a Suez Canal Users Association to oversee the terms of operation, the Egyptian role, and increased revenue for Egypt. Though Egypt denied Israel use of the canal—notwithstanding the 1888 convention and a 1951 UN Security Council resolution criticizing Egypt for such a denial—Eisenhower wanted "to avoid any effort by our allies, the French in particular, to relate Nasser's action to the Arab-Israel quarrel."[24]

As with so much of Eisenhower's approach to Suez, this would prove impossible. Moreover, neither the Soviets nor the Egyptians would go along with our diplomatic solutions. Once the Egyptians demonstrated that they could manage the canal without foreign pilots, Eisenhower felt that there was no legal basis for the use of force and was convinced that forcible intervention would "weaken, perhaps even destroy, the United Nations." With the Russians ever present in his thinking, he feared that if the British and

French acted militarily to retake the canal, the Soviets would "pose as the champion of the underdog, giving support to the newly emerging nations against onetime colonial powers."[25]

So Eisenhower continued to temporize, even as the British and French signaled they were running out of patience. Without informing him, the French began planning with the Israelis for military action against Nasser, and the British became part of the planning in late October. Ironically, at this time, Eisenhower and Dulles were concerned about Israeli military action not against Egypt but rather against Jordan, as terror attacks out of Jordan provoked escalating Israeli counterattacks in mid-October.

When, instead, Israel struck in the Sinai on October 29, 1956, Eisenhower was surprised and angry. He felt betrayed by England and France, and Dulles began to suspect that they had coordinated with the Israelis, noting that for ten days the British and French had not communicated with him."[26] In addition, both countries were quick to protect the Israelis. Prime Minister Anthony Eden told the president in a written message that "Egypt has to a large extent brought this attack on herself" and that Israel was justified in the attack.[27] The British and French also vetoed a UNSC resolution condemning Israel and calling on it to cease firing and withdraw.

In his memoirs, Eisenhower recounts that many of his advisers thought the British and French assumed that "when the chips were down, the United States would . . . go along with" what they were doing on Suez. But Eisenhower never considered joining his allies.[28] He believed we had a duty to oppose aggression—a principle was involved. He would later write that he even considered using U.S. forces to push the Israelis back behind their borders.[29] According to Dulles, the principle, if not observed, might weaken the UN itself, and he said as much in a statement to the UN General Assembly after the British and French exercised their vetoes: "The resort to force, the violent armed attack by three of our members up on a fourth, cannot be treated as other than a grave error, inconsistent with the principles and purposes of the Charter, and one which if persisted in would gravely undermine our Charter and undermine this organization."[30]

As part of the plan concocted with the Israelis, the British and French forces were to be deployed ostensibly to separate the combatants and "protect" the canal. But Eisenhower was determined to stop them. When he was blocked by the U.K. and France in the Security Council, he directed that we submit a tough resolution in the General Assembly calling on all member states to stop all military, economic, and political aid for Israel until it accepted a cease-fire and pulled back to the armistice lines. Separately, he suspended all loans to Israel, and when the British and French persisted with their attack, he put a hold on a desperately needed $1 billion loan to the British and stopped oil shipments to both countries. Under the pressure, Eden was forced to back down. The French soon followed, with both agreeing to a cease-fire and the withdrawal of their forces.

Once the Soviet leadership saw that the United States was opposing the British and the French, its own allies, Premier Nikolai Bulganin sent strong letters to the British, French, and Israelis. He threatened Soviet rocket attacks on London and Paris and implied in his letter to David Ben-Gurion that Israel's survival could be at stake. Eisenhower's position had, paradoxically, made it safe for the Soviets to posture themselves as the party ready to come to the aid of Nasser—and conveniently at a time when Soviet tanks had moved into Budapest to crush Hungary's independence movement and replace its leadership.

After the Bulganin letters, the United States put extraordinary pressure on Israel to accept the cease-fire. Dulles at this point had been hospitalized for what would turn out to be cancer, and Under Secretary of State Herbert Hoover was acting in his place. Hoover called in the Israeli ambassador and told him, "We are on the brink of a World War. Israel's failure to comply with the decision of the [UN General] Assembly is endangering the peace. Israel's position will of necessity have serious consequences, such as the cessation of all government and private assistance, UN sanctions, and perhaps even expulsion from the United Nations."[31]

These were blunt, powerful words. Ben-Gurion would accept the cease-fire and agree in principle to withdraw the IDF. This threat of sanctioning even private donations from the American Jewish community, which at that time dwarfed the loans from the U.S. government, would be repeated by Eisenhower a few months later when Israel resisted the withdrawal of its forces without more specific and formal guarantees of keeping the Straits of Tiran open and of Egypt not sending its forces back into Gaza.

To put this in perspective, all this took place a week before the 1956 presidential election. Eisenhower, in his last speech before the election, declared: "We cannot—in the world, any more than in our own nation—subscribe to one law for the weak, another law for the strong . . . But this we know above all: there are some firm principles that cannot bend—they can only break. And we shall not break ours."[32]

The president meant to stand by our principles of stopping aggression in the Middle East, even if it meant going against our NATO allies. He condemned the nearly simultaneous Soviet intervention in Hungary; however, along with Dulles and Lodge, he would later acknowledge in private to American senators that there was nothing we could have done about that.[33] In the nuclear age, there apparently was one law for those we could pressure and another for those impervious to such pressures.

Yet almost immediately after the cease-fire and the British, French, and Israeli commitments to withdraw their forces, Eisenhower had regrets—at least with regard to the breach that he had opened with our two NATO allies. Not only did he want to repair any damage quickly, it also dawned on him that forcing the British and French to retreat might create a vacuum in the Middle East that could be exploited by the Soviets.

Eisenhower visited Dulles in the hospital after the cease-fire had been accepted. He discussed an upcoming meeting with Eden and his plans to tell the British prime minister that he wanted to "talk about what the Bear will do and what we should do in the face of the Russians' acts. There's no point now in making any recriminations against the British . . . We also need a coordinated Anglo-American intelligence effort in the region."[34] A short time later he would tell Dulles, "I hope that our friends in Europe will see the necessity, as we see it, of beginning confidentially and on a staff level to develop policies and plans whereby the West can work together in making the Mid East secure from Communist penetration."[35]

In early November, after the Israelis agreed in principle to withdraw, Eisenhower dictated two pages of notes on what he felt we might now have to do in the Middle East to "exclude from the area Soviet influence." He felt it important to inform the states in the region what would happen if they fell under Soviet domination; he mused over the idea of providing Nasser's Egypt "an agreed upon amount of arms" in return for not accepting "any Soviet offer." He thought he might have to offer Israel something comparable, as well as a $75 million loan.[36] And he believed the actual use of U.S. forces might prove necessary.

The president's notes suggested the Eisenhower Doctrine, which he would formally adopt two months later. On New Year's Day 1957, he met with key congressional leaders to spell out what he had in mind and to ask for their support in providing assistance—economic and military—to any country in the Middle East that felt threatened by the Soviet Union. He also requested authorization to use American forces if that proved necessary to protect those countries. He emphasized that "the existing vacuum in the Middle East must be filled by the United States before it is filled by Russia."[37]

Shortly before gaining congressional authorization, Eisenhower would exert great pressure on Israel to withdraw from the Sinai. At the time, Prime

Minister Ben-Gurion committed in principle to withdraw, but he made clear that Israel needed several assurances before he would move ahead: first, the Straits of Tiran would not be blockaded again, and Israeli ships would have access to the Gulf of Aqaba and the Israeli port of Eilat; second, Egyptian forces would not return to the Gaza Strip, and the UN forces would administer the area and prevent fedayeen raids into Israel; and third, the United Nations Emergency Force (UNEF) in the Sinai could not be withdrawn simply on request of the Egyptians.

In his memoirs, Eisenhower acknowledges that the Israelis had legitimate concerns but he did not believe they could impose conditions on their withdrawal. Still, he was prepared to offer Israel limited assurances in an aide-mémoire that the State Department conveyed. It stated that while neither the United States nor the United Nations could change the terms of the 1949 armistice, which mandated that Egypt would occupy the Gaza Strip, the United States proposed that "the United Nations General Assembly and the Secretary-General should seek that the United Nations Emergency Force, in the exercise of its mission, move into this area and be on the boundary between Israel and the Gaza Strip." As for the Gulf of Aqaba, the aide-mémoire stated that the United States, on behalf of vessels of United States registry, "is prepared to exercise the right of free and innocent passage and to join with others to secure general recognition of this right." And, assuming that Israel withdrew from the Sinai, Israel would enjoy "a right of free and innocent passage" as well.[38]

Ben-Gurion was not satisfied. He wanted something more formal and explicit. Eisenhower, however, was not prepared to go further—even though Dag Hammarskjöld, the UN secretary-general, had informed the administration that Nasser assured him Egypt would not reoccupy Gaza.

Eisenhower explained later that Dulles believed that to offer the Israelis anything more would "surely jeopardize the entire Western influence in the Middle East, and the nations of that region would conclude that United States policy toward the area was, in the last analysis, controlled by Jewish influence in the United States. In such an event the only hope of the Arab countries would be found in a firm association with the Soviet Union. Should this occur, it would spell the failure of the Eisenhower Doctrine."[39]

With Ben-Gurion insisting on further assurances before withdrawing, Eisenhower sought congressional support for a UN resolution that would impose sanctions on Israel to preclude any private assistance going to it from any country. But congressional leaders, led by Senators Lyndon Johnson and William Knowland, balked, asking, Why put such pressure on Israel when we did not do so on the Soviet Union when it invaded Hungary? With Sam Rayburn, the Speaker of the House, agreeing with them, Eisenhower decided to go to the American public. In a television address, he insisted on Israeli withdrawal, and posed the question, "Should a nation which attacks and occupies foreign territory in the face of United Nations disapproval be allowed to impose conditions on its own withdrawal?" He mentioned the Johnson-Knowland argument and said it would be "a sad day if the United States ever felt that it had to subject Israel to the same type of moral pressure as is being applied to the Soviet Union." He closed his address with the words, "The United Nations must not fail."[40]

At this point, Ben-Gurion gave in to the pressure, but he had his foreign minister, Golda Meir, declare at the UN that Israel would regard any interference with its right of free passage as an attack entitling Israel to exercise its inherent right of self-defense. In an exchange of letters, the United States acknowledged the Israeli declarations on freedom of passage and self-defense, and Eisenhower told Ben-Gurion he believed that "Israel will have no cause to regret" this decision. Eisenhower, mistakenly, was convinced that Nasser would abide by understandings he had reached with Dag Hammarskjöld on Gaza. Shortly after the Israeli withdrawal, Nasser reneged on his assurance and sent his forces back into Gaza. Eisenhower acknowledged that Nasser's "action represented not only a violation of an understanding between him and Secretary-General Hammarskjöld, but evidenced a lack of concern for the goodwill of those powers which had so recently come to his aid."[41] Goodwill might have guided Eisenhower, but clearly not Nasser.

Although the United States had come to his rescue in the Suez conflict in November and then brought about Israel's departure from Sinai, Nasser felt no obligation to repay this support. His reputation had been enhanced in Egypt and the Middle East as a result of the war, appearing as he did to have prevailed over the British, French, and Israelis. The reality that his forces had been defeated by the Israelis was overshadowed by the imagery that he controlled the Suez Canal and that the British, French, and Israelis were all forced to withdraw. In the eyes of the Arab on the street, he possessed mystical powers—even though it was the United States that was largely responsible for his victory. Other Arab leaders knew that, of course, but Nasser played to a broader Arab population that hungered for dignity and freedom from external domination—and he seemed to deliver.

Eisenhower and Dulles now felt that with the Israelis out of the Sinai, they could implement their new policy—the Eisenhower Doctrine. It defined the Soviet threat broadly, and included the right of the United States to act to prevent a regime from becoming a Soviet client. Based on this, CIA operatives, whose coup planning in Syria predated the Eisenhower Doctrine, worked in 1957 to subvert the Syrian regime they saw receiving Soviet arms and drawing too close to Nasser.[42] The CIA failed to produce the coup but was prepared—when asked—to back an Iraqi-Turkish invasion of Syria with Saudi and Jordanian involvement. Notwithstanding the repositioning of our forces and Eisenhower's promise to replace any arms lost, the Iraqis and the Saudis got cold feet and there was no invasion. (Interestingly, before the Iraqis, Saudis, and Jordanians backed out, Eisenhower, fearing that Israel would take advantage of this action to move into the West Bank, went to Ben-Gurion and specifically sought an assurance of Israeli restraint—an assurance he received.)[43]

It may seem ironic that Eisenhower, who had been ready to sanction Israel for invading Egypt, was now encouraging an invasion of Syria by its neighbors. He rationalized this contradiction by saying that the Arabs considered themselves a large confederation and had the right to act against a regime that threatened them. But Loy Henderson, the deputy under secretary of state, was struck, after a trip to the area, by "a surprising amount of rivalry among the Arabs."[44] Moreover, President Eisenhower was hoping that the king of Saudi Arabia could become a focal point around which to build an Arab alternative to Nasser. To his regret, he found that King Saud, the son of Ibn Saud, who had died in 1953, was not up to the task.

Nasser's star, however, continued to rise, particularly with the formation of the United Arab Republic, a union that joined Egypt and Syria in January 1958. The UAR seemingly heralded a move toward the achievement of broader Arab unity, but in actuality only deepened regional divisions as Nasser sought to undermine the Hashemite monarchies in Iraq and Jordan and the Lebanese government led by President Camille Chamoun.

In fact, a crisis in Lebanon had erupted in May over Chamoun's effort to amend the Lebanese constitution and serve a second term as president. Chamoun, who had been one of the few Arab leaders to openly embrace the Eisenhower Doctrine, charged that the UAR was fomenting instability and seeking to take over Lebanon. He asked whether, if requested, the United States would intervene. Dulles was reluctant. He feared a backlash, and the administration was not prepared to act at this point.[45]

But its hesitancy came to an end on July 14. On that day, there was a military coup in Baghdad led by Abdul Karim Qassim, who looked like a Nasser clone. In an instant, the Hashemite monarchy in Iraq was removed in a frenzy of violence in which the body of the long-serving prime minister,

Nuri as-Said, was dragged through the streets of the city. Nasser seemed triumphant. The Eisenhower administration was stunned. In the president's words: "I was shocked to receive news of a coup in Baghdad against the Hashemite monarchy. This was the country that we were counting on heavily as a bulwark of stability and progress in the region . . . This somber turn of events could, without vigorous response on our part, result in a complete elimination of Western influence in the Middle East." And, he added, we had to intervene "to stop the trend toward chaos."[46]

Eisenhower sent U.S. forces into Lebanon, justifying it in terms of the request by President Chamoun, who did, in fact, ask the United States to intervene within forty-eight hours. The British sent forces at the same time to Jordan to shore up King Hussein, and even though we materially supported the British in Jordan, we turned down their request for a joint operation. Interestingly, for the British to get to Jordan, particularly with the Saudis denying them access through or over the kingdom, they needed the Israelis to grant them overflight rights. The Israelis, who had been treated by the Eisenhower administration as a liability given the fear that any cooperation would trigger a backlash from the Arabs, were now being counted on to facilitate the British intervention. Eisenhower would note the irony of Jordan getting indirect help from its supposedly implacable enemy, Israel.

With the Soviets demanding that Israel deny the British access to their airspace, Prime Minister Ben-Gurion on August 2—after two weeks of permitting overflight—sent a message to both the British and the Americans asking them to discontinue the flights. This led to a tough exchange between Dulles and Ben-Gurion.

While Dulles accepted the Saudis' denial of support, he was outraged by the same decision by the Israelis. He chastised them for giving in to Soviet threats, telling Ambassador Abba Eban that there "were wide political implications in giving the U.S.S.R. a sense of power in the Middle East by such subservient actions as Israel seemed prepared to take."[47] After receiving Dulles's message, Ben-Gurion wrote the secretary of state, reminding him that the United States had given others security guarantees but none to Israel, even though it was "surrounded by foes who receive abundant arms from the Soviet Union and who receive Western arms as well, and yet we are not intimidated. I must however admit that we are concerned because up to now we have not been successful in receiving arms assistance from the United States."[48] In effect, Ben-Gurion was saying, You expect us to stand up to the Soviets, but you provide us no support either verbally or materially.

In the end, the Israelis extended overflight rights for a period of time, we helped sustain the British logistically, and the United States successfully carried out its intervention in Lebanon—and at low cost. Ambassador Robert Murphy, who was sent to try to work out a political deal, succeeded diplomatically in ending the political crisis in the country. Chamoun was allowed to complete his term on September 23, 1958, and he was succeeded as president by Fouad Chehab, the outgoing chief of the Lebanese armed forces.

Notwithstanding the fears that triggered our intervention in Lebanon and the British entry into Jordan in the fall of 1958, Eisenhower seemed to shift his view of the region afterward. With Iraq now under the sway of another Arab nationalist, with Jordan's King Hussein seen as inherently weak, with the Saudis less willing to challenge Nasser at this point, and with Chehab—not Chamoun—now in charge in Lebanon, the administration made a judgment that the best way to combat the Soviets was to get the Arab nationalists on our side. Though the president had viewed Nasser skeptically and Dulles had seen him as a fanatic, their preoccupation remained with the Soviets and their earlier fear that his reliance on the Soviets might make him their tool seems to have abated after Lebanon. Was it because we feared that the Arab monarchies were too weak to compete with the Arab nationalists? Was it because Dulles was now gravely ill? Was it because we saw Nasser becoming "progressively less aggressive"—as Eisenhower would say about the Egyptian president in 1959?[49]

The combination of the perceived weakness of our Arab friends and Dulles's absence and then death in May 1959 probably contributed the most to the shift. The evidence of change emerged one week after the last of the American troops were withdrawn from Lebanon. On November 4, 1958, President Eisenhower signed national security policy directive 5820/1, "US Policy Toward the Near East." Its core assumption was spelled out in its opening paragraphs:

> The most dangerous challenge to Western interests arises not from Arab nationalism per se but from the coincidence of many of its objectives with many of those of the USSR . . . It has become increasingly apparent that the prevention of further Soviet penetration of the Near East and progress in solving Near East problems depends on the degree to which the United States is able to work more closely with Arab nationalism and associate itself more closely with such aims and aspirations of the Arab people as are not contrary to the basic interests of the United States.[50]

In other words, our traditional Arab friends who had been in Nasser's crosshairs did not share the aims and aspirations of the Arab people. This was no doubt news to King Hussein, Crown Prince Faisal, who had taken over a number of King Saud's powers, and the leaders of Morocco and Tunisia. But in roughly the last year of the Eisenhower administration the impulse was to accommodate the Arab nationalists, who were seen as representing the wave of the future. The fact that they were also competing with each other—with Nasser soon at odds with Qassim in Iraq—did not alter the administration's approach: it continued to view the region in terms of the nationalists versus the monarchs.

There is one last point worth noting about Eisenhower's policy: his administration resisted all Israeli requests for advanced weapons of any kind. We would not arm Israel (except for one hundred recoilless rifles). But we were prepared to provide arms to Iraq after the coup, even though Qassim's words were anti-Western—and Assistant Secretary of State William Rountree faced demonstrations when he visited Baghdad in December 1958—particularly because the administration still hoped it might keep the new regime from a Soviet embrace.[51] That hope would prove groundless. Still, when it came to supplying U.S. arms, to Eisenhower, Iraq was a more acceptable recipient than Israel.

When Prime Minister Ben-Gurion met with President Eisenhower in New York in March 1960, his agenda focused on finally receiving advanced weapons from the United States.* Nasser was amassing more arms, and the radical regimes in Syria and Iraq had become a more threatening landscape. Ben-Gurion spoke about the dangers to Israel—the Jewish people had been fighting to survive for four thousand years and "the Israeli Republic is our last stand." It was a question of remaining as a free people or being "exterminated." He enumerated all the advantages the Egyptians had in different categories of air, ground, and naval arms over Israel. Israel had a desperate need for antiaircraft missiles given the numbers of Egyptian bombers, their payload, the number of Egyptian airfields from which attacks could be launched, the new bombers Egypt would soon be receiving from the Soviets, and the vulnerability of Israeli air bases—which needed to be protected to permit the Israeli air force to cover the mobilization of Israel's reserves so necessary in light of its small standing army. Ben-Gurion specifically asked for the Hawk antiaircraft missile.[52]

---

* No Israeli prime minister would be invited to the White House until Levi Eshkol met Lyndon Johnson in 1964.

Eisenhower forwarded the request to the State Department, at the same time offering two reasons for his continuing hesitancy to provide arms to Israel: first, he did not want the United States to become a party to the arms race in the region lest we lose our ability to promote peace between the sides; second, the United States should not become a partisan in supporting any party in the Middle East.[53]

In keeping with the president's reluctance, the State Department informed the Israelis a month later that Hawks could not be made available because of the needs of U.S. forces. Interestingly, Christian Herter, who had replaced John Foster Dulles as secretary of state, was initially sympathetic to Israel's request, believing that the Hawk was a defensive weapon and there was an Israeli justification for it. Moreover, he was uncomfortable with what he felt was the dishonesty of our response to the Israelis—Hawks could have been made available to Israel by 1961. But Herter soon fell in line with the orthodoxy of the administration as his department offered a full set of arguments as to why providing the Hawks would be a terrible idea—ranging from the fear of compromising the technology in the Hawk given Soviet penetration of Israel to the risk of Nasser moving closer to the Soviets if he saw us providing arms to Israel.[54]

All of Eisenhower's distancing from and pressure on Israel apparently counted for very little. After all, at the end of Ike's eight years in office, the United States could not afford to provide a defensive weapons system to Israel without pushing Nasser into a Soviet embrace. Apparently, massive arms deliveries from the Soviet Union to Egypt did not constitute an embrace—or justify weapons for Israel under the logic of the Eisenhower Doctrine.

The Eisenhower-Dulles Mind-set and Assumptions

Presidents and their secretaries of state are bound to have broadly shared outlooks on national security needs. Even if there are some differences in perspective, secretaries of state usually fall in line with their boss. But Eisenhower and Dulles came with worldviews that were very similar, and Eisenhower's impulse was to offer his general thinking and guidelines and have Dulles formulate and carry out the policy—and Dulles did that.

Both were determined to counter the Soviet threat. Both believed in international law. Both saw the Middle East and the Arabs as central in the competition with the Soviets, with Eisenhower at one point saying publicly that "as far as sheer value of territory is concerned, there is no more strategically important area in the world."[55] Geopolitical centrality and oil explained its value, with both men believing "that the prosperity and welfare of the entire Western world is inescapably dependent upon Mid East oil."[56] Both also believed that foreign policy and national security should be immune from political considerations—and that the Truman administration had violated that basic precept when it came to the Middle East. How else could one explain that George Marshall, Robert Lovett, George Kennan, Charles Bohlen, and Dean Acheson had clearly opposed partition and Jewish statehood, and yet Truman had nevertheless recognized Israel?

As far as Eisenhower and Dulles were concerned, domestic politics, not the country's overall interests, had determined Truman's decision. As noted earlier, in his first trip to the Middle East, in 1953, Dulles was determined to show the Arabs that our approach was no longer "subject to Jewish influence."[57] In 1955—in the immediate aftermath of the Soviet-Egyptian arms deal and at a time when Eisenhower was recovering from his first heart attack—Dulles organized a high-level meeting with Vice President Nixon and key cabinet officials to try to neutralize political criticism of the administration's policy in the Middle East. As he explained to the group, "We are in the present jam because the past Administration had always dealt with the Middle East from a political standpoint and had tried to meet the wishes of the Zionists in this country. That had created a basic antagonism with the Arabs. That was what the Russians were capitalizing on."[58]

In a conversation with Henry Luce, the media mogul, who was trying to dissuade him from having the United States vote for sanctions against Israel, Dulles said, "If we do not go along with sanctions that will be the end of any hope for us in the Middle East . . . I am aware how almost impossible it is in this country to carry out a foreign policy not approved by the Jews. Marshall and Forrestal learned that. I am going to try to have one."[59]

Eisenhower fundamentally agreed, referring to "our citizens of the eastern seaboard emotionally involved in the Zionist cause," who were likely to react negatively to his response to Israel's "aggression" against Egypt. But he was determined not to be influenced by political considerations and—like Dulles—felt our position in the Middle East depended on it.[60] He justified his demand in 1957 that Israel withdraw from the Sinai unconditionally in terms of our need to signal that Jewish influence did not control U.S. policy. This mind-set remained throughout his presidency. When he met with Nasser in New York in September 1960, Eisenhower explained that he acted the way he did during the Suez War because despite the looming election and the "Jewish vote," he would not let politics undermine our interests in the Middle East.[61]

What stands out, however, is not just that Ike and Dulles were determined to prevent political considerations from entering their policy calculus but also that they believed the key to our competing successfully with the Soviets in the Middle East was distancing from Israel. It was not enough not to show a bias toward Israel; it was necessary to make clear there was space between us. That is why both agreed that we must not provide Israel arms. That is why they insisted that Israel must not be a part of any regional pact, even though the Israelis offered us bases and their forces. That is why both stood firm that we should penalize the Israelis when they transgressed— whether it was trying to divert Jordan River water, retaliate for fedayeen attacks, or attack Egypt in concert with the British and French.*

Embedded in their attitudes was another premise: the Arabs would be natural partners if we could create the right distance from Israel or remove it as an obstacle to our ties. That is why Dulles suggested to Eisenhower that if he could just get through the 1956 "political campaign without giving in to Zionist pressures for substantial arms to Israel, this would encourage the Arabs and have a very good effect on them."[62] It is why Eisenhower could say, even at the time of Lebanon's intervention, that "except for Israel we could form a viable policy in the area," as if Israel were the reason for the Nasserist coup in Iraq or Chamoun's desire for a second term.[63] For the Eisenhower administration, from the outset, Israel had been a liability. In the words of Dulles's first assistant secretary for the Bureau of Near Eastern Affairs, Henry Byroade, it was "the major stumbling block to good relations between the U.S. and the Arab states."[64]

The mind-set of the administration was so deeply ingrained that even when Israel provided things of value to us, the information was exploited often without acknowledging up the chain that the Israelis had been the source. The CIA had developed a relationship with its Israeli counterpart, the Mossad, during the Truman administration. James Jesus Angleton would remain the agency's link to the Mossad from 1951 until 1974. He was completely disconnected from the Middle Eastern section of the CIA, at least in part because of the collective view that Israel had nothing to tell us about the

---

* In his retirement, Eisenhower came to regret the decisions he had made during the Suez Crisis in 1956–57, seeing his actions as having only weakened our allies and emboldened Nasser, though, as is often the case, such policy regrets seldom translate into lessons learned. Makovsky and Ross, *Myths, Illusions, and Peace,* pp. 44–45.

Middle East and because Angleton was not in the habit of revealing all he was getting from the Israelis—and was very protective of his relationship.[65] Throughout the Eisenhower administration and beyond, Mossad provided extensive intelligence on what was going on behind the Iron Curtain. But as Efraim Halevy, the former head of Mossad, told me, this was a one-way flow of information from 1951 to 1967. Israel provided information, while getting none in return. One Israeli intelligence coup was the delivery of Khrushchev's so-called secret speech to the Communist Party of the Soviet Union in February 1956 in which he denounced Stalin. The administration was desperate to get hold of it, and Mossad delivered it to Angleton.[66]

Even though Eisenhower knew some of what the Israelis had done, it did little to alter his view that our interests were tied to the Arabs, and the Israelis made it difficult for us to have a better relationship. If nothing else, this meant that Eisenhower and Dulles tended to view the Israelis with suspicion. They perceived Israel as inherently aggressive and geared toward expansion. Recall Dulles's comment to the Lebanese about readiness "to prevent aggression by Israel." Consider also Eisenhower's response to a question at a 1954 press conference about whether we might provide Israel military assistance: "We are not rendering anyone assistance to start a war or to indulge in conflict with others of our friends."[67] He did not make similar comments about providing arms to Arab states. It was Israel, in his words, that was trying to ensnare us as its protector.

The conviction that Israel had an expansionist agenda may well have been cemented by a 1953 top secret State Department report on Israel, which concluded that Israel was not yet economically viable but was continuing to call for the ingathering of Jews to Israel. This would lead, in the words of the report, to "pressures to expand Israel's frontiers into the rich lands of the Tigris and Euphrates Valleys and northward into the settled lands of Syria."[68] U.S. policy was focused on trying to shrink Israel's size to accommodate the Arabs.

Both Eisenhower and Dulles believed that the solution for Israel was also to accommodate the Arabs. Eisenhower thought Israel was too worried about the threat from the Arabs. It needed "to woo Arab goodwill."[69] Similarly, Dulles at one point asked the Israelis to "play the part of a good neighbor to the Arabs."[70] At a different juncture he suggested that they "review their policies from the viewpoint of international harmony" and adopt a "temperate, moderate mood which would promote international goodwill."[71] And to the Senate Foreign Relations Committee he said that for its national defense, Israel should rely on "collective security" and the UN.[72] This was essentially a means of justifying our refusal to provide them arms (if only they behaved differently, they would not need these arms). It was part and parcel of an approach geared toward attracting the Arabs, even if the Arab rejection of Israel and the use of fedayeen attacks gave the Israelis no reason to think that goodwill would beget anything except increased threats to the state's survival.

Such an approach may have justified our distancing from Israel, but it also depended on the Arabs responding. Eisenhower observed that Nasser was the "complete stumbling block" on the Anderson mission. He also assumed that the Arabs would favor peace and not use Israel as an issue on which to compete with each other. But no one on the Arab side was prepared even to hint at acceptance of Israel, much less deal with it. And yet so deeply ingrained were the presumptions on what we needed in the Middle East that it did not change the president's view on what Israel needed to do.

These core assumptions about how to manage the region included an overly simplistic view of the Arab world that failed to come to grips with the implications of the inter-Arab competition. Kermit Roosevelt and Miles Copeland were convinced that Nasser embodied the authentic views of the Arabs and calibrated our policy to be on his good side. They believed that a friendly relationship with Nasser would lead naturally to achieving our objectives in the Middle East. For them, support for the Baghdad Pact and Hashemite Iraq would create a rival to Nasser and add to his suspicions of our friendship; they thought it a terrible mistake to revoke the offer to finance the Aswan Dam and embarrass Nasser. Copeland responded dramatically to this decision and the way it was conveyed: "The secretary of state has gone mad!"[73] They did not favor Eisenhower's effort to find and promote alternatives to Nasser in the region. Roosevelt would later alter his views toward Nasser and become a staunch opponent in the 1960s. But during the Eisenhower administration, he was part of a small group that was partial to Nasser, even at a time when the president and the secretary of state saw him as a threat.

While there was some disagreement over which potential Arab partners to pursue to further the goal of keeping the Soviets at bay in the region, there was firm unanimity among policy makers on the need to distance the United States from Israel. Unlike in the Truman administration, there was no strong advocate for a relationship with Israel. There was no Clark Clifford or David Niles. No one in the White House was offering a countervailing viewpoint. That should come as no surprise, because for Eisenhower, there was no place for political considerations in his policy toward the Middle East.

Instead, there was a powerful groupthink when it came to Israel. No one seemed to draw any lessons from the reality of ongoing Arab competition. Eisenhower certainly recognized the competition, writing in his diary in March 1956 (seven months before Suez), "I suggested to the State Department that we begin to build up some other individual as a prospective leader of the Arab world—in the thought that mutually antagonistic personal ambitions might disrupt the aggressive plans that Nasser is evidently developing."[74] He tried after Suez with an invitation to Saudi Arabia's King Saud to come to Washington, but the king refused. Indeed, while all such efforts failed, we remained riveted on Israel as the cause of our problems in the Middle East. We did not look at the inter-Arab rivalry as something that determined the priorities of individual Arab leaders. For Nasser, leading the Arab world dictated a certain approach. As Eisenhower observed, this would make him unwilling to end the conflict with Israel. But it also had implications for how Nasser dealt with other Arab leaders, and they with him. They were not partners; they were rivals, and they often sought to subvert each other.

The number-one priority for the Arab regimes was survival. If the focus of a regime was building up its security apparatus, it would look to whoever could provide the arms. However, this fact did not seem to penetrate the mind-set of the Eisenhower administration. The collective focus was on the Soviet Union; in the eyes of the national security apparatus, it was Israel that made it hard for the Arabs to cooperate with us against the Soviets.

But the Soviets were not the focus in the Middle East; priorities were local. Before Nasser emerged as the embodiment of Arab nationalism, Dulles found in his meetings in Egypt in 1953 that the Egyptians were preoccupied with ending the British occupation of the Suez Canal zone—not with Israel. General Naguib described the British—not the Jews—as the "source of all our ills" and later clarified this by saying, "After the British get out I am sure that I can reach an agreement with Israel."[75]

Similarly, while the Iraqis, Jordanians, and Saudis chose not to intervene militarily to overthrow the Syrian regime, their interest in the first place was clearly not about Soviet arms going to Damascus; rather, their concerns were that the new Syrian leaders were too oriented toward Nasser. It was Eisenhower who worried about the Israelis in this scenario, not the Arabs.

Their preoccupation with survival and security meant those Arab leaders who depended on us for their protection would seek more from us regardless of our ties to Israel. Ibn Saud had done so after Truman recognized Israel—actually *increasing* cooperation with us through the Arabian-

American Oil Company. His son King Saud would seek more American arms during Eisenhower's administration, regardless of ongoing complaints about Israel. Indeed, at a time when President Eisenhower thought the Saudis were prepared to act against the Syrian regime in 1957, the king raised his concerns about possible Israeli naval activity in the Gulf of Aqaba and complained about the "slowness of our arms deliveries" and the need to accelerate them—something Eisenhower acted to implement.[76]

Eisenhower and those around him were incapable of seeing that Israel would not prevent Arab states from preserving what they wanted in the relationship with the United States. So long as the Arabs felt that we would stand by them if they were threatened by their neighbors, this would trump other considerations, including Israel. What damaged the United States was the perception that it would not stand by its friends. Eisenhower heard this from an unexpected source in 1959, when the Lebanese prime minister, Rashid Karami, a Sunni generally supportive of Nasser's nationalism, visited the White House. The prime minister told the president that U.S. behavior during the Suez conflict had led him to believe that America would never "resort to force to support friends."[77] Eisenhower related this story in his memoirs to show how our use of force in Lebanon in 1958 had corrected this impression and had a favorable effect; ironically, it also indicated how badly he had misread the consequences of our behavior during Suez.

Eisenhower and Dulles presumed to know Arab sensitivities and priorities, and were overly defensive about Israel as a result. Eisenhower's description of a conversation he had with Tunisian president Habib Bourguiba three weeks after Suez on November 21, 1956, at the White House, is revealing: "I mentioned Israel, expressing the hope that our interest in the existence of this postwar state in the Middle East would not poison American relations with the Moslem nations, whether with the older states or new ones, like Tunisia. Bourguiba replied, 'My attitude regarding Israel will never, in any way, adversely affect Tunisian relations with the United States."[78] Eisenhower goes on to say that he was at pains to show how interested we were in Muslim culture, religion, customs, and the like. There is no evidence of his having heard what Bourguiba said about Tunisia preserving its relations with us irrespective of Israel. Clearly, at the time, Iraq, Jordan, Lebanon, Saudi Arabia, Libya, and Morocco shared this priority.

This is not to say that our Arab friends at the time were happy about Israel. They, too, would condemn Israel and in public completely reject it. This is the essential point to keep in mind: no Arab state at this time was prepared to make peace with Israel. None would respond to our entreaties on peace. Their Arab competitors used any perceived softening vis-à-vis Israel against them—and that made them worry about their stability and security. So dealing with Israel was out for the Arabs. But relations with us were a separate matter; they did not depend on what we did with Israel.

No senior official ever wondered why, when the United States pressured Israel, we never benefited with any Arab state. None of the Arab leaders we already had a relationship with was prepared to do anything beyond what he was already doing with us. Nasser, after we urged Israel to withdraw from the Sinai, not only continued his pursuit of Soviet arms, he also retreated from his commitments to Dag Hammarskjöld on Gaza. Arabs with whom we had no ties showed no interest in drawing closer to us. Their priorities were simply elsewhere. Instead of affecting the Arabs' behavior, Eisenhower merely raised their expectations. Arab leaders came to expect us to pressure Israel, and in subsequent administrations, they would hold up the Eisenhower administration as a model to be emulated.

Theoretically, one could argue that if we got something from Arab leaders for such distancing or pressure, it might be worth doing it. But we never did.

Eisenhower failed on most of the objectives he set for himself in the Middle East. He was unable to keep the Soviets out of the area. Instead of being strengthened, U.S. and Western influence was weakened. The number of U.S. friends in the area declined. And we made no headway on peace. Ironically, Eisenhower's policy reflected what those who had so opposed Truman wanted us to do vis-à-vis the Arabs. And yet courting the Arabs through pressuring Israel bought us nothing. But once again, no one asked whether there was something wrong with our assumptions about the Arabs and what mattered in the area.

President Kennedy would view the Eisenhower legacy in the Middle East as a failure. As Warren Bass observed, Kennedy saw a Middle East in which the Soviets had made gains in Cairo, Damascus, and Baghdad, the Arab kings were jittery about Nasser's rise, and Israelis felt a distinct chill. He believed he could do better in the region—with both the Arabs and the Israelis.[79]

3

THE KENNEDY ADMINISTRATION: BREAKING TABOOS AND PURSUING A NEW BALANCE

For John F. Kennedy, the Middle East was an interest but not a preoccupation. Berlin, Cuba, the Congo, Vietnam, China (and its possible possession of nuclear weapons), and of course the Soviets more generally commanded his attention. Unlike the Eisenhower administration, Kennedy did not see the Middle East as the central arena for competition with the Soviets. In this respect, Kennedy was more like Truman—and not just because they were Democrats. There was no circle of containment to be closed around the Soviet Union in the Middle East.

After all, the Soviets were already in the Middle East. Therefore, it was too late for a strategy to prevent their penetration—an aim the Eisenhower administration had clearly failed to achieve. The question was, What could be achieved in the Middle East? Kennedy and his advisers saw new social and political forces emerging in the developing world that were not interested in being part of either the West or the East. Within the Kennedy administration there was a sense that we could relate to such forces and affect their behaviors—and win in our competition with the Soviets.

In the thousand days of the Kennedy administration, there was no grand strategy for the Middle East. There was an impulse, however, to engage the Arabs without distancing the United States from Israel. Grand breakthroughs might not be possible, but managing the area and avoiding conflict could be.

During Kennedy's presidency, there would be no war between the Arab states and Israel. Instead, this period was marked by inter-Arab turmoil, with us caught in the middle.

Concern for Israeli Security, Outreach, and the Pursuit of Nasser and Peace

Not surprisingly, the strategy began with a new effort at outreach. The president sent personalized letters to Arab heads of state. According to Myer ("Mike") Feldman, deputy counsel to the president in the White House, Kennedy sent letters to thirteen Arab leaders, and although there was a basic text, the letters were tailored to each leader; the president went through "eight or ten drafts . . . before he was satisfied with it." According to Feldman, Kennedy "wanted to give the impression that he was seeking a dialogue with them . . . and that they should feel free to write him personally and not even through the regular State Department channels. And, he wanted to show that he was sympathetic to all their legitimate aspirations. At the same time, he did not want to give the impression that he was siding with them in their conflict with Israel."[1]

While the president would say in the letters to Nasser and the others that there was no easy solution to the Arab-Israeli issue, he spoke of economic development and how the ideas of Lincoln, Wilson, and Franklin Roosevelt naturally lent themselves to respect for "the emergence of vigorous independent Arab states, respected as sovereign equals in the international community."[2] The letters clearly were designed to highlight our natural connections to the Arab people and our desire for a genuine friendship.

For Robert Komer, the NSC official in charge of the Middle East, and the State Department, there was another purpose to these letters. Shortly after the administration came into office, the Egyptian ambassador to the United States met with Secretary of State Dean Rusk and told him that even though Egypt shared America's opposition to communism, Soviet help was needed to counter the Israelis and their nuclear program. The Arabs worried that the Kennedy administration would follow the path of the Truman administration, which they perceived to be favorable to Israel. (Eisenhower and Dulles had told them as much.)[3] The letters, in Komer's words, were designed to reassure and blunt "the natural fears of the Arabs that any new Administration and particularly a Democratic one" might resemble Truman's and not Eisenhower's.[4]

It is hard to miss the irony here: Eisenhower was seen as having failed, as having gained nothing from the Arabs. And yet supposedly the Arabs wanted his policies. Komer and the State Department felt the need to reassure them in this regard, and the president, as part of outreach to the Arabs, was prepared to accept this presumption. His letter to Nasser went so far as to refer to our posture during "the critical days of 1956," an unsubtle way of suggesting that he, too, would be prepared to stop the Israelis, or at least not be influenced by domestic politics.

But there was something different in Kennedy's approach. Even prior to sending these letters, the president had agreed to meet Prime Minister David Ben-Gurion in New York in May 1961. Yes, he was reaching out to the Arabs by sending a message of friendship and emphasizing his readiness to work with them on economic development—and to address the Arab-Israeli issue—but he was also going to see the Israeli prime minister. Unlike Eisenhower, who would not see the Israeli leader until his last year in office, Kennedy would see him in his first, and the theme of balance in the relationship—and not public distancing from Israel—would shape the policy.

At President Kennedy's meeting with Ben-Gurion on May 30 at the Waldorf-Astoria in New York, the Israeli leader had two principal items on his agenda: Nasser and Hawk missiles—and the two were inextricably related.[5] Reprising an argument he had made with Eisenhower, Ben-Gurion argued for receiving these antiaircraft missiles as a means for offsetting the Egyptian advantage and limiting Israeli vulnerability. He also suggested that Kennedy seek at the summit in Vienna the next week with Khrushchev a joint U.S.-Soviet statement committing the two to preserving the territorial integrity of *all* states in the Middle East, which Ben-Gurion suggested could make war less likely. This, too, was a proposal the Israelis had raised during the Eisenhower administration as a backdoor way of gaining an American commitment to Israel's security and the sanctity of its borders.

While Kennedy did not offer Ben-Gurion any new commitments in this meeting, his tone was different from Eisenhower's. He agreed that "Nasser will make our lives as difficult as possible," but in a theme that would persist throughout the administration, Kennedy justified his letter and outreach to Nasser as a means of potentially influencing and tempering his behavior—and that was also in Israel's interest. (Years later, President Obama would use a similar argument to justify his outreach to the Muslims early in his administration.) On the arms request, Kennedy echoed arguments of the past when he suggested that providing Hawk missiles could trigger an arms spiral in the region and might provoke the Arabs to seek their own SAMs.

And yet Kennedy also sounded a very different note. He said he did "not want to see Israel at a disadvantage" and would not want Israel to be in "such a position of inferiority that an attack on it would be encouraged."* When Ben-Gurion argued that Israel was already in a position of inferiority, Kennedy again took note of the danger of an arms race, but then he summarized their discussion on this issue, saying, "We are reluctant to give Israel missiles and you understand that, but we would be disturbed if Israel should get into a situation that would invite attack. We will keep the matter under continuing review in our Administration, I can assure you."[6]

The Eisenhower administration never acknowledged that Israel might have a justification for weapons—after all, it was supposed to use its goodwill and the support of the international community to counter Arab threats. Kennedy, by contrast, was creating a rationale to provide the Hawks if he deemed that Israel's deterrent required the weapon. For Kennedy, outreach to both Arabs and Israelis was now under way. The United States could have relations with both. With the Arabs, he had signaled a wish to connect with their desire for independence; with Israel, he had conveyed an appreciation for their security needs.

To understand the broad approach of the administration to the Middle East, it is worth noting the National Intelligence Estimate (NIE) issued on June 27, 1961. Titled "Nasser and the Future of Arab Nationalism," the NIE concluded that the "long-term outlook for the conservative and Western-aligned regimes is bleak." Much like Eisenhower's national security directive on November 4, 1958, Nasser and Arab nationalism were seen as the wave of the future. But the 1961 NIE made clear that Nasser was facing real economic problems, his military dependence on the Soviets was not seen as buying the Russians much, and while he would be very mindful not to be dominated by either East or West, Nasser would "remain [the] foremost leader" of militant Arab nationalism and its "symbol for the foreseeable future."[7]

The NIE seemed to lend credence to the argument that there were potential benefits to reaching out to Nasser. After the NIE, Robert Komer at the NSC wrote to Walt Rostow, the deputy national security adviser, and said we should pursue Nasser with economic assistance not because we could outbid the Soviets but because "we must live with him and he must live with us."[8]

---

* This view was a profound departure from the attitudes of both Presidents Truman and Eisenhower on how arming Israel might affect the region.

The logic of pursuing Nasser was made more compelling when, in August, his warm and favorable response to the president's letter arrived. Unlike the responses from the other Arab leaders, which had come earlier and were filled with complaints, Nasser's message expressed appreciation for the president's outreach and emphasized that the only real problems were Palestine and Israeli expansionism. He complained about past American policies and the illogic of pursuing the Baghdad Pact, noting that its collapse showed the wrongheaded nature of our past policies. He urged the president to enact a new approach. Those who were enthusiastic about the outreach to Nasser saw a real possibility.

But in September, the Syrians seceded from the UAR. The coup was engineered by Syrian businessmen and their allies in the military—both of whom had chafed under the heavy hand of the Egyptians. Nasser had approached the union not as one of two equal partners but as Egypt as the leader and Syria as a supplicant. As such, he simply shipped senior Egyptian officials to Damascus to run the military, the economy, and political life. With Nasser about to enact far-reaching nationalization of Syrian businesses, key Syrians carried out a coup against the Egyptians in charge.

In the early hours after the coup, the Kennedy administration was at a loss about what this would mean for U.S. policy. Having begun to see Nasser as the wave of the future, they were uncertain how to respond. However, there was no such doubt among the Saudis, Jordanians, Lebanese, or Israelis. All saw a profound weakening of Nasser as a good thing. His ideology and his appeal were suffering a body blow. Suddenly, Nasser's goal of the Arab world in his image of pan-Arab unity was set back. Yet the relief and glee of our traditional Arab friends and the Israelis were not shared in the administration. Initially, there was apprehension that Nasser might militarily intervene to preserve the union. There was worry about a regional war if the Jordanians sent forces to shore up the Syrians in the face of Egyptian threats or intervention. And, echoing fears during the Eisenhower administration, Kennedy was concerned that the Israelis would take advantage of Jordanian actions and annex the West Bank. The State Department cabled instructions to our ambassador in Jordan to make clear to King Hussein that he should stay out of this and do nothing to exacerbate the situation. A similar instruction was sent to our ambassador in Israel to warn the Israelis against adding to the uncertainty by moving or increasing the readiness of their forces.[9]

The State Department also sent instructions to Cairo to convey that it was business as usual for us. Komer wrote Rostow that this was a time for us to be extra nice to Nasser. We did not rush to recognize the new regime in Damascus even though King Hussein urged us to do so; our ambassador to Jordan told him that this could spark a regional conflict "and quite possibly World War III."[10] More than anything else, what seemed to guide the administration initially was the fear that Nasser's loss of power was less an opportunity than a danger and that it was important to cool things so that a regional conflict would not erupt. The level of concern actually led, remarkably, to a message from President Kennedy to Nasser on October 3, lauding him for his "efforts to stabilize the situation by peaceful means."[11] In the aftermath of this message, the administration concluded that Nasser had accepted he could do nothing about the coup, and the sense of crisis passed.

So the U.S. approach to Nasser remained. With the passing of the crisis, Komer wrote to McGeorge Bundy, the national security adviser, and Walt Rostow, his deputy, convinced that this was "the best opportunity since 1954 for a limited marriage of convenience with the guy who I think is still, and will remain, the Mister Big of the Arab World."[12]

Even though Nasser was insecure in Cairo—making arrests to shore up his power and guard against a coup—he remained the "Mister Big of the Arab World" to many in the administration. During the fall and winter of 1962, Kennedy decided to increase U.S. economic assistance to Egypt. In fact, during his administration's three years, we would provide roughly $500 million in economic assistance, two-thirds of which would come from funds that were part of a developmental assistance program that sold excess foodstuffs overseas. (The aid was roughly double the amount the Truman and Eisenhower administrations together had provided Egypt.)

In February 1962, Chester Bowles, the former governor of Connecticut who was now the president's envoy to the third world, visited Cairo. He saw real potential in trying to wean Nasser away from troublemaking in the region by focusing him on domestic development. In a cable sent while on the trip, he wrote, "If Nasser can gradually be led to forsake the microphone for the bulldozer, he may assume a key role in bringing the Middle East peacefully into our modern world."[13] The administration would target developmental, technical, and financial assistance to Egypt. The Egyptians, in response, would send their minister of the economy to Washington for talks on expanding our economic aid to Egypt. There were those in the administration—in the State Department and the White House—who wanted not only to expand our economic support for Nasser but also to cement the relationship by having him make a state visit to Washington.

But enthusiasm for Nasser was not universal. The king of Saudi Arabia came to Washington and saw President Kennedy on February 13, shortly before Bowles's visit to Cairo. King Saud told Kennedy that Nasser was "a Communist who presents a real danger to the Arab World."[14] Similarly, at this time, the French retained their hostility to him and opposed IMF loans to Cairo. Of course, Ben-Gurion continued to see Nasser as a grave threat to Israel. He argued that economic assistance from the United States would be diverted to acquire arms from the Soviets.

Perhaps because of these factors and limited enthusiasm for Nasser in the Congress, President Kennedy favored outreach but remained wary of the Egyptian president. Komer wrote Bundy in late February that Kennedy was "still in an anti-Nasser mood." Nonetheless, during the spring of 1962, the United States continued to strengthen ties, and Nasser seemed responsive. With Egypt clearly in mind, Bowles went so far as to say publicly that "the Middle Eastern nations . . . are becoming less focused on conflicts with their neighbors and more interested in their own internal development." There was, he added, "a kind of quiet political and economic relaxation which, with a measure of good luck, may gradually make for lessening tensions and greater opportunities for all concerned."[15]

Not surprisingly, at this point we began to make more of a push to defuse the Arab-Israeli conflict; since we were engaged with Nasser and considered him the key Arab leader, it made sense to see what was possible.

The focal point of the effort was on Arab refugees. Even as a senator, Kennedy had expressed concern about them.[16] In his initial letters to Arab leaders, Kennedy had made a reference to the refugee issue and later had raised it with Ben-Gurion in his meeting. As Mike Feldman observes in his oral history interviews, Kennedy's approach to peace was generally practical. He favored building bridges where possible, including on issues like water and desalinization. Still, although his expectations were low, Kennedy was willing to make a cautious test on the refugee issue.

Joseph Johnson, president of the Carnegie Endowment, was selected to probe the possibilities of reaching some understandings. With Johnson serving as a U.S. special representative on the UN's Conciliation Commission for Palestine, a body set up in 1948, Kennedy could maintain a low profile on any peace efforts. In September 1961, Johnson set out on a fact-finding mission to the area. The Israelis were generally fearful of anything that hinted at giving the refugees a right to return to Israel. Being mindful of Israeli concerns, Johnson sought to create a step-by-step approach with a pilot project involving a small number of refugees. The Israelis feared a slippery slope, particularly since the refugees were going to be asked where they wanted to go. The Jordanians feared the opposite: that the refugees might simply want to be repatriated in their host country.

Johnson wrote an initial report and asked for comments. The Israelis did not respond, but the Arabs did, and Johnson incorporated at least some of their comments into his next draft. By the summer, according to Feldman, Johnson felt he had developed a workable proposal and wanted to know where the White House stood.[17] When he presented his proposal to the president, though, Kennedy's opinion was that neither the Israelis nor the Arabs would accept it.[18] Johnson had been joined in the meeting by Robert Strong, the deputy assistant secretary of state for the Bureau of Near Eastern Affairs, who argued that the proposal was sound, and if properly presented to the Israelis, they might accede.[19]

As a result, Kennedy decided that Feldman, whom he often relied on as an emissary of the American Jewish community and the Israelis, should be the one to present it to them. The president needed to know first whether the Israelis could accept this proposal before going to Nasser with it.[20] This required secrecy: Feldman would go to Israel under the cover of taking a vacation. If Ben-Gurion accepted the proposal—which Feldman described in essence as "the Israelis taking those who, under free choice, chose to come to Israel and the Arabs taking those refugees who, under free choice, chose to go to their countries"[21]—Feldman would communicate with our ambassador in Cairo, who would then approach Nasser.

Interestingly, according to Feldman, the president remained skeptical, asking "It's free choice for who?" A question that Ben-Gurion immediately seized on, fearing that Arab states would force the Arab refugees to insist on going to Israel. Nonetheless, Feldman succeeded in getting Ben-Gurion and Golda Meir to agree to take 10 percent of the refugees if the Arabs would take 90 percent. The key was Feldman's emphasis on that part of the Johnson report that "stated clearly that Israel would not be required to take more than they could readily absorb."[22]

On this basis, Feldman reported that the Israelis would accept the Johnson plan provided the language remained precisely as he had given it to Meir and Ben-Gurion.[23] After informing the State Department of what the Israelis could accept, he cabled our ambassador in Egypt, John Badeau, to inform Nasser. In their meeting, Nasser listened and offered only limited comment, and this was interpreted in the State Department as a positive sign. As Feldman recalls, "At that point, well, we thought that there was a pretty good chance of solving the refugee problem."[24]

Kennedy did not share the optimism. Being largely silent and noncommittal did not translate in Kennedy's eyes into an agreement. His skepticism was well-founded. Although Nasser was open to a process of resettlement and repatriation in Israel and the Arab world, his actual comments, while limited, should not have been interpreted as encouraging: he simply said there should be an unlimited right of return for refugees in order to supplant the "basic Zionist concept" with a "bi-national state."[25] Notwithstanding this position, Robert Strong and his State Department colleagues saw an opening and began to work with Johnson to make his proposal more acceptable to the Arabs. In September at the UN, he shared the new draft with Golda Meir. She was livid. She called Feldman, who went to see her in New York. She showed him the new proposal which, by their mutual count, had sixty-two changes in it. What the State Department, according to Feldman, regarded as minor alterations, the Israelis saw as fundamental. Meir told Feldman, "This is not the plan we agreed to in Israel so you can't hold us to that." And she added that "as it is phrased now we have to object to it violently because this does not have the kind of safeguard against taking too many refugees."[26]

Feldman asked Meir not to publicly reject the proposal at that point. He assumed—correctly—that the Arabs would reject it when it was presented formally at the UN. It was better, in Feldman's eyes, that the Arabs appear to be the recalcitrant side. At this point—with both Arabs and Israelis opposed—Kennedy saw no reason to continue to push the Johnson plan.

Hawks for Israel, Yemen, and Tension over Israel's Nuclear Program

According to Feldman, the State Department still hoped to revive the plan in the context of the sale of Hawk missiles to Israel. For the secretary of state and others, the Johnson plan and the Hawks were linked. They felt the Israelis should get the Hawks only if they did something meaningful on peace. When Feldman met with Ben-Gurion and Meir, the first thing he told them was that the United States would provide the missiles. They were "ecstatic" to hear this news. But the reason for his trip—and its secrecy—was to make the case for the Johnson refugee proposal. The strategy of telling Israel's leaders about the Hawks at the beginning of the meeting was designed to create a more favorable context for raising the refugee issue.

Why did the Kennedy administration decide to provide the missiles and thus break the taboo on providing advanced arms to Israel? Several factors explain the about-face. First, the president had made clear that though he was wary of triggering an arms race, he also took into account the importance of preventing Israeli vulnerability. The Israelis had kept up the drumbeat on their need for the Hawks, given the bombers and fighter aircraft the Soviets were providing Egypt. Shimon Peres, Ben-Gurion's deputy in the Defense Ministry, made a visit to Washington in May 1962, and his meetings in the Pentagon and the White House had an effect.

Second, there was a real change in the views of the civilian leadership of the Pentagon. Secretary of Defense Robert McNamara, Assistant Secretary of Defense Paul Nitze, and Bill Bundy (Nitze's deputy and brother of McGeorge Bundy) became convinced that the Israelis had a legitimate need. Komer would take note of the change the next month: "Nitze and MacN think mil. bal. has changed."[27] What he was getting at is that the balance had changed against the Israelis—and this marked a real shift in attitude. Unlike in its prestate days when the Jewish community in Palestine was seen as weak and in need of rescue from the Arabs, the persistent theme of the national security establishment about Israel, particularly after the Suez War, was that it was militarily stronger and not in need of any arms from us. This had suited the State Department, which saw only high costs in providing arms to Israel.

But McNamara, Nitze, and Bundy recognized that the continuing flow of Soviet weapons to Egypt and Iraq had shifted the balance. A month prior to Shimon Peres's trip to the United States, Bundy wrote to Phillips Talbot, the assistant secretary of state for the Bureau of Near Eastern Affairs, that he was "a little concerned whether we are getting into an unduly inflexible position on sales to Israel of sophisticated equipment." Sounding like Kennedy on the importance of preserving the Israeli deterrent, he continued, "The increasing Soviet deliveries to Egypt highlight the problem, which is largely one of preserving a military balance under which neither side would be tempted to attack the other."[28] Shimon Peres played on the theme of imbalances and how the Hawks could help reduce Israel's vulnerability—and Bundy, during Peres's trip, conveyed to his State Department colleagues that given the threat now posed by the Egyptian air force, the Pentagon believed that Israel needed an effective defense for its air bases and thus had a "valid military basis" to ask for the Hawks.[29]

Third, the theme of balance figured not just militarily but politically as well. Outreach to Nasser had its share of critics domestically. Nasser's public rhetoric generally retained its anti-Western character, and yet we were justifying public monies to go to Egypt. Providing arms to Israel could temper criticism of aid to Egypt coming from Israel's supporters, particularly in the Congress.

Kennedy did not base his decision to provide the Hawks on political considerations. Still, he could see how to take advantage of the decision once it was made. The provision of Hawks would not be publicly released to the press until September. Prior to the announcement, Kennedy wanted Jewish leaders from around the country and key Israeli supporters in the Congress to be briefed. Mike Feldman would be largely responsible for the outreach.[30]

To be sure, President Kennedy was not immune to concerns about how the Arabs—Nasser, in particular—would react. He wanted Nasser to know about the Hawks before the sale became public knowledge. Ambassador Badeau and Robert Strong went to see Nasser once they had heard from Feldman on the Israeli reaction to the Johnson plan. Whereas Feldman had led with the Hawks to create the context for his discussion on refugees, Badeau and Strong now led with the Johnson plan and our effort to tackle the refugee issue before informing Nasser about the Hawks for Israel. Badeau reported that Nasser did not get overly exercised. When the news of the sale leaked a month later, on September 26, and it was revealed that Nasser had been consulted in advance—which would make Nasser appear to be colluding with us—his mood changed. But even though his press attacked the United States for the sale, Nasser did not lose interest in preserving the assistance he was receiving from the United States.

The anticipation of a terrible price to be paid for the United States helping Israel turned out to be unjustified. To be sure, the State Department had sent out a cable saying the Hawk was a defensive weapon and this would not be a precedent for future arms to Israel. But given State Department fears that our position could be undercut in the area—and even the president's concern that Nasser might walk away from our efforts at outreach to him— the Arab reaction once again tended to indicate that their bilateral relations with the United States were largely independent of the U.S.-Israel relationship.

To be fair, there was another development in the region as the news of the Hawk sale broke. The longtime monarch in Yemen, Imam Ahmad bin Yahya, died on September 19, 1962, and on the 26th, the day the news of the Hawk sale became public, Crown Prince Muhammad al-Badr, Ahmad's son and heir to the crown, was ousted by military officers. Al-Badr fled to Saudi Arabia. When Secretary of State Rusk saw the Saudi crown prince in New York at this time (both were in town for the opening of the UN General

Assembly session), Faisal did not raise the Hawks sale. The upheaval in Yemen was his preoccupation and priority. Back in Cairo, Nasser had been quick to recognize the new Yemeni regime and its self-proclaimed revolutionaries. They declared themselves a progressive vanguard identified with Arab nationalism, and Nasser, after the humiliation of the UAR split one year earlier, was only too ready to offer them support. Faisal saw this as a profound threat to his kingdom. He feared that Nasser was seeking to gain a foothold in the Arabian peninsula. Faisal charged that Nasser intended to make Saudi Arabia his next target—and the Voice of the Arabs radio station, Nasser's mouthpiece in Cairo, was saying as much.

Faisal visited Washington the next week. When he met with President Kennedy, he again did not raise the issue of Israel or the Hawks sale. He was riveted instead on the Egyptian threat. The Saudis and Jordanians had been leery of the administration's outreach to Nasser from the outset. Already in June, the State Department, in a memo to McGeorge Bundy, had warned about Saudi perceptions of the outreach, saying that "the Saudis now appear to feel our aid to the UAR implies a lessening of the U.S. concern for Saudi Arabia."[31] Now Faisal told the president that the threat in Yemen was coming from the Egyptians, that the Soviets and the Egyptians were using our aid to threaten the monarchies. Much like Ben-Gurion, who believed that Nasser could use our aid to leverage his support from the Soviets, the Saudis, too, saw Nasser using us and not the other way around.

The Saudis wanted reassurance that the United States would pressure Nasser to stop. But the administration felt the Saudis needed to be more open to reform. This could lessen the threat from the outside—a threat we were interpreting as fed at least in part by the repressive nature of Saudi Arabia and the other conservative monarchies. Kennedy suggested as much to Faisal.

Faisal was not interested in discussing internal reform or the sale of Hawks to Israel. He wanted new American commitments toward Saudi security: provision of arms and declarations of backing for the kingdom. Kennedy promised to accelerate F-5A aircraft deliveries and naval visits to Saudi ports to demonstrate our support.*

The Saudis were our leading Arab supplier of oil. But Nasser was still seen as a modernizer and a harbinger of the future in the region. Outreach to him was still the policy—a policy that now became much trickier as Nasser,

---

* The similarities with Obama's need to reassure the Saudis today about our outreach to Iran and a possible nuclear deal are striking.

seeing a chance to recoup the luster of being the beacon of Pan-Arabism, sent thousands of Egyptian troops to Yemen to shore up the new regime against the royalists who were fighting it from the hinterlands. Very quickly, a proxy war was emerging in Yemen that pitted Nasser against the Saudis and the Jordanians who were backing the tribes resisting the new regime.

This proxy war soon began to escalate. Nasser not only deployed more than twenty thousand Egyptian troops to Yemen within the first six weeks of the fighting but also began to bomb across the Saudi border to try to disrupt the supplies the Saudis were providing the royalists. Faisal refused to discontinue support for the royalists, believing at a minimum it would frustrate Nasser's designs on Saudi Arabia. Much as the United States did during Vietnam, Nasser quickly fell victim to the idea that if he could just disrupt or stop the supplies coming from the outside, Egypt would defeat the insurgency—or, at least, intimidate the Saudis into ending their support.

The United States was caught in the middle. We were still wedded to Nasser, but the Saudis were the oil kingdom, and oil remained the core of our vital interests in the region. As the Egyptians continued bombing, the Saudis became nearly hysterical in demanding American support—even as they and the Jordanians became more suspicious of our outreach to Nasser. We offered more assurances, joint exercises, and ship visits. More than anything, however, Kennedy wanted a political solution that would not merely defuse the Yemen conflict but end it. The administration viewed the ousted monarchy in Yemen as one of the most regressive regimes in the region and was willing to accept what it perceived to be a more modern alternative. The problem, of course, was how the Saudis, Jordanians, and Israelis read such acceptance. In their eyes, it signaled a readiness to legitimize a Nasser victory, which constituted a direct threat to them.

Both the leading State Department officials and Robert Komer favored recognition of the new Yemeni regime led by Abdullah Sallal. Mike Feldman recalls Komer pushing hard for recognition, making the case that this would enhance our influence with Nasser and make him more "amenable to suggestions that we would make [on Yemen]." For his part, Feldman felt that even if we were to recognize Yemen, "we should get very firm guarantees from Nasser as to what he would do."[32]

Recognition would give the Egyptians what they wanted. It was bound to be seen by the Saudis and Jordanians as a betrayal, and by the Israelis as a boon for Egypt. But the administration saw it as the means to producing a political outcome. In letters the president would send to Nasser, Faisal, Hussein, and Sallal, Kennedy proposed that in return for recognition of the

Sallal regime, Egypt would withdraw its forces in phases, the Saudis and Jordanians would withdraw from the frontier, and Sallal would threaten neither his Arab neighbors nor the British position in Aden.[33] The Saudis were convinced that Nasser could not be trusted and wanted us to withhold recognition until the Egyptian forces were withdrawn.

Nonetheless, we proceeded to recognize the new regime—and Nasser did not withdraw his forces. The Saudis complained about Nasser's perfidy and continued to supply the royalists. Komer, who had been one of the drivers of the outreach to Nasser and of recognition, revealed his frustration with the Saudis and his view of the region in a memo to Bundy: "It's one thing to defend Saudis against aggression. It's another to declare we choose the kings over the bulk of the Arab world; that would be the real way to lose our oil."[34]

Over the next few months, the Egyptians continued to strike Saudi targets. In response, we offered more support to the Saudis, including a squadron of F-100s to fly what amounted to a deterrent mission. The United States also pushed a new diplomatic initiative to try to resolve the conflict. Ellsworth Bunker was sent as an envoy to try to broker a deal—the essence of which was not dramatically different from what Kennedy originally outlined in his letters. In April, after wrangling over the sequence, Nasser and Faisal agreed that Egyptian forces, which now totaled forty thousand, would begin to be withdrawn, the Saudis would cut off their material support for the royalists, and a twenty-kilometer demilitarized zone would be set up on each side of the Saudi-Yemeni border, with the DMZ to be supervised by the UN. Shortly after the deal was finalized, "Kennedy wrote Nasser to thank him for his 'constructive and statesmanlike approach.'"[35]

Once again Nasser did not uphold his end of the bargain. Feldman said that Kennedy had the "feeling that he had before that, that Nasser was completely untrustworthy."[36] But this was not the view of Komer and the State Department. As Feldman would later recount, people in the "State Department used to say that 'Oh Nasser's going to do this. Don't pay any attention to what he's saying publicly. He really is going to reduce his troop commitments' or 'He really does want peace,' or 'He's just making these noises toward Saudi Arabia and toward Israel and toward other nations because that's good politics in Egypt.' But Kennedy felt he had to judge him by his actions."[37] They continued to believe we must maintain our ties to him and would seek to explain away his duplicity.

Despite the State Department's optimism, in the president's mind, Yemen undermined our ability to maintain the outreach to Nasser. The Israelis were not bystanders to Nasser's war on Yemen. In recounting the history, Efraim

Halevy described to me how the Israelis provided material support and training to the royalists—who had no hesitancy to accept help from the Israelis. Through Shimon Peres, the Israelis were also the first to inform us that the Egyptians were using chemical weapons in Yemen.

Aside from Yemen, much was happening in the region that seemed to favor Nasser and his designs. In the beginning of April 1963, Peres met with President Kennedy and called attention to the pan-Arab winds blowing in the region—and warned that Israel could not tolerate the threat reaching Jordan. To put the Peres warning in historical context, Qassim was ousted in a February 1963 coup in Baghdad. In 1958, he had been seen as a Nasser clone, but he soon became a rival, as he arrested and executed those he accused of being Nasser's agents. Ba'athist officers, whose ideology was Pan-Arabism and Arab socialism, carried out the coup against him. A month later in March, Ba'athist officers in Damascus also engineered a coup in Syria. Suddenly, pan-Arabists seemed to be on the march again. While the Ba'athists would later become Nasser's greatest rivals and critics, they were not hostile to him at this point.

On the contrary, they began to call for a restoration of the UAR, pushing to include Iraq in this new superstate. Talks on union led to an announcement on April 17 of a tripartite agreement to join the three states. The fact that this announcement called for a "military union" to liberate Palestine understandably set off Israeli alarm bells. Ben-Gurion wrote to Kennedy, pointing to the aggressive intent of the new union, emphasizing that U.S. and Western financial assistance to Egypt made it easier to use Soviet arms against Israel. He stressed that Hawks alone, given the new Soviet weapons flowing to these three states, would not be a sufficient deterrent.[38]

Adding to the atmosphere were the Nasser- and Ba'athist-instigated riots against the king in Jordan—for the downfall of the "dwarf king" and for Jordan to join the new UAR. Kennedy, according to Feldman, feared Israel would preemptively move into the West Bank in anticipation of Hussein's ouster, and then Egypt would respond, and we would suddenly have a wider regional war. Kennedy's priority was to prevent such an outcome. Much like Eisenhower in 1957, and our earlier warning to Israel at the time of the Syrian secession from the UAR in September 1961, Kennedy first focused on the need for the Israelis not to act. Perhaps because of his meeting with Peres earlier that month and now the Ben-Gurion letter, the president feared imminent Israeli action. In describing the crisis meetings held, Feldman said Kennedy felt he needed to stop Israel, and to that end even considered sending troops to push the Israelis back if they sought to take the West

Bank. Feldman points out that Kennedy directed the 6th Fleet "to move toward Israel [but fortunately] we got word Hussein was reasonably secure, and they didn't have to go all the way."[39]

In a conversation at the time between McGeorge Bundy and Under Secretary of State George Ball, Bundy lent credence to the point that the president felt strongly about the need to convince the Israelis not to move into the West Bank. But Bundy said, "I don't see the President going to war with Israel to recover the West Bank." The Israelis needed to see he was very serious, but, Bundy wondered "if anyone [was] in a position to say that to the Israelis. The trouble with Mike [Feldman] is that he is an unreliable channel, and the trouble with the rest of us is they don't trust us . . . The President is the only man who can say things that they will believe."[40] Clearly, Bundy's words reveal more than only a need to convey a point to the Israelis; Feldman was not trusted by others in the White House and State Department given what was perceived to be his closeness to the Israelis, and the Israelis didn't trust others in the White House.

For all the president's concern about the Israelis, however, he also understood that Nasser had to stop trying to subvert Hussein and he, too, needed to be warned about the fact that he was playing with fire. Ironically, Kennedy decided not to threaten Nasser with direct action. Instead, the United States conveyed to the Egyptian president that it would not stop the Israelis. In other words, Kennedy used the threat of Israel's power to deter Nasser.

The crisis cooled with King Hussein again showing his mettle and staying power. The proposed three-state union failed to materialize, with bitter recriminations among Egypt, Syria, and Iraq as to who was responsible for the collapse. To add to Nasser's difficulties, Yemen would not go away. Thus, the administration's outreach to Nasser became less and less sustainable, particularly as congressional opposition to providing financial support to Egypt became more pronounced. Komer and his counterparts in the State Department perceived an Israeli hand behind the growing congressional opposition to maintaining financial assistance to Egypt and wanted to see greater reciprocity in the relationship.

Reciprocal Relations

The president felt strongly that the relationship with Israel should be a two-way street. Before deciding on the Hawks, he told Feldman, "If we're going to give Israel the Hawks [—and] I'm inclined to think that we have to—let's see what we can get from the Israelis."[41] Later, in December 1962 when he saw Foreign Minister Golda Meir, he emphasized our commitment to Israel and the special character of the relationship, but he also made it clear that our relationship needed to be balanced and we expected something in return. He drew a very clear line on Israel's nuclear program.

To set the context for his expectation on the nuclear program, President Kennedy started by describing our ties to Israel in a way that would have been unimaginable under Eisenhower (or Truman, for that matter). The United States, he said, had "a special relationship with Israel in the Middle East really comparable only to that which it has with Britain over a wide range of world affairs." Addressing the need for balance, he went on to say that "for us to play properly the role we are called upon to play, we cannot afford the luxury of identifying Israel—or Pakistan or certain other countries—as our exclusive friends, hewing to the line of close and intimate allies (for we feel that about Israel though it is not a formal ally) and letting other countries go." He added that our interest and Israel's are "best served if there is a group of sovereign countries associated with the West. We are in a position then to make clear to the Arabs that we will maintain our friendship with Israel and our security guarantees." He assured Meir that if there was an invasion of Israel, "it is quite clear . . . that the United States would come to the support of Israel."[42]

However, as special as our relations were, they needed to be "a two-way street." Ultimately, Israel's security depended on how it dealt with the Arabs, and the president felt it important that Israel "give consideration to our problems" with what was going on at Dimona, the location of Israel's nuclear reactor. The president said very directly that he was "opposed to nuclear proliferation," and he had no interest in "prying into Israel's affairs." Nevertheless, the United States was "concerned [with the reactor] because of the over-all situation in the Middle East."[43]

The issue of nuclear proliferation had been important to President Kennedy from early in his administration; he had, in fact, mentioned the Israeli reactor in his first meeting with Ben-Gurion and would continue to press the issue in letters. If anything, the Cuban missile crisis heightened his concern. He wanted the United States to be able to take a closer look at the reactor at Dimona in order to credibly claim that the Israeli program was peaceful. After much prodding, in September 1962, Ben-Gurion had allowed two American members of the Atomic Energy Commission, with very little notice, a forty-minute visit to Dimona. The tour was informal and tightly controlled by the Israelis, but even though the American scientists had not been allowed to enter one building, their conclusion was that Israel did not have a program for developing nuclear weapons at that time.

Kennedy was clearly not satisfied, which is why he raised the issue with Golda Meir in their December meeting, two months after the missile crisis. He explained that he was serious about stopping nuclear proliferation. He saw great dangers in it generally, and especially in the volatile Middle East. The Israelis had been raising their concerns about the Egyptian missile program and the role of German scientists in it, and Meir went so far as to charge that they were helping with a budding nuclear effort in Egypt as well. While the intelligence community found little evidence that the Egyptians were making much headway, they would not say the same about the Israeli nuclear program. The French were now reporting more about their own concerns, having helped the Israelis develop Dimona. And the U.S. intelligence community's assessment was that if Israel developed such weapons, it could be catastrophic for our interests in the region.

The view expressed by John McCone, the new head of the CIA, was that the Israelis might very well be making substantial progress toward a weapons capability—and if they succeeded, Israel would become more inflexible, force the Arabs to move even closer to the Soviets, give them a reason to blame us for the Israeli weapons, and lead the Soviets not necessarily to provide nuclear weapons to the Arabs but to make dire threats against Israel. McCone's conclusion was that Israeli nuclear weapons would dramatically strengthen the Soviet position in the vital Middle East and do "substantial damage to the U.S. and Western position in the Arab world."[44]

While McCone's words echoed the traditional national security apparatus's arguments about Israel, they resonated with the president because of his deep concern about proliferation. He decided to try a quiet initiative on arms control between Israel and Egypt and asked John J. McCloy to shuttle between the two leaders. Much like the Anderson effort in the 1950s on peace, this, too, failed to produce anything. Thus, in the spring of 1963, the president also became more insistent on getting Ben-Gurion to agree to biannual inspections of Dimona.

But to Ben-Gurion, an Israeli nuclear capability was the ultimate deterrent to Arab aggression. He wanted to be responsive to the president, but he was unwilling to abandon the project. He delayed his responses and played for time. He tried to shift the focus to Israel's need for security guarantees from the United States and his desire to have them formalized. At a May 8 press conference, Kennedy spoke about security for "Israel and her neighbors" and made the point that the United States was against the use of force or the threat of force in the region and would back UN action or "adopt other courses of action on our own" to deal with any such threats. Clearly, he was trying to address Ben-Gurion's concerns.

He was, however, still not getting a response. Worse, according to our ambassador to Israel, Ben-Gurion seemed to be backing off permitting inspections. Having lost patience, the president sent Ben-Gurion a blunt letter on May 18. In his frustration with Israel's nonresponsiveness, he warned that notwithstanding our "deep commitment to the security of Israel," our support "would be seriously jeopardized in the public opinion in this country and in the West as a whole if it should be thought that this Government was unable to obtain reliable information on a subject as vital to peace as this question of the character of Israel's effort in the nuclear field."[45]

Kennedy was the first American president to speak of a special relationship with Israel, to talk explicitly of our commitment to its security, and to overrule the prohibition on the provision of arms. Yet he was now saying that the relationship would be jeopardized if Ben-Gurion would not open up the reactors at Dimona for inspections. Ben-Gurion's response fell short of what the president sought. He offered not twice-yearly inspections but annual visits, a schedule that Kennedy felt was inadequate to keep tabs on Israel's program. After all, a great deal of progress can be made in a year. This produced another tough letter from Kennedy on June 15. For reasons driven largely by the Lavon Affair, Ben-Gurion resigned on June 16.*

Levi Eshkol, Israel's new prime minister, in an August response, wrote that Israel was ready to agree to visits by American representatives. While Eshkol did not explicitly agree to inspections twice a year, he agreed to a visit before the end of 1963 and to work out an agreeable schedule of visitation. Kennedy took the answer as a yes—and Lyndon Johnson would inherit the issue and essentially choose to fudge it. After Johnson, American presidents took Israeli nuclear weapons as a given but to be used only as a last resort. (Ironically, years later, Arab leaders would tell me that they assumed

---

* The conventional wisdom is that Ben-Gurion resigned principally over challenges from within his own party over how to assign blame for failed and embarrassing espionage operations in Egypt that became known as the Lavon Affair. The announcement came on the heels of the public dispute with the United States over the nuclear issue, which may have been a factor; however, the resignation was seen primarily in light of the Lavon Affair, both by Ben-Gurion's supporters and his opponents in Israeli public life. See Anita Shapira, *Ben-Gurion: Father of Modern Israel,* trans. Anthony Berris (New Haven: Yale, 2014), pp. 227–28.

Israel had nuclear weapons, but they, too, perceived them only as an ultimate deterrent. None of them felt particularly threatened.)*

Assumptions, Mind-sets, and Diversity
Within the Administration

If there is one word that characterizes Kennedy's mind-set toward the region, it is "balance." The president wanted a balanced approach to the Arabs
and Israel. Kennedy's words during the meeting with Golda Meir reflect his
assumption that it was in our interests and Israel's for the United States to have
relations with both sides. Feldman said that Kennedy believed that in addition to good relations with Israel, we needed to maintain our presence in Arab
states "to exert some measure of influence on them in the direction of peace
in the Middle East, in the direction of helping American interests there."[46]

But balance, after Eisenhower's distancing from Israel, actually meant
moving toward the Jewish state, and Kennedy did a great deal in this regard.
It is not only that he provided arms. To most other nations, the Pentagon
wanted cash on delivery. But when the Israelis told Mike Feldman that they
could pay only on credit, he found a precedent of the United States selling
arms to Australia on a ten-year 3.5 percent loan basis, and he went to Kennedy with this information. The president informed the Defense Department that Israel would be treated the same way as Australia.[47] Similarly,
when the State Department and the Agency for International Development
opposed developmental assistance to Israel because of its relatively high per
capita income, Feldman interceded again with the president, pointing out
that Israel needed the aid because it also had the "highest per capita debt" of
any country in the Middle East and was helping the United States indirectly with its technical assistance in Africa and Latin America. The president approved $45 million for Israel, the amount Feldman suggested that
Israel needed.[48]

Kennedy was also supportive on policy matters, reversing the Eisenhower position on Israel's use and development of the Jordan River—over
which Eisenhower had suspended loans to Israel. Similarly, whereas the
Eisenhower administration had not accepted Israel's claims over all of the Sea
of Galilee opposite Syria, Kennedy did so.[49]

---

* It is a measure of how differently they see Iran that the possibility of Iran crossing the
nuclear weapons threshold is perceived as a real threat.

Kennedy's mind-set was fundamentally different from Eisenhower's. He saw Israel as a natural American ally, as he told Meir. In a speech to the Zionist Organization of America (ZOA) on August 26, 1960, when he was still a candidate for the presidency, Kennedy declared that Israel "has not been a Jewish cause—any more than Irish independence was solely the concern of Americans of Irish descent . . . Friendship for Israel is not a partisan matter. It is a national commitment."[50] It had certainly not been for Eisenhower. As president, Kennedy would send a similar message to the ZOA in 1962, saying that our friendship with Israel reflected a simple reality: "We are committed to all free societies that seek a path to peace and honor individual right."[51]

These statements suggest that Kennedy saw in Israel a country with which we shared basic values. It was a democracy and it cherished freedom. One could argue that Kennedy was motivated more by political imperatives than by basic values—after all, the Jewish vote had been important in getting Kennedy elected in what had been a very close election, and his 1960 statement to the ZOA was made when he was a candidate. Kennedy, himself, was to say to Ben-Gurion in their meeting at the Waldorf, "I was elected by the Jews of New York. I have to do something for them. I will do something for you."[52]

It is fair to say that Kennedy understood the political value of helping Israel. He told Mike Feldman, after he made the decision on the Hawk missiles, to make sure that "those people who should know about it, know about it." Feldman arranged for American Jewish leaders to come to the White House, and while he did the bulk of the briefing, the president spoke to them "for maybe five minutes [and] expressed his feeling about why this was essential and why the decision was in the best interest of the United States."[53]

But Kennedy was prepared to make decisions that were not politically motivated on Israel and the Middle East. His outreach to Egypt was not a popular political move, but he persisted in it not just because the State Department and advisers like Robert Komer continued to view Nasser and the nationalists as the wave of the future. Kennedy was affected by his own reading of what was happening in the third world. In his acceptance speech at the Democratic convention in 1960, he said that "more energy is released by the awakening of these new nations than by the fission of the atom itself."[54] He would try to connect with this awakening, just as the Obama administration would try to connect with the awakening it faced in the Middle East in 2011.

He was prepared to take decisions that the Israelis—and their political supporters in the United States—might not like. In 1961, he approved a UN resolution condemning Israel for its retaliation following a Syrian attack. Similarly, he allowed his UN ambassador, Adlai Stevenson, to oppose a resolution that called for direct negotiations between the Arabs and Israelis. He saw the latter as a futile gesture, and on the former he overruled Feldman's opposition, telling him he was reluctant to oppose both Secretary of State Dean Rusk and Stevenson.[55]

Kennedy was not unconcerned with the political costs he paid. In part that reflected his desire to preserve a low profile on the Johnson proposal on refugees. He explained, "We should find out what Israel will do. I don't want to get into a costly fight without getting something. I'm still living with [the] residue of [the] December vote [on condemning Israel]. [I don't] want to live with [the] residue of another fight for years and years."[56]

In many ways, Mike Feldman's position as deputy counsel to the president was designed to help manage Kennedy's relationship with the Jewish community. But Kennedy used Feldman for more than that. He wanted someone around him who was open to Israel and aware of its needs. Kennedy used Feldman as his liaison to the Jewish community, and he also used him to transmit messages to the Israelis and chose him, as noted earlier, to present the Johnson proposal on refugees to Ben-Gurion. That said, as Warren Bass observes, Feldman was not granted a security clearance; he was not trusted by Bundy or Komer and would not play a role as important as Clark Clifford had with Truman.[57] Still, despite misgivings about him among some officials, Kennedy valued his perspective on Middle East issues. Feldman later recounted that when he started at the White House, the president asked him

> to go into the Middle East problems; I asked him whether he really meant that I should do this because I said quite frankly that I had an emotional sympathy with Israel, and I was sure this would color any advice that I gave him, and maybe he'd want somebody else. And, he said to me, "No," he said he would expect that I would have those sympathies and he would think less of me if I didn't, and that he wanted me to go into it and to keep him advised in anything that was happening that he ought to know about.[58]

If nothing else, Kennedy seemed to want to be sure he had debates on Middle East issues. Unlike during Eisenhower's time, Kennedy had a diversity of views around him—"the best and the brightest"—and there was no one person, certainly not his secretary of state, who reflected his perspective. Feldman represented one point of view, and while he may not have been the president's central adviser on these questions, both Komer and Rusk complained about his feeding Kennedy's suspicions about Nasser.

Rusk and his State Department represented a distinctly different set of views. Their attitudes were essentially a continuation of those of the Eisenhower administration. At one point, Rusk said that a military alliance or security guarantees for Israel would pointlessly wreck America's delicate web of Middle East ties.[59] He acquiesced in the sale of the Hawks—after initially opposing them—but did not want this to be a precedent or to see the relationship develop further. He permitted a discussion on regional issues to be conducted with the Israelis in November 1963 as an alternative to having to respond to further Israeli weapons requests or the provision of a security guarantee to Israel. His assistant secretary for the Bureau of Near Eastern Affairs, Phillips Talbot, similarly argued that impartiality would necessarily preclude a military relationship with Israel because it would be exploited by Moscow—and a new security guarantee for Israel was "both unnecessary and undesirable."[60] Feldman described the mind-set of Talbot as one in which "the United States had nothing to gain by being pro-Israel; they had everything to gain by being pro-Arab, so why not cultivate the Arabs?" Feldman went on to say that the State Department view, reflected in all their papers, was that the Arabs had oil, a large population, and controlled a geographical crossroads area important for communication and transportation. The Arabs could help in all these areas, the Israelis in none.[61]

Kennedy wanted to make the White House the locus of decision making in foreign policy. In this, his NSC played a central role, beginning a trend in shifting weight in the making of U.S. foreign policy from the State Department to the White House. Robert Komer, who was brought to the White House from the CIA, became one of the strongest advocates for outreach to Nasser—and, as noted earlier, in seeing Nasser, not the Arab kings, as the political force with which we needed to identify. He saw the Israelis as constantly trying to undercut the outreach. He was not opposed to the Hawks and even to more security assurances to Israel—provided we got something in return. In one memo he sent to the president at a time when the Israelis were pressing for more security assurances and when Kennedy wanted responsiveness on the nuclear issue, Komer wrote, "Given the Hawk/refugee episode of last year, we want to avoid giving if possible before we've taped down the quid pro quos."[62]

Like the State Department, Komer had wanted to get much greater Israeli responsiveness to the Johnson plan in return for our providing the Hawks. In a December 1962 memo to the president, Komer pushed to have Kennedy demand more from the Israelis on the Johnson plan. He justified this on the grounds that Kennedy had done more to respond to Israeli security concerns than either Truman or Eisenhower and had gotten nothing in return, going so far as to say, "We have promised the Israelis Hawks, reassured them on the Jordan waters, given a higher level of economic aid (to permit extensive arms), and given various security assurances. In return, we have gotten nothing from our efforts . . . The score is 4–0."[63]

Komer wrote a memo for the record on a meeting with the number two in the Israeli embassy in Washington, Mordechai Gazit, the day before the assassination of President Kennedy. In the meeting, Komer again revealed much about his mind-set. On the one hand, he lamented the Israeli impulse to push for more and more from us in a way that would make us appear so pro-Israel as to undercut our ties with Arab states. On the other, when Gazit pushed back and accused the United States of trying to keep Israel at "arm's length," Komer blasted him for getting much from us and giving little, saying it was "strange to me that Israel was so consistently coy about describing its own defense plans and programs to its guarantor, banker, and strongest friend in the world." He complained that the United States was "expected to subsidize Israel, both privately and publicly, to support her to the hilt on every issue, to meet all of her security requirements, and to defend her if attacked. In return, we did not even know what she intended to do in such critical fields as missiles and nuclear weapons."[64]

Komer's attitude reflected much of what President Kennedy felt on the nuclear issue and on his desire to preserve a balanced relationship in the region. While Komer may well have overstated our role as banker—certainly the Germans at this point were far more important to Israel's economic development—he captured the reality that we had clearly reversed the Eisenhower approach. A major part of the national security bureaucracy was unhappy that Kennedy had done so. The prevailing State Department attitudes had not changed, and the mind-set of the CIA remained basically shaped by the presumption of the high costs that association with Israel imposed on us in the region.[65] However, the civilian leadership at the Pentagon had changed in its attitudes, with McNamara at one point going so far as to suggest that Israel's security perimeter might need to be the Jordan River.[66]

The point is that Kennedy had carried out a significant change in our posture toward Israel. He introduced a whole new lexicon into presidential public references to Israel—and that new terminology was guided by our interests in the region and not just the political considerations here at home.

Still, while Kennedy believed in the change he carried out, he was sensitive to the price we might pay with the Arabs. In seeking a new balance, he did not want to appear too pro-Israel. Indeed, just as he was not prepared to host Nasser at the White House, he also decided not to invite Ben-Gurion to Washington, which would lend credence to the Arabs' complaints.[67] Moreover, in October, in his last letter to Prime Minister Levi Eshkol, in which he turned down a request that Ben-Gurion had made several months earlier for a U.S. pledge to come to Israel's defense much like the ones we had with NATO allies, Kennedy explained that informal arrangements would have to suffice.* "A bilateral security relationship such as Mr. Ben-Gurion suggested would, I fear, have a distinct contrary effect." Kennedy added that the Arabs had no doubt about how the United States "would respond to unprovoked aggression by them," and that we had a "constant and special . . . concern for the security and independence of Israel." But he was also not prepared to simply dismiss the arguments that Rusk and others made about endangering our ties to the Arabs if we went too far with Israel.[68]

John Kennedy built a relationship with Israel even as he kept it within certain bounds. He showed that we could provide Israel arms without losing our relationship with the Arab Middle East. His administration confronted the Soviets in the cold war and had to deal with what Malcolm Kerr called the "Arab Cold War," but Kennedy understood that neither precluded a relationship with Israel. His one blind spot was a failure to ever fully understand the meaning of the inter-Arab conflict, either in terms of what was possible for the United States with different Arab countries or what it meant about what was possible in U.S.-Israeli ties. Kennedy's successors would also grapple with the consequences of the inter-Arab conflict, and they, too, would fail to understand its implications for both our possibilities and limitations in the region.

---

* From early on, Ben-Gurion believed that Israel needed the support of a major power, both for deterrence and to counterbalance the flow of arms to the Arabs. Though he was devoted to the principle that Israel should never rely on others to fight its wars, he also understood the realities of power, particularly given the nature of the cold war.

4

LYNDON BAINES JOHNSON: EMOTIONAL TIES BUT CONSTRAINED BY VIETNAM

Lyndon Johnson was consumed by Vietnam. The Middle East intruded as an issue commanding serious presidential time and attention only on rare occasions. The one exception was sustained presidential involvement during the period before, during, and briefly after the Six-Day War in 1967, when Israel fought Egypt, Jordan, and Syria. Even then, it was primarily the fear of the United States being dragged into a war—one that could produce a U.S.-Soviet escalation—that imposed itself on the president. It is, perhaps, indicative of the preoccupation with Vietnam that President Johnson asked his leading Middle East expert at the White House, Robert Komer, to assume responsibility for the pacification program in Vietnam in March 1966. Though Komer had not worked on Asian issues and, as he acknowledged, knew little of Vietnam, he had Johnson's confidence. The president wanted someone he trusted to take charge of all the nonmilitary aspects of our policy on Vietnam. Clearly he saw little cost in taking his lead expert on the Middle East and putting him in charge of a major part of his Vietnam policy.

In general when it came to the Middle East, Johnson continued the Kennedy policy of managing ties with Israel while also promoting relations with the Arabs. For Johnson, however, the conservative Arab monarchies were our natural friends, and he sought to be responsive to their security needs. Providing arms to these Arab states also required responding to

Israeli arms requests—though there remained deep opposition in much of the national security bureaucracy to doing so. Johnson proceeded, nonetheless, to build on Kennedy's legacy, by providing for the first time offensive as well as defensive weapons to Israel.

The one area where Johnson departed from Kennedy's policy on the Middle East was on Nasser. The outreach to Nasser had largely lost its impetus even prior to Johnson assuming the presidency. Congress was resisting financial assistance. While not cut off, appropriations were already being reduced in 1964 because of the Yemen conflict and Nasser's threats against the Saudis. For Johnson, Nasser was not a natural partner. Indeed, according to Robert Komer, he was "very anti-Nasser." Although he had drawn close to Komer during a trip to the Middle East in 1962 when he was vice president, LBJ would "needle" him: "Komer, you're a Goddamned Nasser lover too. You're one of those guys who used to tell Kennedy to give all that wheat to Nasser and look what it got us."[1] In Johnson's eyes, it bought us only trouble. The Egyptian president threatened the Saudis, continued to bomb across the border in the ongoing war in Yemen, called for the removal of the U.S. air base in Libya, and was an implacable enemy of Israel. Everywhere Lyndon Johnson looked, Nasser was on the wrong side.

Under such circumstances, Johnson had little appetite for continuing the assistance to Egypt. Though Secretary of State Rusk had said earlier in 1964 that it was hard to see that any "benefits had as yet been derived from our attempts to reach an understanding with Nasser,"[2] he argued that we needed to maintain U.S. influence in Egypt and allowed PL 480, Food for Peace Programs, in which aid was given to Egypt to purchase American wheat, to continue even after Nasser permitted a mob to burn the USIS library in Cairo.[3] In so doing, he not only earned the ire of the president but Johnson now also required that all recommendations on assistance to Egypt be sent to the White House for his review.[4]

At the same time, Johnson sought to bolster our ties with the conservative Arab regimes from North Africa to the Arabian peninsula. The United States would provide financial assistance and arms. It was, however, King Hussein's need for weapons in Jordan that would lead to a promise of more arms to Israel.

Following the Arab League Summit of January 1964, and its creation of the United Arab Command, King Hussein informed our ambassador that he was under pressure to provide Soviet weapons to Jordan's armed forces. Unless he could acquire arms from the United States, he would be forced to accept Soviet equipment "either through the UAR or directly from the

Soviet Union."*5 Letting one of our conservative Arab partners and Israel's neighbor open the doors to the Soviets would shift the balance in the Middle East against us. The president couldn't accept this risk and made the decision to provide tanks to Jordan.

Even if it would serve U.S. and Israeli interests to keep Jordan out of the Soviet orbit, Johnson could not ignore the impact arms for Jordan would have on Israel's security. And so he used the Jordan arms sale to justify providing offensive weapons to Israel for the first time. The Israelis, following the Arab Summit, had come to the Johnson administration and requested tanks to counter the buildup of Arab forces and the large-scale Soviet provision of weapons to Egypt. Even though there had been no serious reaction to the sale of the Hawks, the basic assumption that providing arms directly to Israel would undermine our position in the region remained as strong as ever. In a meeting in January 1964, McGeorge Bundy told the Israeli ambassador that it would "be hard for us to maintain our present position in the Middle East" if we were to help Israel to build up militarily at this point.[6]

The assumption was echoed by the intelligence community, which weighed in with a Special National Intelligence Estimate (SNIE) titled "Implications of US Military Aid to Israel." The SNIE argued that selling tanks to Israel would arouse Arab suspicions of a pro-Israel bias and spur anti-American actions in every Arab state, including the "harassment of US diplomatic establishments and of oil companies, revocation of some military transit rights, and increasingly anti-US positions in international forums."[7] While noting that Arab self-interest would restrain reactions somewhat, the SNIE argued that the sale would lead the Israelis to expect that we would side with them on other issues, and reinforce their intransigence toward the Arabs. Ultimately, the SNIE concluded that the United States would lose its leverage to settle disputes in the region.[8]

The only one to challenge the prevailing national security establishment views was Mike Feldman, who remained as deputy counsel, then special counsel, to the president until 1966. He argued for the sale and zeroed in on the argument that it would trigger great Arab hostility, saying, "I am somewhat skeptical of this argument. I have heard it in connection with every

---

* Nasser had called the Arab Summit to confront the Israelis for diverting water from the Sea of Galilee to irrigate the Negev. He found a means of seizing the mantle of Arab leadership in the formation of the United Arab Command, ostensibly without immediately going to war, knowing that this would take time. The UAC was composed of the thirteen member states of the Arab League. Its purpose was to establish a unified Arab military command.

American action designed to give comfort to Israel." He pointed out that even those Arabs we gave assistance to often supported the Soviets, particularly in the United Nations. Sounding like Clark Clifford in 1948, he said he was "more inclined to believe that firmness will attract respect than that concessions will win their favor."[9]

Johnson initially decided that the United States would not provide tanks directly to the Israelis but would help them obtain British or German tanks at an affordable price. In time, we worked out a deal for the Israelis to buy U.S. tanks from West German stockpiles and we would then replenish the German stocks. Additional tanks from Great Britain and modernization kits from the United States also would be part of the deal. All this was contingent on the deal remaining secret to minimize Arab reaction. When word of it leaked in Germany, the Germans backed out, and we then provided the tanks directly to Israel.

Seeking Israeli Reciprocity

Still, Bundy wanted a quid pro quo from the Israelis, with Israel agreeing not to develop missiles and nuclear weapons. Johnson, feeling the Israeli arms request was justified on its own merits, was satisfied with the Israelis permitting us to inspect their nuclear facilities. In time, Johnson would accept an Israeli pledge that Israel would not be the first to introduce nuclear weapons into the region. This was considerably less than those around him—Bundy, Komer, and Rusk—wanted on the nuclear issue or on the principle of reciprocity more generally with the Israelis.

As noted earlier, Komer had consistently harped on the need for the Israelis to be more responsive to our concerns. In this case, he sent a memo to Mike Feldman to argue that in return for our help, we needed some responsiveness on our concerns: "I do hope that you can get across to our Israeli friends that our relationship cannot be so much of a one-way street. Our underwriting of their security necessarily gives us a legitimate voice in their policy. All get and no give is unsatisfactory as a basis for our relationship."[10]

The need for reciprocity also helps to explain why President Johnson sent two senior officials—Averell Harriman and Robert Komer—to Israel once he made the decision on tanks for Jordan. They were to explain that we needed to provide arms to Jordan to shore up the king, and that we wanted Israeli help with the Congress to avoid opposition to the sale.

The core of the Harriman-Komer mission was to convince the Israelis that in return for their help on arms for Jordan, we would provide Israel weapons. Indeed, Harriman, on behalf of the president, asked Prime Minister Eshkol to "put these matters into proper perspective for the key leaders of the [American Jewish] community. This was an essential part of our relationship."[11] If Israel did so, Harriman said that the president would be willing "to consider the direct sales of military equipment Israel needed at an appropriate time and with appropriate coordination of the publicity problem. This represented a major change in U.S. policy." Even though Harriman added that we still preferred that the Israelis get their arms from other Western sources, he was offering, on behalf of the president, a departure from our policy—though he was also making clear that all this needed to remain secret.

Prime Minister Eshkol was not happy with the message. The arms to Jordan would be very public. Israel was supposed to ensure there was no domestic U.S. opposition to the sale, and in return Israel was getting a vague commitment, which had to remain secret. Eshkol resented that Israel would be treated as a silent partner while it was helping the United States carry out a public arms sale to its neighbor—a neighbor that threatened Israel. But Harriman insisted that a public announcement of direct arms provisions to Israel would cause "an explosion" in the Arab world.[12]

While the discussions were not easy, the Eshkol government would do its part. Israel's friends in Congress did not oppose the Jordanian tank sale, and President Johnson fulfilled the commitment that had been conveyed. Indeed, Komer, who remained in Israel for several days after Harriman left, tied down the Israeli commitments by becoming much more specific in our offer: if Israel's needs could not be met by the Europeans, the United States would provide tanks and aircraft directly. And, in fact, in 1965, the Johnson administration would provide 210 tanks to Israel, and in 1966, would finalize an agreement to sell forty-eight Skyhawk bombers to Israel—a sale that we would actually announce several months after reaching the agreement despite Harriman's insistence on secrecy. Once again, and notwithstanding the dire predictions, the sky did not fall.

Komer described reaching these understandings as a very tough process, and at one point he sent "word back to Bundy, 'For God's sakes let me come home, I'm getting nowhere with these guys.'" But the president insisted that he stay until the deal was done. Bundy, recalls Komer, "sent me back a two-line back-channel message, 'The President says you can stay there until you bring home the bacon' . . . Lyndon Johnson kept me there!"[13] "Bringing home the bacon" may have been an ironic expression to use in describing diplomacy with the Jewish state, but Komer stayed and delivered.

Interestingly, notwithstanding Komer's views on the need for the relationship to be a two-way street, he also felt there was a strategic rationale for providing the arms to the Israelis. His counterparts in the State Department did not share this view, but it is noteworthy that Komer believed it and said President Johnson did as well: "We didn't give things to the Israelis because we loved them. We didn't give things to the Israelis because there's a great big constituency that any Democratic President is very sensitive to—Republican Presidents, too, but Democratics [*sic*] more so. There were some very sound strategic reasons for our positions and LBJ hoisted them aboard like a shot."[14]

In other words, politics may have argued for getting Israeli help to gain acceptance of the Jordanian arms sales, but strategic considerations mandated providing arms to the Israelis once this was done. If there was an imbalance of arms in the region, that would reduce Israeli deterrence and thus make war more likely—a rationale that Kennedy had first understood and articulated. Moreover, with Soviet arms flowing to the Egyptians, Syrians, and Iraqis, there had to be a counterbalance both for the sake of stability and to protect American interests in the region.

For LBJ, this seems to have been instinctive. I will say more about President Johnson's mind-set and that of others, but it is important to keep this strategic rationale in mind as we look at the most important event in the Johnson presidency on the Middle East: the 1967 Six-Day War.

Missing in Action: President Johnson and the Chain of Events Leading to the Six-Day War

The Israelis had reluctantly withdrawn from the Sinai in 1957. Though not going as far as Ben-Gurion wanted, the United States offered assurances on maintaining the United Nations Emergency Force presence in the Sinai and on keeping the Straits of Tiran open as an international waterway for free passage to Israeli vessels.

Nasser, having seen the UNEF as an infringement on Egyptian sovereignty, initially resisted the introduction of the UN forces into the Sinai but then acquiesced. He may have violated his promise to Secretary-General Dag Hammarskjöld on not reintroducing Egyptian presence into Gaza, but in order to get Israeli forces out of the Sinai, he accepted the deployment of the United Nations Emergency Forces. The UNEF's presence in Sharm el-Sheikh, at the tip of the Sinai, permitted all shipping, including Israeli, to pass through the Straits of Tiran and enter the Red Sea.

For all his rhetoric, Nasser understood that his military had been soundly defeated by the Israelis. He had no interest in a war that would produce an Egyptian military defeat. From that standpoint, the UNEF presence was convenient. But there was bound to be an inherent tension given his regional ambitions and the use of the conflict with Israel as a rallying point for his leadership of the Arabs. Indeed, if he justified every move as being part of the struggle with Israel, how could he not come to the aid of those who were engaged in tit-for-tat battles with Israel? This was not a theoretical question. Syria had ongoing incidents with Israel over Syrian firing into the demilitarized zones that had been established as part of the armistice agreement in 1949 between Israel and Syria.

Following the breakup of the UAR in 1961, Syria was plagued by coups that placed increasingly radical regimes in power—regimes that not only increased the incidents of firing from the Golan against Israeli kibbutzim in the Hula Valley but also sponsored terror attacks in Israel. Israel retaliated, triggering Syrian taunts against Nasser: While the Syrians were regularly battling Israel, where was he? By 1965, the Soviets had grown closer to the Syrians—arming them and assuming the role of Syria's protector—and Prime Minister Eshkol resisted pressures from Yitzhak Rabin, the chief of staff of the Israel Defense Forces, to hit the Syrians far harder.

In the fall of 1966 and again in May 1967, the Soviets warned of Israel mobilizing forces for an attack on Syria—in each case, the warning was erroneous.[15] And yet the May warning would set in motion Egypt's mobilization, the entry of its forces into the Sinai, its request that the UNEF be removed, the subsequent blockade of the Straits of Tiran, and the effective undoing of the arrangements that had kept the Egyptian-Israeli conflict basically under control after the Suez War of 1956.

Nasser may have wanted to keep the conflict with Israel in "the ice-box," but he could no longer have it both ways, simultaneously using the conflict with Israel for his regional pretensions while preventing it from erupting into all-out war.[16] From his high-water mark with the formation of the UAR in 1958, Nasser had been riding a losing streak in the region. The UAR collapsed with the Syrian secession in September 1961. He had become embroiled in the war in Yemen, which required nearly seventy thousand of his troops, sapped his already weak economy, had him fighting a proxy (and at times direct) war against the Saudis, and offered little prospect of success. In 1963, the Tripartite Agreement for a wider union with the new Ba'athist governments of Iraq and Syria collapsed in a stream of recriminations and led to an ongoing propaganda war with these so-called progressive regimes.

But the rhetorical invective hurled by—and against—Nasser was not limited to Iraq and Syria; it was mirrored by the monarchies in Saudi Arabia, Jordan, Morocco—and Iran. Nasser was involved in an ongoing war of words with nearly every other regime in the region.

Nasser, of course, was not the only one trying to have it both ways. Indeed, King Hussein, unlike Nasser, was quietly cooperating with the Israelis and even secretly meeting with them from time to time. Nonetheless, when he could not prevent guerrilla raids or attacks that killed Israelis, the Israelis would retaliate against Jordan. And in public he would answer every charge against him by asking why Nasser was not fighting the Israelis. His on-again, off-again prime minister, Wasfi al-Tall, would say that unlike Egypt, he would rather die than let UN forces on his territory.[17]

Meanwhile, the revolving Syrian regimes were trying to have it only one way. Lacking any legitimacy, they tried to keep the focus on fighting the Zionists. Believing that the Soviets would protect them, they saw great merit in attempting to trigger a wider war. Nasser and Hussein might not want an actual war, but the only thing Arabs could agree on in public was the need to fight Israel and avenge Palestine. Thinking he might reduce Syrian hostility, Nasser forged a defense pact with the Syrians in 1966. This tied him to them in a way that would force him to react to the Soviet warnings that the Israelis were making preparations for an attack on Syria, particularly as the pace of Syrian-sponsored Palestinian attacks into Israel increased.

In early April, a Syrian barrage from the Golan Heights triggered Israeli air attacks against the Syrian artillery positions. Syrian aircraft scrambled to engage the Israeli planes, and this led to, first, air combat above the Golan, and then to an aerial dogfight over Damascus in which the Syrians lost six planes and the Israelis none.

In May, with the temperature rising in Israel over the continuing guerrilla raids, and the Israeli rhetoric becoming more threatening, the Soviets decided to pass information to the Egyptians that the Israelis were massing ten to twelve brigades on the border for an assault on Syria between May 16 and 22.[18]

In response, Nasser mobilized his forces. On May 14, he ordered the bulk of the Egyptian forces into the Sinai. The Johnson administration, preoccupied with Vietnam and mindful of Syrian provocations, was interpreting events through a very different lens. Harold Saunders, who had replaced Komer as the senior Middle East official on the NSC, wrote a memo on May 15 making the case for a visit to Cairo to try to repair relations with Nasser. Saunders stated, "Nowhere in the Arab world is there cooler calculation that now is not the time to take on Israel" than in Cairo. He went on to say that the problem was Syria, and the answer was an "in-and-out raid on Syria" by the Israelis in which we would effectively say to the Israelis, "Do what you have to, but make sure it's quick and limited." Rostow agreed and passed this memo to the president, saying, "We sympathize with Eshkol's need to stop these [Palestinian] raids and reluctantly admit that a limited attack [on Syria] may be his only answer."[19]

The timing of Saunders's memo is remarkable. Rostow gave it to the president the day *after* the Egyptian mobilization. Our support for a very limited Israeli move into Syria might have made sense in a context where Nasser was truly quiescent. But he had moved his most important divisions into the Sinai. For the U.S. officials, the assumption that Nasser did not want a war was so deeply ingrained that his movement of forces was still seen initially in symbolic terms.

By May 16, Nasser had requested removal of the UNEF. It was only at this point that the administration understood that something bigger was afoot. Still, we were largely immobilized in terms of responding. Nasser's request to U Thant, secretary-general of the UN, was ambiguous; it did not explicitly ask for the removal of the entire UNEF presence and said nothing about Sharm el-Sheikh—where the UN presence ensured that the Straits of Tiran were kept open and the Gulf of Aqaba remained free for the transit of all shipping to Eilat, Israel's only port on the Red Sea. U Thant responded to Nasser that either all of the UN forces must go, or they all must stay—he would not pull them out partially and leave them in a vulnerable position.[20]

With such a choice, Nasser's posture was bound to be that they all must go. His decision to send his forces into the Sinai had already captured the imagination of Arab publics throughout the Middle East. Nasser was once again a hero—with all his erstwhile rivals in the area who had been vilifying him now suddenly declaring their support and their readiness to join him in the coming battle.[21] All the UNEF would have to go.

Hereafter, U.S. diplomacy was more energized, with letters from President Johnson sent first to Eshkol on May 17 and later to Soviet premier Aleksei Kosygin. But we were effectively missing in action on the critical days of May 14–16. What emerged in the nearly three weeks until the Israelis launched their preemptive attack on June 5 was an American priority of trying to avoid a war. And yet once the UNEF withdrew and the Egyptian forces occupied Sharm el-Sheikh and blockaded the straits, war was nearly inevitable.

The combination of Egypt sending six divisions into the Sinai and blockading the straits completely reversed the outcome of the 1956 war. Israel was now facing a massive Egyptian military force on its border without the blocking presence of the UNEF. Its port of Eilat was cut off from the world. The status quo that had prevented war had been shattered.

Given Johnson's desire to prevent another war while the United States was mired in Southeast Asia, the administration should have immediately reacted to Nasser's mobilization of forces and request for the UNEF to be withdrawn. When U Thant responded that it was all or nothing, the record shows that there is no sign of an urgent U.S. attempt to alter his ultimatum.[22]

It was U Thant's predecessor, Dag Hammarskjöld, who had stipulated that there would be a process within the UN to review whether the mission of the UNEF had been completed in answer to any Egyptian request or demand that the forces be withdrawn. Gideon Rafael, the Israeli ambassador to the UN, went to U Thant and told him of Hammarskjöld's promise. Rafael reported that U Thant professed ignorance of any such promise.[23]

In fact, Hammarskjöld's pledge had also been included in a letter to Secretary of State Dulles. We could have leaned on U Thant and said he did not have the authority to reverse a commitment of his predecessor. We could have moved to have a special committee review the request as part of the process of having the General Assembly consider it. The committee could have taken weeks or even months to make a finding on the legality of the request, which would have slowed the Egyptian move to war.

But we did none of these things. Our UN ambassador was Arthur Goldberg, a jurist of international standing as a former Supreme Court justice. He went to Ralph Bunche, U Thant's deputy, and showed him Hammarskjöld's letter to Dulles, which Bunche said he didn't remember.[24] Goldberg would later say that he had "always faulted U Thant for not playing a waiting game, and also Ralph Bunche—but Ralph was getting older and sick—for acceding to Nasser's request."[25]

President Johnson had a similar reaction. Later, commenting on U Thant's decision, he would say it was "an action that shocked me then, and that still puzzles me." The Egyptians were also surprised, with the Egyptian ambassador to the United States, Mustafa Kamel, telling us that his government had hoped and expected that U Thant would "play for time."[26]

If preoccupation with Vietnam distracted the administration, U Thant's decision changed the circumstances. Suddenly the president and others feared there could be a war. However, even here, as William Quandt points out, President Johnson did not send a message to Nasser until May 22. The delay is significant. Nasser's forces moved into Sharm el-Sheikh on May 19, but he did not close the straits until midnight of May 22. Quandt plausibly suggests that Nasser was waiting to see what the U.S. and Israeli responses would be before deciding to announce a blockade. But in this time period, Nasser saw no public statements or even private warnings from the United States. For Quandt, knowing that closing the straits after the 1956 war was an unmistakable casus belli for Israel, this period of U.S. passivity toward Nasser helped to produce the war—the very thing the president was determined to avoid.[27]

To be sure, once President Johnson and his administration understood there was a crisis, their main objective was, as Johnson himself would later write, to go "full-out to forestall war." But their initial priority was preventing Israel from responding militarily to Egypt's actions. In his first letter to Prime Minister Eshkol, Johnson voiced themes that he would repeat throughout the crisis, emphasizing the importance of restraint and the need not to strike first if Israel wanted our support: "I am sure that you will understand that I cannot accept any responsibilities on behalf of the United States for situations which arise as the result of actions on which we are not consulted."[28]

Perhaps, Johnson felt we could affect Israel but was less certain of our ability to influence Egypt directly. His letter to Kosygin appears geared toward the Soviets using their influence on Egypt so that we might work together to avoid a war. Ironically, it is Eshkol who asks in his response to LBJ's May 17 letter for the president to reaffirm the U.S. commitment to Israeli security and convey that commitment to the Soviets, clearly believing that this might get the Soviets to restrain the Egyptians. To that end, President Johnson in his letter to Kosygin made a general statement about our support for Israel. He went on to suggest a "joint initiative of the two powers to prevent the dispute between Israel and the UAR and Syria from drifting into war," and closed with a plea that the United States and the Soviet Union use their "influence to the full in the cause of moderation."[29]

If the president believed that the best way to avoid a war was to have the two superpowers share responsibility to prevent it, this might have made sense. But by emphasizing cooperation to avoid the *drift* to war, LBJ was signaling that our primary concern was not to reverse Egypt's actions but to manage the response to them. Implicitly, while we supported Israel, we would work to restrain Israel from striking first, and the Soviets would do the same with Egypt. In other words, there was no reason for Nasser or Kosygin to believe that Egypt's changing the status quo was highly risky for Egypt. On the contrary, with Nasser's popularity in the Arab world now soaring, and the Soviets effectively backing him, Egypt could achieve a great deal at little risk.

The problem was that changing the status quo came at a high cost to Israel. It could not accept the reality of multiple Egyptian divisions on its border with no UN presence in between. Interestingly, Arthur Goldberg, who said he knew war was inevitable after Nasser sent his troops into the Sinai, understood this would require Israel "to mobilize its troops and keep them mobilized for an indefinite period. They have a civilian army. Indefinite mobilization would bankrupt the country."[30] LBJ was seeking to avoid an Israeli preemptive strike, but this became harder after Nasser announced his blockade of the straits.

After having regained his exalted status, Nasser was not about to back down and risk losing all he had gained. For its part, Israel now faced the strangulation of the port of Eilat, its gateway to Asia. Moreover, when it withdrew from the Sinai in 1957, Israel had declared that blocking the straits would be interpreted as an act of war. As such, Johnson now had to reverse Nasser's action, not just prevent an escalation of the crisis.

At the outset, the Israelis showed administration officials the commitments that President Eisenhower had made at the time the Israelis had withdrawn from the Sinai. We had stated clearly that if the straits were closed, we would recognize that Israel had a right of self-defense to reopen them, and we would act to ensure the right of free passage through this international waterway. When no one could actually find a record of the commitments, the president asked Walt Rostow, his national security adviser, to visit Eisenhower in Gettysburg. As LBJ wrote later, "I wanted to know precisely how Eisenhower had viewed the matter at the time, so I sought his views and invited any statement he might care to make. General Eisenhower sent me a message stating his view that Israel's right of access to the Gulf of Aqaba was definitely part of the 'commitment' we had made to them."[31]

The president now felt obligated to open the straits, yet he also wanted to forestall any Israeli military action that could embroil us in a conflict that we could not afford. His letter to Nasser had been written prior to the closing of the straits but was delivered only afterward. If Egypt's president had worried about possible U.S. reactions to this move, he need not have. The letter reiterated Johnson's priority: he urged Nasser to "avoid war," spoke of America's basic friendship and understanding of "the pride and aspirations of your people," and conveyed that if we could get "through these days without hostilities," he would send his vice president, Hubert Humphrey, "to talk to you and other Middle East leaders to try to resolve all problems."[32]

It was only after the closure that the president made his first public statement against what the Egyptians had done. Previously, our messages had not criticized Egypt for mobilizing its forces or for moving its major divisions into the Sinai or for asking the UNEF to withdraw. Now Johnson felt the need to state clearly the U.S. position: "I charged that Nasser's blockade was 'illegal' and 'potentially disastrous to the cause of peace.'"[33] He also declared that his administration was committed to the territorial integrity and freedom of all states in the area.

Even though Johnson's statement went beyond anything he had said to this point, for the Israelis it fell short in two respects: Israel had sought a clear statement of America's commitment to its security and an indication of what we might do in response to Egypt's action.

There was nothing on the latter and only a general statement on the territorial integrity of all states on the former. Johnson did, however, communicate to the Israelis that they should wait forty-eight hours before taking any military action. Prime Minister Eshkol, wanting to avoid any possible replay of the U.S.-Israel crisis of 1956–1957, and to prevent internal pressure on him to act militarily against the Egyptians, decided to send his foreign minister, Abba Eban, to Washington to be sure of the United States' commitments and support.

Countdown to War

Eban began his meetings in Washington on May 25 while President Johnson was in Canada. LBJ had other reasons to be there but used his visit to solicit Canadian support for a multinational convoy to challenge the Egyptian closure of the straits. The convoy idea grew out of a plan to go to the UN and produce a process that Dean Rusk later described as follows: "We looked upon it as involving two stages: one, a declaration by the Maritime powers— by a considerable number of Maritime powers, maybe a dozen—that the Strait of Tiran was an international waterway, and that innocent passage through the Strait of Tiran was available for all nations . . . The second stage was the possibility of forcing ships through the Strait of Tiran even against Egyptian opposition."[34]

Eban was told about this plan to open the straits, and he was also warned against Israel taking any precipitous military action. Even though Nasser had taken steps to fundamentally change the status quo—and in the president's public words acted "illegally"—it was Israel that we felt needed to be stopped. According to Walt Rostow, our task was to ensure that Eshkol did not "put a match to this fuse."[35] In fact, when Eban told Rusk that Israel's intelligence indicated an imminent Egyptian attack, the secretary of state responded, "I do not wish to assume that your information is meant to give us advance notice of a planned Israeli pre-emptive strike. That would be a horrendous error."[36]

Robert McNamara, still the secretary of defense, recalled years later both the preparatory discussion that LBJ had with his main advisers prior to seeing Eban and then the meeting itself. The president, McNamara said, "was trying to prevent this [a war] from happening and in any event he didn't want the Israelis to preempt, which we were beginning to feel they might." He went on to say that President Johnson had asked Secretary Rusk and himself to join him in the family quarters of the White House for the meeting with Eban, and that in that meeting "Johnson really worked him over to try to persuade him to persuade his government not to preempt."[37]

In Johnson's preparatory meeting with his advisers, he asked them: "If you were in Eban's place and we told you we were relying on the UN and a group of maritime powers, would that be enough to satisfy you?" The "big question was whether we will regret on Monday not having given [Eban] more today?" Only Abe Fortas—a member of LBJ's kitchen cabinet—seemed to be inclined to convey more to Eban. But the desire to avoid war, and the fear that we might pay heavily with the Arabs, seemed to affect others. Rusk said, "If Israel strikes first, it would have to forget the U.S."[38]

In Johnson's account of his meeting with Eban, he left little doubt that he tried to reassure him about ending Egypt's blockade, telling him, "You can assure the Israeli Cabinet we will pursue vigorously any and all possible measures to keep the Strait open." But for us to be able to take such measures, LBJ explained that he needed to go through a progression of moves, starting with the UN. Eban and the Israeli government needed to understand that he, the president, could not act alone; he needed to show he had exhausted all other possibilities in order to be sure Congress and the American people would be with him if we needed to take direct actions to open the straits.[39] Eban's account of the meeting is more revealing of Johnson's feeling constrained, quoting the president as saying, "I am not a King in this country . . . I do not have one vote and one dollar for taking action before thrashing this matter out in the UN." Only after that could a convoy be launched, and then, according to Eban, Johnson said, "I'm not a feeble mouse or a coward and we're going to try."[40]

While Johnson skips this in his account, he does return to his clear message to Eban that Israel should not be the one to initiate war: "The central point, Mr. Minister, . . . is that your nation not be the one to bear the responsibility for any outbreak of war . . . Israel will not be alone unless it decides to go alone." According to Johnson, Eban then asked if he would be wrong if he was to say to Prime Minister Eshkol that "your disposition is to make every possible effort to assure that the Strait and the Gulf will remain open to free and innocent passage[.] I assured him he would not be wrong."[41]

Johnson went on to say that Eban could assure Prime Minister Eshkol that "within the limits of my constitutional position, I would make a maximum effort to that end." Although this sounded like a real commitment, Johnson was limiting it with his caveat. Moreover, the meeting did not end on this seemingly reassuring note. Instead, the president repeated his point that Israel would be alone only if it decided to act alone, and he then gave Eban an aide-mémoire that had been drafted by Rusk that reinforced this point with blunt language: "I must emphasize the necessity for Israel not to make itself responsible for the initiation of hostilities. Israel will not be alone unless it decides to go alone. *We cannot imagine that it will make this decision.*"[42]

Once again, the American priority was clear. Still, the president seemed to be giving the Israelis every reason to believe that we would open the straits. However, the next day, when Eban saw Arthur Goldberg in New York, and Eban recounted what the president told him, Goldberg pulled no punches in telling him not to count on this as a commitment: "You owe it to your government, because lives are going to be lost and your security is involved, to tell your cabinet that the President's statement means a joint resolution of Congress before coming to your aid, and the President can't get such a resolution because of the Vietnam War."[43]

Was Goldberg undercutting the president's message of reassurance? Undoubtedly, he was. But Eban, perhaps because of the weight of Johnson's words about not taking military action, chose not to convey Goldberg's message when he briefed the Israeli cabinet on May 28. Instead, Eban stressed the fact that the president would never support preemption but would endeavor to open the straits. Three messages arrived from Washington that reinforced Eban's argument. The first conveyed the president's readiness to use "any and all measures in his power" to open the straits. The second, reflecting Johnson's reaction to a Soviet message that Israel, not Egypt, was about to strike, concluded with a warning from the president: "Pre-emptive action by Israel would make it impossible for the friends of Israel to stand at your side." And the third, from the secretary of state, stated, "With the as-surance of international determination to make every effort to keep the Strait open to the flags of all nations, unilateral action on the part of Israel would be irresponsible and catastrophic."[44]

These were not ambiguous or subtle diplomatic messages. The warnings were unmistakable, even if the promises were less tangible. Though split, the

Israeli cabinet decided to give the Americans time to open the straits. How-ever, when Eshkol subsequently sought reassurance on Johnson's readiness to take "any and all measures," the president became uneasy about what he was now actually committed to doing. According to Goldberg, President Johnson called him and asked, "Do you understand I made a commitment to go to war with Egypt with the Israelis if Nasser doesn't get out of the Sinai?" Goldberg assured him that he had been "very careful" and his qualification on constitutional powers meant he had made no such commitment.[45]

But the president did not go only to Goldberg. Uneasy that the Israelis would hold him to a commitment that he might not be able to fulfill, he in-structed Walt Rostow to clarify again that his assurance of action had to be consistent with our constitutional processes. When Rostow conveyed this to the minister Ephraim "Eppy" Evron, the number two in the Israeli embassy in Washington, Evron asked whether he had been wrong to believe that the president was personally determined to act. Rostow responded by essen-tially telling Evron to use his own judgment in this regard.[46]

For Israel, there were other unsettling signals. The Israeli request for a number of weapons to shore up their position got no response. In the Eban meeting with the president, the Israeli ambassador, Avraham Harman, had raised the idea of creating a military liaison—or clear point of military contact for Israel in the crisis. Though Johnson seemed sympathetic in the meeting, again, there was no follow-up response. To make matters worse, very few countries were signing up to be part of the convoy—or Regatta, as it was being called—to breach the Egyptian blockade. In fact, only the British and the Dutch seemed ready to participate. When the declaration was presented at the UN on the right of free passage through the Gulf of Aqaba, only eight countries were prepared to support it—and that included the United States and Israel.

There was no sense of urgency and very little momentum for action to open the straits, despite the fact that the Arab world was coalescing around Nasser militarily. King Hussein went to Cairo on May 30, the time of Esh-kol's letter to Johnson seeking reassurance. The Jordanian monarch signed a defense pact putting his armed forces under Egyptian command. He was prepared to allow Iraqi, Syrian, and Saudi forces into Jordan as well. The mil-itary noose was tightening. Moreover, rhetoric throughout the Arab world was reaching a fever pitch—invoking the looming battle to avenge the Pal-estinians and annihilate Israel. Syrian leaders declared shortly after Egyp-tian troops moved into the Sinai that the "war of liberation will not end except by Israel's abolition."[47] On May 29, Nasser declared before the National

Assembly: "If we were able to restore conditions to what they were before 1956, God will surely help and urge us to restore the situation to what it was in 1948."[48] Iraq's President Abdel-Rahman Aref put it simply: "Our goal is clear—to wipe Israel off the face of the map. We shall, God willing, meet in Tel Aviv and Haifa."[49]

At the same time, Israel's citizen army had been mobilized, bringing the country in many respects to a standstill. Those not in the IDF were digging defensive trenches around and within cities. Pressures built on Prime Minister Eshkol to act. The military leadership was telling him that the Arab buildup of forces all around them would result in increased Israeli casualties for every day that went by without preemptive action. Domestically, doubts about Eshkol grew, and he faced mounting demands to broaden the government. He finally relented, agreeing to form a national unity government with the opposition and to appoint Moshe Dayan—the hero of 1956— as defense minister.

The messages from the United States' ambassadors in the Middle East took account of the war fever, and their counsel was clear: accept the new status quo and forget about what we committed to Israel. Our ambassador to Jordan suggested that we "not honor" our commitments to Israel. He said that if Israel launched a war, the Arabs would be convinced that we encouraged it, and this would "wreck every interest we have in North Africa and the Middle East." Hugh Smythe, our ambassador to Syria, averred that on "scales we have Israel, an unviable client state whose ties, value to [the] US [is] primarily emotional, balanced with [the] full range [of] vital strategic, political, commercial/economic interests represented by Arab states."[50] Their messages were echoed by others, all emphasizing the terrible price the United States would pay if it acted on its commitments to Israel.[51]

No wonder that President Johnson looked for a way out. Robert Anderson, who had been Eisenhower's envoy, visited Cairo and, working with our embassy, arranged to see Nasser. While Nasser was completely unyielding on his position on the blockade of the straits or Egypt's presence in the Sinai, he was prepared to send his vice president, Zakaria Mohieddin, to Washington for discussions on June 7. Recall that President Johnson, in his May 22 letter to Nasser, raised the possibility of sending Vice President Humphrey to Cairo if hostilities could be averted. In agreeing to send Mohieddin to Washington, Nasser appeared to be signaling that there could be a diplomatic way to settle this short of war.

Mohieddin's visit to Washington was announced on June 3—and took the Israelis by complete surprise. They saw it as another delaying tactic. The

Israelis feared the Egyptians would drag this out and, in the worst of all worlds, the Johnson administration would agree to an outcome in which Israel would be the loser.

The announcement of the visit only confirmed what had become inevitable in Israel: once Dayan joined the government as defense minister on June 1, Israel was going to preempt. This came two weeks after LBJ's initial letter to Eshkol, eight days after we had asked the Israelis to hold off for forty-eight hours on any military action, two days after Hussein's visit to Cairo on May 30, and also after Eshkol had sent Meir Amit, the head of the Mossad, to Washington for one last effort to understand our position.

Amit met with his intelligence counterparts as well as Secretary Mc-Namara and his aides in the Pentagon, and he was not encouraged. He noted a decided lack of enthusiasm about the Regatta. It was not only that we had essentially no takers to be part of the convoy to break the blockade, but the Pentagon itself had no interest in doing it. It was a diversion of assets that we could not afford, and there was great uncertainty over how long we would have to keep naval forces there. Amit interpreted all this as not just that the Regatta would never take place but also that the United States preferred Israel to act. Much as we will see during the Reagan administration—when Ariel Sharon felt he had received a "green light" from Alexander Haig to act militarily in Lebanon—Amit felt McNamara was giving Israel the go-ahead. Amit quoted McNamara as saying, "I read you loud and clear" in response to the Mossad chief's statement that he was going to return to Israel and recommend that Israel launch a military strike.[52]

McNamara later claimed that he would not have consciously sent such a signal, given our concerns that an Israeli preemption would provoke Soviet intervention and require us to intervene to save Israel.[53] But there is no mistaking Amit's interpretation. Moreover, there clearly were those in the administration who had come to the conclusion that it would be better for Israel to act to break the blockade than for us to do so. The presumption that we would pay a terrible price in the Arab world if we challenged the Egyptian blockade was widely shared—and not only among our ambassadors in the region. In Johnson's preparatory meeting before seeing Eban, Lucius Battle, assistant secretary of state for the Bureau of Near Eastern Affairs, said, "Whatever we do we are in trouble. If we fail to stand by Israel, the radical Arabs will paint us as a paper tiger. If we stand by Israel, we will damage ourselves seriously with all the Arabs."[54]

Since the Regatta was not going to take shape, and since diplomacy was unlikely to work, the only answer to Battle's dilemma was for Israel to take military action. In a White House memo on the eve of the war, Harold Saunders made the case for it while adumbrating Battle's description of our no-win situation in starker terms. Saunders explained that restraining the Israelis now would force us to make a long-term commitment to Israel's security—something he did not favor—while breaking the Egyptian blockade meant identifying fully with Zionism and forcing the Arab moderates into Nasser's arms: "The only other choice is to let the Israelis do this job themselves. We ought to consider admitting that we have failed and allow fighting to ensue."[55]

Eshkol was unwilling to wait any longer for American action.

The War, Its Aftermath, and Johnson's Parting Gift to Israel

On the morning of June 5, Israel launched a preemptive strike against the Egyptian air force. While it sought to avoid war with Jordan, Hussein's forces would attack Israeli forces in Jerusalem, and the Syrians, who had done the most to provoke war, fired salvos from the Golan Heights but did little more. By June 10, in what would be called the Six-Day War, Israel had captured the Sinai, Jerusalem, and the West Bank—separating it from the rest of Jordan—and the Golan Heights from Syria. In so doing, Israel exposed the emptiness of the Arab rhetoric and dealt a death blow to Nasserism and Pan-Arabism. More than shattering the very concept of Arab unity, Israel also destroyed much of the arsenal that the Soviets had provided to Egypt and Syria.

On the first day of the war, we supported the idea of a cease-fire. The Soviets were generally supportive of Nasser's position and he rejected the cease-fire, insisting that Israeli forces must be withdrawn. In addition to being in shock at the scope of the Egyptian losses on day one—most of the Egyptian air force had been destroyed in the opening Israeli air force attacks—Nasser may well have been counting on the kind of American intervention that had saved him in 1956. But Lyndon Johnson was not Eisenhower. He found it difficult to fulfill Eisenhower's commitments to Israel; he was not, however, now going to rescue Nasser.

In fact, no one, not even those most sensitive to our position in the Arab world, were inclined to help Nasser after he accused U.S. aircraft of having taken part in the air attacks in Egypt. Instead, Johnson was prepared to support a cease-fire resolution in the UN Security Council that included Israeli withdrawal of forces—but only if, in the words of the resolution, it required all parties to refrain from "acts of force regardless of their nature," and only if it mandated the lifting of the blockade of the straits and the withdrawal of Egyptian as well as Israeli forces from the Sinai.[56]

Johnson seemed most concerned that Israeli preemptive action might provoke a U.S.-Soviet confrontation. And yet it was Premier Kosygin who activated the hotline in the early hours of the war.* In his initial message on June 5, Kosygin was seeking our support for a cease-fire and for us to use our influence with Israel to that end. Johnson was open to cooperation but only if Egypt had to act as well.

The hotline would be used three times during the war. Johnson used it on June 8 in the aftermath of the Israeli attack on our ship the USS *Liberty*. The *Liberty* was an electronic eavesdropping ship, and we initially thought the Soviets had attacked it. We soon concluded that the Israelis had done it by mistake.[57] But Johnson, worried that the Soviets could misinterpret the movement of our planes and ships to rescue the surviving crew, sent a message over the hotline to convey what we were doing. Kosygin again initiated its use on June 10, when the Israelis were seemingly moving toward Damascus. The Soviet premier warned that if Israel did not stop, Moscow would make an "independent decision" and would take "necessary actions, including military." Johnson describes this moment as one of great gravity and near silence in the Situation Room. He ordered the 6th Fleet to move within fifty miles of Syria to show we would not countenance a Soviet intervention. At the same time, we leaned heavily on the Israelis to stop all military operations—and they did.[58]

When the war was over, Israel had vanquished the Egyptian, Jordanian, and Syrian armies, and was now occupying what had been Egyptian, Jordanian, and Syrian territories. It had captured huge amounts of Soviet weaponry. After Nasser's false claim that the United States had bombed the Egyptian air fields,[†] Egypt, Syria, Iraq, Algeria, Yemen, and Sudan had broken relations with the United States.[59] In other words, all the radical Arab states broke with the United States but none of the conservative or moderate Arab states did so.

After the defeat, Nasser offered his resignation, but millions of Egyptians poured into the streets of Cairo to plead with him not to leave. The

---

* This was the first time the hotline had been activated, and McNamara was surprised to find that the terminal was in the Pentagon, not the White House.

† The State Department would come to refer to this dubious claim as the "big lie." Though Israeli radio, as early as June 8, released a recording of a conversation between Nasser and Hussein hatching the story of Western collusion with Israel, the story would stick, even after Nasser retracted the accusation in an interview in *Look* magazine, saying that he never made such a charge but merely repeated information from King Hussein.

shock of losing the war was bad enough; the prospect of losing a leader who had become a symbol of the new Egypt was too much to bear.

President Johnson concluded that it was time to try to resolve the Arab-Israeli conflict—not settle for a new fragile truce. As he later wrote, "This time I was convinced we could not afford to repeat the temporary and hasty arrangements of 1957. As we worked for a ceasefire, we began to frame principles of a settlement on which the United States could stand." As he would not accept a cease-fire during the war calling on Israel to withdraw without commitments from the Egyptians, he again would present principles that needed to be accepted and fulfilled if there was to be Israeli withdrawal after the conflict. In other words, he would not ask Israel to withdraw and get nothing in return.[60]

On June 19, LBJ publicly presented principles to guide withdrawal and a peace agreement.[61] Several of these would become embedded in UN Security Council Resolution 242, adopted in November 1967. The Soviets would agree, and 242 would be the basis for negotiations. Its principles would become encapsulated in the phrase "land for peace."

One of Johnson's principles that did not get incorporated into 242 was limiting the arms race in the area. Johnson met Kosygin after the war and pressed for a U.S.-Soviet agreement to limit and control the flow of arms to the Middle East. The Soviets rejected any limitations, as their response to the Arab losses of Soviet-provided arms was to double down and start a massive resupply of more advanced arms, equipment, and advisers to Egypt and Syria.

For his part, President Johnson was finally prepared to demonstrate the warmth of U.S.-Israeli ties. He had been the first president to host an Israeli prime minister at the White House in 1964.* In January 1968, Johnson invited Prime Minister Eshkol to visit him at his ranch in Texas—highly prized for what it symbolized about the close, personal relations that the president had with a foreign leader. Considering that no Israeli prime minister had even been invited for a formal White House visit prior to Eshkol's trip in 1964, for fear of an Arab backlash, the invitation to the ranch was another indication that LBJ would not hide the United States' relationship with Israel and its leaders.

Advanced arms, however, were still a ticklish matter. At the ranch, Eshkol raised the issue of Soviet aircraft and armor going to Egypt and Syria—not only replacing all their losses but also substantially adding to the quality

---

* At that time, he was following through on President Kennedy's invitation to Levi Eshkol to make a state visit.

and quantity of the weapons Egypt and Syria would now have. The Israeli prime minister then requested F-4 Phantom fighter-bombers to offset the Soviet arms deliveries. While LBJ asked for the details, both Rusk and Mc-Namara, who took part in the meeting, made it clear that they were hesitant. Johnson said he still wanted to see if the Soviets would agree to a limitation on arms supplies; if they would not, Johnson promised to sell Phantoms to the Israelis.

Both the State Department and the civilian side of the Pentagon resisted the sale after Johnson's qualified promise to Eshkol. In the Bureau of Near Eastern Affairs, the arguments were familiar: the provision of the Phantoms would complicate our relations with the Arabs, imposing costs on us but no benefits; the Israelis did not need them; their provision would make the Israelis even less flexible on the diplomacy—and if we were to provide them, we should get an Israeli commitment to withdraw from the Sinai first. This was at a time when there was no hint of Arab interest in peace with Israel. On the contrary, only five months before at the Arab League Summit in Khartoum, Nasser had declared his famous three nos—no to recognition of Israel, no to negotiations with Israel, and no to peace with Israel. Yet at the State Department, the focus remained far more on Israel's intransigence than Nasser's—and Rusk et al. opposed the F-4 sales.

Only the chairman of the Joint Chiefs of Staff, Earle Wheeler, agreed with LBJ that the Israelis had a legitimate need for the Phantoms. In fact, he argued that the combination of Israeli losses and the Soviet supplies to the Arabs threatened to place Israel "in an inferior military position."[62] With overwhelming congressional support for the Phantoms and with both presidential candidates—Humphrey and Nixon—declaring theirs, on October 9, 1968, Johnson directed the secretary of state to initiate discussions with the Israelis on the planes. On December 28, the administration, in its waning days, announced that the first F-4s would be delivered to Israel by late 1969. Once again, when it came to providing advanced arms to Israel, President Johnson had overridden bureaucratic resistance and responded to Israel.

The President's Mind-set, the Instincts of Key Advisers, and the Legacy of the Administration

President Johnson felt a basic attachment to Israel. Rooted in his reading of the Bible, he understood the historical struggle of the Jewish people. In Israel, he saw their redemption. In a speech to the B'nai B'rith in September

1968, LBJ said, "Most, if not all of you, have very deep ties to the land and with the people of Israel, as I do, for my Christian faith sprang from yours. The Bible stories are woven into my childhood memories as the gallant struggle of modern Jews to be free of persecution is also woven into our souls."[63]

But it was not just the Bible and its prophecies that affected Johnson; it was also our shared values. As he said in a toast to Israel's president, Zalman Shazar, in a 1966 visit to the White House, "Our Republic, like yours, was nurtured by the philosophy of the ancient Hebrew teachers who taught mankind the principles of morality, of social justice, and of universal peace. This is our heritage, and it is yours."[64]

LBJ did not speak in the same way about the Arab states we supported. We might have practical reasons for such support, but Johnson did not connect to them emotionally. Israel was different. He identified with the Jewish state and saw it as a natural ally. Moreover, the Israelis, unlike the Egyptians and other Arabs, supported us against the Soviets. They were not critical of what Johnson was doing in Vietnam—something that was not true even of many of our European allies. For Johnson, Vietnam and Israel were alike in one important respect: both were small countries threatened from the outside. As such, he was highly distrustful of those who were hawks on Israel and doves on Vietnam, including many American Jews. Harry McPherson, who had replaced Mike Feldman as the liaison to the Jewish community, would quote LBJ as complaining about the many prominent Jews who criticized him on Vietnam and in the same breath told him to do more for Israel: "Dammit, they want me to protect Israel, but they don't want me to do anything in Viet Nam."[65]

Jewish pressure provoked his anger at times, particularly because, in his eyes, he had overridden bureaucratic opposition to support for Israel. At the outset of the Six-Day War, the State Department spokesman, Robert Mc-Closkey, stated that our position was "neutral in thought, word and deed"—a statement that made Johnson sufficiently unhappy that he directed Rusk to correct it. But that did not satisfy some of Johnson's Jewish supporters, who felt it signaled American disengagement at Israel's greatest moment of need. They began to press Johnson to send a strong message of support to a pro-Israel rally to be held across from the White House, fearing the rally might otherwise turn against the president. His aides Larry Levinson and Ben Wattenberg, who were both Jewish, urged him to do this as well. In his frustration, LBJ shouted at Levinson, "You Zionist dupe! . . . Why can't you see I'm doing all I can for Israel. That's what you should be telling people when they ask for a message from the President for their rally."[66]

Like Truman, who had similarly erupted in a cabinet meeting, Johnson was annoyed by pressure that he felt was unfair. Yet it did not change his fundamentally sympathetic position toward Israel—and one that, much like Harry Truman's, had him resisting the advice of the national security establishment and his chief foreign policy advisers, who were worried about losing our position in the Arab world. Although they were not the unified front that Truman faced, the instincts of the leading national security advisers were clearly different from Johnson's. Walt Rostow, who was Jewish, reflected a traditional mind-set about Israel, including the suspicion that Israel sought to prevent the United States from preserving its friendship with key Arab states. After the Israeli raid on the Jordanian village of es-Samu in November 1966, Rostow said Israel was trying to undermine King Hussein "so that it could then have a polarized situation in which the Russians would be backing the Arabs and the U.S. would be backing Israel, and Israel would not be in an embarrassing position where one of its friends among the Great Powers would also be a friend of an Arab country."[67]

Dean Rusk's attitudes toward Israel were long-standing. Going back to 1948, he had opposed the partition plan. As secretary of state, he had opposed the Hawk sale until Kennedy made it clear he would go ahead with it. He sought to undo the Komer commitment on planes to Israel as part of the deal for selling tanks to Jordan, telling his assistant secretary, "While we wish to avoid specific discussion on bombers or attack aircraft, we do not think this is what Israel needs for defense or what we would wish to sell."[68] His most blunt messages to the Israelis were before the 1967 war, warning of the consequences of their initiating military action. And when the French proposed four power talks in place of going to the UNSC both before the war and after it, Rusk was opposed because "the United States would be cast in the role of the lawyer for Israel."[69] Needless to say, he felt that would be very damaging to the United States. Later, when he recounted how Johnson had asked him to correct the press spokesman's statement on our being neutral, he said, "But actually it was not as bad a statement as that—it just excited some of the Jews in our own country."[70]

To be fair to Rusk, he did feel that in order to persuade the Israelis not to preempt, we should offer them a package of arms and money to make it easier to sustain their mobilization of the IDF. There is, however, little evidence that he pushed very hard to make it happen. Moreover, he opposed providing Phantoms and other arms to the Israelis after the war. After Johnson had approved the sale of the Phantoms, Rusk, without any consultation with the Israelis, and apparently without clearing it with the White House, also informed the Egyptians that as part of a package of steps on a settlement, we favored full Israeli withdrawal from the Sinai. The Rusk package would effectively offer the Egyptians full withdrawal for nonbelligerency, not peace, with Israel. William Quandt suggests that Rusk did this to offset what he anticipated would be a strong Arab backlash to the Phantom sale.[71] Others saw it more as a means to rebuild our relations with the Arabs.[72]

McNamara was far less of a player on these issues than Rusk. He had been reluctant to support the Phantom sale, but it was concluded after he had left the administration in 1968 and had been replaced by Clark Clifford. Clifford's assistant secretary of defense, Paul Warnke, tried very hard to condition the sale to Israel's joining the Nuclear Non-Proliferation Treaty and, barring that, to Israel's commitment not to develop a nuclear weapon. Ultimately, he was overruled by Johnson.

The Pentagon generally was preoccupied with Vietnam and focused little on the Israelis. Wheeler supported the Phantom sale in 1968—and like others saw the value of the captured Soviet weapons that the Israelis permitted us to exploit—but the last thing he and those in the uniformed services wanted was to be distracted from Vietnam. They were dead set against the Regatta idea. Their focus and their forces were elsewhere and they weren't interested in helping the Israelis in opening the straits. They effectively were saying let the Israelis do it but make sure they don't come to us for anything. Wheeler, in the discussions prior to Abba Eban's meeting with the president, even suggested that the Israelis keep the IDF mobilized for two months, ignoring the psychological and economic strains on the society and trying to make the case that there was no great urgency to respond to the Israeli demands to get the straits open.

The greatest antipathy toward Israel was in the Bureau of Near Eastern Affairs of the State Department. There, Israel remained a strategic liability. The collective mind-set before the Six-Day War was that we should simply accept, in the words of Charles Yost, that Nasser had created a new status quo—and Israel should understand that it needed to accept it as well.[73]

Remarkably, while Yost and the others in NEA saw the great cost of fulfilling our 1957 commitments to Israel, they dismissed the consequences of retreating from our word. They seemed incapable of understanding that the new status quo that they believed we—and the Israelis—should accept was not likely to last for long. On what basis would Nasser, having coerced a victory over the Israelis—and us—be able to withstand the pressure for an all-out assault on Israel? Even if Yost and others thought Israel was strong enough to defend itself, their posture of accepting the new realities with six Egyptian divisions on Israel's border made the next war only a matter of time—and ensured that there would be little respect for the United States and the commitments it made.

Once again, an important part of the national security establishment saw only the terrible consequences of the war for us with the Arabs. Moreover, in most departments of the government, the preoccupation was to address Arab concerns. President Johnson emphasized the importance of the two sides meeting directly to make peace, saying, "It is hard to see how it is possible for nations to live together in peace if they cannot learn to reason together."[74] But the proposal Rusk conveyed to the Egyptians made no mention of direct talks—after all, it was an Israeli desire. In speaking about the need to pursue a settlement, Eugene Rostow, Walt's brother and a senior official in the State Department, captured the broad sentiment about the need to restore our position in the Arab Middle East: "Our only hope is that in the end we'll get peace under our resolution and under our auspices, which ought to *restore our position* in the Middle East."[75]

What is remarkable about Rostow's statement is that he was generally more sympathetic toward Israel. There clearly was a feeling that the war had damaged our position with the Arabs. True, all the radical regimes, with whom we had very poor relations before the war, broke their diplomatic ties to us. However, our traditional friends in the Gulf—Saudi Arabia, Kuwait, Oman; in the Fertile Crescent—Jordan and Lebanon; and in North Africa—Morocco, Tunisia, and Libya—all still looked to the United States. And, of course, our relationship with non-Arab Iran remained close. With all the countries that depended on us for their security, nothing had changed.

The United States had imposed an arms embargo shortly after the war in the hopes that the Soviets would join us and work out agreements on limiting arms transfers to the region. When the Soviets instead went on a binge providing arms to their client states, the administration lifted the embargo. This led to the Phantom sale to Israel in late 1968. But well before that time, U.S. arms began flowing again to Saudi Arabia, Jordan, Tunisia, Morocco, Lebanon, and Libya. In 1963, our arms sales had been valued at $44.2 million. By 1968, these sales had risen to nearly $1 billion—a growth of more than twenty times in five years. And the arms to Israel made up only a small fraction of our overall weapons trade.[76]

Obviously, providing the Israelis tanks and planes in the mid-1960s had not harmed our relationships with those Arabs who also got their arms from us. This did not change after the 1967 war. However, no one asked *why* the dire consequences that were predicted did not materialize. No one wondered *why* the Arab countries that got their arms from us still wanted that to continue.

It didn't seem to occur to anyone that Arab priorities centered around their security and that getting U.S. arms implied an American commitment to them.

It was as if the costs we suffered with those who were not our friends in the region—Egypt, Syria, Iraq—colored the view of the foreign policy establishment about what had happened as a result of the war. The consensus view, as expressed by Eugene Rostow, was that we had to restore our position in the region—and this view would be held very strongly in the Nixon administration as well.

Once again, the inter-Arab competition drove Arab priorities, but this was somehow submerged in the minds of most senior policy makers. Johnson was not prepared to let that determine what he would do with Israel. He not only approved the Phantom sales, he also changed the character of our intelligence cooperation with Israel.

Efraim Halevy told me that from 1951 to 1967, intelligence flowed essentially one way: Israel provided information, and got precious little in return. After the war, that changed. Johnson liked those who supported us. Israel had enticed the defection of an Iraqi pilot with his MIG aircraft in 1966, and the Israelis allowed us to examine the plane. But that was a pittance compared with the intelligence bonanza of all the captured Soviet military equipment from the war. Thereafter, Johnson made the intelligence exchanges a two-way street.[77]

Johnson, like Truman, was a friend of Israel. With a kitchen cabinet that included Abe Fortas and Clark Clifford—and UN ambassador Arthur Goldberg—he did not have a unified phalanx of hostile advice toward Israel. Still, he had to overcome the instincts of many senior officials. Of greater significance, he had to contend with the constraints Vietnam imposed on him, both practically and politically, particularly when it came to the possible use of force. He responded to many Israeli needs and requests both before and after the war. The irony is that he basically felt unable to act on the commitments that the Eisenhower administration had made in 1957. This friend of Israel largely failed the Israelis at a critical moment.

For Israel, it raised lasting questions about whether the Jewish state could count on any commitments or guarantees from the outside. As we will see, it did not lead Israel to give up seeking such assurances, but it made most Israelis believe such outside commitments could never be a substitute for Israel's ability to act on its own. The war and its outcome—which continue to shape the landscape of the Middle East to this day—left the Israelis feeling far more secure than ever before. But challenges would come soon enough.

5

NIXON AND FORD: DYSFUNCTION, WAR, AND INTERIM AGREEMENTS

Richard Nixon presided over a policy characterized by mixed messages, primarily to the Israelis. This general dysfunction, particularly in his first term, stemmed from Nixon's reluctance to overrule his secretary of state, William Rogers. To the Israelis, Nixon conveyed his understanding of their needs and offered reassurances, even seemingly distancing himself from the policies he was permitting Rogers and the State Department to implement. Those policies over the first two years of the administration included holding up arms to Israel, pressuring the Israelis to make concessions on peace that they resisted, and often acquiescing to threatening moves by Egypt and the Soviets.

Nixon's national security adviser, Henry Kissinger, frequently warned against the consequences of offering concessions that received no response from the Arabs or the Soviets—and, if anything, fostered an impression of American weakness. As in earlier chapters, I will offer an overview of the key events and actions pursued by the administration. However, because this administration is characterized by far greater division and dysfunction on its Middle Eastern policy than its predecessors, there is value in first framing the divide and explaining the context for its policy.

The starting point is Nixon's acceptance of the State Department view that our position in the Middle East required us to rebuild our ties with key

Arab states and work with the Soviets. To begin with, Nixon felt a strong need to restore our position in the Arab world, and he gave responsibility of managing our outreach to the Middle East to Rogers and the State Department. As Nixon later explained, "I did this partly because I felt that Kissinger's Jewish background would put him at a disadvantage during the delicate initial negotiations for the reopening of diplomatic relations with the Arab states."[1] To be sure, we had lost relations only with those states, such as Egypt and Syria, that had already been hostile to our interests in the region. But Nixon believed that the Soviets were gaining there and we were not. "It was," he explained, "clearly in America's interests to halt the Soviet domination of the Arab Mideast. To do so would require broadening American relations with the Arab countries."[2] And for him, Kissinger's Jewish identity might cost us with the Arabs. Nixon was determined to take Arab sensibilities into account regardless of the effect on Israel.

Consequently, while Nixon would not entrust other policies to the State Department, he gave his secretary of state responsibility for the Middle East. In the initial months of the administration, the State Department succeeded in pushing an active policy on peace—one that Kissinger believed had us largely negotiating with ourselves—and in adopting a policy that distanced us from Israel.

Much like when Eisenhower and Dulles came into office intent on correcting what they viewed as Truman's overly supportive posture toward Israel, so, too, this new administration purposely created distance.

Kissinger did not favor distancing from Israel, but he did share the view that we needed to find a way to improve our position with Arab states like Egypt. As such, the dysfunction came not from our desire to improve our position with the Arabs but how to do it. For Rogers and the State Department, it was a given that our problems stemmed solely from the Soviets being able to take advantage of the Arab-Israeli conflict; the answer, therefore, was to extract concessions from the Israelis that would allow us to restore our ties with Nasser.

Kissinger, on the other hand, did not want the Soviets to appear able to produce concessions for the Arabs. Early in the administration, he did not believe the situation was ripe for peace. In his words, "The prerequisite of effective Middle East diplomacy was to reduce the Soviet influence so that progress could not be ascribed to its pressures."[3] But he accepted that at some point Arab countries like Egypt would need to see that only we—and not the Soviets—could help them recover their land lost to Israel. In other words, he, too, would try to extract Israeli concessions—once the right conditions were created. He, too, felt peace could deny the Soviets their position in the region and that "once the . . . moderate Arabs had turned to us, we had to move decisively to produce diplomatic progress."[4] But Kissinger did not want us to pressure Israel "on behalf of countries which, with the exception of Jordan, had broken relations with us, pursued policies generally hostile to us, and were clients of Moscow."[5] Those were the wrong conditions, and he would resist the State Department's initiatives based on that logic.

Nixon felt we needed to be active in pursuing Middle Eastern peace, in part to improve what he saw as our damaged position with the Arabs, and in part because he worried about the risk of another war. His comment during a press conference one week into his presidency illustrates this:

> I believe we need new initiatives and new leadership on the part of the United States in order to cool off the situation in the Mideast. I consider it a powder keg, very explosive. It needs to be defused. I am open to any suggestions that may cool it off and reduce the possibility of another explosion, because the next explosion in the Mideast, I think, could involve very well a confrontation between the nuclear powers, which we want to avoid.[6]

Nixon thought that the Johnson administration had been much too passive on this issue. It had not only cost us but also was dangerous. His impulse toward activism ran against Kissinger's preference to wait for the conditions to be ripe to work on peace in the region. President Nixon, who in Kissinger's words "still believed that the Soviet Union had been the political victor of the 1967 war," was not persuaded by what Kissinger called "my strategy of patience."[7]

Nixon was not prepared at the outset of his administration to wait either to shape the conditions for activism on Middle East peace or to allow them to evolve on their own. As a result, he was responsive to Rogers's efforts to immediately launch peace initiatives.

The Rogers Plan: Chasing Nasser and Getting Rebuffed

Rogers immediately pushed a Middle East peace initiative, working with the Soviets to develop principles that we might then get our respective friends—the Israelis and the Egyptians—to accept. In theory, these two-power talks would enable both nations simultaneously to use their leverage to forge a peace settlement.

There was, however, an inherent asymmetry: the United States was prepared to push the Israelis and try to accommodate the positions the Soviets said were required. But the Soviets merely represented the Egyptian positions. As Yitzhak Rabin, Israel's ambassador to the United States, later said, "At no stage in the talks did the Russians adopt any position that had not previously been agreed upon with the Egyptians, whereas basic American positions were not coordinated in advance with us."[8]

Kissinger understood this dynamic but was unable to stop it, even as he complained that we were "endlessly asked to modify our positions" without any real change from the Soviets.[9] As such, the principles we discussed with the Soviets evolved, with us first saying that the final border "should not reflect the weight of conquest," then that we did "not exclude the international border" as the appropriate outcome on territory, and finally accepting the position the Soviets insisted on: the 1967 lines had to define the borders.[10]

Rogers and Kissinger were at odds on the very logic of the approach. Rogers felt we must break the deadlock on the peace issue lest our position with the Arabs suffer. Kissinger felt the deadlock hurt the Soviets more than us, showing that "the Soviets could not produce anything" and that if Nasser or other Arabs wanted their land back, they had to come to us.[11]

Kissinger tried to persuade Nixon that we were essentially chasing after the Soviets and Nasser. He argued that Nasser had asked us for a gesture, and we had been responsive, launching active diplomacy and delivering a very forthcoming position on the border that the Israelis hated. But not only had Nasser not responded to our gesture, he also had launched a war of attrition against the Israeli presence along the Suez Canal.[12] While Nixon told Kissinger he was doubtful that Rogers could produce anything, he allowed him—and Joseph Sisco, his under secretary doing the negotiations—to continue to make accommodating moves in the talks with the Soviets.

As the regional environment deteriorated, Rogers and the State Department pushed to offer more. To be sure, there was a growing sense in the administration that our position in the region was eroding. In September 1969, a Nasserist regime came to power in Libya with Muammar Qaddafi's coup—which led to the expulsion of our presence from the country, including from our large air base. Added to the instability in Lebanon and growing pressures on Jordan, the Libyan coup fostered a perception among our regional friends that the radicals were on the move and we were doing nothing about the changing balance of power. As Kissinger recalled, "Our friends, moderate leaders in the Middle East—King Hussein, King Hassan of Morocco, Prince Fahd of Saudi Arabia, the Shah of Iran, and the Lebanese—told us either directly or through envoys of their despair at the growing radicalization of the region."[13]

In the fall of 1969, much like today, America's friends felt that they were losing—and that the United States was passive in response. Not surprisingly, Rogers's answer to the pleadings of our friends was to try to remove the conflict with Israel as a lever against us. His instinct was to press Israel. It was in this context that President Nixon met with the new Israeli prime minister, Golda Meir, during her visit to Washington in September.

While Rogers seemed focused only on extracting Israeli concessions, Nixon's message to Prime Minister Meir had a very different tone. Nixon spoke of Israeli security and only in that context would he urge possible Israeli flexibility toward the Arabs. According to Kissinger, Nixon told Meir that he favored "a strong Israel because he did not want the United States to have to fight Israel's battles—which was exactly Mrs. Meir's view as well."[14] Kissinger added that Nixon thought "Nasser would become moderate only if faced by overwhelming power."[15]

Here Nixon's suggested approach was significantly different from the one the United States had been pursuing. He indicated he would be responsive to Israel's arms requests and seemed to reinforce this point when he told Prime Minister Meir that he was "more sympathetic to Israeli concerns than [was] his bureaucracy." As long as he was president, "Israel would never be weak militarily."[16] Rabin, who was in the meeting, said that Nixon went even further when he admitted that he was not enthusiastic about the State Department's diplomatic approach—one the prime minister had complained about in a letter to Nixon prior to the meeting—and he even suggested to her a separate channel of communication of Rabin to Kissinger rather than Foreign Minister Abba Eban to Secretary Rogers.

Perhaps this was Nixon's way of trying to build Golda Meir's confidence in him as a genuine friend of Israel, hoping this would make her more responsive to his requests. One indication that this is what he had in mind was the "hardware for software" formula that he suggested in the meeting: the United States would provide arms to Israel in return for Israeli flexibility during the negotiations.[17] Nixon's approach indicated a clear pattern of sending messages that differed from those of his secretary of state.

Nixon might have meant what he said to Meir, but his words at this point had little real meaning, as no arms were forthcoming. Moreover, shortly afterward, he approved Rogers's request to concede on the border and to issue what became known as the Rogers Plan. Some of the principles in the plan were designed to take account of Israeli concerns.* The plan, however, ultimately failed to define security needs or arrangements that addressed Israeli requirements. It offered nothing on the content of peace, failed to provide for direct talks or recognition of Israel, and stated explicitly that secure borders should be established at the international frontier that had existed between Egypt and Palestine at the time of the mandate.

The plan was conveyed privately on October 29, 1969, and the Israeli response—also private—was as swift as it was negative. Rabin told Kissinger that Israel rejected the plan and complained that we had preempted possible negotiations and "determined the border already." He also asked what had happened to the promised arms supplies. Despite the good words from the president, the Defense and State Departments were nonresponsive and resisted all discussions on weapons for Israel.[18]

Neither the Soviets nor the Egyptians responded to the Rogers Plan for more than six weeks. Only after Rogers gave a speech on December 9 in which he described the core elements of the plan did Egypt react—and the reaction was negative, claiming that what the United States was offering was a trick designed to create an impression of impartiality.[19] In Kissinger's words, "Contrary to what Nasser had led us to believe earlier, accepting the pre-war frontiers did not improve our relations with him," much less render a positive response to the plan.[20] The formal Soviet rejection came only on December 23, 1969.

Rogers and the State Department had predicted positive responses from both the Soviets and the Egyptians. Ironically, the only thing that the Soviets, Egyptians, and Israelis agreed on was that they rejected the Rogers Plan. But failure was not seen as necessarily the worst thing. Even after the rejection of the plan, the secretary of state persuaded Nixon to authorize a similar proposal to Jordan—meaning that the border between Israel and Jordan should essentially be what it was prior to the 1967 war.[†]

---

* Israeli withdrawal would take place only after agreement on all elements; the state of war would end on the date the agreement went into effect; the parties to the agreement were responsible for preventing military or paramilitary attacks from their territory.

† The State Department's argument was that this proposal "would give the US a balanced position in the eyes of the world and might provide a starting point for later negotiations even if [it] failed now." (Kissinger, *The White House Years*, p. 374.) The same argument was made in May 2011 and again in 2014 for President Obama to give a Middle East speech laying out our best judgment on peace. The idea was that even if it failed, it would become the starting point or standard for subsequent negotiations.

Significantly, the State Department went ahead with this proposal even after Rogers met with Eban and Rabin, and was briefed on the secret contacts between Israel and the Jordanians.[21] They pleaded with him not to make the proposal. It would preempt the possibility of Israeli-Jordanian negotiations by putting Jordan in a position where it could not accept less on the border from the Israelis than what the United States was offering.[22]

Kissinger was opposed to the proposal. He likened the State Department's approach to a "gambler on a losing streak" who doubles down.[23] Once again, however, he was on the losing side of the argument. In his memoirs, Nixon explains his support for the Rogers Plan in language that also reveals, in more sophisticated terms, why he would have accepted the doubling-down approach:

> I knew that the Rogers Plan could never be implemented, but I believed that it was important to let the Arab world know that the United States did not automatically dismiss its case regarding the occupied territories or rule out a compromise settlement of the conflicting claims. With the Rogers Plan on the record, I thought it would be easier for the Arab leaders to propose reopening relations with the United States without coming under attack from the hawks and pro-Soviet elements in their own countries.[24]

If Nixon hoped the plan would lead to a reopening of relations with Nasser or the Syrians, he was disappointed—they rejected our outreach and actually drew closer to Moscow.

Kissinger explained this turn of events: "Nasser counted on us to extricate him from the consequences of his recklessness in 1967. But he was unwilling to relinquish his role as champion of radical Arab nationalism, which forced him into a strident anti-American posture on almost all international issues."[25] The pattern of Arab leaders being driven by their needs and priorities—not ours—remained just as strong during the Nixon years as it had during the tenures of his predecessors.

Nasser Turns to the Soviets, and We Withhold Arms from Israel

Rejecting the Rogers Plan, Nasser now faced a growing problem. He had initiated a war of attrition to raise the cost to Israel of occupying the east bank of the Suez Canal. Israel, however, built the Bar-Lev Line—a string of hardened bunkers along the canal—to withstand the Egyptian artillery bombardments. Moreover, Israel's very concept of deterrence required not merely absorbing Arab attacks but also delivering withering responses to show that the price of such attacks would be tenfold what was inflicted on Israel. So Israel pounded all the Egyptian cities along the canal in response and later launched deep penetration raids around the outskirts of Cairo.

Nasser could not back down without appearing to surrender to Israeli military pressure. After the humiliating defeat of 1967, he had guided the Khartoum Arab League Summit two months later to declare "no to negotiations, no to recognition, and no to peace" with Israel. Rather than forcing Nasser to stop the war of attrition, therefore, the deep-penetration raids in fact drove him toward the Soviets for protection. He sent a delegation to Moscow after the raids started in December and then he went himself in January to ask the Soviet leadership directly for massive Russian military assistance.

The Nixon administration—as divided as ever between Kissinger and the State and Defense Departments—saw the Israelis producing greater entrée for the Soviets. As such, Nixon would decide not to provide arms to Israel even as unprecedented quantities of Soviet arms and military personnel flowed into Egypt.* The Soviets were providing not only offensive and defensive weapons systems but also the most advanced SAM-2 and SAM-3 batteries and missiles in the Soviet arsenal. These systems required extensive Soviet forces to man them and effectively created a Soviet air defense umbrella for the Egyptians.

Kissinger argued for a tough U.S. response. He saw a threshold being crossed: for the first time, the Soviets were providing direct protection in an area outside of the Soviet bloc. In his words, "We had no choice but to resist, regardless of the merits of the issue that triggered the action."[26] Even if Israel's deep-penetration raids created the opening for the Russians, Kissinger argued that no response or even a weak one now would be interpreted as acceptance of this new Soviet behavior—and that in turn could lead to a dangerous miscalculation down the road. As a result, Kissinger sought a "review of our plans in case the Soviets threatened Israel with retaliation [and] asked for measures to prevent the attrition of the Israeli air force."[27]

Both the State and Defense Departments opposed such measures, argu-

---

* The most significant weapon being withheld was the F-4 Phantom aircraft promised at the end of the Johnson administration.

ing that Israel had brought this on itself and that "large-scale aid to Israel would, at that juncture, 'blow the place apart.' "[28] It was in this context that Rogers announced on March 23 that the United States would not be responding to the Israeli request for arms.*

Kissinger worried that denying arms to the Israelis at a time when the Soviets were shipping qualitatively new weapons and personnel to Egypt could lead to an Israeli preemption—particularly given the Israeli fear that the threat would become worse if they held off. Once again, however, Nixon went along with the prevailing opinion in the State and Defense Departments. Later he explained that he had hoped to "slow down the arms race without tipping the fragile military balance in the region." He also felt that "American influence in the Middle East increasingly depended on our renewing diplomatic relationships with Egypt and Syria, and this decision [to withhold arms from Israel] would help promote that goal."[29]

In other words, in the face of unprecedented Soviet arms deliveries to Egypt, we would not ship arms to Israel, because to do so would *feed* the arms race and damage our ability to restore relations with Egypt and Syria. The year before, according to Kissinger, we had chased after the Egyptians and failed to alter their behavior. Yet holding back on arms to Israel while the Soviets crossed new thresholds was still seen as somehow offering us a chance to restore our position with radical Arab states. The logic of distancing from Israel was driving U.S. policy with the expectation that it would yield us something with Nasser and the Syrians. Once again, it did not.

To be fair, our friends King Hussein and King Hassan had written letters to the president asking the United States to hold off on providing new arms to Israel, arguing it would make them more vulnerable to internal radical pressures. All these factors—Israel's deep-penetration raids, the appeals of Hussein and Hassan, and Nixon's sense that the Soviets "became the Arabs' friend and the U.S. their enemy"—likely contributed to Nixon's decision.[30]

For Kissinger, few things could have made less sense: "Less than a week after the introduction of Soviet combat personnel into the Middle East, and three days after canceling the cease-fire discussions with [Soviet Ambassador] Dobrynin, the United States had publicly denied additional planes to Israel."[31] Shortly afterward, Under Secretary Sisco went to see Nasser in Cairo, hoping to build on our latest effort to take his concerns into account.

---

*Nixon had announced on January 30 that he would make a decision on the Israeli arms request in thirty days; those thirty days became nearly two months and yielded a public rejection.

But Sisco got nowhere. Worse, we learned from Rabin on April 24 that Soviet pilots were now flying air defense missions over Egypt.

On April 30, Rabin met with Kissinger and President Nixon, the latter ostensibly joining the meeting to answer Israel's concerns about Soviet behavior in Egypt and the continuing hold on U.S. arms for Israel. According to Rabin, Nixon explained, "Some sections of the administration are strenuously opposed to supplying arms to Israel at this time. I won't identify them, but believe me, they have spared no effort in trying to convince me. You can be sure that I will continue to supply arms to Israel, but I shall do so in other, different ways. The moment Israel needs arms, approach me, by way of Kissinger, and I'll find a way of overcoming bureaucracy."[32]

In the face of this remarkable image of an American president thwarted by his own cabinet, Rabin told Nixon that by depriving Israel of arms even as Russians man SAM-3s with their own personnel, he was sending a message to the Soviets that they could go further with impunity. Nixon responded by saying, "You can be sure that you'll get your arms."[33]

U.S. arms to Israel, however, would not be coming anytime soon. A few weeks later, in May, Nixon met with Eban and Rabin and emphasized the need for a political answer to the threat: "We want to help you and you have to help us without harming yourselves or us. Damn the oil. We can get it from other sources. We have to stand beside the decent nations in the Middle East. We will back you militarily, but the military escalation can't be allowed to go on endlessly. We must do something politically."[34]

While Nixon was again attempting to reassure the Israelis, his real message was that we needed to find a diplomatic way out of the current war of attrition. Rogers shortly offered an initiative to do so.

Stop Shooting and Start Talking

In June, Rogers proposed that the sides—Egypt and Israel (and Jordan)— "stop shooting and start talking." The idea was to establish a ninety-day cease-fire that would enable negotiations to begin on the basis of UN Security Council Resolution 242. Kissinger was dubious of renewing "our compulsive peace initiatives of the previous year" but again could not prevent Rogers's proposal. It would be presented to both sides on June 22, 1970.[35] Rabin was told that U.S. arms deliveries depended on Israel accepting the proposal, and Nixon wrote to Meir stressing that Israel not be the first to turn it down.[36]

Meir wrote back to Nixon July 1, neither accepting nor rejecting, but saying that SAM-2s and SAM-3s "were being installed to cover the Suez Canal" and as this was going on, "We were being told [by the administration] that the balance of power has remained intact." She said, Kissinger recalled, that "Israel would have no choice but to bomb these installations," with a direct Israeli-Soviet clash likely.[37]

In an interview the same day, Nixon threatened action if the Soviets upset the military balance in the Middle East.[38] Prior to the interview, Kissinger delivered a background briefing in which he spelled out our aims: "We are trying to expel the Soviet military presence, not so much the advisors, but the combat pilots, and the combat personnel before they become so firmly established."[39]

On July 22, one month after receiving the stop shooting and start talking proposal, Egypt accepted it. Perhaps the Nixon and Kissinger statements made both the Egyptians and Soviets more mindful of the risks they were running. Or, as Kissinger suggested, maybe they accepted the cease-fire because they thought it would give them cover for moving the surface-to-air missile complex forward to the Suez Canal area with minimal risk.

To encourage the Israelis to accept the cease-fire, the president wrote a letter to Prime Minister Meir on July 24. Rabin described the letter as a "latter-day Balfour Declaration" and felt it was so favorable that Israel could not reject the initiative. Among other points in the letter, the president said that "our position on withdrawal is that the final borders must be agreed upon by the parties by means of negotiations under the auspices of Ambassador [Gunnar] Jarring. Moreover, we will not press Israel to accept a solution to the refugee problem that will alter fundamentally the Jewish character of the State of Israel or jeopardize your security."[40]

The Israelis interpreted the letter as contradicting the core of the Rogers Plan on borders. Kissinger would write that while the letter assured the Israelis that we would not force them to accept the Arab definition of 242—namely, full withdrawal—the State Department had given the Arabs the opposite impression when the cease-fire proposal was presented to them.[41] Regardless, both sides accepted the proposal, but not before Israeli and Soviet-piloted aircraft engaged in several dogfights the last week of July.

On August 7, the cease-fire went into effect. The terms included a military standstill of forces in a fifty-kilometer zone on each side of the Suez Canal. As such, the Egyptians/Soviets were not supposed to move the SAM-2s and -3s to the canal. But as Kissinger expected, almost as soon as the cease-fire was in effect, the Soviets began to move the batteries forward. The Israelis cried foul very quickly.

The administration, however, was not inclined to jeopardize the cease-fire and impending negotiations over what the Israelis alleged to be violations. Initially, there was reluctance at the State Department to acknowledge there had even been violations. Rogers and his colleagues were not alone in this regard. Melvin Laird, the secretary of defense, tried to belittle the violations, saying at one point, "I think the important thing for us now is to move forward towards negotiations and not debate what went on twelve hours before or twelve hours afterward."[42]

The violations were far more serious than that, however. On August 17, Rabin brought evidence of extensive violations to the attention of President Nixon, along with a protest: "Now we are expected to enter into negotiations . . . But how can we think of negotiations when the Egyptians brazenly violate the present agreement and the United States will not stand by us? Who will guarantee that the Egyptians will stick to their part of any future bargain?"[43] Obviously not the Soviets, who were the ones moving the batteries and violating the agreement.

Nixon responded that "Israel must understand that I have no illusions about Soviet motives. Perhaps even I understand them better than Israel itself. We have launched our ceasefire initiative with no preconceived notions as to Soviet goodwill. On the other hand, it was important that the initiative be made so that it is on the record." In effect, Nixon was seeking to show that Israel was not the aggressor. Echoing Johnson prior to the Six-Day War, he wanted Israel to show restraint, telling Rabin, "If our peace initiative fails, everyone should be able to recognize who is at fault. And I hope it will not be Israel."[44]

Much as in 1967, this was small comfort to Israel. It was supposed to swallow the violations so the United States would be in a better position to support Israel and to prevent the cease-fire from collapsing. For his part, Rogers, eight days after the president's meeting with Rabin, was continuing to argue that the violations did not justify jeopardizing the cease-fire or the start of negotiations. However, our intelligence confirmed the scope of the Soviet/Egyptian violations, and as compensation to the Israelis, Nixon authorized the immediate shipment to Israel of a dozen F-4 Phantoms, Shrike air-to-ground missiles, and other electronic countermeasures—still well short of the Israeli requests. Our responsiveness to the outstanding Israeli requests would change by October, because Israel would help us rescue Jordan during what came to be called "Black September."

The Jordan Crisis, Anwar Sadat Emerges, and Kissinger's Ascendancy on the Middle East

Long-brewing tensions in Jordan became acute as a result of the kingdom's support for the cease-fire. As early as June, there had been an assassination attempt against the king, and he had taken personal command of the military. As tensions grew, Kissinger began contingency planning at the NSC for possible evacuation of American citizens and requests from Hussein for assistance. To Kissinger, our weak response to the Soviet deployment of thousands of military personnel to Egypt only upped the stakes in Jordan. As events in September spiraled into a crisis—and Hussein's survival seemed increasingly at risk—Kissinger and the president came to view Jordan much as Eisenhower had viewed Lebanon in 1958.

Kissinger feared that a Jordanian implosion would "radicalize the entire Middle East."[45] For Nixon, Hussein's fall would set in motion a chain of events leading potentially to a nuclear abyss: "We could not allow Hussein to be overthrown by a Soviet-inspired insurrection." If that happened, "the entire Middle East might erupt in war: the Israelis would almost certainly take pre-emptive measures against a Syrian-dominated radical government in Jordan; the Egyptians were tied to Syria by military alliances; and Soviet prestige was on the line with both the Syrians and the Egyptians . . . It was like a ghastly game of dominoes, with a nuclear war waiting at the end."[46]

On September 6, members of the Palestinian Front for the Liberation of Palestine hijacked four civilian airliners. They flew three of the planes to a remote location in Jordan and the other to Cairo and held five hundred passengers hostage, demanding the release of fedayeen imprisoned in Israel, Switzerland, and West Germany.[47] For King Hussein, the hijackings were the last straw.

Through the British, he informed us on September 15 that he had formed a military government and intended to dismantle the fedayeen presence in Jordan. As he was readying his action, he wanted to be sure that if he needed assistance, the United States would provide it. As the hostage crisis unfolded, we had moved a number of aircraft and naval forces closer to the region and raised the readiness level of the 82nd Airborne. Militarily, however, we were still bogged down in Vietnam, with a domestic backlash over the decision in May to move forces into Cambodia. As a result, our military options were limited. Israel, obviously, also had its own high stake in Hussein's survival and was far more capable of intervening or threatening to intervene.[48]

From the moment of the hijackings, everyone at senior levels in the administration understood the ramifications. However, Rogers believed at the outset that Hussein was unlikely to move militarily against the Palestinians, that deploying American troops was impractical, and that "Israeli intervention might be his death warrant."[49]

Nixon, at least initially, shared Rogers's view about the costs of Israeli intervention. But Kissinger disagreed, believing that only Israeli forces could stop either the Iraqi or Syrian military from intervening on behalf of the fedayeen against the king. Nixon preferred American intervention over Israeli, and at one point he wrote Kissinger, saying that "he opposed any Israeli military moves unless he specifically approved them in advance, which he strongly implied he would never do."[50]

On September 17, when King Hussein ordered his army into Amman to act against the fedayeen forces, fighting broke out all around the country. The Jordanian forces quickly gained the upper hand. Nixon approved the movement of additional forces, as well as aircraft and helicopter carriers.

By the following day, it appeared the situation had stabilized. The Jordanian army retained its upper hand, and neither the Iraqis nor the Syrians made moves to intervene. But on September 19, several hundred Syrian tanks crossed into Jordan. In addition to issuing a tough public statement demanding an immediate withdrawal of Syrian forces and conveying a blunt private message to the Soviets, we ordered additional troop movements. By the next day, the scope of the Syrian move became clearer. King Hussein was desperate, asking for immediate air strikes. From an early point after the hijackings, Kissinger had been chairing a senior interagency group called the Washington Special Action Group (WSAG) that brought the decision-making process into the White House. The senior cabinet officials and their deputies took part in the discussions, and Kissinger took their recommendations to the president. With Hussein's request for air strikes, the reality of what we could and could not do militarily became clear. Kissinger argued that the Israelis were far better equipped than we were to strike a blow against Syrian ground forces—and at this point the WSAG, including Secretary Rogers, favored asking the Israelis to move if the situation on the ground required it.

Nixon changed his position from what it had been only days before. On Sunday evening, he authorized Kissinger to approach the Israelis. Kissinger would have several conversations with Rabin, initially requesting Israeli reconnaissance flights, and later President Nixon decided to support Israeli ground operations if King Hussein accepted them.[51] At the time, Kissinger offered the Israelis certain assurances—replacing Israeli material losses and deterring the Soviets. Shortly after, when the Israelis mobilized two brigades on the Golan Heights, we put the 82nd Airborne on full alert and sent a U.S. reconnaissance plane from one of our carriers to Tel Aviv—an act designed for the Soviets to see.

By Tuesday, September 22, the balance on the ground changed, making actual Israeli intervention unnecessary. Whether because of internal differences, Soviet pressure, or fear of taking on the IDF—or a combination of all three factors—Syrian air forces were not committed to Jordan, and Jordanian aircraft attacked the Syrian tanks, inflicting significant losses. Soon the Syrian forces were withdrawn, and the crisis was over.

On September 25, the administration conveyed a formal message to Israel:

> According to the latest available information, the forces which invaded Jordan have withdrawn to Syria. We believe that the steps Israel took have contributed measurably to that withdrawal. We appreciate the prompt and positive Israeli response to our approach. Because circumstances will be different if there is another attack, we consider that all aspects of the exchanges between us with regard to this Syrian invasion of Jordan are no longer applicable, and we understand that Israel agrees. If a new situation arises, there will have to be a fresh exchange.[52]

Along with our appreciation, Rogers asked that the assurances and pledges of support that the president had offered two days earlier be formally revoked lest they serve as open-ended commitments.*[53]

The United States may have needed the Israelis, but for those like Rogers within the administration, there should be no mistaking our view of Israel—and the need to be leery of making commitments to it. Contrast this posture with Rabin's interpretation of the outcome of the Jordanian crisis and how he now thought Israel was perceived by the Nixon administration. Suddenly, "in the eyes of many officials in Washington," Rabin said, "we were ... a valuable ally in a vital region during times of crisis."[54]

---

* In fact, Kissinger intervened to walk back Secretary Rogers's personally drafted message, considering it an "especially abrasive and unnecessary affront to the Government of Israel in the light of the cooperative attitude they maintained throughout the recent crisis." Although Kissinger recommended that the president "clean the slate with respect to commitments made this week," he counseled doing so in a way that would "avoid an unnecessary irritant and would not jeopardize future cooperative action if required." This approach was reflected in the formal message sent to the Israelis.

It was not just the reality of the role that Israel played, it was also the message that Kissinger separately relayed from the president to Rabin that reinforced this impression. According to Rabin, Kissinger said that the president would "never forget Israel's role in preventing the deterioration in Jordan and in blocking the attempt to overturn the regime there." Kissinger went on to say that "the United States is fortunate in having an ally like Israel in the Middle East. These events will be taken into account in all future developments."[55]

That message, like so many from Nixon, played to the warmth of the relationship with Israel. Moreover, in the aftermath of the Jordanian crisis, Nixon finally approved the Israeli arms request that had been on hold since January. Much had transpired in the intervening nine months, including strong domestic criticism for Nixon's withholding military assistance to Israel, particularly in the face of the Soviet buildup in Egypt.

Even though he withstood this pressure to provide Israel arms, Nixon deeply resented the criticism he faced for doing so. In his memoirs, he spoke of the "unyielding and shortsighted pro-Israeli attitude prevalent in large and influential segments of the American Jewish community, Congress, the media, and in intellectual and cultural circles." He described the "wave of criticism in the media and in Congress when my decision to postpone the Phantom deliveries was announced" and his annoyance that "a number of the senators who were urging that we send more military aid to save Israel were opposing our efforts to save South Vietnam from Communist domination."[56] Here he sounded much like Lyndon Johnson, equating Israel and South Vietnam, though in this case Nixon was providing military aid to the South Vietnamese and denying it to Israel.*

Sadat Emerges and Israel Equivocates

At the end of the Jordanian crisis, one development in particular created an opening for us. At a moment when King Hussein, an American friend, defeated radical forces with the crushing of the fedayeen and the withdrawal of Syrian forces from Jordan, the very face of radical Arab nationalism in

---

* Nixon was sensitive to criticism of his policy on Israel. He would use John Mitchell, his attorney general, and Leonard Garment, a White House counsel, to reach out to the Jewish community leaders. Often he used them to convey messages that distanced him from Rogers's policies in the first two years of the administration.

the region, Egypt's Gamal Abdel Nasser, died. With his death, an era came to an end. Anwar Sadat—at the time a man so discounted that he was referred to as "Nasser's poodle"—would replace him. Even Kissinger saw Sadat initially as "an interim figure who would not last more than a few weeks"—a judgment he would later describe as one of his "wildest misjudgments."[57] Soon afterward, Hafez al Assad, the commander of the Syrian air force who had refused to commit it to cover the Syrian ground incursion into Jordan, seized power in Damascus. With Jordan now stable, the PLO expelled and adjusting to a new haven in Lebanon, and both Egypt and Syria focused internally, this might logically have seemed a time to take stock of what had just transpired in the region and how we should deal with it.

Instead, Rogers wanted to push "stop shooting and start talking." While Israel had generally respected the cease-fire, it had not been willing to start negotiations given the Egyptian/Soviet violations. Then the Jordanian crisis diverted attention from what had been happening between Egypt and Israel. At this point, with the cease-fire holding and the war of attrition no longer active, and the Soviets largely on the sidelines, Rogers and the State Department wanted to launch the talks that the UN special envoy, Gunnar Jarring, was supposed to conduct.

Kissinger thought the approach had limited prospects when the region was in dramatic transition. But the State Department was, in his words, unwilling to forgo its "eager diplomacy," reflecting an unfortunate trait: "Policies well established in our government tend to appear (and sometimes to be) impervious to change."[58] Kissinger seemed ready for a change and thought that Nixon would be, as well, particularly in light of how events had played out in Jordan. But Nixon's predilection to pursue Middle East peace had not changed. Again, he went along with the State Department effort to get the talks going.

Perhaps he was also inclined to support the State Department because he had approved arms packages for Israel in October that included $500 million in a supplemental appropriation to cover Israel's expenditures. Nixon was acting on his formula of hardware for software. To that end he exchanged letters with Prime Minister Meir in December 1970 on initiating the talks based on UNSC Resolution 242. Meir sought assurances against Soviet intervention, against being pressured by us in the negotiations, and against anti-Israeli resolutions in the Security Council. Nixon was not willing to guarantee the use of our veto in the UNSC, but he was willing to deliver twelve F-4 Phantoms and twenty A-4 Skyhawks during the first six months of 1971. After some initial hesitation, at the end of December, Meir agreed to take part in the Jarring talks—which Sadat had already accepted.

Remarkably, the White House was not aware that the State Department had been encouraging Jarring and the Egyptians to base the talks on the same parameters as the Rogers Plan. There was no reason to believe that the Israeli reaction would be any different than it had been a year earlier, even as the Egyptians were still focused on full Israeli withdrawal, not a peace treaty with fully normalized relations.[59]

After several missteps, on February 8, 1971, Jarring presented a questionnaire to both sides. It dealt with the full range of issues, but there was one mirror-image question: Were the Egyptians willing to make peace with Israel if Israel withdrew to the international border? And if Egypt was prepared to make peace, would Israel be willing to withdraw to the international border? Sadat answered a week later, and for the first time he committed Egypt to making peace with Israel in return for full Israeli withdrawal. For the Israelis, this was not the forum to give such an answer—that should be reserved for the give-and-take of direct negotiations with the Egyptians.

While Egypt's response was maximal in many ways—requiring Israeli full withdrawal on all fronts and the right of return for Palestinian refugees, there was no escaping that Sadat was crossing a threshold. Rabin saw Rogers after the Egyptian response had been conveyed but before the Israeli government had come up with its reply. Rogers warned Rabin about an evasive or negative response; Rabin responded that Israel could not go back to the 1967 lines. Rogers replied, "It's just a matter of time before you are forced to face the necessity of making concessions for peace!"[60] A few weeks later, Rabin met with Sisco and conveyed Israel's formal response—which disappointed even Rabin in its vagueness and failure to express what Israel needed. Sisco's reaction, as Rabin described it, was to say that Israel was again undermining "the United States' standing in the Middle East and weaken[ing] the influence of circles in Cairo and Amman that were truly striving for a peaceful settlement."[61]

The administration's frustration with the nonresponsiveness of the Israelis was palpable. When Nixon saw Zalman Shazar on March 8, he told the Israeli president, "I understand the difficulties Israel faces in exchanging something concrete—territories—for promises and guarantees. But you should remember that your pipeline of military supplies is liable to dry up. Under no circumstances will that happen as long as I am president of the United States. But I won't serve forever."[62] In his own way, Nixon was signaling both his understanding of Israel's anxieties and his deep concern with the Israeli posture—and the potential consequences for Israel with the United States.

When Eban visited Washington a short time later and saw Kissinger, the national security adviser's frustration boiled over. Kissinger went beyond what Nixon and Sisco were saying and challenged Eban to explain why the Israelis could not formulate answers to Jarring's questions; indeed, if they could not tell Jarring, why not at least tell us what they could do?

Though Kissinger had not been enthusiastic about this diplomatic undertaking, he felt the Israelis owed us an answer, and he pushed hard to get them to reveal what they could do on peace. As Eban and Rabin equivocated, he became increasingly frustrated:

> Gentlemen, would you, at long last, tell us, your friends, what you really want? Are you prepared to withdraw to the international border in return for peace? Yes or no? What are your terms? Sharm? What else? If not to the international border, how far *are* you prepared to pull back? And when? In return for what? . . . What are your positive proposals? You don't have to accept our position on every subject. But by the same token, you can't totally reject all proposals without advancing some of your own! No one understands you. No one knows what you want. There is serious fear that all you *really* want is to evade any settlement that requires concessions on your part so that you can remain along the lines you hold at present!

Upon hearing that the Israeli position on some of the lesser issues might be formulated in another seven to ten days, Kissinger blew up: "What kind of relations do you want with the United States? You ask for close, frank, intimate relations, but you don't tell us what you think or want. Intimacy is feasible only on a reciprocal basis. So go ahead, formulate your positions on an overall settlement and a partial settlement and clarify them to us, at least."[63] Kissinger's words echo Komer's suspicions and earlier remarks on reciprocity in the U.S.-Israel relationship—these very same points and themes would be repeated countless times in the following decades.

With signs that Jarring's mission was going nowhere, Sadat revealed that he was willing to embrace the idea of a partial settlement. He announced publicly in February that he could accept an interim step that would involve the reopening of the Suez Canal and a partial, not full, Israeli withdrawal—as long as this was linked to a commitment to full withdrawal later.

Here, again, the State Department and Kissinger were split. State's approach never really departed from the Rogers Plan's focus on final borders. Rogers might embrace the idea of a first, partial step involving the reopening of the canal, but, like Sadat, he wanted it linked to the end-game. For his part, Kissinger felt there was logic in a step not tied to full withdrawal—it could at least get the process started and produce something. This achievement could stand on its own and set the stage for further negotiations that could lead to, but not mandate, further withdrawals— an approach he would, in fact, adopt after the 1973 Yom Kippur War.

Rogers remained convinced that we could forge an agreement along his preferred lines and wanted to travel to the Middle East in May 1971. Given the gaps between the parties, Kissinger felt it was a mistake for the secretary of state to take a high-profile trip that would only "intensify the current stalemate." He wanted Sadat to perceive the onus for the stalemate to be on the Soviets, not us. The trip would shift responsibility, and his worst fears about the trip would, in fact, materialize.[64]

Just prior to Rogers's trip, Sadat purged his vice president, Ali Sabry, and all those in the Egyptian regime who were tied to the Soviets. In return, he expected Rogers to come with an agreement in hand to reopen the canal as part of a larger understanding. When he did not, Sadat shifted course and, on May 27, 1971, concluded a Treaty of Friendship and Cooperation with the Soviet Union.[65]

Nixon's reaction to Sadat's signing of the Treaty of Friendship is revealing for what it again says about his instincts. In response to Kissinger's assessment that the treaty might give the Soviets a veto over future negotiations, add to their long-term influence, and make them more likely to engage in hostilities if they erupted again, Nixon said, "We must not allow this to be a pretext for escalation of arms to Israel. We should assist only in response to incontrovertible evidence of Soviet military aid which we evaluate as significantly changing the balance of power."[66] Nixon's words demonstrate his sensitivity to reacting reflexively to the Soviet-Egyptian move, given his continuing concern about the costs to us with the Arabs of doing more for Israel; they also reflect his basic belief that we must guard against any significant shift in the balance of power lest that, too, lead to an increased risk of conflict.

Still, in the aftermath of the Treaty of Friendship and Rogers's failed trip, Kissinger was given responsibility for executing Middle East diplomacy. He would later write, "Nixon did not believe he could risk recurrent crises in the Middle East in an election year. He therefore asked me to step in, if only to keep things quiet."[67]

The remainder of 1971 and 1972 set the stage for transformative events in the Middle East in 1973 to 1975. Starting at this point, Sadat was the driver of those events. On July 18, 1972, Sadat asked all fifteen thousand Soviet advisers to leave Egypt. He blamed the Russians for adopting a "no war-no peace" posture in the Middle East and called on them to "enable Cairo to develop an adequate military option for use in the future."[68]

Shortly after the expulsion of the Soviet advisers, Kissinger received a message from the Egyptians indicating their willingness to have confidential talks, their seriousness about a limited agreement along the Suez Canal, and their desire to hear new ideas from the United States. Though Kissinger exchanged messages, he did not agree to meet with his Egyptian counterpart, Hafez Ismail, until February 1973. And, when they did meet, Kissinger saw no great urgency in offering new ideas.

Nixon was much more eager than Kissinger to change the dynamic in the Middle East. This had been true at the outset of his presidency in 1969 and remained true early in his second term. He wrote in his diary on February 3, 1973, of his desire for Kissinger to be much more active on Middle East peace and the reasons for his hesitancy:

> Henry has constantly put off moving on it [the Middle East], each time suggesting that the political problems were too difficult. This is a matter which, of course, [I] will have to judge. He agreed that the problem with the Israelis in Israel was not nearly as difficult as the Jewish community here, but I am determined to bite this bullet . . . He just doesn't want to bite, I am sure because of the enormous pressure he's going to get from the Jewish groups in this country.[69]

In a press conference on September 5, one month before the October 1973 war, Nixon showed his concerns about the stalemate in the Middle East and spoke at length about the need to resolve it. He explained that he had instructed Kissinger to make [progress toward] "the settlement of [that Arab-Israeli] dispute" the highest priority. Unlike his earlier diary entry, however, he said publicly that both sides were responsible for the paralysis on peace and emphasized the need for movement: "Israel simply can't wait for the dust to settle and the Arabs can't wait for the dust to settle in the Mideast. Both sides are at fault. Both sides need to start the negotiating." And then, for the first time, he mentioned concerns about oil: "Now one of the dividends of having a successful negotiation will be to reduce the oil pressure."[70]

Nixon's comments at this press conference are particularly striking because of their similarity to what he said in a private meeting with Brezhnev during their summit on June 23, 1973. In the minutes of his meeting at San Clemente, Nixon told the Soviet leader, "I want you to know I consider the Arab-Israeli dispute a matter of highest urgency." And when Brezhnev still pressed for agreement on principles, Nixon said, "We can't abstractly beat the issue to death. We don't owe anything to the Israelis. That means I am interested in a settlement. We will work on it. We can make some progress in moving this problem off dead center . . . I am prepared to move towards a settlement."[71]

On October 6, 1973, one month after his press conference, the administration was taken by surprise by the Arab attack on Israel on Yom Kippur. We assumed that Egypt and Syria knew they could not win a war with Israel and would not launch one in which they would suffer a devastating defeat. Yet they did so, and it did not go the way we or the Israelis anticipated. Israel would win a military victory but at tremendous cost.

The 1973 War and the Onset of Arab-Israeli Diplomacy

The Egyptian-Syrian coordinated attack on Yom Kippur—the Day of Atonement, when Israel comes to a standstill—caught both the Israelis and Americans unprepared. As recently as the day before, the CIA had reported that war in the Middle East was unlikely."[72] Like most cases of strategic surprise, it was not a lack of information of a coming attack; it was the misreading of the information that was available. Faulty assumptions about Israeli prowess, Arab military ineptitude, and the certainty of an Arab humiliation if they went to war created a prism through which Egyptian and Syrian moves were misread.

The ongoing delivery of advanced Soviet weapons, and large-scale exercises in the spring of 1973 that might have readied the Egyptians for the attack across the canal, were seen as posturing. When Egypt again prepared exercises just prior to the war, Israel chose not to mobilize its forces because of the expense and the impending holiday.

Golda Meir believed that Israel's superiority permitted it to absorb an initial attack and that in doing so it would avoid political problems with the United States and the rest of the world. Through the first days of the war, the Israelis believed that they could reverse the reality on the battlefield quickly. Indeed, in a message from Israeli Prime Minister Meir to Kissinger on the second day of the war, October 7, she relayed that "our military people estimate . . . that we are engaged in heavy battles but with our reserves of men and equipment the fighting will turn in our favor."[73] She asked us to postpone any move in the UN toward a cease-fire for a few days because "I have reason to believe that by that time we will be in a position of attack rather than defense . . . I would not have come to you if I did not think the situation would improve within the next few days."[74]

Kissinger and the president were prepared to support the Israeli request for delay at the UN because the Israelis had been the victim of aggression. But they both also wanted the United States to be in the position of peacemaker, and this required relations with the Arabs. The president told Kissinger on October 7, "One thing that we have to have in the back of our minds is we don't want to be so pro-Israel that the oil states—the Arabs that are not involved in the fighting—will break ranks."[75] Three days later, in a briefing that the president and Kissinger gave the congressional leadership, they said the following:

NIXON: As the war ends our role must be such that we can play a constructive role in diplomatic initiatives to get a real settlement.

KISSINGER: If we can keep our posture, we will be in the best position that we have ever been to contribute to a settlement.

NIXON: Our goal is not domination of anyone, but to be a peacemaker. So the United States must retain the strength to play a peacemaker role. We must, when the war ends, be in a position to talk to both sides—unlike 1967.[76]

For Nixon, this was not a new theme. As noted earlier, he felt that the Six-Day War had been a loss for us. In his view, it had cost us with the Arabs; we had become too pro-Israeli and had to reach out to the Arabs. Here was a chance to reverse this. Nixon's long-standing preoccupation fit with Kissinger's view that the Arabs had to see that only we had the influence to affect Israeli behavior and produce withdrawal.

But this required a stalemate in the conflict. The war could not end with an unmistakable Israeli victory where, once again, the Arabs were humiliated. Nixon would later write, "I believed that only a battlefield stalemate would provide the foundation on which fruitful negotiations might begin. Any equilibrium—even if only of mutual exhaustion—would make it easier to reach an enforceable settlement." To be sure, his constant worry of escalation with the Soviets and a desire to preserve the gains made toward détente also guided this view: "I was also concerned that if the Arabs were actually to start losing this war, the Soviet leaders would feel that they could not stand by and watch their allies suffer another humiliating defeat as they had in 1967."[77] In Nixon's mind, Israel could not be allowed to win decisively.

In a meeting with the secretary and deputy secretary of defense, the chairman of the Joint Chiefs of Staff, and the director of Central Intelligence, the key members of the Washington Special Actions Group, Kissinger reflected Nixon's view, explaining that we were guided by two objectives from the outset of the war. First, we must maintain "contact with both sides. For this, the best outcome would be an Israeli victory but it would come at a high price, so we could insist that they ensure their security through negotiations, not through military power. Second, we attempted to produce a situation where the Arabs would conclude the only way to peace was through us."[78]

With Kissinger's back channel to Sadat, he and the president believed that the Egyptian president was ready to make peace if he could emerge as having restored Egypt's dignity. Kissinger would communicate with his counterpart, Hafez Ismail, throughout the war. And toward the goal of achieving a stalemate—the key to postwar diplomacy—we withheld arms to the Israelis during the first week of the war. William Quandt, who was the senior director on the NSC for the Middle East, would later write, "The resupply of arms to Israel had been deliberately delayed as a form of pressure on Israel and in order not to reduce the chances of Sadat's acceptance of the ceasefire proposal."[79]

To be sure, we were also sensitive to broader Arab reactions. Kissinger later referred to Secretary of Defense James Schlesinger's opposition to a significant resupply of Israel, particularly because it might "blight our relations with the Arabs for a long time."[80] To a certain degree, he shared these concerns. On October 9, Kissinger raised the issue of the increasingly desperate Israeli requests for arms, saying we would have to decide how to handle these requests, but that to "meet them would immediately drive the Arabs wild."[81]

Kissinger's focus was on a cease-fire resolution. Anatoly Dobrynin, the Soviet ambassador, told Kissinger that Sadat was ready to acquiesce to such a resolution and that they would support it. On October 12, Kissinger explained to the British ambassador why Britain needed to introduce the resolution in New York the next day: The Egyptians "do not want to be in the position of having asked for it. But they apparently would accept it if the Security Council passed it without their indicating that they wanted it."[82]

Sadat, however, had not in fact agreed to a resolution. He thought he was winning the war and therefore did not see the need to turn to diplomacy at this point. So the United States had to switch gears. It was not just that Sadat rejected an advantageous cease-fire resolution, but that the Soviets were carrying out significant resupply of arms—estimated to be seven hundred tons of military supplies a day—to the Egyptian and Syrian militaries. Our resupply to Israel was still moving in fits and starts and was composed of consumables like ammunition and not weapons—even though at the end of the first week the Israeli losses in planes and tanks were staggering: seventy planes lost and forty grounded, and as many as eight hundred tanks out of commission.

The ground rules had changed: the Soviets were not reciprocating our restraint; and we could not allow Soviet arms to defeat American arms. For both Nixon and Kissinger, this was axiomatic. Near the end of the war, Kissinger explained the thinking behind this dramatic shift to his senior staff at the State Department: "We could not tolerate an Israeli defeat . . . The judgment was that if another American-armed country were defeated by Soviet-armed countries, the inevitable lesson that anybody around the world would have to draw is to rely increasingly on the Soviet Union."[83]

Though both Kissinger and Nixon would later refer to our restraint in resupplying the Israelis in the first week of the war in their messages to the Arabs, the administration at this point no longer withheld military matériel or tolerated foot-dragging by the Pentagon—to the point where the Israelis told Kissinger that they had halted their offensive on the Syrian front because of lack of ammunition.[84] But this would all change now: Nixon insisted on it.

Kissinger, who only the day before had told William Clements, the deputy secretary of defense, that he did not want to go all out on resupply to the Israelis, now told Schlesinger, "For pressure we will begin a massive supply effort and stop it only with a ceasefire." In the same meeting, Kissinger still worried about an outcome in which the Arabs were crushed, said, "The worst outcome would be if the Arabs appear to be impotent. The best outcome would be if the Arabs come to believe that we are the only ones who can solve the problem."[85]

This would happen only if the United States massively resupplied the Israelis so that the Arabs and the Soviets understood how far we would go—and the Israelis would see how much they depended on us. Nixon was preoccupied by Watergate, but he told the Pentagon to "send everything that can fly" to get arms and material to Israel. The United States drew weapons out of its stocks for the Israelis, sent a $2.2 billion aid package for Israel to Congress, and over the next few weeks conducted a total of 550 flights airlifting military material to the Israelis. Within the first few days of the airlift, the United States was quickly able to provide far more than the Soviets were providing to the Egyptians, Syrians, and Iraqis combined.[86]

The tide of the war had already turned between the Israelis and Syrians, and in the coming week it would turn on the Egyptian front as well. Though the cost would be very high, the Israelis outflanked the Egyptians and crossed the canal to the West, gradually encircling the Egyptian 3rd Army. They wound up literally on the road to Cairo. By the time Sadat understood what was happening on the ground and sought a cease-fire, the Israelis were far less willing. But we now had great leverage on the Israelis given the scope of our resupply.

Oil Embargo, Near Confrontation with the Soviets, and Diplomacy Begins

Although managing the Arabs and preserving contact with them had been a major preoccupation of Nixon and Kissinger, the Arab members of OPEC announced on October 17 that they were banning oil exports to the United States (and some other countries), and two days later they announced they would reduce by 5 percent their production of oil and continue that reduction on a monthly basis until Israel had withdrawn to the 1967 lines. This announcement came after a meeting that Nixon and Kissinger had with foreign ministers from Saudi Arabia, Morocco, Kuwait, and Algeria, in which the president committed very strongly to working for a peace settlement. In fact, Nixon told the ministers he knew they believed that the United States was "politically influenced too much on the side of Israel," but he promised them in very blunt terms that "I am not now, nor have I ever been, nor will I ever be affected by domestic politics in my search for peace in the world."[87] Given what was happening with the Watergate investigation, this was an extraordinary statement. Nixon went on to say that the military security situation of this "tragic war" had now created conditions "where we can use our influence to get negotiations off dead center in moving toward a permanent, just, and equitable peace such as you want." While he could not guarantee to persuade the Israelis to retreat to the 1967 borders, he said we would "work within the framework for Resolution 242"—and he concluded by say-ing, "We will make a major and successful effort."[88]

On October 20, Kissinger flew to Moscow to discuss a cease-fire. That night, Nixon carried out what became known as the Saturday Night Massa-cre: he had Archibald Cox, the independent counsel who had insisted that Nixon turn over the White House tapes to Congress, fired—over the opposi-tion of his attorney general and deputy attorney general, who refused to implement his order to fire Cox and quit in protest. Kissinger obviously pre-ferred to be in Moscow, conducting serious diplomacy, than in Washington during a time of deep domestic crisis. Nixon, too, had an interest in a diplo-matic success at this moment, hoping it might remind the American public of his indispensability.

Eager to end the war—and perhaps also desperate for a success—Kissinger agreed to a cease-fire resolution with the Soviets without any con-sultation with Israel. The resolution, UN Security Council Resolution 338, called for a cease-fire, implementation of Security Resolution 242 in all its parts, and negotiations under appropriate auspices. Kissinger resisted the Soviet efforts to tie the cease-fire, or the 242 reference in the resolution, to withdrawal to the 1967 lines. Upon arriving in Israel from Moscow, how-ever, he was greeted by an unhappy Israeli leadership. The Soviets and Egyptians might have become eager for a cease-fire, but the Israelis wanted to foster the impression of an unmistakable military victory. They knew nothing about the Kissinger discussions in Moscow at the time or about the guidance that the president would send Kissinger after he arrived in Mos-cow saying it was time to go for a full settlement.[89] Kissinger largely ignored this guidance, which he felt was too ambitious for the moment: a cease-fire was necessary to set the stage for diplomacy; only later could an approach to peacemaking be adopted.

For the Israelis, the job of setting back the Egyptian military was not completed—and yet the resolution now jointly presented in New York by the United States and the Soviet Union called for a cease-fire on October 22, within twelve hours of Kissinger's arrival in Israel. In addition to the cease-fire, Prime Minister Meir was deeply suspicious of the language on Resolu-tion 242. She feared that speaking of implementing 242 *in all its parts* would be interpreted by the Arabs and the Soviets as requiring Israel to return to the 1967 lines. Kissinger explained that the pressure from the Arabs on oil supplies meant there was no choice but to bring the fighting to an end. He tried to explain why the resolution was in Israel's interests: it would end the fighting, with the Israelis having made gains on both fronts, against Egypt as well as Syria. Nowhere was 1967 or withdrawal mentioned, though the Soviets had pushed hard for both and Kissinger had said no. And, finally, the resolution would provide for direct negotiations under the appropriate auspices, which had always been the Israeli position and had always been rejected by the Arabs. Kissinger added that Israel might keep improving its military position until he returned to the States, though technically this would be after the cease-fire was due to go into effect.

The next two days, however, did not result in the end of the war but instead led to a near confrontation between the United States and the Soviet Union, as well as great pressure on the Israelis not to destroy the Egyptian 3rd Army and to respect the cease-fire. Israel acted on Kissinger's suggestion of improving its position on the ground while he flew to Washington; the Israelis tightened the noose around the 3rd Army and prevented its resupply. So when the Israelis began to observe the cease-fire, the Egyptians felt the need to break the 3rd Army out of its encirclement. However, each move by the Egyptians was not only repelled by the Israelis but also was used to further change the disposition of their forces on the ground—this in turn left the 3rd Army in an even more vulnerable position and threatened Sadat's tenuous "victory."

The Egyptian and Soviet messages became increasingly desperate. Brezhnev sent several messages on October 23 and 24 to Kissinger and the president beginning to question whether he had been misled by Kissinger. Finally, on the 24th, in an extremely blunt message to the president, he called for the joint intervention of Soviet and U.S. forces to enforce the cease-fire. If we were not willing to join the Soviet forces, they would act unilaterally.[90]

Nixon not only rejected Brezhnev's message, he also ordered a worldwide alert of U.S. forces to reinforce the point. But at the same time, he sent Prime Minister Meir a very tough message, which he later described as *Godfather*-like: we gave the Israelis an offer that they "could not refuse."[91] Cease all military activity or we will cut off all assistance. Overruling her military's resistance, Meir reluctantly complied.

With the cease-fire finally holding, Egyptian and Israeli generals met in what became known as the Kilometer 101 talks to cement the cease-fire and the provision of supplies to the Egyptian forces. For Kissinger, this was step one. If the United States was to show that only through us could something be done, we would have to become the broker of an agreement.

The war marked a new beginning for American involvement in an environment marked by two new realities. First, after the euphoria of the Six-Day War, Israel was now in a mood of self-doubt and vulnerability—fed by both their unmistakable dependence on U.S. arms and the Arab oil leverage. Second, the Arabs had successfully used the oil weapon for political effect for the first time, with the Europeans sufficiently fearful that many of our allies, including the British and the Germans, would deny access and overflight for the U.S. resupply effort to Israel lest they incur Arab wrath.*

Kissinger Begins His Shuttles as the Oil Weapon Is Employed

On November 1, less than one week after the cease-fire finally went into effect, Golda Meir arrived in Washington. She expressed her extraordinary gratitude toward President Nixon for what the United States had done. However, with more than 2,500 soldiers killed—a terrible toll that left nearly every family in Israel touched directly or indirectly by the losses in the war—she was also deeply reluctant to ease the encirclement of the Egyptian forces without exacting something from Egypt, starting with the release of the Israeli POWs. Kissinger had assured her that would happen after the adoption of the cease-fire.[92]

Before seeing Nixon, she vented to Kissinger, "It's ridiculous. They start a war and lose. And they want us to hand it to them."[93] Kissinger warned this was not the time to resist or be inflexible, explaining that it "won't take much to get the US Government to support a return to the '67 borders."[94] The mood in Washington toward Israel had soured because of the Arab employment of the oil weapon, and the more traditional instincts within the government were reemerging. In referring to the "psychological climate" Meir would find here, Kissinger told her, "It is now fed by our allies and it is supported by every single official in the Government. What I've tried to explain to you is that the war has liberated all these tendencies."[95]

In his meeting with her, Nixon sounded a similar theme, emphasizing that Israel needed to ease the pressure on the Egyptian army and move on peace: "The point is that now it is imperative to realize that if hostilities break out over an unreasonable Israeli position, we are not going to lose our respect for Israel, but it will be difficult for us—not because of the Russians

---

* Germany was allowing its ports to be used until this was publicly reported, and then it, too, denied us access.

but because of the Europeans, Japanese, and some Americans."[96] He went on to say that the United States would not "stab Israel in the back" or negotiate behind its back. "But we are going to try very hard to get a reasonable peace settlement," said Nixon. "Your interests require it. Our interests require it. The world's interest requires it. These US-Soviet confrontations are not pleasant."[97]

Immediately after Meir's visit, Kissinger departed for what would be the first of eleven trips to the Middle East over the coming year and a half. His meetings with Sadat would produce agreement on a step-by-step approach to peace, meaning there should be initial disengagement agreements that would launch a negotiating process. By November 10, he had achieved an initial set of understandings, signed by Egyptian and Israeli generals, that provided for an easing of the Israeli encirclement of the 3rd Army, a corridor for supplies, and the release of the Israeli and Egyptian POWs. On this same trip, Kissinger jetted to Saudi Arabia to see King Faisal, who also agreed to the step-by-step approach, but he would not budge from the position that the embargo on Arab oil shipments to the United States would continue until Israel withdrew to the 1967 lines.[98]

By March 1974, the Saudis and the Arabs had backed off of this position, but it is, nevertheless, worth putting in perspective the Arabs' use of the oil weapon. Prior to the war, Arab members of OPEC had been seeking to change the price of oil in the market. The war provided a perfect political pretext. Their announcement of the 5 percent reduction in supplies and then their embargo on sales to the United States reduced the supply of oil available worldwide and bid up the price. Instead of $3 a barrel, suddenly the oil states were getting $11 a barrel—an immediate economic windfall.

Kissinger, in his conversations within the government, made it clear that we would not allow the Arabs to use oil to coerce us. He told his staff, "We will be as hard as nails on oil. We will tell them that if they want our auspices [diplomacy] they have to stop their oil threats—that we will do nothing under pressure."[99] Yet he was soon pursuing negotiations notwithstanding the embargo. Moreover, Nixon signaled that we had little choice but to give in to their pressure, and that they had good reason to believe that using oil as a political weapon would lead us to lean on the Israelis. How else could one interpret what he told a delegation of governors visiting Washington: "The only way we're going to solve the crisis is to end the oil embargo, and the only way we're going to end the embargo is to get the Israelis to act reasonable . . . I hate to use the word blackmail, but we've got to do some things to get them [the Israelis] to behave."[100]

This statement, reported in *The Washington Post*, was certainly more blunt than what he had said before the war, but it was consistent with the comments he made in his September press conference when he linked the absence of peace to possible oil pressure. His private correspondence with Sadat and other Arab leaders left little doubt that he saw a clear connection between oil and our Middle East diplomacy.[101] Even after the embargo was lifted in March 1974, Nixon continued to link peace and oil, saying that he was "confident that the progress we are going to continue to make on the peace front in the Mideast will be very helpful in seeing to it that an oil embargo is not reimposed."[102]

The irony is that the linkage had been presumed in the national security establishment from President Roosevelt's time. One of the arguments against supporting partition had been that it would provoke the Arabs to cut off the oil spigot. But this had never happened. Finally, this argument seemed to be borne out. Finally, we really were paying a price for supporting Israel—or so it seemed.

But if this was actually the case, why would the Saudis insist that they would not end the embargo until the Israelis pulled back to 1967 and then drop it by March? Put simply, the Saudis did not see it in their interests to preserve the embargo. True, Anwar Sadat promised Kissinger that he would get the Saudis to lift it in January as part of Kissinger's shuttle efforts that led to the first disengagement agreement. But the Saudis did not respond at that time. Nor did they respond when Hafez al Assad asked them not to lift the embargo before Kissinger brokered a similar disengagement agreement on the Syrian front. Such an agreement would not be reached until the end of May 1974, more than two months after the embargo had ended.

The Saudis had both economic and national security reasons for lifting the embargo when they did—and these had nothing to do with Israel. The Saudis had to worry about the effect of the price hike on the health of the global economy. An economic slowdown could lead to a decrease in demand for oil—which did in fact happen with the global recession of 1974–1975. Saudi oil ministers from 1974 until today have preached about the need for "balance" in the oil market, declaring that their own well-being depends on not driving the price so high that demand for their principal resource dampens and alternatives to oil begin to look more attractive.*

---

* The Saudi actions in 2014 and 2015 to drive down the price to preserve their market share and reduce the incentives for exploiting shale bear this out.

But there were also profound security reasons for Saudi behavior. The Saudis looked to the United States as the guarantor of their security. So long as the oil embargo continued, they ran the risk that we would not engage in defense cooperation; we certainly could not have politically justified selling arms to the Saudis as long as they refused to sell us oil—and the Congress needed to approve such arms sales. Just as the Saudis and the other Arabs who were acquiring arms from us prior to and after the 1967 war did not want our arms sales to them to stop, so, too, would the Saudis after the 1973 war not want any disruption in the supply of U.S. weapons to the kingdom. Indeed, with their newfound revenues, their appetite for arms went up. So once again, their own interests trumped concerns about the Israelis, and the Saudis and the other Arab oil-producing states dropped the boycott.

Even more to the point, the Saudis actually increased the scope of their cooperation with us. With their vast new monies, they set about building a civilian infrastructure. Whom did they want building their highways, pipelines, petrochemical industry? The United States. We, of course, were eager to recycle the petrodollars and set up a Joint Commission on Economic Cooperation with the Saudis in June 1974. Our trade with Saudi Arabia went up by 700 percent between 1972 and 1976. True, they could use Kissinger's active diplomacy, which would produce three disengagement agreements in 1974 and 1975 to justify increased cooperation, but none of these agreements came close to meeting their initial demand of Israeli withdrawal to the 1967 lines.

Even after the Saudis lifted the embargo, our sense of vulnerability, alongside their continuing complaints about the Israelis, tended to preserve the image that we must push the Israelis lest we pay the price again. Longstanding assumptions about U.S.-Arab relations had, in the minds of many, been confirmed. That the Saudis had abandoned the oil weapon of their own accord, based on their interests and their desire for a strong relationship with the United States, simply did not penetrate the collective psyche of the administration. The proof of this reality: Nixon's comments on the linkage to peace *after* the lifting of the embargo.

Kissinger did succeed in finally producing an interim agreement along the lines of what he had originally envisioned in 1971. The first interim agreement involved an Israeli pullback of its forces from both sides of the canal and Egypt rebuilding the cities along it. Concluded in January 1974, it became known as the Sinai I agreement, and it involved Kissinger shuttling back and forth between the Egyptians and Israelis.[103] Kissinger's shuttle diplomacy replaced the Geneva Conference, which was cochaired by the United States and the Soviets and would meet only once.*

Unlike Rogers, who had focused on the end state of negotiations—a fixation that precluded any negotiations starting—Kissinger adopted the posture that gaining an agreement had value on its own. He could use it to change the climate, show understandings were possible, and provide a basis for additional negotiations. He could also use it to show that only American diplomacy could produce anything. The conceptual difference between an incremental approach and a comprehensive one would be debated throughout different administrations—with the incremental usually, but not always, winning out.

Kissinger also applied such incrementalism to the Syrian front, reaching a disengagement agreement after thirty-two days of onerous shuttling between Israel and Syria.† All this was achieved against the backdrop of a deteriorating political environment at home. Watergate was increasingly destroying the president's hold on his office, and Nixon was desperate for a diplomatic success. He insisted that Kissinger not leave the area without an agreement.

Both sides frustrated Kissinger. Assad constantly reopened issues, and the Israelis haggled over every meter. At one point, he blew up at the Israeli delegation, declaring that he was "wandering around here like a rug merchant in order to bargain over 100 to 200 meters . . . I'm trying to save you, and you think you are doing me a favor when you are kind enough to give me a few more meters."[104] More fundamentally, Kissinger thought the Israelis failed to see the bigger picture and what was at stake. He was trying to prevent a reemergence of the conflict, which "would benefit the Soviet Union" and put pressure on Sadat "to rejoin the battle." In this same spirit,

---

* Prime Minister Meir was reluctant to go to Geneva, and Kissinger pressured her by saying at one point that the "whole [U.S.] government is against you" and that "if there is a war, my opinion is that the President will oppose you." Meir asked, "Even if the Egyptians attack?" and Kissinger replied "Yes." *Foreign Relations of the United States* (*FRUS*) 1969–76, vol. 25, no. 398, "Memorandum of Conversation," December 16, 1973, pp. 1101 and 1105. http://history.state.gov/historicaldocuments/frus1969-76v25/d398.

† The agreement provided that Israel would not only withdraw from its advanced positions on the road to Damascus but also pull back beyond the city of Quneitra, the Syrian "capital" of the Golan Heights. The Israelis would remain in the Golan Heights and the Syrians would accept separation of forces and limited deployment zones, a UN monitoring presence, and a U.S. provision of aerial reconnaissance to each side. The reconnaissance mission has been conducted by the United States since 1974 and is called Olive Harvest.

he is reported to have said at one point, "You're always looking at the trees, and you don't see the woods! If we didn't have this negotiation, there'd be an international forum for the 1967 frontiers."[105] Kissinger was dealing with a Labor—not a Likud—government, but his criticisms of Israeli inflexibility and lack of strategic vision would be repeated countless times in the future; his arguments echo through the years in the voices of successive presidents and secretaries of state.

Nixon scheduled a trip to the Middle East almost immediately after Kissinger's successful mediation, hoping that this could bolster him politically. He was obviously thinking of his domestic position but also genuinely thought he could build real momentum toward peace. In Egypt, he was greeted by crowds that actually exceeded Israel's entire population, and he wrote about how moved he was by the reception—no doubt contrasting this support and respect with his criticism at home. For him, the Arab part of the trip was the highlight, as he saw the potential for the United States to make major new inroads; prior to the trip he referred in his diary to our having "apparent success in weaning the Arabs away from the Soviets," and his journey convinced him that the United States could actually succeed in this objective.[106] Yet the trip was too late in his presidency to affect the realities of peacemaking. Less than two months after his return to Washington, he would resign the presidency.

Ford and Kissinger: One More Interim Agreement and Tension with Israel

Gerald Ford assumed the presidency in a time of economic difficulty and with the country reeling from the resignation of its president. Ford's pardon of Nixon may have been necessary to spare the country the ordeal of a trial of a former president, but it greatly damaged Ford's authority. Kissinger's star shone brightly at this time, and Ford largely deferred to the secretary of state in foreign policy—and certainly in the Middle East. Indeed, Ford, who had been a staunch supporter of Israel during his entire career in the House of Representatives, now adopted a much tougher posture toward the Israelis. This pressure emerged at the time that Kissinger initially failed at producing a second disengagement agreement in the Sinai.

In his memoirs, Ford's description of his approach to Israel reflects the continuing desire to extract reciprocity from the Israelis—an impulse clearly seen with Kennedy, Johnson, and Nixon.

Every American President since Harry Truman had willingly supplied arms and funds to the Jewish state. The Israelis were stronger militarily than all their Arab neighbors combined, yet peace was no closer than it had ever been. So I began to question the rationale for our policy. I wanted the Israelis to recognize that there had to be some *quid pro quo*. If we were going to build up their military capabilities, we in turn had to see some flexibility to achieve a fair, secure, and permanent peace.[107]

Although Ford is wrong about the history of American provision of arms to Israel—Truman and Eisenhower did not do what Ford describes— he captures the strong conviction that the United States needed something in return from Israel for our support.

Ford was prepared to apply great pressure on Israel in pursuit of another disengagement agreement in the Sinai. Initial discussions in November 1974 did not lead anywhere, and Kissinger waited until March to launch another shuttle. This turned into a struggle over several issues: the depth of the Israeli withdrawal and the extent of the Egyptian advance; the fate of the Israeli early-warning stations in the key Sinai passes and the Abu Rhodeis oil fields; the duration of the agreement; and Egypt's readiness to commit to nonbelligerency and the nonuse of force.

Much as he had during the Syrian shuttle, Kissinger complained about the Israelis missing the big picture. As failure loomed, he lamented to them that

> an agreement would have enabled the United States to remain in control of the diplomatic process. Compared to that, the location of the line eight kilometers one way or the other frankly does not seem very important. And you got all the military elements of nonbelligerency. You got the "nonuse of force." The elements you didn't get—movement of peoples, ending of the boycotts—are *unrelated* to your line. What you didn't get has nothing to do with where your line is.[108]

For Kissinger, Israel was damaging its interests and ours, and we would have a hard time defending it. He told Rabin that the "Soviets will be happy and there will be an immediate Arab-Soviet demand to reconvene the Geneva Conference. Under the circumstances, I can't promise you anything about American policy."[109] While Kissinger only implied a threat, he had Ford make an explicit one in a letter that arrived the night before the secretary of state ended the shuttle:

I wish to express my profound disappointment over Israel's attitude in the course of the negotiations . . . Failure of the negotiations will have a far-reaching impact on the region and on our relations. I have given instructions for a reassessment of United States policy in the region, including our relations with Israel with the aim of ensuring that overall American interests . . . are protected. You will be notified of our decision."[110]

Ford's blunt words failed to make the Israelis cave on what the United States was asking on behalf of Sadat. Rabin recounts that rather than making the members of the Israeli cabinet reconsider their collective position, it had the opposite effect.[111]

When Kissinger ended the shuttle, he made explicit the "reassessment" of relations with Israel, telling reporters, initially under the guise of being a "senior official," that Israel was to blame for the breakdown of the talks, that the Rabin government was weak, and that a reassessment was called for given the impact on U.S. interests.[112] In his memoirs, Ford explained why Kissinger focused so clearly on Israel: "Henry was deeply disappointed by the Israeli attitude. He was worried that Sadat, who had gone along with many of our suggestions, would never work with us again."[113] All along, the Kissinger strategy depended on our producing for moderate Arabs like Sadat. The problem was that he was paying with Israeli currency—not our own—and the Israelis felt they were not getting much in return for giving up territory.

Rabin found his own way to fight back. In addition to allowing Ford's threatening letter to be leaked, he encouraged Israel's friends on the Hill to react to the pressure on Israel. They produced a letter signed by seventy-six senators—covering the spectrum from left to right—which, among other things, called on the administration to meet Israel's urgent military and economic needs and to stand firm with Israel in the search for peace. These should form the basis of the administration's "reassessment."

When Ford met Rabin two months later, in June, he expressed his displeasure with the leak and with the letter from the senators. He threatened Rabin that if Israel was not prepared to be more flexible on withdrawal in the Sinai, then the United States would give up on negotiating an interim deal with Egypt, reconvene Geneva, go for a comprehensive agreement with all of Israel's neighbors, and leave Israel to fend for itself in that forum. Returning to Geneva conjured an image of Israel isolated in a setting where, rather than negotiating bilaterally with its neighbors, the Israelis would face a common front—and without the certainty of U.S. protection. While Rabin implies that he pushed back in the face of unreasonable pressure, he in fact offered new concessions on the Sinai passes if the United States would take charge of Israel's early-warning stations there.*[114] When Kissinger offered new proposals in response to the Israelis showing flexibility, both Israel and Egypt signaled an agreement was possible.

On August 31, 1975, a deal was reached. To gain Israeli cabinet approval of the agreement, Rabin told Kissinger that he needed American assurances. The resulting Memorandum of Agreement was far-reaching economically, militarily, and diplomatically. Not only would the United States provide the roughly $2 billion in aid the Israelis had requested for the coming year, we also promised to compensate them economically for the oil given up in the Abu Rhodeis field and to meet Israel's oil needs if they could not be met otherwise. Further, the Memorandum of Agreement promised to consult regularly on Israel's economic and military needs while requesting assistance for Israel from the Congress on an annual basis—an important new precedent. Militarily, we agreed to review Israel's request for the F-16 fighter, with the implication that we would be responsive. This was an impressive list of commitments.

The diplomatic assurances were also of enduring significance. They included commitments not to undertake diplomatic initiatives on peace without first "consult[ing] fully with the Government of Israel" and not to recognize the PLO or deal with it so long as it did not "recognize Israel's right to exist and [did] not accept Security Council Resolutions 242 and 338." All the key elements of the agreement were embodied in a presidential letter from Ford to Rabin—with one important additional proviso on Syria and the Golan Heights: if the United States ever adopted a position on the final status of the Golan Heights, we would give "great weight" to Israel's maintaining a presence there.[115]

Presidential letters are significant and traditionally bind succeeding administrations. When I served in later administrations, I saw how these commitments affected their behavior. Kissinger promised a great deal to gain the second interim agreement in the Sinai. It should come as no surprise that Rabin, even as he recounted his battles with Kissinger, also attested to how much he did for Israel's security.

The Sinai II agreement marked the end of Kissinger's achievements on peace in the Middle East. To cement ties with the Arabs—and given continuing concerns about another oil embargo—the Ford administration

---

* The Gidi and Mitla passes held the key to strategic movement of ground forces throughout the Sinai.

provided significant arms to the Saudis and also began to talk about dealing with the Palestinian issue. Notwithstanding the pledge not to negotiate with the PLO, Kissinger approved congressional testimony by Harold Saunders, which hinted this could change. Saunders, who now worked for Kissinger in the State Department, stated that the Palestinians were the heart of the conflict. Saunders acknowledged that we did not yet have "the framework for a negotiation involving the PLO," but he added that "it is obvious that thinking on the Palestinian aspects of the problem must evolve on all sides. As it does, what is not possible today may become possible."[116]

The testimony was meant to send a signal at a time when the Ford administration was eager to show responsiveness to the Arabs. The administration would do so not only with a $7.5 billion arms sale to Saudi Arabia, weapons to Jordan, and the first sales to Egypt of C-130 Hercules transport aircraft. It also criticized Israel's settlement policies. William Scranton had been appointed to replace Daniel Patrick Moynihan, an outspoken defender of Israel and, as our ambassador to the UN, the leader in opposing the "Zionism is Racism" resolution. Scranton would give a speech on March 23, 1976, at the UN criticizing unilateral Israeli measures in the territories and referring to the settlements in the occupied territories—including Jerusalem—as "illegal." He added that they were an "obstacle to the success of the negotiations for a just and final peace between Israel and its neighbors."[117]

Thus it was the Ford administration that first labeled Israeli settlements illegal; Carter, too, would describe the settlements as illegal. Reagan would alter our posture to say simply that they were an obstacle to peace. This posture, treating settlements as a political and not a legal issue, would be embraced by all succeeding U.S. presidents.* What is striking is that the Ford administration's position was articulated by Scranton in an authorized speech with a Rabin Labor-led government in power, and Labor's approach to settlements was far more limited than Likud's.[118] And yet, as part of the effort to show sensitivity to the Arabs, the Ford administration adopted this stance.

Mind-sets and Lessons from Nixon and Ford

Nixon's mind-set was complicated. On the one hand, he saw the Six-Day War as a loss for the United States and a gain for the Soviets. In his eyes, we

---

* As we will see, President Obama would move back in the legality direction in the first year of his administration.

had to improve our position with the Arabs, and this meant reaching out to those who had broken relations with us—Egypt and Syria and their radical nationalist governments at the time. Fundamentally, according to Kissinger, Nixon felt that Israel's policies created problems for us in the region. In this sense, he was much like Eisenhower and Dulles. And yet, unlike them, for all his talk of being impervious to domestic politics, Nixon was mindful of the need to manage them and Israel's supporters in the United States. Moreover, he was a deep believer in the balance of power globally and the need to play power politics vis-à-vis the Soviets, which meant standing by Israel because we could not have Soviet arms defeat American arms.

Nixon wrote in one of his long memos to Kissinger in 1970, "Our interests are basically pro-freedom," and "we are *for* Israel because Israel . . . is the only state in the Mideast which is *pro*-freedom and an effective opponent to Soviet expansion." But he went on to equate Israel with South Vietnam—which was hardly pro-freedom but was part of the power equation in our competition with the Soviet Union.[119]

Nixon's instincts thus led him in two different directions: distancing from Israel—which meant withholding arms as an attempt to wean the Arabs away from the Soviets—and yet a readiness to stand by Israel in its hour of need in 1973. After the war, he was prepared to pressure the Israelis. Indeed, he saw oil as leaving us little choice.

For Nixon, U.S. pressure was justified by a view reminiscent of Roosevelt's that a Jewish state could not survive the hostility of so many millions of Arabs, and that only a peace settlement could save Israel. He wrote Kissinger relatively early in the administration that "I am beginning to think we have to consider taking strong steps unilaterally to save Israel from her own destruction."[120] And, later, just before his trip to the Middle East in June 1974, he wrote in his diary, "Whether Israel can survive over a long period of time with a hundred million Arabs around them I think is really questionable. The only long-term hope lies in reaching some kind of settlement now while they can operate from a position of strength."[121]

Kissinger was on the same page with Nixon on power politics. He shared the view that we could compete with the Soviets by showing the Arabs that only the United States could move the Israelis and deliver concessions. But he wanted it to benefit us and not the Soviets, and he wanted something from the Arabs in return. He could not understand chasing after the Egyptians as long as Nasser led Egypt. He understood that Nasser's desire to be the leader of "progressive, anti-imperialist forces" internationally required an anti-American posture. No amount of distancing from Israel or U.S.-produced Israeli concessions would alter his behavior. Indeed, Nasser's own self-definition and priorities precluded a change in Egypt's fundamental posture.[122] So Kissinger would try to convince Nixon of the folly of the Rogers–State Department thinking and of the certainty that their initiatives would fail, leaving the Arabs in the Soviet court.

Kissinger had seen the value of Israeli power when it came to saving King Hussein of Jordan in the crisis in September 1970; Nixon's own instincts about the costs of collaborating with the Israelis left him opposed to using Israeli threats or intervention until it became clear that Israel had the means and we did not. Nixon understood that we must save the king. Rogers, too, acquiesced in the end, but his own attitudes and those of his department made them certain that no Arab leader could "afford" to be saved by the Israelis. In an instance that surely demonstrates how deeply this mind-set was embedded in the psyche of State Department officials, Kissinger recounts the Jordanians going to the deputy chief of the U.S. mission in Amman in September 1970 to ask about possible Israeli reactions to a threat to Jordan: "Reflecting the State Department attitude, our chargé responded to renewed Jordanian queries about Israeli intentions with the extraordinary statement that he could not imagine Jordan's accepting help from its enemy Israel against a fellow Arab country."[123]

Survival was the first priority of most Arab leaders, and if the Israelis could make the difference, they would seek such help. Yet this did not occur to this official or many like him. They accepted the narrative in the region that Israel was a pariah and any association with it was the kiss of death. That mind-set was so rigidly in place that our chargé did not recognize that the question itself indicated the Jordanian desire to receive such help. Generally, many in the State Department could not "imagine" circumstances where Israel could actually be of help to us or serve our interests. Similar views existed in the CIA, and they were even more extreme, going so far as to debate whether we should support Hussein as he faced threats from Arafat and the Palestinians prior to the crisis in September 1970.[124]

While Kissinger could not shape Middle East diplomacy in Nixon's first term, he would come to dominate Middle East policy in the second and during Ford's term in office. Sensitivity to Arab oil leverage would drive our diplomacy, even though Kissinger wanted to avoid any real linkage between oil and diplomacy. However, after the war, the continuing fear of a resumption of an embargo certainly drove Nixon, and Ford also seemed mindful of it. In the Pentagon, the concern about another oil embargo and its effects led the chairman of the Joint Chiefs of Staff, George Brown, to make a revealing statement in a public lecture one year after the 1973 Yom Kippur War. He stated that if there was war in the Middle East, "You can conjure up a situation where there is another oil embargo and people in this country [the United States] are not only inconvenienced and uncomfortable but suffer and they get tough-minded enough to set down the Jewish influence in this country and break that lobby."[125] Brown reflected a conviction that our provision of supplies to Israel had resulted from Jewish pressure and not our interests. He saw a clear cost to us. He saw damage to our relations with the Arabs who held the oil threat over our heads. For him, it was domestic political pressures that cost us unnecessarily.

Starting with Kennedy, there was certainly more attention paid to the domestic supporters of Israel than existed during Eisenhower's time. Johnson would go so far as to offer tanks and jets to Israel for the first time to get Israeli/Jewish support for arms to Jordan. But domestic considerations and the so-called Jewish lobby did not stop Kennedy from reaching out to Nasser—notwithstanding Israeli opposition; they did not lead Johnson to fulfill our commitments to Israel after Nasser blockaded the Straits of Tiran in 1967; they did not prevent Nixon from withholding arms to Israel even as the Soviets provided unprecedented weapons to Egypt or from withholding resupply in the first week of the Yom Kippur War when Israeli losses were staggering; they did not prevent Ford from announcing a reassessment of relations with Israel after the failure of Kissinger's first effort to broker a second withdrawal in the Sinai.

That said, during the Ford administration, Israel's supporters became more vocal and their efforts with the Congress became more organized and effective. At the same time, the traditional fears of the costs of alienating the Arabs finally seemed to materialize with the oil embargo. Our vulnerability, and the European hysteria in response to the cut-back in oil supplies during the Yom Kippur War, convinced much of the national security establishment that the costs of association with Israel were simply too high and, therefore, we must press Israel to concede territory. James Schlesinger said at one point during the war that it was one thing to protect Israel, something else to protect its conquests.

Kissinger was not exaggerating when he told Meir that anti-Israel "tendencies" were reemerging in the government. The great irony, of course, is that once again what ultimately drove the behavior of key Arab oil countries like Saudi Arabia were their own interests. To be sure, they had no love for Israel. Our association with Israel and its relations with us could put the Arabs on the defensive—and they hated being put on the defensive. Their leaders often repeated that if only Israel did not create problems, everything would be fine. I heard these words often in meetings with different Arab leaders and officials over the years, and certainly they were standard fare for all those who did business in this part of the world.

Yet again, those Arab countries that felt their interests depended on ties to the United States made sure to preserve those relations and security links, regardless of what we were doing with Israel. The Saudis, as noted above, canceled the oil embargo after five months and sought massive arms sales from us; they embraced a joint economic commission designed to foster greater U.S. economic investment in Saudi Arabia as a way of binding us closer together. They did all this even though we neither forced the Israelis to withdraw to the 1967 lines nor addressed the Palestinian issue as they demanded.*

Distancing from Israel in the first two years of the administration once again bought us nothing with those Arabs with whom we sought to restore ties. It created only greater demands. The improvement in our ties to Egypt emerged from the change in leadership from Nasser to Sadat in late 1970, not from our distancing. On the contrary, as Sadat admitted, the United States held 99 percent of the cards and that is why he made peace. Here again, the irony was lost on those who could see our relationship with Israel only in terms of its cost: it was our strong ties to Israel that gave us influence, not our distancing from it. The Soviets, by contrast, had no relationship with Israel, and so once the war ended, their utility to Sadat plummeted. That reality would dawn on the Carter administration, but not immediately.

---

* One other factor that led the Saudis to drop the embargo was their concern that Iran was gaining market share at their expense.

6

THE CARTER PRESIDENCY: THE PURSUIT OF PEACE AND CONSTANT TENSION WITH ISRAEL

If there is one word I would use to describe the Carter administration's relations with Israel it is "irony." No administration was more committed to pursuing Arab-Israeli peace, and no administration offered Israel more as a consequence of brokering Israel's first peace treaty with an Arab neighbor. And yet no administration was more consistently critical of Israel in private and public. For President Jimmy Carter, Israel seemed to be a constant irritant. It frustrated his designs for Middle East peace, but he would spend more time on this issue than any other in his presidency. Later he would write, "Looking back, it is remarkable to see how constantly the work for peace in the Middle East was on my agenda, and my mind."[1] As he would also say, many other issues might claim his attention, but "the Middle East question preyed on [his] mind."[2]

Israel was at the heart of that preoccupation because Carter could not achieve his objective of peace without Israeli acquiescence. In his eyes, the Israelis were resisting what he thought was fair, necessary for Israel, and, most important, essential to safeguarding U.S. interests in the region. Ironically, Carter's devotion of time and attention to Middle East peace did yield the singular achievement of his presidency—the Egyptian-Israeli peace treaty in 1979 after the Camp David Accords—yet other developments and crises in the region not only threatened our interests but ultimately doomed his presidency. The fall of the shah in Iran, the taking of the American hostages at our embassy in Tehran, the Soviet invasion of Afghanistan, and the Iraq-Iran War all combined to produce a dramatic rise in the price of oil and showcased American impotence in a way that led to Carter's loss to Ronald Reagan in the 1980 presidential election.

Each of these crises surprised the administration, and not one of them could have been prevented by Arab-Israeli peacemaking. It is hard to escape the reality that Carter was so preoccupied with Arab-Israeli peace that he paid scant attention to Iran and the cascade of problems triggered by the fall of the shah.[3]

James Schlesinger, Carter's first secretary of energy, later complained that the Iran issue "was not effectively brought to his [Carter's] attention." With Carter and his advisers focused elsewhere, principally on the Egyptian-Israeli peace talks, Schlesinger recalled that "when I made my own rounds in November and December of 1978, the top topics [Iran] appeared to me to be reasonably novel in the eyes of . . . all the President's political advisors."[4] Schlesinger prefaced this observation by saying not only had he received a letter from one of his former subordinates in the Defense Department telling him in March 1978 that "the Shah is in mortal peril" but also that Carter came to the issue late and with ambivalent feelings about the shah.[5]

There was no such ambivalence about Arab-Israeli peace. It was the strategic preoccupation of Carter and his key advisers Zbigniew Brzezinski and Cyrus Vance, his national security adviser and the secretary of state. Brzezinski, who tended to define international relations in broad architectural terms, believed that the world had moved into a "new post-Eurocentric era" and the Arab-Israeli issue resonated strongly not just in the Middle East but also throughout the third world.[6] Solve it and the United States would appeal to the Arabs, reduce the risk of another Saudi-OPEC-led oil embargo, freeze the Soviets out of the Middle East, and identify with the aspirations of those in the developing world—or so Carter, Brzezinski, and the rest believed. Indeed, Carter would say at the White House dinner for the crown prince of Saudi Arabia in May 1977 that "there is an increasing realization that peace in that region means to a great degree a possibility of peace throughout the world."[7]

Like the Nixon administration, which in 1969 began with a sense of urgency about launching a diplomatic initiative on Middle East peace, the Carter presidency decided that it must immediately push high-level diplomacy to end the Arab-Israeli conflict. Unlike the Nixon administration, however, where Kissinger was at odds with Rogers and those in the State

Department about how to proceed, there was no basic division in the Carter administration. The White House and the State Department were on the same page. Brzezinski, Vance, and their leading aides all shared the same basic assumptions and attitudes about strategy toward Middle East peace. Brzezinski observed in his journal early in the administration that "Cy, the President and I are very much on the same wavelength insofar as the Middle East is concerned."[8] Later he would say that the American team was "remarkably united," and Vance praised the State and NSC aides working in "total harmony" on this issue.[9]

That harmony stood out because Brzezinski and Vance diverged so sharply on other issues. When it came to dealing with the Soviet Union or the approach to Iran as the shah's position deteriorated, they were completely at odds. But that was not the case on peace in the Middle East. They agreed on its primacy and on the fundamental need to change Israel's behavior and address the Palestinians as the core of the conflict.

Brzezinski was probably the most convinced that a "showdown" with Israel—a word he repeatedly used in his journal entries—was inevitable. But Carter used this word frequently as well. For the national security establishment in the Carter administration, it was Israel we had to pressure; it was the Arabs we had to embrace. Too close identification with Israel would cost us with them and provide the Soviets openings in the region—and, of course, peace was seen as the means to freeze the Soviets out of the area.

The built-in suspicion of Israel's motives expressed in previous administrations was widely shared among Carter and those around him. Prior to Carter's first meeting with Prime Minister Yitzhak Rabin in March 1977, early in the administration, Brzezinski described the collective mind set about Israel:

> We expected Israeli opposition, for it was our feeling that the Israelis were essentially playing for time, and were more interested in preserving an exclusive relationship with the United States than in moving toward a broader peace in the Middle East. We were determined to retain close links with Israel, but we knew that we had to widen our relations with the more moderate Arab states, to build on what had been achieved by Nixon and Kissinger in Egypt, and to intensify our collaboration with Saudi Arabia.[10]

Bear in mind that this expectation was held at a time when the Labor Party, not Likud, still dominated Israel. Rabin, not Menachem Begin, was prime minister. The interest in drawing closer to the Saudis reflected an awareness of our dependence on Middle East oil and the deep fear within the Carter administration of another oil embargo. Peace would remove that possible threat. Peace would also allow us to live up to our commitment to Israel's security without paying a price in the area. In what would become a mantra in future administrations as well, peace was seen as the best guarantee of Israel's security.

At one level, such a mantra is a truism. Yes, if Israel had true peace with its neighbors, it would be secure. But for the Israelis, this mantra was more tautology than reality. They did not see signs that their neighbors were prepared for genuine acceptance of the Jewish state in their midst. It was Israel's military strength that lessened Arab temptations to resort to war and that conditioned its neighbors to the reality of living with Israel and giving up the idea of its destruction. In time, perhaps, genuine peace might become possible. As such, the Israelis across the political spectrum had their own mantra: security was the best guarantee of security. To them, this was the only way to promote and sustain peace.

Carter never accepted the Israeli view, but he understood later that in order to achieve a peace treaty between Israel and Egypt he would have to offer Israel significant security assistance—and he did so. He offered assistance to the Egyptians as well, and those commitments to Israel and Egypt on military and economic assistance have endured since the peace treaty of March 1979. They have formed a critical baseline for U.S. policy since that time.

Moreover, while Carter may have been riveted on peace to the exclusion of other regional issues, he would become much more focused on security concerns late in the administration. In another irony, it is Carter who, after the December 1979 Soviet invasion of Afghanistan, enunciated the Carter Doctrine in January 1980, in which he declared that the United States would never permit an outside power to gain control over the Persian Gulf. Once again, it may well have been oil that guided the policy, but the fact remains that it was the Carter administration—an administration that had focused on peace to the near exclusion of everything else in the region—that laid the foundation for our ongoing security posture in the broader Middle East. The plans were formulated then for what later became the Central Command with the forces and infrastructure needed to project American power to this region.

Even in the last year of Carter's presidency, when the preoccupation shifted from peace to the hostages held by Iran and our need to shore up our security position in the Persian Gulf, the administration continued to look at the Jewish state as more of a liability than an asset. Neither Israel's peace with Egypt nor the sudden Saudi interest in having greater U.S. visibility in providing Saudi security altered this view.

In essence, three distinct periods characterize Carter's policy toward the region: the period until Sadat goes to Jerusalem, when the focus was on re-convening the Geneva conference; the years of managing Egyptian and Is-raeli talks and ensuring they neither collapsed nor produced only a separate peace; and the period after the Egyptian-Israeli peace agreement, when the focus was on Iran and the Soviet invasion of Afghanistan.

Getting to Geneva

Middle East peace was more than a preoccupation as Carter entered the White House; it was, in Brzezinski's words, "an urgent priority of the new Administration. The new team believed that the stalemate that existed in 1977 would gradually fragment with disastrous consequences for world peace as well as for the United States itself."

Like Nixon, Brzezinski worried about a "major U.S.-Soviet confronta-tion" and saw peace in the Middle East as a way to deny the Soviets a foot-hold in this strategic region.[11] Carter shared this concern, but he also focused on oil: "OPEC had considerably strengthened Arab clout in foreign capitals." He did not relish being "isolated along with Israel." And he understood American vulnerabilities, observing that "by the beginning of 1977, we our-selves had become increasingly dependent on foreign oil and therefore more vulnerable to future attempts at blackmail—with our own security directly threatened."[12]

Small wonder, therefore, that Cyrus Vance would say that "President Carter and I agreed that his administration would take an immediate, lead-ing role in breathing new life into the Middle East peace process."[13]

The assessment of the administration's Middle East specialists, Harold Saunders and William Quandt, both of whom had worked for Kissinger, was that the pursuit of interim agreements had "exhausted its potential and that it was time to renew the pursuit of a comprehensive peace."[14] With comprehensive peace as the goal, it made sense to try to reconvene the Ge-neva Conference, where all the Arabs would be present with Israel. Carter decided in a February NSC meeting that we should aim to do so before the end of the year. Vance would make an early trip to the region and start discussions in Israel. Interestingly, Vance felt that we had to start discussions with Israel not because it was an ally or partner but because Nixon and Ford had given "us a rather narrow line to walk in discussing our ideas with Israel before trying them out with the Arabs."[15] In truth, it was not Nixon who had obligated us but Kissinger through the 1975 Ford-Rabin letter that was part of the U.S. assurances to Israel to get them to conclude the Sinai II agreement. That letter also committed us not to deal with the PLO unless it recognized Israel's right to exist *and* accepted UN Resolution 242. As we will see, these commitments constrained the Carter administration but did not prevent it from interpreting them liberally and minimally.

Vance believed that his initial trip to the region was a good beginning; he felt each leader—Arab and Israeli—understood the importance of defining his own position, heard Vance's description of the "views of the others," and accepted "that the United States would seek compromise solutions."[16] Even from this early moment, Sadat was pressing for substantive U.S. proposals, believing only that would produce progress.

Vance saw his trip as preparing the ground for the president's meetings with the Israeli, Egyptian, Jordanian, Syrian, and Saudi leaders over the course of the spring. The idea was for the president to focus on drawing each leader out even while he conditioned them to our views that peace must consist of having normal relations; that the final borders would need to be close to the 1967 lines with only minor modifications but with appropriate security arrangements; and that there would be a need for a Palestinian homeland—not necessarily a state—if the Palestinian issue was to be resolved.[17]

The president's aim in the meetings was to begin laying the substantive basis for Geneva so when it convened we might have already achieved agreement on the basic principles that should guide the negotiations toward a comprehensive peace settlement. His first meeting was with Yitzhak Rabin, the Israeli prime minister. It did not go well. Rabin saw Carter repeating the mistakes of Rogers, seeking to lay out borders that should be negotiated and giving the Arabs no reason to compromise. He saw Carter as leaning far too forward on the Palestinians, and pushing for a Geneva conference that would produce a lowest common denominator on the Arab side. Carter saw Rabin as unresponsive. In his diary entry of March 7, 1977, Carter described his attempt to draw Rabin out on what he hoped to see in a permanent settlement, and he could get nowhere. Carter went on to say that he

> found him very timid, stubborn, and also somewhat ill at ease. When he went upstairs with me, just the two of us, I asked him to tell me what

Israel wanted me to do when I met with the Arab leaders and if there were something specific that I could get Sadat to do. He didn't unbend at all, nor did he respond. It seems to me the Israelis, at least Rabin, don't trust our government or any of their neighbors. I guess there's some justification for this distrust.[18]

Rabin's perceived nonresponsiveness reinforced the preexisting view that Israel was not serious about peace. Unfortunately, the aftermath of the meeting further soured relations. In a press conference on March 9, Carter said that "there may be extensions of Israeli defense capability beyond the permanent and recognized borders"—seemingly embracing the Israeli concept of "defensible borders."[19] But when Rabin publicly claimed that Carter supported the Israeli concept—that borders must be different from the indefensible 1967 lines, which left Israel nine miles wide at its narrowest point—the White House issued a clarification denying it. To make matters worse for Rabin, Carter talked publicly about nearly full Israeli withdrawal to the 1967 lines, and a week later in a town hall meeting in Clinton, Massachusetts, declared that "there has to be a homeland provided for the Palestinian refugees who have suffered for many, many years."[20] The language shocked Israelis and fostered an impression that there was "a crisis . . . in U.S.-Israeli relations."[21]

When combined with Carter's decision to veto the Israeli sale of Kfir jets to Ecuador* and to cancel weapons sales to the IDF, the perception grew in Israel that the Labor-led government had a serious problem with the new administration. In advance of the meetings with Arab leaders, and the Israeli elections, this did not seem to concern the leading officials in the administration. Nonetheless, as Brzezinski noted, it did "arouse Jewish public opinion" and "create the impression that the new administration was "tilting away from Israel."[22]

The positive cast given to Carter's meetings with the Arab leaders deepened this impression. Sadat's visit took place shortly after Rabin's, and it went well. Vance noted that Carter and Sadat almost immediately developed "a special bond of trust and confidence."[23] Carter observed that Sadat early in the meeting had said that full diplomatic relations were not possible "in his lifetime," but he softened his position later in the discussion and also

---

* The United States had a say in the matter because the jets had an American-made engine, and the administration was seen early on to try to reduce arms transfers throughout the developing world.

offered what Carter saw as unprecedented flexibility when he said that "some minimal deviation from the 1967 borders might be acceptable." Sadat completely won Carter over at the end of the meeting, when he made it clear that his priority was peace: "When we talked about military sales to Egypt he said, 'I would rather do without weapons that we need, like the F-5E fighter plane, in order not to endanger the possibilities of a Middle East peace settlement.'"[24]

King Hussein similarly made a good impression. In the meeting with the president, the king acknowledged that Israel needed adequate security but added that "security is less a matter of geography and borders than a state of mind and a feeling of wanting to live in peace."[25] Although this played well with Carter, it was hardly likely to be a source of reassurance to the Israelis, who saw few signs of Arab acceptance of Israel and nothing in Hussein's own behavior that indicated he was prepared to run any risks for peace. Nonetheless, it clearly affected Carter's perceptions. As he wrote in his diary after seeing Hussein, "My own judgment at this time is that the Arab leaders want to settle it and the Israelis don't. The Israeli government has been pretty much in limbo for the last few years. I don't know if the elections in May will help or not, but we are thinking about having someone meet with the representatives of the PLO after the Israeli elections and my final meeting with other Middle East leaders."[26]

Already, Carter was indicating that he might not treat Kissinger's commitments on the PLO as a straitjacket. The notion of reaching out to the PLO fit with the broader approach of making our own judgment of what the appropriate solution should be and then presenting it in the context of the Geneva Conference. Indeed, once Carter finished his meetings with the Arab leaders, the plan was for Vance to go to the region—ostensibly to crystallize our thinking further—and then, in Carter's words, we would "put together our own concept of what should be done in the Middle East . . . and then put as much pressure as we can bring to bear on the different parties to accept the solution we think is fair."[27]

First, of course, Carter had to see Hafez al Assad and then Crown Prince Fahd of Saudi Arabia. He again was encouraged by what he heard—and the contrast with his description of Rabin could not be more striking. Of Assad, a leader with whom I would spend many long hours in the 1990s and whose approach to negotiations was more akin to attrition than any sort of give-and-take, Carter recorded in his diary, "It was a very interesting and enjoyable experience. There was a lot of good humor between us, and I found him to be very constructive in his attitude and somewhat flexible in dealing with some of the more crucial items involving peace, the Palestinians, the refugee problem, and borders."[28] Although flexibility was an attribute that few would ever ascribe to Assad, Carter somehow saw it differently. His enthusiasm bubbled over into his public comments. Following their meeting, Carter said that Assad's "intimate knowledge of the Middle Eastern region" helped him to understand the Middle East—not a statement likely to reassure Assad's Arab rivals, like Anwar Sadat, or any Israeli leader.[29]

Carter's comments on the meeting with Fahd were equally positive: "After meeting with these key Arab leaders, I was convinced that all of them were ready for a strong move on our part to find solutions to the long-standing disputes and that with such solutions would come their recognition of Israel and the right of Israelis to live in peace. I agreed with their most important premise—that the Palestinian question would have to be addressed."[30]

Unfortunately for Carter's plans to press ahead on peace, in May Israel elected as prime minister Menachem Begin, a Likud leader. Unlike Rabin's Labor Party, the Likud did not believe in territorial compromise and claimed the West Bank, an area they referred to by its biblical names of Judea and Samaria. Carter, after watching Begin being interviewed, was concerned that Begin referred to Judea and Samaria as liberated territories in which he hoped to see a Jewish majority emerge: "This statement was a radical departure from past Israeli policy, and seemed to throw United Nations Resolution 242, for which Israel had voted, out the window."[31]

It is hard to escape a sense of irony: Carter had described Rabin as inflexible and unyielding yet now he realized he faced an Israeli leader who represented "a radical departure" from past Israeli policies that Rabin embodied. Moreover, there is no awareness that maybe our posture, by creating a sense of crisis in the U.S.-Israel relationship, might have contributed to Labor's defeat in the election. Interestingly, William Quandt, the senior Middle East adviser on the NSC staff, would later make this very point.[32]

Unlike Carter, who initially worried about the consequences of Begin's election, Brzezinski saw an opportunity. He felt that "precisely because Begin is so extreme, the President will be able to mobilize on behalf of a settlement a significant portion of the American Jewish community . . . This will make it easier for the President to prevail and to have the needed congressional support."[33] He continued to think that we should confront the Israelis, believing that they could not sustain opposition in the face of real U.S. pressure. Emotionally, Carter shared the Brzezinski position but was also well aware of the political costs:

I was increasingly concerned about criticisms of our peace initiatives from within the American Jewish community. My own political supporters were coming to see me . . . and stirrings in Congress were becoming more pronounced . . . Additionally, they were troubled about some of our proposals concerning the Palestinian issue and "dual borders" and my highly publicized and apparently friendly series of meetings with the Arab leaders.[34]

It made sense to find out what was possible with Begin, who would come to Washington in July. Carter's initial impressions of Begin recorded in his memoirs were positive: "I think Begin is a very good man and although it will be difficult for him to change positions, the public opinion polls that we have from Israel show that the people there are quite flexible . . . and genuinely want peace. My own guess is that if we give Begin support, he will prove to be a strong leader, quite different from Rabin, who is one of the most ineffective persons I've ever met."[35]

Begin clearly sought to make a good impression in this initial meeting. According to Dayan, Begin, in preparation for the meetings, adopted positions that represented, for him, very meaningful flexibility. He conveyed to Carter a readiness to go to the Geneva Conference, make significant concessions in the Sinai, and withdraw from the present lines on the Golan to a permanent border. While Israel would not transfer sovereignty to any foreign power in Judea, Samaria, and Gaza, it would also not claim sovereignty at this point. In addition, Begin was ready to negotiate without preconditions on the basis of UNSCR 338, which included Resolution 242, the key resolution on territorial compromise.[36]

This is not to say there was agreement. Begin was not prepared to make a commitment on withdrawal as a price for getting the Arabs to come to Geneva, and he asked that we not make public our position on final borders—though, of course, Carter had already done so.

Also, perhaps with the desire not to spoil the atmosphere, Begin did not respond when Carter spelled out our position that settlements were illegal and settlement building should cease. His silence was significant. For when he returned to Israel, he announced new settlement building—a sign of bad faith in Carter's eyes.

The Carter administration condemned Begin's announcement, referring again to the illegality of settlements. It was in this climate that Vance went to the region in August, hoping to gain agreement on principles that would serve as the substantive basis for negotiations launched at the Geneva

Conference. He discovered, unhappily, that Begin's acceptance of 242 did not apply on all fronts. Moreover, the Israeli government could not accept two key principles that the administration felt were essential for guiding the negotiations: withdrawal to the 1967 lines with minor modifications and a Palestinian entity to enable the Palestinians to achieve self-determination.

These Israeli positions and the Saudi inability to broker an understanding with the PLO on accepting 242—even after Carter and Vance agreed to soften our posture and go along with a PLO reservation on the resolution— led the administration to shift its focus from substance to procedure in the conference.[37] But even that would prove difficult as Syria insisted on a role for the plenary and one Arab delegation for all the Arab parties, including the Palestinians. The Egyptians and Israelis were dead set against such an arrangement, as it would preclude bilateral negotiations. From Sadat's perspective, it would give Syria a veto. Vance found Sadat uneasy with the focus on procedure and once again preferred us to present an American plan on substance.

Secret Diplomacy, the U.S.-Soviet Joint Statement, and Sadat Goes to Jerusalem

Several developments in September and October altered the diplomatic landscape and led Sadat to take a leap and go to Jerusalem. First, Dayan met secretly with Hassan Tuhami, Egypt's deputy prime minister, in Morocco. Shortly after Begin had been elected, the Israelis used the Moroccans to pass intelligence to the Egyptians about a secret Libyan plot against Sadat. When the Egyptians discovered that the information was correct, this surprised Sadat and opened the door to a meeting.[38] Sadat's inclination to work out an arrangement bilaterally with the Israelis had already been revealed when during Vance's August trip, he gave him a draft peace treaty that he was prepared to sign with Israel. He had pressed Vance to seek a comparable draft from the Israelis and others, and then have the United States offer a compromise proposal to bridge the differences. At this time, and without telling the United States, he agreed to the secret meeting between Tuhami and Dayan. Although Dayan in his memoirs says he did not respond to what Tuhami was seeking on the Sinai and on the other fronts, Tuhami gave Sadat the sense that the Israelis would withdraw fully in return for a peace treaty.[39]

Next, Dayan flew to the United States after his secret meeting in

Morocco—not revealing to anyone that he had had such a meeting—to see Vance and Carter. His meetings in Washington revealed very clearly Carter's view that the Israelis were the obstacle to peace. Carter pressed the Israeli foreign minister hard to stop building settlements. Though he said that was not possible, Dayan promised to recommend a reduction of settlement activity in size and scope—with the six additional settlements that Israel planned to build limited to being "carried out within the framework of military camps."[40] After initially resisting Dayan's proposal, Carter reluctantly accepted this plan, believing that construction would be circumscribed within existing military areas. However, a week later, Vance told Dayan that we could not agree to Israel building even in the military camps. Consequently, Dayan felt it was pointless to try to persuade Begin to scale back the settlement effort in this fashion.*

In the private part of their meeting, Carter vented on Israeli settlements and told Dayan, "You are more stubborn than the Arabs, and you put more obstacles on the path to peace." Dayan countered that it was not Israeli settlement activity that prevented peace: "The Arabs had been refusing to reconcile themselves to Israel's existence for thirty years, even when we had lived within the pre-1967 boundaries."[41] Carter was not persuaded by this argument, and, according to Dayan, when he and the president joined others in a larger meeting, Carter went on the offensive:

> Israel was taking an obdurate line whereas the Arabs were flexible; Israel did not really want peace . . . our deeds . . . made it difficult to convene the Geneva conference and impossible to fulfill the 'principal element' of Resolution 242—Israeli withdrawal and peace. My associates were astounded. After four wars and thirty years of Arab refusal to sit with us to discuss peace . . . the Arabs were the "flexible" ones who yearned for peace, and we were the rejectionists.[42]

Unfortunately, the situation between the president and the Israelis would get worse before it got better. On October 1, the administration issued a joint statement with the Soviets, who were cochairs of Geneva. But the Israelis reacted to the statement much the way they had to the Rogers Plan, by criticizing it sharply in public. They saw twin evils: the statement seemingly had the United States both ushering the Soviets back into the

---

* Carter would later say, when this did not happen, that Begin was "breaking his word of honor" on limiting the settlements. Carter, *White House Diary,* pp. 167–68.

Middle East peace process and accepting a new formula on the Palestinians—fulfilling their "legitimate rights"—which the Israelis felt fostered a path toward statehood. But it was not only the Israelis who were unhappy. The statement triggered a torrent of criticism from the media and the Congress against the administration for undoing the Kissinger legacy of excluding the Soviets from Middle East diplomacy. One measure of the scope and depth of the domestic backlash was that not a single senator or representative defended the administration.[43]

In an effort to douse this political firestorm, Carter and Vance met Dayan on October 4 in New York. The meeting produced a U.S.-Israeli working paper that seemingly retreated from the U.S.-Soviet paper as it did not make acceptance of the joint statement a condition for attending Geneva. The meeting, however, was confrontational, marked by blunt exchanges. At one point, Brzezinski described Dayan as saying if there was no agreed formula between us, he would have to acknowledge this to the American Jewish organizations. In response, Carter threatened, "We might have a confrontation unless you are willing to cooperate. But a confrontation would be very damaging to Israel and to the support of the American public for Israel. If there is a confrontation, and if we are cast in a role against Israel and with the Arabs, Israel would be isolated, and this would be very serious. It would be a blow to your position."[44]

Carter's own description in his diary conveys a different impression of the meeting. Even while describing the discussion as "productive," he makes his view of the Israelis crystal clear: "I told the group that there was no doubt that, of all the nations with whom we had negotiated on the Middle East, Israel was by far the most obstinate and difficult. This seemed to cause them [the Israelis] genuine concern and they kept coming back to the point, but of course Cy and Zbig and *all of us know that it's absolutely a fact.*[45]

While Brzezinski was pleased with Carter's tough words to Dayan, he worried that our retreat from the joint statement would convince the Israelis that the United States would never confront them given domestic concerns. Later, he would also cite our retreat as a reason Sadat felt he had to do something dramatic on his own—hence his trip to Jerusalem.[46] While he might have been right, Sadat's frustration with Syria probably drove him more than any other factor—and both Brzezinski and Quandt say we underestimated the enmity between Egypt and Syria.[47] Once again, our focus on Israel tended to blind us to the implications of the inter-Arab rivalry, much as it had in previous administrations.

It was Assad's posture—alongside our determination to go to Geneva—that convinced Sadat that everything would remain stuck unless he took the initiative by going to Jerusalem. Sadat's move took the Carter administration completely by surprise, and their initial response was hesitant. Sadat was undercutting their plans for Geneva, undermining getting to comprehensive peace. In short, he was sabotaging all their efforts to date.

William Quandt said the administration adopted a "fairly reserved public posture" in response. It was not that anyone was suggesting that we thwart Sadat, but, he writes, there "was some concern that negative Arab reactions, coupled with Begin's essential rigidity on the Palestinian issue, would cause the initiative to fall far short of the psychological breakthrough that Sadat sought."[48] Brzezinski said, "I took the position that we had no real alternative but to support the Egyptian-Israeli negotiations; however, we should use our influence to keep those talks from producing only a separate peace which would be inherently unstable."[49]

The Road to Camp David and the Egyptian-Israeli Peace Treaty

Comprehensive peace was the aim of the administration, and Sadat's initiative, which captured the imagination of the world, left the administration without a clear path. Carter described his uncertainty and frustration in his diary two days after Sadat's journey to Jerusalem: "We've still not gotten any report from our ambassadors in either Egypt or Israel—from the President or the Prime Minister. There is general confusion in the Middle East about specifically what we should do next. The same confusion exists in the White House."[50]

To be fair, Sadat had gone to Jerusalem on November 19 with no consultations and no preparation. The Dayan-Tuhami meeting may have convinced Sadat that he would receive a favorable Israeli response to his bold stroke, but he was essentially betting that his visit would psychologically transform the reality in Israel and create a whole new dynamic.[51] Sadat was correct that his readiness to fly to Israel and end an era of Arab rejection—the only reality that Israelis had known—would have an electric effect on the Israeli public. But there were still issues that had to be discussed and resolved.[52]

Begin and Sadat agreed to follow-on negotiations. To that end, Sadat called for an international conference in Cairo in early December. No Arab state would attend—only Israel, the United States, and the UN. Vance traveled to the region on December 10–14, but it was mostly to try to drum up support for Sadat among the Arabs, which Vance found would not be forthcoming unless Sadat "achieved speedy and noteworthy results" on all fronts. He concluded that Sadat's own political future could be jeopardized if there were progress only toward a separate Egypt-Israeli agreement. Sadat told Vance that it was essential now for Begin to respond with a readiness to withdraw to the 1967 borders and address the Palestinian issue in all its aspects.[53]

With concern about Sadat's political survival and fear that Jordan, Saudi Arabia, and other Arab friends of the United States would be unable to withstand the pressure of Iraq and Syria to ostracize Egypt—and maybe also the United States—the administration's message to Begin was that he needed to produce a generous response to Sadat. Begin conveyed that he had proposals to present to Sadat, but before doing so he wanted to visit Washington and discuss them with us.

In fact, Begin sought a U.S. imprimatur on his ideas. In a pattern that would be repeated by many of his successors, he wanted the United States to endorse his ideas to give them greater credence, both regionally and internationally. In later years, I would hear a common refrain from Israeli leaders and negotiators that their ideas couldn't be accepted by the Arabs, but ours could—meaning, of course, that the United States should use its influence to obtain the Arabs' acceptance of their ideas or proposals.[54]

In Washington, Begin faced a mixed reception to his two proposals. On the Sinai he was proposing essentially full Israeli military withdrawal, and on the West Bank and Gaza he was offering an autonomy plan for the Palestinian inhabitants. In his diary, Carter described the Sinai proposal as "acceptable to us and the Egyptians." But even though the autonomy plan was "a step in the right direction," he said Begin's proposal "on the West Bank [was] not acceptable." In his entry the following day, he was somewhat more positive about Begin, referring to areas of agreement on some of the powers of the Palestinian administrative council—the key institution of Begin's autonomy proposal—and even noting that Begin was "much more flexible than we had feared." Still, there were basic gaps between how Carter and Begin viewed autonomy: unlike Begin, Carter envisioned autonomy as transitional and not an end point for the Palestinians.[55]

On the whole, Carter, Brzezinski, and Vance all felt that Begin had taken a step. Unfortunately, when Begin met Sadat, the Egyptian president was deeply disappointed. As far as he was concerned, Begin's proposals fell far short of what he both expected and wanted. He could not sell them to the Palestinians or other Arabs. In his eyes, Begin was not taking full advantage of his bold outreach.

At this stage, with no prospect of Geneva, and with Arab support unlikely until there was substantial progress, the only game in town was the Egyptian-Israeli talks. Though disappointed by Begin's proposals, Sadat agreed to set up political and military committees that would meet and negotiate starting in mid-January 1978. Prior to those meetings, Carter flew to Iran to see the shah; he stopped in Saudi Arabia to talk about oil production and pricing decisions—as well as the peace issue—and then saw Sadat briefly in Aswan as his plane refueled on its way back to Washington.

The shah was strongly supportive of Sadat's initiative but told Carter not to expect any backing from the Saudis. He proved prophetic. Carter, nonetheless, sang the Saudis' praises in the pages of his diary: "Although sometimes they make public statements of concern, their private commitment is absolute to what Sadat is attempting to do. They're deeply worried about a possible conflict in the Middle East that might spill over into Saudi Arabia, strongly anti-Communist, and eager to accommodate us on almost anything I request."[56] That, unfortunately, did not prove prophetic.

After seeing Sadat, Carter in his diary refers to his "strong friendship" with the Egyptian leader and reflects his view that "Sadat and I have no differences between us. Now the main problem is the Palestinian question. We agreed with the Arab position: that Israel ought to withdraw completely from the occupied territories with minor adjustments in the western part, that there should be self-determination of the Palestinians short of an independent nation, and genuine peaceful relations between Israel and each of her neighbors."[57] The last point of "genuine peaceful relations" might have been Sadat's position, but it was not the Arab position at the time.

At the conclusion of their meeting, Carter, seeking to publicly shore up Sadat's position and give a direction to the Egyptian-Israeli talks, laid out three principles: true peace required normal relations between the parties; withdrawal must be from the territories occupied in 1967 to secure and recognized borders; and the Palestinian problem needed to be resolved in all its aspects, requiring recognition of the legitimate rights of the Palestinian people and their participation in the determination of their own future.[58]

The Israelis were not consulted on this language, and they saw a clear U.S. effort to lean forward on the Palestinians. The words did not include "self-determination," but they were meant to get as close to that meaning as possible.

Still, with the political and military committees set to meet within two weeks after the Aswan meeting, the Israelis chose not to make an issue of what became known as the "Aswan formula." But things did not go as planned. Sadat withdrew his delegation from the political committee in Jerusalem, claiming Begin disrespected his foreign minister. The real reason was that he thought the Israelis were haggling over details instead of dealing with the big issues.[59]

Vance met with both Begin and Sadat separately in Jerusalem and Cairo. Begin felt he was being castigated for acting intransigent when, in his mind, he had offered substantial proposals. Sadat, meanwhile, felt Begin had missed the essence of his initiative. Vance understood that two months after Sadat's historic move, there was a stalemate.[60]

Carter decided to invite Sadat to Camp David in the beginning of February to see what could be done. In the days prior to Sadat's arrival, Carter's diary has four entries on Israel, and every one of them is focused on settlements. He describes a meeting with congressional leaders and their growing support for the Arabs because of the Israeli "insistence on the illegal settlements." And then on three successive days—January 30 and 31, and February 1—he speaks of Begin "breaking his word of honor to me that no new settlements would be permitted in the West Bank." He was "concerned by the Israeli settlements," as his "word of honor is at stake with the Arabs." He noted, "We reviewed the transcripts of my meeting with Dayan, and it was very clear that Dayan said that at the end of a year there would be no more than six settlements, all of which would be within military boundaries."[61]

Apart from conflating what Begin and Dayan said—and turning Dayan's willingness to make a recommendation on the settlements into a sacred promise—Carter's preoccupation with the settlement issue is unmistakable. When Sadat came in February, Carter wanted him to focus on the settlements in his public statements while he was here. Sadat, however, arrived with something very different in mind. He told Carter that he had offered the Israelis what they had always wanted—"direct negotiations with Arab leaders, recognition as a permanent entity in the Middle East, and to live in peace"—and he wanted to announce upon leaving Camp David that he was ending the talks due to Israeli intransigence. But Carter did not want the process to end after their meeting. Instead, along with Brzezinski and Vance, he persuaded Sadat to embrace a strategy that would end with the U.S. offering a peace plan.[62]

The essence of the strategy was for Sadat to come out with an Egyptian proposal with some manifestly unacceptable items in it to the Israelis, and then "have the United States step forth with a more moderate compromise solution." Sadat had long wanted us to present a plan, so he was keen on such an approach. It became more refined in the discussions at Camp David, with Brzezinski spelling out a six-point strategy that would lead to our presenting our plan by the end of March or early April.[63]

William Quandt, Brzezinski's aide, described the plan as depending on Sadat making a fairly tough proposal so we could be seen as arguing with both sides before presenting a compromise—this, Quandt said, "would help protect Carter's flank at home, since one-sided pressure on Israel could not easily be sustained."[64] Notwithstanding the Ford-Rabin letter of 1975, the Carter administration was not consulting with the Israelis before presenting a peace initiative; on the contrary, it was colluding with President Sadat both because it trusted his commitment to peace and feared for his political survival if his initiative failed. And, unlike Sadat, Begin was perceived to be unwilling to take the steps necessary for peace.

The plan seemed very clear, and yet it was not carried out. Quandt and Brzezinski largely agree on why the plan's proposed calendar was not met. Both agree Sadat did not stick to the script, though Quandt says the problem was that the Egyptian president tended to ignore the themes of 242 and Israeli settlements, "making it appear that Carter was being more pro-Arab than Sadat himself."[65] However, the bigger impediment to the plan was the administration's decision to seek congressional approval for the sale of F-15s to Saudi Arabia and to Israel, and F-5s to Egypt. The administration basically hoped by making it a package deal—Israel would get F-15s provided the Saudis and Egyptians got their planes as well—they would defuse the opposition in the Congress.

But Carter and his team in the White House misjudged Congress's reaction and were quickly embroiled in a deep controversy over the planes for the Saudis. It would take them until May 15, 1978, to gain congressional approval of the sale, and that sidetracked them from the plan worked out with Sadat.

If peace was the preoccupation, why would the administration announce the sale on February 14, immediately on the heels of working out a plan with Sadat? The answer, as Brzezinski explains, is that the Saudis were insisting. The Saudis' priority was F-15s and their security, not peace or Carter's requests—and we were going to be responsive to Saudi Arabia.

Though the need to gain congressional acquiescence on the arms sale diverted the administration from the plan for several months, it continued—at least privately—to push the Israelis on settlements and to be responsive to

Sadat's needs on the Palestinians. Both these themes were emphasized first in Dayan's February visit to Washington and then in Begin's in March. Vance told Dayan that we "would not support Israel in pushing Sadat to make a bilateral agreement with Israel that failed to deal with the West Bank and Gaza."[66]

Begin's visit was delayed. On the day the prime minister was to depart Israel, March 11, a PLO team based in southern Lebanon carried out a terror attack, seizing a taxi, shooting at cars, and hijacking an Israeli bus in what became known as the Coastal Road Massacre. To this day, that attack constitutes the single worst terror event in Israel's history in terms of the number of fatalities—thirty-eight civilians dead, including thirteen children. It sent a shock wave throughout the whole of Israel. Three days later, Israel responded by sending significant forces into Lebanon and seizing the territory up to the Litani River, which lies roughly ten miles north of the Israeli border, with the aim of clearing it of any PLO/Fatah presence.

While Carter conveyed condolences to Israel for the deaths, the United States would condemn the Israeli response.[67] We also sponsored a Security Council resolution demanding Israeli withdrawal and the creation of a UN Interim Force in Lebanon (UNIFIL) to move into Lebanese territory to monitor the area that Israel would vacate.

Carter, of course, could not know that UNIFIL would be ineffectual. But his special revulsion over the Israeli attack into Lebanon—less so the PLO terror attack into Israel—is unmistakable. His diary entries on March 16 and 21 reveal his views: "I notified the Israelis that we would introduce a resolution in the United Nations calling for their withdrawal, and for UN forces to keep the peace in Lebanon. They're using our equipment illegally to invade a foreign country." He continued: "The response was excellent regarding our resolution calling for Israeli withdrawal from Lebanon . . . The Israelis did their best to prevent our sponsorship of the resolution. They grossly overreacted in Lebanon to the terrorist attack on some Israeli citizens, destroying hundreds of villages, killing many people, and making two hundred thousand Lebanese homeless."[68]

Carter's dismissing the terrorist assault as an attack "on some Israeli citizens" shows no understanding of the impact on the Israeli public, or of the enormous pressure on Begin to respond in a way designed to prevent future such attacks. This was at a time when he was trying to press Israel to be far more forthcoming on the Palestinians for Sadat. He was aware of Israeli security needs in the abstract, even noting in a diary entry ten days earlier that it might be "necessary to offer a United States–Israel security treaty" to get them to be more flexible on peace.[69] But his seeming indifference to Israeli casualties was bound to limit the appeal of such offers. Why would the Israelis think that Carter would understand or agree on what they would see as a threat? Indeed, Carter's indifference to Israeli casualties is reflected in another diary entry on November 10, 1977, when he railed against Israeli retaliation over what he referred to as an attack on "some small Israeli village." In this instance, there were three Israelis killed and three wounded in Nahariya—an event that dominated the news in Israel but did not merit mention of Israeli casualties for Carter.

It was in this atmosphere of condemnation of Israel and the passage of the UN resolution demanding Israeli withdrawal from Lebanon that Begin came to Washington to see Carter on March 21–22. Vance described the meetings as "confrontational and unproductive."[70] Carter told Begin on the twenty-first that "the obstacle to peace was Israel's intention to retain perpetual control over the West Bank."[71] Two days later he told top Senate leaders, "We cannot support Israel's policy which is incompatible with the search for peace."[72] The PLO attack had been aimed at undermining the Egyptian-Israeli peace process. In that sense, it appeared to have been a success.

Carter would later say that throughout the spring there was no change in the Middle East situation except for increasing strains between the United States and Israel over the Israelis having not yet withdrawn from Lebanon and our pressing the F-15 sales for the Saudis. The president was not indifferent to the political cost he was paying, noting that he had "serious political problems among American Jews."[73] He even spoke of being in a "quandary" as to what to do given the political price he was paying.[74] Nonetheless, with the F-15 sale finally approved, the administration could get back to trying to break the stalemate between the Egyptians and Israelis. Brzezinski would explain that by mid-June, a four-week scenario was devised, starting with an Egyptian proposal, a foreign ministers' meeting, and then a U.S. effort to break the expected deadlock.[75]

The meeting of foreign ministers took place in mid-July at Leeds castle in the U.K. Vance and Carter's descriptions of this meeting vary widely. Vance felt that the informal discussion between Dayan and Muhammad Ibrahim Kamel—the Israeli and Egyptian foreign ministers—on the practical arrangements for an interim period of Palestinian self-rule was useful, with Kamel suggesting that the Israelis should negotiate the final outcome with those Palestinians elected in the territories.[76] By contrast, Carter wrote in his diary, "Cy sent me a report on the meeting in Leeds, where the Israelis again insisted that they would keep the West Bank. Kamal [*sic*] got emotional about the Israeli intransigence."[77] Whatever the actual tenor of the Leeds meeting, it did not produce a breakthrough.

Carter decided it was time to go for broke. He explained in his diary that Sadat was showing signs of walking away from his own initiative, noting that he was "meeting with the radical Arabs to try to repair his fences with them, which is not a good omen."[78] Carter even said that he was concerned "Sadat might precipitate a conflict in October."[79] With this in mind, he sent Vance to see Sadat and Begin with long personal letters inviting each to a summit at Camp David—he felt it was time for an "all or nothing gamble."[80]

The Camp David Accords

Carter prepared himself for this roll of the dice by going to Camp David a few days before the participants. He told Begin in their initial meeting at Camp David that he had "the right, and had the duty, to put forward compromise proposals." By Carter's account, Begin "insisted repeatedly that the Israelis see any American proposal before it was presented to Sadat, and claimed that he had an official commitment from President Ford—referring to the Ford-Rabin letter of 1975—that this procedure would be followed."[81]

Like Kissinger earlier, and future American negotiators, Carter was enormously frustrated by the Israeli hesitancy to reveal real positions and needs. At one point, as described later, he almost shouted:

> What do you actually want for Israel if peace is signed? How many refugees and what kind can come back? I need to know whether you need to monitor the border, what military outposts are necessary to guard your security. What else do you want? If I know the facts, then I can take them to Sadat and try to satisfy both you and him. My problem is with the issues that do not really relate to Israel's security. I must have your frank assessment. My greatest strength here is your confidence—but I don't feel that I have your trust . . . You are as evasive with me as with the Arabs.[82]

Although Ezer Weizman, Israel's defense minister, replied, "We wouldn't be here if we didn't have confidence in you," in reality there were doubts about Carter—over his readiness to accept Israel's needs and not push for more—and uncertainty about how far they themselves were willing to go on some issues.[83] Israeli wariness was endemic, given the risks. Nonetheless, Carter would push, and by the fourth day at Camp David, September 9, he was ready to present a U.S. draft based on the proposals he had received from both sides. From this point forward in the summit, Carter and Vance and their supporting team would go over each successive draft, incorporating comments and trying to reconcile them and our perception of what our team believed each side actually needed. The work on the draft that would address the Palestinians and the West Bank and Gaza, titled "Framework for Middle East Peace," was tortuous. It would go through twenty-three revisions before agreement was reached.[84]

Interestingly, given the difficulty of reaching agreement on the Framework, it was Carter who early in the second week of the summit told Vance, Brzezinski, and the other members of the U.S. team that their "preoccupation with the West Bank–Gaza complex of issues" was causing them to overlook the "chance to negotiate an Egyptian-Israeli peace treaty." He said that the United States must not lose this "unique opportunity" for a bilateral peace agreement, and then the president "sat down in his lodge to draft the framework of a peace treaty between Israel and Egypt."[85]

Key differences on each of the frameworks would bedevil the negotiations until nearly the end of the summit. On the "Framework for Middle East Peace," the most difficult issues to overcome were on Resolution 242 and its principle of nonacquisition of territory through force and its applicability to the West Bank; transfer of authority to Palestinians and the resolution of the final status of the West Bank and Gaza; and the freezing of settlement activity. On the draft Egyptian-Israeli peace treaty, the two sides differed over the disposition of Israeli settlements and the airfields the Israelis had built in the Sinai. There were points of near breakdown, with Carter having to persuade Sadat on September 15, two days before the final agreement, not to leave, leveraging their personal relationship and promising him that if there was no agreement at the summit, Israel could not treat Sadat's concessions in the drafts as something it could pocket.[86]

A breakthrough came on Saturday, September 16. That day, Begin—who had said he could not accept the withdrawal of Israel's small settlements in the Sinai, an absolute Sadat demand—agreed to have the issue decided by the Knesset, Israel's legislature, as part of their vote for the agreement. On the key issue of the 242 language, the U.S. team came up with a new formulation, saying this was the basis for talks between Israel and Jordan. Begin could accept this because he felt Jordan had no rights on the West Bank—and the United States in turn dropped the explicit reference to the nonacquisition of territory through force. Thus the U.S. team created the appearance of applicability on all fronts without including explicit language to that effect.

No such cleverness would work on the settlement freeze. In a late-night session Saturday lasting six hours, Carter was fixated on the need for a freeze. Carter and Vance both believed that Begin had finally relented and agreed to sign a letter expressing that "no new Israeli settlements would be established" for the duration of the talks on autonomy.[87] Yet according to Aharon Barak, a member of the Israeli delegation who was in the meeting, Begin agreed only to consider a freeze.[88] On Sunday, Begin conveyed in writing that he agreed to a settlement freeze for ninety days—the time the Egyptian-Israeli framework specified for talks to conclude the bilateral peace treaty. In other words, Begin tied the freeze to the peace treaty, not to the time it would take to negotiate Palestinian autonomy. Carter rejected this draft later that day but proceeded with the White House ceremony with Carter, Begin, and Sadat approving the Camp David Accords that evening. (Begin sent a letter to Carter the next day repeating his commitment to a ninety-day freeze.)

At times in any negotiations, particularly those that are exhausting, when the stakes are very high and everything else seems to be agreed, two sides hear what they want to hear and decide to fuzz the differences or live with ambiguity. Was that the case this time? Carter is adamant that his interpretation is correct, writing, "My notes are clear—that the settlement freeze would continue until all negotiations were completed—and Cy Vance confirms my interpretation."[89] Stuart Eizenstat, who was Brzezinski's counterpart on domestic policy issues in the White House, recounted a conversation he had with Carter in the Oval Office several months after Camp David in which Carter told him that Begin had agreed to a settlement freeze for five years and was now going back on his word. Eizenstat, who typically played no role on national security issues, responded that there "was no way Begin's politics would permit such a promise." Carter remained insistent that he was right.[90]

Aharon Barak maintains that this was a simple misunderstanding and not willful on either side.[91] Regardless, for Carter it was a breach of faith—and it would color his views of Begin and Israel. He would blame Israel for all the subsequent difficulties in gaining Arab support and turning the Camp David Accords (CDA) into a final Egyptian-Israeli agreement. Again, his diary entries illustrate what he was thinking. On the day after Camp David, he wrote, "It became obvious that Begin was making an ass of himself with his public statements. Sadat, of course, was very responsible and moderate."[92] The next day, September 19, he recorded, "In the privacy of the Oval Office, with Rosalynn present, I told him [Begin] how extremely damaging his statements were, and asked him to restrain himself. He made a non-committal reply. A flap developed between us on the West Bank settlements. He's trying to welsh on the deal."[93] Two days later he wrote that Begin "has already done enough damage to the peace treaties—denying the agreement we worked out Saturday night, on which I have a complete record and a perfect memory."[94] Later, on October 27, Carter wrote, "I sent Begin and Sadat a congratulatory message after they received the Nobel Peace Prize jointly. Sadat deserved it; Begin did not."[95]

His anger toward Begin and some of the harshness of his private remarks should not detract from Carter's accomplishments. He is the hero of Camp David, and the agreements would never have emerged without him. He played the role of mediator, often explaining and defending each to the other. He literally drafted the Egyptian-Israeli part of the accords and held the summit together at the moments when it might otherwise have collapsed. (It helped that Sadat could not afford to have it fail and that Dayan was prepared to leave if Begin would not concede on the settlements in Sinai.)

The CDA would provide the basic framework for how to deal with the Palestinian issue in subsequent American and Israeli administrations. The George H. W. Bush administration would only slightly refine the framework and embed it in the invitation letter to the Madrid Conference in 1991. Yitzhak Rabin would insist in the secret Oslo talks that the essential elements from the CDA framework provide the basis for the Declaration of Principles that would be signed at the Clinton White House in September 1993. It was Camp David that created a five-year transition period to determine the permanent status of the West Bank and Gaza, called for the Israeli military to withdraw to specified security zones, mandated an interim self-governing authority be elected by Palestinians in the territories, and required negotiations on the permanent status issues of borders, security, settlements, refugees, and Jerusalem by the third year of the transition.

Though Carter could not negotiate Palestinian autonomy in his single term in office, I would mediate in the 1990s on a framework that was largely a legacy of his administration. While he did not actually deliver an agreement—or even negotiations—between the Israelis and Palestinians, he was able to produce an Egyptian-Israeli peace treaty that served as the basis for the regional order for decades. Notwithstanding the mandated ninety-day period to conclude the Egyptian-Israeli treaty, it would take six months to achieve the agreement. Once again, Carter played a central role, this time traveling to Egypt and Israel and taking a week to finalize the agreement in March 1979.

To reach agreement, Carter assured Begin of several things: he pledged additional military equipment; he guaranteed that if there was any problem with oil supplies from Egypt, we would make sure that the gap would be filled; and he would ask the Congress for substantial financial assistance for Israel, which in the end would be $3 billion a year for Israel and $2 billion a year for Egypt.[96]

The Egyptian-Israeli treaty was signed at the White House on March 26, 1979. Carter, feeling that he could no longer afford the time or the political cost of his deep involvement in the peace negotiations, appointed Robert Strauss as our Middle East negotiator on May 1, 1979. Strauss, the former chairman of the Democratic National Committee, had had a successful tenure as Carter's special trade representative. He was politically savvy and would make sure that nothing in the negotiations would cost the president politically at a time when Carter's focus was shifting to his reelection. While Carter would recede into the background on the negotiations, his interest did not waver. He remained convinced that we should find a way to draw the Palestinians into the autonomy talks between the Israelis and Egyptians. To that end, he once again sought to modify UNSC Resolution 242 to see if we could attract the PLO. Though Strauss believed this was a mistake, he presented it to Sadat and Begin—both of whom rejected the idea.[97] But Andrew Young, the U.S. ambassador to the UN, did not give up on the idea, and in August 1979, when the United States held the rotating chair of the UNSC, he met secretly with the PLO's UN representative without informing either the president or the secretary of state. When the news of the meeting leaked, Young initially denied it to Vance but then acknowledged what had taken place. Apart from the political firestorm that was ignited, Vance felt this was an act of insubordination and demanded that Young be fired, something Carter reluctantly felt obliged to do.

This was not the last self-inflicted political wound that Carter would suffer over an Israel-related issue. Unfortunately for him, another took place prior to the New York primary—this time involving Jerusalem. Because of a misunderstanding, Donald McHenry, Young's replacement, voted for a UNSC resolution that called on Israel to dismantle existing settlements and cease on an urgent basis all the building of new ones, including in Jerusalem. Vance, Brzezinski, and the White House were prepared to support the UN resolution provided it contained no references to Jerusalem. Vance mistakenly told Brzezinski there were none. At a time when Carter was leading Ted Kennedy by a wide margin in the polls in New York, and with a good chance to force him to drop out of the race, the Kennedy campaign seized on the UN vote—causing an immediate sensation. Carter clarified publicly that the vote had been a mistake. However, the damage was done. The sizable Jewish vote in New York went decisively against Carter, and he lost the primary. Kennedy stayed in the race, and Carter saw this as one of the factors that cost him the 1980 election.

Whatever interest Carter may have had in the autonomy negotiations had long since been overshadowed by his political needs and the Iranian hostage crisis, which began on November 4, 1979, when fifty-two Americans were taken hostage and held for 444 days. Even prior to the hostage taking, he had asked Strauss to leave as the negotiator and take over his troubled reelection campaign earlier in the fall.

Iran and Security: The End of the Carter Administration

The Iranian Revolution replaced the shah's friendly regime with one fundamentally hostile to the United States—and Israel—led by Ayatollah Khomeini. As noted earlier, the Carter administration was caught largely by surprise. Brzezinski recalled that his aide, Gary Sick, had reported to him in 1978 about the growing signs of instability, and he referred to a dinner he had with the Iranian ambassador on August 2, which, he said, "convinced me, if I needed further proof, that the Shah was in trouble."[98] But for someone who later made the case for supporting a military coup, it is amazing that Brzezinski did so little about Iran at the time. There were no urgent meetings on Iran or efforts to figure out what our options were until November 1979 when the turmoil and the shah's indecision had taken on a life of their own—by which time it was too late.

The president and Brzezinski were distracted because they had defined other issues, principally Middle East peace, as their top strategic priorities.[99] As Brzezinski later explained, "Our decision-making circuits were heavily overloaded. The fall of 1978 was the time of the Camp David process and its aftermath."[100] Even when the administration's recognition of the problem became more acute in late October, with turmoil and labor unrest cutting Iranian oil exports from 5.8 million barrels a day to 1.9, and Brzezinski warning Carter that "unless the Shah can combine constructive concessions with a firm hand, he will be devastated," Carter's diary reveals neither a sense of deep urgency nor an awareness that we might be required to take dramatic action.[101]

By contrast, in the midst of very troubling events in Iran, Carter wrote in his diary on November 12, "I spent almost all day on the Mideast peace negotiations, which are apparently coming apart."[102] Iran also was coming apart, but it did not command the same amount of attention from Carter. In fact, even during the fateful days of late December when the shah was agonizing about what he should do, crack down as his military was demanding or leave, Carter's entries reflect his worry and frustration but not deep consideration of the issues and alternatives. Yet in the same period he describes intensive discussions with Vance at Camp David on the agenda for 1979: "The Middle East dispute was the heaviest political burden, even above SALT and China-Taiwan. It was very time-consuming and it would have been a relief to all of us to be rid of the responsibility for such frustrating and thankless negotiations."[103]

His diary entry of December 29 says he and Vance "reviewed the Mideast question in minute detail, and decided that we would continue to move aggressively on it and not postpone the difficult discussions, even though they were costly to us in domestic politics."[104]

If Iran factored in these discussions, it did not merit Carter's mentioning it. Maybe this is just another example of how the Middle East "preyed" on his mind. Or maybe, as Schlesinger argues, Carter came late to Iran and was grasping for how to deal with it.

Brzezinski and Secretary of Defense Harold Brown, however, were deeply concerned about the strategic consequences of the fall of the shah. Indeed, for both of them, as Brzezinski wrote later, "The collapse of Iran, and the growing vulnerability of Saudi Arabia dictated the need for such a wider strategic response."[105] Brzezinski says that the Saudis, Egyptians, and smaller Gulf states privately conveyed "their sense of relief" once the president announced what became known as the Carter Doctrine in January 1980.[106] Though Carter articulated the doctrine only after the Soviet invasion of Afghanistan a month earlier—which might account for the sense of relief that Brzezinski refers to—the United States then began to deploy more military presence in the region. In March, the president approved sending a carrier to the Arabian Sea and two AWACS aircraft to Saudi Arabia.

Brzezinski and Brown traveled to Saudi Arabia in 1979 and 1980 in order to offer reassurances about security, and by the fall of 1980, Brzezinski points out that the Saudis were asking not only for deployment of U.S.

early-warning aircraft to Saudi Arabia but also for increased air defense and intelligence support, and we were responsive.[107] The scope of our security cooperation grew, to include long-range security planning and upgrading of Saudi military capabilities—notwithstanding that we had produced a separate Egyptian-Israeli peace treaty.[108] Even though Brzezinski had feared that a separate Egyptian-Israeli agreement would alienate the other Arabs, it obviously had very little effect on the Saudis' perception of their need for a relationship with us. Once again, their own needs, their own priorities on security, trumped other considerations.

In truth, we needed each other. We wanted the Saudis to increase oil production to reduce the surge in prices, and they needed us to ensure their security. But we acted as if we needed them and they did not need us. Schlesinger would say that Carter did not know how to deal with the Saudis, lamenting that we would ask for Saudi permission to fill our Strategic Petroleum Reserve instead of simply doing it. He quoted a "high-level Saudi" who came to see him and asked, "Can't you get your government never to ask us [for] permission in the kingdom? We are a little country, we are weak, we are dependent on you for our survival, the great power of the free world, and when you . . . ask us permission to do something that you can do . . . we get alarmed about our security."[109]

This mind-set was alien to Carter and those around him. Pressing the Israelis, accommodating the Saudis, and believing both postures would help us in the Middle East reflected the basic instinct. By definition, Israel could not be seen as an asset but only as a liability to our relations with the Arabs. Distancing from Israel rather than identifying with it would help us with the Arabs—or so it was believed.

I would see this mind-set in action even though I was not part of the decision-making circles. The Carter administration was the first one in which I served. From my vantage point in two different offices in the Pentagon, working on security issues in the Middle East and the Persian Gulf, I saw clearly the instincts and assumptions that guided the approach of the president's leading advisers.

Three examples stand out. One involved Harold Brown's response to an analysis of Persian Gulf security that I helped write. After the fall of the shah, Brown decided that the new strategic situation required us to reassess what we might need to protect our interests in the Persian Gulf. He directed the office of Program Analysis and Evaluation (PA&E) to do the work. I was part of a small group under the guidance of Deputy Assistant Secretary of Defense Paul Wolfowitz, who drafted a Limited Contingency Study for the

Persian Gulf. Our analysis identified what the United States needed to be able to project our forces to the region and support them in response to a number of different threats.

While lauding the study and tasking follow-on work to it, Secretary Brown questioned why we included a particular contingency—an Iraqi threat against Saudi Arabia.* Brown could not conceive of Iraq being a threat to Saudi Arabia—reflecting a more general mind-set of the national security establishment that didn't envision an inter-Arab conflict; it was focused on the Arab preoccupation with Israel. In fact, Brown at the time said that Brzezinski and others would not take that part of the study seriously because of its implausibility.

The other two examples related to Israel and involved me directly. In the fall of 1977, the Israelis made an arms request known as Matmon C—an extensive request for arms over a ten-year period. It was designed to offset expansive advances in Arab weaponry. In a meeting in what the Joint Chiefs of Staff call the "tank"—a secure facility in the Pentagon—I joined representatives from other offices in the Pentagon, the State Department, the intelligence agencies, and the National Security Council from the White House. This was a meeting of midlevel officials who had been asked to recommend to the senior members of the administration how to respond to the Israeli request. The collective view of those assembled quickly became apparent: the Israelis did not need this weaponry because they could defeat any combination of Arab states, and supplying the weapons would damage us with the Arabs.

As the youngest and most junior person in the meeting—I was twenty-eight at the time—I did not initially speak up. Finally, I interjected that I thought the discussion was focused on the wrong measure for evaluating the request: the measure should not be whether Israel could defeat any combination of Arabs, but rather whether these arms would make a war less likely by enhancing Israeli deterrence. If deterrence failed, would the weapons reduce our need to provide resupply to the Israelis during the war, something that would lessen the price we might pay with the Arabs? And in the event of conflict, would the weapons make rapid war termination more likely, something that would reduce the risk of escalation and superpower confrontation that we had seen during the 1973 war? All three of these

---

* This contingency and our conclusions on what would be required to counter it would be drawn upon heavily a decade later in the George H. W. Bush administration when Iraq invaded and occupied Kuwait in 1990.

measures, I suggested, reflected our interests and should be used to guide our response to Matmon C.

I will never forget the silence in the room and the looks I received from the others assembled there. The unspoken thought, *He must be Jewish*, for why else would he raise such questions, was followed by a patronizing comment that I did not grasp that things were more complicated than I was suggesting. I said in response, I was identifying three measures for weighing the request while others were oversimplifying by trying to reduce the question to whether the Israelis could win or lose a war with the Arabs. At this point, I was told by the senior military person there that the Arabs don't believe in deterrence. This defied any logic. I asked, if that were the case, why weren't the Arabs constantly launching large-scale wars against Israel knowing that would wear it down?

My arguments were not persuasive, and every office represented except mine recommended a negative response without considering the issues I raised. In the end, the administration decided it would not approve a ten-year request from Israel; instead, Israeli arms requests would be evaluated on a case-by-case basis.*

The third example took place after the Egyptian-Israeli peace treaty and after I moved from PA&E to the Office of Net Assessment in the Pentagon. Andrew Marshall, the director of Net Assessment, along with James Roche, a cerebral naval officer, led a secret dialogue with the Israelis. The talks had been initiated during the last year of the Ford administration.[†] Out of these discussions came new insights on battlefield surveillance, the use of drones and standoff weapons, the development of active armor to protect our tanks and armored personnel carriers, and how improvements in command, control, and the integration of tactical intelligence could produce significant force multipliers.

When Harold Brown became secretary of defense, he allowed Marshall to continue the exchanges, but with strict oversight on the issues to be discussed—and with the admonition that there must be absolute secrecy

---

* As part of the Egyptian-Israeli peace treaty, the Israelis would receive many of the items from the Matmon C request.

† Shimon Peres, the Israeli minister of defense, had approached Donald Rumsfeld, the U.S. defense secretary, and suggested that a discreet dialogue be launched. The discussion focused on how the Israeli military had adapted our weapons to be more effective in combat against Soviet weapons and doctrine, as well as on how the Israeli defense establishment was creating innovations in equipment and doctrine to marry arms and concepts in the new battlefield situations.

about its existence. The dialogue was approved by the White House, but the circle of people who knew about it in the administration was kept to a minimum to reduce the risk of exposure. At Net Assessment, I was responsible for developing the issues, agendas, and our presentations in the meetings.

The Israeli side was led by Deputy Defense Minister Mordechai Tsipori. But General Abrasha Tamir, the head of planning for the IDF—and a close confidant of Ariel Sharon—was the key Israeli player. When I joined the discussions in the summer of 1979, the Israelis were keen to expand the dialogue to cover possible contingencies in the region with an eye toward joint U.S.-Israeli planning. Brown allowed us to identify possible conflicts, accepting our argument that we might gain insights into potential problems in the area, but he was adamant that there could be no joint planning.

The meetings were held two to three times a year and alternated between the United States and Israel. In advance of each meeting, I would draft Marshall's memos to the secretary, laying out what we would say, and then report on what we had discussed and learned in each session. Brown's guidance typically came in written responses to Marshall's memorandum. But if I wanted to understand more about what lay behind Brown's guidance, I would speak to Frank Kramer—or he would reach out to tell me the parameters within which we must operate in the discussions with the Israelis.

Kramer was the principal deputy assistant secretary for the Office of International Security Affairs in the Office of the Secretary of Defense. His boss, David McGiffert, designated Kramer to keep watch on what we were doing. Brown wanted to ensure that we did not cross red lines in the administration's approach to Israel or the Middle East, and McGiffert shared the basic suspicions that the Israelis were always trying to ensnare us into more of an exclusive relationship with them.

Kramer was more sympathetic than his boss to the value of the dialogue. Nonetheless, he would remind me that we needed to be careful to avoid anything that might lead to joint actions with the Israelis. By then, the shah had fallen, the Egyptian-Israeli peace treaty had been signed, a civil war was raging in Yemen, and our planning for more robust power projection capabilities to the Gulf had begun, so I probed to see if we could discuss with the Israelis how they might contribute to U.S. responses in certain scenarios. Kramer's reply was unambiguous: "No way. Brzezinski and Vance will never accept this. They are convinced it would kill us with the Arabs." I asked him which Arabs. The Egyptians, who now had a peace treaty with Israel? The Jordanians, who'd actually sought Israeli intervention in the September 1970 crisis with Syria? The Saudis, who probably knew the Israelis provided arms to the Royalists they backed in Yemen in the 1960s? I said there were lots of ways the Israelis could discreetly help—from providing intelligence to actual logistical support, including providing captured Soviet arms to those the Saudis wanted us to back in the current Yemen civil war but who had no experience with our arms. I added that the more any Arab regime felt its survival was at stake, the more it would be open to help from the Israelis—or at least would not quibble if we turned to the Israelis.

Kramer did not challenge my arguments. But he told me there was no way to convince the White House or the State Department—much less his boss—who felt that Arab hostility to Israel was so great that it would damage our position in the area. He went on to say that the "collected wisdom" of Brzezinski and Vance was that any cooperation with Israel must be very limited and invisible. I asked, "Do they really believe that our Arab friends think we are so stupid to give the Israelis $3 billion a year"—the assistance we promised in the aftermath of the Egyptian-Israeli treaty—"and not get anything for it?" And he answered that they simply had a different view of what the Arabs could tolerate with regard to cooperation with Israel, and their instinct was not to test this at a time when even Egypt was being ostracized for its peace treaty with Israel. The instinct Kramer described fit well with Jimmy Carter's mind-set and his attitude toward Israel.*

Carter's Mind-set and Approach

The conviction that cooperation with Israel cost us in the region can explain much of Carter's policy, but it does not fully explain the hostility that he frequently expressed toward the Israelis. I asked Stuart Eizenstat, who had worked for Carter when he was governor of Georgia, ran the policy operation in his presidential campaign, and would become his senior domestic

---

* Three months into the hostage crisis in Iran, we were meeting in Israel, and Tsipori offered Israeli help if we undertook any kind of rescue mission into Tehran. He told us that the Israelis had some Farsi-speaking units, and they were prepared to put them at our disposal. Tsipori added that Israel had conducted long-range rescue and special operations missions and what they had learned from these experiences might be of use to us. Marshall checked with Brown on his return and was told that we would not take the Israelis up on their offers. After Desert One, the failed rescue attempt in April 1980, Tsipori, expressing the deep regret over the aborted mission—saying any failed use of American power hurt all of America's friends in the region—offered to conduct a lessons-learned study of the mission to avoid similar failures in the future. Brown also declined this offer.

policy adviser at the White House, if he could elucidate. Eizenstat, who is Jewish, offered an interesting explanation. According to him, Carter came to the issue of the Middle East with few preconceived ideas. He was, in Eizenstat's words, heavily influenced by Brzezinski, whose attitudes toward Israel were clear. He considered Israel largely an impediment to U.S. interests in the region; we needed to cultivate the Saudis, we needed to compete with the Soviets, and the Israelis made those objectives difficult. Peace was necessary to cement our relations with the Arabs and deny the Soviets a role—and Israel would make peace only if it was forced to do so by U.S. pressure. Vance and those key aides working on the issue—Saunders, Alfred Atherton, and Quandt—might have been a little softer in their approach to the Israelis, but basically they shared those attitudes. There was, according to Eizenstat, no one on the national security side whose views toward the area were different.

Eizenstat added one point: Carter's regret that he had not played a large role in the civil rights movement. As such, he related to those who were victims internationally and was deeply motivated to do something about that. This moral impulse helped to explain his commitment to human rights—and unquestionably affected his view of Israel and the Palestinians.[110]

On this particular point, a number of comments by Carter lend credence to Eizenstat's explanation. For example: "Since I had made our nation's commitment to human rights a central tenet of our foreign policy, it was impossible for me to ignore the very serious problems on the West Bank. The continued deprivation of Palestinian rights was not only used as the primary lever against Israel, but was contrary to the basic moral and ethical principles of both our countries."[111] Another Carter comment may be even more telling: "On one of my walks with Sadat, we discussed that my being from the South gave me a sensitivity to the problems of the Middle East. My region had suffered, lived *under an occupying power*, for generations had been torn apart by racial prejudice, and was resurgent."[112]

Carter's work on Middle East peace seemed to have a missionary, redemptive cast. Human rights more generally were important to him, and Schlesinger, for one, said it informed his ambivalence toward the shah. But it is interesting that he did not make human rights an issue with the Saudis or, for that matter, with Sadat. He could be selective.

Ironically, before Iran took the American hostages on November 4, 1979, Carter recognized that Iran's revolutionary regime might be killing thousands, but this did not prevent him from trying to work with it. Consider his description of the period after Khomeini emerged but before the embassy was seized: "You have to remember from roughly March until through October of '79 we had increasingly good relationships with Iran, even including Khomeini." We used this period to extract all Americans because, in his words, "thousands of people were being killed in Iran."[113] While one might argue that we used these "increasingly good" relations to get the Americans not associated with the embassy out of the country—and given our ties with the shah, there were large numbers—Carter was trying to explain why the United States was surprised by the seizure of the hostages. In other words, he saw no contradiction in his stance toward Iran, even as the regime was killing thousands.

This is not to suggest that Carter did not care about human rights; he surely did. But like any president, he made choices about where and how he would act on his concerns. Israel's occupation and his guilt about not having done more during the American civil rights movement help explain why this issue was so important to him and why he seemed to reserve special hostility for Israel. He saw Israel as the country occupying Palestinians and as the one mainly responsible for the perpetuation of the conflict.

Two last observations about the Carter administration are worth noting. First, Carter made frequent references to the political costs to him of pursuing peacemaking, and Brzezinski often referred to the political clock ticking and the need to apply pressure on Israel before electoral considerations became dominant. However, Carter was prepared to absorb the political costs until he began campaigning. When he sent Vance to the region in December 1978 to try to meet the ninety-day timetable for concluding the Egyptian-Israeli peace treaty, he told him, "I would be willing to lose my election because I will alienate the Jewish community, but I think it is important to prevent the Arabs falling under Soviet sway. Thus, if necessary, be harder on the Israelis. If there is a breakdown, we will have to go with Sadat."[114] Here is the quintessential Carter, mindful of the political costs, revealing his stakes as he saw them in the Middle East, and reflecting his basic instinct on where we needed to position ourselves.

Second, Carter, Brzezinski, and those around them fundamentally misread our Arab friends. They feared they would walk away from us—or believed we could accommodate them by leaning on Israel and selling them arms. But the Saudis did not walk away from us because of a separate peace between Egypt and Israel. They became nervous when the United States "let" the shah fall. Reagan would come in and assure them we would not let the same thing happen to them. They depended on us for their security, and that was their priority. True, peace would make them feel less vulnerable to the radicals. But it would not make the radicals go away or remove the threat of the Islamic Republic of Iran, whose mullahs challenged the legitimacy of monarchies. It would not reduce their need for American arms, which tied our security to theirs. The Saudis and others would rely on us even if they did not want our presence in their countries to become a magnet for attacks against them.

Peace was important, but its pursuit did not save Carter in the Middle East. Indeed, his preoccupation with it made him miss the emerging threats in the region. As Steven Spiegel observed, "The rise of anti-American Islamic fundamentalism in Iran, the hostage crisis, the Iran-Iraq War, the Soviet invasion of Afghanistan—all these foreshadowed a wider conflict that the Carter team, with its focus on the Palestinian question, was ill-equipped to address."[115] Reagan would pay less attention to the Palestinians, convinced that the Soviets were the source of instability and the lack of peace in the region. He would see Israel through a different lens—as a natural partner. Even though there would be very strong divisions within the Reagan administration, including on ties to Israel, his administration would mark a fundamental turning point in America's relationship with Israel.

7

THE REAGAN ADMINISTRATION
AND THE POLICY OF DUALITY

President Ronald Reagan's approach to foreign and national security policy could not have been more different from Jimmy Carter's. Unlike Carter, the focal point was not north-south relations but on the Soviet Union—the "evil empire" that challenged our interests and our values around the globe. He saw the Soviet Union on the march. It was our duty to stop it, reverse its momentum, and force it into decline. Reagan presided over a dramatic increase in defense spending and a colossal buildup of our military capability. As he competed with the U.S.S.R., he sought to play on its vulnerabilities and the vulnerabilities of its proxies.

For Reagan, Israel was a natural partner. Prior to his presidency, but after the Islamic revolution in Iran, he spoke of Israel's reliability and strategic importance to us in the Middle East: "The fall of Iran has increased Israel's value as perhaps the only remaining strategic asset in the region on which the United States can truly rely . . . Only by full appreciation of the critical role the state of Israel plays in our strategic calculus can we build the foundation for thwarting Moscow's designs in territories and resources vital to our security." Later, during his campaign for the presidency, he said that Israel "has the democratic will, national cohesion, technological capability and military fiber to stand forth as America's trusted ally."[1] For Reagan, however, it was not just Israel's strategic value that created his connection to the Jewish state. He had an emotional attachment to Israel, which stemmed from the searing images he had seen in film of our liberation of the concentration camps.

Former secretary of state George Shultz told me that Reagan, who had made training films for the military during World War II, saw the early movies that our soldiers made as they liberated the camps. He told Shultz he "saved" these because the evil was so "unbelievable that people won't believe that this ever happened." According to Shultz, the Holocaust and these images "shaped Reagan's belief that we had an enduring moral commitment to Israel and nothing—no disagreements with Begin or Shamir—could or would detract from that obligation."[2] In his memoirs, Reagan describes this feeling in detail:

> I've believed many things in my life, but no conviction I've ever held has been stronger than my belief that the United States must ensure the survival of Israel. The Holocaust, I believe, left America with a moral responsibility to ensure that what had happened to the Jews under Hitler never happens again . . . My dedication to the preservation of Israel was as strong when I left the White House as when I arrived there, even though this tiny ally, with whom we share democracy and many other values, was a source of great concern for me while I was president.[3]

There were periods when Israeli behavior was a source of great concern to Reagan. So much so that during the early years of his presidency, there were moments of deep tension in the relationship. The policy of the Carter administration might have been riddled with irony, but "duality" defined the Reagan presidency. Reagan was the first president—indeed, the only president—to suspend aircraft deliveries as a *punishment* for Israeli behavior; yet he was also the first American leader to institutionalize and formalize strategic cooperation with Israel.[4] The formal undertakings that Reagan established with Israel strategically in the area of military, intelligence, counterterror, and security cooperation would create a baseline for all subsequent American presidents. Indeed, even those subsequent presidents who might not have instinctually viewed Israel as a strategic asset would respect these undertakings and build on them.

While Reagan punished Israeli actions that he felt damaged our interests, he did not alter his basic view of Israel or the value of cooperation with it. That cannot be said of every player in his administration, however. Secretary of Defense Caspar Weinberger and others in the Pentagon did not share

the president's view. Weinberger, reflecting more traditional national security establishment attitudes, saw Israel as a liability. He was quick to favor
far-reaching sanctions when he felt Israel's actions cost the United States in
the region. According to George Shultz, during the worst of the Lebanon
conflict in 1982, when Israel laid siege to Beirut, Weinberger advocated that
we "sever relations" with Israel.[5]

Conversely, there were some in the State Department—initially around
Secretary of State Alexander Haig and later George Shultz—whose instincts reflected the president's on Israel. They saw Israel as a strategic asset.
Like the president, they tended to see the world through the lens of competition with the Soviets and the need to counter Soviet and Soviet-proxy
threats. Haig, for example, recognized a new reality in the Middle East.
There was, he argued, "in a real rather than a theoretical sense, a strategic
consensus in the region" built around common Egyptian, Saudi, Jordanian,
and Israeli fears of terrorism, Islamic fundamentalism, and the Soviet
Union.[6] Haig was not indifferent to the difficulties that the Arab-Israeli
conflict imposed on fostering regional cooperation, but he believed that at
least tacitly we could build on these common concerns to try to amelio-
rate conflicts in the region—and in any case this did not preclude our ability to work with the Israelis openly to combat Soviet or Soviet-inspired
threats.

Weinberger saw only cost in our relationship with Israel. He did not include the Israelis in the strategic consensus that Haig saw. Instead, he felt we
could strengthen our presence in the region to combat possible Soviet
threats by excluding Israel and providing arms to the Saudis and others. In
his later years, Weinberger tried to soften the perception that he was anti-
Israel, saying in one interview, "My big point was, constantly, that we needed
more than one friend in the Middle East. The thing we could do that would
help Israel the most was not to give them money and not arms, but to give
them friendly neighbors. And the only way you could ever get that was by
demonstrating the fact that we wanted to have strong, friendly relationships
with a number of Mideast countries."[7]

In his eyes, this required providing the Arabs weapons, and Weinberger
did not believe that selling arms to the Saudis and others—but not to the
Israelis—was bound to heighten Israeli fears even if his goal was to achieve
balance in the region. Weinberger would not mourn Haig leaving the administration in June 1982 and would subsequently explain the secretary of
state's departure as a result, at least in part, of his uncritical support of

Israel: "Haig was a one hundred percent supporter of Israel on all issues, and many felt he left because our policy in the Middle East was becoming more even-handed."[8]

It is true that Haig left at a time of deep tension with Israel over its siege of Beirut. But the divisions within the administration did not ease after Haig's departure. In fact, Shultz and Weinberger remained at odds over Lebanon, the use of force there and, most fundamentally, our policy toward the Soviet Union. They would later both argue against providing arms to Iran to try to gain the release of American hostages held by Hezbollah in Lebanon, but this was the exception that proved the rule: their disagreements tended to dominate policy making in the Reagan administration. And it is no surprise that they would also disagree on policy toward Israel and strategic cooperation with it.

When Shultz replaced Haig, there was no reason to expect Shultz and Weinberger to be at odds on the Middle East; they had worked together at the Bechtel Corporation, which had major construction contracts in Saudi Arabia. But their attitudes, particularly toward Israel, could not have been more different. For Weinberger, Israel was a problem and he felt no commitment toward it. For Shultz, it was a special country. I would see this firsthand later in the administration.

Initially, in the Reagan administration, I served as a civil servant from 1981 to 1984. Later, after spending two years back in the academic world, I returned as the senior Middle East policy adviser at the National Security Council in the White House. Before being hired in that position, I needed to receive Secretary Shultz's blessing. Though he and Admiral John Poindexter, the national security adviser, would have profound differences on Iran-Contra, the admiral had agreed that Shultz needed to be comfortable with whoever was in that position, especially given Shultz's work on the Middle East peace issues. I met with Secretary Shultz for an hour and a half in his office, discussing the full range of Middle East issues, before receiving the formal job offer. I would get to know him as I accompanied him on his trips to the Middle East and see up close his feeling for Israel and the continuing duality in the administration.

The duality I will describe was not limited to divisions on policy; there also was a duality in time. The period from 1981 until 1983 was marked by tension in the U.S.-Israel relationship. For the remainder of Reagan's presidency, although there were some differences, the relationship was characterized by far-reaching support.

The Period of U.S.-Israel Tension: 1981–1983

Ronald Reagan entered office expecting a close relationship with Israel. But the Israeli government led by Menachem Begin would take a number of decisions that surprised, unsettled, and, at times, angered him. The first had less to do with an Israeli initiative and instead involved their leadership's reaction to one of ours—our decision to sell AWACS aircraft to the Saudis. Reagan inherited a commitment made by the Carter administration to provide airborne early-warning aircraft to the Saudis along with additional equipment on the F-15s that Carter had sold them. During the transition, Reagan said that Jewish groups were urging him to cancel the sale, and he concluded that the United States should review the possible sales before making a decision.[9]

Reagan put the AWACS sale in a larger context, believing that we needed to shore up the Saudis and to show that we would stand by our friends, particularly in the aftermath of what he saw as the Carter administration's "decision to look on while the shah of Iran was removed from power."[10] Reagan considered the sale as a way to demonstrate our credibility to the Arabs and, in his words, "I also wanted to send a signal to our allies and to Moscow that the United States supported its friends and intended to exert an influence in the Middle East not just limited to our support of Israel." Interestingly, Reagan also felt that we needed to make the sale to "convince the Arabs that we could be fair." He thought that if we proved our fairness, it would help us "bring the warring parties together and negotiate a peace" in the Middle East.[11]

Given the stakes and his own perception that the sale could ultimately help in peacemaking, it was a source of deep concern—and even distress—that the Israelis opposed the sale. When the administration officially notified the Congress of its decision on April 21 to sell the AWACS to the Saudis, the Israeli cabinet denounced the decision and Prime Minister Begin informed our ambassador of Israel's "unreserved opposition."[12]

In his diary, Reagan expressed his dismay:

> I'm disturbed by the reaction and the opposition of so many groups [to my support of the AWACS sale]. First of all it must be plain to them, they've never had a better friend of Israel in the W.H. than they have now. We are striving to bring stability to the Middle East and reduce the threat of a Soviet move in that direction. The basis for such stability must be peace between Israel and the Arab nations. The Saudis are a key

to this. If they can follow the course of Egypt the rest might fall in place. The AWACS won't be theirs until 1985. In the meantime, much can be accomplished toward furthering the Camp David format.[13]

Two points bear mentioning. First, Reagan attached great weight to the sale because of its potential to move the Saudis on peace. And yet the Saudis had opposed Camp David and at this point were still ostracizing Egypt for having made a separate peace. In fact, the sale of F-15s by Carter had produced no responsiveness on peace and had actually diverted Carter from the timetable he had worked out with Sadat to push a peace proposal.

Second, by investing such hopes in the sale, Reagan had to make sure that he could prevail over congressional opposition. As he later put it, Israel and its supporters "created a donnybrook in Congress that I believed we could not afford to lose."[14]

Reagan ended up having to invest an enormous amount of personal time and effort to win this battle with the Hill, a battle that was not resolved until October 1981. While he would eventually win the vote in the Senate, 52–48, his frustration with what he perceived as Israel's attempt to block an important national security objective of ours spilled over during a press conference on October 1: "It is not the business of other nations to make American foreign policy."[15] This was a remarkably tough statement. President Reagan was calling out Israel and effectively saying it was illegitimate for it or its friends to oppose what was in the United States' interests. The specter of "dual loyalty" hung over this statement and is a testimony to Reagan's basic attachment to Israel that it did not become a defining moment for his relationship with Israel and American Jewry.

Frustration was not the sole cause of Reagan's comment at the press conference. He felt Begin had betrayed a promise. Begin had made an official visit to the United States in September and met Reagan for the first time at the White House, a meeting that Reagan believed had gone very well. Although they didn't reach an understanding on AWACS, the Israeli prime minister promised that he would not campaign against the sale during his visit. Yet an annoyed Reagan learned that "almost immediately after he left the White House, Begin went to Capitol Hill and began lobbying very hard against me, the administration, and the AWACS sale—after he had told me he wouldn't do that."[16]

Reagan wrote these words after his presidency, even though Alexander Haig would say that Sam Lewis, our ambassador to Israel, had accompanied Begin to his meetings in the Congress and felt that Begin had been true to his word. He did not raise the AWACS sale but had simply responded when asked about Israel's position.[17]

The White House, however, heard otherwise. James Baker, the president's chief of staff, had received two different reports and informed Reagan that Begin had been lobbying in the Senate and had called on the Reverend Jerry Falwell to help defeat the AWACS sale.[18] As noted, Lewis said the first report was not true, and when Haig called Falwell, he "denied that he and Begin had even discussed AWACS."[19] Nonetheless, Baker took the rumors as gospel. Haig's efforts to show them to be untrue had little impact—perhaps, because Haig was seen by others in the White House to be supportive of Israel. I would see this pattern of believing rumors about Israeli lobbying against the policies and political interests of the president repeated in the future. In fact, in each of the subsequent administrations in which I held a senior position—Bush, Clinton, and Obama—there was angst about Israeli political efforts. I was often the one asked to do something about "what my friends were up to." While I cannot say there was never any truth to the reports of Israeli political activity, they were almost always exaggerated. Nonetheless, they were typically taken at face value.

Reagan, like his successors, believed the Israelis had crossed a line. But it was not only AWACS and the political reaction to the sale that caused Reagan "concern" in 1981. Even before he overcame congressional opposition to the AWACS sale, there were other Israeli actions that provoked American responses and criticisms. In each case—fighting in Lebanon, the strike on the Osirak nuclear reactor in Iraq, and the bombing of downtown Beirut—Reagan felt sympathy for the Israelis. However, the administration was surprised by each of these actions and concerned about the impact on U.S. interests.

In the first instance, Israel shot down two Syrian helicopters in April over the Bekaa Valley in Lebanon. The Syrians responded by moving SAM-6s into the area—a move that breached the tacit redlines that Israel and Syria had respected since 1976.[20] The Israelis made it clear that they would bomb the Syrian SAMs. To avoid a war, Haig told the Israelis that we could get the SAMs removed by diplomatic means. He asked the president to send Philip Habib, a retired senior diplomat, to the area to negotiate an understanding. But the conditions that produced the potential for escalation in Lebanon involved both internal Lebanese conflicts—Syria was intervening on the side of the Muslim forces against the Christian Phalange militia—and PLO mortar and rocket fire into Israel from southern Lebanon. Clashes involving PLO fire and Israeli retaliations against Palestinian positions in Lebanon were becoming more severe. Habib shuttled between the parties for three months before concluding a cessation of hostilities agreement. On July 24, the agreement set in motion a process that was supposed to deal with the internal conflicts in Lebanon, remove the Syrian missiles, and end the PLO fire against Israel. In fact, it produced none of these outcomes, but at the time, it was a relief to President Reagan and Secretary Haig—and Habib was seen by the White House as a miracle worker.

The agreement came one week after Israel, in the midst of Habib's shuttling, bombed the PLO headquarters in downtown Beirut. The attack was condemned internationally and caught us by surprise—but it was not the first surprise that the Begin-led government sprung that summer. Earlier, on June 7, three days after Begin had met with Sadat as part of a process to build relations in advance of Israeli withdrawal from Sinai, the Israelis conducted an air raid that destroyed the Osirak nuclear reactor in Iraq. There had been no advance warning to the Reagan administration. The Israelis feared that the reactor would soon go online, and if they attacked after it was operating, significant radiation would be released into the atmosphere. Menachem Begin made the decision to carry out the attack, believing a sworn enemy of Israel could not be allowed to acquire the means to build a nuclear weapon lest Israel face an existential threat.

The Reagan administration condemned the attack and announced it was suspending the delivery of F-16 aircraft in response. Haig explained that "this was a startling and dangerous action" by Israel and "the Arabs would suspect collusion." He added that "American equipment, delivered to the Israelis for defensive purposes only, had been used in the attack," and he felt the need to state that "there would be consequences."[21] But Haig also acknowledged mixed feelings about the administration's punitive response, saying that the "suspicion that Iraq intended to produce nuclear weapons was hardly unrealistic," and that Begin's actions "might well be judged less severely by history than by the opinion of the day."[22] Reagan's views were similar to Haig's; he, too, "had no doubt that the Iraqis were trying to develop a nuclear weapon." As such, he said he understood Begin's "fear but [felt] he took the wrong option." In his diary, Reagan wrote that Begin "should have told us and the French. We could have done something to remove the threat."[23]

Like Haig, he felt the need to do something since Israel had used U.S. weapons for offensive purposes, technically violating the terms of the agreement under which we provided the F-16 aircraft to the Jewish state.[24] With Weinberger and Vice President George H. W. Bush arguing for a total cutoff of assistance, the president decided to put a hold on the aircraft deliveries to Israel. Reagan's initial anger at Israel was tempered when he learned a week after the attack that Begin had not acted totally without warning. He had raised the Iraqi nuclear threat—and the need for action—with the Carter administration.[25]

Even before learning that the Israelis had consistently warned the Carter administration, Reagan felt the United States needed to limit its response because we could not be seen as "turning on Israel. That would be an invitation for the Arabs to attack."[26] He noted, however, that the Israeli attack added fuel to the "AWACS bonfire." The Saudis now said that since the Israelis had overflown their airspace, they had an even greater need for the aircraft. Weinberger, who was the strongest proponent of the sale and of penalizing Israel, admitted years later that he had been wrong about the blowback that we would get from the region for the Israeli attack: "That was a bolt from the blue, and obviously I was afraid we were going to unite a great many of the Moslem countries, even more so than they were then. It turned out it didn't have as many of the damaging side effects as I feared."[27]

Weinberger would go on to say that "it was an extraordinarily skillful job."[28] But Israel's military prowess meant little to him when he was secretary of defense because he believed the risk of alienating the Arab states precluded any cooperation with the Israelis. Haig, however, was focused on countering the Soviets in the eastern Mediterranean or even in the Persian Gulf, a strategy for which the Israeli military infrastructure could be advantageous. Toward this end, he wanted to develop strategic cooperation with the Israelis and designated Robert C. "Bud" McFarlane, the counselor in the State Department, to be the point person.

The Origins of U.S.-Israel Strategic Cooperation

Haig called on the Policy Planning Staff (S/P) and the Bureau of Political-Military Affairs (PM) in the State Department to develop the concepts to support McFarlane's efforts.* I would write many of the conceptual papers laying out the logic and options for strategic partnership with Israel for McFarlane and his office. I did not, however, take part directly in the discussions he had with David Kimche, the director-general of the Israeli Foreign Ministry. Their discussions, which began in March 1981, as well as the memos

---

* In the State Department, the Policy Planning Staff was referred to as S/P. The S stood for the secretary's office; the P was for "Planning." I would serve as a staff member of S/P from 1981 to 1982, and would head it in the Bush 41 administration.

I helped draft from S/P and PM, provided the framework for McFarlane's meeting with Prime Minister Begin in Israel in April 1981.

Howard Teicher, who worked for McFarlane first at State and later at the NSC, has described well the essence of what Haig had in mind on strategic cooperation with Israel—and where it diverged from what Begin and certainly the Israeli Defense Minister, Ariel Sharon, sought. Haig wanted "to enhance America's ability to project power to southwest Asia [the Gulf] and deter Soviet expansionism, while reducing Israel's tendencies to act unilaterally in order to enhance Arab receptivity to the U.S. regional strategy." Begin and Sharon desired "a strategic relationship based on greater Israeli freedom of action and independence from the constraints of subordinating Israel's interests to those of the United States."[29] Sharon was convinced that Israel was the only country in the region that offered the United States any real military capacity to help counter Soviet advances in the Gulf, and the United States should be prepared to cut the Israelis the slack to do what was necessary.[30]

Despite these different approaches, the April discussions in Israel produced a "detailed agenda for political-military planning," which included a "framework of ideas for cooperation, including joint military planning, prepositioning of military equipment, a schedule of exercises, and global political cooperation."[31] The foundation for this relationship was the work done in the secret strategic dialogue I had been running for Andrew Marshall during the Carter administration. Weinberger wanted nothing to do with such discussions, but Haig understood their potential value and knew that Reagan shared his view.

While McFarlane was focused on future cooperation, he also raised concerns about Israeli military operations that affected U.S. interests. In the wake of each Israeli unilateral action—the Osirak raid and the bombing of the PLO headquarters in Beirut—McFarlane sought greater Israeli understanding of our needs, explaining that "while the United States did not expect Israel necessarily to consult before operations were conducted, the administration certainly expected Israel to take into account American interests before decisions were implemented."[32] This point was particularly important for the administration because the Begin government seemed indifferent to the costs its actions imposed on us.[33]

Still, by September, with the congressional battle over AWACS looming, the president was eager to assuage Israeli security concerns and develop a genuine strategic partnership. When Begin in their meetings at the White House in September suggested that since we shared the same strategic views, "why don't we formalize this in some kind of agreement?" Reagan was quick to agree. Begin saw Secretary Weinberger after his meeting with the president, and told him that he and President Reagan had "just decided to formalize a defense agreement." According to Sam Lewis, who was in the meeting, "Cap almost swallowed his gum!"[34]

Weinberger sought to minimize whatever real military cooperation would be formalized within the emerging memorandum of understanding on strategic cooperation. The agreement, finalized in early December 1981, stated that the United States would cooperate with the Israelis on threats from outside the region—but would not coordinate with them on their conflicts with the Arabs.

Having helped to conceptualize strategic cooperation with Israel, I knew how difficult it was to overcome the resistance to it from within the Pentagon. With this MOU, however, I felt a fundamental threshold had been crossed, and from this point forward we had a framework that would allow us to build a genuine military partnership. Unfortunately, seventeen days after concluding this agreement, Prime Minister Begin once again acted unilaterally. With no real notice even to his own government, he extended Israeli law and administration to the Golan Heights. What Begin described as a technical move was seen by the rest of the world and portrayed in Israel as the annexation of the Golan—effectively ruling out any negotiation with Syria.

Reagan described Begin's action as a violation of UN Resolution 242, and the administration reacted harshly. It suspended not only the recently concluded MOU on strategic cooperation but also F-16 shipments—again.*

Begin exploded over the twin penalties. He called in Ambassador Sam Lewis and, in a fit of anger, called our effort to convince Congress to permit the AWACS sale to Saudi Arabia an "ugly anti-Semitic campaign." He asked scathingly, "Are we a vassal state of yours? Are we a banana republic? Are we 14-year-olds who, if we misbehave, we get our wrists slapped?"[35] Begin, who was recovering from a broken hip, used his condition to make it clear Israel would not bow to U.S. pressure: "The trouble is, I can't bend my leg. But you know me by now, Sam—a Jew bends his knee to no one but to God."[36] When I read Lewis's cable of his conversation, I wondered if Begin even thought about the impact of such words on President Reagan.

I worried about the consequences for the MOU, a document that for the

---

* The administration had lifted the hold on F-16 deliveries after the AWACS sale had gotten through the Congress.

first time put the relationship with Israel on a basis not just of shared values but of shared interests as well. Grounding the relationship in interests as well as values was important for those of us in the administration who felt the need to counter the traditional assumption embedded in the national security establishment that our real interests lay only with the Arabs. Now there was reason to wonder whether the MOU and strategic cooperation would survive. My worry deepened when I read the letter Begin sent to President Reagan following his meeting with Lewis. Begin decried our penalties and said, "The people of Israel lived without the memorandum of understanding for 3,700 years, and will continue to live without it for another 3,700 years."[37]

At this time, Lewis reported that Begin had not been satisfied only to blast our actions rhetorically. He felt the appropriate response to our penalties should be an Israeli military action, one that would also meet an Israeli need. Thus, according to Lewis, Began sought to gain cabinet approval to launch a major military incursion into Lebanon to clear out the PLO terrorists. It was as if he intended to show us that if you penalize us, we have little to lose and we will take other steps that might draw your wrath but will solve a problem we face. The Israeli cabinet was not ready to take such a step—and risk a more severe U.S. response.

Even though Begin did not succeed with the cabinet at this point, Ariel Sharon, his defense minister, began to brief Sam Lewis and visiting American officials on a far-reaching plan to drive the PLO out of Lebanon and pave the way for a pro-Western, Christian government to take over. From December onward, we were being put on notice that Israel would act at some point in Lebanon to change the landscape.[38]

In fact, Begin had raised this possibility earlier with Haig at the funeral of Anwar Sadat in October 1981. He told Haig then that Israel was planning a military move into Lebanon, without drawing Syria into the conflict. Haig responded, echoing LBJ prior to the Six-Day War, by saying, "If you move, you move alone. Unless there is a major, internationally recognized provocation, the United States will not support such an action."[39]

Similarly, in response to "credible reports" that Israel was preparing to root out the PLO in Lebanon, Reagan urged Begin "to exercise restraint" and "appealed for Israel not to go on the offensive unless it was the victim of a provocation of such magnitude that the world would easily understand its right to retaliate." Reagan says that Israel essentially told us, "Mind your own business."[40]

The Lebanon War

The war itself was triggered by an act of terror. On June 3, 1982, in London, Palestinian gunmen shot the Israeli ambassador to Britain. The Israelis retaliated the next day by bombing the sports stadium in Beirut, empty except for the vast stores of PLO arms, which exploded spectacularly. On June 5, PLO mortars and rockets hit twenty towns in the north of Israel—and notwithstanding a plea from Reagan for restraint, a plea he made from the G-7 summit being held at Versailles, on June 6 Israel launched a campaign that it called Peace for Galilee.

The Israelis stated that their aim was to clear an area stretching forty kilometers above their border of the entire PLO armed presence. While that was the declared objective, Israel quickly moved beyond the forty-kilometer zone, and by June 11, it had closed the Beirut–Damascus highway, isolated Syrian forces, destroyed eighty-seven Syrian aircraft (and lost none), connected with the Christian Phalangist troops, trapped the PLO leadership, and cut off West Beirut—the Muslim part of the city.

By June 13, the Israeli forces completely encircled the Lebanese capital. The world watched as Israel tightened the noose on Arafat and the PLO, who now sought to hide among the population. Though aware of the potential problems if the conflict dragged on, Haig saw a great strategic opportunity:

> Israel's military incursion also created circumstances in which it was possible, during the fleeting moments in which the former equation of power had been overturned, to remove all foreign troops from Lebanon and restore the powers of government to the Lebanese. Beyond that a settlement in Lebanon would have significant consequences for Arab-Israeli peace: Syria and the PLO, the heart of the Arab opposition to Camp David, had been defeated.*[41]

Like Sharon, Haig saw the potential to transform the Middle East chessboard. Unlike Sharon, he wanted to take advantage of the new equation to advance a solution to the Palestinian conflict in the West Bank and Gaza.

---

* Because the Israelis, and Sharon in particular, warned that they would have to go into Lebanon—and Haig saw the potential strategic gains if they did so—the perception that we had given the Israelis a green light took hold. In his memoirs, Haig argued that we had done no such thing.

Sharon, on the other hand, thought he would defeat Syria and the PLO, and make peace with Lebanon possible. These victories would fundamentally change the balance of power in the region and permit Israel to maintain its position in the West Bank and resolve the Palestinian question by having Jordan become a Palestinian state. Haig felt the destruction of the PLO's military power "negated" the Israeli argument against granting autonomy to the Palestinians of the West Bank and Gaza. He even told Prime Minister Begin in their last meeting at the White House, on June 21, 1982, that after the resolution of the Lebanon problem, the United States expected that "Israeli settlement activity in the West Bank would come to an end and rapid progress toward an agreement on autonomy would be realized."[42]

They might have diverged on the meaning of the strategic opportunity that was created, but they agreed that with Israel poised on the outskirts of Beirut, the only way to force the PLO to leave Lebanon was to convince its leaders that the United States would not hold Israel back. Diplomacy now required effective coercion. PLO leader Yasser Arafat must know that no one could save him, and that if he did not exit Beirut, he and the PLO would not survive the Israeli onslaught. For this to work, the message from the United States had to be consistent and convincing—and it was not.

From the very outset of the Israeli move into Lebanon, Reagan had urged a cease-fire. On June 8, unbeknownst to Haig, who was traveling with the president at the G-7 summit, the president was poised to act on a recommendation to support a UN Security Council resolution that would condemn Israel and threaten sanctions if it did not immediately withdraw from Lebanon. The recommendation had been sent by the crisis group chaired in Washington by Vice President Bush, and Haig was told nothing about this until the last minute by William Clark, the national security adviser. When Haig went to the president and explained the implications of a resolution that condemned only Israel, made no reference to any provocations against it, and made the imposition of sanctions likely, Reagan instructed Haig to reverse the instructions—with fifteen minutes to spare. The pattern repeated itself when a harsh letter was drafted for the president to send to Begin, demanding an immediate cessation of all military action, with Haig again learning of it only at the last minute and deflecting it. Habib was ushered in to see the president, without Haig present, and told what to do in Lebanon—all this orchestrated by Clark, who sided with those wanting to put pressure on the Israelis to cease and desist in Lebanon.

Haig later argued that his efforts were undercut. At key moments, when there were signs that Arafat was ready to give in, a countervailing message would indicate that we would stop the Israelis. When Bush and Weinberger led a delegation to Riyadh for the funeral of King Khalid of Saudi Arabia on June 16, they told King Fahd that the United States would not allow Israel to go into Beirut and that the president would be tough with Begin when he visited the United States the following week. They went so far as to say that the United States was not controlled by Israel and promised that our policy would change.[43]

Haig worried that this message would lessen the pressure being applied to the PLO. So he issued his own statement, emphasizing that all foreign forces must leave Lebanon and that, given the events that led to the crisis, careful analysis was required "before any value judgments would be appropriate"—implying there should be no rush to judgment about what the Israelis were doing.[44] The next day Weinberger publicly differed with him, equating the Israeli actions with Argentina's aggression in the Falkland Islands the previous year. For Haig, the mixed messages took all the heat off Arafat. Indeed, he notes that Arafat, the same day that Bush and Weinberger were in Saudi Arabia, agreed to negotiate the PLO's disarmament and their submission to Lebanese governmental authority. The next afternoon, however, "We heard that the PLO was hardening its position; the Lebanese attributed this change to Saudi advice"—advice that came after hearing from Bush and Weinberger.[45]

No doubt, our mixed messages gave Arafat room to maneuver—and he did. But the Israelis, having committed themselves so thoroughly and already having paid a high price in casualties, could not let him remain in Beirut. They were determined to make it impossible for him to stay.*

The siege lasted until August. Israeli bombing and manipulation of the supply of electricity and water in Beirut was condemned as all this played out on television—and increasingly imposed a price on Israel's relationship with the United States. As Reagan's anger grew over the course of the siege, he said of Begin, "Boy, that guy makes it hard for you to be his friend."[46]

Although Reagan was unhappy with the Israelis, he also resisted, at least at this juncture, the instincts of Bush and Weinberger. On the contrary, in his diary on June 16—the same day Bush and Weinberger were in Saudi Arabia conveying a different message—he indirectly described the value of Israeli coercion as he explained that the Lebanese president, Elias Sarkis,

---

* While the Saudis and other Arabs pressed us to get the Israelis to end the siege and allow Arafat to leave, no one was willing to take him and his fighters. Eventually, Tunisia agreed to host Arafat and the PLO, but this came only at the bitter end.

couldn't say this openly, but "he apparently wants Israel to stay near until the P.L.O. can be disarmed, then he wants to restore the Central government of Lebanon . . . and get all foreign forces to withdraw from Lebanon. The world is waiting for us to use our muscle and order Israel out. We can't do this if we want to help Sarkis, but we can't explain the situation either."[47]

Reagan seemed to share Haig's strategy, but he allowed the mixed messages to be sent. On June 22, the day after Reagan met with Begin at the White House, Clark conveyed to the Saudi ambassador that the Israelis would not go into Beirut. And two days later, Clark had Larry Speaks, the White House press secretary, say that the Israelis had promised not to go into Beirut—which was not true and was certain to take the pressure off of the PLO.

Reagan found Haig difficult to deal with. Haig had tendered his resignation a number of times in the first eighteen months of the administration. He had wanted to be the "vicar" in foreign policy and as a result constantly fought with the White House about decision making. He never established a close relationship with the president and was largely isolated from everyone else in the first few weeks of the Lebanon conflict. When Haig's frustration led him again to offer his resignation—perhaps as a ploy to get the president to grant him more control of the policy and its execution—Reagan had enough. He accepted the letter of resignation and announced on June 25 that Haig had resigned.

The president asked Haig to stay on and manage the Lebanon crisis until George Shultz was confirmed by the Senate.[48] For Reagan, the pictures of the ongoing and often intensive Israeli barrages on Beirut took a toll; one, of a baby who had lost her arms from Israeli bombing, weighed very heavily on the president. He told Foreign Minister Yitzhak Shamir in an August 2 meeting, and Begin in a written message on August 13, that this picture had become the symbol of the war.*

George Shultz became secretary of state in the middle of July. He described Reagan's meeting with Shamir in August as "grim," with the president warning Shamir, "If you invade West Beirut, it would have the most grave, most grievous consequences for our relationship."[49] Reagan and Shultz felt strongly that the only feasible way to get the PLO out was to preserve a cease-fire and permit Phil Habib to negotiate the details of their

---

* It mattered little that UPI admitted several weeks later that the photo had been doctored and the baby had not lost her arms; the truth was that a baby was suffering and the image of brutality stuck with Reagan. Spiegel, *The Other Arab-Israeli Conflict*, p. 417.

departure; conversely, Begin and certainly Sharon were convinced that Arafat would never leave if he was not forced to do so under unrelenting military pressure.

Here was a perennial divide about what works in the Middle East. Similar arguments would be repeated in the future between American and Israeli leaders—during the first and second intifadas, in the wake of terror acts by Hezbollah and Hamas, and during debates over what might lead to a resolution of the Iranian nuclear program. But with Israel trying to coerce Arafat by bombarding an Arab capital city—and with the world watching— President Reagan's threshold of tolerance was tested beyond its limits. Shultz agreed: "Israel's bad behavior at this time and after the PLO's withdrawal" left us little choice.[50]

From August 2 to 12, Begin repeatedly claimed that Israel was only returning fire, while Habib called in desperation from Beirut to say that Israeli bombing was making it impossible for him to talk to anyone, to do anything, or for anyone literally to move in the city. Reagan describes warning Begin on August 4 that if the "disproportionate bombing of West Beirut" did not stop, "he could expect a drastic change in Israel's relationship with the United States."[51] There was another warning on August 12, following an Israeli barrage of the city lasting fourteen hours—an onslaught that Reagan said "sickened" him and led him to phone Begin and say, "It [has] to stop or our entire future relationship [will be] endangered." In response, Begin agreed to order "an end to the barrage and [pleaded] for our continued friendship."[52]

The barrage did stop on the twelfth. But the Israelis moved their forces into new neighborhoods in West Beirut, which Habib said limited his ability to negotiate. Reagan now followed up with a written message the next day in which he made clear he had run out of patience with Israel's misleading assurances. It was time for the IDF to "stop these massive eruptions [in response] to any provocation."[53]

In fact, over these days, it was Ariel Sharon acting largely on his own, even misleading Begin and the Israeli cabinet about what he was ordering.[54] Finally, after Reagan's threat, the cabinet voted 16–2 to stop the bombardments and to cease fire. Habib reached agreement on Arafat's departure on August 19, and Reagan announced that day that we would join the French and Italians in overseeing the withdrawal of the PLO from Beirut. Our collective forces would be called the Multinational Forces (MNF).

The siege had profoundly troubled President Reagan and led to repeated warnings about the future of the relationship. Unlike Jimmy Carter, Ronald

Reagan deeply believed in the Israeli relationship both for reasons of interests and values. And yet the threats he made between August 2 and 13 might have been what Carter often contemplated, but they went well beyond anything that Carter actually conveyed to Israel's prime minister. Reagan felt the Israelis lied to and ignored us, and engaged in unacceptable actions. Like Shultz, he felt they took our support for granted. This tension may not have changed Reagan's commitments to Israel's security, but it compelled him and Shultz to spring a surprise of their own on Menachem Begin.

The Reagan Plan

Shultz recounts that shortly after he was confirmed as secretary of state in July, President Reagan, in one of their early conversations, encouraged him to tackle Arab-Israeli peace. As Israel's siege of Beirut continued into its second month, Reagan saw value in taking steps after this crisis was over to deal with the more fundamental issues of peace. Reagan wrote later that when the shooting stopped, "George Shultz and I regarded this moment in the explosive history of the Middle East as a possible golden opportunity to make a fresh start toward achieving a long-term settlement of the region's problems. We decided to offer the framework for a new peace initiative."[55]

Shultz convened a small core group in July to begin a discreet effort to forge such an initiative. All the members of the group were sworn to secrecy on the content of the meetings to ensure frank discussions without damaging leaks.[56] His charge to the group was: "When the last ship sails out of the port of Beirut with the last PLO fighter on board, we must be ready to move on the larger Palestinian issue, or we will have lost any chance of turning the course of this war into an avenue toward peace. We must avoid the trap of putting the peace process to one side until Lebanon's problems are solved."[57]

Shultz invited a lively debate on all the issues and then decided what he would recommend to the president. Ultimately, he would disagree with those like Bob Ames of the CIA, who argued that this was the time to recognize the PLO and make them part of the process.* Much like Haig, Shultz

---

* Unbeknownst to Shultz, Ames had set up a liaison relationship with the PLO as early as 1969; he had even met Arafat on a number of occasions. He deeply believed that the Palestinian issue was the core of the Middle Eastern problem, and while his dialogue,

felt recognition would reward the PLO—which he regarded as neither reliable nor practical—and refused to let the organization seem victorious in Lebanon. While the Reagan Plan reflected much that was in the Camp David Accords—it, too, called for a transition period—it diverged in one important respect. Unlike the Camp David Accords, which kept the status of the West Bank and Gaza open, making either Palestinian statehood or Israeli annexation possible, this initiative proposed a Palestinian entity in association with Jordan.

The Reagan Plan required withdrawal from most of the West Bank and Gaza—but not all of it, because for this administration, Israel's security also had to be addressed. When Reagan finally gave the speech presenting the plan on September 1—the same day that Arafat and the last of the PLO troops exited Beirut—he included a telling sentence in the text. After referring to Israel's pre-1967 borders being "barely 10 miles wide at its narrowest point" and the "bulk of Israel's population living within artillery range of hostile Arab armies," Reagan added, "I am not about to ask Israel to live that way again."

But he clearly was committed to the "land for peace" element of UNSC Resolution 242 and felt it must be applied to the West Bank and Gaza. This is also why the plan called for a freeze in the establishment of new Israeli settlements during the transition period so as not to tighten Israel's grip on the territory. Embracing land for peace and advocating a freeze of settlements would guarantee, in Shultz's words, that we were on a "collision course with the Israeli leadership." Shultz understood that Begin would resist the plan and felt the president must know what he was accepting.[58]

Given Jordan's centrality to the plan, Nick Veliotes, the assistant secretary for the Bureau of Near Eastern Affairs, flew secretly to Amman to present the initiative to King Hussein on August 20, eleven days before Begin would be briefed by Sam Lewis. Veliotes reported that the king reacted positively to the plan and would shortly respond in writing to it. Above all else, he said that Hussein wanted assurances that we would stay the course and stick to our opposition to both Palestinian statehood and Israeli sovereignty in the West Bank and Gaza, as well as our support for the political association between the Palestinian entity and Jordan.[59] Shultz received the king's formal written response within twenty-four hours after Veliotes's discus-

---

first with Ali Hassan Salameh and later with Hani al-Hassan, would lead to the PLO providing security for our diplomats in Lebanon, it never achieved the political breakthrough he sought. Kai Bird, *The Good Spy*, pp. 84–267.

sions with him, but it conveyed a very different message from the one the assistant secretary heard and reported. In Shultz's words, before the king could do anything, the United States "had to get wide Arab support, go far toward meeting PLO needs, and make clear that this initiative was not linked to Camp David."[60]

Veliotes and Ames both claimed it was a good response and were confident Hussein "would come around." Shultz, not prone to wishful thinking or inclined to put the best face on the Arabs' positions, would say the letter amounted to a no. The king was asking us "to stay the course but was not going to get on course himself."[61] Even when our ambassador to Jordan, Dick Viets, cabled that the king was giving the initiative a "green light" and would be going to the Saudis, the PLO, and the Egyptians to seek their support to cooperate with us, Shultz was skeptical, saying that although his "Arabist advisers" saw the king as being forthcoming, his view was that Hussein would support us only if he had a broad Arab consensus behind him, and that was unlikely to be forthcoming. At this time only King Hussein had been briefed—though without Shultz knowing, Ames would convey to Arafat a two-page summary of the Reagan plan before Begin was presented it.[62] Notwithstanding the Ford-Rabin letter, which obligated us to go to the Israelis before presenting any peace initiative, the administration had not done this. Why?

There are probably two explanations. First, the anger over Israel's behavior during the course of the siege was very high, and the impulse to be attentive to a leadership that misled us was correspondingly low. Second, the well-founded presumption was that Begin would reject the proposal and probably try to get his friends in Congress and the American Jewish community to put pressure on the administration to "block the initiative."[63]

They were certainly right about Begin's rejection, though they underestimated how bitter he would be. Sam Lewis briefed Begin on August 31, the day before Reagan gave the speech, and the Israeli prime minister was surprised. No doubt, he was hoping for a respite after finally producing withdrawal of PLO forces from Lebanon. Riveted on the price Israel had paid in casualties—not his lost credibility with Reagan—he could focus only on what he saw as an American betrayal. The United States had betrayed its commitment to come to Israel first; we were walking away from the Camp David Accords that left the final status issues to be resolved by the parties after the transition period and not by the United States stating its position when it had not even consulted with Israel. Even before the president's speech, Begin and his cabinet vehemently rejected the Reagan Plan, without even waiting for the Arab leaders' reaction. Begin publicly denounced it, then conveyed his anger to Reagan: "We have chosen for the last two years to call our countries friends and allies; such being the case, a friend does not weaken his friend, an ally does not put his ally in jeopardy; this would be the inevitable consequence for the positions transmitted to me on Aug. 31 to become a reality. I believe they won't."[64]

The Arabs felt little need to respond publicly to the Reagan Plan, but they would also not embrace it. Indeed, when an Arab summit convened in September, it adopted positions completely at variance with it: calling for a Palestinian state; reaffirming the PLO as the sole legitimate representative of the Palestinians; and demanding Israeli withdrawal to the June 4, 1967, lines.

The Reagan Plan would gain us nothing with the Arabs, but would not mark the low point in U.S.-Israel relations.

The Multinational Forces and the Ups and Downs of Lebanon

On September 14, Bashir Gemayel, the Christian president-elect in Lebanon, was killed by a huge bomb that destroyed the building in which he was giving a speech. Lebanon was thrown into new turmoil. The Phalange blamed the Palestinians, even though no one knew who was behind the bombing. The Israelis suddenly moved their forces back into Beirut—ostensibly to provide order—and surrounded the Palestinian refugee camps in the southern part of the city. Starting the night of September 17 and stretching into the 18th, Phalange forces entered the Sabra and Shatila refugee camps and indiscriminately killed men, women, and children in a rampage triggered by their desire to avenge their assassinated leader. Israeli forces permitted their entry to the camps and stood by as the killings continued.

We had given assurances as part of the PLO pullout of forces that Palestinians would be protected in the camps. If tensions were running high with the Israelis after the president presented his peace plan, they became even worse at this point. A new reality had just been created in Lebanon, and the administration felt responsible—and blamed the Israelis. After the Gemayel assassination, Shultz had a very tough exchange with Moshe Arens, in which the Israeli ambassador said, "Without Israeli forces in Beirut now, all hell would break loose . . . You want Israelis to clean up the mess while you Americans stay clean with the Arabs!" And Shultz responded, "The occupying power of a city is responsible for everything that takes place there; Israel should not want such a responsibility, nor can it possibly fulfill it."[65] The slaughter in the camps had made Shultz's words prophetic.

While Begin convened the Israeli cabinet, which subsequently issued a communiqué denouncing as "blood libel" the accusation that Israel was responsible for what a "Lebanese unit" had done in the refugee camps, a storm of protest against the government's policy in Lebanon erupted. Four hundred thousand Israelis demonstrated in Tel Aviv—10 percent of the entire population—demanding a change. As a result of the public outcry, Begin appointed a commission of inquiry chaired by the president of the Israeli Supreme Court, Yitzhak Kahan—what became known as the Kahan Commission—to investigate what had happened in Sabra and Shatila.[66]

President Reagan decided to send our own forces back into Beirut with the French and Italians, reconstituting the MNF, after demanding that the Israeli forces leave the city. The Israelis withdrew, remaining in the surrounding areas and close to the airport, where our contingent of forces— U.S. Marines—would deploy.

Weinberger resisted any serious patrolling or active role for our forces. The division between him and Shultz and Habib, who was now charged with helping the Lebanese reestablish their independence as he negotiated the withdrawal of Israeli and Syrian forces from Lebanon, would become even wider. Shultz and Habib felt the U.S. forces, with their French and Italian counterparts, needed to play an active role in filling the vacuum, providing law and order and helping the Lebanese reconstitute their army so at some point Lebanon could be responsible for its own security. Weinberger wanted our forces simply to hunker down and stay put at the airport—let others play the role Habib sought.

Amin Gemayel, Bashir's brother, was elected as the new Lebanese president with very active Saudi backing. The Saudis assured us that the Syrians would withdraw their forces from Lebanon if we could get the Israelis to withdraw from the country—and Habib focused on trying to produce an agreement on withdrawal even as he mediated among the different Lebanese groups in an effort to shape a working political consensus.[67]

At this point, I became Andrew Marshall's deputy in the Pentagon's Office of Net Assessment. Marshall and I visited Israel in late 1982 with the express purpose of working out an agreement with the IDF on the military, operational, and doctrinal lessons from the war—a war in which Israeli tactics had worked effectively against Soviet arms and in which Israel had employed drones to gain a different picture of the battlefield.

We met those Israelis who had been a part of the earlier strategic dialogue that we had conducted to try to work out a protocol for sharing information. On an *ad referendum* basis, we concluded an agreement: the Israelis promised to provide complete access to their own lessons-learned review, permit the U.S. Army to send specialists to look at Israeli weapons modifications and examine newly captured Soviet equipment, and let us assess their new tactics employed in the war, particularly integrating real-time intelligence with targets to be hit on the battlefield. (The latter reflected the development and use of drones, which proved to be an eye-opener for our forces.)

Though our agreement was technical and contained no political references, Weinberger vetoed it; he was not interested in having any agreement with Israel at this time. Tension seemed to define the relationship. Weinberger, never a fan of working closely with Israel, was not going to be the one to signal any improvement.

At roughly the same time, in December 1982, while Reagan and Shultz were traveling in South America, Israel's friends in Congress pushed a supplemental bill to provide an additional $250 million to help Israel pay for the costs of the Lebanon conflict and its continuing presence there. President Reagan and Secretary Shultz actively opposed the add-on, with Shultz saying we "fought it hard" and Shamir calling the president's opposition "an unfriendly act."[68] Both the president and the secretary felt that Israel's actions in Lebanon, and its resistance to Habib's efforts to get the IDF to withdraw, demanded that Israel not get additional assistance at this time. And, as Shultz would say, the "supplement . . . was approved by the Congress as though President Reagan and I had not even been there."[69]

From the time of the PLO's withdrawal, Habib had emphasized that the future of Lebanon depended on getting all foreign forces out. So long as Israel was there, Syria had a pretext to stay. In September, with his forces having suffered terrible losses, Hafez al Assad had committed to King Fahd of Saudi Arabia that Syrian forces would be withdrawn if the Israelis left. For Habib, this became a mantra: if Israel withdrew, everything could fall into place in Lebanon. In a lunch with Reagan after the president's return from his Latin American trip in December, Habib said that as long as the Israelis refused to withdraw from the country, "the Arabs would cite their refusal as proof that they didn't want peace, and that it was a waste of the Arabs' time to negotiate with Habib." Reagan instructed Habib on his return to the area to tell Begin that "Israel's intransigence might cost it its special relationship with America."[70]

Once again, Reagan was threatening the future of the relationship. Only this time, he was doing it not during the heat of Israeli military actions but simply in response to his negotiator's portrayal of Israeli obstinacy—an obstinacy that was being portrayed as the source of Arab nonresponsiveness in Lebanon and on peace more generally. After the events of the preceding year, Reagan was accepting this assessment uncritically. This president, who had written in his diary that Israel had never had a better friend in the White House, had moved far from that instinctive position of support.

Yet the direction began to shift in 1983, starting with the findings of the Kahan Commission Report on Sabra and Shatila in February, which recommended the dismissal of Ariel Sharon and the censure of a number of senior Israeli officials.[71] The Israeli cabinet voted 16–1 to accept the findings of the Kahan Commission, and Sharon resigned. He was replaced by Moshe Arens, who set out immediately to defuse tensions with the United States and to put the relationship back on track.

But there were other developments that contributed to the new trajectory in U.S.-Israel relations. The bombing of the U.S. embassy in Beirut on April 18, 1983, in which sixty-three people were killed, including Bob Ames, led Shultz to go to the region and broker an agreement between the Israeli and Lebanese governments. Reached after Shultz shuttled for two weeks, the accord, which became known as the May 17 Agreement, provided for the Israelis to withdraw from Lebanon if the Syrians did so as well.

Though not a peace agreement, Shultz felt he got what he needed: an Israeli commitment to withdraw, which would allow the Arabs and the international community to press Assad to live up to his commitment to the Saudis eight months earlier. Unfortunately, in the intervening period, the Soviets had rebuilt the Syrian armed forces and deployed new and advanced long-range SAM-5s, manned by Soviet crews, and so now Assad felt far less vulnerable. What's more, he had forces, including Hezbollah, a radical Shia group set up, funded, and trained by the Iranian Revolutionary Guard, and the Druze militia, which would either do his bidding or could be coerced to do so.

At this point, Assad rejected the May 17 Agreement, claiming Israel gained from it and that Syria had been invited into Lebanon to restore order in 1976; he did not regard the Gemayel government's request to withdraw to be legitimate. With domestic pressure building in Israel to withdraw as the IDF kept taking casualties in Lebanon, now, paradoxically, we wanted the Israelis to stay. Shultz felt Israel's presence was essential at this point because "only if the Arabs saw that Israel would not leave unless Syria agreed to go would the plan have a chance of succeeding."[72]

But Assad would not budge; he also refused to deal with Phil Habib. The president appointed Bud McFarlane to take Habib's place in July 1983.[73] Unfortunately, by that summer, Assad had gained increasing leverage, and as Walid Jumblatt, the Druze leader, told the Saudis, he could not withstand the pressure from the Syrians to subvert the May 17 Agreement.[74]

The next month, the situation worsened dramatically. On August 28, Prime Minister Begin resigned. At this point, he was a broken man. The combination of his wife's ill health and the deteriorating Lebanon conflict, with IDF casualties at this point exceeding two thousand, left Begin in a state of deep depression. Within a week, the Israelis pulled out of the Shouf—the area overlooking Beirut—and the situation for our forces became far more perilous, and we soon began to take casualties. McFarlane pushed for our forces to become more aggressive. He argued not just for returning fire against the Syrian-backed militias that were lobbing artillery shells on our Marines hunkered down at the airport, but also to be prepared to take on Syrian forces more directly so Assad would see he was running big risks. With Weinberger opposed, McFarlane's request was denied.

Shultz favored McFarlane's approach, believing that otherwise Assad would continue to feel that it was costing him nothing to apply pressure and coerce Gemayel. Shultz and Weinberger were completely at odds, and President Reagan hesitated in the face of their division.

But that division within the administration hamstrung us. With his situation weakening, President Gemayel conveyed that he would form a new national unity government, but the price of doing it would be to walk away from the May 17 Agreement. Reagan plaintively asked Shultz, "Are we going to let the Syrians and the Soviets take over?"[75] For Shultz and McFarlane—who had replaced Clark as national security adviser in October 1983—the answer was no. The new Middle East envoy, Donald Rumsfeld, agreed with them, and collectively they believed we could prevent such an outcome only if Assad could be made to see that he was going to pay an unacceptable price. But Weinberger and the Joint Chiefs remained reluctant to be drawn more heavily into Lebanon and a conflict with Syria.

On October 23, we suffered a trauma in Lebanon when a Hezbollah suicide truck bomber crashed through the gate of the U.S. Marine barracks at the Beirut airport, blowing up the facility and killing 241 American troops. In the period after the attack, Reagan was buffeted by conflicting advice. Weinberger pressed for us to pull out of Lebanon to avoid getting involved in the increasingly messy civil war. Reagan, however, felt instinctively that was the wrong thing to do: it would mean the "sacrifice of those marines had been for nothing," and we would be inviting the Soviets to "supplant the United States" while allowing the Syrians to be the "biggest winner."[76]

Nonetheless, and notwithstanding his instincts, he was largely paralyzed by the division of his top advisers. Indeed, after an NSC meeting he wrote in his diary, "We're a divided group. I happen to believe taking out a few batteries [that had been firing at our forces] might give them pause to think. Joint Chiefs believe it might drastically alter our mission and lead to major increases in troops for Lebanon."[77]

The Joint Chiefs were on the same page as Weinberger when it came to the use of force, and Reagan was hesitant to overrule his secretary of defense and the uniformed military. By January, and over the opposition of Shultz, McFarlane, and Rumsfeld, the president decided to side with Weinberger and Vice President Bush and withdraw our forces. Reagan saw the futility of committing more deeply to a conflict in which our Lebanese allies were becoming progressively weaker. The only way to reverse the trend in Lebanon was for us to dramatically escalate the conflict—and Reagan wasn't ready to take this path.

Abdel Halim Khaddam, the Syrian foreign minister, mocked Rumsfeld in a meeting in Damascus by saying, "You Americans are short of breath." This would become a slogan repeated by our Arab friends in the aftermath of our withdrawal, a euphemism for America's lack of staying power.*[78]

Syria's unwillingness to withdraw from Lebanon and its increasing manipulation of direct and indirect threats against our forces did have one significant consequence: it pushed the president and Shultz to refocus on our common interests with Israel. With Sharon gone and the balance of forces shifting against us—and Israel's acceptance of the May 17 Agreement—President Reagan wanted to reestablish strategic cooperation. Though Weinberger resisted, our office in the Pentagon was informed by the NSC staff in the summer of 1983 that we should consider how we might activate the suspended MOU on strategic cooperation—and how cooperation might be used to pressure Syria. Our review of this went nowhere until after the bombing of the Marine barracks in October. Soon thereafter, the president decided to send Larry Eagleburger, undersecretary of state for political affairs, to see Yitzhak Shamir, who had replaced Begin as prime minister. Eagleburger conveyed that "the President and everyone in the administration want to sit down with you and really talk about strategic cooperation . . . You and

* Osama bin Laden would later cite our withdrawal from Lebanon in explaining why the United States could be defeated.

we have a long-standing special relationship. This is the time for defining it."[79] Menachem "Mendy" Meron, the director-general of the Israeli Defense Ministry, would say later that this took Israel by surprise.[80] Discussions began immediately on how to give institutional expression to strategic cooperation.

On November 29, 1983, Prime Minister Shamir visited the White House, and President Reagan announced the formation of a Joint Political Military Group (JPMG) with Israel, which would "examine ways in which we can enhance U.S.-Israel cooperation. This group will give priority attention to the threat to our mutual interest posed by increased Soviet involvement in the Middle East." The administration was particularly concerned about a growing Soviet military presence in Syria that in many ways recalled the Soviet role in Egypt during the war of attrition in 1970.[81]

The first JPMG meeting took place in January 1984, and Admiral Jonathan Howe, head of the Bureau of Political-Military Affairs in the State Department, and Mendy Meron were its first cochairs. The JPMG would be the institutional umbrella for what would become increasingly wide-ranging security cooperation between the United States and Israel. Officials from the State and Defense Department established different working groups with their Israeli counterparts to improve military-to-military communication, plan cooperation in research and development, foster greater ties to and procurement from Israel's defense industries, conduct joint plans and military exercises, and examine how best to preposition equipment and ammunition in Israel. The meetings of the umbrella JPMG would take place twice a year. It spawned many other groups throughout the national security establishment, including in the intelligence community.

Notwithstanding Weinberger's continuing fear that we would pay a terrible price for any security cooperation with the Israelis, there was little practical Arab reaction. Indeed, much as was the case after the Six-Day War, when no Arab state receiving U.S. arms wanted anything to change, the announcement of the JPMG had no impact on our security relationships with any Arab state. According to Howard Teicher, who was on the NSC staff and involved in cooperative programs with a number of Arab states, "None of Washington's Arab military allies decreased the level of their ongoing joint planning or cooperation with the United States."[82]

While Arab leaders might not have liked it, none were particularly surprised by our cooperation with Israel. They wanted the United States to support their security and survival needs—with more arms, intelligence assistance, and commitments to counter their enemies. Once again, this reality prevailed, and Weinberger's fears about the consequences of strategic cooperation with Israel did not materialize because those Arab leaders who depended on us saw no alternative to that dependence. No one could take our place. They were drawn to us not by values but by interests. They might urge us to press Israel to change its policies or not to embarrass them by asking for certain forms of public security cooperation, but they were not going to make what mattered to them dependent on what we did with Israel.

For President Reagan, the shifting realities on the ground led him again to see Israel as an asset for competing with the Russians in the Middle East. He saw the Soviets as troublemakers and the Syrians as their clients. When they would not withdraw from Lebanon and began to threaten our forces and friends in Lebanon—with more Soviet arms and personnel in Syria— Reagan went back to his roots. He focused on how Israel could help us in a region where the Soviets aimed to supplant us and threaten our friends.

During the remainder of the Reagan administration, we built on the institutional framework for strategic cooperation and added significantly to our help to Israel. The change was dramatic. We concluded a Free Trade Agreement. At the initiative of George Shultz, we provided Israel an infusion of $1.5 billion per year above the annual Camp David allotment in 1985 and 1986 to help Israel deal with hyperinflation. Shimon Peres was the prime minister in a national unity government at that time, and he agreed to a series of economic reforms that Shultz required in order for us to provide the additional grant assistance. These monies and the reforms succeeded in reducing Israel's staggering inflation of 1,260 percent in 1985 to 15 percent in 1986.

In 1987, Congress also got involved, designating Israel a "major non-NATO ally." Israel was now permitted to use what would become nearly $500 million a year of our assistance to purchase weapons from its own defense industries. (The idea had originated in our strategic dialogue as a way of further developing the Israeli defense and R&D establishment.) Finally, in 1988, the last year of the Reagan administration, a new MOU was concluded that provided a more formal basis for all the political, economic, and security cooperation that now characterized the relationship.

Clearly, the relationship had taken a fundamental turn from 1983 and was put on an entirely new plane. Of course, differences remained. But our focus now was on the Soviets, the Iraq-Iran War, terrorist threats—and Israel was a natural ally. On peace, especially after Peres's rotation from

prime minister back to foreign minister in 1986, differences reemerged.*
But peace was George Shultz's domain and he had his own doubts about the
Arabs—cemented by the experience in Lebanon. He continued to pursue
peace initiatives but tempered how far he would push the Israelis, considering the neighborhood and his own conviction that Israel must not be forced
to accept positions that it felt threatened its security.[83]

No Progress on Peace, but Eventual Recognition of the PLO

Shultz had hoped that the Reagan Plan would provide a fresh start in the
region. It did not. The predictions of those he referred to as the Arabists
consistently proved to be wrong about the PLO and the Arabs more generally.
Arafat's vacillation and hints of moderation persisted and led Shultz to say
with some frustration, "I would hear again and again from credible people
that the PLO and Arafat were 'about to change.'" Only it never seemed to
happen.[84]

Instead, he focused on bringing Jordan into the process. This, too, would
prove to be a frustrating experience. From the effort to launch the Reagan
Plan in 1982 until 1988, there was an on-again, off-again effort to bring King
Hussein into negotiations with the Israelis. Throughout this period, the king
held secret meetings with Israeli leaders, but they never led to an opening for
negotiations. Initially, the king said he must have Arab backing to join the
process—and this was not forthcoming. Then, from 1983 to 1986, he sought
to work out a common approach with Arafat in which there would be a joint
Jordanian-PLO delegation to meet first with the United States and then with
Israel—always premised on the PLO meeting our conditions of recognizing
242 and Israel's right to exist. Arafat would indicate flexibility, then retreat;
Hussein would threaten to move without him, and then, fearing the consequences of acting alone, the king—even on the brink of getting into talks—
would back off. Finally, from 1986 to 1988, King Hussein, having given up on
Arafat, would seek to enter negotiations under the cover of an international
conference. In the end, nothing would materialize on the peace process
before the end of the Reagan administration—other than our initiation of
a dialogue with the PLO in the waning days of the Reagan presidency.

---

* The dead-heat election in 1984 produced a national unity government in which Peres
served as prime minister from 1984 to 1986 and then swapped jobs with Shamir and
became foreign minister from 1986 to 1988.

I was involved in Shultz's efforts from 1986 to 1988. My frustrations over the dysfunctions of our Lebanon policy led me to leave the Pentagon for an academic post at UC Berkeley in June 1984. I rejoined the government as the special assistant to the president and senior director for Near East and South Asia on the National Security Council staff at the end of May 1986, becoming a political appointee for the first time. I was part of the small team that Shultz used to support his diplomacy on peace.

My first role in Middle East diplomacy took place six weeks after I assumed my position at the NSC, and it was with the vice president, not Shultz. Vice President Bush took a trip to Israel, Jordan, and Egypt, and as the senior aide on the Middle East at the White House, I went with him. Richard Murphy, who was now the assistant secretary of state for NEA and Shultz's most senior adviser on the Middle East, was also on the trip. During the trip, I suggested that the vice president seek to produce a statement of common principles among Israel, Jordan, and Egypt. Since Jordan had no overt ties to Israel, such a statement would be unprecedented. Murphy and others on the trip were skeptical and thought the vice president should not risk trying and failing. But I persuaded Bush to let me try to put it together, arguing that because Shimon Peres would soon be giving up the prime minister's position and swapping out with Yitzhak Shamir as part of the government's rotation agreement, Peres would want guidelines that would permit him to carry out peace diplomacy; Shamir would not want to give Peres an excuse to void the rotation agreement; Mubarak and Hussein would both want Shamir, far more conservative than Peres, to be bound by some understandings—and both might also want to give Vice President Bush an achievement, particularly if he followed Reagan as president.

I succeeded in negotiating the statement, which cemented my relationship with Bush. It called for an end to the conflict, direct negotiations based on UN Resolutions 242 and 338 as the basis for achieving peace, and new mechanisms for launching multilateral talks, including an international conference. The king soon made the international conference his focal point for any movement on peace and the key to entering direct talks with the Israelis. Shamir, now prime minister, was dead set against an international conference. He saw it as a way to avoid direct talks, not facilitate them, and he was convinced that it would not be a forum for negotiations, but rather a tribunal against Israel. Unlike bilateral negotiations, which required the Arabs essentially to recognize Israel, it would allow them to perpetuate a fiction that they were not dealing directly with the Jewish state.

Peres's position was clearly different from Shamir's. Shultz, too, felt there were ways to address Shamir's concerns by creating a "properly structured" conference that would serve only as an opening and would lead to bilateral talks. Shultz's views were supported by a profound shift in leadership in the Soviet Union, with Mikhail Gorbachev and Eduard Shevardnadze the new president and foreign minister. Shultz told Reagan that Shevardnadze agreed that an international conference should pave the way to bilateral talks but play no other role.[85]

Against this backdrop, Peres met secretly in London with King Hussein on April 10, 1987, and they produced an agreed-upon document. Peres sent his aide, Yossi Beilin, to Washington to brief Shultz on the agreement, letting him know in the process that Prime Minister Shamir knew nothing about the agreement and that Peres and Hussein were requesting that Shultz make the understanding an American initiative. Shultz felt that if the agreement was real, it was very promising.[86]

The first issue, of course, was to determine if the Jordanians would give us a comparable readout of what had been agreed. Very shortly, they did so. While Shultz was attracted to the content of the agreement, he felt—legitimately—that we could not make it an American initiative, since we had not negotiated it. Instead, he suggested that Peres brief Shamir on the agreement, after which Shultz was prepared to call Shamir and convey his support and his readiness to come to the region to follow through.

Peres did brief Shamir, and Shultz followed up. But Shamir rejected the agreement, saying that it was a conference and thus inherently inconsistent with fostering real bilateral negotiations. Soon thereafter he sent Moshe Arens to see Shultz to complain about the impropriety of Israel's foreign minister going behind the prime minister's back. Impropriety aside, Shultz felt that there was a real opportunity with the Jordanians, but he was not going to force the Israeli prime minister to pursue an initiative he opposed, and he turned his attention elsewhere.

It remained elsewhere until near the end of the year, when an Israeli truck accidentally hit several Palestinians in Gaza and triggered what became known as the first intifada—or uprising. Frustrations had grown in the West Bank and Gaza in the face of ongoing Israeli settlement activity, the lack of any prospect of an end to Israeli occupation, and the preoccupation of the region not with the Palestinian issue but the Iran-Iraq War. The PLO played very little role in the largely spontaneous uprising. It was the Palestinians in the occupied territories who, without guns or bombs, were resisting with stones thrown by young people. Arafat was left to try to piggyback on what the "children of the stones" were responsible for creating.

The national unity government in Israel, with Shamir the prime minister, Peres the foreign minister, and Yitzhak Rabin the defense minister, had no easy answers. Rabin, when he saw that IDF coercion did not end the intifada, came to feel the only solution was a political one. He was prepared to support an effort to alleviate conditions for the Palestinians and tie this to a broader negotiation. Unlike Peres, Rabin felt we should find an approach to negotiations that Shamir might accept. From these days, I would begin to forge a relationship with Rabin.

Shultz wanted to bring the intifada to an end. Picking up on Rabin's notion of changing the conditions in the territories, he began to emphasize "quality-of-life" initiatives, and I would help develop these from my perch at the NSC, working very closely with his special assistant, Charlie Hill. But the secretary raised another idea. He suggested a shared sovereignty arrangement where there might be a more functional approach to issues of security and economy—and Israelis, Palestinians, and Jordanians might divide up the responsibility, particularly in parts of the West Bank like the Jordan Valley. In addition, he suggested an "interlock" approach in which the relationship between the interim period and the negotiations on final status called for in the Camp David Accords and the Reagan Plan would be accelerated by setting a six-month target to reach an agreement on self-government for the Palestinians—with the final status talks to begin regardless of whether or not an interim agreement had been achieved in that time frame.[87]

Shultz made several trips to the region in the first half of 1988, trying to change the dynamic on the ground and get talks started. I joined him on these trips and even ended up taking a separate trip with Phil Habib to Amman to see King Hussein. None of our ideas were accepted, and by the late spring, the administration's efforts on the peace issue had largely run their course. However, there would be one last development that would not be finalized until after George H. W. Bush had been elected—and that was recognition of the PLO.

Even during the summer of 1982, at the height of the siege in Beirut, when the anger level toward Israel was high and many were arguing for us to recognize the PLO, Shultz rejected the idea. He saw little sign of moderation in Arafat or the PLO. With the advent of the intifada, Arafat's hints about recognizing 242 increased. He was on the sidelines of the uprising and needed to prove his relevance. If anything, Arafat's desperation increased our leverage with him, suggesting that there should be no easing of our conditions for direct talks. Shultz supported this position even though once again some in NEA argued that only by dealing with Arafat might we be able to ease the intifada. Shultz would not budge, and little came of this until the fall of 1988.

By this point, I had left the NSC. Vice President Bush had asked me to become the senior foreign policy adviser to his campaign for the presidency, and I agreed to do so on August 1, 1988. During the fall, as I was caught up in the campaign, I became aware of a new initiative that had been launched outside the Reagan administration, involving Sweden as the go-between with Arafat.[88]

In November, when the PLO issued the Algiers Declaration, accepting the original partition plan, which called for the creation of a Jewish and an Arab state in Palestine, I assumed that Arafat would finally meet our conditions for dealing with the PLO. When I told James Baker that this was probably going to happen, I added that the Israelis would hate the idea of us talking to the PLO—even if they had explicitly met our conditions. Baker told me that he and Bush hoped it would be done during the transition so the new administration would simply inherit this and not have to make the decision. I sensed it was not just political expediency that led the vice president to favor recognition of the PLO but also the belief that it would improve our position in the Middle East.

In December, after a few false starts, Arafat finally made a public statement and signed a letter that had been coordinated with Shultz and that met our terms. In response, Shultz authorized a dialogue to be held only through our embassy in Tunis and only with nonsenior PLO figures. We could now talk to PLO representatives but only in a very limited format. Shultz still wanted to see behaviors—not just words—that made clear that PLO terror had been relegated to the past. Prime Minister Shamir was apprised of this development but understood there was little he could do about it at this point in the Reagan administration.

Iran-Contra

Iran-Contra was the worst scandal of the Reagan presidency. In covertly providing monies to the Contras in Nicaragua, laws were broken. Adding to the outrage was the fact that we were trading arms to the Iranians in order to get Hezbollah to release American hostages in Lebanon. The excess money that the Iranians were charged for the arms—mostly TOW antitank missiles—was then transferred to the Contras. To his dying day, Ronald Reagan insisted he never intended to trade arms for hostages, but he reluctantly acknowledged that is how it came to be perceived. Reagan by his own admission was preoccupied with getting our hostages released and rationalized the provision of arms because he believed that we were dealing with moderates in the Iranian elite who wanted to reach out to the United States, end the "tyrannical theocracy imposed on them by Khomeini," stop the war with Iraq, and create a new day in Iran and in the Persian Gulf.[89]

There is little need here to tell the whole story, but no discussion of the U.S.-Israel relationship during the Reagan presidency would be complete without describing this episode at least briefly.[90] In part this is because the Israelis were the initial channel to the Iranians. In the summer of 1985, David Kimche, the director-general of the Israeli Foreign Ministry, who had a deep intelligence background, approached Bud McFarlane with information that the Israelis had opened a channel to moderate Iranians who were politically important and who had an interest in building ties to the United States. He thought this channel might be helpful in getting our hostages released. Shultz, informed by McFarlane of the approach, was initially skeptical but agreed we should listen to what the Iranians had to say. He learned only later that the Iranians were seeking weapons and that, in fact, a central player in this was a shady Iranian arms dealer, Manucher Ghorbanifar. At that point, he told McFarlane to end the discussion.

But President Reagan was enthusiastic. One reason was the Israeli involvement, which seemingly made the initiative legitimate. "We had great respect for Israel's intelligence abilities," he wrote, and the Israelis were telling us that the Iranians they were talking to were opposed to terror. Moreover, "I was told that Israeli Prime Minister Shimon Peres was behind the proposal," and those "involved . . . were close to Peres." For Reagan, "Here was a bona fide opportunity to shape the future in the Middle East."[91]

Shultz was not reassured by the Israeli involvement. On the contrary, he felt the Israelis had interests that diverged from ours: we were trying to block arms from going to Iran and Iraq, and Israel was "glad to see their enemies demolishing each other and, beyond that, wanted to maintain at least a subterranean relationship with Iran and thereby with Iranian Jews."[92] But he was cut out—and so was I.*

---

* As the senior Middle East adviser at the National Security Council, I was certainly involved with Iran, but I was kept out of the operations side of the NSC and so I knew nothing about what was going on. This was the reason I survived the shake-up that took place at the NSC when the full story of Iran-Contra came out. John Poindexter and Oliver North were not only fired but also prosecuted. Frank Carlucci became the new national security adviser and Colin Powell became his deputy. Others on the NSC staff

There is one other point about Iran-Contra that is worth noting because of possible connections to contemporary developments. Amiram Nir, Peres's counterterrorism adviser, was one of those who accompanied Bud McFarlane when he traveled to Tehran in late May 1986 and famously brought a cake and a Bible. The trip produced neither the expected meetings with senior Iranian leaders nor the release of hostages. But it did not end the effort—quite the contrary. Subsequently, there were meetings with the nephew of Iranian power broker Akbar Hashemi Rafsanjani. Nir was the critical link to the Iranians. As part of his outreach to the Iranians, Nir apparently met with Hassan Rouhani separately in Paris and recorded their encounter. At the time, he was one of those "moderates" who Nir said wanted to take Iran in a different direction—in no small part because of the high cost of the war with Iraq and the Iranian desire not only to gain American arms but also end the U.S. tilt toward Iraq. Indeed, while Shultz would say that our policy was not to provide arms to either side, the fact is we provided advanced radars to the Iraqis that had a force multiplier effect, and the Reagan administration also provided agricultural credits to Iraq to help their economic situation during the war.

According to transcripts of his meeting with Nir, Rouhani gave the following advice on how to deal with Ayatollah Khomeini: "If we analyze Khomeini's character, we will see that if someone strong stands opposite him, he will retreat 100 steps; and if he is strong and someone weak faces him, he will advance 100 steps." He warned that we would face troubles all over the world if we were not resolute with Khomeini.[93] Was Rouhani trying to prove his credentials as a true moderate who wanted a different course? Can we be sure the transcript is accurate, or that the meeting was even with Rouhani? There are questions here, but one thing is for sure: there were those in the administration who were convinced that they were dealing with moderates who were determined to chart a different course in Iran—and Rouhani was identified as one of those figures. Today, Rouhani is Iran's president. When I discuss the Obama administration's approach to Iran, we will return to Rouhani and how he and others are perceived today, and how, interestingly, this time it is the Israelis who doubt the presumed moderates in Iran.

---

were let go as well, and the role of the NSC itself would change as a result. Carlucci brought in Robert Oakley, a long-serving, well-respected foreign-service officer, to be in charge of the broader Middle East. I was placed in charge of the Arab-Israeli issues but now reported through Oakley to Carlucci and Powell—though Oakley, in fact, would treat this more as a paper line of command than an actual one. I continued working with Shultz and his team just as I had before.

Reagan's Mind-set

Reagan and Shultz viewed Israel through a lens of shared values. With Begin and Sharon's departure, the end of Israeli "surprises," and Syria's role in our debacle in Lebanon, Reagan returned to his instincts toward Israel. Shultz shared Reagan's emotional attachment to Israel, often speaking of his "visceral support."*[94] Reagan and Shultz were drawn to Israel and saw it as a natural partner. Caspar Weinberger did not. He reflected the traditional attitudes of the national security bureaucracy, seeing Israel as a burden. He resisted Shultz on a range of issues, including Israel.

In fact, division and duality continued to define the Reagan approach to the Middle East until after Iran-Contra and Weinberger's departure as secretary of defense in November 1987. When Frank Carlucci replaced Weinberger and Colin Powell became the new national security adviser, they would have a daily breakfast with George Shultz to coordinate policy—and our approach was no longer characterized by division on the Middle East or Israel.

Both Carlucci and Powell were prepared to accept the new strategic approach to Israel, even though they did not necessarily share the same instincts as Reagan and Shultz. From my vantage point at the NSC, I saw that neither romanticized the region. They felt no special attachment to Israel or the Arabs. They saw a strategic imperative in having relations with both. In this, they of course reflected Reagan's broader approach to the region. Indeed, Reagan was convinced that "it was essential to continue working with moderate Arabs to find a solution to the Middle East's problem, and that we should make selective sales of American weapons to the moderate Arabs as proof of our friendship. In this I was constantly frustrated, following the AWACS sale, by strong resistance from Israel's supporters in Congress. That undermined our efforts to improve relations with the moderate Arabs."[95]

In keeping with what started in the Kennedy administration, Reagan truly wanted to be on good terms with Israel and the Arab states, believing this was both necessary for peace in the region and possible. This was logical, but also difficult to achieve. Unlike his predecessors, however, Reagan did not see a contradiction between cooperating with Israel on matters of

---

* Shultz explained to me how his experiences with Joseph Levy, a student at the University of Chicago, and Teddy Kollek, the mayor of Jerusalem, convinced him that Israel was an extraordinary country that produced extraordinary people.

security interest to us and having good relations with the Arabs. Until Carlucci and Powell arrived, there were those in his administration, particularly Weinberger and some in the uniformed military, who reflected the assumptions of the past and thought the two objectives were incompatible. Reagan and Shultz would prove otherwise and create a baseline for all succeeding administrations. That new baseline did not mean the countervailing assumptions would go away—there was still a perceived high cost to us of cooperation with Israel—but subsequent administrations, even in the face of crises in the relationship, would not undo the institutions of strategic cooperation that were established by Ronald Reagan and are surely an enduring legacy of his Middle East policy. No doubt Reagan, who viewed Israel as a country of shared values, would be pleased by such a legacy.

He would be less pleased with the evolution of the political influence of Israel's organized supporters on U.S. policy. As noted above, it was not unusual for him to express his unhappiness with the efforts of Israel's friends in the Congress. And by the time of Reagan's presidency, groups supporting Israel, like the American Israel Public Affairs Committee (AIPAC), had become far better organized and more effective. It's tempting when we read his complaints to overstate the influence of these supporters of Israel. In reality they have never driven basic policies, even as presidents have become more mindful of them. To be sure, the congressional capability to respond to Israel's assistance needs or initiate programs that benefited the Jewish state had become far stronger by Reagan's time. But Congress's ability to block actions presidents want to take was far more limited. Carter could overcome opposition to the sale of F-15s to the Saudis and Reagan would do so as well with the AWACS.

The ability of organizations like AIPAC to affect Congress because of their great political reach throughout the country certainly became more apparent during the Reagan presidency. That political influence would be felt even more strongly during the Bush administration—but here again, when an administration really felt it must adopt a certain posture toward the region or Israel, it succeeded in doing so despite congressional opposition. We will certainly see this during Bush's loan guarantee dispute with Israel in 1991–1992.

8

GEORGE H. W. BUSH AND ISRAEL: DISCORD AND RESPONSIVENESS

George H. W. Bush's instincts when it came to Israel were very different from those of his predecessor. Unlike Ronald Reagan, he did not have an emotional attachment to Israel. In his eyes, it was not a special or unique relationship; there was no intangible link or sense of moral responsibility generated by the Holocaust. That is not to say that President Bush shied away from the commitments we had made to Israel's security. On the contrary, he told Prime Minister Yitzhak Shamir early in their first meeting after becoming president that the United States was "unshakable in our commitment to Israel."[1] Later in his administration, when he was trying hard to persuade the Congress to delay action on an Israeli request for $10 billion in loan guarantees—with the Israeli government pushing hard on Capitol Hill to act on it—he would say that "nobody has been a better friend to Israel than the United States, and no one will continue to be a better friend than the United States."[2]

He meant those words. George H. W. Bush was very much a man of principle who believed that commitments made must be commitments fulfilled. But he also felt that Israel needed to take better account of our interests—and be a better friend to us. Bush was a traditionalist when it came to U.S. national interests, and he acted based on how he saw those interests best served. He would not betray our commitments to Israel, but he

believed our interests required us also to have good relations with the Arabs. He agreed with what Richard Nixon told James Baker during the transition period after Bush's election: "Reagan has been the most pro-Israeli
President in history. It's time for some evenhandedness [*sic*] out there."[3]

The Middle East was not a priority for Bush at the outset of the administration. East-West issues commanded his attention early on. Mikhail Gorbachev's leadership in the Soviet Union opened new possibilities in Europe.
Indeed, redefining the superpower relationship, pursuing arms control, and
managing military modernization in NATO during a time of change
represented real challenges, particularly at a point when for many Europeans, Gorbachev's posture argued for reducing military spending and
modernization. Bush wanted to know that perestroika and new thinking
constituted a new day in the U.S.S.R. and were not merely a more clever way
of splitting the West and competing with it. If perestroika was for real, he
was ready to transform the relationship with the Soviet Union, but Soviet
intentions had to be tested, not assumed. Here was where the United States
needed to be putting its attention and effort.

His new secretary of state, James Baker, and national security adviser,
Brent Scowcroft, were completely in sync. Neither felt there was much to be
gained by pursuing an active agenda on the Arab-Israeli conflict. Baker told
me during the transition period that he thought there was little prospect for
diplomacy leading anywhere between Arabs and Israelis, and that he was
"not going to fly around the Middle East like George Shultz had done." These
would prove to be famous last words: Baker ultimately traveled far more
often to the Middle East than Shultz. Baker resisted going to the Middle
East until after Saddam Hussein's invasion and occupation of Kuwait in
August 1990. Even then he did not engage in peacemaking efforts in the
area until after the Gulf War, traveling to Israel for the first time more than
two years after becoming secretary of state, in March 1991.

In the Bush administration, I would become part of James Baker's inner
circle at the State Department and assumed a much more central role in
policy making than I had in previous administrations. Ironically, I had
gotten to know Bush before Baker. After accompanying him on his 1986
trip to the Middle East, Bush asked to see me on a regular basis, and soon,
his chief of staff, deputy chief of staff, and pollster were asking me to suggest
themes for his speeches and to outline what I thought our foreign policy
priorities should be.[4] In late spring of 1988, Vice President Bush asked if I
would leave the NSC staff and become the senior foreign policy adviser to
his campaign for the presidency, and I did in July 1988.

I got to know Baker during the campaign but began to brief him seriously on foreign policy only after Bush won the 1988 election. Though I had been a lifelong Democrat, I joined the Bush campaign because I liked and respected him. I had been impressed during the 1986 trip to the Middle East with how he dealt with the leaders he met—Peres, Hussein, and Mubarak. He put them at ease and had a facility discussing the issues. To be sure, the fact that he allowed me to negotiate an understanding with them and trusted my judgment added to the appeal of being part of his administration. After he won the election, I was soon offered positions by both Scowcroft and Baker—with Scowcroft asking me to join him at the NSC as deputy national security adviser. Although Scowcroft's offer was more senior than going to State as the head of the Policy Planning Staff—the position that George Kennan had once held—I felt the action would be with Baker and was inclined to go with him.

Before deciding, the president-elect called me and said he knew about the two offers. He said, "I know that Jimmy Baker may put a lot of pressure on you to go with him, and if you want to go with him that would be fine, but you should go where you want to go and not where you feel pressured to go." I still chose to go with Baker, but the call meant a great deal to me, and it was very revealing about President Bush—his personal touch, his outreach, his concern for those around him, and his sense of what was proper and right. He had a strong code of how one should behave. It was this strict sense of propriety that would affect his relationship with Israeli prime minister Yitzhak Shamir. They would get off on the wrong foot and would never recover because President Bush felt Shamir misled him and betrayed his word.

Bush carried certain legacies from the Reagan administration: he hated the infighting between first Haig and Weinberger and then between Shultz and Weinberger. From the outset of his administration, he expected his people to operate as a team—disagreements and debates were fine, but there would not be dissension, competing leaks, or ongoing resistance once decisions were made. The first and second tier of officials worked together informally and reflected this guidance. Baker and Secretary of Defense Richard Cheney, for example, had been close for twenty years. Although they often disagreed on arms control and policy toward the Soviet Union, once the president made a decision, the issue was settled. Baker had senior Defense Department officials on his trips who could represent Cheney's views, even as they supported Baker fully in the steps he decided to take. Those of us who were the senior officials working for Baker, Scowcroft, and Cheney

developed our own informal channels that mirrored our bosses' and ensured that we thrashed out the issues in advance of many of their meetings.
On the Middle East, there were debates, but once the decisions were made,
they were implemented.

On substance, there were other legacies. In one meeting, the president
explicitly said he remembered the Israeli onslaught against Beirut, with its
forces entering the city, and that was not a mistake he would allow the United
States to make. In the run-up to the Gulf War, he repeatedly told Baker, "I
don't want American troops going into an Arab capital."[5] Unlike his son,
Bush would not send U.S. forces into Baghdad in large part because of the
Israeli experience in Beirut.

The legacy of Israel's behavior in Lebanon and elsewhere during the
Reagan administration was also very much on Bush's mind in his first
meeting with Shamir. When the two met alone, Bush raised two issues. The
first bore directly on the past, when he told Shamir it was "important that
Israel and the United States avoided surprising one another." He especially
"did not want to learn of an attack by Israel on Syria or Iraq."[6] Bush was
warning that he wanted no repeat of what the Reagan administration had
experienced during its first two years, with the Israeli bombing of the
nuclear reactor in Iraq and the subsequent invasion of Lebanon.

The second issue was Israeli settlement activity. Bush's views on settlements were not acquired from Reagan. Baker observed that "the President
was of the very strong belief that the settlements were simply wrong."[7] For
him, the West Bank and Gaza were occupied territories, not disputed lands
as the Israeli government saw them. It was wrong for Israel to be populating
them with settlements. No doubt, the fact that expanding settlement activity made it appear that the Israelis had no intention of withdrawing from
the West Bank and Gaza—something that ruled out the land for peace
premise of UNSC Resolutions 242 and 338—also factored heavily in President Bush's thinking.[8]

Three weeks prior to Shamir's visit to Washington, the president met
with Foreign Minister Moshe Arens and told him that "the creation of any
new settlements in the occupied territories would pose a tough issue for us."
He said it was important that "the PM appreciate the significance of this issue
here and avoid surprises."[9] Bush was putting Shamir on notice.

Notwithstanding his warning, Israel announced new settlements in the
intervening period. As a result, Bush told Shamir that he had been "greatly
upset by the fact that soon after the visit of [Foreign Minister] Arens here,
Israel went ahead and started up new settlements." He went on to say that

this was "an issue of great concern to us." Shamir's response was that "settlements ought not to be such a problem."[10] While Shamir may have felt he was telling the president that he should not let this issue concern him so much, the president heard something very different: Bush told Baker after the meeting that he believed "the spread of settlements would be halted."[11]

Thus Bush felt that Shamir lied to him when, two weeks after his visit to Washington, new settlements were announced in the West Bank. For Bush, it was not just a case of mendacity; far worse, in his eyes, was the fact that he deliberately met Shamir alone in order to talk to him, leader to leader, in an atmosphere designed to promote honesty and trust and not to embarrass him or force him to concede something in front of others—and this was Shamir's response. Few things more clearly signified bad faith to the president, and he would not get over it.[12] I would see the impact on Bush in all his subsequent meetings with Shamir, where the president's normal graciousness—so much a part of his persona—was simply absent. Indeed, in these meetings Bush often adopted a confrontational style—something completely out of character for him. Bob Gates, who served as the deputy national security adviser for Bush before later becoming his CIA director, was asked in an oral history interview whether there was any leader Bush "actively disliked," and he responded by saying Shamir.

> But I will say this. Every President I worked for, at some point in his presidency, would get so pissed off at the Israelis that he couldn't speak. It didn't matter whether it was Jimmy Carter or Gerry Ford or Ronald Reagan or George Bush. Something would happen and they would . . . rant and rave around the Oval Office. I think it was their frustration about knowing that there was so little they could do about it because of domestic politics and everything else that was so frustrating to them. But he did not, I think, care very much for Shamir . . . I can't think of any others.[13]

Gates may well be right that every president expressed frustration with the Israelis and had concerns about the political fallout of confronting certain Israeli behaviors, but that, of course, did not prevent them from criticizing or challenging Israeli behaviors in public. Ford did the "reassessment" of relations with Israel; Carter publicly condemned Israeli settlement activity; Reagan criticized the Israelis over the siege of Beirut and for their efforts in trying to block the AWACS sale; and Bush publicly challenged the Israelis on settlements. Over the years, I, too, heard presidents express the sentiments that Gates described, but I also heard their frustration with other countries and their leaders. There might not be the same domestic political considerations at play, but there were other concerns, and those would preclude a public response against an egregious act by one of our other friends, whether it was the Saudis or the French.

Regardless, George H. W. Bush's problems with Yitzhak Shamir would affect his approach to the prime minister—and prevent his giving him the benefit of the doubt on any issue. I experienced this directly with the president at different points during his term. But in the first year, other than the visits of Middle East leaders—and what would become an initial effort on the peace issue that required an occasional phone call—President Bush's focus was on Europe and the Soviet Union. Mine, too, was dominated by our efforts to deal with Gorbachev, key European arms control, and NATO-related issues, and, after the fall of the Berlin Wall in November 1989, German unification. But unlike Bush, Baker, and Scowcroft, I thought there were factors in the Middle East and with the Soviets that required an initiative by us and also created a possible opening. During the first fifteen months of the administration, we pursued a peace initiative, one that Baker later described as guided by "moderate activism" on our part. Our effort eventually fell victim to the collapse of the Israeli national unity government and the emergence of a narrow right-wing coalition led by Shamir. Had Saddam Hussein not invaded and occupied Kuwait in August 1990, I have little doubt that there would have been a crisis between the United States and Israel on the peace issue at some point during the Bush administration.

Instead, the Gulf War and our approach to its aftermath produced a very different trajectory. To be sure, there was tension and denial of Israel's request for $10 billion in loan guarantees until Yitzhak Rabin replaced Shamir as prime minister. Following Rabin's election in July 1992, we agreed on the terms for providing the loan guarantees. The financial assistance represented only one small part of what the Bush administration would do to respond to Israel's most basic strategic and political needs.

Indeed, the record of what the administration provided Israel is extensive:

- It maintained assistance at $3 billion a year and in the aftermath of the Gulf War furnished an additional $650 million to compensate for damages caused by Scud missile attacks, a figure well above the actual damages inflicted.
- The JPMG and its subsidiary groups continued to meet and expand

areas of cooperation in joint R&D ventures, exercises, training, pre-
stocking of materials, and military contracts.

- Two Patriot missile batteries were deployed on an emergency basis to
  Israel after Iraq struck Israel with Scud missiles early in the Gulf War,
  requiring the unprecedented deployment of seven hundred American
  troops to Israel to operate the Patriots.
- A direct communications link, Hammer RICK, was established for
  the first time between the offices of the U.S. secretary of defense and
  the Israeli minister of defense.
- The president and the secretary of state continued high-level efforts to
  get the Soviets to allow the Jews in the U.S.S.R. to immigrate to Israel,
  and the floodgates on emigration literally opened.
- President Bush secretly arranged for Ethiopian Jews to be flown to
  Israel, and Secretary Baker persuaded Hafez al Assad to allow Syria's
  Jews to leave.
- The administration mobilized and led the effort to repeal the odious
  "Zionism is Racism" resolution at the United Nations.
- The administration was, in James Baker's words, "instrumental in
  helping Israel establish diplomatic relations with forty-four countries,
  including the Soviet Union."[14]
- It produced the Madrid Conference, which ended an era of diplomacy
  through denial and broke the taboo on Israel being able to talk to its
  Arab neighbors.
- It destroyed the military capabilities of Iraq, Israel's most implacable
  Arab foe in the region at the time.

For a president who lacked the emotional attachment of Ronald Reagan
and who had a basic problem with Israel's prime minister for most of his
term in office, this is a remarkable record of responsiveness to Israel. It hardly
seems to fit the advice that Richard Nixon provided James Baker about the
need to be more "evenhanded" and less pro-Israel. Nor does it fit the image
of the Bush administration in the Jewish community as anti-Israel. How
can one account for this seeming dichotomy?

Two explanations stand out. First, the Bush administration did a great
deal for the Arabs. It liberated Kuwait from the Iraqi occupation and removed Saddam's threat to the Gulf states. Its use of power to respond to
threats made it far more credible than previous administrations in the eyes
of most Arab leaders. With the decline and then collapse of the Soviet
Union, the United States was now seen as the only superpower and one that

proved it would exercise its power if it felt its interests or friends were threatened. That perception trumped in the eyes of the Arabs what the Bush administration did for Israel. Of course, the Bush administration did not go easy on Israel in public. When it had differences with Israel, it did little to hide them, and its clear resistance on the loan guarantees to the Likud-led government demonstrated a readiness to take on Israel's supporters in the United States. It was not reluctant to manifest its differences with Israel both out of belief in its position and due to the benefits it presumed it would gain from the Arabs.

This leads to the second explanation: the tone of the discourse with Israel and its supporters in the United States was tough. There was much less outreach to the Jewish community and its leaders—and to the extent there was outreach, it came not from the president or Baker but from me and others, like Richard Haass, who served on the NSC staff as the senior Middle East aide to Scowcroft and the president.*

I appeared before a large Jewish audience in 1992. After reciting the litany of what the Bush administration had done for Israel, I was asked, "If things are so good, why do I feel so bad?" The feeling was rooted in public statements by President Bush and Baker. In May 1989, Baker had given a speech to AIPAC that was serious and substantive. It called on both Arabs and Israelis to take steps toward each other. Among other things, he said that it was time for Israel to "lay aside, once and for all, the unrealistic vision of a greater Israel."[15] It was legitimate to say this to an audience that consisted of Israel's most activist supporters. But if one was going to make tough statements about Israel, they needed to be balanced not just by calling on the Arabs to take parallel steps of acceptance of Israel—which Baker did—but also by speaking about our unique ties to Israel, the values that bind us as democracies, an awareness of Israel's history and its vulnerability, and ongoing Arab rejection.

Before the speech was finalized, I went over the draft with Baker and Harvey Sicherman, the member of my staff who was the principal drafter of the speech. When Harvey and I saw that Baker had taken out all the notes of warmth and acknowledgment of the United States' unique relationship with Israel, we both argued that those needed to be put back in. Baker replied that Bush would see that language as pandering and would instinctively oppose it—and it had to come out. In vain, I protested that this would be

* Like me, Haass is Jewish.

self-defeating: "You want this audience, and the Israeli public, to hear your message about what Israel needs to do for peace and that a policy of expanding settlements and annexation won't serve Israel's well-being. But you will lose them because they won't see any basic understanding of Israel's predicament or attachment that makes our commitments to Israel's security seem real."

Baker said he knew the president and what he could accept, and the language he edited out would never pass muster in the White House. As it turned out, the speech was portrayed as the "toughest ever given to a Jewish audience." That image came to define the Bush administration and its approach to Israel in the eyes of the Jewish community.[16]

In 1992, Ed Koch, the former mayor of New York City, added to the perception of the Bush-Baker hostility to Israel. Koch sought to explain it by claiming in his *New York Post* column that Baker had said, "Fuck the Jews, they don't vote for us anyway."[17]

While Baker's real and imagined statements fostered a certain image of the administration in the Jewish community, it was President Bush's press conference on the loan guarantees on September 12, 1991, that cemented this perception. He was making the case that Congress should defer consideration of loan guarantees for Israel lest they derail our effort to put together a peace conference. At one point he referred to "powerful political forces" he was up against and that he was facing "something like a thousand lobbyists on the Hill working the other side of the question. We've got one lonely little guy down here doing it."[18] In the Jewish community, Bush's words seemed to suggest that Israel's supporters did not have a right to lobby and that they were working against our national interests.

Bush later apologized to the Jewish leaders, saying he never intended for his words to be taken that way. He repeated this to me before I made an appearance at the president's Conference of Jewish Organizations. But the damage was very difficult to undo. Tom Dine, the director of AIPAC, led off his national conference in March 1992 by saying, "September 12, 1991, will be a day that lives in infamy for the American pro-Israel community. Like an Indian elephant, we don't forget!"[19]

Ronald Reagan had made a demonstrably tougher statement—raising the ugly specter of dual loyalties in his comments about the opposition to the AWACS sale—but because he conveyed an unmistakable commitment and emotional attachment to Israel, it did not stick. With Bush, it did. He would receive only approximately 11 percent of the Jewish vote in 1992.[20]

The irony is that Bush and Baker did a great deal for Israel and built upon the foundation of strategic cooperation that Reagan had established.*

To fully understand the dynamics of the U.S.-Israel relationship during the George H. W. Bush years, it is useful to take a closer look at the key developments and policies as they related to the U.S. approach to Israel. Four stand out: the effort to produce an Israeli-Palestinian dialogue from 1989 to 1990; the Gulf War, both in terms of excluding Israel from the coalition and then the steps taken to ensure it would not retaliate against Iraq after Scud missiles were fired into Israel; the postwar diplomatic effort that produced the Madrid Peace Conference; and the loan guarantee imbroglio in 1991.

Trying to Produce an Israeli-Palestinian Dialogue—Baker's Five Points and Their Demise

James Baker moved to the transition office in the State Department in December 1988. He asked Robert Zoellick and me to organize most of his early briefings within a small, trusted circle of advisers.[†] The initial discussions involved my briefing Baker on the changes, possibilities, and challenges in the Soviet Union and Zoellick doing the same on Europe. Following these, I did a similar briefing on the Middle East. At the outset of my Middle East briefing, Baker made his comment on not flying around like Shultz, saying that to be a successful secretary of state, he could not be engaged in quixotic pursuits. He saw only failed efforts in the Middle East, and he was not about to join the ranks of those who had failed. He well remembered the Reagan Plan, and as he recounted later in his memoirs, he was convinced that "even the most intensive application of diplomacy would be a wasted investment."[21] I told him that he might want to ignore the Middle East, but it would not ignore him. Sooner or later, the Middle East would impose itself

---

* Bush, on the other hand, had much more credibility with friendly Arab leaders because he demonstrated his willingness to use force against an aggressive Iraq, an image the Saudis and others see lacking in President Obama's reaction to the Iranians in the region today.

† Larry Eagleburger, who would become the deputy secretary of state, Robert Kimmitt, who would become the under secretary of state for political affairs, Margaret Tutwiler, who would become the assistant secretary of state for public affairs, and Janet Mullins, who would become the assistant secretary of state for legislative affairs, joined Zoellick and me in many of these early discussions. Zoellick would become the counselor and later under secretary for economic and agricultural affairs.

on him, and it was better to try to shape the environment than respond at a point when he had no choice but to act and his options were more limited.

The key, I argued, was to recognize what was possible and build a strategy accordingly. Even though peace seemed unlikely anytime soon, the intifada created a new reality. Israelis increasingly realized there was no military answer to the Palestinian problem; Palestinians in the West Bank and Gaza understood the intifada needed to produce something tangible; and, in Tunis, Arafat was anxious to prove his relevance after the Palestinians in the territories had launched the intifada without him. An international conference might not be immediately relevant to these circumstances, but steps on the ground that could change the dynamic between Israelis and Palestinians were essential. With that in mind, I suggested a twofold approach. First, defuse the intifada by brokering parallel steps—Israel releases prisoners, stops military sweeps of villages, and lifts restrictions on commercial activity, and Palestinians accept local cease-fires and end strikes. Second, once the situation on the ground was defused, prepare elections to produce Palestinians who could negotiate with the Israelis to, at a minimum, establish self-rule.

Baker saw great benefit in this approach, which could transform the landscape without requiring a high-profile U.S. initiative. He felt he could use these ideas with the Europeans—who he knew would be pressing for U.S. action.* Moreover, with Bush following the pattern of his predecessors and inviting Middle East leaders to Washington in the spring, Baker felt this approach could provide a focal point for those discussions. He asked me to convey these ideas directly to the Israelis and let them know that if they were not responsive to them, they needed to come with ideas of their own.

I conveyed this to Eli Rubenstein, a close aide to Prime Minister Shamir whom I knew well from his earlier stint as the deputy chief of the Israeli mission in Washington. In essence, I told Rubenstein that we could not beat something with nothing. The Europeans were poised to push for an international conference if we did not have an approach. If the prime minister did not like what I was suggesting, he needed to come with ideas that were credible and we could sell.

"Sell" is the operative word here and would set a pattern for much of our approach to peace in the Bush and Clinton administrations. We would take Israeli ideas or ideas that the Israelis could accept and frame them in a way

---

* Interestingly, U.S. peace initiatives have often been driven by concerns about the Europeans.

that might increase their appeal to the Arabs, all the while trying to scale back Arab expectations. There was a reason this pattern emerged: the Arabs were not about to initiate anything. They believed that what they were getting from the Israelis was rightfully theirs, and so it was up to Israel, and us, to offer up something tangible. In many ways, this is a process that Kissinger had begun; he wanted the Arabs to understand that only we could produce accommodations from the Israelis and that they needed ties to us if they were to get their land back.

One could argue that if the Arabs reached out to the Israelis on their own, they would not need to work through us. But the political psychology in Arab countries defined this as surrender. Only Anwar Sadat had been prepared to challenge it. And even though Sadat had gone to Jerusalem, he needed the United States and its president to invest heavily to produce an agreement that led to the recovery of Egypt's land. Had there been other Arab leaders like Sadat who would take the initiative, we might not have needed to forge such an approach. But there were not. Moreover, the Israelis were now led by the enormously cautious Yitzhak Shamir, who wanted Arab acceptance of Israel first, and even then doubted that it would buy Israel very much. His instinct was to move very slowly, give up the minimum, and stretch out the time for doing so. He talked earnestly of his interest in and commitment to peace, but saw risks in every move—and far less risk in standing pat. Still, he was convinced by Eli Rubenstein that he needed to come to Washington with an initiative—and he did.

Shamir's initiative had four elements: it would strengthen the Egyptian-Israeli peace, initiate direct negotiations with other Arab states to end the state of war, launch an international effort to alleviate the living conditions in the Palestinian refugee camps, and plan for elections in the territories to elect Palestinians to negotiate with Israel.

Baker candidly told Shamir that while we would support every part of his initiative, the only element that we could sell in the near term was the election idea. This, he explained, we could present as opening a "political pathway" to dealing with the Palestinians—and given the intifada and the perception internationally that Palestinian political needs must be addressed, this would have "traction." Shamir, in turn, was prepared to work with us on the election idea and accepted our language that it could launch a "political negotiating process."

Shamir wanted to use elections to select Palestinians from the territories who might talk to Israel about limited autonomy. We had a broader definition in mind. We wanted to use elections to foster a preelection dialogue between Israelis and Palestinians to change the realities on the ground. Such a dialogue, we believed, could produce mutual steps by Israelis and Palestinians that would change the environment and make it possible for elections to take place. Moreover, any real discussion geared toward preparing elections would begin to get at larger political questions: Who could run in the elections? Would Palestinian Jerusalemites be eligible to vote or to run? Where would the IDF be deployed during this period and how would they operate? What would be possible after the election and be on the table for negotiations?

Shamir sought to limit the scope of our questions. But we would use these questions to demonstrate that the election idea could launch a meaningful political process between the Israelis and Palestinians. We would use them to convince the Europeans and President Mubarak of Egypt and King Hussein of the merits of the approach—and we sought to gain PLO acceptance of it as well. Of course, any discussion with the PLO made Shamir deeply suspicious. He saw it as a murderous organization determined to destroy Israel. He was willing to accept our idea now of a preelection dialogue as a way of creating a Palestinian alternative to the PLO. While we understood that the intifada was homegrown and had created a pressure on Arafat, we also believed that Palestinians from the territory would not enter a dialogue or take part in the elections if the PLO opposed them doing so.

Thus there was an inherent tension between what the administration now sought to do and what Shamir was prepared to accept in the pursuit of the initiative he brought to Washington. We soon found the PLO imposing absurd strictures. It would support elections only after Palestinian statehood was accepted as a principle—meaning Israel had to concede the PLO's major objective first in order to allow an election or preelection talks. The only way around this was to get Egypt to convince Arafat to allow the initiative to go forward and support a preelection dialogue with Palestinians from the territories.

Elsewhere, I have told the full story of Baker's five points.* It is sufficient here simply to summarize what occurred and how it affected Bush and Baker. Egypt's president, Hosni Mubarak, did not act to pressure the PLO until Baker made it clear that he would turn his own diplomatic focus elsewhere—and pay little attention to the Middle East—unless the Palestinian position became more reasonable. In response, the Egyptians engaged with Arafat and also secretly colluded with the Labor side of the Israeli

* See *The Missing Peace.*

national unity government and forged a ten-point proposal under which Israelis and Palestinians would negotiate to set up elections and then hold talks afterward.* Several of the points—territory for peace, halt to settlement construction, and Jerusalemites eligible to vote and run in elections— were acceptable to Shimon Peres, the head of Labor, but were anathema to Shamir. Since both Shamir's original proposal and Egypt's ten points were about holding elections for the Palestinians in the West Bank and Gaza, we suggested that the logical way to reconcile the two proposals was to produce a preelection dialogue between Israelis and Palestinians from the territories.

The problem remained which specific Palestinians would participate in such a dialogue and how we could get it launched. To overcome these problems, Baker hosted a meeting in New York with Moshe Arens, Israel's foreign minister, and the Egyptian foreign minister, Esmat Abdel Meguid. I was the only other person in the meeting, and we were able to reach a number of understandings, including that we would work with the Egyptians and Israelis to produce a list of Palestinians the Israelis could meet.

However, when Arafat balked at what he saw as an Israeli veto, President Mubarak decided to force the issue and simply issued an invitation to the Israelis to come to Cairo and sit with a Palestinian delegation. Unfortunately, this triggered a governmental crisis in Israel, when Peres insisted on accepting the invitation and Shamir rejected it. To avert the collapse of the government, Arens called Baker and asked him to issue what had been privately worked out in the trilateral meeting, declaring that if the secretary presented this as a formal American proposal, Peres would feel obliged to accept it and the crisis would end. Baker agreed, and I drafted what became known as Baker's five points, and they were formally conveyed to Arens.†

---

* The 1988 election produced another national unity government, with Likud and Labor. Likud led this government with Shamir as prime minister, Yitzhak Rabin as defense minister, Moshe Arens as foreign minister, and Shimon Peres as finance minister. Peres remained the head of the Labor Party.

† Baker's five points were (1) Egypt and Israel agreed that an Israeli delegation should conduct a dialogue with a Palestinian delegation in Cairo. (2) The United States recognized that Egypt could not substitute itself for the Palestinians and would consult with the Palestinians on all aspects of the dialogue. (3) The United States understood that Israel would attend the dialogue only after a satisfactory list of Palestinians had been worked out. (4) The United States understood that Israel would come to the dialogue based on its "initiative." The Palestinians would come prepared to discuss elections and negotiations in accordance with the Israeli initiative but would be free to raise issues for how to be successful in each. (5) The United States would host a meeting of the Israeli and Egyptian foreign ministers in Washington to facilitate the process.

To our surprise, however, when the five points leaked in Israel, Shamir rejected them publicly, saying on October 16 that he would not compromise with the Palestinians even if it meant the collapse of his government and a confrontation with the United States. Notwithstanding what Arens, his Likud foreign minister, was telling us, he seemed to be rejecting the very idea of going ahead.

We decided that Bush should talk to Shamir, and Baker joined him for a phone call the next day. On the phone, Shamir told the president that "we're fully committed to our peace initiative—to the spirit *and* the letter of it." Bush, increasingly distrustful of Shamir, replied, "There *is* a perception that Israel is moving away from your own position," and he added that "Jim Baker's five points meet your concerns and protect Israel. You know *who* you will be talking to, and what you'll be talking about . . . We're not trying to force you to talk with the PLO. But we *do* wish there could be less delay in responding factually to us on these points. If you give us a positive response, then Israel and the United States can move forward together. If you don't respond, we have to interpret that you *don't* want to go forward." Shamir argued, "We are not pulling away from our initiative, but we will not meet with the PLO."[22]

Bush persisted, pressing to see what Shamir was willing to do to implement his "*own* initiative," with Shamir essentially suggesting only that Arens should talk to Baker. Bush became increasingly frustrated and very bluntly said, "I've just read the wire story quoting you about a confrontation with the United States. If you want that—fine."[23] Shamir did not respond, but it was clear to me that both Bush and Baker were about to give up on our effort to launch a preelection dialogue and, perhaps, forgo trying to do business with this Israeli prime minister altogether.

Sallai Meridor was Arens's right-hand man. He and I had begun to work closely together to try to ensure that our bosses would have productive discussions. I called Sallai and told him unless we could get an Israeli yes on Baker's five points, we were shortly going to be out of business. Meridor promised to see what he could do, indicating that cabinet approval with some reservations was probably the most that was possible. And that is what transpired: the Israeli cabinet voted to approve the five points with reservations.

It would take several weeks, but Egypt would produce a second yes from the PLO.

But we soon discovered the Palestinian yes carried conditions—with the Egyptians telling us the Palestinians would not launch the dialogue unless there was an outsider and a Jerusalemite on the Palestinian delegation. Both conditions were rejected by the Israelis. Once again, we faced an impasse, only now, it was at a point when Baker and I were intensively focused on dealing with the new reality created by the removal of the Berlin Wall. We were in the midst of making an enormous effort to persuade the Soviets—and the British and French—that Germany must be unified within NATO.

Occupied elsewhere, Bush and Baker had little time and even less patience for a stalemate. If Egypt and Israel wanted something to happen, they would have to create a solution. Yitzhak Rabin, the defense minister in the unity government, privately conveyed two ideas to me to overcome the impasse: Israel would allow a "dual addressee" and two deportees from the territories to be on the Palestinian delegation.* Rabin told me Shamir would accept these ideas, and while I was prepared to run them by the Egyptians, Baker felt the need first to talk to the Israeli prime minister.[24] Shamir confirmed that he was aware of Rabin's ideas and had no problem with our seeing if the Egyptians would accept them.

However, when the Egyptians came back with a yes, and Baker phoned Shamir with the "good news," Shamir was hesitant, saying, "Let's not rush." When he pointed to his upcoming Likud Party conference and suggested that Arens come to Washington for more talks, Baker and I exchanged glances, with me mouthing, *The dog ate his homework.* Shamir was unmistakably stalling, and we were not convinced it was only because of the upcoming Likud conference. Indeed, when Baker called Arens after this conversation with Shamir, he was astonished to learn that Arens knew nothing about Rabin's ideas. While clearly embarrassed and unhappy to learn about them from the secretary of state, he was, nonetheless, ready to come to Washington to work with Baker to try to resolve everything.

Sallai and I met beforehand and worked out a formula that Baker and Arens accepted and that Arens said he would try to sell to Shamir and would, in any case, support in the cabinet. If nothing else, this meant it would gain cabinet approval.[25]

There was a new surprise on Saturday, March 3—only it came from our side. President Bush was meeting Japanese prime minister Toshiki Kaifu in Palm Springs, and in answer to a question in their press conference, he said, "We do not believe there should be new settlements in the West Bank or East Jerusalem." At this delicate moment, the president unexpectedly, and

---

* The deportees would be allowed to return to the territories, and the dual addressee would be someone who lived in Jerusalem but maintained an address outside it. In this way, the Palestinians could claim they had outsiders and a Jerusalemite at the talks and the Israelis could say they were talking only to those from the territories.

for the first time, referred to settlements in East Jerusalem. His comment was not planned. We learned only later that John Sununu, the White House chief of staff, had raised Israeli building in East Jerusalem with him earlier in the week. Jerusalem was sensitive at any time, but particularly now, when we were crafting an indirect way to deal with it, the last thing we needed was for Jerusalem to become an issue. Shamir leaped on the Bush comment and said he could not support the American approach. When Peres pushed for a vote on the American formula, Arens was true to his word; he and two other members of Likud split. With Shamir in opposition, the cabinet voted 9–3 to accept the American approach. Shamir was not prepared to proceed and Labor called for a vote of no confidence in the Knesset. The Shamir-led government fell by a vote of 60–55, with the five members of the Ultra-Orthodox Shas Party abstaining.

The fall of the Shamir government was greeted with no tears in Washington. Bush had no trust in Shamir. Baker had lost what little he had. With Shimon Peres seemingly able to put together a Labor-led government, we expected movement on the Israeli-Palestinian-Egyptian dialogue. But we were in for one last surprise. On the day of the vote in the Knesset to establish the new government, the ninety-six-year-old ultra-Orthodox Rabbi Elazar Shach in New York inveighed against the Aguda Party (an orthodox party) joining a Peres-led government, and two members of Aguda refused to vote for the Labor-led coalition. Suddenly, Peres was just short of the necessary majority. On June 11, 1990, after three months of going back and forth, Shamir—and not Peres—was able to form a narrow right-wing coalition. Gone were Rabin and Peres from the government—and with them any hope of being able to move forward on the peace initiative that had started in February 1989.

Shamir sent a message to Baker shortly after forming a government that he was serious about peace. A highly skeptical Baker asked me perfunctorily to check with Eli Rubenstein to see if Shamir would accept the formula we had worked out with Arens—and the answer came back he was not. It was in this context that Baker famously answered Congressman Mel Levine that when the Israelis were serious they could call the White House switchboard at "202-456-1414."

The Gulf War: Coalescing with the Arabs

I was with Baker in Irkutsk for a two-day ministerial with Eduard Shevardnadze when Bob Kimmitt, the under secretary for policy, called to say that it appeared Iraq was about to invade Kuwait. Iraqi threats against Kuwait had been mounting over the preceding few weeks, but President Mubarak, King Fahd, and King Hussein all said that Saddam was only posturing: "These pressures were Saddam's way of doing business."[26] The White House, the Bureau of Near Eastern Affairs in the State Department, and the intelligence community thus discounted the prospects of an invasion. As Bob Gates observed later, their views had a great impact on us: "The truth of the matter is, the people who knew it best, the leaders, who lived in the region, who knew the language, knew the culture, knew the history, were all . . . saying nothing was going to happen."[27]

In order to secure final Soviet agreement on German unification in NATO, we had been engaged simultaneously in a number of parallel negotiations with the Soviets, Germany, and other key members of NATO. Later, Baker would explain that the administration was "grappling with one of the most revolutionary periods in world history." The great changes taking place in Europe—as well as unanticipated events like the Chinese killing of dissidents in Tiananmen Square in June 1989—created an environment in which, in Baker's words, "none of us considered policy toward Iraq to be an urgent priority. And it was simply not prominent on my radar screen, or the President's."[28]

But it would be forced onto our radar screen when we received the report that Saddam's forces were poised to move into Kuwait. Baker immediately conveyed this information to Shevardnadze. The Soviet foreign minister did not buy it. Shevardnadze, like many of our own officials, was convinced that "Saddam is a thug, but he is not crazy, and it would be crazy for him to launch another war." This, too, had been part of a collective mind-set: following Iraq's recent war with Iran, which had cost hundreds of thousands of lives and destroyed the Iraqi economy, it would be crazy for Saddam to go to war again. But that was obviously not Saddam Hussein's calculus.

The next morning, August 2, 1990, Bob Kimmitt reported to Baker that Iraq's forces had invaded Kuwait. When Baker reported this to Shevardnadze, he was deeply embarrassed, now finding himself in the awkward position of hosting Baker in the Soviet Union and being caught totally unaware of the invasion of a Soviet client state in which several thousand Soviet personnel, security and nonsecurity, were present. His being blindsided by those within the Soviet security apparatus about the invasion contributed to his joining with us not only in condemning Iraq but also in pushing Gorbachev to support what became a united front in the UN Security Council to impose sanctions and ultimately the use of force to reverse the Iraqi aggression.

At this juncture, as the ministerial in Irkutsk ended, Baker flew to Mongolia and I joined Shevardnadze on his plane back to Moscow. On our five-hour flight, I spoke with Shevardnadze and Sergei Tarasenko, Shevardnadze's chief aide,* and said that the Iraqi invasion was a grave danger to international security but it also offered us the chance to demonstrate to the world that the cold war was truly over. We needed to seize this moment and give content to "new thinking," and show that this was an era in which the United States and the Soviet Union would be partners and work to end conflicts, not perpetuate them. We must, I argued, be on the same side and act in unison.

Both were taken with the sense of possibility. Once in Moscow, at the suggestion of Peter Hauslohner, a member of my staff, I proposed a joint U.S.-Soviet statement. Notwithstanding opposition from within the Soviet Foreign and Defense Ministries that made the negotiations uncertain until the last minute, Shevardnadze would deliver, and Baker returned to Moscow to issue a tough joint statement on August 3.

With the Soviets on board, it certainly was easier for President Bush to declare on August 5 that "this will not stand. This will not stand, this aggression against Kuwait."[29] Bush quickly adopted a strategy to isolate Iraq, build international pressure on it, impose painful sanctions until and unless it withdrew unconditionally from Kuwait, and deter any further aggression. But this strategy depended not just on no Soviet vetoes in the UN but also, and more important, on successfully deterring an Iraqi move against Saudi Arabia. With little blocking the Iraqi forces from moving across the Saudi border and seizing the Saudi oil fields in the northeastern part of the country, it was essential to deploy U.S. forces, starting with tactical air wings, to the kingdom.

In Bush's initial conversation with King Fahd, the king "evaded the question" of accepting U.S. forces, even when the president pressed for an answer.[30] Instead, the king spoke of working with the team the president would immediately send, headed by Secretary of Defense Cheney. For any Saudi king, whose title is the Custodian of the Two Holy Mosques, accepting

---

* Sergei Tarasenko and I worked together much the way I worked with Sallai Meridor. However, because Baker and Shevardnadze were meeting so often, our communication was even more frequent and intensive as we worked the agenda and objectives in advance of each get-together.

overt protection on Saudi soil from "nonbelievers" is not simple. As Bandar bin Sultan, the Saudi ambassador to America, later explained to me, he had met with the king—his uncle—before Cheney arrived and worked to overcome his reservations. The king understood the need for U.S. forces and wanted to see Saddam defeated, but he was wary of the possibility of American forces occupying Saudi Arabia and the image that he was hiding behind them.

It was not just Bandar's persuasion that moved the king, however; it was also Bush's own personal credibility. As Cheney later explained, "I could remember going to talk to King Fahd when I asked him for approval to deploy the force to Saudi Arabia. His basic response was . . . 'Okay, we'll do it. We'll do it because I trust George Bush and because I know when it's over with, you'll leave.'"*31

Concerns about U.S. ties to Israel never factored into the conversation with the Saudis. The same was true with Egypt, the other Gulf states, and even Syria, when Baker began his trips to shape an Arab coalition aligned against Saddam Hussein. The Arab leaders were all focused on Saddam's betrayal—this was especially true of Fahd and Mubarak—and the need to ensure his withdrawal.

Saddam, seeing that he was very quickly isolated internationally and in the region as well, sought to make Israel the issue. Ten days after he occupied Kuwait and referred to it as the nineteenth province of Iraq, he claimed his occupation was linked to ending Israeli occupation of Palestinian lands. He implied that he had gone into Kuwait to raise the issue of Israeli occupation. In doing so, he sought to make himself the champion of the Palestinians. While Palestinians in the territories would later cheer Iraqi Scud attacks on Israel, no one took Saddam's claim seriously, but it did make Arab leaders like Fahd and Mubarak determined that Saddam should not be able to claim that he had achieved anything for the Palestinians.

Both Arab leaders were very blunt in saying this to Baker during his initial trip to the region in early September, which I joined. During our very intensive discussions in the Gulf and Egypt, both Fahd and Mubarak had been adamant that Saddam must not only lose but also be seen to lose. They also made it clear that we must not talk about the peace issue at this stage, lest it appear that Saddam's actions drove us to it. Here were our most important Arab allies at the time imploring us to avoid the trap of "linkage"—

---

* Bush would call the king and commit to withdrawing U.S. forces as soon as the conflict was over.

tying our actions toward Iraq to the Arab-Israeli issue. Their priority at this point was dealing with the threat of Saddam Hussein, not the Palestinian issue.

With their admonition ringing in my ears as we flew to Helsinki—where Bush was meeting with Gorbachev for a summit and where we would negotiate another joint statement on Iraq in the name of the two presidents—I drafted a joint communiqué for Bush and Gorbachev to issue at the conclusion of the summit.* Baker liked it. We met the president there but had little opportunity to brief him on it before he and Scowcroft met with Gorbachev. Baker and I went into a simultaneous meeting with Shevardnadze and Tarasenko. Baker showed our draft statement to Shevardnadze, who was prepared to accept it as written but said Gorbachev might want to add something general on the peace issue. When Baker pointed out that we needed to avoid any hint of linkage and that the peace issue could be addressed only after we had undone Saddam's occupation of Kuwait, Shevardnadze agreed.

However, when we got together with the president following his meeting with Gorbachev, he said that the Soviet president had insisted that any joint statement needed to show we also cared about Arab-Israeli peace. We therefore had to commit ourselves to holding an international conference soon. Bush's briefing made clear that he had raised no objections to Gorbachev's argument, and his intonation implied that he was ready to include a commitment to the conference in the statement. Believing this would be a disaster, I blurted out, "You can't do that. This will absolutely undercut what we're trying to do. We'll put the moderate Arabs in a position where Saddam is delivering for the Palestinians and they're not. If we create linkage, he can claim victory. And, if he does that, we will have undermined our friends in the area and we are going to face a Middle East that is far more dangerous than we've ever seen."

The president was taken aback. He initially started to get mad at me, but Baker intervened. Even though he would later write that I was "impassioned almost to the point of intemperance,"[32] Baker told the president, "You are wrong on this and Dennis is right." He then pointed out that we had drafted a statement without any reference to an international conference and Shevardnadze had accepted it. Bush said he doubted that Gorbachev was going

---

* It built on their earlier joint statement, pledging continuing joint efforts to produce Iraq's unconditional withdrawal from Kuwait and suggesting that additional action might be required for us to achieve that objective.

to accept anything less than a reference to the conference. When Baker persisted, saying we have a draft without it so "don't worry about it," the president's reply cast a pall over the room and poignantly conveyed the pressure and responsibility that was weighing on him: "Well, I've *got* to worry about it. I put all those kids out there. Nobody else did it—*I* did it. And I've gotta take every step to be sure that I don't put their lives at risk needlessly. If I can get them out of there without fighting, I'll do it."[33]

No one responded for a few minutes. When John Sununu broke the silence by saying, "Maybe we can put a reference to an international conference in there," Baker told him to "get off of it," and President Bush then said, "Look, Jimmy, if you can get the statement without it, fine."[34]

We succeeded in doing so, making only a private commitment that we would work with the Soviets on a regional peace conference after Saddam had withdrawn from Kuwait. Again, in another example of President Bush's character, late that night as he was flying back to Washington, he called Baker and thanked him and asked him to thank me for saving him from making a mistake. He understood "linkage" would be a mistake. It would never come up again prior to the war.

Preventing Israeli Retaliation

Baker did not include Israel on any of his trips to the region. His focus was on producing and maintaining an Arab coalition against Iraq. Any public discussion with Israel was seen by the administration as potentially playing into Saddam's hands: he would try to make this an issue of the United States and Israel against Iraq and not the world against Iraqi aggression. We were in the odd position of Baker going twice to Damascus but not to Jerusalem before the Gulf War began.

I was opposed to Baker going to Damascus, thinking that Assad's bitter historical rivalry with Saddam Hussein meant, by definition, that he would support the coalition against Iraq. In his memoirs, Baker recounts that because of my opposition to his going to Damascus, he dropped Syria from his itinerary for the September trip. He would add it to the planned trip only after President Bush asked him to go.[35]

According to Baker, Bush had opposed the decision during the Reagan administration to cut off contacts with Syria after the debacle in Lebanon in 1984. Now he told Baker, "I think you should consider going to Syria. I don't want to miss the boat again."[36] Bush's instinct had been to reach out to the

Syrians before, and at this point he could see the virtue of including Syria, a so-called Arab nationalist state, in the coalition. In terms of the Arab street, it made sense and certainly added to the image of Saddam's isolation from the key Arab states.

Just as the Arab street argued for Syria's inclusion, it argued for Israel's exclusion. But Israel was a part of the region. Secretary Cheney and my former boss Paul Wolfowitz, who was now the under secretary of defense for policy, believed that we needed to keep Israel in the picture—even if our cooperation remained discreet. Bush and Baker's antipathy toward Shamir reinforced their instinct to keep Israel in the shadows at this juncture. But the president accepted Cheney's argument that if we wanted the Israelis to be cooperative and not create problems, we needed to be working quietly with them. Shortly before we departed on Baker's September trip to the region, therefore, Cheney hosted a senior Israeli defense delegation, led by David Ivri, at the Pentagon. Ivri, the director-general of the Defense Ministry, told Cheney he believed that if it took a war to remove Iraq from Kuwait, Saddam Hussein would surely attack Israel. Cheney responded by ordering the sale of advanced Patriot antiaircraft missiles on favorable terms to Israel.[37]

Beyond the sale of the Patriots, the Pentagon sought Israeli assessments of Iraqi capabilities and target lists. While the Pentagon saw benefit in quiet cooperation with Israel, there was an enduring suspicion in the White House and parts of the intelligence community that Israel might try to take advantage of the crisis to attack Iraq. Though I argued that Israel had little reason to do so, President Bush was sufficiently concerned about the possibility of an Israeli preemptive strike that when Shamir came to see him in December 1990, with the UN-imposed deadline for Iraqi withdrawal from Kuwait a month away, the president's main preoccupation in the meeting was to elicit a promise from the prime minister that Israel would not carry out a preemptive attack.[38]

Baker did not raise Israel during his discussions in the Arab capitals until his November trip. At that point, he pressed for commitments that if Iraq struck Israel and the Israelis retaliated, all of our Arab partners would stick with us. He wanted clear understandings we could hold the different Arab leaders to, and we achieved them. In our meeting on Israel with Saud al Faisal, the Saudi foreign minister, and Prince Bandar, Bandar immediately said, "no problem," but Prince Saud said that only the king could decide on the question of Israel hitting Iraq. I asked if he realized that we were talking about Iraq launching rockets against Israel and Israel reacting, not initiating the conflict, and Saud said, "Yes, I understand, but that is a complicated issue" and only the king can decide that. As we finished our meeting, Bandar grabbed me by the arm and whispered, "Don't worry." Bandar was right; the king would have no problem with Israel retaliating if it was attacked by Iraq first—nor would any of the other Arab leaders with whom Baker raised the issue.

Despite these assurances, the closer we got to war, the more President Bush wanted to be sure that the coalition would not come apart. He feared that Arab leaders would not be as steadfast once we were actually bombing Iraq, an Arab country, and that if Israel hit Iraq, even in retaliation, Arab leaders would come under great pressure from their populations. He did not want to put these understandings to the test.

With that in mind, the president sent Larry Eagleburger, the deputy secretary of state, and Paul Wolfowitz to Israel on January 12, 1990, three days before the UN deadline on Iraqi withdrawal and three days after Baker's failed meeting with Iraqi foreign minister Tariq Aziz in Geneva.[39] War now seemed inevitable. The Eagleburger-Wolfowitz mission was to ensure that Israel would not strike Iraq preemptively or even in retaliation. They carried a letter from President Bush to Prime Minister Shamir that asked Israel not to get involved in the fighting even in response to an Iraqi provocation. Eagleburger and Wolfowitz sought to amplify the arguments in the letter, saying that it was best for Israel to stay out of the fight: we would be destroying Iraq's warmaking capability and, thus, neutralizing one of its biggest threats. Israel would not need to put its forces at risk.[40] When Shamir and Arens asked if they were being asked not to strike back even if Israel took casualties, the Eagleburger-Wolfowitz answer was twofold: we are a superpower and can inflict far more destruction on Iraqi targets, and we will offer you an American "aerial umbrella" with U.S.-manned Patriot missile batteries deployed until the Israeli ones can "be up and running on their own."[41]

The Israelis turned down the offer of U.S.-manned batteries because, as Eagleburger would later say, "the Israelis have always had the view that they would defend themselves."[42] Shamir reacted with the frustration of someone who had been excluded from the coalition over the preceding five months and was now being told not to exercise his right of self-defense, saying, "You are treating us like some black sheep of the family that you want to pretend doesn't exist, like someone with a social disease." To which Wolfowitz responded: "Here is the president of the United States, for the first time in American history, offering to deploy American troops to protect Israel. This is a very public connection."[43]

Both were correct. The Israelis focused not just on their sense of exclusion but also on the impact that forbearance in the face of direct provocation would have on Israeli deterrence. They feared it would seem as though they were so dependent on the United States that America could make decisions on Israel's security. The Bush administration, on the other hand, wanted nothing to undermine its strategy on Iraq and felt that it was taking care of Israel's needs in the process.

Reality quickly imposed itself on us both. The U.S. bombing campaign against Iraq began on the evening of January 16, 1991. The very next night, Washington time—early in the morning of January 18, Israel time—Iraqi Scuds were fired against Israel, hitting targets in Tel Aviv and Haifa. Arens immediately called Cheney and requested the electronic codes—called IFF codes—that allow the identification of friend and foe aircraft. In addition, he asked us to get the Saudis to open up a corridor for Israeli aircraft to fly through to attack western Iraq. Cheney raised Arens's request with Baker, who spoke to the president. Bush asked him to call Shamir and push Israel to withhold any response at this point.

The Saudis might have been willing to accept an Israeli retaliation against Iraq, but that did not mean they were prepared to allow their airspace to be used for it. Moreover, Bush and Baker were convinced that if the Israeli attacks came through Jordan, the Jordanians would try to shoot down Israeli aircraft, inevitably widening the war and shattering the coalition against Saddam.[44] As a result, they were not prepared under any circumstances to give the Israelis the IFF codes.

On that first night of the Scud attacks into Israel, Baker tried to convince first Arens and then Shamir that it was not in Israel's interest to respond. He repeated many of the Eagleburger-Wolfowitz arguments, adding that Israel's strategic interests were better served by not letting Saddam transform the conflict. In his initial call with Shamir, Baker was also able to report that we had F-15s over the Scud launch sites in western Iraq and added, "There is nothing your air force can do that we are not doing. If there is tell us and we'll do it." Shamir was concerned less with what we were doing than with the message he might send about Israel. In his words, "Israel has never failed to respond." It was for Shamir a "terrible problem for us."[45]

The prime minister called Baker back, waking him in the middle of the night, and said that Israel had to respond to the attacks on Tel Aviv and Haifa. The secretary bluntly replied this "would be a disaster for Israel," telling him not to "make it more difficult for us to do the job for you." When Shamir agreed that it was not in Israel's interest to provoke the other Arab nations but that he could not rule out launching a retaliation, Baker told him, "You cannot do this, Prime Minister. It's not in your interests. We'll respond to whatever needs you have, but you can't do this."[46] We were asking the Israelis to override what was a basic impulse of their self-reliance.

To show we meant what Baker said and also to give the Israelis a reason to hold off, the president now sent Eagleburger and Wolfowitz back to Israel. Their mission was to ensure the Israelis did not retaliate, and to offer, within certain bounds, whatever assurances and material assistance and support was needed to prevent their acting. Arens would continue to ask for the IFF codes and other items.[47] These requests would not be accepted, but we would respond to the Israelis in a number of other ways: providing ongoing intelligence, accepting Israeli advice on targeting, and diverting U.S. air and special operations forces to go after the Scuds in western Iraq.

The Israelis now very quickly accepted the deployment of U.S. forces to man two Patriot batteries—with nearly forty giant C-5A transports arriving from Germany on January 19 to deliver the missiles, their radars, and the required seven hundred personnel to operate and maintain them. The Patriots were far more effective against attacking aircraft than against incoming Scud missiles, but their deployment was significant psychologically in Israel and made it a little easier for Shamir to withstand the enormous pressure he was under from the IDF and his ministers to retaliate. Baker believes our withholding the IFF codes was the reason Shamir did not do so; I suspect, however, the prime minister's inherent caution may also explain why he exercised such restraint.

Brent Scowcroft was close to President Bush and no fan of Shamir's, but he would later say that "whatever other problems may have arisen between us and Shamir from time to time, on this occasion he showed himself a strong, stalwart ally."[48] Interestingly, Shamir's restraint also had an effect on how at least some of the Arabs looked at Israel. Prince Bandar would tell me shortly before our first postwar trip to Saudi Arabia that the Saudis needed to look anew at the region and understand who were the kingdom's friends and who were its foes. Israel had not acted as an enemy, and in difficult circumstances had acted with restraint, showing respect for the needs of others. Yasser Arafat and the PLO had taken a different path, supporting Saddam Hussein—no doubt thinking it would share in the war booty of Kuwait. "Saudi Arabia would not forget what each had done," Bandar assured me.[49] Soon after the war, we would try to capitalize on this perception to initiate a peace effort.

The Road to Madrid

Within a week of the war ending, Baker launched an intensive effort at peacemaking that would lead to the Madrid Peace Conference. Baker made eight trips to the region over the next eight months to produce the taboo-breaking event.

The president and Baker had withstood any effort at linkage between Iraq and the Arab-Israeli conflict, but they felt obliged to act on peace, in part because they had quietly committed to Gorbachev that we would do so after removing Saddam from Kuwait. To be sure, they also believed there was an opportunity. In the aftermath of the war, the United States had unprecedented credibility with the Arabs: the president had declared that Iraqi aggression would not stand, and he mobilized the world behind a plan to make sure it did not. For the Israelis, we had taken care of one of their greatest military threats.

Earlier in November, I had met Eitan Ben-Tsur, the director-general of the Israeli Foreign Ministry. We talked about the likelihood of war with Iraq and what should be done in the aftermath on peace. Ben-Tsur felt that you couldn't just repeat the effort for an Israeli-Palestinian dialogue; you needed an Arab state negotiation with Israel as well. This idea gave rise to the "two-track concept" I would present to Baker: we would pursue both Israeli-Arab and Israeli-Palestinian tracks of negotiations. Having just fought a war with the Arabs against "an Arab brother," they should be prepared to join us now in trying to make peace. We could not ask the Israelis to negotiate with the Palestinians from the territories, who had cheered as Iraqi Scuds hit Israel, without showing that their Arab state neighbors were prepared to talk peace. But we could also tell the Israelis that the Arabs could not make peace with Israel unless there was a peace track for the Palestinians. The Arabs were angry at Arafat for siding with Saddam Hussein. Largely isolated in the Arab world and financially cut off by the Gulf Arabs, Arafat's spoiling capability was reduced. As part of the two-track approach, I suggested mutual confidence-building steps to create a better context for negotiations and a regional, not international, conference to launch the talks.[50]

Baker accepted this approach. I joined him in briefing the president in Houston before our first postwar trip to the region to get his blessing for our presentation of this concept to the Middle East leaders Baker would shortly see. Ironically, while Bush was enthusiastic about this initiative, Brent Scowcroft was not, skeptical that anything would result from it. Baker asked

Larry Eagleburger to talk to him before we saw the president, to ask him not to oppose it.[51] In the Houston meeting, Scowcroft expressed his doubts that it would work but agreed that Baker should make the effort.

From the outset, it was clear that both Arabs and Israelis wanted to appear responsive to Baker—the demonstration of American power had produced this commonality in both sides. Initially, the Saudis, Egyptians, and even the Syrians were open to the idea of two tracks, Israeli negotiations with Palestinians from the territories and not the PLO, and a regional peace conference to launch negotiations. The Israelis, too, were eager to hear about the indications that the Arab states were open to peacemaking with them— and not pushing the PLO—and a regional event immediately prior to the talks. Both sides were open to the idea of mutual confidence-building steps, but it quickly became apparent that each side was focused not on what it might do but what it wanted the other to do.[52] If we focused on producing parallel tangible steps, it was clear that little would happen soon and we might lose the moment to get anything done.

Since our broad aim was to break the taboo on direct talks, Baker focused principally on getting to a conference for launching talks—and quickly this became a struggle over the modalities of the conference rather than the substance of talks.* Between April and July 1991, Baker would be caught between the diametrically opposed views of Assad and Shamir on holding a conference: Assad wanted it under UN auspices, to be continuous, decision making, and based explicitly on the principle of land for peace. Shamir wanted a one-time event, with no UN role or presence and no preconditions. In multiple trips—in March, April, and May—we sought to come up with a compromise between these opposing positions, with the issue of Palestinian representation still to be worked out.

The differences on modalities of the conference were in many ways a surrogate discussion. Both Assad and Shamir were seeking to gain an advantage in advance of the negotiations, each hoping to shape them in a way that would increase his leverage. Assad hoped to isolate Israel in a conference and wanted to enter discussions without having conceded to bilateral talks. Shamir wanted Assad to accept bilateral talks and appear to concede on recognition of Israel. In effect, each was posturing, preferring to delay any discussion on substance and thus avoid hard decisions on the conflict itself.

---

* Sixteen years later, Secretary of State Condoleezza Rice would move similarly from trying to create substantive agreement in advance of holding a conference at Annapolis to simply convening the event.

Baker found the discussion on modalities frustrating, particularly as it seemed so far removed from the conflict itself, and he made it clear to both sides that he would not continue his efforts forever. He also made clear that if the discussions were to break down, he would be sure to let the world know whom he held responsible—in his words, on whose doorstep he would leave "the dead cat."

Interestingly, no one wanted to be blamed for a breakdown of our peace effort—something that also has its echoes over time. In this case, following a presidential letter at the end of May laying out our proposed compromise on the terms of the conference, we received a "no, but" from Shamir and no response from Assad. Baker mobilized Saudi, Egyptian, and European pressure on the Syrians to respond affirmatively and put the onus on the Israelis. After six weeks, Assad relented and sent a letter agreeing to the U.S. proposal.

Armed with Assad's yes, Baker traveled to Jerusalem in late July and Shamir told him Assad said yes because "he thinks I will say no." Baker agreed, and got the Shamir yes as well.

At this point, we had a Syrian and an Israeli yes for the conference but we still needed to produce a joint Jordanian-Palestinian delegation that was acceptable to Shamir. Getting the Palestinians on board, given the divisions in the territory and Arafat's effort to show his relevance, was no simple matter—and would take us literally until the last minute. Between the end of July and the convening of the conference on October 31, we were consumed with negotiating the terms of the invitation letter, the letters of assurance, and the composition of the Jordanian-Palestinian delegation.

While the concept was a two-track negotiation, in reality, we were creating three different sets of talks: bilateral negotiations between Israel and its neighboring Arab states, multilateral talks between Israel and Arab states in the wider ambit of the Middle East, and bilateral talks between Israel and the Palestinians from the territories. I had put special emphasis on the multilateral talks because this was a way to show the Israelis that peace could bring wider acceptance in the region.

What were the key moments on the way to Madrid? Several are worth noting because they highlight the challenges that had to be overcome with the Saudis, Syrians, Israelis, and Palestinians to produce the conference and the negotiations that followed it. Baker's first postwar trip to the region was to Saudi Arabia; this was the moment of our maximum leverage with the Saudis, and we needed to go to Israel showing that the region was now different and the Saudis and other Arab states were prepared to make peace. Baker and I met King Fahd and Bandar alone. Baker explained the two-track concept and the tangible steps we would like each side to take. He then told the king: you put your trust in the president in wartime, now it is time to do so on peace. The king did not respond on the specific steps but poignantly, and for the first time that we had ever heard, he said that if a homeland could be found for the Palestinians, he was prepared to accept full diplomatic and economic relations with Israel.

This was a big break. But on our third trip to the region, in a dinner with Foreign Minister Saud al Faisal, the prince told Baker that while the Saudis would support our efforts, it was not appropriate for them to attend the peace conference. Baker was shocked and appalled, knowing it would pull the rug out from under us with the Israelis, and angrily told the Princeton-educated Faisal that it might be okay for them "to hold our coat in war" but it was unacceptable that they would not be there for us as we tried to make peace. Later, with the king, Baker was less blunt but still said, "We were there for you. We need you to be there for us. How can we be partners in war but not in peace? If you can't do this, what do I say to your friend George Bush?"[53]

Bandar was not in the kingdom for this visit and had been unavailable to us in Washington before the trip, claiming back troubles. He did not return either my calls or Baker's, which I took as a worrisome sign. Either he was incapacitated physically or—more problematically—he was incapacitated politically. On our return to Washington, and without telling Baker, I saw Bandar privately at his imposing mansion overlooking the Potomac River in McLean, Virginia. I told him that the visit had been a disaster. For the sake of our relations, we had to alter the image that the Saudis were retreating and would not play any role on peace after we had effectively rescued them in war. Bandar understood but needed a creative way to get around the Saudi decision not to attend the conference. I offered him an idea: the Gulf Cooperation Council (GCC)—made up of Saudi Arabia, Bahrain, the Emirates, Kuwait, Qatar, and Oman—could send an observer or observers to the conference. Under this guise, the Saudis would be present and everyone would know it, since they dominated the GCC. Following the conference, there was no reason why the Saudis could not then attend the multilateral talks because those dealt with regional issues. Bandar loved the idea and said he could get it done if the request came directly from the president.

President Bush made the request, asking Bandar to have the Saudis announce that the GCC would attend the conference and join the multilateral discussions afterward. Bandar delivered three days later, enabling Baker to tell Shamir that the Saudis would be at the conference and at the multilaterals if Israel was prepared to do its part to launch the process.

We had similar ups and downs with the Syrians, which, at one point, actually put the achievement of getting the Saudis into the multilateral working groups at risk. Baker's talks with Assad were all marathons; they were in themselves like a war of attrition. His readiness to accept Baker's proposal on the conference reflected Assad's understanding that in a unipolar world, he needed a relationship with the United States. Still, we were not out of the woods. At this point, our tough meetings with Assad and his team of advisers—including Farouk al-Shara, his foreign minister, and State Minister Nasser Qaddour—focused on both the letter of assurances and the invitation to Madrid. After the first day of grudging discussions, Assad seemed to make the multilateral talks the key sticking point. He argued that they constituted normalization with Israel while Israel was still holding Syrian land. He would not go to them; worse, he was not prepared to accept the letter of invitation unless it made clear that the multilaterals would not start their work until the bilateral peace agreements were achieved.

We broke late that night and repaired to Baker's suite to strategize. He said he would give on this one if he had to. I argued emotionally against this, saying we had built a concept on there being a wider orbit of peace and this had been one of our key sources of pressure on Shamir. Domestically within Israel, he could not look like he was forgoing a chance to integrate Israel into the region when it might finally be possible—and that is precisely what the multilaterals offered. Fifteen Arab countries were prepared to participate in them. But for Baker, the key was to get the bilateral negotiations launched, and if it took abandoning the multilateral negotiations to hook Assad, so be it. In his view, Shamir could not say no to bilateral talks.

To this day, I don't know why Assad did not hold out on this, since Baker's suite was surely bugged.[54] The next morning, Assad seemed to be quibbling about everything—but not the language on the multilaterals, which we had modified to say they would be organized two weeks after the conference but not actually convened then. With each new issue Assad raised, Baker was becoming more impatient. At one point he had had enough, angrily shouting, "It is a good letter. If you don't like what we're doing, and you think you can get the Golan back without sitting with Israel, then go ahead and get it back."

Even taking a brief break did not improve Baker's mood. When Assad raised another quibble, Baker looked like he was about to explode. Nasser Qaddour—an Alawite like Assad—said to him in Arabic, "Take care, he is

really angry." Assad, in language he would repeat five years later in a negotiation with Warren Christopher and me, said, "Why? We are negotiating!"
But when he looked at Baker, he could see that the secretary had reached his
limit, and suddenly Assad said that we were in agreement: "I guess these are
all the issues." I scribbled Baker a note, "Take the money and run," and we
were done with the Syrians.

But we were not done with the Israelis and Palestinians. The issue of
Palestinian representation had been with us from the time of the five-point
exercise. It was a different world after the Gulf War, but we still needed
Shamir to accept Palestinians from the territory that he could sit with. Until
the end, we struggled on formulating the list of Palestinians who would be
part of the joint delegation. Baker rejected Shamir's demand that any par-
ticipating Palestinians renounce the PLO—an impossibility—but later he
would verbally promise that the Palestinians would be those Shamir could
accept. Interestingly, when Baker made this commitment to Shamir—at the
moment Shamir was accepting the compromises on the conference in
August—Yossi Ben Aharon, Shamir's chief of staff, said that would not be
sufficient. Shamir cut him off, saying, "Jim Baker's word [is] good enough."

Their relationship after the Gulf War was clearly different. Still, we now
had to produce what Baker had promised. There could be no Palestinian
from Jerusalem on the delegation. To solve this I came up with the idea that
a Jordanian on the joint delegation could come from Jerusalem. Shamir accepted this; he would not question the credentials of any Jordanian and understood that including someone on the delegation who came originally
from Jerusalem would help symbolically. This compromise was not, however, a simple sell to the Palestinians from the territories. It fell to me to tell
Faisal Husseini that he would not be able to attend the conference. This pill
was bitter for him. As we sat alone and I explained that we simply would
have no process if he were on the joint delegation, he began to weep. A
member of the famous Husseini family of Jerusalem, Husseini had a stature
like no other Palestinian in the territories.* He often led delegations to see
Baker, but now he was being excluded from substantive talks. The Egyptians
and Jordanians pressed both Arafat and Palestinians from the territories to
come up with a list, and until Baker's last trip, we were still without one.

Finally, as we returned to Jerusalem from Damascus on October 16, we

---

* Faisal's uncle was Haj Amin al Husseini, the former grand mufti of Jerusalem, notori-
ous for siding with the Nazis and spending the war years in Germany before later going
to Cairo.

got news that Husseini and Hanan Ashrawi, a Christian from Ramallah and a leading Palestinian intellectual, were meeting with the Jordanians. A list of twenty names of those who would make up the Palestinian side of the joint delegation soon appeared in the Jordanian press. That night Baker and I saw Husseini and Ashrawi alone at our consul general's house in West Jerusalem. Rather than wrapping everything up, they raised new issues on Jerusalem—this after Baker had agreed to meet the Palestinians who would be on the delegation at our consulate in East Jerusalem and promised that in our letter of assurance to the Palestinians we would not recognize the Israeli annexation of East Jerusalem. Both moves caused the Israelis great angst. So when they opened up an issue Baker thought we had closed, he exploded: "With you people, the souk never closes, but it is closed with me. Have a nice life." And he walked out. They sat in stunned silence and then asked me what to do. I was not prepared even to talk to Baker unless they dropped what they had raised and finished the list. They agreed. When I found Baker pacing in the back of the residence, he was in no hurry to return.

In the end, the Palestinians provided us only a partial list. Until the last moment, they debated who should be on the delegation, trying to balance different factions and representatives from the West Bank and Gaza. Baker actually announced the invitations to Madrid when we still had only a partial list. After the announcement, the Palestinians reached out with the rest, with names we knew, and asked if we could announce that they were the first to respond to the invitation. When I told Baker this as we were flying out of Israel, he only laughed and said, *"I guess we closed the souk."**

The Loan Guarantees: Conflict, Rejection, and Eventual Approval

No administration would do more to help ensure that Jews—whether in the Soviet Union, Ethiopia, or Syria—who wanted to get to Israel could do so. But with the gates opening in the Soviet Union, with 12,900 allowed to enter Israel in 1989 and 185,200 in 1990, there was inevitably going to be a clash.[55] President Bush was opposed in principle to Israeli settlement activity in the

---

* In *The Missing Peace*, I describe what happened in the three days of the Madrid Conference. None of the parties gave good speeches, with the Egyptian foreign minister, Amr Moussa, acting so hostile to Israel we threatened not to let him speak again on the second day. But the conference did launch direct bilateral talks on its last day.

West Bank and Gaza. Prime Minister Shamir, on the other hand, headed a government that saw it as Israel's right to build settlements for Israelis everywhere, not only drawing no distinction between lands inside the June 4, 1967, lines and those outside it, but also actually providing financial incentives in the form of subsidies, tax benefits, and mortgage breaks for building in the territories.

Israel first came to the Bush administration in 1990 requesting $400 million in loan guarantees, which meant the United States would ensure there was no default on the loans and permitted the Israelis to get the loans at far more favorable rates. Given Baker's publicly stated concerns that the loan guarantees could not be used for a purpose that was counter to U.S. policy on settlement activity, David Levy, Israel's foreign minister, offered to provide us assurances in order to make it possible for us to respond to the Israeli request.

Working with Eitan Ben-Tsur, I negotiated a draft letter for Levy to send Baker pledging to keep the United States informed of new settlement activity and promising to undertake "best efforts" to itemize what was being spent on settlement activity in the West Bank and Gaza. Baker and Levy approved our draft.

Baker and I went to explain to the president the meaning of the letter and why we felt it permitted us to provide $400 million in loan guarantees. I made the case that with the assurances we received in the Levy letter, we would know what the Israelis were spending on settlements prior to our providing the $400 million. If spending on settlements went up after the loan guarantees, we would know it—and the Israelis would be jeopardizing any future guarantees. I told Bush that the Shamir government knew the $400 million was a small down payment on what Israel would need given the number of Soviet Jews poised to immigrate, adding that "the prime minister would not be stupid enough to put what he will need down the road at risk."

This persuaded Bush, and I turned out to be dead right on the $400 million being a small down payment. The Israelis came back to us in 1991 for an additional $10 billion in loan guarantees. But I was dead wrong about Shamir not putting the larger request at risk by increasing the settlement activity. Israel did precisely that—and my credibility with the president on this issue was now shot. Not only did the Israelis increase their settlement activity—by some estimates threefold—but they also never provided us the information that was promised.

In retrospect, I was probably naïve. Likud governments went to great lengths to disguise their spending on settlements in the territories, particularly because more was being expended on them than on development towns within Israel, cities on Israel's periphery built, at least initially, to house Jewish refugees from the Middle East, which were often underserved. Levy may have made his promises in good faith, but he could not deliver on them. At no point did Shamir do anything to restrain settlement building, even when Ariel Sharon, then the housing minister, announced new settlements every time Baker arrived on his visits. Needless to say, this aroused Baker's ire, and Shamir told the secretary he was not happy about these announcements.

But why would Shamir run the risk of jeopardizing the $10 billion request by so clearly violating the promises in the Levy letter? Perhaps the politics of the coalition explain why Shamir did so little to rein in Sharon. I suspect, however, that there is another explanation for why I was wrong. Shamir felt that after he withheld retaliation to the Iraq Scud attacks, we owed him. His finance minister, Yitzhak Moda'i, called on January 22, less than a week into the war, for the United States to provide Israel an aid package of $13 billion—$10 billion in loan guarantees and $3 billion for damages caused by a war we were still in the early stages of fighting. Shamir may have realized the timing was premature, but the next month, the administration agreed to release the $400 million in loan guarantees and to provide Israel $650 million in compensation for damages from the Scuds. In return, Israel promised to defer their request for the additional $10 billion in loan guarantees until Congress returned from its summer recess in September.

Of course, in the interim the Gulf War ended and our efforts on peace commenced. For Shamir, however, his need for the loan guarantees remained urgent, particularly with Soviet Jewry arriving now in huge numbers. He had agreed to defer and he felt now he was owed. Bush, however, felt that we had met our obligations and that, once again, Shamir was guilty of betraying a promise in the form of the Levy letter. Moreover, by August we had Syrian and Israeli agreement on the modalities of the conference, and we were now working on the letter of assurances and the Palestinian delegation; the last thing we needed was to allocate $10 billion in loan guarantees to Israel, an allocation that Baker worried would only highlight the settlement issue. The Arabs had neither raised the subject of settlements nor demanded a freeze on them as a condition for attending the conference. Baker did not want this to suddenly become a complicating question.

He asked Janet Mullins, the assistant secretary for legislative affairs, to check on the Hill to see whether we could quietly reach an agreement to defer the issue until after we had convened the peace conference. She reported that AIPAC had been very active and essentially lined up broad support to press ahead in September on the loan guarantees. To delay, she told Baker he would need to convince AIPAC to hold off. Baker invited Tom Dine, the executive director of AIPAC, to his office to make the case for delaying and asked me to go to the Hill and talk to a few key senators—Democrats and Republicans—to get their opinion. It became clear that unless the Israelis agreed to defer the issue, we would have a fight on our hands. Baker wasn't thinking only of the Arabs: he did not want a fight that might complicate the political realities in Israel. So after leaving for vacation, he called Shamir from Wyoming on September 1. Baker made the case for delaying another 120 days to get us beyond the convening of the peace conference. In their initial conversation, Shamir appeared sympathetic to Baker's argument. He asked to call Baker back in a day or two. When he did, Shamir had changed his mind. Given Israel's budget situation, he wanted to go ahead on the loan guarantees now. That said, he would discuss the issue with Baker when he arrived in Israel in two weeks' time.[56]

Baker still hoped we might be able to work out an understanding, but events conspired against us. AIPAC pressed ahead and planned a massive lobby day on the Hill on September 13, to push the legislation to approve the loan guarantees. President Bush's position soon hardened, and he expressed his frustration both privately and publicly. Unbeknownst to Baker and me, Senator Robert Kasten of Wisconsin—the ranking Republican on the Finance Committee and a strong supporter of Israel—saw the president at the White House. He was one of the senators Baker had asked me to meet, and Kasten, after discussing the loan guarantees with Bush, would tell the president that I had conveyed a position that was different from his—that Baker was ready to do a deal on the issue.

At the time, I was with Baker in the Soviet Union. This was a sensitive visit, the first after the coup attempt against Gorbachev in August 1991. Only Boris Yeltsin's intervention had saved Gorbachev, but as we met with Gorbachev and Yeltsin—and leaders of the Soviet republics who were now all more assertive—it was clear we were in an entirely new situation: the Soviet Union might not survive. I was literally writing these words at one a.m. for Baker's night note to the president, when Baker came into my room. To describe such a visit as unusual would be an understatement. Few things would wake Baker during the night once he had gone to sleep and, furthermore, if he had wanted to see me, he would have asked me to come to his room.

He greeted me with "We have a problem, pal," showing me a note he had just gotten from the president. Essentially, it said: Jimmy, I know you are working hard with all the tumult with Gorbachev and don't mean to bother you. But I saw Bob Kasten and he said that Dennis told him we are ready to do a deal on the loan guarantees. That is not my position and I hope on your trip that is not what you plan to do with Shamir. The rest referred to talking about all this when Baker got back and wishing him the best.

After I read the note, Baker asked me what I'd told Kasten, and I explained that I had echoed what he had told Tom Dine—that we sought a delay of 120 days, that the last thing we needed was to make settlements an issue with the Arabs before the peace conference or to roil the politics in Israel, and that we would address the loan guarantees early next year and hopefully reach an understanding. Baker nodded and said, "I know my friend [the president], and he is steamed. I won't even try for an understanding now with Shamir and I will have to be tough on the issue."

This is part of the backdrop to the Bush press conference on September 13, where he described himself as being one lonely guy in trying to delay the loan guarantees. But it is not the full story. As we flew from the Soviet Union to Israel, Tom Friedman, who was part of the press corps that traveled with Baker, wrote a piece in *The New York Times* in which he said that Baker had been able to convince the Arabs on settlements, but not Bush. Baker, ever sensitive to any appearance of a gap between himself and the president, became even tougher on the loan guarantees as a result—and I was no longer in a position to affect it.

Several points are worth noting about the loan guarantee issue. First, notwithstanding AIPAC's position, the administration succeeded in deferring a decision until 1992, after the peace conference. Once again, when it really mattered to the president and he made the issue one of our national security priorities, his administration triumphed and the "Jewish lobby" did not.

Second, Baker held firm, not just on the deferral but also on not agreeing to any deal prior to the Israeli election in May 1992—even though Israeli ambassador Zalman Shoval and I informally worked out a deal where, in return for providing $2 billion, or one year's worth of loan guarantees, the Israeli government would commit to no new settlement starts. But Baker was not buying, partly because he did not trust Shamir on anything related to settlements and partly because he believed this might help Likud in the election. Rabin's victory in the election can, in part, be attributed to the administration's reluctance to provide the loan guarantees.

Third, this issue is noteworthy because it echoes beyond the Bush administration, particularly with the approach toward settlements taken early on by the Obama Administration. While Tom Friedman's suggestion that Baker had convinced the Arabs on settlements but not Bush may have been an exaggeration, it did reflect a reality that Bush felt deeply about this issue. We would see a virtual replay with Obama when his call for a settlement freeze with the Netanyahu government would later be described by Palestinian president Mahmoud Abbas as putting him "up the tree and removing the ladder." Indeed, Abbas rather openly said he had never made it a condition for negotiations—it was the Americans who had done so. Could he, the Palestinian president, care less about settlements than the Americans?[57]

Bush concluded the $10 billion loan guarantees with Israel after Rabin became prime minister. But he would not soften our conditions. With Rabin, we reached agreement in August 1992, with a dollar-for-dollar reduction from the loan guarantees for the estimated cost of what the Israelis were expending on settlements. That said, Bush trusted Rabin and felt that we could rely on his word. And Rabin, in turn, trusted Bush and Baker. Given their response in the Gulf War, he saw them as ready to use American power—for him always the sine qua non in the relationship with the United States.

Encapsulating the Bush Approach to Israel

George H. W. Bush viewed Israel as he did any other state. He believed in outreach to the Arabs and thought we should have more balance between our relations with the Arabs and Israel. He also felt it was wrong to pander. We would stand by our commitments to Israel but, by the same token, he expected them to stand by theirs. Bush was true to his word, and our military and security cooperation with Israel would proceed, particularly on joint military developments like the Arrow ABM defense system, but generally with a preference for less visibility—unless, of course, it was to provide Patriot missile batteries with U.S. presence during the Gulf War. Bush's delivery on issues important to Israel—countries recognizing Israel, immigration to the Jewish state, repealing the Zionism is Racism resolution at the UN, and breaking the taboo on direct negotiations between Israel and its Arab neighbors—was truly remarkable.

And none of what the Bush administration actually did with Israel cost it with the Arab states. Was it because Bush was prepared to be tough with

Israel on the issues on which it disagreed? Was it because he made a serious effort on peace? Was it because with the collapse of the Soviet Union, the United States was the only superpower—and retaining good relations with it mattered? Or was it because the Bush administration also delivered on what mattered to Arab leaders, reflecting their genuine preoccupation with security and their own survival? To some degree, perhaps, all of these factors were at play. But with leaders who ultimately lack basic legitimacy and feel vulnerable as a result, their preoccupation with their own survival almost always trumps other concerns. The Bush administration was perceived to be reliable on what mattered most to them.

In summing up the mind-set of the Bush administration and its relationship with Israel, one might say that the substance was good, the tone was difficult, and the readiness to disagree in public was clear. The administration was comfortable with this mix—it allowed us to fulfill our obligations toward Israel and position ourself well in the region. Reflecting the pattern of administrations responding to the perceived failures of their predecessors, the Clinton administration set out to change the tone of the relationship with Israel, and the results would be dramatic.

9

THE CLINTON ADMINISTRATION AND ISRAEL: STRATEGIC PARTNERS FOR PEACE

Bill Clinton inherited a new international context. America's power was unrivaled and even peace in the Middle East now seemed possible. As the president-elect surveyed the global landscape in late 1992, he understood that the United States was the world's only superpower. Russia was in a state of economic free fall and navigating a difficult process of internal transformation. The Arab states knew that diplomacy was their only option vis-à-vis Israel, and they needed to work through the United States to recover their lands. Moreover, Arab leaders recognized now that they ran little risk in pursuing diplomacy after the defeat of Saddam Hussein—the most radical among them—in the Gulf War. Finally, while the Iranians might pose a threat to the Arab states, they had been terribly weakened by their eight-and-a-half-year war with Iraq.

But it was not just the new reality of global and regional power that made pursuing peace an option whose time had come. Israel was now led by a government that made the pursuit of peace a priority. Unlike Yitzhak Shamir, who feared the risks associated with peacemaking, Prime Minister Yitzhak Rabin feared the consequences of not making peace when the strategic realities in the region had shifted. He believed it was imperative to expand the circle of peace with his immediate neighbors, recognizing that the weakness of Iraq and Iran would not last forever and that it was essential to isolate them in the region while they were too weak to prevent it. Rabin saw the strategic value of peacemaking with Syria—the only country that posed a conventional military threat to Israel—but had promised as a candidate that he would conclude an interim agreement with the Palestinians within nine months of assuming office. For him, the intifada meant that the Palestinians must not be ignored, even if he saw them posing more of a political and psychological problem than a military one. And while Rabin seemed no more willing than Shamir to engage the PLO, he was not alone. Arab leaders were still penalizing Arafat for his backing of Saddam Hussein and remained unwilling to push for his inclusion in the talks.

If all this were not enough, the prohibition on direct talks between Israel and its neighbors had been ended. The Madrid Conference had established bilateral and multilateral negotiations in the Middle East, and Clinton saw the need, the opportunity, and the mechanism to act on Arab-Israeli peace.

Bush had helped to create these circumstances. Clinton understood that, but he also understood that Bush had paid a political price by creating the appearance of constantly pressuring Israel. Unlike Bush, Clinton tended to be more attentive to the political realities in which he and his counterparts operated: he would not repeat the mistakes of Bush on the settlement issue, for instance. Truth be told, he was instinctively more sensitive not just to his own political needs but also to those of his Israeli counterparts. It was easier when he had Labor leaders like Rabin, Peres, and Barak, all of whom were prepared to take real risks for peace. It would be more difficult with Benjamin Netanyahu as Israel's prime minister, given his solidly right-wing base and his grudging approach to peace. President Clinton hesitated to confront Netanyahu, however—even when his secretary of state and national security adviser counseled that such a confrontation was necessary to move the process and preserve our credibility.

Given the changed landscape, peace would be very much the focal point of relations with Israel throughout the Clinton presidency. Reagan had seen strategic partnership with Israel measured largely in competition with the Soviets and their proxies in the Middle East, and Bush had been preoccupied with the transformation of East-West relations until he confronted Iraq in the Gulf War—and tended to downplay any role for Israel. Clinton would measure the partnership in terms of our making it easier for Israel to take risks for peace. This would be his point of departure because he saw an opportunity to make peace and also because he believed it would transform the region.

To be sure, every previous president had felt that the conflict between

Arabs and Israelis complicated our interests and relations in the Middle East. Ending this conflict would remove an irritant with the Arabs and reduce the costs to us of standing by Israel. Carter tended to see this conflict as the be-all and end-all in the region until, of course, Iran proved otherwise. For Reagan, the terrible siege of Lebanon forced an interest in Middle East peace, but the lack of any movement returned his focus to larger strategic threats; Israel was more partner and asset than liability in his eyes. Clinton entered the White House focused on domestic issues—after all, the theme of his campaign against Bush was "It's the economy, stupid." However, he understood there was an opening and he wanted to act on it. Martin Indyk, who would become a senior adviser on the Middle East, has described his briefing Clinton during the campaign about the rare moment that existed in the region, telling him that if he were elected he would be able "to put his immense influence as the leader of the dominant power in the Middle East behind Rabin as he moved forward," and he "could achieve four Arab-Israeli peace agreements in his first term as president." Clinton "looked [him] in the eye and said, 'I want to do that.'"[1]

Unlike Jimmy Carter, Clinton was motivated not by his fears of renewed conflict but by his hopes of what could be achieved. Still, in the first years of his administration, he was active only as the events presented themselves. Later, he became driven by a deep sense of responsibility. The assassination of Prime Minister Yitzhak Rabin on November 4, 1995, would have a searing effect on Clinton. In his first meeting as president with Rabin in March 1993, when the Israeli prime minister told him he had a mandate to take risks for peace, Clinton replied, "If you're going to do that, my role is to help you minimize those risks."[2] Many may say that Clinton was driven by his desire for a legacy, but I saw something different: I saw a man on a mission. It was far less about his legacy and far more about his fulfilling his side of the bargain: Rabin had done his part and paid for it with his life. Clinton owed a debt and had a responsibility as a result. He would act to fulfill the Rabin legacy—and his actions, some well considered, some not—from 1995 onward, whether at Wye River or at Geneva with Assad or at Camp David with Barak and Arafat or in the waning days of his administration with the Clinton parameters, reflected someone who was prepared to put himself on the line in order to try to settle the conflict.

How, considering my close relationship to Bush and Baker, did I come to be with Clinton nearly every step of the way as he raised the stakes of his own involvement in Middle East peacemaking and made this the centerpiece of the U.S.-Israel relationship? Needless to say, I did not expect to be asked to stay in the new administration, especially after I went with Baker to the White House in August 1992 when he was asked to rescue Bush's re-election campaign.[3] Immediately after the election, Baker allowed me to return to the State Department.[4] I would work with Larry Eagleburger, who had succeeded Baker as the secretary, and my role was to help him wrap up the START agreement and oversee the transition to the Clinton team. I did briefings for Brian Atwood and Peter Tarnoff, who had been designated to run the transition at the State Department on behalf of the incoming administration. To my great surprise, Tarnoff approached me about ten days before the end of the Bush administration and asked if I would be willing to stay for three to six months as a senior adviser to incoming secretary of state Warren Christopher. I would have direct access to the secretary, could write memos to him on any subject, take part in briefings of him on the Middle East, and accompany him if he traveled to the area.

Having played such a central role in putting together Madrid and the bilateral and multilateral negotiations that it launched, I did not want to see that process go off the rails, and I agreed to stay for a transitional period. I was treated very well by Christopher. I saw him regularly and joined him on his trip to the Middle East in February. I was also part of a small group briefing President Clinton before his first meeting with Rabin. Still, my role was basically that of a kibitzer. After having shaped policies and been allowed to implement them, the position was unsatisfying. As a result, I approached Christopher after Rabin's visit and said I felt it was time for me to move on. He asked if I would stay until June, and I agreed. His chief of staff, Tom Donilon, tried hard to dissuade me from leaving, offering different jobs and finally asking me, "What is the one position you could not say no to?" I told him I could not say no to being the administration's chief negotiator on the Arab-Israeli conflict. But I also told him that given the bureaucratic crockery in the State Department he would have to break, it made no sense for Christopher to offer me the position.[5]

Much to my surprise, shortly before I was to leave in June, the secretary told me that he had proposed and President Clinton had accepted that I be put in charge of Arab-Israeli diplomacy. I would report directly to him. I'd have the staff I needed, and the Bureau of Near Eastern Affairs would take my direction on the issue and provide whatever support I wanted. Suddenly, I was no longer a kibitzer. But I was also inheriting an environment shaped by a series of other people's moves.

My Inheritance

Christopher traveled to the Middle East in February. Negotiations at the time were suspended on all tracks as a result of an Israeli decision, after a number of terror attacks in Israel, to deport four hundred members of Hamas from the West Bank to Lebanon; Lebanon, however, would not take them, and the deportees remained stuck in a no-man's-land just above the Israeli border, where they became a media sensation. All the Arab delegations in the bilateral talks suspended their participation in the negotiations pending a resolution of their status. Christopher would work out an agreement with Rabin that resolved their fate.*

Notwithstanding the deportee issue, Rabin's priority during Christopher's trip was Syria, not the Palestinians. Unlike the Palestinians, Syria posed a strategic threat to Israel. With more than four thousand tanks, Syria represented the only serious conventional military threat to Israel and was building up its missile force with chemical weapons. End the conflict with Syria—the self-proclaimed beating heart of Arab nationalism—and the Jordanians and Lebanese would feel able to follow suit, and the Saudis and other Gulf states would likely normalize relations with Israel as well. This would leave the Palestinians with no leverage and a need to make peace—or so Rabin's logic went. In fact, he was pushing on an open door with Clinton, who quickly embraced the Syria-first strategy.

I saw it in the discussions we had with Clinton in preparation for his meetings with Rabin a few weeks after Christopher's trip. Rabin had not only laid out the logic of Syria first but also had told Christopher when they were meeting alone that he would ask the president two questions: Would Israel have to withdraw fully from the Golan Heights? Would the United States be prepared to replace Israeli forces there?

When Christopher returned from his trip, there was a White House meeting of principals at which President Clinton presided and the secretary reported on his Middle East visit. Martin Indyk has described the meeting and Christopher's unusually forceful presentation, in which he went over the Rabin questions and the secretary's belief that there was a tremendous opportunity to make progress on Middle East peace. Clinton asked Colin Powell, who was still the chairman of the Joint Chiefs of Staff, what it would take to secure Israel if it withdrew from the Golan Heights. Powell replied

---

* Rabin agreed to a phased return of the deportees over eighteen months, and the talks resumed.

that given the military value of the Heights—a value no military officer would want to surrender—it would take a U.S. brigade of roughly four thousand personnel to show we meant business and had a credible fighting force.[6]

Powell was speaking about a military force—not monitors like those we had inserted into the Sinai as part of the Egypt-Israel peace treaty.[7] Clinton reacted by saying, "It would be worth it," and he added, "We shouldn't minimize the advantage of concentrating on Syria first. If we have a chance to do that we ought to take it while pushing on the other tracks, too."[8]

In his subsequent private discussion with Rabin, when Clinton asked him if he thought it was possible to achieve a peace agreement with Syria "without full Israeli withdrawal from the Golan Heights," Rabin simply said no. When the president told him that he was prepared to guarantee a peace agreement by inserting an American brigade, Rabin reflected his instinctive reluctance to have others guarantee Israeli security: "I know it can't be done without U.S. forces, but I hate the idea." However, when the president asked if the security arrangements were satisfactory and backed by U.S. forces and "you have a genuine Syrian offer of peace, . . . would Israel then be prepared to withdraw fully from the Golan," Rabin answered, "I don't exclude the possibility."[9]

That was as much as Clinton could expect at this point.[10] While the president may have been optimistic—no doubt in part because of Rabin's readiness to take risks for peace—he was also aware of the unpredictability of the region. Rabin was forced to return early from this trip because of Palestinian stabbings of Israelis in Jerusalem, reminding everyone that even though the focus was on Syria, the Palestinians could not be wished away. Ironically, Rabin may have come with a Syria-first strategy in mind, but he arrived in Washington with a proposal on the Palestinians. He saw Secretary Christopher before meeting with the president, and privately to the secretary he proposed that Faisal Husseini come to Washington as the head of the Palestinian delegation. The idea, Rabin told Christopher, must not come from him, but he would accept it as an American proposal.

This was a dramatic proposal. I had been the one to tell Husseini in 1991 that he could not come to Madrid because he was a Jerusalemite. Rabin did not want it to appear that he was suddenly putting Jerusalem on the table. But he increasingly understood that the Palestinians talking to his negotiators in Washington were not empowered.

Rabin was trying both to bolster the Palestinians from the territories by having Husseini lead their delegation and to test whether it was possible to get around Arafat. As would often be the case in the Clinton administration, we took Rabin's suggestion and made it our own, proposing that Husseini come and lead the Palestinian delegation. Arafat, understanding that he was being sidelined, insisted that Husseini come to Tunis and he kept him there, away from Washington—making all too clear that Husseini did not have an independent standing and could not make decisions unless the PLO chairman allowed him to do so. Rabin concluded that there was no way to avoid dealing with the PLO if he wanted to achieve anything on the Palestinian track.

The administration was not there yet for several reasons. First, there was no impulse to get out in front of the Israelis. Rabin was ready to take risks for peace and there was no sense that we needed to push him—both the president and the secretary's instinct militated against such pressure.[11] Second, the dialogue with the PLO had been suspended in June 1990 because of an aborted act of terror in Tel Aviv and Arafat's refusal to expel its perpetrator, Abul Abbas, from the PLO Executive Committee. Clinton had no interest in renewing contact with the PLO. Third, there was no pressure to open a direct dialogue from any Arab leaders. And, last, Clinton's interest was still far more on the Syrian track than the Palestinian one.

After Rabin's visit, however, little developed on either track. The Syrians remained insistent that they would not discuss a framework agreement with the Israelis until the Israelis agreed in principle to full withdrawal from the Golan Heights. And, as noted, the Faisal Husseini idea had produced only a trip to Tunis for him and nothing more.

It was in this context that I became the administration's chief envoy on Arab-Israeli issues in the middle of June and would take my first trip to the Middle East in July. The diplomacy was stuck, and my first challenge was to change the dynamic and see if I could generate movement on at least one of the tracks. Though I knew that the president had a Syria-first preference, I took the view that we needed to get something moving. As much as the president had shown interest in the area during the preparation for Rabin's visit, he was preoccupied domestically with the economy and getting a budget deal done with Congress. Internationally, he was focused on his first summit with Boris Yeltsin and the G-7 meeting afterward. The former related to one of his priorities in foreign policy—helping the transformation in Russia—and the latter was tied to our economic well-being. In addition, the G-7 meeting was bound to highlight Bosnia and the failings of our policy at this time. Whatever his concern about producing a breakthrough in the Middle East during his presidency, he was not riveted on the peace issues at this juncture. No doubt, Christopher had sold him on making me the chief envoy as a way of showing there would be consistent attention on the issue by someone who had produced success for Bush, and that I could set the stage for those moments when Christopher's intervention could make a difference.

Warren Christopher saw the Middle East as his preserve and wanted someone who could make things happen and bring him in as necessary. I worked closely with Martin Indyk, the lead Middle East specialist at the NSC, not only because of our friendship and his talents but also because he could ensure there would be no problems at the White House for anything I might seek to do. Until Indyk became our ambassador to Israel in 1995, he joined me and the team I put together on my trips to the region. On the first trip, I sought to push ideas on early empowerment for Palestinians and to find out whether any of the back channels we now knew the Israelis had with the PLO were bearing fruit. In addition, I wanted to see if I could create momentum on the Israeli-Syrian track by conveying messages back and forth between Rabin and Assad. While I would report on a letter Rabin had gotten from Arafat, Christopher was far more interested in the exchange of messages I initiated between Rabin and Assad. He was eager for me to return to the region to build on this indirect dialogue.

Before I could do so, fighting erupted between Hezbollah and Israel. From a distance, with me in Washington and Christopher traveling in Asia, the two of us mediated a cease-fire, using Syria as the address for communicating with and influencing Hezbollah to end the fighting.

We succeeded in reaching an understanding in which both sides would stop firing at civilian areas. Implicitly, the cease-fire agreement meant that Rabin understood that Hezbollah would continue to attack the Israeli security zone in southern Lebanon but could not do so from civilian areas without drawing an Israeli response—and when Farouk al-Shara, Assad's foreign minister, confirmed this understanding with me, we had a deal.* Christopher and I went to the region the following week, the first week of August, expecting that we would take my write-up of the understandings and formalize them with Rabin and Assad. But we were in for a surprise.

The "Pocket"

Upon arrival, Rabin asked to see Christopher and me alone, without the rest of the team. He had only Itamar Rabinovich, his ambassador to the United

---

* The deal would hold from 1993 until 1996.

States, with him. He said he had something sensitive he wanted to raise with us: the cease-fire agreement, he said, might indicate that Assad was ready for something larger and more strategic. Sometimes, out of crises come opportunities, and he wondered if that was the case now. With that, Rabin asked us to convey to Assad that he would be prepared to commit to the United States (not Syria) that Israel would withdraw fully from the Golan Heights provided Israel's needs were met and that Syria's acceptance was not contingent on any other agreement—meaning one between the Israelis and Palestinians. He defined Israel's needs:

1. Normalization of relations, with full diplomatic ties and an exchange of ambassadors after the first phase of withdrawal—with withdrawal spread over five years.
2. Trade and tourism as an integral part of the normalized relationship.
3. Satisfactory security arrangements, with the United States manning the early-warning sites in the Golan.
4. Israel's water needs recognized and safeguarded.

Assad should understand, Rabin went on, that the proposal we were conveying must remain completely confidential; if it leaked, Rabin would deny it ever even existed.[12] If Assad could accept this, Rabin wanted to move quickly to an agreement. Christopher understood the significance of what we were being asked to convey. Before leaving, the secretary asked Rabin if he expected anything to happen with the Palestinians, and the prime minister made a cryptic reference to the secret talks—but was dismissive of them.

The next day, we went to Damascus to see Assad. He immediately acknowledged that what Christopher conveyed was "very important." But almost as quickly, he began to negotiate. He did not like the word "normalization"—"normal peaceful relations" was better; he could not mandate trade and tourism, but he would not block them; he accepted that there had to be satisfactory security arrangements, but these had to be mutual; and water was important to both sides, not only one. As for the agreement not being contingent on any other peace settlement, he could not move alone without Lebanon—Syria had special relations with Lebanon, and he said, without the hint of a smile, that he did not anticipate there being a problem with an Israeli-Lebanese agreement if Syria had already made peace with Israel. Finally, he said five years for withdrawal was much too long; he noted that the disengagement agreement in 1974, where Israel withdrew from the outskirts of Damascus to Kuneitra on the Golan Heights, took only twenty-two days. He envisioned a short period for withdrawal. Christopher and I pointed out this was a permanent agreement—not an interim disengagement—and therefore it was not surprising that a different standard would guide withdrawal. But Assad persisted and asked for an explanation from Rabin.

Assad was, in effect, already negotiating through us. While he would accept the need for confidentiality, he treated what we brought as the beginning of a process, not its conclusion. Rabin was looking for a quick response that suggested rapid movement to agreement—after all, he was making a historic move. But Assad did not move in leaps. Neither Christopher nor I knew there was about to be a breakthrough with the Palestinians. Rabin knew and had not told us; no doubt, he decided to make this move with Assad less because of the cease-fire agreement we had just worked out and more to see if his strategic preference of moving on Syria first was possible. A different kind of response from Assad—one designed to say let's get this done quickly—would have probably altered Rabin's approach to accepting the Declaration of Principles with the PLO. But Assad would not be prepared to move quickly until the end of 1999, when his own health was failing and long after Rabin had been assassinated. In fact, throughout the process, Assad's instinct was to move slowly. Negotiations were always a process of attrition with him, and at this point, as we would shortly discover, Rabin was not going to wait for him.

Oslo and the Signing at the White House

Our focus after the trip was to begin the negotiations between the Israelis and Syrians in the new context provided by what we now referred to as the "pocket." We knew the negotiations would not be simple, but we had crossed a threshold because the essence of what Assad wanted—the land—he now knew he could get. The secretary and the president believed we would be able to produce a historic breakthrough between Israel and Syria. In fact, there would be a breakthrough at this point—however, it would be between the Israelis and the PLO. Their history of mutual denial and rejection was about to be replaced by mutual recognition.

Warren Christopher and I had both gone to California on vacation after our Middle East trip, with the expectation that I would begin to host informal Israeli-Syrian talks upon our return. On August 25, however, I got a message from the State Department operations center that Prime Minister

Rabin was urgently trying to reach Christopher, and that the secretary wanted me to join him on the call. Rabin came on the line and said that an understanding had been reached with the PLO in Oslo. He wanted Shimon Peres and Johan Holst, the Norwegian foreign minister, to fly to meet us as soon as possible. He was interested in our reaction to the Peres-Holst briefing of this understanding. Rabin's tone was still skeptical, implying that he was reserving judgment pending our reaction. He emphasized the sensitivity of the possible agreement and wanted the meeting to remain secret. Christopher, who had a home near Santa Barbara, said we could meet at Point Mugu naval station, a base that Peres and Holst could fly to with few people knowing.

Holst and Peres met us on August 27, and both were clearly nervous, apparently fearing we might not be supportive, since this had been done without us. Holst emphasized that Israel had reached a historic understanding but only the United States could mobilize the international support—political and economic—that was now needed. He then turned it over to Peres to brief us on the content of the deal. While he spoke, I was quickly reading the document that Peres's aide, Yoel Singer, had given me.[13]

Peres emphasized the historic nature of the agreement: Israel had a choice to follow either "the logic of power or the logic of wisdom in dealing with the Palestinians." His government had chosen the latter path and agreed on this Declaration of Principles, which he said stood on its own. It did not require mutual recognition of Israel and the PLO, but the two sides were ready to work out the terms of this as well. He then said that massive economic support would be needed to build the peace and, echoing Holst, said only the United States could produce this. Therefore, he suggested that the United States announce it had brokered the agreement and host the signing ceremony.

Christopher thanked Holst and Peres for their briefing. He felt it inappropriate for us to claim to have brokered the agreement but asked for a few minutes alone with me to go over the document and give a more considered response. Christopher's request did not relieve their anxiety. As soon as they left, he turned to me and asked what I thought. I said it is surely historic. I then summarized what was in the Declaration of Principles, adding that it turned an existential conflict into a political one. While telling him we had to support it, I added that we should be mindful that it was more about aims and aspirations than clear-cut agreements. The hard work would begin now, and I suggested that I press Peres on two points. First, there was no way the Declaration of Principles could stand on its own. There had to be mutual recognition—otherwise who was the agreement between and who would bear responsibility for it on the Palestinian side? Second, if we were to host the signing ceremony, Peres must understand we have our own requirements when it comes to the PLO. Our dialogue had been suspended since 1990. Arafat must clearly renounce terror and violence and commit to act against those who engaged in it or we would not be able to deal with the PLO, much less invite its representatives to Washington.

Christopher agreed and then asked whether I thought the White House should host the event. Yes, I said. Whatever difficulties lie ahead, this is transformative. These two national movements competing for the same space are now effectively saying they are going to figure out a way to share it: "This is huge." Christopher required no persuasion and thought President Clinton would also get it "instinctively."

When we rejoined Peres and Holst, Christopher congratulated them on this historic breakthrough, and their relief was palpable. Peres quickly agreed on the need both for mutual recognition and for Arafat to make the commitments on terror and violence—though, in a harbinger of things to come, working out the terms of both were not easy and were not concluded until September 9.*

Christopher had been right about Clinton, who in fact grasped the significance better than I did. I say that in two respects. First, he was very sensitive about keeping Assad on board, wanting him to know of our continuing commitment to a Syrian-Israeli deal and comprehensive peace. It was not just that Syria-first was still his preferred option; he was more concerned that Assad have a stake in not disrupting the Israeli-Palestinian negotiations.[14] Second, unlike me, Clinton felt Rabin and Arafat had to be at the event. Peres told us that given Arafat's responsibility for terror acts in Israel over many years, it was too much for the Israeli public to see Yasser Arafat at an event at the White House. Instead, he suggested that he and Abu Mazen— the putative number two in the PLO—attend and sign the document at the ceremony. I did not question his logic. Nor did Martin Indyk, who had been in touch with Rabin's aide, Eitan Haber, and Itamar Rabinovich, who repeated what Peres had told us. But Clinton had different ideas: when asked by the press if there were any circumstances in which Yasser Arafat might attend, he responded that it was up to the PLO and Israel to decide who would come, and "whoever they decide will be here is fine with us and we

---

* Israel and the PLO would exchange letters of mutual recognition on September 9, and Arafat's commitments on violence would be embodied in his letter to Rabin.

will welcome them."[15] This meant that Arafat, who craved the recognition—still bearing the stigma from the Gulf War—would attend the signing and Rabin would have to be there as well.

Clinton later explained his reasoning: "In fact, I badly wanted Rabin and Arafat to attend and urged them to do so; if they didn't, no one in the region would believe they were fully committed to implementing the principles, and, if they did, a billion people across the globe would see them on television and they would leave the White House even more committed to peace than when they arrived."[16]

The president saw the two leaders, not surprisingly, through a political and psychological lens. He was right to do so. But that was part of his persona and how he operated as president in dealing with other leaders. He also saw this conflict in emotional terms, at least in part because of his deep religious beliefs.

He called on religious symbolism at important moments, perhaps to gain perspective and strength for himself, but also to convey deeper meaning about the events he was addressing. It is telling that when he could not sleep the night before the September 13 event, he recounts: "I got my Bible and read the entire book of Joshua. It inspired me to rewrite some of my remarks, and to wear a blue tie with golden horns, which reminded me of those Joshua had used to blow down the walls of Jericho. Now the horns would herald the coming of peace that would return Jericho to the Palestinians."[17]

Clinton wanted to maximize the effect of the day; he knew it would be hard for Rabin emotionally to shake Arafat's hand, but the symbolism of the handshake was essential. He would raise it in private before the ceremony and he would literally envelop the two leaders, an image that was captured in what became an iconic photograph.

In Arafat, Clinton saw someone who was ready to shake hands with Rabin, even while he did precious little to reach out to Israelis in his speech. By contrast, Rabin gave, in Clinton's words, a magnificent speech in which he reached out to his adversaries rhetorically but found it hard to touch Arafat. He would ask Rabin after the ceremony why he was making what were obviously difficult decisions for him on peace, and this no-nonsense Israeli leader would tell him that the territory Israel occupied since 1967 was no longer a source of security for Israel—just the opposite, it was a source of insecurity.[18]

In many respects, Clinton was awed by Rabin, and that day certainly added to his emotional connection with him. Consider how he described his feelings toward him as a result of September 13, 1993: "I had admired Rabin even before meeting him in 1992, but that day, watching him speak at the ceremony and listening to his argument for peace, I had seen the greatness of his leadership and his spirit. I had never met anyone quite like him, and I was determined to help him achieve his dream of peace."[19]

When Rabin told Clinton that to manage the political fallout from the Oslo agreement he needed to put the Syrian negotiations on hold for four months and he hoped we would manage Assad during this time, the president readily accepted this role. If that meant calling Assad to reaffirm our commitment to Syrian-Israeli peace, inviting the Syrian foreign minister to the White House for a bilateral meeting in the fall of 1993—an unprecedented visit for a country that was on our terrorism list—or going to see Assad in Geneva in January 1994, he would do it. True, Clinton saw the virtue of the Syrian track, but he was willing to manage it in a way that met Rabin's political needs. In his eyes, Rabin was the one taking the hard steps—it was Israel that was being asked to give up tangibles for intangibles. No previous president was attuned to Israel's political dynamics and pressures the way Clinton was.[20]

After Clinton's meeting with Assad in Geneva, there were many other developments and events in the Middle East over the next several months that required a great deal of effort and management. However, except for phone calls we would ask the president to make at select moments, Clinton's involvement was kept to a minimum. Even when Dr. Baruch Goldstein, an Israeli settler, gunned down twenty-nine Palestinians as they prayed in Hebron's Ibrahimi Mosque on February 25, 1994, Christopher and I worked first to prevent a collapse of the process and then orchestrated the resumption of talks.*

We similarly helped Israelis and Palestinians overcome their basic conceptual differences on the responsibilities and role of the Palestinian Authority (PA) and brokered the conclusion of the Gaza-Jericho Agreement, which was signed in Cairo on May 4, 1994, the instrument that established the PA.

Interestingly, at the same time we were helping to mediate the Gaza-Jericho

---

* To end the crisis and restore the negotiations, I flew twice to Tunis with an Israeli team to see Arafat on successive weeks. The talks, two-way and three-way, were highly emotional, but during the second round with Amnon Shahak, the number two in the Israeli military, the talks took on a different cast, with Arafat more willing to deal. Arafat would always find it easier to deal with the Israeli military, considering them the real Israel; he, the self-described only "undefeated general in the Middle East," sought their acceptance.

agreement in the first week of May, we faced a private drama in the Syrian track. Assad, for the first time, insisted that full withdrawal meant to the June 4, 1967, lines, not merely to the international border, and he would not continue discussions on any other issues until Rabin accepted this. Rabin refused, and we were stuck.[21]

Over the next two months, from May until July, I presented countless formulas for overcoming the differences on the definition of full withdrawal. Suddenly, in mid-July, the Israeli ambassador, Itamar Rabinovich, came to lunch with Christopher and accepted a way out of the impasse.

Why did Rabin accept a formula at this point that was available weeks earlier? Here we see the dynamic of different negotiating tracks—sometimes creating a spur to an action and other times requiring reassurance. In this case, the president was soon to host Rabin and the king of Jordan at the White House and announce the Washington Declaration—a declaration that King Hussein would publicly say ended the state of war between the two countries and committed both to finalizing a peace agreement within three months.

The king had made some initial gestures toward the Israelis after the signing of the Israeli-PLO Declaration of Principles on September 13, with an agreed framework for discussions and three-way meetings with us on developing joint economic projects. But little developed on these until after the May 4 agreement that set up the Palestinian Authority in Gaza and Jericho. It was the latter that motivated the king, suddenly, to act. With Arafat in Jericho, close to Jordan, his influence in the West Bank and potentially even in Jordan could affect the kingdom.

Much like with the Oslo breakthrough, we were again surprised. Christopher and I returned to the region two weeks after the May 4 ceremony, and Rabin told the secretary that he wanted me briefed on secret talks he had just had with Hussein in London. Efraim Halevy, his Mossad channel to the king, told me that Hussein had agreed to start drafting a peace treaty and for the first time to have Jordanian officials meet publicly in the Middle East with Israelis. Halevy, knowing I was to host a trilateral Israeli-Jordanian-U.S. meeting in the State Department in the coming week, wanted to see if the Jordanians would follow up on the agreement.

On my return to Washington, I called Fayez Tarawneh, the Jordanian ambassador to the United States, who told me that the king had instructed him to accelerate the drafting of a peace treaty and to move on the projects as well. Something was clearly happening, but the key turning point was provided once again by President Clinton. King Hussein visited Washington a few weeks later, in the middle of June, and the message from Fayez was that he wanted to know what he would get materially from us for accelerating peace with Israel. He was seeking debt forgiveness and F-16s, and I had to tell Fayez and the Jordanian prime minister that only a dramatic move on peace—such as Hussein meeting Rabin in public and/or signing a peace treaty—could produce anything close to what they were seeking.[22]

Clearly by prearrangement, Halevy was also in town during the king's visit. Though the meeting with the president had not yet taken place, Halevy told me that our meetings with the king's delegation, in which I spelled out what we could and could not do, were leaving a sour taste in the king's mouth. I understood that the Jordanians were using the Israelis to try to pressure us to provide them more.* Still, I tried to maximize what we could offer the king and told Fayez that the meeting with President Clinton would be crucial in this regard. Specifically, I said it would help if he could provide us some itemized requests that were within the ballpark of what we could do on debt restructuring (not forgiveness), food aid, provision of excess military equipment from NATO, and so on. His letter was well crafted, and Indyk attached it to the memo prepping the president for his meeting with the king.

In briefing the president before the meeting, Indyk and I explained the psychological and political significance of holding a three-way meeting at the ministerial level in the region and the importance of giving the king enough materially to produce such a meeting. But Clinton's sights were higher: he wanted a Hussein-Rabin summit. We told him that Hussein, at a minimum, would need to know that he would receive debt forgiveness, something very expensive and politically costly for us.

Clinton wowed Hussein in the meeting. Without as much as a note, he went through all the items that Fayez had included in the letter and explained what we could do. It was vintage Clinton: he demonstrated that he was immersed in the details of Jordan's needs, that he was prepared to do much to help the kingdom, and that to overcome the limits he faced in the Congress, he needed an unmistakable symbol of reconciliation such as the king publicly meeting Rabin. Coming from me, it sounded analytical. Coming from the president, who was demonstrating his awareness of Hussein's needs and his emotional commitment to meet them, it sounded empathetic

---

* At one point, I asked Efraim, "Are you really asking us to commit to F-16s at a time when you don't have a peace treaty?" He said no, but we needed to find a way to give the king more. I told him fine, let him do more with you.

and compelling. The king was "thrilled" with the meeting—both Fayez and Efraim used the same word in briefing me about his reaction and both conveyed that the king was thinking about the president's suggestion.

Nothing, of course, is automatic in the Middle East. The king did not immediately move on the idea of meeting Rabin. However, on July 4, he sent a secret message saying he would agree to hold a three-way U.S.-Israeli-Jordanian ministerial meeting in the region. Then, five days later, he pulled a Sadat, announcing to the Jordanian parliament that he would be prepared to meet Rabin if it would help meet Jordan's needs on peace.

Having made a decision to cross a political Rubicon, he now didn't hold back. We proceeded to check discreetly to see if the king would accept a sequence where Christopher would go to the area first to prepare the summit and then hold it in Washington for maximum effect on the Congress. While we faced some coordination problems with the Israelis on the orchestration of the sequence of events, we overcame those and Rabin and Hussein met at the White House on July 25. The president and the two leaders unveiled the Washington Declaration, formally ending the state of belligerency— which Hussein, much to the delight of Rabin and the Israeli delegation, said meant, in practical terms, the end of the state of war.*

The declaration laid out immediate steps, including opening a border crossing at the Wadi Arava within two weeks, and a timetable for completing a peace agreement within ninety days. Notably, it also gave "high priority" to preserving Jordan's historic role in the Muslim holy sites in Jerusalem—a clear signal from both Israel and Jordan to Arafat that Jordan would play a role in the resolution of this most emotive of all the issues in the conflict. Here was Rabin showing he could play one track off against the other. By the same token, as noted above, his readiness to have us convey to Assad that full withdrawal meant June 4, 1967, at this point was clearly designed to preserve the Syrian president's stake in the process and give him no reason to threaten Hussein as he now moved on peace with Israel. President Clinton, always mindful of keeping Assad on board, called the Syrian leader before announcing the summit he would host with Rabin and Hussein.

The actual signing of the Israeli-Jordanian peace treaty took place in the Wadi Arava. The president made the historic event part of a regional tour, speaking to the Jordanian parliament and the Israeli Knesset after the signing.[23] He also stopped in Damascus as well as Kuwait and Saudi Arabia.

---

* A less legalistic and a politically more meaningful formulation for the Israeli public than "ending the state of belligerency."

For the president, the focus of this trip was peace. He needed to reassure the Israeli public, who had experienced a terrible suicide bus bombing in Tel Aviv eight days earlier. He was also intent on giving the Israeli-Syrian track a push. Much like during the Bush administration, there was an internal debate over whether Damascus should be included on the trip, though in this case it was about a presidential and not a secretarial visit.

The president's political advisers did not want him to go, but Clinton felt that he needed to do so. He was convinced that the only way to move Assad was with a personal meeting. Unlike during Bush's time, when I had opposed Baker visiting Damascus, I agreed that the president should go—and certainly Walid Muallem, the Syrian ambassador, was telling Indyk and me that Assad must not be excluded on this trip if we wanted to keep him committed to peace. However, both Indyk and I felt that President Clinton should get something for the visit. He would take criticism for going to Damascus—where Assad permitted Hamas and Islamic Jihad, groups that were responsible for acts of terrorism, including the most recent bombing in Tel Aviv, to maintain a presence. Muallem, after considerable effort, was able to tell us that if Assad were asked a question about terror at the press conference, he would say that he condemned it "whether it occurred in Beirut, Ramallah, or Tel Aviv." Muallem also indicated that Assad privately would give the president something on the two key issues on which we had been stuck in our private negotiations: a longer timetable for withdrawal and an Israeli diplomatic presence prior to the completion of full withdrawal.

Had we achieved these objectives, the trip would have produced firsts from Assad. Unfortunately, we were disappointed. Assad made some limited moves in private, agreeing to extend the withdrawal timetable to sixteen months and saying that four months before the withdrawal was complete the Israelis could establish a liaison office in Damascus. True to form, however, Assad linked the two points, meaning that Rabin would have to accept the sixteen-month timetable if he wanted to get the liaison presence prior to final withdrawal. Had this been accompanied by the public condemnation of terror acts in Israel, we could have gone to Israel with an achievement that would have resonated with the Israeli public and helped Rabin. But Assad did not hold up his end of the bargain. When Rita Braver of CBS News posed an accusatory question on terrorism at the press conference, Assad fell back on his rote instincts, blaming the Israelis for acts of terror because of continuing occupation. Christopher, Indyk, and I were livid, telling Farouk al-Shara and Muallem that Assad had embarrassed the president of the United States—and that they needed to fix it. Shara said Assad had been angered by the question because it was "rude." President Clinton, though mindful of the criticism he was sure to be subjected to, was almost philosophical afterward. He would tell me, "I knew people like him [Assad] in Arkansas—afraid of change and overly rigid because of it. I know what it takes to affect a guy like this, and my job is to work on him and get him to the point where he can move."

To be sure, Clinton was disappointed that he had lost an opportunity to arrive in Israel with momentum for peace and the potential to make life politically easier for Rabin, particularly after the Tel Aviv bus bombing that killed twenty-one Israelis. Still, he remained undaunted, convinced that we could do this—or, more likely, he could do this—and that it was essential to try. This impulse would become even stronger after Rabin's assassination. At this point, however, it was more of an impulse than a mission.

That would come later after the low point of the process. In the meantime, after extensive negotiating, we would reach an agreed Aims and Principles Non-Paper on security arrangements between Israel and Syria. Both sides referred to it as a "procedural breakthrough." With the Israelis and Palestinians we would soon get a substantive one.

The Interim Agreement, the Assassination, and Bill Clinton's Sense of Mission

After the Gaza-Jericho Agreement had been concluded and Arafat returned to Gaza from exile in Tunis, the next milestone to be achieved was the negotiation of the Interim Agreement that would establish the Palestinian Authority in the West Bank. Gaza bordered only the southwestern tip of Israel; unlike the West Bank, it was not rich in Jewish history, did not provide Israel strategic depth, and did not lie adjacent to Israel's major population centers. Negotiations for the Interim Agreement were bound to be long, difficult, and highly controversial in Israel.

Neither President Clinton nor Secretary Christopher was much involved in the talks. Their focus remained on Syria. The president, again, met the Syrian foreign minister in Washington as we managed this track and moved toward finalizing the Aims and Principles Non-Paper. We then had the Israeli and Syrian military chiefs of staff meet again in Washington—only this time the meeting was announced—and the president saw them in the Oval Office. Since the Israeli-Syrian talks were always three-way, I was a part of every meeting. That was less true of the Israeli-Palestinian track, which, having grown out of the Oslo process, had largely been bilateral, involving us mostly when the sides were stuck. But I would be drawn more and more into these talks as progress on the Interim Agreement proved difficult.

The two negotiators, Uri Savir and Abu Ala, created their own more informal back channel and they found it useful to involve me—at least in part to have me play a role with both of their leaders to give them greater space to negotiate. Essentially, I became their advocate with each leader.

Deciding on the scope of Palestinian responsibilities, where the IDF would be operating, the role of Palestinian police, when Israeli redeployment of its forces would take place, and how to avoid any contact between Palestinian security forces and Israeli settlers were enormously complicated. It would be early July 1995 before key concepts were accepted, principally involving the agreement on dividing the West Bank into three areas (A, B, and C) and defining the respective authorities within each.[24]

Once again, the timing of breakthroughs would be dictated by developments on the other tracks. Arafat approved the conceptual agreement creating areas A, B, and C shortly after the Israelis and Syrians had announced their procedural breakthrough. But the Israeli-Palestinian talks would slow again until there was a new stalemate on the Israeli-Syrian track. At this point, Rabin pushed the Israeli-Palestinian talks, but Arafat began to drag his feet. With the backing of the president and the secretary, I convinced Arafat that we needed to finish the Interim Agreement before the end of September lest Congress not renew our waiver authority to preserve a PLO office in Washington. He took my threat very seriously, and it was after this, on September 15, that he agreed to go to Taba where, over a period of ten days characterized by crises to the last minute, an agreement was finalized.[25] The rudiments of a Palestinian state were now being put in place.

In contrast to Rabin's awkward unease in the presence of Arafat on September 13, 1993, the president saw something very different during the signing ceremony. Before the ceremony, Clinton was in the Oval Office with Rabin, Arafat, Mubarak, Hussein, and Peres, and I had to interrupt their meeting. One final issue had come up, and the negotiators felt that I should resolve it with the two leaders; it had to do with whether the Palestinians would have a police station outside of Hebron on a road that was in dispute as to whether it was area B or C—if it was the latter, the Palestinians could not have the police station there. I asked Rabin and Arafat to join me in the small kitchen just behind the Oval Office, where the president often dined. When I explained the issue, Arafat said whatever the prime minister accepted would be good enough for him. Rabin, on the spot, said that the police station could be there. They shook hands and the issue was settled—and I later explained to the president what had happened. Clinton subsequently wrote about that kitchen agreement: "It was the handshake even more than the official signing that convinced me that Rabin and Arafat would find a way to finish the job of making peace."[26]

But Rabin would not get the chance to finish the job. In an increasingly ugly environment in Israel, in the weeks before and after the conclusion of the Interim Agreement, the right wing organized repeated and violent demonstrations with the ultranationalist and religious part of the settler movement. Rabin was depicted as a Nazi and portrayed as a traitor for giving away the land God had given to the Jews. Then, on November 4, 1995, after Rabin addressed a massive rally in Tel Aviv in support of peace, he was assassinated—six weeks after the signing in Washington.

All of us involved in this process were shaken to our core by the assassination—Clinton especially. He had come to revere Rabin. He saw him as a leader engaged in an ennobling struggle; the president saw himself as his partner in this epic battle for peace. Clinton's own words capture the depth of his feelings about Rabin and the effect the assassination had on him:

> In the two and a half years we had worked together, Rabin and I had developed an unusually close relationship, marked by candor, trust, and an extraordinary understanding of each other's political positions and thought processes. We had become friends in that unique way people do when they are in a struggle that they believe is great and good. With every encounter, I came to respect and care for him more. By the time he was killed, I had come to love him as I had rarely loved another man.[27]

The president felt he now had a duty to finish the job Rabin had started. He had to complete his legacy. Once again, he would use the Bible to express his feelings and to inspire others. In his eulogy for Rabin in Jerusalem, Clinton would cite the Torah portion of that week in which God tests Abraham's faith by seeing if he would sacrifice his son Isaac—Yitzhak in Hebrew—if so commanded. And now, the president would continue, "God tests our faith even more terribly, for he has taken our Yitzhak. But Israel's covenant with God, for freedom, for tolerance, for security, for peace—that covenant must hold. That covenant must hold. That covenant was Prime Minister Rabin's life's work. Now we must make it his lasting legacy."[28]

Clinton understood that his task in Jerusalem was not just a public one. He had to embrace and spiritually revive Shimon Peres, Rabin's successor, who had lost his rival and partner of fifty years. He was devastated—and yet Clinton, with the simple gesture of enveloping him in a tight bear hug, seemed to literally lift Peres up. It signaled that Clinton was his partner the way that he had been Rabin's.

Shortly after, they got into a practical discussion, with the president confiding in Peres about Syria and asking him questions about how he planned to proceed politically given the circumstances and what could he, the president, do to help. Peres's visage began to change—the sadness remained but an unmistakable aura of determination accompanied it—and Clinton left him with no doubt that whatever he needed from the United States, he would have.

In the coming months, Clinton demonstrated this repeatedly, in the face of severe challenges and without regard to the demands of domestic politics. Rabin's assassination had discredited the right wing in Israel, and Peres had decided to call for early elections, which would, he hoped, give him an unassailable mandate to pursue peace. But suddenly, everything changed. Hamas and Islamic Jihad carried out suicide bombings on successive Sundays on the same bus in Jerusalem, and a day after the second bombing there was an attack in Tel Aviv that killed children wearing costumes for the Jewish holiday of Purim. We put great pressure on Arafat to crack down on the Hamas infrastructure in Gaza, but he was doing too little. The Israelis now felt they had no security and were asking themselves, Was this the peace that Peres spoke about?

I went to the White House and told the president we were about to lose Peres and the peace process. We needed a dramatic initiative that not only put pressure on Arafat to change his behavior but also demonstrated to the Israeli public that the Rabin-Peres peace process had transformed the region—and put Israel, for the first time, in a position in which it was neither alone nor without partners in fighting terror. To do this, I argued, we needed to organize a summit in Egypt that brought leaders from around the world and the Middle East together with Peres to produce an action plan for dealing with the groups responsible for the terror. Mubarak and the president should cohost the summit, and Peres should be showcased meeting with Arab leaders, including those who did not have relations with Israel, like the Saudis. Afterward, the president needed to go to Israel and use his unique standing—a standing that had been cemented by the way Israelis reacted to his eulogy for Rabin three months earlier—to reassure Israelis about the future. I concluded by saying, "This must happen within days."

As soon as I finished speaking, Rahm Emanuel and the other political advisers in the room, speaking almost in unison, said I was crazy. They argued that it could be a disaster politically for the president, especially as he was heading into the 1996 election: "You could go there and there could be more bombs while you are there or immediately after the trip. You will have accomplished nothing. Don't do this. This is the last thing you need." Clinton turned back to me and asked if we could pull this off. I told him that I already had the Egyptians and Saudis on board provided he went. Can this save Peres and the process? he asked. I replied, "I don't know, but without it, the peace process won't survive." With all of his political advisers opposed, Clinton said, "Let's go."[29] He took the risk, and even though it shored up Peres's position at the time, Peres would still lose a very close election to Benjamin Netanyahu in May 1996.

Several months later, in September, only two months before our elections, another crisis emerged. Only now Netanyahu was the Israeli prime minister, and against the advice of all his senior security officials, he had not blocked Ehud Olmert, the mayor of Jerusalem, from opening a tunnel in the Old City of Jerusalem. The security officials had argued this would trigger violence. And it did. Arafat seized on the tunnel opening to put pressure on Netanyahu. Until this point he had continued to act against Hamas and Islamic Jihad, but Netanyahu, once he became prime minister, had effectively frozen the political process. Now Arafat decided to show Netanyahu that he could not be taken for granted: he enflamed passions by—falsely—declaring that the tunnel was undermining the foundation of Haram al-Sharif (Temple Mount), the location of the al-Aqsa mosque and the Dome of the Rock. Violence spiraled out of control, and at one point fifteen members of the IDF were killed by a mob in Nablus that included Palestinian police.

I knew from talking to Netanyahu that he could not resist for much longer the pressures to use dramatically more force to suppress the Palestinians. He wanted to avoid such a scenario and was seeking our help to defuse the situation. Most significantly, he was not using the killing of Israeli soldiers as a reason to walk away from Oslo—a process he had run against in the election campaign.

Once again I went to the president and said that only his dramatic intervention would give all sides a reason to pause and step back. Otherwise, I feared what Netanyahu might be driven to do. I suggested that he invite Netanyahu, Arafat, Mubarak, and Hussein to the White House to discuss how to end the crisis and resume negotiations—negotiations that had not moved forward since Netanyahu's election four months earlier. Predictably, the president's political advisers literally screamed that this was crazy. Two months before the election, with a strong lead in the polls, why take the risk of a big failure at the White House? In response, Clinton asked if we could "get Bibi to close the tunnel." Probably not, I said. He won't want to appear to have retreated in the face of violence or American pressure. If we don't do this, I argued, Netanyahu will soon employ far more massive force to suppress the Palestinians, and who knows where that leads? Over the unanimous opposition of his advisers, the president agreed to hold the summit meeting at the White House, which did in fact lead to an end to the violence and the resumption of negotiations.[30]

Clinton would do what was necessary to preserve the pursuit of peace, ignoring political advice and similarly rejecting the path of political correctness. Earlier, he did all he could to help Peres in the May election, an election that pitted Rabin's successor against an opponent (Netanyahu) who was running against Oslo. Apart from inviting Peres to Washington just prior to the onset of the official campaign in Israel, the president heaped praise on him and held a prominent signing ceremony to enact the U.S.-Israel Counter-Terrorism Cooperation Accord. If that was not enough, he also announced an additional $50 million in emergency counterterrorism assistance to Israel.[31]

Netanyahu and the Politics of Preserving Peace

Clinton would never have the relationship with Netanyahu that he had with Rabin or Peres. Netanyahu had won despite all the predictions, even from his own party, that Peres would win—and over Clinton's public opposition.* The new Israeli leader arrived at the White House for his first meeting with Clinton feeling that having defied expectations in Israel and internationally, he knew best. In their initial meeting, Netanyahu lectured the president on the region and how to deal with the Arabs. As soon as the meeting ended, Clinton turned to me and asked, "Who does he think the superpower is?"

---

* Given his fear that Netanyahu would undo the Rabin legacy, Clinton expressed overt support for Peres in a speech the week before the Israeli election in which, with little subtlety, he spoke of the stakes in the election and U.S. readiness to be there for Israel as it took risks for peace. His interviews the day before the election struck a similar theme.

Still, it was less the initial arrogance that worried him and more that in Netanyahu he saw someone who was, at best, grudging about peace. Unlike Rabin and Peres, who felt they must take the initiative on peace, Netanyahu was elected because he would not rush after the Palestinians or the Arabs. They would have to prove themselves to him.

While pursuing peace was not easy with Rabin and Peres, Clinton saw they were willing to take risks for peace, and his responsibility was to support them and minimize those risks. Emotionally, he connected with them and considered them his partners. Netanyahu was a different story; Clinton would have to push and prod if progress was to be made. Nonetheless, while the prime minister was different and more difficult to work with, for Clinton the mission had not changed, and in his words, "I was eager to determine whether and how he and I could work together to keep the peace process going."[32]

In truth, it was a bumpy road. Initially, Netanyahu let the negotiations lapse on both tracks.[33] The negotiations with the Palestinians resumed after the White House summit in September 1996; Netanyahu accepted negotiations over Israel's commitment in the Interim Agreement to the redeployment of Israeli forces in the West Bank city of Hebron. Netanyahu—unlike Rabin and Peres—wanted us to participate in the talks, typically preferring to speak with us and have the United States negotiate with the Palestinians. Arafat liked this, as he felt it would make it more likely that we would bring Netanyahu along.

Interestingly, even while he was campaigning in the two months before the November election, the president wanted to be kept in the loop of my efforts to revive negotiations on Hebron. With the election looming, I even asked Clinton to make calls to both leaders in order to break through an impasse on security issues. The calls were useful, but the talks dragged on. I carried out two twenty-three-day shuttles in the area before finally producing agreement on Hebron, on January 15, 1997, five days before the beginning of Clinton's second term. Though the redeployment had been part of the Interim Agreement, Netanyahu's base in Likud was strongly opposed to it. With the agreement, Likud now "owned" Oslo. Clinton understood the significance of the agreement and foresaw its impact on Netanyahu, observing that he "was constrained politically in what he could do beyond the Hebron deal."[34]

In fact, Netanyahu felt the need to compensate his political base for doing the deal on Hebron. In what would become a pattern in the future—

both during this tenure as prime minister and again during the Obama administration—he would announce new settlement construction anytime he took a step toward the Palestinians in order to manage his base, signaling that he was not departing from Likud's basic ideology. In this case, he built in Har Homa, an area in southeastern Jerusalem that the Palestinians saw as cutting off any potential contiguity between Bethlehem and Jerusalem. It was bound to trigger a backlash among Palestinians, and when it was compounded by Netanyahu's approach to Israel's obligation to carry out a further redeployment (FRD) by March, we suddenly had a crisis in the talks.*

Clinton was sympathetic to the politics of Netanyahu's coalition and understood that it was hard for him to move. Both at this point and later, he accepted Netanyahu's need to compensate. When the prime minister came to see him after the Hebron deal in February, the president chose not to pressure him on Har Homa. Instead he made the case that we could argue for his position with the Palestinians and the international community if he could do a credible FRD of 10 percent of the territory or "something very close to it." Netanyahu acknowledged the argument while sitting with the president, but when he faced opposition from within the coalition—over what amounted to actually turning over additional land in the West Bank to the Palestinians—he told us he could do only a tiny fraction of what we wanted. His offer of 2 percent from area C gave us little to work with, and it was rejected by the Palestinians.

Notwithstanding countless efforts that eventually involved combining the first and second FRDs, the talks on redeployment dragged on from March 1997 until late October 1998, at Wye River, when we would produce an agreement. But the intervening eighteen months were marked by sturm und drang. Netanyahu resisted our efforts to break the stalemate if it required him to move significantly on the FRDs or to take a step like working out terms to open the Gaza airport—also a commitment in the Interim Agreement—without first getting significant moves from the Palestinians on security, incitement, and the PLO Charter. His demands were clear, but his readiness to take steps was not. Clinton would be frustrated even as he acknowledged Netanyahu's problems. He would say, "Psychologically,

* The Interim Agreement mandated three FRDs; they represented what was supposed to be the process of devolving authority and responsibility over an increasing area of the West Bank to the Palestinian Authority. The first was to take place in March 1997 and the third by March 1998.

Netanyahu faced the same challenge Rabin had: Israel had to give up something concrete—land, access, jobs, an airport—in return for something far less tangible: the best efforts of the PLO to prevent terrorist attacks."[35]

Madeleine Albright and Sandy Berger, the secretary of state and the national security adviser, were far less sympathetic than the president to Netanyahu's politics. Both felt Netanyahu was not serious and, in Sandy's words, "was playing rope-a-dope with us." They believed he had no interest in pursuing peace. Worse, they saw him complicating our life in the region and making it harder, for example, to sustain sanctions and pressure on Iraq, with the Arabs finding it difficult to accept that Iraq was subjected to sanctions while Israel was not. Over the months of stalemate, both Albright and Berger became more insistent that we press Netanyahu, and confront him if necessary, to move the process along. Partly they believed that he would back down and partly they believed such a posture would preserve our credibility in the region.

Their impulse to confront him grew as they were subjected to increasing pressure and criticisms from the Europeans that something must be done on peace, and that if we did not do it, they would have little choice but to find ways to act that would put them at odds with us. I was not indifferent to the pressure we were getting from others, nor was I immune to the frustration they felt; after all, I was on the front lines dealing with Netanyahu and Arafat. But I had made a judgment about Netanyahu, particularly after the Hebron deal, that we could slowly move him on peace.

During this period, Berger and Albright argued that only ultimatums would work with Netanyahu. But President Clinton was uneasy, even calling me in the spring of 1998 when I was away at a retreat for my synagogue, asking for arguments on why it did not make sense to confront the prime minister. His hesitancy made me reluctant to threaten what we would do if Netanyahu was not responsive.

Did Clinton believe that Netanyahu understood how to navigate Israeli politics better than we did? Was he concerned about our domestic politics and did not want to provoke the pro-Israel community? Was he convinced that the way to move Netanyahu was by embracing him rather than by confronting him? Did his basic discomfort reflect his view of Israel and his recognition that the United States was Israel's only real friend in the world? Maybe all of these concerns led him to be less inclined than any of his presidential predecessors to publicly put pressure on Israel. Of course, the Israeli press would play up all signs of difference to portray troubles in the relationship, but the president was very careful to avoid public statements that created a sense of crisis.[36]

Despite Clinton's sympathetic approach to Netanyahu, by the fall of 1997, all our efforts to revive negotiations between Israel and the PLO had failed. At that point, two developments changed the dynamic. First, in September, Israel missed the date for the second FRD, meaning that neither the first nor second further redeployment had been carried out, as stipulated in the Interim Agreement. And second, Israel's attempt to assassinate the Hamas leader, Khaled Meshaal, in Amman had required the president's intervention to persuade a furious King Hussein not to break off relations with Israel.[37]

After the Meshaal affair, in Clinton's eyes, Netanyahu needed to demonstrate that he could do something right.[38] Netanyahu knew that the president had prevented the embarrassment of a loss of relations with Jordan, and we decided to tell him that our focus must now be on his doing two further redeployments as part of a package that included the Palestinians performing on security. Initially, he did not resist, and we set in motion a number of meetings between Secretary Albright and me with Netanyahu and Arafat separately, in Europe, as a prelude to meetings each of them would have in January 1998 with the president at the White House.

But nothing came easily. Netanyahu withheld how much he would do on the FRDs, even as he tried to impose two new conditions: dropping the Interim Agreement's requirement for a third FRD and getting the PLO to convene the Palestine National Council (PNC) to revoke the amended PLO Charter, which rejected Israel's right to exist.[39] Meanwhile, Arafat was resisting new demands on security and expected substantial Israeli redeployments.

President Clinton met Netanyahu on January 20 and Arafat two days later. The meetings were noteworthy because of what he offered to each— and because on the 21st, the news about Monica Lewinsky broke. Prior to the meetings, I briefed the president on each leader's approach and Netanyahu's new conditions. Even though I explained that one required us to unilaterally change an agreement the president had signed and the other required us to ignore that Peres had accepted the PLO's 1996 annulment of the offending articles of the charter, the president was again sensitive to Netanyahu's political difficulty in moving on the FRDs. He wanted to find a way to make it easier for him, partly because of how long we had been working on this issue.

To be fair, Clinton approached both leaders the same way. Previously, he had asked me about possible inducements we could offer each of them at a point when we simply had to find a way to break through. With Netanyahu, I said we could offer a defense treaty, raising Israel's status to that of a formal ally. With Arafat, I said we could offer our support for a state at the right moment. I did not expect Clinton to play either of these cards at this point, but he did, in fact, in his private meetings—the former to try to get Netanyahu to agree to do a third FRD and the latter to try to get Arafat to drop it.

It was not simply Clinton's style that led him to make these offers. With Israel, the treaty fit his concept of the relationship and our obligations—and if this was not only a way to reassure Netanyahu but also to give him a political achievement, so much the better. With the Palestinians, he felt we were going to get to statehood anyway. If this offered Arafat comfort and legitimacy, why not use it to get over the hump?

The Lewinsky affair may well have triggered his impulse to offer Arafat statehood at this point. When the story exploded publicly, Clinton, while denying an "affair," told the press that he was busy doing his job, having spent until after midnight with Prime Minister Netanyahu working the peace process. The bold move with Arafat the next day showed that he was not distracted and could offer a big idea even as he was asking the chairman to forgo the third FRD. He wouldn't make any headway on either issue. But Clinton's style was to press ahead, and during the course of 1998, this would remain true. The problem was that Arafat and Netanyahu, at least initially, wanted to see if the president was politically wounded.

Over the next few months, I worked both leaders. After much give-and-take, we were at an impasse on the size of the FRD. Netanyahu would not go above 11 percent and Arafat not below 13 percent.* I overcame the difference by raising a new idea: we would use the "green areas" to bridge the gap. Because there could be no construction in these environmental areas, I persuaded Netanyahu that the PA could get 13 percent, but they would be able to build on only 11 percent, and he could, therefore, claim he had done less than what we had been demanding. Having come up with the idea meeting alone with Netanyahu, I had not cleared it with Albright, Berger, or the president. But Clinton loved it, saying that Netanyahu "could claim he held out" and "gave up less than everyone else would have."

---

* We had gotten Arafat to come down to 13 percent from the 30 percent he originally wanted. We had selected 13 percent because Netanyahu had told me he could do the "lowest teen." Only later he said the lowest teen meant 11 percent.

We still had to convince Arafat, but this is how we finally solved the 13 percent problem on the FRDs. That still left us the security and other outstanding issues from the Interim Agreement to be resolved—and these included the airport, seaport, Israeli prisoner releases, and safe passage. These would all be part of what turned into an eight-day marathon at the Wye River Plantation on the eastern shore of Maryland at the end of October, where we would finalize an agreement on the FRDs and security.

Wye River, Netanyahu's Government Collapses, and Ehud Barak Is Elected

The Aspen Institute owns the Wye River complex, about ninety minutes by car outside Washington, DC. Arafat, Netanyahu, and their delegations joined Secretary Albright, me, and our delegation at Wye with Clinton appearing every day but spending the night only at the end—a final night in which there was no sleep, only negotiations. What matters for the story of the Clinton administration's relationship with Israel is not the details of the discussions at Wye but what drove the president. He was determined that we not leave without a deal. I reassured him at the outset that even though we would inevitably confront crises in the talks, we would succeed. I explained that the image had taken hold in Israel that Arafat and the Palestinians were responsive—terror acts had stopped—and Netanyahu's government was essentially paralyzed and incapable of making any decisions on peace. I said that if Netanyahu left Wye without an agreement, he would confirm that image: then his government would collapse and there would be new elections. As for Arafat, I judged that he would hold out until the end on most of the issues to be sure he had gotten the maximum and given the minimum, but he, too, was not going to leave Wye without an agreement. He valued his relationship with Clinton and knew an agreement was important to the president.

Clinton had an amazing capacity to convince each side that he was in its corner. While he let me orchestrate the tactics and the details of the negotiations—and the last day he and I would sit with the two leaders separately to work the issues—he also held private one-on-one discussions with each. There was a moment when he blew up at Netanyahu for seemingly disrespecting Arafat; however, that was so unusual that Sandy Berger pleaded with me not to give the president a reason to calm down after Netanyahu had asked me to intercede. Sandy felt that Clinton needed to keep the heat on Netanyahu to be able to close the deal. The president remained heavily focused on Netanyahu's politics on the one hand and the personal relationship with Arafat on the other.

Several points are worth noting in this regard. First, at the end of the sixth night, the president asked Berger and Albright to leave the two of us alone for a few minutes. Clinton wanted to talk about Jonathan Pollard, the Israeli spy who had been in prison for espionage since 1985. He asked, "Is it a big political issue in Israel? Will it help Bibi?" I told him yes, because Pollard was seen as an Israeli soldier and the ethos in Israel is that you never leave a soldier in the field. While saying that I thought there were good reasons to release Pollard, particularly because he had received a harsher sentence than those who had committed comparable crimes, I was also against linking the issues. Netanyahu did not need Pollard to do this deal. If he was thinking about linking Pollard to the peace issues—which I believed was a mistake—the president should save him for permanent status. Clinton disagreed, saying, "I usually agree with you, but this stalemate has lasted so long that it has created a kind of constipation. Release it and a lot becomes possible. I don't think we can afford to wait, and if Pollard is the key to getting it done now, we should do it."

We would have a crisis at the end of the talks when Netanyahu agreed to the final compromises, assuming that the president had committed to release Pollard as part of the deal, only to discover that Clinton had agreed only to review the case.[40] It took several hours before Netanyahu signed the deal with the proviso that he would change the makeup of the Palestinian prisoners he would release.

Second, on the last day of the talks, Yitzhak Molcho, Netanyahu's negotiator, suggested to me that we allow the leaders and their aides to meet without us to discuss the outstanding issues. During their meeting, they agreed to resolve the PLO Charter issue by having President Clinton attend a PNC meeting in Gaza in which the members would vote to revoke the charter in his presence. The charter was the last major issue that we needed to resolve and it seemed that the two sides had come up with an answer. But Berger was dead set against it, fearing the potential for a major embarrassment for the president. At the time, we were all in the tent area attached to the Wye Center, and Netanyahu rushed over to me and said, "Dennis, this will work, don't let Sandy talk the president out of it." We were still discussing this when Clinton, after listening to Sandy's arguments, came over to Netanyahu and me and asked for my reaction. "If the two parties agree," I said, "we should make it happen, not make it harder for them." Clinton agreed. If the politics demanded this for Netanyahu and Arafat, he would do it, saying, "Look, I know how to work a crowd; I can get them to respond."

Third, Clinton would play on Arafat's desire to bring the U.S. president to Gaza as part of the implementation of the agreement. He intuitively understood how this would give the Palestinian Authority and Arafat a more exalted, statelike status. But he also understood it gave Arafat an incentive not only to close the deal but to implement it as well and be on his best behavior prior to the president's visit—lest he put the visit at risk.

Notwithstanding the drama with Pollard at the end, we would have a ceremony at the White House, and both leaders—along with a cancer-stricken King Hussein—were gracious and hopeful.* Netanyahu, however, would face a backlash from the right and made a serious political mistake. He could have used the agreement to call for a national unity government with Ehud Barak to embrace Wye and to deal with the major decisions that would be called for in the pending permanent status negotiations. Barak would have joined and 80 percent of the country would have supported a unity government. But Netanyahu instead sought to accommodate those on the right who opposed the deal, seeking new assurances from us, and eventually getting cabinet approval of the Wye agreement but with no Likud ministers supporting him.

Clinton seemed to be riding high after the agreement. The Democrats gained seats in the midterm elections, and increasingly it appeared that he would face only a censure resolution in the House of Representatives over the Lewinsky affair. This, unfortunately, changed while we were en route to Israel for the president's trip to oversee the midpoint implementation of the Wye agreement. During our flight, two articles of impeachment were voted by the House.

Though Clinton was distracted—during a three-way meeting with Arafat and Netanyahu I saw him scribbling "focus on your job, focus on your job, focus on your job"—he once again performed brilliantly. His speech at the PNC after the delegates had voted to rescind the charter was largely ad-libbed as he used little of the prepared script. Instead, he sounded like a preacher in acknowledging the deep sense of Palestinian grievance but calling on them not to let their hurt blind them to what peace with Israel could mean for Palestinians. He would similarly inspire an Israeli audience.

Netanyahu did not fare as well. He was now hamstrung by the politics of

---

* Hussein had visited Wye on the penultimate night and appealed to everyone there to finish the job.

his coalition. Sharon told me during the course of the trip that the government could no longer function, and it was time for either new elections or a national unity government. Not long after Clinton's visit, the government lost a no-confidence vote. Elections were set for May 1999.

Clinton survived the impeachment assault, but Netanyahu did not survive the election, losing in a landslide to Ehud Barak. Israel was again led by the Labor Party, and Barak announced that he would fulfill the legacy of Yitzhak Rabin.

Barak and Clinton: Partners to the End

It took time for Barak to form his government. Prior to visiting the White House on July 15, he signaled that he did not want to meet me or the secretary before seeing the president alone—he wanted no filters to the president.

With Clinton, Barak made clear he was ready to push for deals with both the Syrians and the Palestinians in fifteen months. He needed the president's full engagement, telling both Clinton and me separately that Assad would do a deal only with the president, not with the secretary of state or the envoy. Barak wanted an open line to the president, and he would have it.

Clinton once again had a partner in peacemaking, and he was ready to do whatever it took to be responsive. He saw in Barak a leader prepared to move fast, to take great risks, and to finish the job that Rabin had started. He would ignore the warning signs on this first visit—Barak did not want to embrace the Rabin pocket commitment on the June 4, 1967, lines with Syria, and he was backing away from the time line on FRDs in the Wye River agreement.

Barak appealed to the president on each, saying there might be a different way to deal with the Syrians and we should explore the possibilities. He would meet his obligations in Wye, but he first wanted to see if it was possible to persuade Arafat to negotiate a framework agreement on all the core issues. I flagged the difficulties with each of Barak's requests, but President Clinton was willing to grant Barak a license.

These initial discussions set a pattern that we would see for the remainder of the Clinton presidency: Barak would have big ideas and was convinced of his tactics, but he needed our help in implementing them. The president would be sympathetic to Barak's objectives and risk taking, and would pledge our help—even when it required us to carry much of the load and necessarily produced resistance from the Syrians and the Palestinians. Notwithstanding what Barak told the president about moving on both tracks, he was, in fact, interested primarily in Syria, and he initially viewed the Palestinians as a managerial problem—with us left to do the management.

On both tracks, Barak had great ambitions tempered only by his desire to avoid prematurely exposing any concessions. He feared his Arab partners would do nothing in response, and he would be a "*friar*"—a sucker—and lose the Israeli public in the process. One of his mantras with both the president and me was that he could not afford to lose his political capital with the Israeli public by appearing too ready to concede while having little to show for it.

Consequently, on the Syrian track he resisted reaffirming the Rabin pocket—even though we knew that was the sine qua non for Assad, and the Israeli public knew nothing about it. We would effectively lose the period from July until December 1999 as Barak sought alternatives to conveying that he accepted the Rabin pocket.

During this time, President Clinton persuaded Assad to have two secret trilateral meetings that I would host and orchestrate between Uri Saguy and Riad Daoudi, the Israeli and Syrian negotiators, first in Zurich and then in Bethesda.[41] In these meetings, Saguy would be constrained by Barak from going as far as he wanted, even as Daoudi signaled flexibility on the border. We hit a roadblock when Farouk al-Shara suffered an aortic aneurysm in early October. As Assad's health deteriorated, he had Shara assume the management of the peace issue, and with his foreign minister now incapacitated for some time, we were stuck.

Barak, mindful that Assad was becoming increasingly frail, feared we could lose the opportunity with Syria. After agreeing to work out a formula on the Rabin pocket that Albright and I could present to Assad, Barak changed his mind. With me in Jerusalem at the time and preparing to meet Albright in Damascus the next day for discussions with Assad, Barak called President Clinton and insisted that we could not present the formula to Assad. Instead, the president needed to shock Assad by flying to Damascus and presenting Barak's reaffirmation of Rabin.

The president's instincts led him to tell Barak he was open to doing it. He had not demurred or said he needed to check with Sandy, Madeleine, or me. Sandy and Madeleine were vehemently opposed, seeing this as exposing the president to risk and possible embarrassment. It would let Assad decide whether what the president was offering was good enough.

In the end, Clinton's presence in Damascus would not be required. The next day, December 7, Assad surprised us. Even though we did not raise the Rabin pocket, Assad, in response to our question about whether his recent letter to President Clinton signaled a retreat, suddenly dropped all conditions for resuming talks. More significantly—and completely out of character— he agreed on the spot not only to resume formal public talks with Israel but also, for the first time, to raise the negotiations to the political level. These would involve Shara, who had now sufficiently recovered, meeting Barak. Barak was surprised and now pressed us to move quickly to an endgame negotiation in an isolated place. Once again, we complied with his request.

Unfortunately, after we had arranged the talks in the setting and format Barak insisted on, the prime minister's enthusiasm diminished. He decided that his politics ruled out making any concessions even as the Syrians moved on every issue in meetings first at Blair House and then again two weeks later in the eight days of negotiation at Shepherdstown, West Virginia. Indeed, Barak, who had been willing to have Clinton fly to Damascus to reaffirm the Rabin pocket, retreated even on this, insisting that he could neither say this to Shara directly nor have Clinton do it on his behalf in Shepherdstown.

Why did President Clinton tolerate Barak's posture? Why would he not say to him, If you want my help, and if you want me to continue my efforts, I need you either to reaffirm the Rabin pocket directly or allow me to do it— otherwise you are on your own. That was simply not Bill Clinton. He had great sympathy for Barak's political predicament. He understood that the large number of Russian immigrants had changed the Israeli political calculus, saying "they had come from the world's largest country to one of its smallest ones," and they didn't believe in "making Israel even smaller."[42]

Clinton believed he had to cut Barak slack, not, in his words, "jam him." This guided him both at Shepherdstown and at Camp David. Clinton told Barak that, as a general, he knew more about security than he would ever know, but Barak was new to politics and that was one thing Clinton understood. Writing later about the Shepherdstown talks and Barak's unwillingness to concede anything, Clinton described his attempt to convince Barak that results mattered more than momentary poll numbers: "People hire leaders to win for them." If he succeeded in making real peace with Syria, that would count for something over time, but if he failed because he was holding out now, his good poll numbers of the moment would vanish within days. "As hard as I tried, I couldn't change Barak's mind."[43]

The Syrian track formally came to an end on March 26, 2000, in a meeting that President Clinton had with President Assad in Geneva. I say "formally" because Assad had checked out shortly after the Shepherdstown talks. At this point, he now doubted Barak, but it was public criticism of Shara by the writers' union in Damascus over concessions made to Israel at Shepherdstown that led Assad to walk away from pursuing a peace agreement. The writers' union had no power and was an obvious front for more powerful forces in the regime. Assad read the criticism as directed at him, and suddenly he felt that the pursuit of peace would jeopardize his ability to transfer power to his son. Given his health, succession—not peace—was Assad's priority. This became clear to Clinton when Assad delayed their meeting in Geneva and then rejected Barak's readiness to withdraw to the June 4, 1967, lines based on a mutually agreed border—the very thing that he had been asking the president to produce.

With an agreement with Syria no longer possible, Barak was eager to press ahead—but once again on his terms and at his pace. He unilaterally withdrew from Lebanon on May 23, 2000, fulfilling the promise he had made during the electoral campaign. He then told us he wanted to move quickly to a summit with the Palestinians, even though he had failed to fulfill a number of standing commitments to Arafat—on a redesignation of a number of villages as part of an understanding on further delaying the redeployments called for in the Wye River Memorandum. I warned the president that Barak was repeating the pattern we had seen on Syria, demanding that we rush to a decisive meeting without making clear what he was—or was not— prepared to do. Clinton was now caught between Barak pressing him to call an immediate summit, and Berger, Albright, and me all saying that we could not go to a summit until we knew much more about each side's positions and whether and how they might be bridged. The president accepted our logic but was also attracted to Barak's arguments regarding the sustainability of his coalition, which looked increasingly fragile at this point.

Given the duality of his instincts, the president would tell Barak he would call a summit but not until we had more details. Since Barak was pushing for the meeting, we focused more on finding out what he was prepared to do. Both in my meetings with Barak and the secure phone calls the president had with him, we sought to draw him out, following the path that so many previous administrations had tried with earlier Israeli leaders. Once again, we would say, Tell us what you can do, your limits, what you must have on each issue—borders, security, refugees, and Jerusalem. We won't share this with the Palestinians; this is just for us. Like his predecessors, Barak would resist, fearing that either through inadvertent hints or suggestions, we would give away his redlines, and he would be forced to go farther. Still, between my conversations with him and his colleagues, and our continuing reluctance to convene the summit, we did learn more about what was possible on the Israeli side.

I was still hesitant, however, because, as I told the president, "Arafat makes decisions only one minute to midnight. Why would he make decisions now when he knows you will remain in office another seven months?" And Clinton would tell me, "Yes, but Barak may not be there." The president felt we had to move soon, and Sandy Berger explained that Clinton had another consideration: he wanted to do the summit before the Republican and Democratic Party conventions lest it look like he was trying to steal the thunder of Gore and Bush. If we did not do this in July, we would not have a summit, period.

In retrospect, I should have taken these admonitions less seriously. After all, Clinton would push until the end of his presidency for a deal. But there was no ignoring Barak's precarious political position and his incessant pressure on the president to convene a summit. Barak was convinced that the pressure cooker effect of a summit meeting would force each side finally to make decisions. Notwithstanding my doubts, if given the choice of no summit or a summit, I, too, came down on the side of proceeding—and on July 3, at Camp David, Berger, Albright, and I met with the president.

Our meeting took place in his study in Laurel, the cabin where he received visitors. In a room that was full of his memorabilia that effectively encapsulated his political career, the president suddenly turned wistful and wondered whether he was doing the right thing in going to a summit. He had spoken to Rahm Emanuel, who had left the White House and returned to Chicago, and Emanuel had said the summit was a high-risk venture and it might end up hurting Al Gore.

Suddenly, the tables were turned. Now it was the president expressing doubts and unease about convening a summit. Berger and Albright were forceful in pressing him to move ahead, with the secretary of state saying we would be judged poorly by history if we let our fears prevent us from going the extra mile. I agreed. Earlier in the year, both Ami Ayalon, the head of Shin Bet, Israel's internal security service, and Shaul Mofaz, the chief of staff of the IDF, had asked me to push Barak to move on the Palestinians because they said it was only a matter of time before violence erupted. They cited deep frustration on the Palestinian street—a function of the corruption of the PA and the absence of statehood. They both felt the Israeli public would accept far-reaching concessions, but not once violence reemerged. We had a dress rehearsal of the violence in May when Palestinian riots broke out on the anniversary of Israel's founding. I knew we had an Israeli government that was prepared to go further than ever before, and if we did not go for the summit, we might lose a historic opportunity.

There is no need to run through the details of Camp David here.* What is important to note is President Clinton's instinct on how to deal with Barak and with Israel generally. We had fine-tuned a strategy and choreography for the meeting, but Barak rejected our plan, which called for the president to present parameters to the leaders on day one and, after two days of receiving comments from the two sides, put an American draft agreement on the table at the beginning of day three. The president was not prepared to proceed over Barak's objection. In Clinton's mind, Barak was the one doing the bulk of the giving, and he had to ease him to that point. Our strategy for the summit now had to be developed on the fly.[†] Clinton was convinced that he understood Barak's psychology as well as his politics, and this was the best way to deal with him. The irony is that only at the end of the eighth day of the summit, when the president became fed up with Barak's reticence, did he say he would have to announce the failure of the summit unless the Israeli leader finally told us his bottom lines—proving that the pressure cooker worked on him but not on Arafat, who would reject the offer.

Would things have worked out differently if we had stuck to the strategy we had going in? We will never know. Barak showed he would resist any discussion until he thought the time was right. And Arafat was unwilling to move at all, either because he was incapable of doing an end-of-conflict deal or because Barak had insisted on this summit and he was not going to be responsive at this juncture—or because, in his view, after Hezbollah proved that "resistance" worked in Lebanon, he planned for what would be the second intifada.

What we do know is that the president pressed Arafat very hard at Camp David after finally eliciting Barak's bottom lines. When Clinton called it quits on July 26, he spoke to the press with Barak's political needs very much in mind. As he wrote later, "To give Barak some cover back home and indicate what had occurred, I said that while Arafat had made clear that he wanted to stay on the path of peace, Barak had shown particular courage, vision, and an understanding of the historical importance of this moment."[44] The contrast with Arafat could not have been more stark: he had simply

---

* I describe Camp David in great detail in *The Missing Peace*, pp. 650–711.

† Interestingly, the Israeli team by day three would be asking us why we backed off our approach.

shown up, while Barak had been a statesman. The president, at the end of Camp David and in the immediate aftermath, would speak to the Israeli press and "assured the people of Israel that he [Barak] had done nothing to compromise their security" and "they should be very proud of him."[45]

Clinton was surely trying to use his connection to the Israeli public to protect Barak politically. But that was not the full story. The more he would pay tribute to Barak, the harder it was for the Israeli PM to take the low road against Arafat—and the more Arafat might feel the need to prove his own peace credentials: Clinton decided that the game was not over and he wanted to keep the process alive. While we had made only a limited effort with Arab leaders prior to and during Camp David—mostly because Barak insisted that we not expose his flexibility—after the summit, we briefed them on how much was offered by Israel that Arafat had turned down.

This approach seemed to work in the weeks after the summit. Barak did not pay a political price in Israel, with key issues like Jerusalem being demystified for the first time. For his part, Arafat, after initially trying to capitalize on the image of defying us, became defensive and asked the president to send me to the area to prepare for a second summit. Notwithstanding the previous concerns about the impact on the presidential campaign, the president was now willing to consider the possibility. He would accept my recommendation that Arafat must prove his seriousness first by negotiating issues quietly with the Israelis and demonstrating flexibility. We held the line for a few weeks. However, when Barak pressed me to come to work with both sides on a U.S. proposal, the president sent me to the area. By late September, I saw both promising and disturbing signs. There was no doubt that unlike the lead-up to Camp David, the Palestinian negotiators—Mohammed Dahlan, Jibril Rajoub, and Saeb Erekat—were showing signs of genuine flexibility. But in my meetings with Arafat in Ramallah, and in the president's discussion with Arafat in New York, he showed no responsiveness to ideas we had developed on how to resolve Jerusalem. Still, all the Palestinian negotiators were hopeful and pressing us to continue the efforts, and they used the Israeli negotiators and Barak to keep pushing us.

On September 26, 27, and 28, I went back and forth between the two sides at the Ritz Carlton in Pentagon City, and I indicated the direction of what we might propose. Both sides were very hopeful, so much so that Mohammed Dahlan called CIA director George Tenet on the 28th to say there was going to be a deal. His call is particularly ironic because it came *after* Ariel Sharon's visit to the Temple Mount earlier that day, a visit that triggered Palestinian riots the next day throughout the West Bank and Gaza. This was the beginning of the second intifada.

The Israeli crackdown produced large numbers of Palestinian casualties and minimal Israeli ones as the turmoil was contained mostly to the Palestinian territories. We were leaning on Arafat to stop the violence, but he made little effort to do so. After a failed meeting with Madeleine Albright, Arafat, and Barak in Paris, the president attended a summit in Sharm el-Sheikh hosted by Hosni Mubarak. During the summit, an agreement was reached on a plan of mutual steps to calm the crisis—but it would not be implemented by the Palestinians.[46]

President Clinton was aware that Barak, having conceded more than any of his predecessors, was being destroyed politically by the new uprising. But Clinton also believed that our pressure on Arafat was not effective. As a result, he promised at the Sharm summit that if the violence stopped, he would see the PLO leader at the White House in November after the presidential election. Barak favored increased pressure on Arafat, but he also supported White House efforts to revive discussions, believing his only hope politically was to produce an agreement. The violence ebbed, and in the two meetings in November, I proposed and both leaders accepted a back channel between Israeli minister and former chief of staff of the IDF Amnon Shahak and Arafat to see if it was possible to reach practical understandings to stop the violence and address the political issues.

By early December 2000, Amnon's back channel had led to discussions on permanent status between Israeli and Palestinian negotiators. Arafat requested that I meet him in Morocco, where he revealed that he could accept what I suggested the Israelis could probably do on borders, security, refugees, and Jerusalem.[47] When I briefed the president, he asked me why I was not more enthusiastic about Arafat's response, and I told him it was easy for Arafat to agree with me in private, but would he really defend such a deal in public? The president thought he was ready, that he knew he was facing a dead end, particularly with the prospect that the upcoming Israeli elections would produce Sharon, a member of Likud, in place of Barak. "Then where would Arafat be?" he asked.[48]

It was on the basis of my meeting in Morocco that we called for both sides to send their delegations to Washington for intensive discussions to reach agreement. Unlike at Camp David, I outlined guidelines for each issue in the talks, and from December 19 to 21, they tried to reach understandings. On the evening of the 21st, the leaders of the delegations, Saeb

Erekat and Shlomo Ben Ami, said they needed the United States to make a proposal to resolve the differences. The president presented the Clinton Parameters on December 23 to the two sides in the Cabinet Room of the White House. He read them the points and told them I would answer questions after he left. He made it clear they represented not American policy but a bridging proposal, and when he left office in a month, they would leave with him if there was no agreement. Each side had five days to respond; they could negotiate within the parameters but not on the parameters themselves. After leaving the Cabinet Room, Clinton called Mubarak and presented the points to him—and, unlike previously, we explained the parameters to key Arab leaders and lobbied them to press Arafat to accept them.

Our effort was to no avail. While Barak's cabinet voted to accept the parameters on December 27, Arafat gave us no response. Mubarak and others pleaded with us to give Arafat more time. On January 2, 2001, Arafat came to the White House and claimed he was accepting the parameters, even as he explicitly rejected our proposals on Jerusalem and refugees. To avoid damaging Barak politically, we did not publicly announce the Palestinian leader's rejection. Afterward, Barak actually asked the president to come to the area to broker a deal, and Clinton was willing. Nothing was more important to him. He would later write that Madeleine Albright was convinced that if he had gone with her and our negotiator, Wendy Sherman, to North Korea at this time, he would have produced a missile deal there. "Although I wanted to take the next step," Clinton said, "I simply couldn't risk being halfway around the world when we were so close to peace in the Middle East."[49]

I no longer thought that we were so close to peace. But President Clinton did, and he fervently believed that if he brokered the deal even in the last week—and if he stayed behind to sell the agreement to both publics—it would make the difference in the Israeli election.[50] The only reason he did not travel on January 14 or 15, with only five days remaining in his presidency, was that I convinced him to test Arafat and see if he was willing to close first. What was the test? Call Arafat and tell him that if he would meet with Shahak or Shimon Peres for the next twenty-four hours and if after the meeting report that they had agreed on the principal issues, he would come to the region and broker the final deal. Clinton agreed and called Arafat, who demurred; he had to visit Morocco, but the negotiators could meet. I scribbled a note to the president: "It is time to take no for an answer." And he did.

President Clinton felt Arafat had failed him. When Arafat called later to thank him for all his efforts as he was leaving office, and told Clinton he was a great man, the president responded, "Mr. Chairman, I am not a great man.

I am a failure, and you have made me one." He warned Arafat that he was electing Sharon and would "reap the whirlwind."[51] He also warned his incoming successor, George W. Bush, not to trust anything Arafat said, and he did the same with Colin Powell.*

The Clinton Mind-set and Approach

For Bill Clinton, the United States and Israel were strategic partners. During his tenure, all the areas of security cooperation were continued and upgraded. There was expanded counterterror coordination and support and a commitment to increase our provision of advanced surveillance technologies and aircraft, particularly as Israel took risks for peace. As president, Clinton was ready to forge a formal security alliance with Israel—even when he did not feel especially close to Benjamin Netanyahu. There was little doubt about his attachment to Israel. Both Israelis and Arabs were aware of this connection, and yet he paid no price with Arab leaders for it. Similarly, his effort at outreach to Iran after the moderate Mohammad Khatami was elected president came at no price with the Saudis—a far cry from the reaction we have seen to the Obama administration's policies.

To be fair, the Saudis saw Iran as less of a threat then; its nuclear program was largely undeveloped. Khatami stopped Iranian subversion in the kingdom. In addition, Iran did not look like it was gaining in the region and altering its balance of power. If anything, Iraq was more of a preoccupation for both Iran and Saudi Arabia. But that provides only part of the explanation. The deeper explanation is that the United States was still seen as the only superpower—and after an initial period of American hesitancy in Somalia and Haiti, our use of hard power in Bosnia, Kosovo, and Iraq added to American credibility. Once again, perceived U.S. credibility counted for more than anything else with our key Arab friends. To be sure, Clinton's activism in pursuit of peace was recognized as genuine and made it easier not to be defensive about ties to us and what we were doing with Israel. Increasingly, many of the Gulf states also began to cooperate discreetly with the Israelis on security issues during the 1990s.

For the Clinton administration, cooperation with Israel was the rule, even during Netanyahu's tenure. Partnership would extend to all areas but

---

* Clinton told Bush and Cheney on January 20 that depending on Arafat was the "biggest mistake I made in my presidency." Elliott Abrams, *Tested by Zion*, p. 5.

was riveted on the pursuit of peace. The president's views were so clear and his sensitivity to the political needs of Israeli leaders so apparent that there was little dissonance within the administration on policy. While the constituency that saw Israel through a competitive prism did not disappear within the national security bureaucracy, it had less weight than in any other U.S. administration—before or after Clinton. The debates were more apparent during Netanyahu's time, but even there the impulses to pressure the Israeli prime minister were almost always constrained by Clinton's own instincts—and efforts to downgrade cooperation with Israel had no champion in the upper reaches of the administration.

President Clinton himself never felt comfortable putting pressure on Israel. If this inclination was about politics, it had less to do with ours and far more to do with Israel's. Clinton's successor would enter office feeling neither his commitment to pursuing peace nor his emotional attachment to Israel. And yet during the course of his presidency, he would evolve on both—and emerge as one of Israel's greatest friends.

10

BUSH 43:

TERROR, PARTNERSHIP, AND

BUREAUCRATIC DIVISIONS

George W. Bush did not enter the White House preoccupied with the Middle East. Indeed, foreign policy in general had not figured prominently in the campaign against Vice President Al Gore. To the extent it did, Bush spoke about greater humility in our involvement overseas. He was not eager to engage in ambitious pursuits of peace or nation building. During the campaign, Condoleezza Rice, who would be his national security adviser in his first term and secretary of state in his second, wrote that the priorities of a Republican administration would be far different from President Clinton's: great power relations, built on institutions not personalities, and developments in Europe and Asia would take precedence over Clinton's "misguided" attempts to negotiate treaties like Kyoto on climate change or invest presidential capital in conflict resolution in the third world. The Middle East warranted barely a mention in her overview of foreign policy priorities.[1]

How ironic this appears in retrospect. When we think now about the Bush administration, it is not its humility or avoidance of far-flung activism that comes to mind. The war on terror, the freedom agenda, and the debilitating conflict in Iraq are the hallmarks of its foreign policy.

The trauma of 9/11 transformed President Bush's approach to the world. It would have transformed any presidency—and fighting terror would have become a preoccupation for any administration. Not surprisingly, it influenced the president's view of Israel and his identification with its ongoing struggle against terrorism. This is not to say that the president focused heavily on Israel. His preoccupation was largely elsewhere—certainly with Iraq, even before we went to war and all the more so afterward, when we faced an ongoing insurgency there. But Israel was also fighting its own war on terror. The second intifada was characterized by incessant suicide bombings and terrorist attacks against Israeli civilians. Small wonder that after 9/11 this had an effect on Bush. He later wrote about the intifada: "I was appalled by the violence and loss of life on both sides. But I refused to accept the moral equivalence between Palestinian suicide attacks on innocent civilians and Israeli military actions intended to protect their people. My views came into sharper focus after 9/11. If the United States had the right to defend itself and prevent future attacks, other democracies had those rights, too."[2]

As we will see, prior to 9/11, the Bush administration criticized Israeli targeted killings designed either to punish acts of terror or preempt them by going after leaders of those Palestinian groups responsible for attacks. After 9/11, this criticism largely stopped. But it would be misleading to say there was an immediate change in the administration's policies toward Israel. That took some time.

Interestingly, while Bush would be known for his decisiveness, his administration was characterized by profound internal divisions. In many respects, George W. Bush's administration bears similarities to Reagan's. This is true both in terms of the president's eventual attachment to Israel and the deep divides among his central advisers—politically and ideologically. On the Middle East, the divisions were wide and deep. Describing them during the first term, Condoleezza Rice said, "The differences in the administration between the decidedly pro-Israel bent of the White House and the State Department's more traditional pro-Arab view percolated beneath the surface . . . State and the White House were not on the same page and everyone in the region—and in Washington—knew it."[3]

Robert Danin, who worked for Rice on Middle Eastern issues at both the NSC and the State Department, described his experience and the differences in broader terms: "I am on one side of what is a divided administration on this issue [the Middle East]—between a traditionalist, NEA [Near Eastern Affairs] worldview that dominates the State Department, and a totally different worldview that dominates the NSC, the White House, the VP's office, and the Pentagon."[4]

And what was the traditionalist worldview? That the Arab-Israeli conflict dominates the Middle East and there is little that the United States can do in the area or with the Arabs unless we solve the problem. In other words, it is the key to the well-being of the United States position and our capacity to take on the challenges in the region—a view that has been embedded in the national security establishment of every administration since Truman's.

Vice President Cheney and those around him rejected this view: "I did not believe, as many argued, that the Israeli-Palestinian conflict was the linchpin of every other American policy in the Middle East. I saw instead a complicated region in which issues are inter-related and couldn't be com-partmentalized. We did not have the luxury of dealing with them sequen-tially, waiting until the Israeli-Palestinian conflict was resolved before we dealt with the threat that terrorism posed to the United States."[5]

Though Cheney has been portrayed as having great influence on Presi-dent Bush, his views on this—and, as we will see, in other areas—were not always decisive.

I say this because even though 9/11 transformed the Bush presidency and gave the president an unmistakable sense of mission, the traditionalist view of the State Department—one that Cheney debunked—guided our policy toward Israel in the initial period after the attacks on the World Trade Center and the Pentagon. But that posture would not last. After 9/11, as the administration waged its struggle against terror, its policy began to tilt more openly toward Israel.

Over time, there would be periods of tension in the relationship. But such moments were generally kept private and typically did not involve President Bush directly—and when they occurred they were kept within bounds because of Bush's instincts. Bush was a friend of Israel. He saw it fighting the same threats that the United States faced. In May 2008, in a speech to the Knesset, Bush declared that although Israel was a country of just over seven million people, when "you confront terror and evil, you are 307 million strong, because America stands with you."[6] For Bush, this was not just a rhetorical flourish; it had become his mind-set. He would tell Prime Minister Ehud Olmert that he did not want there to be any daylight between the United States and Israel—and he meant it.

The Evolution of the Bush Policy: The Pre-9/11 Period

At the outset of the Bush administration, there was a very strong "anything but Clinton" impulse. And, of course, Clinton was most identified with his effort to negotiate Arab-Israeli peace. During the transition, I kept Colin

Powell, the secretary of state designate, informed of what we were doing to see if we could gain agreement on the Clinton Parameters—an effort that continued until the last week of the administration.[7] Powell told me more than once, "I hope you succeed, because we are not going to make such an effort. My young president thinks it is a fool's errand."

I told Powell I doubted we would succeed because Arafat was not up to it: "He simply cannot end the conflict; it defines him." But I added that Powell could not walk away from this, because the conflict would get dramatically worse. "So you will not be about peacemaking but about managing the conflict and keeping things together until after Arafat passes from the scene."

Powell understood this, but he faced a phalanx that was very much inclined to walk away. The gestalt, as Robert Danin put it, was that "this thing is a loser; the Clinton administration spent too much time on this, and it's not really a priority."[8] Clinton's own parting words to Bush that he had put too much weight on Arafat—and it was the "biggest mistake I made in my presidency"—reinforced the basic instinct of Bush, Cheney, and others around the president.

On January 30, 2001, at his first meeting with the principals of his NSC, Bush's views came through clearly: "We're going to correct the imbalances of the previous administration on the Mideast conflict. We're going to tilt back toward Israel. And we're going to be consistent. Clinton over-reached, and it fell apart. That's why we're in trouble. If the two sides don't want peace, there's no way to force them." Bush then commented on the helicopter ride he had taken with Ariel Sharon in 1998 when he had visited Israel, and how what he had seen then still influenced him now: "Looked real bad down there. I don't see much we can do over there at this point. I think it's time to pull out of that situation."[9]

Colin Powell reacted by saying that to do so would reverse thirty years of U.S. policy and "unleash Sharon" and the IDF. The "consequences of that could be dire, especially for the Palestinians." To which Bush replied, "Maybe that's the best way to get things back in balance. Sometimes a show of strength by one side can really clarify things." The discussion then turned to Iraq and an intelligence presentation on plants producing chemical and biological materials for weapons. The juxtaposition seemed, as Ron Suskind wrote, to have been planned and signaled that the United States "was washing its hands of the conflict in Israel. Now, we'd focus on Iraq."[10]

There is nothing particularly surprising about Bush's comments except the need to correct the "imbalances" and to tilt back toward Israel. The criticism of Clinton in many quarters was that he tilted too much toward Israel, that he was, in the words of my former deputy, Aaron Miller, too much "Israel's lawyer."[11] The imbalance could, of course, refer to a policy that was far too centered on the peace process, which Bush and those around him clearly believed. After all, early in the Bush administration, even the term "peace process" was banned—although Powell argued for some diplomatic activity.[12]

Powell believed, unlike the prevailing sentiment in that first NSC meeting, that "you can't be the American government without a process or without getting involved . . . with no illusions about the personalities we were dealing with, and no illusions that process can be more than process."[13] But a process looked too much like what Clinton had done, and that was simply off-limits in the Bush administration. While Bush would say in his memoirs that he did not blame Clinton for the violence, his words in the January 30 meeting suggest otherwise. Vice President Cheney clearly held that view, later saying, "Bill Clinton had made that mistake at the end of his second term with a high-profile, high-expectations, and high-stakes maneuver that brought Arafat and Israeli Prime Minister Ehud Barak to Camp David for a series of talks that failed tragically and led to the renewed intifada."[14]

At the time, Ari Fleisher, the president's spokesman, made a similar statement from the White House podium: "Actually, I think if you go back to when the violence began, you can make the case that in an attempt to shoot the moon and get nothing, more violence resulted." He added that "as a result of an attempt to push the parties beyond where they were willing to go, that it led to expectations that were raised to such a high level that it turned into violence." Fleisher was forced to retract the statement given the firestorm it quickly produced, but he was clearly reflecting the assumptions that were prevalent at the White House.[15]

Fleisher's remark was triggered by questions posed by the press about the administration's passivity in the face of escalating violence, with terror attacks increasing against Israelis and the Israeli reprisals becoming much tougher. Fleisher's response was a defensive one, trying to suggest that overreaching had produced the violence in the first place. For his part, Powell was hoping to contain the violence and would treat the Mitchell Report, issued on April 30, 2001, as the basis for a policy.*

---

* Mitchell, along with former Senator Warren Rudman, were the cochairs of the Sharm El-Sheikh Fact-Finding Committee, which had been established at the Sharm summit in October 2000 to look into the causes of the intifada and what might be done to stop it and prevent a recurrence.

In fact, prior to the issuance of the report, Powell, according to one of his close aides, brought Mitchell into the office and said, "George, give me something to work with."[16] It is remarkable that Powell on his own was not in a position to shape a policy and needed Mitchell to provide something he could use. In this case, the Mitchell Report offered a set of recommendations, calling on the Palestinians to stop violence and terror and on the Israelis to halt settlement activity, including natural growth.

Drawing a moral equivalence between terror and settlement activity would have been unthinkable after 9/11, but prior to September, the Bush administration was not focused on terror as a central policy challenge. Powell hoped to use Mitchell and his report, alongside Bill Burns, his assistant secretary for the Bureau of Near Eastern Affairs, and CIA director George Tenet, to see if we could work out a security plan. Arafat resisted taking any actions, demanding that security steps be linked to political discussions. And Sharon was insisting that no negotiations could begin until there first had been "seven days of calm."[17]

As the stalemate continued, the violence escalated. Appeals from Arab leaders—including King Abdullah of Jordan, who had ascended the throne on his father's death in February 1999, in an April visit to the White House—would not motivate Bush to become involved. They did lead him, however, to accept Powell's efforts to try to stop the spiraling violence. When Israel, for the first time since the intifada began, sent the IDF back into the A areas in Gaza—the areas where the Palestinians had putative control—Powell publicly criticized Israel. He demanded that the Israeli forces withdraw, and Sharon pulled them back. Powell then called for unconditional cease-fires, but to no avail. He did, however, persuade the president to have George Tenet go to the area, following the June 1, 2001, bombing of the Dolphinarium nightclub in Tel Aviv. And Tenet—who had developed a relationship with the Israeli and Palestinian security services during the Clinton administration—spent a week forging a security plan that called for a sequence of mutual steps by the Palestinians and Israelis.[18] Once again, it was not implemented. Powell was trying, but he had to operate within the frame of not appearing to replicate the Clinton efforts on peace.

When Sharon came to the White House in March, Bush told the press afterward, "I assured the prime minister my administration . . . will not try to force peace." Then, at a dinner in May that the White House gave for Israeli president Moshe Katsav, Bush told one of the Jewish leaders at the event that "the Saudis thought 'this Texas oil guy was going to go against Israel,' and I told them you have the wrong guy."[19]

Powell would make another effort to quiet the violence, and even go to the area in June—but with little White House backing. The basic approach at this point was avoidance: this would ensure that Bush did not look like Clinton, even as it allowed him to avoid political problems with Israel. Before 9/11, Bush was probably driven as much by political considerations in his relationship with Israel as anything else. Bush had lost the popular vote and become president because the Supreme Court brought a Florida recount to a stop. His father had won only 11 percent of the Jewish vote,[20] and he was not going to repeat the political mistakes his father had made with the Jewish community—a point I would hear from my friends in the administration with whom I had served in the Bush 41 presidency.

To be sure, as Itamar Rabinovich notes, unlike his father, George W. Bush was tied to the right wing of the Republican Party and its Christian evangelical base—both of which were strongly pro-Israel.[21] In light of Karl Rove's strategy of cementing their political base, Bush would have strong reasons to show his public support for Israel and ensure that the tone of the relationship was far different from his father's.

Initially, the approach was different. However, Saudi concerns soon began to intrude on policy—and might well have altered the approach to Israel had it not been for 9/11. The Saudis complained about the policy of acquiescing in Israeli actions against the Palestinians—with Crown Prince Abdullah, the de facto leader of the kingdom, unwilling to visit Washington and the Saudis canceling a high-level defense-planning meeting at the last minute. At this point, the president and his advisers became concerned enough about the relationship to have his father call the crown prince. The call in July came after a difficult meeting between Powell and Abdullah in Paris, during which the crown prince showed Powell photos of the consequences of Israeli military actions against the Palestinians. He insisted that the United States do something to stop the suffering being inflicted by the Israelis with U.S. weapons.[22]

With the president sitting next to his father as he made the call, George H. W. Bush, who had enormous credibility with Abdullah because of the First Gulf War, told the crown prince that his son's "heart is in the right place," and that he is "going to do the right thing." The White House revealed details of the call, with a senior official saying that its purpose was to let Abdullah know that the president had "a grasp of the Middle East similar to that of his father."[23]

But the call did not do the trick. The realities on the ground did not improve; terror attacks and bombings did not stop in Israel, and Israeli closures and reprisals continued. Saudi unhappiness soon expressed itself in the form of an implied threat. In August, the crown prince wrote a letter to President Bush explaining that unless the United States got serious about pursuing peace, Saudi Arabia would reevaluate its relationship with the United States.[24]

In response, the Bush administration decided to break new ground on the Israeli-Palestinian conflict. The president sent a letter to Abdullah in which he emphasized the American commitment to a peace settlement and went on to say, "I firmly believe the Palestinian people have a right to self-determination and to live peacefully and securely in their own state."[25] Here was an administration whose approach to peace was "anything but Clinton." Its policy was one of avoidance because it saw the issue as a "loser." It would allow steps to deal only with the security situation, not political issues; it was not going "to force peace." And yet now it was adopting, in response to a perceived threat from the Saudis, a posture that no previous American president had held: self-determination and statehood for the Palestinians.

Statehood might not have seemed to be much of a leap. Recall that the Clinton Parameters—though a bridging proposal and not formally U.S. policy—would have provided for statehood.[26] Still, in adopting statehood as our explicit policy, the president was crossing a threshold. But even that paled in comparison with his readiness to embrace the Palestinian right to self-determination—a readiness stated directly and with no qualifications. How was self-determination to be defined or fulfilled? How could it be made to fit with Israeli rights and Jordanian rights? There was a reason that no previous administration had adopted such a position—after all, an unqualified right of self-determination for Palestinians might well deny Israeli and Jordanian rights of self-determination and undermine their very existence.

With little or no consideration of the consequences, the administration and the president were making an enormous leap. Moreover, President Bush was asking nothing from the Saudis in return. He was not saying that the United States was prepared to support Palestinian statehood *provided* Saudi Arabia make a comparable commitment about its readiness to recognize Israel and accept its right to exist; or provided the Saudis would condemn acts of terror against Israel and press Arafat to act to fulfill his obligations on security.

It is hard to escape the conclusion that, fearing a rupture with the Saudis, the administration panicked. These fears about "losing" the Saudis go back to William Eddy's warnings to President Roosevelt—and they have certainly been embedded in the psychology of much of the national security establishment since the creation of the State of Israel. For reasons of oil, security, and even financing the needs of other key American friends, the Saudi relationship has been central to our regional posture. More generally, the Saudis have been the balancer in the oil market—the swing producer. The historic bargain that characterized the relationship between the two countries was that the United States would provide for Saudi security and the Saudis would ensure a stable supply of oil.

The perceived consequences for U.S. access to oil and our position in the region produced, at the first sign of trouble, the phone call from the president's father. Then the Abdullah letter triggered a policy leap that seemed to defy all the prior assumptions of the administration. Those who might have questioned such a response to the Saudis were not informed of the president's major shift. In fact, those in the vice president's office who raised questions after the fact—Scooter Libby, Eric Edelman, and John Hannah—learned of the president's letter only after it had been sent. Condoleezza Rice had joined with Secretary Powell to handle the incoming letter and its response strictly as an NSC–State Department exercise. Not surprisingly, this later provoked a strong protest and deepened the sense, in the words of Eric Edelman, of "the bureaucratic tribalism" affecting policy at the time.[27]

What is striking is that none of those in the State Department and the NSC who assessed the implied ultimatum from the crown prince seemed to ask what the Saudi threat of reevaluating its policy toward us meant practically. Would it really lead to a change in Saudi oil production policy? Was that not driven by Saudi needs for a stable oil market? Would it really mean that the Saudis would depend on someone else for their security? Who could be an alternative to the United States, particularly at a time when America was the world's only global power? Was this a credible threat?

Those questions were not asked. Instead, the administration broke new ground, and with the president's private promises, Abdullah dropped his threat. It was as if Abdullah wanted to see if he could privately move us, and seeing that he could, he was satisfied.

In August, following the crown prince's letter, the administration became more openly critical of Israel on its policy of targeted killings of Palestinians. It did so in a context in which Israel suffered fifteen terror attacks during that month after suffering twelve in July. Despite the attacks, on August 27, in response to the Israeli killing of Mustafa Zubari, the leader of a radical Palestinian faction, State Department spokesman Richard Boucher said, "Israel needs to understand that targeted killings of Palestinians don't end the violence but are only inflaming an already volatile situation and making it much harder to restore calm." While Boucher repeated the administration's refrain that the Palestinian Authority needed to take "sustained and credible steps" against those carrying out terror acts, he also specifically called on the Israelis to alter their approach to the Palestinians more generally: "If the situation on the ground is to improve, then Israel must also take the economic and security steps that are necessary to alleviate the pressure, the hardship and the humiliations of the Palestinian population."[28]

Three days prior to this statement, President Bush had called on the Israelis to show "restraint." But he had also said that "the Israelis will not negotiate under terrorist threat. It's as simple as that." Was Boucher's much harsher comment on the Israelis another example of the split between the State Department and the White House? Perhaps, but one official said that the word "humiliations" in Boucher's statement had come from the White House to describe the effect of Israeli actions on the Palestinians.[29]

9/11, Initial Israeli Fears, and the Transformation of Policy

The attacks of September 11, 2001, transformed the Bush presidency. An administration that had no clear identity in foreign and national security policy prior to 9/11 now had one. A president who lacked a clear footing in the first eight months of his administration found his mission, his confidence, and his voice. He would combat the evil of terrorism as the primary threat to the United States and its values. There was no alternative to fighting this war that had been imposed on us, and there could be no compromise with the terrorists or those who supported them. Bush's blunt, no-nonsense style of speaking fit the moment. This was not a time for nuance.

His approach was embodied in what he later described as the Bush Doctrine: "First, make no distinction between the terrorists and the nations that harbor them—and hold both to account. Second, take the fight to the enemy overseas before they can attack us again here at home. Third, confront threats before they fully materialize. And, fourth, advance liberty and hope as an alternative to the enemy's ideology of repression and fear."[30]

Understandably, in the initial period after 9/11, the president was riveted on who was responsible for the attack, whether there could be more attacks coming, and what our reaction needed to be. The Arab-Israeli issue and the intifada and Israel's strategy for dealing with it did not rank high on his list of concerns. But the State Department and parts of the intelligence community fell back on historic assumptions that always seemed to be lurking in parts of the national security establishment. For them, this terrible attack needed to be understood in the context of the deep antipathy that Muslims felt toward the United States, an anger that stemmed from our support for Israel. If we were not so supportive of Israel, we would not be the victim of such hatred and the terrorism that resulted from it—or so their thinking went.

It mattered little that Osama bin Laden's desire to attack the United States was not driven by Israel. He was far more motivated by his desire to remove "iniquitous" Arab regimes that we backed—the Saudis, the Egyptians, the Jordanians—which he felt survived only because of the United States.[31] But the consensus in the State Department at this time, as Elliott Abrams points out, reflected the traditional view that we paid a price for our association with Israel—and for that reason we needed to push Israeli-Palestinian peace.*[32] Reflecting this mind-set, Secretary of State Powell told the president shortly after 9/11 that "we need a serious Arab-Israeli peace initiative."[33]

Daniel Kurtzer, who was the U.S. ambassador to Israel, suggests that this instinct existed in the administration as a whole, not just the State Department. It was fed by the assumption that "to garner as much regional support as possible for its counter-terrorism efforts," the United States must show it was addressing the Palestinian conflict.[34] Powell made the case for a peace initiative by telling Bush that the Europeans were also pressing us to engage in the "peace process." In effect, the argument he was making was that the Europeans (and the Arabs) would be more responsive to our entreaties to join us in fighting terror if we were seen as responsive to them on promoting Middle East peace.

Abrams says the president was not impressed by Powell's argument, saying, "You know when I hear the Europeans talk about Israel, they just sound anti-Semitic."[35] And yet notwithstanding Bush's instinct, in his first phone call to Prime Minster Ariel Sharon after 9/11, he asked Sharon to have Foreign Minister Peres meet Arafat, even as Palestinian bombings and terror attacks were continuing in Israel. Later Steve Hadley, the deputy national security adviser, would explain that pressing Sharon in such a manner was important to Secretary Powell.[36]

In their phone conversation, Sharon, while expressing great sympathy for the United States, did not agree to the meeting. When Kurtzer met with Sharon afterward and pressed him to act on the president's request, "Sharon

---

* Elliott Abrams was a senior director in the NSC at this time. He would become the lead official in Middle East issues and would later be appointed a deputy national security adviser.

demurred, saying he feared the United States would then ask Israel to do more."[37] He would ultimately reconsider, allowing Peres to hold the meeting on September 26. And in another sign of taking American concerns into account, Sharon gave a speech three days before the Peres-Arafat meeting in which he expressed acceptance of a Palestinian state for the first time. But terror attacks continued in the days after his speech and the Peres-Arafat meeting.

In light of this pressure from the United States, it's easy to understand why Sharon on October 4 inveighed against the Western world engaging in a 1930s-type policy of appeasement in which Israel would be asked to pay the price for winning over the Arabs. Declaring that "Israel will not be Czechoslovakia," Sharon made clear that "we can rely only on ourselves." He went on to "call on the Western democracies, and primarily the leader of the Free World—the United States: Do not repeat the dreadful mistake of 1938, when enlightened European democracies decided to sacrifice Czecho-slovakia for a 'convenient temporary solution.' Do not try to appease the Arabs at our expense—this is unacceptable to us."[38]

Needless to say, equating George W. Bush with Neville Chamberlain—particularly after 9/11 and before we had yet held anyone to account for the attacks—was bound to trigger unhappiness in Washington. Ari Fleischer, the White House spokesman, responded: "The President believes that these remarks are unacceptable. Israel can have no better or stronger friend than the United States and [no] better friend than President Bush."[39] Still, as Abrams notes, there was a salutary result from Sharon's speech and the White House's reaction—now there would be much more frequent contacts between American and Israeli officials, specifically between Condoleezza Rice and two people close to Sharon, Danny Ayalon and Arie Genger.*[40] Effectively, the White House was creating for the first time in the Bush presidency a direct channel with the prime minister's office. In fact, Condoleezza Rice, the national security adviser, not Colin Powell and the State Department, now became the keeper of the Israeli relationship. She would use the channel regularly to avoid public misunderstandings and to keep Sharon in the loop of what we would be doing.[41]

For example, Rice let Ayalon know beforehand that the president, while principally addressing the scourge of terrorism in his speech to the UN

---

* Danny Ayalon served in the prime minister's office and would subsequently be appointed the Israeli ambassador to the United States. Genger, an American citizen who was born in Israel, had been a friend of Sharon's for several decades.

General Assembly on November 10, would also call for two states: Israel and Palestine. Rice also told him: "Don't lobby the Hill. It's not going to work."[42]

In the wake of Sharon's provocative speech and new efforts by the Bush administration to reach out to Israel, there was a series of terror attacks, and an Israeli minister, Rehavam Ze'evi, was assassinated by Palestinian gunmen at his hotel in East Jerusalem. The Israeli responses included arrests as well as targeted killings, and this time there was no U.S. criticism.

This silence, however, did not mean there was a consensus within the administration—not on how to conceive of the Israelis in relation to the war on terror, and not on our approach to dealing with the Palestinian conflict. There were those who remained convinced that we could not elicit support to fight terror in the region and internationally unless we defused the conflict between the Israelis and Palestinians. For them, this conflict remained a centerpiece around which terrorists could be recruited globally and hostility toward the United States mobilized, particularly among Muslims. The secretary of state certainly held this view. Powell, the hero of the Gulf War and the one person of real stature in the cabinet, was focused on the Israeli-Palestinian conflict, and his view mattered to the president. Not only was President Bush prepared to call for two states in his November 10 speech to the United Nations, he also would approve of Powell making a speech nine days later in which he would offer a fuller explanation of our support for two states and the steps both Israelis and Palestinians would need to take.

Others in the White House, and especially in the vice president's office, saw the war on terror differently. This was a battle of ideas, a struggle within Islam itself between extremists determined to fight all nonbelievers, including other Muslims, and anyone who stood for greater moderation and coexistence with other faiths. This was not about Israel and the Palestinians; this was about fighting the radical Islamists on their own terms—destroying them and their bases militarily—and getting governments in the Middle East and elsewhere to stop radical imams from preaching hate and justifying the use of violence.

Clearly, there was not a common vision in the administration about how to approach the Middle East. Eric Edelman recalls that Powell wanted the president to deliver the speech that he gave—and this was rejected in the White House. In addition, as Edelman observed, there was considerable debate over the content of the secretary's speech before it was finalized for delivery. Even before Bush called for two states in his UN speech, there was resistance from Cheney's office. Scooter Libby, Eric Edelman, and John Hannah all raised questions about the value of declaring support for Palestinian statehood in the midst of an intifada and without getting anything for it.[43] For the president, however, having privately conveyed our support for Palestinian statehood to Crown Prince Abdullah in his August letter, there was no reason to hold back on saying this publicly. Moreover, he probably agreed with Powell's argument that pronouncing our support for Palestinian statehood would gain us some benefits with the Arabs.

If this was the expectation, he would be disappointed. Rice, too, having favored the President's call for Palestinian statehood, later observed that Bush's declaration elicited little from the Arabs: "This initial failure to credit the president's stance was an important lesson too: whatever you do for peace in the Middle East, it is never enough for the Arab parties."[44]

Still, Powell, in his speech, offered a fuller explanation of our support for two states and called on Palestinians to stop terror and on Israelis to be willing to "end its occupation." But the real focus of the speech was on halting the violence between Palestinians and Israelis. To that end, he announced the appointment of retired Marine Corps general Anthony Zinni—not as a peace envoy but as his senior adviser on the Middle East, charged with "helping the parties achieve a durable cease-fire and to move along the lines of the Tenet security work plan and the Mitchell Report."[45] Arafat, however, was not willing to play ball, and Zinni's presence, rather than leading to a de-escalation of the intifada, was accompanied by a surge of suicide bombings in Israel.*[46]

While the cumulative effect of the bombings on Bush was significant, there was one event that decisively changed his attitude about Yasser Arafat. On January 3, 2002, the Israelis intercepted the *Karine A*, a ship that was smuggling large quantities of Iranian arms and explosives to the Palestinians. The ship's captain admitted Arafat knew all about the vessel's mission. Although Arafat denied that he had anything to do with the arms, Bush later wrote: "We and the Israelis had evidence that disproved the Palestinian leader's claim. Arafat had lied to me. I never trusted him again. In fact, I never spoke to him again. By the spring of 2002, I had concluded that peace would not be possible with Arafat in power."[47]

This, however, was January, and Bush's decision to call for a new leadership for the Palestinians would not take place until his speech on June 24. The turn away from Arafat was not immediate and it was resisted by the State Department and Colin Powell and even Condoleezza Rice, at least

* With high casualties on November 29 and December 1, 2, 9, and 12, 2001.

initially. At this stage, even Vice President Cheney, who was more skeptical than Powell or Rice about Arafat, was willing to deal with him directly.

The vice president visited the Middle East from March 12 to 19, ostensibly to talk to the Arabs about Iraq. Cheney's staff did not plan for a meeting with Arafat. But Bill Burns, the assistant secretary of state traveling with him, and General Zinni both argued that the vice president needed to see him. Although John Hannah and Scooter Libby strongly advised against meeting Arafat under any circumstances, Cheney felt he should go along with Burns and Zinni's requests.[48]

Two points are worth noting here. First, more than two months after the *Karine A*, the vice president agreed to see Arafat, even though March was a month of nearly nonstop suicide bombings in Israel, with attacks occurring even during Cheney's trip in the area. To be sure, the vice president had been subjected to pressure from Arab leaders to see Arafat and to urge the Israelis to allow Arafat to travel to the planned Arab summit in Beirut on March 28, where Saudi Crown Prince Abdullah's peace initiative was going to be presented and adopted.[49] Second, the vice president was willing to see Arafat not only at the end of the trip in Cairo, but also, if it was going to take Arafat several more days to accept a proposed cease-fire in writing, he was prepared to return to the region a week later. In the end, Arafat rejected the proposal and the vice president did not return to the area. His readiness to do so, however, demonstrates vividly that the *Karine A* may have been a psychological turning point for President Bush but not a practical one in terms of dealing with Arafat and the Israelis on the intifada.

Two Speeches: The Low and High Points in the Relationship

The suicide bombing at a Passover seder at the Park Hotel in Netanya was the last straw for Sharon. Earlier in March, in the face of nearly continuous attacks, Sharon had dropped his insistence that there be seven days of calm before direct talks with the Palestinians could resume. But enough was enough. Sharon now prepared to launch a military campaign—Operation Defensive Shield—to clean out the infrastructure of terror in the West Bank.[50] Sharon sent the IDF back into the cities—the A areas of the West Bank. He would also surround the Muqata, Arafat's Ramallah headquarters, and effectively tighten the noose around the chairman. The Palestinians accused the Israelis of carrying out a massacre in the old city of Jenin with claims of five hundred dead, which turned out to be wildly exaggerated.[51] Nonetheless, the image of the IDF moving through the cities and refugee camps of the West Bank was terrible.

Condoleezza Rice describes "a full-blown Middle East crisis and a deepening split with Israel, . . . and the Arab world was roiling. We were under enormous pressure to rein in the Israelis."[52] She also portrays the split between Cheney and Rumsfeld on one side and Powell on the other. Vice President Cheney and Secretary of Defense Rumsfeld believed "the Israelis had a right to crush the terrorists who were attacking them. The President shared this view but acknowledged Colin's point that the inevitable carnage among innocent Palestinians was also a serious problem and that the credibility of the United States was deteriorating."[53]

Bush decided to give a speech on April 4, and as if reflecting the conflicting attitudes in the administration, the speech had different parts to it. He spoke of the terrible and serious challenge Israel was facing as it rooted out terrorist nests; he recognized Israel's right to defend itself; he declared that Arafat had not consistently opposed or confronted terrorists as he was obligated to do. Yet he also called on Israel to stop the incursions into Palestinian cities and to pull back from those it had recently reoccupied. He emphasized again his support for two states and urged Israel to stop settlement activity. Finally, he announced that he was sending the secretary of state to the region.

In a meeting prior to giving the speech, Bush told his principal advisers, "You know I've got to do something and I think Colin has to go over and try to break this open."[54] Rumsfeld thought the trip was a mistake, and during the course of the trip, the president and the vice president would veto moves that Powell sought to make.[55] At one point, Powell even hinted to Arafat that he did not have full support from within the administration to meet with him, and if the chairman did not stop the attacks, he would be the last American official to see him. This may have been a tactic, but the opposition Powell faced was real. The secretary wanted to be able to announce that a peace conference would be convened, and he let the press know that a conference might help to defuse the conflict.

The vice president was dead set against this strategy. As Cheney later wrote, "At a press briefing in Israel, Secretary Powell decided to float the idea of an international conference on the Israeli-Palestinian issue. The president had not agreed to this, and it was a bad idea. Giving Arafat a place on the world stage would only legitimize him at a moment he was making it clear that he had chosen the path of terror."[56] In this instance, Cheney and President Bush were on the same page.

Powell sent the White House a draft paper he wanted to get Sharon and Arafat to accept that involved steps to stop the violence and provide for the subsequent convening of a peace conference. Rice describes trying to convince Bush to accept Powell's proposal. The president was "adamant" in his opposition, and she "called Colin, who was still in the region, to tell him that the draft statement he'd sent to Washington was dead on arrival."[57] Powell felt he was being set up to fail after being asked to travel to the region. Cheney explains that this marked a turning point in the relationship between the White House and the Powell State Department: "Looking back, I believe that Secretary Powell's trip to the Middle East in the spring of 2002 was a watershed moment in relations between the State Department and the White House. Both Powell and his deputy, Richard Armitage, seemed to take the fact that the White House had been compelled to walk back Powell's announcement of a Middle East conference as a personal affront to the secretary."[58]

Despite these tensions in the administration, the White House was putting very real pressure on Sharon and facing resistance from him. The president on April 4 had called for Israel to stop its offensive in Palestinian cities and pull out. But the Israelis continued their operations into the West Bank. On April 8, Bush said publicly, "I meant what I said to the Prime Minister of Israel. I expect there to be withdrawal without delay."[59] Rice followed up on the president's message with a call, saying, "now means now," and she repeated this publicly.[60] Still, Sharon did not stop. There was an air of crisis in the relationship between the United States and Israel.

By the time Powell returned to Washington, Sharon had withdrawn from some areas, but the noose around Arafat in Ramallah remained tight. The secretary reported on his trip to the president at a meeting in the White House on April 18. During the meeting, he and Cheney argued about where our focus should be in the region. The vice president told Powell, "Don't get completely consumed with Arab-Israeli issues." The secretary replied, "You're dreaming if you don't think the Arab-Israeli conflict is central to the region—central to whatever we want to do in Iraq. Don't underestimate the centrality of this crisis."[61]

Here was a debate on what mattered in the region and what would affect the war on terror and our position in the Middle East. Powell embodied the belief that seemed to have animated the approach of every administration since Truman's at one time or another. Cheney, on the other hand, was not arguing that the conflict was meaningless, just that our ability to affect it was limited and we could not allow it to prevent us from dealing with our other needs in the region. Powell, like so many of his predecessors, was saying it was impossible to deal with those other needs without addressing this one.

And where was the president? When Bush and Powell met with the press after Powell's briefing on his trip, he surprised both his secretary of state and national security adviser by saying that "Israel started withdrawing quickly after our call from smaller cities on the West Bank. History will show that they've responded." And he added—much to Powell and Rice's chagrin—"I do believe Ariel Sharon is a man of peace."[62] Powell asked Rice afterward, "Do you have any idea how this plays on Arab TV? The Israelis are just thumbing their noses at the president. Why is he giving Sharon a pass?" As Rice notes, "The State Department went into overdrive trying to explain what the President had 'meant to say.'"[63] Rice, too, at the time thought the President had "done long-term damage to our relations" with the Arabs, particularly with the Israelis "continuing to lay waste to the West Bank and Gaza."[64]

Steve Hadley later said that the president had a "gut feeling" for leaders and how you invest in them so they will respond to you. Sharon, in Hadley's words, would know that he had to live up to what Bush was saying.[65] But it was not just this. Here was a sign that Bush really had given up on Arafat— maybe not on the Palestinians but on Arafat. Here was also a sign that in the debate between Cheney and Powell, he was tilting toward Cheney.

Bush faced an early test of the Cheney theory at a meeting with Crown Prince Abdullah the following week at the president's ranch in Crawford, Texas. At one point the crown prince was ready to leave in frustration, since apparently he had expected Bush to force Sharon to withdraw Israeli forces from Ramallah prior to his arrival at the ranch—and if that failed, the president would call the Israeli prime minister on the spot and press him to act. When he did not—and the two delegations took a break—Gamal Helal, who served as the interpreter and adviser in the meetings, reported to the president that the Saudis were simply going to leave, cutting the meeting short. Bush asked Rice whether it mattered if they left. She replied, "It would be a disaster."[66]

Bush asked to see the crown prince alone. With only Helal present to interpret, they talked and then took a drive around the ranch. Bush speaks of seeing a wild turkey and Abdullah taking it as a good omen—and the mood changed. Bush would say that the visit ended well, attesting that "for the rest of my presidency, my relationship with the crown prince—soon to be king—was extremely close."[67]

But it wasn't only the turkey that improved the mood. Abdullah explained to Bush that the image of Arafat, an Arab leader, surrounded by Israeli forces and under siege while he was seeing the president of the United States was intolerable for him. In response, Bush promised that, though it might take some time, he would work to end the siege of Arafat.[68] In fact, Condoleezza Rice called Danny Ayalon while Abdullah was still at the ranch, and two days later she told Ayalon that "the President [has] instructed me to say that there had better be some movement within twenty-four hours or he [will] publicly criticize Israel and the prime minister in the harshest terms."[69] There would be some movement on April 28, and by May 2, the Israelis would withdraw from around the Muqata.

The episode is revealing. In a sense, Cheney was right: we did not need to subordinate our policy needs in the Middle East to resolving the Arab-Israeli conflict. But it would be a mistake to think that the Saudis or others would not be affected by the potential for embarrassment on the Palestinian issue if we appeared indifferent to it. It is noteworthy that ultimately the president's word that he would get the Israelis to end the siege was critical to Abdullah. Ironically, our ties to the Israelis were and are a source of potential embarrassment for the Saudis but also an attraction because only the United States is seen as capable of affecting Israeli behavior.

Even if belatedly, Bush did affect Israel in this instance. Moreover, the sense of crisis that had been triggered by Operation Defensive Shield produced a consensus in the administration that something needed to be done after the Israelis pulled back from the West Bank cities. As Rice recounts, Powell and the State Department again proposed a peace conference and the president again said no. Nevertheless, the president also felt that "we needed a game-changer."[70]

Bush had already come out in favor of statehood, but this appeared to be essentially a political decision driven in no small part by his August 2001 promise to the Saudis. By the spring of 2002, it became much more of an emotionally driven belief, reflecting Bush's emerging commitment to the freedom agenda—a commitment that would not be fully articulated until closer to the decision to launch the war in Iraq in 2003. Already at this point, Bush was becoming convinced that the Palestinians needed a state of their own:

> With no state, Palestinians lacked their rightful place in the world. With no voice in their future, Palestinians were ripe for recruiting by extremists. And with no legitimately elected Palestinian leader committed to

fighting terror, the Israelis had no reliable partner for peace. I believed
the solution was a democratic Palestinian state, led by elected officials
who would answer to their people, reject terror, and pursue peace with
Israel.[71]

Bush decided on his game changer: he would give a speech that laid out
the content of the state the Palestinians needed and call not just for reform
but also a new leadership. His idea sparked, as he put it, controversy within
his administration. Cheney and Rumsfeld were against the speech because
they felt that calling for the state in the midst of the intifada would look like
we were "rewarding terrorism." Powell was against it because calling for a
new leadership would "embarrass Arafat and reduce the chance for a negotiated settlement."[72]

Rice describes the drafting of the speech and its clearance process as an
"interagency nightmare," with the speech going through thirty drafts.[73]
Robert Danin calls it really two speeches in one, reflecting the fundamentally different views of the White House and the State Department.[74] Those
differences revolved around Arafat and whether the president should actually call for a new leader, something the State Department strongly resisted
until the end. Ultimately, the speech reflected what the president wanted to
say—and, as Steve Hadley recalls, Bush went over it carefully, approving
each amendment.[75] At one point before delivering the speech, the president
remarked, "Wouldn't it be amazing if democracy in the Middle East sprung
first from the rocky soil of the West Bank?"[76]

Bush's speech on June 24 made a detailed call for Palestinian reform and
institution building and offered full-throated U.S. support for the creation
of a state if "Palestinians embrace democracy, confront corruption and
firmly reject terror."[77] Not surprisingly, however, it was not his insistence on
Palestinian reform and statehood that produced the headlines but his demand that Arafat must go. Even with Arafat's rejection of the Clinton Parameters and his continuing responsibility for terror, he was the acknowledged
leader of the Palestinians. As Bush later wrote, "While I considered Arafat a
failed leader, many in the foreign policy world accepted the view that Arafat
represented the best hope for peace."[78]

Condoleezza Rice recalled that "the Arabists in the State Department
were appalled too. One [U.S.] diplomat who was serving in the Middle East
told a reporter at a cocktail party that he could no longer do his job thanks
to 'that speech.'"[79] He was not alone. In Rice's words, there were "howls
of traditionalists at the time" in response to the president's speech.[80] He was

breaking the mold and no longer saying that a Palestinian state could come into being if it was led by a terrorist and rooted in corruption. Bush was not going to create one standard for us in the war on terror and another for the Israelis. He might genuinely believe a Palestinian state was needed and should be supported by the United States, but it could not emerge from a terror campaign.

In Sharon's eyes, there was now a complete meeting of the minds with the president. Interestingly, when the Saudi, Jordanian, and Egyptian foreign ministers came to see Bush in July, they were not resisting his calls for change in the Palestinian leadership—once again reflecting that the "Arabists" had misread their "clients." Instead, Marwan Muasher, the Jordanian foreign minister, asked the president how he was going to act on the vision he had laid out. Muasher suggested a "roadmap" to turn the words of his speech into reality. Initially, the president did not accept the Muasher proposal. But ten days later, when Muasher joined King Abdullah in a meeting at the White House, President Bush accepted his argument and suggested that Muasher work with Bill Burns of the State Department on developing it. The Roadmap to Peace emerged from this meeting.

The Roadmap to Peace, the Iraq War, and Two Summits

Steve Hadley described the Roadmap as the "State Department's baby." Doug Feith, who was the under secretary of defense for policy, said the Roadmap was the State Department's effort to retake the policy initiative on the peace issue and undo the president's speech: "I remember having people at the State Department say to me, the purpose of the Roadmap is to win back in operation what was lost at the strategic level in the fight over the June 24 speech."[81]

To be sure, Bill Burns, who had negotiated the Roadmap along with his deputy David Satterfield, viewed it differently. He saw an opportunity to take the president's words and do something with them—and gain European and Arab support in the process.[82] But we would not involve the Israelis in drafting the Roadmap. In fact, the Israelis would be presented the draft only when Sharon came to see the president in October 2002. Notwithstanding the Ford-Rabin letter of 1975 pledging that the United States would present no initiative on peace without first discussing it with Israel, the Israelis were surprised with a paper that had been negotiated without their input.

For an administration that had been so close to Israel, this may seem unusual. But the Roadmap grew out of the president's speech, Sharon was very happy with the administration's approach, and the real focus of the White House at this point was Iraq.

Recall that in the fall of 2002, the president and the vice president were preoccupied with preparing the ground for war with Iraq. Starting in September, they launched a full-court press to pass congressional resolutions authorizing the use of force, and with 9/11 still casting a large shadow psychologically and politically, they succeeded in getting the necessary support on the Hill. Reversing the pattern of his father, who galvanized UN and international support for the Gulf War before going to the Congress, Bush focused on the domestic base before turning to the UN. Colin Powell took the lead on the international stage, and by November he produced UN Security Council Resolution 1441. Unlike UNSC Resolution 678 at the time of the Gulf War, UNSC 1441 would be interpreted differently by the United States and the French and the Russians.[83]

The international divisions also played a big part in the development of the Roadmap. British prime minister Tony Blair faced opposition domestically over a perceived rush to war in Iraq, and he was largely alone in Europe. His hawkish approach could be bolstered if he could show that although he supported Bush, he was also able to influence him on the issue that mattered far more in Europe: Israeli-Palestinian peace. In his memoirs, Blair describes himself as sounding like a broken record with President Bush, emphasizing the importance of addressing the Israeli-Palestinian peace process: "To me this was the indispensable soft-power component to give equilibrium to the hard power that was necessary if Saddam were to be removed."[84] As one senior official admitted at the time, there was deep concern about Blair's public standing and a belief that the Roadmap would provide him evidence that the Palestinian issue was going to be dealt with.[85] John Hannah, Cheney's aide, said President Bush looked at the Roadmap as an "alliance management tool in the context of Iraq," while the State Department saw it as "diplomacy on the Palestinians being back in the game."[86]

Still, the Israelis were surprised when presented with the Roadmap draft during Sharon's visit to Washington in October. Sharon asked for time to consider it. He chose not to fight the initiative and instead decided to interpret it as affirmation of what he felt was always necessary: nothing could happen on negotiations until the Palestinians carried out all their security responsibilities. When Sharon's coalition with the Labor Party fell apart in November, he asked the United States to wait to formally present the Roadmap until after the Israeli vote. When it was released months later, the Israeli government accepted it—with fourteen reservations.[87]

For Powell, there was now a mechanism for pursuing Israeli-Palestinian peace with the State Department in the lead—and the secretary, in an NSC meeting on December 18, 2002, told the president that the Roadmap was a "pretty good product." Elliott Abrams, who had just become the lead official in Middle East issues at the NSC, attended the meeting, and he later wrote that the president and the secretary "were not on the same wavelength."[88] Bush worried that the security dimension was being watered down and made it clear that we could not appear to be rushing forward regardless of whether terror attacks had stopped and security reform had actually been adopted. For him, as long as Arafat remained in power, it was hard to see anything changing. Powell seemed to think that the mechanism of the Roadmap could operate even if Arafat were still there—or so Abrams concluded.

At this time, when speaking to Arab and European visitors who raised doubts about Sharon, Bush would reply that he believed Sharon would do the right thing, and that if he did not he would be voted out in Israel. For George W. Bush, democracy was self-correcting. If democracy took root among the Palestinians, this process would work there as well. The president's faith in democracy would guide him later after Arafat's death in November 2004 and led to the administration's insistence that legislative elections be held in 2006, which would produce a Hamas victory.

In the meantime, Bush wanted to work around Arafat, and this affected the formal adoption of the Roadmap. We would, together with the other members of the Quartet—Russia, the EU, and the UN—hold back its release as a form of leverage on Arafat to appoint a prime minister. The idea was that Arafat would become more of a figurehead and his prime minister would control the real levers of power. Arafat resisted making the appointment. But under pressure, particularly from Arab leaders and the Europeans who continued to deal with him, he acquiesced and appointed Mahmoud Abbas (Abu Mazen). The appointment was real, but Abbas's power was not.

In June 2003, Bush went to the region with the aim largely of bolstering Abbas's position. At the time, he looked triumphant. We had defeated the Iraqi army in three weeks, Saddam Hussein was in hiding, the insurgency had yet to emerge—and the president had given his "mission accomplished" speech. American hard power seemingly had been used to begin the transformation of the Middle East by implanting democracy. Condoleezza Rice, in April, had begun quietly to think about something big to follow the war. Robert Danin, who had just begun working at the NSC, recalls that Rice convened a small group in her office and told them that we have "broken the Middle East and now we have to show we can put it together again." Her next step was to push Israeli-Palestinian peace.[89]

This is what produced the idea of two summits: first one in Sharm el-Sheikh and then one in Aqaba. The first would be hosted by President Mubarak of Egypt and attended by Crown Prince Abdullah of Saudi Arabia, King Abdullah of Jordan, King Hamad of Bahrain, Prime Minister Abbas, and President Bush. The purpose was to create an Arab embrace of Abbas and boost his standing while also winning the endorsement of the Roadmap. The summit in Aqaba, also on the Red Sea, was hosted by the Jordanian King, and Prime Minister Sharon would attend with Abbas and President Bush. With American power at its perceived zenith, no one quibbled over the summit communiqués that we had drafted—a reminder that much like in the immediate aftermath of the Gulf War, the tendency of Arab leaders was to be responsive to what the United States asked in moments of its ascendancy.

In Aqaba, Bush met with both Sharon and Abu Mazen separately before bringing them together. Sharon was at pains to emphasize the sequence built into the Roadmap, making clear that Israel could not make concessions and then find it was still living under the threat of terror, and Bush was emphatic in response that the Roadmap meant Israel need not negotiate until the terror threat was removed. With the Roadmap calling for Palestinian statehood by 2005—and for the permanent status issues to be negotiated in phase three—Sharon raised the subject of the Palestinian refugees and why there must not be a "right of return" for them. Bush's instinctive reply was, "No shit—here come three million people!"[90]

While Bush was reassuring, even disarming with Sharon, he also urged him to act in a way that would strengthen Abbas. And with Abbas, according to Abrams's account of the meeting, he spoke movingly about the meaning of a democratic state of Palestine and how it could be a model for the Middle East. He promised to press Israel to be responsive on Palestinian needs and that it would be our policy to "make him and his new government steadily stronger."[91] The problem was that Abbas did not control the levers of power—Arafat did, and he was not going away. The Palestinian leader was keen to show that Abbas could do nothing unless he let him do it.

Adding to the difficulties in launching the Roadmap, immediately following the two summits, attacks in Israel quickly resumed. Hamas carried out an attack that killed four Israeli soldiers, and Israel retaliated by attempting to assassinate Abdel Aziz Rantisi, a Hamas leader. They failed this time, killing and wounding a number of noncombatants in the process.* Focused on trying to strengthen Abbas, Bush uncharacteristically criticized the Israeli action, making clear at this point that he was against such targeted killings: "I am troubled by the recent Israeli helicopter gunship attacks. I regret the loss of innocent life. I'm concerned that the attacks will make it more difficult for the Palestinian leadership to fight off terrorist attacks. I also don't believe the attacks help the Israeli security."[92]

Bolstering Abbas made sense, but it ignored the reality that he did not have the means to stop the attacks, even though he favored doing so. Rice saw the effort on the Roadmap quickly bog down, and portrayed it as a mutual problem: "I would learn valuable lessons about how frustrating it can be to get the Israelis to actually carry through on promises relating to the Palestinians." But, she added, the "Palestinians were frustrating too. Abbas meant well, but Yasser Arafat would soon grow jealous of the prime minister's new international stature. When the cautious Abbas tried to carry out reforms, he'd find resistance from Arafat's security chiefs and from the old guard of the ruling party, Fatah . . . Then, on September 6, 2003, Abbas abruptly resigned."[†][93]

Israeli Disengagement and the April 14, 2004, Letter

Sharon came from the founding generation of the State of Israel, and as such he was not afraid to take big moves that he thought could shake up the strategic landscape. He had done so—disastrously—in the Lebanon war during the Reagan administration. But now, in the late fall of 2003, with Abbas out, Arafat still in power, terror attacks continuing unabated, and the U.S. initiative on the Roadmap going nowhere, pressures were building in Israel to do something.[‡] So he began to consider moving the pieces on the chessboard as they related to Israel and the Palestinians. His solution was "disengagement." He laid out his initial ideas secretly to Elliott Abrams in Rome on November 18, 2003: he would pull out of Gaza unilaterally and not as part

---

* They succeeded ten months later, in April 2004.

† Abbas's public comments blamed the Israelis but at the same time implied criticism of Arafat. And, as he told me at the time, Arafat had threatened his life.

‡ For him, the Geneva Accords, which had been negotiated between former Israeli officials and quasi-official Palestinians, were a symptom. He didn't like their content, but what worried him more was that they were a harbinger of things to come so long as there was a vacuum.

of a negotiation with the Palestinians. Everything was stuck, and he would "unstick" it by leaving Palestinian territory.[94]

In its response, the administration was split. The State Department saw unilateralism as essentially an end run around the Roadmap. Steve Hadley notes that Secretary Powell was "really quite critical" of Sharon's move, but he acknowledges that even Condoleezza Rice was "a little uncertain."[95]

President Bush's reaction was immediate and positive: "If Sharon does it, I'll support him." When Hadley asked why he supported it, Bush responded, "It is a bold move. It is going to shake things up. It is going to shake up the status quo. It is going to force the Palestinians to respond."[96]

Not surprisingly, Sharon faced opposition from his own base over his decision to pull out of Gaza. As he and Dubi Weissglass, his longtime lawyer and closest adviser, explained to Rice, Hadley, and Abrams, he was not getting anything from the Palestinians, so he needed to show his public that he was getting something from the United States—particularly at a time when terror attacks were continuing in Israel. He wanted American support on key permanent status issues: the scope of withdrawal, recognition of the large settlement blocs in the West Bank, and an understanding that Palestinian refugees would not be returning to Israel. In the State Department, as Bill Burns observed, there was concern that in return for withdrawing from Gaza, the United States would now prejudge the outcome of key permanent status issues in Israel's favor. As Condoleezza Rice later wrote, we needed to get something in return from the Israelis if we were going to give them assurances; at a minimum, we needed to know that the Gaza withdrawal would be the beginning of the process and not its end—that withdrawal from Gaza first would not be withdrawal from Gaza only.[97]

The need for mutual understandings led to negotiations headed by Rice and Dubi Weissglass and an exchange of letters. In Bush's April 14, 2004, letter, he addressed a number of Sharon's requirements: on settlements and borders, he said that "in light of new realities on the ground, including already existing major Israeli populations centers, it is unrealistic to expect that the outcome of final status negotiations will be a full and complete return to the armistice lines of 1949." In this language, Bush acknowledged the large settlement blocs, using the euphemism "existing major Israeli populations centers"—and made it clear that we did not expect withdrawal to the borders that existed prior to the 1967 Six-Day War. On refugees, he said, "It seems clear that an agreed, just, fair, and realistic framework for a solution to the Palestinian refugee issue as part of any final status agreement will need to be found through the establishment of a Palestinian state, and the settling of Palestinian refugees there, rather than Israel." In other words, Palestinian refugees should settle in their state rather than Israel—indeed, the logic of establishing a state for Palestinians was at least in part designed to settle the refugee issue once and for all.[98]

The Bush letter also offered assurances about our commitment to Israeli security even while it stated that Israel needed to be able to defend itself by itself—language we would subsequently use in the Obama administration. At the same time, the letter spoke of the Roadmap and explained that resolving the issues in question must be negotiated and "mutually agreed." The headlines from the letter, which the president read out loud in Sharon's presence, seemed to miss this point and focus instead, as Rice would later write, on how the United States had now "legitimized" settlements and "rejected" the right of return.[99]

As Rice notes, Arab reaction to the April 14 letter was negative, with the Jordanians arguing that the president "would need to give assurances to the Arabs just as he had to the Israelis."[100] He would do so by emphasizing that no final status issues had been prejudged because mutual agreement was still required. The letter did help Sharon, though he faced significant internal opposition, losing a Likud referendum on the withdrawal from Gaza. Yet he went ahead anyway, carrying out the evacuation in August 2005. Even though Abbas had now replaced Arafat, who had died the previous November, Sharon still doubted that negotiations would lead anywhere. Considering the stalemate, and the opposition of Likud to further unilateral moves, Sharon would decide to leave his party and create a new one, Kadima.

But that would not come until November 2005. Disengagement, rather than the Roadmap, would be the path for the remainder of 2004, and would continue after President Bush was reelected.

Condoleezza Rice Becomes Secretary of State and the Balance of Power Shifts in the Administration

Bush had decided that if he was reelected, he would replace Colin Powell with Condoleezza Rice. In his memoirs, he writes, "I admired Colin, but it sometimes seemed like the State Department he led wasn't fully on board with my philosophy and policies."[101] For his part, Powell had hoped to stay longer.[102] According to Bob Woodward, he understood that "the White

House saw the State Department and its diplomats as appeasers. Cheney, Rumsfeld and Rice to some extent, would not allow State to engage in diplomacy because diplomacy was considered a weakness."[103]

Ironically, in her confirmation hearings, Rice announced, "The time for diplomacy is now," implying it had not been the guiding principle of the administration until this point but it would be her motif as secretary of state. Almost immediately, she made fence-mending trips to Europe and Asia. In Europe, she went out of her way to emphasize a common approach on the Iranian nuclear issue.[104] Diplomacy and alliance management might not have been Bush's hallmark of the first term, but for Rice it would guide the second. Unlike Powell, she would have the running room to pursue this agenda.

In fact, as the second Bush term evolved, Rice became the dominant player in the administration. In the first term, she never enjoyed decisive influence on Iraq or the war on terror. In these areas, which were Bush's priorities, Cheney and Rumsfeld were far more influential. But the deteriorating conditions in Iraq and the consequences for President Bush's political standing and credibility made it possible for Rice to assume a more central role. As one former senior official in the Bush administration put it: "As Iraq slides and goes downhill, Cheney's standing with the president goes in the same trajectory. I don't know if the president blames him or him and Rumsfeld . . . but what is happening in Iraq and the sense that the war is going badly . . . all that begins to work against the VP as well. The bottom line is that there has been a shift in the balance of power within the administration away from Cheney by the fall of 2006."[105] The shift was clearly to the new secretary of state.

It was not only diplomacy in general that she was determined to emphasize in the second term; she was focused on the achievement of statehood for the Palestinians.[106] She felt there was an opportunity in the wake of Sharon's decision to withdraw from Gaza and with Abbas assuming the presidency of the Palestinian Authority after Arafat's death.[107] Her motivation may well have stemmed from her previously stated view that we had broken the Middle East and now we needed to show we could repair it. Nonetheless, old habits die hard, and she did not act to guarantee the success of Israel's withdrawal. Maybe the enduring "anything but Clinton" mind-set precluded the hands-on management that would have committed heavily to ensuring that the Israeli withdrawal would not only go smoothly but also be coordinated in a way that enabled the Palestinian Authority to assume appropriate responsibilities and thus share credit for the disengagement.

To be fair, Sharon was not keen on coordinating with the Palestinians, lest their actions determine what he could do—and indeed Abbas was leery of assuming responsibilities. But this was all the more reason why the United States should have been the bridge, orchestrating what each side would say, pressing for dry runs on handovers, defining the areas where PA security forces would deploy and how they would interact with the IDF, and mediating the borders and passage arrangements months before the withdrawal to anticipate inevitable operational problems. Rice would negotiate the borders and passages agreement only two months *after* the Israelis had withdrawn, more or less guaranteeing that there would be breakdowns after the withdrawal and that her agreement would never be implemented in practice.

The stakes were huge in making the Gaza withdrawal a success on the ground, but little was done in advance to deal with the likely problems, and the results were predictable. As chaos reigned in Gaza, Hamas gained, and the seeds of its eventual takeover were sown—both because it could take credit for driving the Israelis out through "resistance" and because the PA was clearly inept at handling the realities on the ground after the Israelis left.

When Sharon visited Bush at his ranch in April 2005 and they talked about the planned Israeli withdrawal in five months, the president saw Gaza as a precedent for the West Bank. But, as Elliott Abrams notes, Bush also saw the other side of the coin: "If this experiment failed, if the Palestinians could not rule Gaza, Sharon would have proved to the world that moving forward in the West Bank was not possible." Bush would go on to tell Sharon that he was not interested in moving toward a final status agreement if there was no prog ress in Gaza.[108] He would not stick to that position, but Sharon was no longer prime minister in the last years of the administration when there was a push for the very agreement that he said would not be an objective if Gaza failed.

Sharon succumbed to a second massive stroke in December 2005. His deputy prime minister, Ehud Olmert, replaced him and subsequently was elected prime minister—on a platform of "convergence" that called for an additional disengagement in the West Bank if a negotiated agreement proved unattainable with the Palestinians. That seemed far more likely after Hamas won the elections for the Palestinian Legislative Council on January 25, 2006, over Fatah, 44–41 percent.[109]

Though President Bush had been a proponent of the elections and believed that Hamas would ultimately fail, his only comment on an NSC memo about Hamas was to say that there should be no daylight between America and Israel.[110]

Olmert came to see Bush after his election, in the spring of 2006, and they quickly bonded. Bush had much more personal chemistry with Olmert than with Sharon. He admired Sharon and saw him as a real leader, but Olmert had an easygoing, colloquial style much like his own. Olmert agreed to try negotiations first, and to meet with Abbas. But it was also clear that if Abbas would not fight terror or if he proved incapable of doing a deal, he would move unilaterally. Already, during this visit, Rice raised with Olmert the idea of going to a peace conference by the end of the year. Olmert was cool to the idea, telling her, " 'I'm not going to negotiate with 20 Arab countries at the same time . . . I am ready to sit with Abu Mazen; until now he turned down all my attempts to meet with him . . . So, if he needs some kind of an international umbrella to help get into touch with me, that's fine.' And, so she said, 'OK, we'll talk about it.' But then, you know, Lebanon came, and everything's changed."[111]

Rice's Turning Point: The Lebanon War

Did everything change with Lebanon? Not for George Bush. But Condoleezza Rice's views of Israel and of our priorities did change—or, perhaps, they simply became more explicit.

On July 12, 2006, Hezbollah orchestrated an ambush across the Israeli border that was covered by an initial barrage of mortars and rockets. Its forces killed eight Israeli soldiers and kidnapped two wounded ones who would subsequently die. Considering that Israel had withdrawn from Lebanon in May 2000, it is not difficult to understand why Israel struck back hard on July 13. But that is only part of the explanation for an Israeli campaign that was designed to hit Hezbollah very hard from the air—and set in motion a war that dragged on for a month.

On June 25, Hamas, using a tunnel under the border, had attacked from Gaza into Israel and killed two Israeli soldiers and kidnapped a third, Gilad Shalit, who would be held for five years. With the Hezbollah attack on July 12, Olmert felt the need to reestablish the image of Israeli deterrence—and his own strength. He was not Sharon, whose credibility on security was never in question within Israel or outside. For both internal and external reasons, Olmert had to show there was a severe consequence for testing Israel this way. But there was another reason for him to act: his priority had been the Palestinians, and he had intended to pursue a policy of unilateral withdrawal from a major part of the West Bank if negotiations proved unavailing with Abbas. After the attacks from both Gaza and Lebanon—the two areas where Israel had withdrawn unilaterally—he had to either reestablish Israeli deterrence or risk weakening the justification for withdrawal from parts of the West Bank, an area that was not only emotionally part of Israel's heritage but literally touched the most populous areas in Israel.

Initially, there was unanimity within the administration and internationally that Hezbollah had provoked Israel. For President Bush, the issue was very clear: "The Israelis had a chance to deliver a major blow against Hezbollah and their sponsors in Iran and Syria," and he very much hoped they would do so.[112] Hezbollah had acted just as the G-8 summit was convening, and Rice took the lead in drafting the communiqué that laid the blame on Hezbollah, expressed concern about the toll on civilians, urged Israel to exercise restraint while affirming its right to defend itself, and called for a cease-fire on terms that would be sustainable. The last point was central to the administration's views; it did not want a cease-fire "on any terms"; it wanted Hezbollah and all militias to be disarmed and the Lebanese government to extend its writ throughout Lebanese territory—which is what the previous UNSC resolutions had called for but had not produced.[113]

One of the administration's success stories at the time was the Syrian withdrawal from Lebanon after the assassination of Prime Minister Rafik Hariri in 2005 and massive popular protests against Syrian influence. Elections had produced a new prime minister, Fouad Siniora, who was moderate and pro-Western. The president and Rice saw Hezbollah's aggression as an opportunity to build the authority of Siniora's new government, but this depended on the Israelis quickly inflicting serious damage on Hezbollah without causing widespread suffering among Lebanese civilians.

Unfortunately, Israel's strategy was marred by unclear objectives and a misguided belief that air power alone could stop Hezbollah's rockets. Following the pattern of past wars with Hezbollah—in 1993 and 1996—the Israeli attacks intensified, destroying Lebanese infrastructure and killing civilians while failing to stop the Hezbollah attacks.

Rice later described her conflicted feelings: "I felt personally responsible for trying to stop it [the conflict]—and very much on the spot. Yet I knew that we had to have the right ceasefire terms so that Hezbollah was not handed a victory for its aggression."[114]

An NSC meeting called by the president on July 19, six days into the fighting, reflected the duality that both she and the president felt. It was necessary for Hezbollah to sustain more losses, and yet there was "a great deal of sympathy for Siniora and the Lebanese people. We agreed to press the Israelis on all fronts to refrain from attacks that punished our allies in Beirut."[115]

Rice traveled to the region after the NSC meeting. There was an inevitable tension with the Israelis. We wanted to protect the Lebanese government, but as Foreign Minister Tzipi Livni told Abrams, "Saving Siniora is not an Israeli goal. He is too weak."[116] The Israelis were focused on reducing Hezbollah's firepower and capacity to threaten Israel with rockets. In theory, this need not have been incompatible with helping Siniora, but practically it was, particularly given Hezbollah's strategy of embedding rockets and rocket launchers in civilian areas. Olmert told the Associated Press in early August that Israel could stop only once there was a "robust military international force" in the south of Lebanon because otherwise "Hezbollah will be there and we will have achieved nothing."[117] Bush favored this idea, saying that we needed "shooters, not school-crossing guards" and a "cease-fire today is a win for Hezbollah, so we would oppose it."[118]

The mood changed dramatically after Israel's mistaken bombing of a three-story building in Qana, which killed twenty-eight people, more than half of them children. At this point, Rice found it intolerable to resist demands for a cease-fire and told Olmert, "Get it over with. After today, you have no ground to stand on. And, I'm not going to let the United States go down with you."[119]

Qana also heavily affected Bush, who later wrote, "I wanted to buy time for Israel to weaken Hezbollah's forces. I also wanted to send a message to Iran and Syria: They would not be allowed to use terrorist organizations as proxy armies to attack democracies with impunity. Unfortunately, Israel made matters worse . . . I started to worry that Israel's offensive might topple Prime Minister Siniora's democratic government."[120]

Once again there were real divisions within the administration. In his memoirs, Bush describes a "heated" disagreement in an NSC meeting in which Cheney argued for "[letting] the Israelis finish off Hezbollah," to which Rice replied, "If you do that, America will be dead in the Middle East."[121] Bush decided in Rice's favor, reasoning that "if America continued to back the Israeli offensive, we would have to veto one UN resolution after the next. Ultimately instead of isolating Iran and Syria, we would isolate ourselves."[122] Moreover, as Rice later recounted, Bush felt that "too much was at stake to allow the war to continue—including our posture in Iraq and his desire for a push toward Palestinian statehood."[123]

Rice would negotiate UN Security Council Resolution 1701, and it would end the war, permit the deployment of Lebanese army forces to the Israeli border in place of Hezbollah, create a deployment of a significantly expanded UNIFIL force in southern Lebanon, and seek to prevent the rearmament of militias. The last item was a spectacular failure, as Hezbollah would not only be rearmed but also would dramatically expand its arsenal of rockets from fewer than ten thousand after the war to at least fifty thousand within a year.[124] Israel would once again see the failure of international forces to safeguard Israeli security, cementing the historic view that Israel could only count on itself for its own defense.

In describing her state of mind after the war, Rice cited an opinion piece that said she would have to make sense of a crumbling order in the Middle East. She would later write, *"That's absolutely right,* I thought. *I have to, and somehow I will."*[125] Much like George Shultz after Israel's summer-long siege of Beirut in 1982, Rice's answer was to focus again on the Israeli-Palestinian conflict. Earlier, she had felt this was necessary after the removal of Saddam Hussein to show the world that the United States was going to repair the region. Now it was her priority again, and her colleague Philip Zelikow, whom she had appointed counselor in the State Department, delivered a speech in September 2006, a few weeks after the end of the Lebanon war, which offered the strategic rationale for a revived initiative on peace: "For the Arab moderates and for the Europeans, some sense of progress and momentum on the Arab-Israeli dispute is just a sine qua non for their ability to cooperate actively with the United States on a lot of other things that we care about . . . That means an active policy on the Arab-Israeli dispute is an essential ingredient to forging a coalition that deals with the most dangerous problems."[126]

Abrams, from his perch at the White House, was furious about the speech, engaging in what he describes as "a poison-pen email exchange" with Zelikow because he felt the speech "was very far from the president's policy."[127] But the speech captured Rice's views.[128]

Zelikow offered the traditionalist view of what mattered in the Middle East and what needed to guide our policy. For the vice president and for Abrams, now a deputy national security adviser, it was wrongheaded. The argument that we needed the Arabs for Iraq and other matters, and we would not get them unless we were to "push the Israelis into some peace deal," assumed that Arab leaders would, as Abrams put it, change their policies "on Iraq or Iran or Afghanistan if you muscle the Israelis."[129] That logic might have seemed "downright silly" to Abrams, but Rice, who earlier was critical of the traditionalist views, was making the policy and this now reflected her mind-set.[130]

Previous Arab-Israeli wars had triggered new initiatives on peace: Kissinger after 1973, Shultz after 1982, and now Rice after 2006. In each case, the war had captured the attention of the world and put us at odds with our European allies while also placing our Arab friends on the defensive. In each case, American presidents—Nixon, Reagan, and Bush—had stood by Israel but also put pressure on it to stop the conflict. Also in each case, the secretary of state felt the need to launch a peace initiative, believing either there was an opportunity because war had reshaped the landscape—certainly Kissinger felt this—or that the American image required repair.[131] Rice now quietly began to press the idea of an international conference while also firmly telling the Israelis that we had a "strategic imperative to find an Israeli-Palestinian solution" lest we not get help from the Arabs on Iran.[132]

In January 2007, Rice went to the region to see Egyptian President Hosni Mubarak, King Abdullah of Saudi Arabia, and the other Arab leaders of the Gulf Cooperation Council. Her purpose on the trip was to explain President Bush's decision to initiate the "surge" in Iraq, our desire to talk to Iraq's neighbors, including Iran, and her efforts now to make a push on Israeli-Palestinian peace. And what was their focus? Iraq and Iran, not the Palestinians. Mubarak and Abdullah, in Rice's words, were thrilled to hear the president was doubling down on Iraq, having worried that the United States would "cut and run, leaving them to face chaos in Iraq and enhanced Iranian influence in the region."[133] The same was true of the other Arab leaders, who wanted to know why Rice wanted to talk to the Iranians about Iraq's future. When Rice moved on to discuss her efforts on the Israeli-Palestinian conflict, "the GCC ministers were pleased, but there wasn't a lot of discussion. *This is pretty interesting*, I thought. *The Israeli-Palestinian issue has fallen down the list of priorities. Iran is number one, two, three, and four.*"[134]

Once again, we see the actual priorities of Arab leaders: their security. Notwithstanding Rice's argument with Cheney only a few months earlier about us being "dead in the Middle East" if the war in Lebanon continued, Arab leaders continued to define their relationship with us based on their security needs. And yet even Rice's own conclusion that Israeli-Palestinian peace had fallen down in the list of *Arab* priorities did not alter her view of its importance, or the strategic rationale that continued to guide her. In 2007 and 2008, Rice pushed for peace as a priority for us in the region, hoping that the Israelis', Saudis', and others' preoccupation with Iran would make it easier for them to consider peacemaking.[135]

Initially, in 2007, she sought to produce an agreed set of principles for how to settle the core issues of the conflict. Much like John Kerry's objectives in 2013 and 2014, Rice wanted to lay out a "political horizon" for how to end the conflict, and have it agreed on and then endorsed at an international conference.

She pressed Olmert on the core issues—repeating what Kissinger, Carter, and Clinton had done with previous Israeli prime ministers. She faced similar resistance, even though she, too, promised not to share the Israeli bottom lines with the Palestinians. Note Elliott Abrams's account of an exchange between Olmert and Rice: "I am ready to leave most of the West Bank and do a deal on Jerusalem, he [Olmert] said to Rice; why do you need more? I need to know more, more detail, she answered. Which are the major blocs, and what are the borders for each? This is just for me; I will not tell the Palestinians your positions. But we do need to structure a process; let's start the discussion to create a sense of movement and progress."[136] Olmert, much like his predecessors, was not interested in sharing, convinced it would not satisfy her and also determined to keep her out of the negotiations. He would go along with the conference idea but not the political horizon.

When Rice realized she could not get the Israelis and Palestinians to agree on the core principles, she scaled back her aims and initiated what became the Annapolis Conference to serve as a forum for launching final status negotiations.

Bush was willing to go along with her approach even though it explicitly contradicted what the president had told Sharon at the ranch in 2005—that if the pullout from Gaza failed to produce quiet along Israel's frontier and Palestinian responsiveness, we would not push for final status negotiations. But Sharon was gone and Rice was now calling the shots on much of the national security agenda. Rumsfeld's resignation in November 2006 had tilted the decision-making process on national security further in her direction. Her instincts now put special emphasis on diplomacy, and that would also manifest itself in the debate over what to do about al-Kibar, the secret nuclear reactor being built in Syria.[137]

The Debate and Decision over al-Kibar

In April 2007, the Israelis not only informed the White House about the reactor North Korea was building in Syria but also asked that the United States destroy the facility.*[138] The Israeli information triggered a vigorous debate over how the United States should respond that basically pitted

---

* Meir Dagan, the head of Mossad, came to the White House along with Olmert's two key aides, Yoram Turbowicz and Shalom Turgeman. They provided a full dossier of materials to Steve Hadley and the vice president in Hadley's office.

Cheney against Rice and Robert Gates, now the secretary of defense. Cheney argued that we should support the Israeli request. The plant was a "clear and distinct target," and destroying it would "send an important message not only to the Syrians and North Koreans, but also to the Iranians."[139] Rice and Gates strongly opposed this view. But Gates was against not only a U.S. strike. He opposed an Israeli military strike as well, saying, "If we let the Israelis take care of the problem, we would be regarded as complicit or a coconspirator and that this option also ran the risk of igniting a wider war in the Middle East and an unpredictable reaction in Iraq." He went so far as to argue that Olmert must allow us to handle the issue, and that the president should tell the Israeli prime minister "very directly that if Israel went forward on its own militarily, he would be putting Israel's entire relationship with the United States at risk."[140]

The alternative that Rice and Gates favored was publicly exposing the Syrian reactor to the world and going the diplomatic route of using the International Atomic Energy Agency and the United Nations to build an international consensus to force the Syrians to shut down the reactor. Bush sided with Gates and Rice, but when he informed Olmert of his decision, the Israeli prime minister's response was blunt. Israel could not live with the Syrian reactor, and going to the IAEA would produce that result. Israel would have to act militarily, but he said it was essential that the information not be leaked so Israel could preserve surprise. The president not only promised that we would remain "buttoned up" but also acknowledged that Israel had a right to protect its national security.[141]

Bush's reaction to Olmert's position was, "That guy has guts."[142] But that was not Gates's or Rice's reaction. Gates felt Olmert was telling us that if "we didn't do exactly what he wanted, Israel would act and we could do nothing about it. The United States was being held hostage to Israeli decision-making." From Gates's standpoint, our strategic interests in Iraq, in the Middle East, and with our other allies were being put in Israel's hands, and this was unacceptable. According to Gates, Rice agreed, and when he said he would talk to the president again and try to reverse his acquiescence to Olmert, Rice said, "Use my name and count me in."[143]

President Bush, however, was not prepared to confront Olmert. Gates believes that the president shared Olmert's view that the Syrian reactor was an existential threat to Israel, and he was thus ready to let "Israel do whatever it wanted."[144] Israel destroyed the reactor on September 6, never publicly admitting what it had done, and we would respect Israel's request for secrecy both before and after the attack, only months later revealing what had happened.

Gates later acknowledged that "a big problem was solved and none of my fears were realized."[145] It is noteworthy that both Gates and Rice, much like Weinberger at the time of Israel's attack on the Iraqi nuclear reactor at Osirak, had expected terrible blowback in the region if the Israelis militarily struck al-Kibar. Weinberger, like Gates, admitted years later that his fears had not materialized.

Neither Gates nor Weinberger—nor, for that matter, Rice—asked why what they feared didn't happen. What did it say about the region and our understanding of it? Was it possible that none of Iraq's or Syria's neighbors were unhappy about Israel's actions? Did they see the Israeli actions actually improving their security? The lack of blowback in each case spoke volumes about the real priorities of Arab leaders. But, as in previous cases, the administration's priorities in the region at the time did not change. Indeed, Rice remained invested in a Middle East peace conference and remained determined—from September 2007 until the end of the administration—to produce on it.

Iran, Defense Cooperation, and Signs of Dissonance

Gates had been convinced that an Israeli military attack on the al-Kibar complex would trigger a wider war with Hezbollah and Syria and jeopardize our position in Iraq. Though his fears turned out to be unfounded, he would use similar arguments in making the case against responding to new Israeli arms requests in May 2008. Gates felt that the Israeli military requests would, if satisfied, greatly enhance Israel's ability to strike Iranian nuclear sites. As he later wrote, the debate over the request was "a reprise of the debate over the Syrian nuclear reactor the year before." Once again, it would basically pit Gates against Cheney, with Gates maintaining that "Iran was not Syria—it would retaliate, putting at risk Iraq, Lebanon, oil supplies from the Gulf and the end of the peace process, as well as increasing the likelihood of a Hezbollah war against Israel."[146] Gates recalled that Cheney disagreed with everything he said, arguing that the "United States should give Israel everything it wanted. We could not allow Iran to get nuclear weapons. If we weren't going to act, he said, then we should enable the Israelis."[147] Gates was pretty sure that Rice did not favor accommodating Israel's request, but she was less clear-cut in this meeting, having made the point that we should not leave an ally in the lurch.

Gates decided to communicate privately with Bush. He told the president that America's vital interests could not be held hostage to Israel's decisions and that we should not risk what we had gained with the surge in Iraq or risk the lives of our soldiers there "on an Israeli military gamble in Iran."[148]

Unlike in the Syrian case, the Israelis were not telling us that they were going to attack the Iranian nuclear facilities. Gates, nonetheless, saw the arms requests as presaging such action, and his basic distrust of Israel's intent to act "irrespective of our interests" led him to adopt this posture.[149] President Bush was sufficiently convinced by Gates that he chose not to approve the Israeli arms requests.

Despite this rejection, Bush had real concerns about Iran, and he was sensitive to Israel's worries. Although he did not respond to this particular request, he did order an expansion of our bilateral intelligence sharing and cooperation with the Israelis to slow down the Iranian program. Steve Hadley created a small team with the key people from Defense and CIA to meet with him and the head of Mossad and Israel's Directorate of Military Intelligence because "we wanted to have Israel right on the same page with us, partly because we felt they had information and capabilities that we wanted to take advantage of, and also because we felt that they were also an independent actor," and we did not want them going their own way.[150]

Collaboration in the intelligence areas was extremely close, but there was room for improvement in defense cooperation. At one point, there had actually been a breakdown in the defense relations because of Israeli military sales to China, which triggered deep anger within the Pentagon. Eric Edelman, who replaced Doug Feith as the under secretary of defense for policy, said that when he assumed this office in 2005, "the relationship was very bad."[151]

Edelman worked to repair the relationship. Nevertheless, there was a hangover effect. As Amos Gilad, a senior Israeli Defense Ministry official, described it to me early in the Obama administration, the issue was not what we would provide to the Israelis; rather, it was that the United States did not appear to be taking into account the impact on Israel of the sale of advanced weapons to the Saudis and the Emirates.

Gates addressed this. In April 2007, he was the first secretary of defense to visit Israel during the Bush administration. He pledged to maintain Israel's qualitative military edge at the same time that he asked Olmert "not to oppose the sale of military equipment, including weapons, to Saudi Arabia." In arguments he would repeat during the Obama administration, Gates made the case to Olmert—and later to Netanyahu—that "Saudi Arabia was focused on the threat from Iran, not on acquiring capabilities to threaten Israel."[152] Israelis in the Defense Ministry worried about the impact of these sales on Israel's qualitative edge but would not make them an issue with the Congress.[153]

Notwithstanding these tensions between the Pentagon and Israel's Ministry of Defense, Bush was, in fact, very responsive to Israel's security needs. He directed Gates to replenish Israel's arms in the aftermath of the Lebanon war. More important, during Olmert's June 2007 visit to Washington, he agreed to the prime minister's request to put U.S. military assistance to Israel on a new, enduring footing by signing a ten-year memorandum of understanding.[154] Similarly Rice, regardless of personally difficult relations with Olmert after Lebanon, directed her under secretary for political affairs, Nicholas Burns, to renew strategic cooperation discussions with the Israelis—and he would both negotiate the terms of the MOU and conduct what he described as "close, open and intensive" discussions on Iran and a number of other issues. He later explained that Rice wanted him to keep the Israelis completely apprised of what we were doing on Iran in the discussions we joined with the British, French, Russians, Chinese, and Germans—the so-called P5+1 talks—and he did so.[155]

During the last year of the Bush administration, the quiet cooperation with the Israelis on Iran continued. But most of the effort was geared toward supporting the negotiations between the Israelis and Palestinians that had been launched at Annapolis. The negotiations took place at two different levels—between Tzipi Livni and Abu Ala, the heads of the two negotiating teams, and in private meetings between Abbas and Olmert. Rice joined Livni and Abu Ala from time to time, pressing them to reach agreements; there were serious talks but no agreements. Livni, although she agreed to a definition of what constituted the lands occupied by the Israelis in 1967, did not agree to be more specific on borders because she felt the Palestinians were not forthcoming on security. Rice was not part of the private Abbas-Olmert meetings, and Olmert, at one point, proposed to cut through everything and offered his bottom lines on all the issues. He did so not as a starting point for negotiations but to conclude them. As Olmert later told me, Abbas did not say yes or no, he simply never responded.[156]

Bush and Rice's hopes in the Annapolis process would not be realized. But the two were generally in sync, particularly during Rice's tenure as secretary of state. While disagreements were rare, there were two that were noteworthy. Aside from Bush's decision to acquiesce in Olmert's approach to the al-Kibar nuclear reactor, the president would not go along with Rice's response to the conflict in Gaza at the end of his presidency.

By way of background, in the summer of 2008, after intensifying Hamas rocket fire into Israel and tough Israeli reprisals, the Egyptians brokered a truce. It frayed, with intermittent rocket fire out of Gaza, but generally held—until December 19, when Hamas declared the truce over and proceeded to fire eighty-eight rockets into Israel. More were fired over the coming week, and in response, Israel launched a massive surprise bombardment, starting on December 27, against Hamas infrastructure throughout Gaza. The Israeli assault was the opening of a military campaign against Hamas in Gaza that the Israelis called Operation Cast Lead.

Rice saw the events through a prism in which she perceived legitimate Israeli responses inevitably getting out of hand because the Israelis did not know when to stop. In June 2006, after the Israeli withdrawal from Gaza, she described her general view of Israel's approach:

> The problem was that the Israelis always seemed to overreach. Initially, there was some sympathy for a response but sooner or later the inevitable Al Jazeera pictures of civilian misery would turn the tide of public opinion. Israel, determined to damage Hamas and to send a message of deterrence, was never sufficiently aware of when it was running out of time before it, and not the terrorists, was considered the aggressor. It was the job of the United States—and the secretary of state in particular—to walk the fine line that affirmed Israel's right to self-defense and protected U.S. interests with a broad set of allies and friends. Every secretary of state since 1948 has had to do that. I sometimes wonder how many more of us will come and go before that challenge goes away.[157]

Here again, in the waning days of the administration, Rice defended the Israelis at first but then switched course, seeking UN Security Council intervention to help end the conflict with a resolution. The Israelis were dead set against a Security Council resolution. Hadley, reflecting Bush's view, assured Olmert that our policy was to keep the issue out of the UN, but this was not Rice's position; she did not want us to be between the Israelis and the UN. She told Hadley that an American veto would weaken our Arab allies.[158] In the end, she actually negotiated the terms of the resolution with the British, the French, and the Arabs—and it did not mention Hamas or its rocket fire. Abrams described an unhappy call with Rice in which he complained of how unbalanced the resolution was, and President Bush subsequently instructed the United States to abstain from the vote on the resolution, even though his secretary of state had negotiated it.[159]

The Bush Approach

George W. Bush presided over an administration divided on many issues, including our relationship with Israel and how it affected our position in the region. His administration and its policies toward Israel were distinctly different before and after 9/11. Yet even after 9/11, a fundamental divide persisted between the White House and the State Department over where Israel fit in the region, with Colin Powell representing the long-standing traditionalists' view that resolving the Palestinian issue was the key to our posture and relations with the Arabs. President Bush at first acquiesced to positions Powell advocated at certain moments but increasingly decided against them. Significantly, however, this mind-set and approach returned in the last years of the administration—and in fact carried new weight—when Condoleezza Rice, who was clearly primus inter pares, became secretary of state. Rice's views appeared to evolve, particularly during her tenure as secretary.

Given all that had gone wrong in Iraq, Rice and Gates were concerned with repairing our position in the region—and mindful of avoiding new conflicts. Gates went so far as to argue that we should threaten the future of our relationship with Israel if it acted militarily against Syria's nuclear reactor, an issue Israel saw in existential terms. Bush might have accepted Rice's new priorities along with Gates and Rice's arguments about not striking al-Kibar militarily, but the president's belief in Israel's right of self-defense meant he would not stand in the way of its acting to take out the Syrian reactor. And he fundamentally would not buy the argument that our position in the region and our ability to protect our interests there could be damaged or limited by our ties to Israel—or by our not resolving the Palestinian issue.

In his speech to the Knesset in May 2008, the president explicitly said, "Some people suggest that if the United States would just break ties with Israel, all our problems in the Middle East would go away. This is a tired argument that buys into the propaganda of our enemies, and America rejects it utterly."[160] He strongly favored the emergence of a democratic Palestinian state, believing that it could have a positive effect across the region. Still, notwithstanding his support for Rice's emphasis on promoting peace in the last years of his administration, he did not address peacemaking in this speech. Rice later noted with regret that this was a missed opportunity, saying, "Somehow the President should have used the moment to challenge the Israelis to make tough decisions—the peace process wasn't even mentioned."[161]

Were Rice's attitudes so different from Bush's toward Israel? She was clearly far more concerned about balance between Israel and the Arabs. Even in the first year of the administration, she observed that Palestinian terror against Israeli civilians "led the President to tilt toward Tel Aviv." And she added, "I think I convinced Colin that any attempt to chart a new course in 2001 was likely to result in an outcome that would be so pro-Israeli as to inflame an already bad situation."[162] She also believed in the centrality of the Palestinian issue to our position with the Arabs, accepting the logic that we could gain little cooperation on Iraq or Iran without dealing with it. Here her own experience in her January 2007 trip, when Arab leaders hardly raised the Palestinian issue, did not alter her assumptions.

Her commitment to the Palestinian issue also seems to have been driven by her identification with the Palestinian sense of victimhood. At one point, when Israeli defense minister Ehud Barak was asking why she was so committed to holding an international conference, Rice answered by emphasizing that Palestinians required permits on certain roads, and that smacked of the segregation she had experienced as a child in Jim Crow Alabama.[163] Rice drew the civil rights analogy again in her closing comments at the Annapolis Conference: "I grew up in Birmingham, Alabama, at a terrible time for black people. I think I know what it's like for a Palestinian mother to tell her child that she can't travel on that highway—because she is Palestinian. And the anger and humiliation that comes with that. My mother had to do that—because I was black and there were places that I couldn't go just because of the color of my skin."[164]

She went on to display her empathy for Israeli concerns as well, saying, "But I know too what it's like for an Israeli mother to put her child to bed and not know if a bomb will kill him in the night."[165] Rice seems to have genuinely felt for both sides in making the case for peacemaking. She indicated her frustration with Israel at different points. She was deeply unsettled by the Israeli assault on Lebanon, and she challenged the "old Israeli claim that 'there was no Palestinian partner for peace.'" She got angry when the Israelis did not fulfill their promises to the Palestinians.[166] Still, there was something fundamentally positive about her view of Israel that she also expressed even as she noted her frustration: "And whatever the problems, I reminded myself constantly that even if Israel's leaders were sometimes a nightmare to deal with, this important ally of ours was the only democracy in the Middle East. Our relationship really was based on more than strategic interests; we were friends, and that mattered."[167]

At the end of the day, George W. Bush was the president. At times, the president went along with policies that did not reflect his own view of how we should deal with Israel. But he kept any differences with Israel within certain bounds. He seemed intuitively to see Israel facing the same threats as the United States. Israel was our friend and deserved our support. At the very end of his administration, Israel was trying to destroy the ability of Hamas—an organization pledged to Israel's destruction, committed to terror, and aligned with the Iranians—to fire rockets against it. Ultimately, it was the sense of common struggle with common foes that meant Israel and the United States would stand together, and there would not be—and should not be—daylight between us. Bush's successor would see the world, and the U.S.-Israel relationship, quite differently.

11

OBAMA AND ISRAEL: SUPPORT FOR SECURITY, LITTLE CHEMISTRY, AND CONSTANT CHALLENGES

Barack Obama approached the presidency with great ambitions to set America on a new course. Nowhere was that more true than in his approach to the Middle East. The United States was engaged in two wars—in Iraq, a war of choice that Obama had opposed from its beginning, and in Afghanistan, a war that he declared was one of necessity that had been imposed on us. He felt the United States must be seen differently in the Middle East and around the world. If George W. Bush came into office determined to be "anything but Clinton," Barack Obama arrived at the White House determined to pursue an "anything but Bush" policy. Between the Iraq War and the global economic crisis, the American brand was tarnished. Our example and our appeal had been diminished. Obama believed he could reestablish both.

I met Obama in 2005 when he asked me to come to Chicago and speak to a group who supported the Hope Fund.* The participants were from around the country and on the left side of the political spectrum. He asked me to speak about Iraq and the Middle East. At the time, I was struck by how, on these issues, he deliberately chose not to appeal to the base instincts

---

* The Hope Fund offered college scholarships to Palestinian refugees in the United States.

of those in attendance, who clearly wanted him simply to call for a pullout from Iraq and to find malfeasance in the Bush administration. In this encounter, and later when I joined him on a 2008 trip to Israel and Europe, I found Obama very thoughtful and became a strong supporter of his candidacy.

I took a position in the administration soon after the inauguration. Hillary Clinton approached me during the transition period and asked me to join her at the State Department to run Iran policy from there. Shortly afterward, I was asked by General Jim Jones to join the National Security Staff (NSS) at the White House, to be in charge of a new office called the Central Region.[1] Both positions would allow me to shape our approach to Iran, which I felt was the linchpin for what would happen in the region and our place in it. Even though working in the White House would give me more direct access to the president as well as more responsibility for all issues in the broader Middle East—including the Arab-Israeli conflict—I felt the State Department position would allow me largely to play the same role because Iran cut across every other issue. Israel saw the Iranian nuclear program as an existential threat, and working closely with the Israelis on Iran would be essential. Benjamin Netanyahu was almost certain to be elected as the new Israeli prime minister, and it was unthinkable that he would consider taking risks on peace with the Palestinians if he did not feel secure about Iran. We therefore needed to reassure him on Iran if we were to move him on peace. And since all America's key Arab friends were preoccupied with Iran—far more so than with the peace issue—our approach to Iran was going to be the centerpiece of what we would be doing with them.

Assuming that President Obama and the White House would be preoccupied with the financial meltdown, I decided to go with the new secretary of state. I knew her and felt certain she would dominate the policy process much like Jim Baker during Bush 41. I expected the State Department to be the locus of conceptualization and implementation in foreign policy—and Clinton's weight would ensure that.

That turned out to be wrong. This is not a reflection on Hillary Clinton; her talent and capabilities were clear from day one. But the Obama administration from the outset was White House centered and driven. President Obama was the decision maker, and everything—not just the financial crisis—was going to run through him. Whereas during the Bush 43 administration, the United States could go to war in Iraq without ever having debated the pros and cons, in the Obama administration, every issue would be vetted in a process—and that process would be directed out of the White

House. Had I read the landscape correctly, I would have chosen to take the job at the NSS.

As it turned out, I would move to that White House position on July 1, 2009—but not because I sought it. On the contrary, with no advance notice, General Jones called me after President Obama returned from his trip to Saudi Arabia and Egypt in June. He told me only that the president wanted to see me the next morning. When I queried him on what the meeting was about, Jones said, "He will tell you." Only shortly before I arrived for what turned out to be a one-on-one meeting with President Obama in the Oval Office did Tom Donilon, the deputy national security adviser, inform me that the president would tell me that he needed me to come to the White House. "To do what?" I asked. Donilon, like Jones, would say only, "He will tell you." In our meeting, President Obama told me that he needed me to "quarterback" Middle East issues. Currently, he said, those who have responsibility for the problems in the region were "far too stovepiped." Connections between regional problems were too often missed. "You see how decisions on one set of problems affect others, and I need you here to do that, to manage the issues more generally," the president said.

When I asked him specifically what I should be trying to manage, he said, "everything." I asked whether George Mitchell was aware I would play this role, and he told me not yet. But he added that while he wanted me to work everything from Iran to the Arab-Israeli issue, "Mitchell is the envoy, you are not." By that time, the approach to the peace issue had been launched, and was not, in my view, on a good path. I had been involved with the discussions on Israel only as they related to Iran—though, interestingly, nearly every time I was in a meeting with President Obama prior to June, he asked me something about Israel.

That said, I clearly understood the context in which the president was operating and his belief that big changes were required in our foreign policy. We were estranged from our traditional allies. Our economic house was not in order, and repairing it was necessarily a big part of mending our image internationally. Moreover, our body politic was weary from wars that cost us so dearly in blood and treasure. For Obama, it was essential to restore America's standing and leadership, but not because he necessarily thought we were the "indispensable nation."[2] Rather, if we wanted others to share the burdens of confronting the international challenges facing all of us, we needed to be seen again as a good ally, a responsible and cooperative actor internationally, not one prone to shoot first and act without regard to the concerns of others.

An interview the president gave years later revealed the outlook that was guiding his thinking from early on: "In today's world, where power is much more diffuse, where the threats that any state or peoples face can come from non-state actors and asymmetrical threats, and where international cooperation is needed in order to deal with those threats, the absence of international goodwill makes you less safe."[3]

For Obama, we needed to be less arrogant and listen to others. Tom Donilon, whose role was critical from the beginning because he ran the interagency deputies meetings, explained why the administration needed to operate differently from its inception: "We came into office at a period of very significant diminution of American influence, prestige and power in the world. And our principal strategic goal was the restoration of that position."[4]

In addition to repairing the international financial system and the United States' image generally, Obama entered office with two preoccupations in national security: preventing the spread of nuclear weapons and transforming our relations with Muslim-majority countries. The first meant doing all we could to ensure the safety of nuclear materials by strengthening the nuclear Non-Proliferation Treaty (NPT) so terrorists or rogue nations like Iran could not acquire nuclear arms. The second meant reaching out to Muslim countries and undoing the perception during the Bush years that the United States was at war with Islam.

Obama was especially concerned about this view of the United States. He was convinced that it fed the terror threat we faced, making it easier to recruit the very terrorists we had to fight. The rhetoric—"the war on terror" and "Islamofascists"—had to change. And we had to close Guantánamo Bay and end abuses like those committed at Abu Ghraib and bring the Iraq War to a conclusion. As David Remnick observed, "If George W. Bush's foreign policy was largely a reaction to 9/11, Obama's has been a reaction to the reaction."[5]

Obama started by trying to forge a new beginning with the Muslim world. During the campaign, he promised to give an early address in a Muslim country to start a dialogue with Muslims internationally. Transforming our relationship with the Muslim world mandated a related priority: peace between Israel and the Palestinians, a conflict that in Obama's view compounded our troubled relations with Muslims. He acted quickly on that priority by announcing the appointment of George Mitchell as our Middle East peace envoy on the second day of the administration in a ceremony at the State Department.

Where Did Israel Fit in Obama's Approach to the World?

Put simply, the Obama administration's national security priorities almost guaranteed that Israel would be a problem. Restoring relations with our European allies would inevitably mean being more responsive to their concerns and priorities. Their preoccupation with Middle East peace and their collective view that Israeli occupation and settlement activity—not Palestinian behavior—were responsible for the conflict argued for pressuring Israel. Similarly, the new emphasis on international norms was also certain to create problems with the Israelis because of the broad consensus that Israel's settlement activity was a violation of international law. Finally, the need to reach out to the Muslim—and effectively the Arab—world had its own implications for how we should be dealing with Israel, or so the president and those around him believed.

Each of the priorities suggested potential complications in our relationship with Israel. But it was the outreach to Muslims that led President Obama to see value in demonstrating some distance from the Jewish state. During the transition, Tom Donilon asked me to write a memo on where to give the speech to the Muslim world. I made the case for Egypt, but I strongly felt that if the president gave a speech in Egypt, he had to go to Israel on the same trip. Otherwise he would convince the Israeli public that our outreach to Muslims came at Israel's expense.

Only later when I queried him on why the president had decided not to go to Israel after Cairo did Donilon tell me that two key aides, Denis McDonough and Ben Rhodes, had persuaded the president against doing so.[6] They argued that it would look too traditional: he would be doing what every other president felt obliged to do. Obama was different, and the Muslims needed to see he was different. If he was going to reach out to Muslims—and do so in Cairo—he would devalue the effort and "mix the message" if he then went to Israel as well.

The president's emphasis on extending a hand to Muslims was evident immediately. Six days into the administration, Obama gave an interview with Al Arabiya. He gave a speech in Turkey in early April on the back end of his trip to Europe and previewed some of the themes he would raise in his June speech in Cairo. He traveled to Saudi Arabia before stopping in Cairo, visiting three Muslim countries—all the while bypassing Israel. He was certainly breaking the mold, and the Cairo speech was designed to acknowledge Muslim grievances while also creating distance from Israel.

The president spoke not of "terror" but of "violent extremism." The war on terror was interpreted by many Muslims as a war on Islam, and he wanted to change the terminology. He declared that "Islam is not part of the problem in combating violent extremism—it is an important part of promoting peace." In addition, Obama consciously addressed deep-seated perceptions in the Arab Middle East of historical mistreatment by the West by referring to how colonialism "denied rights and opportunities to many Muslims" and how, during the cold war, "Muslim-majority countries were too often treated as proxies without regard to their own aspirations." Not surprisingly, he also made strong statements on the Palestinian issue, speaking of the "daily humiliations—large and small—that come with occupation" and declaring that the "situation for the Palestinian people is intolerable."[7]

While he vigorously confronted Holocaust denial, a potent theme in Arab countries, he implied that it was the Holocaust—and not the historic yearning of the Jewish people and its historic links to the land—that produced Israel. For Israelis, as Obama was addressing the narrative of Muslims in general and Palestinians in particular, he was dismissing theirs. He also used new terminology to make clear his opposition to Israeli settlement activity, saying for the first time that the "United States does not accept the legitimacy of continued Israeli settlements."[8]

That the president's distancing from Israel was deliberate and tied to the desire to reach out to the Muslims was revealed in a meeting Obama held with Jewish leaders on July 13, 2009. Malcolm Hoenlein, the longtime executive director of the Conference of Presidents of Major Jewish Organizations, expressed concern about the administration's position on Israel. He said, "If you want Israel to take risks, then its leaders must know that the United States is right next to them." President Obama disagreed: "Look at the past eight years. During those eight years, there was no space between us and Israel, and what did we get from that? When there is no daylight, Israel just sits on the sidelines, and that erodes our credibility with the Arab states."[9] Much like previous administrations—Eisenhower, Nixon, and Bush 41—Obama was consciously distancing from Israel because he believed our relations with the Arabs, and Muslims more broadly, required it.[10] The expectation of benefits drove the policy of distancing, just as it had in the past. But what of the costs? At a time when he made Israeli-Palestinian peace a priority, why was the possibility of alienating the Israeli public not considered?

Several factors account for the failure to think through the consequences of distancing. In the first instance, there was little debate on our approach at the time. Tom Donilon, by his own admission, was focused on Iran, Afghanistan, and the Russia and China "reset." Denis McDonough, Ben Rhodes, and

General Jones were all in agreement on the outreach to the Muslims, and this trumped any concerns about the impact on the Israelis. Rahm Emanuel, the president's powerful chief of staff, was seen by Obama as an expert on Israel—Obama even telling the Jewish leaders that "Rahm understands the politics there [Israel] and he explains them to me."[11]

But Emanuel carried a memory of Netanyahu from the Clinton administration, when he was one of President Clinton's senior political counselors.[12] From that experience, he was convinced that with Netanyahu, little could be achieved on the Palestinian issue without pressure. By early summer of 2009, however, he became more concerned about the way the president was perceived in Israel and in the Jewish community—and by what he saw as little responsiveness from the Arabs. This contributed to his pushing to bring me to the White House to diversify what the president was hearing on Israel and the Middle East.

Secretary Clinton, though more sensitive to the Israeli reaction, felt it was futile at the outset to fight what she saw as a collective mind-set around Obama. She believed that the more she could build her credentials with the president, the more responsive he would be to her. She spent much of the first year of the administration trying to prove she was the good soldier—toeing the official line and endeavoring to do what she believed Obama wanted. Still, by June, she, too, like Emanuel, was prepared to tell the president that the approach was not working and we needed to show greater sensitivity toward the Israelis.

Clearly, the president had his own instincts. He accepted the view embedded in every administration that our problems with the Arabs and Muslims were largely connected to the Palestinian issue. General David Petraeus, the head of Central Command, reflected this mind-set—and at this point also the president's thinking—in "cleared" congressional testimony he gave in March 2009:

> Israeli-Palestinian tensions often flare into violence and large-scale armed confrontations. The conflict foments anti-American sentiments due to a perception of U.S. favoritism for Israel. Arab anger over the Palestinian question limits the strength and depth of U.S. partnerships with the governments and peoples in the AOR [area of responsibility] and weakens the legitimacy of moderate regimes in the Arab world. Meanwhile, al-Qaeda and other militant groups exploit that anger to mobilize support.[13]

Leaving aside whether Arab leaders might have other domestic reasons for wanting to limit the scope of their partnership with us, this argument tied the terrorism we faced to Israeli occupation and certainly justified making an effort to resolve the Palestinian issue—and it was persuasive to the president. Still, Obama's instinct to simultaneously distance from Israel and move on peace contained a built-in contradiction, and no one around him pointed this out.

Later, when I got to the White House and emphasized outreach to the Israeli public in order to mitigate its fears over his pursuit of better relations with the Arabs, the president asked, "Doesn't the Israeli public see that if I can succeed in reducing Arab hostility it would be good not just for us but Israel as well?" I answered that they needed to see him reaching out to them first and then he could explain that point—which Obama would, in fact, do when he finally gave an interview to the Israeli press eighteen months into the administration.

By not reaching out, he did little to indicate that he understood the centrality of security to Israelis. And yet in discussions I had with him, I had no doubt he was genuinely committed to Israeli security. Moreover, while he might believe that real security for Israel would come only when it had peace, the president accepted that one could not expect Israeli leaders to make serious concessions and run risks unless they knew their security needs would be met. His initial trip to Israel in 2006 as a senator affected him; his key Jewish supporters influenced him; and his visit in July 2008 to Sderot, the Israeli town constantly hit by rockets out of Gaza, moved him. He often said in our meetings, even when he was criticizing an Israeli action, that we had to be sure that we were addressing Israel's security requirements.

This sentiment was captured in an interview he gave in 2014. Even though the observations were offered in his second term, I had heard him make similar statements far earlier, when we were meeting on issues involving Israel: "Here's what I would say: The U.S. commitment to Israel's security is not subject to periodic policy differences. That's a rock-solid commitment, and it's one that I've upheld proudly throughout my tenure. I think the affection that Americans feel for Israel, the bond that our people feel and the bipartisan support that people have for Israel is not going to be affected."[14]

So Obama had an instinctive commitment to Israel's security—and he acted on it. But there was an additional reason that Obama was very attentive to Israel's security needs, and it can be encapsulated in one word: Iran. Blunting the Iranian nuclear program was one of Obama's national security priorities. Even before the election, I had an exchange with him on Iran and Israel in which I told him I thought he would need to move quickly to try to set back the Iranian nuclear program, lest the Israelis, who saw it as an existential threat, feel the need to act militarily on their own against it. He agreed, saying if he were elected, this was an issue he would have to be dealing with from day one.[15]

He did, in fact, attach a very high priority to dealing with the Iranian nuclear program and to dissuading the Israelis from striking. This preoccupation fostered very close collaboration with the Israelis on security issues. Much as Steve Hadley described working closely with the Israelis because they had something to contribute and to keep them from going their own way on Iran, so too did Obama approve intensive cooperation across the full range of military, intelligence, and security programs with Israel. Robert Gates later wrote that notwithstanding the "frosty" political and diplomatic relationship between Obama and Netanyahu, "the defense relationship remained strong and in every dimension would reach unprecedented levels of cooperation."[16] Iran was not the sole explanation for this, particularly given Obama's genuine commitment to Israel's security, but it was a major contributor.

From my perspective as an original author of strategic cooperation back in the Reagan administration, I can say that the scope of the security collaboration went beyond what any previous administration had put in place. Here, we see the parallels with the Bush 41 administration, where there was extraordinary responsiveness to Israel on its core strategic needs, even as the tone of the relationship in public could be discordant. The Obama administration was marked by a similar duality—strategic responsiveness and public differences.

The strategic responsiveness was reflected in multiple ways. During Obama's first term, there were high-level visits and meetings of senior intelligence, defense, and/or military officials literally every week, either in the United States or Israel. Notwithstanding the severe budgetary problems the administration faced, the president not only preserved all previous financial commitments made to Israel on security but also authorized additional spending for the Israeli Iron Dome short-range missile defense system that had proved so effective against Hamas rockets out of Gaza. Similarly, the president approved a new approach to evaluating, upgrading, and systematizing how to maintain Israel's qualitative military edge (QME). And that led to an unprecedented effort with the Israelis in evaluating the impact of arms sales to the Arabs on the QME and the U.S. government providing more compensation to Israel when such sales were made. Last, the president directed even closer overt and covert cooperation with Israel on the Iranian nuclear program.[17]

At the same time, much like the Bush 41 administration, Obama's approach to Israel would be characterized by a public disagreement on settlements. When George Mitchell made his initial listening tour of the region, the Arab leaders he met with may have been most concerned about Iran, but when he asked about the one step Israel could take that would make a difference, the answer was a freeze on settlement activity. Like Bush, Obama felt the Israeli settlement activity was simply wrong. In addition, he felt it was a good issue on which to distance the United States from Israel, because—as he told one adviser before I moved to the White House—he could "demonstrate that he could change Israeli behavior on the ground" and strengthen U.S. credibility with the Arabs.[18]

In his Cairo speech, Obama said that Israeli settlements were not legitimate. Soon after I arrived at the White House in the summer of 2009, he used this language in a meeting. I pointed out that he was changing our historical posture. Since the Reagan administration, we had opposed Israeli settlement activity as an obstacle to peace, as a political problem but not as a legal one. Using words like "legitimate" or "legitimacy" ran the risk of turning it into a legal problem, which would complicate any political process we were trying to pursue. The president was surprised by my comment. While he did not use that terminology again in our in-house meetings, it found its way back into his September 2009 speech to the United Nations General Assembly. When I tried to change it in the draft, Denis McDonough told me the president had used the formulation before and he could not look like he was retreating from it. I told him any conceivable deal would have to involve Israeli settlement blocs remaining in the West Bank, with the Palestinians being compensated for the blocs with territorial swaps from within Israel. If the president is saying, "America doesn't accept the legitimacy of continued Israeli settlements," he undercuts the justification for blocs and the swaps, the one substantive requirement for a peace agreement. Despite my argument, in McDonough's view, the president could not be seen to be retreating, and the language remained in the speech.

As time went by, I witnessed a tempering in President Obama's views on how to approach Israel and the peace issue as he was exposed to a more diverse discussion. He also became convinced of the need to create a connection with the Israeli public. The president would eventually go to Israel in March 2013 and give speeches that addressed Israeli concerns—the way he had addressed Muslim concerns in 2009. Had he given the speeches in 2009 rather than 2013, they would undoubtedly have had a very different effect. After his trip, polls in Israel showed his visit had reversed the negative impressions of him, but they had not fostered the inherent trust that was so important to establish—and not just for the peace issue but for Iran as well.

It was on Iran where the president, even in the first year, was directing us to work very closely with Israel. He understood that Israel needed to recognize how serious we were in making this a priority and that we were committed to doing whatever was necessary to stop the Iranian nuclear program. Private cooperation and assurances were certainly important, but if the Israeli public was to be a constraint on Israel acting unilaterally against the Iranian nuclear facilities, they needed to believe that we took the threat seriously.

For the first two years of his administration, the president thought a lot about Iran and the peace process. While outreach to the Muslims and the Arabs had provided a point of departure for his orientation toward the Middle East, Iran and Israeli-Palestinian peace were specific policy areas where choices and decisions had to be made. Both issues made Israel's behavior a central preoccupation. There was a paradox here. On Iran, Obama instinctively understood that if he were to dissuade the Israelis from preempting militarily, he needed to reassure them. An embrace, more than pressure, made sense. By contrast, on the peace issue, he saw the Israelis as the ones who needed to move and make things easier for the weaker party, the Palestinians. This made him much more open to the logic of pressure.

Much like Condoleezza Rice during the Bush administration, Obama saw a linkage between the issues and believed it could be used to move the Israelis. Since the Saudis, Emirates, Egyptians, and Jordanians shared Israel's concerns about Iran, there was the potential for a strategic realignment in the region if the Israelis were ready to make serious concessions in trying to resolve the conflict with the Palestinians—or so he believed.

The notion of strategic convergence had deep roots. Alexander Haig had raised it in 1981 in the Reagan administration, believing it could help move both Arabs and Israelis. By putting their differences in perspective, they could make concessions toward each other that would enable them to counter a greater danger to both. I had my doubts. I suggested in our internal discussions that getting Arabs or Israelis to make concessions to each other was unlikely—they had never been motivated by a common threat to do so. Both sides compartmentalized. They could covertly cooperate, but neither was prepared to pay a political price internally because of the greater common threat they both faced.

Nonetheless, Netanyahu might be induced, I argued, to take hard steps on the Palestinians if he had a commitment from the president to act militarily against the Iranian nuclear threat if diplomacy failed. The president—for understandable reasons—was not prepared to make such a commitment. Although Obama was ready to cooperate closely with the Israelis on Iran, he was not going to tie his hands on the use of force. By 2010, the president was focused far less on the possible link between Iran and the peace issue and far more on isolating the Iranians and showing the costs of their continued nuclear development in defiance of the international community. To be sure, other developments in the area would grab his attention and affect how he perceived the region and how Israelis and Arabs alike would perceive him.

The Arab Awakening and the Evolution of Obama's Approach

The upheaval in Arab countries in early 2011 became the president's new preoccupation. He saw it as an opportunity to transform the Middle East; it offered him a chance to alter our approach to the area and embrace the forces that promised to bend the arc of history in the direction of justice—one of the president's favorite quotes from Martin Luther King. When Obama had come into office, the need to be the anti-Bush meant that, unlike his predecessor, democracy promotion would not be the guiding principle of our policy in the Middle East. That smacked too much of trying to impose our values on the Arabs. And in his Cairo speech, Obama made clear we would not do this.[19]

But as the demonstrations in Egypt gathered increasing momentum, Obama's instincts were to align with the forces of history, and these forces seemed to be in the street and not in the presidential palaces. Obama at this point was drawn to those demonstrating for their rights. This time, it was not about us; it was not about the Israelis. The demonstrators embodied the antithesis of al Qaeda—they were producing change through peaceful means.

In these early weeks of the demonstrations, the president chaired or dropped by several meetings of his national security team. More than once

I heard him say that the way we were thinking about the region was "out of date" and that we should not be on the wrong side of the revolutions taking place.

Two points are worth noting here. First, events in the region moved very quickly. Mubarak was ousted only eighteen days after the January 25 demonstrations set in motion a train of events that led Egypt's military leadership, much like its counterpart in Tunisia, to make clear they would not save the Egyptian president. The Egyptian military cared about saving itself as an institution. With Mubarak out, it was as if a political tornado swept through much of the region. Demonstrations and protests erupted within days in Algeria, Bahrain, Jordan, Morocco, Oman, and Yemen. The ability to instill fear, the essential currency of authoritarian regimes, seemingly had been lost.

Second, at this stage, with the regional turmoil buffeting only the Western-oriented regimes—the uprising in Syria had not yet begun—key American friends were appalled. The Saudis, the Emirates, and the Israelis were all saying the same thing: they felt President Obama had pushed Mubarak out. They were completely convinced that the president and the administration were encouraging change without any idea of where it was going—or of the high likelihood that the Muslim Brotherhood would be the main beneficiary.

Indeed, it was the president's public statement after a phone call with Mubarak that fostered an impression that he was determined to drive the Egyptian president out and even "humiliate" him. The president's demands that the transition "must begin now" and Robert Gibbs's comment the next day that "now means yesterday" had an impact the president never intended.[20] Even as sophisticated an observer of the United States as my friend Dan Meridor, a senior Israeli minister, asked me in the prime minister's office in Jerusalem, "Why did the president have to push Mubarak out? Why did he have to say anything publicly?"

Leaving aside the simple reality that America could not remain silent in the face of two million people in the streets in Cairo, Obama was hoping to help manage events. I was in the Oval Office for his first phone call to Mubarak, and the president was respectful, even as he tried to persuade Mubarak of the seriousness of the situation. Mubarak was in a state of denial, telling Obama, "I understand my people . . . In a few days it will all be over." And, if it isn't? Obama asked. Mubarak simply repeated that it would all be over in a few days. Little did he know how right he was.

It was Obama's hope to avoid turmoil in Egypt—and Mubarak being pushed out precipitously—that led him to call for transition. He believed the promise of political change could defuse the emotions of the moment and make a manageable transition possible.

But the Israelis, Saudis, and Emirates all feared change in Egypt. For Israel, the peace treaty with Egypt was the linchpin of its strategic force posture and doctrine. A cold peace with Egypt had endured under Mubarak, and there was great fear about what would come next if he were driven out. If the Muslim Brotherhood—a group that rejected peace with Israel—came to power, what would happen? This prospect was profoundly unsettling to Israelis and made them deeply suspicious of the change taking place. The Saudis felt similarly. They saw Egypt as the bulwark against the two threats that Saudis most feared: Iran and the Muslim Brotherhood.[21] In truth, the president was aware of these fears and wanted us to work closely with the military to manage the transition after Mubarak, but he was less fearful of the Muslim Brotherhood—not because he felt they were democrats, but because, as I would hear him say, the Islamists in Indonesia had evolved and he felt that could be possible in Egypt as well.

This more benign view of the Muslim Brotherhood penetrated much of the State Department as well as the intelligence community. Unlike the president, who drew on the Indonesian example, Middle East experts within the administration, reflecting a long tradition across different administrations, once again tended to look at the Muslim Brotherhood through a particular prism. The Brotherhood was a real social force. It was the wave of the future; we could work with them as they learned to govern. Once again, the instinct to see the more extreme as the more authentic guided much of the analysis. Just as the Arab nationalists in the 1950s and 1960s captured the imagination of much of the national security establishment—and produced arguments that we needed to accommodate them—so too would the Muslim Brotherhood now get characterized in internal memos in the Obama administration.[22]

From the beginning of the transition in Egypt, both Tom Donilon, who had replaced General Jones as national security adviser, and I were skeptical that the Muslim Brotherhood was capable of changing. We saw our interests—and values—being served by getting the Egyptian military to manage the transition so that the Muslim Brotherhood could not exploit its superior organization over all other political actors. Unfortunately, Field Marshal Mohammad Tantawi, the head of the Supreme Council of the Armed Forces who removed Mubarak, rejected our advice. Tantawi seemed to feel he could manage the Brotherhood. But he would be forced out by President Mohammad Morsi not long after he came to power in the June

2012 presidential election. We were no more successful in trying to influence Tantawi to reach out to the Israelis. This would change after Tantawi and Morsi were gone.

When Field Marshal Abdel Fattah el-Sisi, the force behind the military's removal of President Morsi in July 2013, took power, Egyptian cooperation with Israel on security would be transformed and reach unprecedented levels.[23] The jihadi terror threat in the Sinai, which Sisi saw as largely driven by the Muslim Brotherhood and Hamas, compelled the Egyptian military to cooperate extensively with Israel. Though still reluctant to expose the relationship in public, there was a sea change in terms of actual security cooperation.

By contrast, Tantawi had not only kept security cooperation to the bare minimum, he was also slow to react when, in September 2011, a mob breached the building housing the Israeli embassy in Cairo.* President Obama intervened, making it clear to the Egyptians that our relationship was at stake if Tantawi did not protect the Israelis and bring the situation under control.[24] The president's intervention, which likely saved Israeli lives, tempered Israeli criticism about the American approach to the Arab Spring—at least for the moment.

Ironically, the Jordanians, the Emirates, and other Gulf states increasingly were expressing to the Israelis their concerns about the Obama administration's approach to the upheaval in the area. These Arab leaders believed that the Israelis could push the administration to change its approach to the uprisings. On a number of occasions, Saudi officials explained to me their misgivings about U.S. policy and drew attention to the fact that the Israelis had similar worries, with one senior Saudi telling me, "The Israelis explain it better than we do."

I sometimes pointed to the irony of Arab leaders trying to use Israel to influence an administration that had felt it was necessary to distance itself from Israel in order to reach out to the Arab world. While I hoped to provoke questioning of traditionalist assumptions about the region, there was little interest in introspection among Obama's inner circle. Instead, there was a tendency to read these Arab efforts simply as being driven by a resistance to change—and a presumption that the Israelis shared the reluctance of our traditional Arab friends to accept the need to be more responsive to popular attitudes in Arab countries.

---

* Demonstrations over an anti-Islamic video had erupted against the U.S. embassy and spread to an assault on the Israeli embassy.

The Arab Awakening would not prove to be a springtime for the region. The images of courageous protesters in Tahrir Square that captured the imagination of the world quickly turned into a revolt in Libya, a civil war in Yemen, and an ugly sectarian war in Syria—a war in which the regime would become, in the words of Saudi King Abdullah, a "killing machine."[25]

Obama would face more dilemmas as a result of the resistance (or counterrevolutions) by regimes trying to hold on to power in response to societal efforts to oust them. In Libya, the president decided to lead an intervention, but he bound it carefully. On Syria, notwithstanding the humanitarian catastrophe, Obama saw only a quagmire, and he was not about to let us get sucked in.*[26]

While he would come under pressure from the Saudis to do more in Syria, the Israelis were far more ambivalent. The Israeli security establishment saw an opportunity to shift the balance of forces in the region against Iran. Assad's fall would weaken Hezbollah and make it hard for the Iranians to resupply them with arms. But Prime Minister Netanyahu was not where his security establishment was. In conversations I had with him both before I left the administration and afterward, he was far more cautious about Syria, worrying about what would happen the day after Assad fell. He saw chaos along Israel's border and the growth of jihadi forces who might not accept the logic of deterrence that seemed to guide the Syrian regime when it came to Israel. Netanyahu's concern, which he conveyed to President Obama, was focused primarily on the danger of Syria's chemical weapons (CW) stocks falling into the hands of jihadis or Hezbollah if Syria collapsed.

President Obama took Israel's concerns very seriously. He authorized contingency planning with the Israelis to deal with a situation in which centralized control over the chemical weapons stocks in Syria was lost. Intelligence sharing was intensified, and different scenarios and joint responses were planned. On a number of occasions, the president said clearly that the United States did not have vital interests in Syria—but the United States did have an interest in making sure Syrian CW did not proliferate.[27] It was the concern about the possible use or movement of chemical weapons that led

---

* Before I left the administration at the end of 2011, I argued that everything we feared providing lethal assistance would do—heighten the level of violence, break down the central institutions of the state, deepen the sectarian conflict—would all happen precisely because we didn't back the moderate opposition, and it was the radical Islamists who would prevail as a result.

the president to declare, in August 2012, a "redline" on Syria. He said Syria's use of such weapons would "change my calculus."[28]

Declaring a redline should always be done with great care. For one thing, doing so makes any action short of the redline tolerable. For another, once invoked, if the redline is breached, military action is required lest we raise fundamental doubts about our credibility. And that is precisely what happened with the president's redline on Syria's use of CW. Syria breached the line in the spring of 2013, but it took several months to confirm that the regime had done so. To show there would be consequences, Ben Rhodes—not the president—issued a statement essentially saying that since Assad's forces had crossed the redline, we, too, would cross a threshold and begin to provide lethal assistance to segments of the Syrian opposition. The low-key statement in fact highlighted not our resolve but the reluctance President Obama continued to feel about doing more in Syria.[29]

If the hope was that this decision would deter the Assad regime from using its CW, the administration learned on August 21, 2013, that hope was in vain. The Assad regime attacked the Damascus neighborhood of Ghouta with CW—killing fourteen hundred, including four hundred children. Even though Assad denied he had used CW, the evidence was undeniable. The administration indicated it was readying a strike on Syrian targets to demonstrate the costs of violating this international norm.

Obama took international norms seriously; breaking the rules meant a price must be paid. As he had said in Oslo during his acceptance speech for the Nobel Prize, he hoped to find alternatives to using violence against those who broke the rules, but the "words of the international community must mean something." And, he added, "Those regimes that break the rules must be held accountable."[30] Secretary Kerry laid out a compelling public rationale for using force in this case given the "overwhelming evidence" that the Assad regime had used these weapons. Notwithstanding the expectations that we were about to launch strikes, President Obama, in a statement from the White House on Saturday, August 29, made what appeared to be a political U-turn. Though maintaining that he had the legal right to order military strikes, the president said that before taking any military action, he would seek congressional authorization. In a democracy, it was important, he said, to show broad support when using force. Having not hinted that he would seek such support earlier in the week when the administration was laying out its rationale for a strike, the president's statement came as a surprise both domestically and internationally. It had a devastating effect on the United States' friends in the region.

To the Israelis, it was a profound and unsettling shock. Almost immediately after the president completed his statement, I received a call from a senior Israeli official.[31] He said: "We are stunned. This is a terrible day for all America's friends in the Middle East. We may be split here about greater U.S. intervention in Syria, but America cannot draw a line and then pull back. This is a disaster—and particularly for those of us who say we can count on the U.S." He added, "The only hope now is to go to the Russians and see if they will join you in pressing for Assad to give up the CW. Putin might go for that, and it will at least remove the CW threat if it works." I asked if this idea had been raised with the president or with Kerry, and he said, "It will be very soon."

Secretary Kerry would subsequently tell me that he did discuss the idea with Prime Minister Netanyahu, but that he had previously proposed it to the Russian foreign minister, Sergei Lavrov. Regardless of where it originated and with whom—and why the Russians suddenly accepted it—President Obama repeatedly spoke about how he had succeeded with his redline. His threat to use force had led the Russians to agree to the joint initiative to get the Assad regime to turn over their CW for destruction—and it was a model, in his words, for his larger aim of having international norms respected: "The fact that we did not have to fire a missile to get that accomplished is not a failure to uphold international norms, it's a success."[32]

In objective terms, the president's claim that he had fulfilled the purpose of his redline—the destruction of Syria's chemical weapons—and that the planned military strikes would not have produced such a result is surely correct.[33] The problem, unfortunately, is that redlines create objective as well as subjective realities.

The perception in Israel and with America's Arab allies in the region is that the United States established a redline, spoke publicly of military strikes, and then drew back when it appeared there might not be public or congressional support for military action. The subjective reality embedded itself in the minds of Israeli, Saudi, and Emirati leaders and fostered the impression that the Obama administration was not reliable. King Abdullah said as much in private, and one Saudi official was blunt in public: "But this year, for all their talk of 'redlines,' when it counted, our partners have seemed all too ready to concede our safety and risk our region's stability."[34]

The administration's broader approach to Syria also did much to contribute to this perception. The president made it clear repeatedly that "we cannot be involved in someone's civil war." For him, destroying the CW was one thing; the future of Syria and what was happening there on the ground was another. As terrible as the humanitarian toll was in Syria, he believed our interests argued against getting drawn into the conflict there. Moreover, President Obama believed Iran and Russia—not the United States—were losing in Syria, and we should let them pay the price, not pay one ourselves. Note his words:

> I'm always darkly amused by this notion that somehow Iran has won in Syria. I mean, you hear sometimes people saying, "They're winning in Syria." And you say, "This was their one friend in the Arab world, a member of the Arab League, and it is now in rubble." It's bleeding them because they're having to send in billions of dollars. Their key proxy, Hezbollah, which had a very comfortable and powerful perch in Lebanon, now finds itself attacked by Sunni extremists. This isn't good for Iran. They're losing as much as anybody. The Russians find their one friend in the region in rubble and delegitimized.[35]

Ironically, although Prime Minister Netanyahu shared the president's ambivalence about intervention in Syria, he, like Arab leaders, saw Iran and the Russians acting in Syria to change the balance of power in the region at the expense of the United States' partners—and the United States as acquiescing in this aggression. When coupled with the perceived eagerness of the president for a nuclear deal with Iran, particularly after the election of Hassan Rouhani as president in June 2013, the Israelis, the Saudis, and the Emirates had profound doubts about the administration's purposes and aims in the region.

Different Mind-sets for How to Deal with Israel

Tom Donilon, as national security adviser, had maintained high-level channels to the Chinese, his key counterparts in Europe, and the Israelis, Saudis, and Emiratis. He conducted the strategic dialogue with the Israelis focused especially on Iran. His departure from the White House on July 1, 2013, was felt everywhere. But its most profound effect was in the Middle East, where key Arab officials, with whom I maintained an ongoing relationship, told me they no longer felt they got a "good hearing" in the White House and that there was little appreciation for their concerns.

With Israel, the problem was most severe, and I saw it directly. Donilon had developed a relationship with Netanyahu and the senior leadership in the Israeli national security establishment. They collectively felt that he was aware of their concerns and took them into account. In February 2012, he traveled to Israel and spent five hours in a private discussion with the prime minister, focusing principally but not exclusively on Iran. No national security adviser had ever before held such a discussion, and he did it without going elsewhere in the region, which was unprecedented. It was not that he agreed with everything he heard or in any way held back in conveying what was important to President Obama—quite the contrary. Rather, he gave Netanyahu the sense that Israel got a "fair hearing" and his views were taken into account when U.S. actions were considered. Donilon acted in much the same manner with senior Israeli military and intelligence officials, who noted his meticulous preparation on the Iranian nuclear issue and his command of all aspects of the challenge.

Donilon's successor, Susan Rice, would not maintain the same involvement in the dialogue. One senior Israeli commented that Rice was just "checking the box. She showed little interest and little understanding of the issues. The contrast with Donilon was unbelievable."

It was not only that Rice did not invest in the dialogue with the Israelis the way Donilon had. She had very different instincts about the Israeli relationship altogether. Whereas Donilon, much like Steve Hadley before him, believed that the best way to keep the Israelis from going their own way was to work closely with them, Rice viewed the Israelis more competitively. She was prone to see them acting without regard to U.S. interests and frequently undermining them. Surely her time at the UN put her in a position where she saw Israel constantly isolated and the United States nearly always cast in the role of Israel's defender. To be fair, when I was in the administration and asked her to be helpful to the Israelis on issues coming up at the UN, she was responsive.

Still, in the internal debates in the administration, she nearly always took the view that the Israelis were hurting us and never took our needs into account. She embodied the mind-set that we needed to be wary of Israel and not let it exploit differences within the administration. The less we shared with them, the better. Like Denis McDonough, she, too, believed that we needed to manage discussions with the Israelis and not allow them to have multiple channels into the administration, which they would exploit. Suspicion was the point of departure for Rice—and other key figures, like McDonough.

When I first got to the White House in July 2009, I learned that there was great discomfort with the Israelis having these separate channels. McDonough told me we needed to minimize the danger of the Israelis hearing different messages, and we should ensure that if someone like Ehud Barak, the defense minister, was visiting Washington, he should see the vice president, the secretary of state, and the national security adviser in one joint meeting. I explained that was neither practical nor smart. We had an interest in drawing him out on sensitive issues, and the less intimate the discussion, the less forthcoming he would almost surely be. Moreover, I said in those cases where relationships and trust already existed, we could use these channels to help produce more Israeli responsiveness. For Tom Donilon, this view was an article of faith. For Denis McDonough and Susan Rice, it was anathema.

In reality, there were two different mind-sets in the administration on how to deal with the Israelis. One saw that cooperation and collaboration—and drawing the Israelis close to us—would serve our interests and theirs, and make the Israelis more responsive. The other, reflecting a long-standing view held by previous administrations, saw a largely competitive relationship that was basically a one-way street. Sharing with the Israelis offered little and cost much. While the president's impulse to distance the United States from Israel at the outset of the administration fit naturally with those who tended to see Israel in competitive terms, the lineup within the administration on what to do with Israel was not always consistent. Robert Gates is a case in point.[36]

His mind-set toward Israel was deeply rooted, and he fit in comfortably with those in the Obama administration—and its predecessors—who felt there was little reciprocity in the relationship. In fact, during one meeting in 2010, he declared in words that sounded eerily similar to those used by Robert Komer fifty years earlier: "With Israel, it is all give and no get. We give and give and give and we get nothing. It is a one-way street."

Yet precisely because he did not want the Israelis to feel that they might have no choice but to hit Iran, Gates saw the value of reassuring them and gave directions for extensive sharing and cooperation across the spectrum of military-to-military and defense intelligence ties.[37] Gates essentially shared the instincts of McDonough and Rice, but he was also highly practical. On the other side of the ledger, in the first term, Vice President Biden, Secretary of State Clinton, and Tom Donilon were generally of the view that collaboration with the Israelis was in our interests. President Obama's instincts on Israeli security tended to put him in the collaboration camp, but his sense that Israel did not follow the logic of its own interests and was the stronger power when it came to peace also made him sympathetic to the competitive-suspicious school within his administration.

By any objective measure, we did give to Israel—and we also got from Israel. On a government-to-government basis, Israeli intelligence, counter-terror support, and military information provided to us consistently grew over the years. From allowing us to assess and work on captured Soviet equipment to sharing in weapons innovations in active armor and drone technology to developing the tactics on urban warfare and missile defense—we acquired much from Israel that could not be measured only in dollars.

But it wasn't necessarily what policy makers wanted. In effect, they took for granted the security-related benefits that we got from the Israelis. Policy makers focused on whether the Israelis responded to us on the Palestinian or peace issue, particularly because they put so much emphasis on this being at the core of our problems in the region. And, of course, they worried about unilateral Israeli military actions that might impinge on our interests, as when Israel struck the Osirak reactor in Iraq or the al-Kibar reactor in Syria, or the possibility of Israel attacking Iran's nuclear facilities. Over the years, U.S. decision makers understandably defined reciprocity in the rela-tionship as Israel being responsive on what primarily mattered to us—peace and avoiding unilateral military actions.

To the Israelis, however, we sought "reciprocity" on what amounted to fundamental issues relating to their future. Israel would not sacrifice on ex-istential issues just to satisfy the United States, no matter how important the relationship was. As Israeli prime ministers as different as Rabin and Net-anyahu often told me, Israel would take our concerns into account, but our concerns could not be the arbiters of Israel's future. In no small part they said this because they frequently felt that our views of the region were naïve and wrong.

In the summer of 2013, I was reminded of this when seeing Prime Min-ister Netanyahu. He asked me if the president and Susan Rice believed what recently retired General James Mattis had said about the conflict with the Palestinians and its impact on the U.S. position in the region. Mattis, who had been head of Central Command after David Petraeus, echoed com-ments cited earlier that Petraeus had made to the Congress in 2009. Only he went further:

> The current situation is unsustainable . . . We have got to find a way to
> make the two-state solution that Democrat and Republican administra-
> tions have supported, we've got to get there. And the chances for it . . .
> are starting to ebb because the settlements and where they're at are
> going to make it impossible to maintain the two-state option . . . So

we've got to work on this with a sense of urgency. And I paid a military-security price every day as the commander of CENTCOM because the Americans were seen as biased in support of Israel, and that moderates all the moderate Arabs who want to be with us because they can't come out publicly in support of people who don't show respect for the Arab Palestinians.[38]

That Netanyahu would raise Mattis's statement was no surprise. It was remarkable, particularly at a time when the Egyptian military had just removed Mohammad Morsi from office and there was great tumult in Egypt; when nearly 100,000 Syrians had been killed in the civil war, a conflict that was rightly seen as a proxy war between Saudi Arabia and Iran; and when Rouhani was about to be inaugurated in Iran. These were the issues that completely absorbed the leading Arab states at the time. Mattis's comments seemed completely out of touch with the actual concerns of the Saudis et al. Netanyahu was asking: Do the president and those around him not see what is happening in this region? Do they not know what the concerns of the Arabs are? "What I am hearing from them and their concerns about America—could they really view things the way Mattis does?"

I told him I didn't know, but old habits die hard. No doubt many in the administration shared those attitudes. They might not probe deeper and see that the Saudis and Emirates were focused first on the threats to them, whether from Iran or the Muslim Brotherhood, and only secondarily on the Palestinians. I reminded Netanyahu that those states were put on the defensive because of the Palestinian issue, and no doubt this is what Mattis often heard. I understood that much like in the past, the Saudis and others would cooperate with us to the extent that their security required it, and I suspected the president understood that. Still, I went on to explain that just as he was asking about whether we see the region as it actually is, many around the president ask whether he saw what is happening in Israel's backyard with the Palestinians. I asked Netanyahu whether he really thought the status quo was sustainable.

He replied that he was aware of the need to move and that he was ready to run risks, but it was daunting if the United States did not seem to have a firm grasp on what was happening in the region.[39] Our conversation took place before the president's "U-turn" on Syria. I saw the prime minister again the next month, and he was more unsettled about us, but not as unsettled as he would be when we met in November 2013, when he felt we were about to conclude what became known as the Joint Plan of Action agreement with the Iranians.[40]

On Friday night, November 8, 2013, Prime Minister Netanyahu asked me to come by his residence after sundown for an informal chat. I was in Jerusalem, and he wanted to discuss both the talks with the Palestinians and the nuclear negotiations with Iran. As it turned out, I arrived while he was on a secure call with President Obama. When I joined the prime minister after the call, he was as disturbed as I had ever seen him. Earlier in the day, Secretary Kerry had left Israel to go to Geneva to see if an interim deal on the Iranian nuclear program could be concluded. The Israelis had been surprised that such a deal was suddenly on the brink of happening. Only a week earlier, Israel's Iran team was briefed on the status of the talks, but Rice, in keeping with her more competitive, noncollaborative instincts, had not authorized the Israelis to be briefed on the actual state of play in the negotiations.[41] Now the surprise left them alarmed—and Kerry, who had a good relationship with Netanyahu, had not been able to reassure him about the content of the deal. Netanyahu had publicly stated that if the deal was concluded, it would be a "historic mistake."[42] The president had called to change the prime minister's view, in no small part because of the impact that Israel's position would likely have on congressional attitudes toward the emerging deal.

The call had not worked. I was struck by how alone Netanyahu felt. He believed the United States had given up all its leverage in this deal and the sanctions would now collapse of their own weight, taking all the pressure off the Iranians and freezing the situation. The Iranians would be left as a threshold nuclear state, and Israel would be confronted with unpalatable choices. I challenged his conclusions, saying that the sanctions would not collapse because there was much the United States could do to demonstrate the costs to those businesses that might think of breaking the sanctions regime. He acknowledged that I could be right, but what became apparent is that he interpreted what he heard from the president as a loss of will on his part to keep the pressure up. When I asked him why he drew this conclusion, he said because the president felt politics ruled out the use of force and therefore required a deal.

I told him, "I just don't believe the president said or meant that. Maybe he was making the point that the war-weariness of our public requires us to demonstrate we made every effort to give diplomacy a chance and this deal gives us the chance to do so." But the prime minister felt the president was telling him that our domestic reality left him little choice but to do a deal.

I was certain two leaders speaking the same language had talked past each other. I contacted Secretary Kerry to let him know that the prime minister had formed an impression about the U.S. position that needed to be corrected. Kerry quickly followed up with a call. But the problem was a White House problem—and not one Kerry could easily correct. Had Tom Donilon still been the national security adviser, he surely would have understood from the call that there was a problem and he would have immediately spoken to his counterpart. If the misimpression was not corrected, he would have had President Obama make another call.

He had done precisely this in September 2012 when Prime Minister Netanyahu had made public comments challenging our position on the Iranian nuclear issue. Donilon arranged the call and the air was not only cleared but there was a meeting of the minds.[43] By contrast, now there was no call from Rice, there was no follow-up from the president, and the prime minister did not soften his public criticism two weeks later when the actual Joint Plan of Action was concluded. Instead, Rice, reflecting her generally more combative mind-set, would say to Abe Foxman, national director of the Anti-Defamation League, that in reacting to the Joint Plan of Action, Netanyahu's posture was outrageous. In her view, the Israeli leader did everything but "use 'the n-word' in describing the president."[44]

With Donilon gone, the school of thought that saw Israel through the competitive-costly prism became dominant at the White House. Secretary Kerry did not share this mind-set, but he had to contend with it in his own diplomacy. That said, when it came to Iran, there was little dissonance within the administration on its approach, either in Obama's first term or second. However, in his first term, Israel was a constant factor in the administration's considerations and policies on Iran, and it is worth explaining in greater detail how the policy was shaped and how it evolved.

Shaping the Approach Toward Iran

From the outset of the presidency, Obama was focused on establishing what became known as the dual-track approach: be prepared to deal directly with the Iranians but also build our leverage with them. Engagement put pressure on the Iranians in two ways. First, talking to the United States created deep fissures in the Iranian elite. Second, if the Iranians balked at dealing directly with us, it made it far easier for us to mobilize sanctions against them. The hope was to alter Iran's behavior through negotiations, but if the

Iranians would not engage at all, or engaged but would not budge, we would then be able to garner international pressure on them to change course.

Israel was very much a factor in this approach. To forestall Israeli military action against what Israelis perceived as an existential threat, the president understood we needed to show we could apply meaningful pressure on the Iranians that would alter their nuclear program. In his first meetings with Prime Minister Netanyahu, in May 2009, Obama explained the logic of the dual track—which necessarily had to start with the effort at engagement. When Netanyahu asked how much time we would give engagement—clearly fearing that the Iranians might just string us along as they proceeded with their nuclear development—Obama told him that if nothing happened before the end of the first year we would pivot toward sanctions. In order to add to the credibility of our pressure on Iran, the president wanted the Israelis to understand that he meant it when he said "all options are on the table." To that end, we briefed the Israelis on the steps we were taking to act militarily—if it came to that—vis-à-vis the Iranian nuclear program.*

While engagement and possible sanctions were means to affect the Iranians, they were obviously not ends in themselves. The goal was to get the Islamic Republic to roll back its nuclear program, but the administration did not at this time address what it was ultimately prepared to accept in this regard. Robert Gates sent a memo to the president emphasizing we needed to be clear on our objective. Gates wanted systematic discussions not just on our goals but also on different scenarios related to the eruption of conflict, including if the Israelis were to strike the Iranian nuclear program and the Iranians retaliated, what should the United States do—support the Israelis, not support them, threaten Iran, etc. Gates's memo led to a number of highly sensitive discussions among the principals, including some in which the president participated.[15] More than anything else, these discussions provided impetus for enhancing our presence in the region and led to further deployments of missile defenses and an additional carrier to the Persian Gulf. We would add to our capabilities to be ready for any contingency—and in time we would discuss these with the Israelis.

Although we withheld some military and intelligence capabilities that would have made unilateral Israeli military strikes easier, the president's

---

* President Obama directed the Pentagon early in the administration to make sure he could back up his promise. He told a small group of us that if he decided at some point that force had to be used, he did not want to be told we did not have the necessary military means. But he also did not want the way we prepared that capability to leave him with no choice but to use force.

inclination was to be very responsive to Israeli military and intelligence requests. Here there was no dissonance among the president's senior advisers. To the extent there was any disagreement, it had to do with the nature of our objective: Should we prevent Iran from acquiring a nuclear weapon or ultimately be prepared to live with it and contain it after the fact? No one minimized the consequences of Iran acquiring nuclear weapons or a nuclear capability. But there was debate over whether we should use force to prevent the Iranians from crossing the threshold if crippling economic sanctions, isolation, and diplomatic pressure and negotiations failed to do so.

Gates and Mike Mullen, the chairman of the Joint Chiefs, made it clear that we were in two wars in the region and that was quite enough. They were not soft on Iran, but they were not in favor of the use of force if all other means failed to stop the Iranian nuclear weapons pursuit. Secretary Clinton, Tom Donilon, Deputy Secretary of State Jim Steinberg, and I had a different view. But we understood that for coercive diplomacy to succeed— and obviate the need for military strikes—the Iranians had to believe we would use force if diplomacy failed. It was a source of continuing frustration that Gates and Mullen periodically spoke of the terrible costs of an attack on Iran—whether by us or the Israelis. If the costs were so terrible, why would we ever do it? Why would the Iranians believe the president when he said all options were on the table?[46]

The mixed messages triggered Israeli complaints, in no small part because the Israelis understood they were derivative of the more basic disagreement over prevention versus containment of the Iranian nuclear program. The president heard the Gates-Mullen view and also the countervailing view that the problem with containment was that it would fail. We could deter the Iranians from using or transferring nuclear weapons, but the Saudis and others then would feel obliged to get their own weapons. They would not trust U.S. assurances after three administrations—Clinton, Bush, and Obama—had all declared that it was unacceptable for Iran to have them, and it had acquired them anyway. The NPT would probably collapse as a result, and the ground rules of the cold war, where mutual deterrence worked, would not apply in this region because no one in the Middle East would feel they could afford to strike second.

We had debated this issue in front of the president but, as was so often the case, he kept his counsel to himself. Only as we prepared for Vice President Biden's trip to Israel in March 2010 did he reveal what he had decided. President Obama wanted the vice president to provide outreach to the Israeli public and also reassurance on our readiness to deal with the Iranian nuclear threat. We met with the president on successive days in the Oval Office to discuss what the vice president should say about our objective on the Iranian nuclear program in a major speech. Initially, the president was comfortable saying that it was "unacceptable" for Iran to have a nuclear weapon. When I pointed out that "unacceptable" was an observation, not necessarily a policy, he asked what I meant. I said, "It will still be unacceptable after they have it, just as it is with North Korea today." I said he could certainly stick with this position—it is, after all, what both Presidents Clinton and Bush declared.

But Obama felt that was not enough and asked what more we could say. I suggested: "We are determined to prevent Iran from acquiring nuclear weapons." Unlike saying it is unacceptable, which does not require us to act, once you say this, you are making it clear you will act. "This is not about living with a nuclear Iran but preventing it." President Obama wanted to think about it overnight and we would reconvene before we left on the trip. The next morning he told us he was comfortable with "determined to prevent," and this became the language the administration used from that point forward.

It was not until two years later that the president publicly drew a distinction between prevention and containment as our objective. He did it first in an interview with Jeffrey Goldberg and subsequently at the AIPAC conference in March 2012. With Goldberg, he was clear about all options being on the table, that he did not "bluff," and that prevention was necessary because if Iran crossed the nuclear weapons threshold it would trigger "a nuclear arms race" in the Middle East.[47]

Why would the president choose Goldberg and AIPAC to stake out this public position? Some might argue he was trying to shore up his political standing in the Jewish community. Certainly, Jewish leaders were bound to prefer a posture that emphasized prevention and not containment given the existential threat Iran's nuclear pursuits posed to Israel. No doubt he was mindful of the political benefits of articulating this position and denying Mitt Romney an opening on this issue. Still, I suspect he had another reason. Netanyahu was visiting Washington at this point, and the president, I believe, was looking to give the Israeli prime minister a reason not to strike the Iranian nuclear facilities. At this time, Israeli Defense Minister Barak was emphasizing that Iran was on the brink of reaching a "zone of immunity"—representing the point past which an Israeli military strike could have only limited effect. After the president's public statements and his meeting with the prime minister, Netanyahu said that the time left to deal with the Iranian nuclear challenge was measured "not in weeks, but also not in years."

He thus sent a clear signal that the president had more time for diplomacy to work.

By the fall of 2012, Netanyahu was feeling differently. That led to the secure call to Obama in September, which again helped to defer any Israeli consideration of striking on its own. When President Obama visited Israel in March 2013, Netanyahu would say, "I'm absolutely convinced that the President is determined to prevent Iran from getting nuclear weapons. And I appreciate that."[48]

That firm confidence lapsed by the time of my meeting with the prime minister on November 8 of that year. In the intervening time, Rouhani had been elected president in Iran. We had opened a back channel to the Iranians, facilitated by Oman, and that back channel had led us to believe that a deal was possible with Rouhani—particularly given his desire to see sanctions lifted and Iran's isolation ended.[49] The Joint Plan of Action, as key officials in the administration explained to me, reflected the belief that Rouhani was a moderate and could, in time, do the kind of deal we needed. But he could not do it without gaining some limited sanctions relief, which would show the supreme leader, Ali Khamenei, that Rouhani could affect our behavior—and thus build his authority. Netanyahu, for his part, saw Rouhani very differently. He saw no moderation and feared that the deal, rather than leading to a rollback of the Iranian program, would end up freezing it in place as our leverage inevitably eroded. Iran with 19,500 centrifuges would be a nuclear threshold state, and we would no longer be able to prevent it from breaking out at a time of its choosing—or so Netanyahu believed. President Obama disagreed. He felt the Joint Plan of Action allowed us to test the possibility of Rouhani being able to do a deal that would roll back the Iranian nuclear program, and that if it failed to do so, we still had the option of applying pressure—and using force if need be.

After the Joint Plan of Action was agreed, a public gap emerged between the president and the prime minister. But they would act to cool the rhetoric, and the administration would work quietly with Israel on our approach to a comprehensive agreement. However, over the course of 2014, as the administration showed its readiness to accept an industrial-scale Iranian nuclear program and not roll it back, the gap with the Israelis reemerged, and Netanyahu became far more outspoken in his criticism of a possible deal.[50]

Overall within the administration there remained a strong consensus on our policy toward Iran. That would not be the case on the issue of Israeli-Palestinian peace for much of Obama's first and second terms. Here too, it is worth describing the sources of the internal debate and how the policy evolved.

Points of Friction on Peace Throughout the Obama Presidency

Until I arrived at the White House in July 2009 and began to challenge what we were asking of Israelis and Palestinians, there was little discussion within the administration on the approach to peace. There had been no serious internal debate on the wisdom of insisting on a complete settlement freeze—even though it meant asking a "rightist" Israeli government to do what no center or center-left government had ever done.* Hillary Clinton had her doubts about the policy but felt resistance to it was pointless, given the depth of President Obama's views on settlements.

Interestingly, later in 2009, the secretary would find herself the target of criticism from anonymous White House sources when she described the Israeli decision to adopt a ten-month moratorium on new housing starts in settlements as "unprecedented"—objections that seeped out after Arabs and the Palestinians dismissed the moratorium as meaningless because it didn't apply to building in Jerusalem and because existing construction could be completed.† The instinct of those in the White House who saw a competitive,

---

* I made this point to the president at the time of Netanyahu's first visit as prime minister, in May 2009. I was in the Oval Office with George Mitchell to brief President Obama for the meeting with Netanyahu. Mitchell was there to brief on peace; I was there to brief on Iran. After Mitchell said that the key to the meeting was getting Netanyahu to agree to a settlement freeze, the president turned to me and asked for my opinion. Though I had been involved in none of the peace process strategy at this point, I replied, "You are asking Bibi to do what no Labor prime minister has done—not Rabin, not Peres, and not Barak. How is he supposed to explain it?" The president asked Mitchell to answer my question, and the senator said we were trying to reopen liaison offices the Israelis used to have in Qatar, Morocco, and Tunisia, and to get overflight rights for El Al over Saudi Arabia. When the president again asked me what I thought, I said, "You are asking Bibi to take an unprecedented step. He needs drama to justify it—a meeting with the Saudis, something unprecedented on the Saudi side." While our posture did not change after this conversation, I was later told that the president made the trip to Saudi Arabia before his Cairo speech to try to produce a Saudi step we could use with Netanyahu. But he got a very negative response from King Abdullah.

† The moratorium meant no new construction would be permitted for ten months. That was unprecedented, but it applied only to breaking ground on new building. Existing construction would continue, and roughly three thousand units fit this category.

costly relationship with Israel was to be critical of the secretary for crediting the Israeli move, particularly when the Arabs were not prepared to accept it.

The push-and-pull on this issue within the administration was reflected both in what Mitchell could tell the Israelis about the Bush letter of April 14, 2004, which had essentially recognized settlement blocs, and the reaction to an Israeli announcement of new building in Jerusalem during Vice President Biden's visit to Israel. On the former, Mitchell had been instructed (before I got to the White House) to tell the Israelis that the Obama administration did not regard the Bush letter as binding—a position that Dan Meridor told me shocked the Israelis when they heard it. It did not make Mitchell's task of negotiating a limitation on settlement activity (or anything else) any easier, because it suggested that U.S. assurances were good only for the administration that offered them.[51]

On the latter, there was a surprise announcement of new building in the East Jerusalem neighborhood of Ramat Shlomo during the vice president's visit to Israel in early March 2010. It would trigger heated discussion internally and at one point make me a target of leaks from within the administration.

The Biden Trip to Israel in March 2010 and Its Fallout

In the White House, the president and Rahm Emanuel were outraged by the announced plan to build in Ramat Shlomo. They saw it as a slap in the face, which they believed was deliberate and designed to embarrass the United States before the world. Netanyahu was chagrined. He had been blindsided by his own bureaucracy, and he understood how this made Biden look. After the president decided we should "condemn" the Israeli action—language normally reserved for acts of terror—he was still not satisfied with Netanyahu's apology and promise that there would be no building at Ramat Shlomo for at least two years. This came as a surprise to Biden and those of us on the trip with him. We thought the issue was largely behind us because Abu Mazen had told Biden he was satisfied with our public condemnation and the promise on Ramat Shlomo. Moreover, Biden's trip had been all about outreach to the Israeli public, and his speech at Tel Aviv University—which included the language on Iran worked out with Obama—had taken place after the Ramat Shlomo "surprise" and had been very well received.

But the anger at Netanyahu for "dissing" us had led to Secretary Clinton being instructed to call the prime minister and "insist" that he take further actions to correct the Ramat Shlomo decision, and to have the State Department publicly reveal that she had dressed him down in a "tough phone call." All this took place while I was en route back from Israel and after the vice president had gone on to Jordan, and was an additional surprise to those of us on the trip.

I soon heard from Yitzhak Molcho, Prime Minister Netanyahu's closest confidant and adviser, with whom I had long worked closely. He described Clinton's call and said, "Dennis, we need to figure a way out of the mud."[52]

Molcho and I worked together to develop a number of possible understandings on what Israel would do on settlement activity and vis-à-vis the Palestinians, which would be discussed by the president and the prime minister when he visited Washington two weeks later to speak to AIPAC. This meeting, like nearly all their meetings, ended up involving a serious, thoughtful discussion: the president addressed the ideas we had developed and said to Netanyahu that the key was for the prime minister to think about those steps he could take that would show Israel was trying to strengthen its weaker Palestinian partner. He was not asking Netanyahu to do what was impossible, given his coalition, but to think strategically about the benefits of empowering Abu Mazen to do more. Netanyahu agreed, and they broke so the president could have dinner with his family. Netanyahu discussed with his team the steps they could take toward the Palestinians and on settlement restraint.

What had been a serious, thoughtful meeting was soon utterly transformed when the Israeli press interpreted the absence of a photo of the two leaders as a sign that relations were so bad the White House was not prepared to have a public meeting with Netanyahu. If that were not bad enough, some one on the Israeli side stoked things by saying the president left Netanyahu to cool his heels at the White House for a few hours.[53] Notwithstanding the public speculation, and Netanyahu's unhappiness that the White House was doing nothing to dispel the Israeli press's characterization of the meeting, we were in the process of reaching some understandings on moves Israel would take toward the Palestinians. In fact, the basic steps that Molcho and I had originally developed were discussed and expanded by Obama and Netanyahu, and they would lead to further refinement the next day in discussions between Mitchell, Dan Shapiro of the NSC staff, and me with Netanyahu; Molcho; Ron Dermer, the prime minister's aide; and the Israeli ambassador, Michael Oren. Later, we would produce an informal private understanding in which the Israelis agreed not to issue any tenders for construction in Jerusalem for the next four months and to take a number of other confidence-building measures designed to be responsive to what the president had sought.[54]

However, the effort to reach an understanding with the Israelis and end the appearance of a crisis in the relationship was not without its critics within the administration, and I was the target of their wrath in leaks to the press. Despite the fact that Mitchell and I carried on these talks together, anonymous sources described a battle between us. I was allegedly seeking to ease the tension with Israel at the expense of our credibility with the Arabs, while Mitchell was supposedly pushing a hard line. An article by Laura Rozen in *Politico* quoting several officials spoke of an intense debate: "[Ross] seems to be far more sensitive to Netanyahu's coalition politics than to U.S. interests. And he doesn't seem to understand that this has become bigger than Jerusalem but is rather about the credibility of the administration."[55]

With the ugly specter of dual loyalty appearing in the first posting of Rozen's article, Denis McDonough came to my defense. In the updated version of the article the next day, he rejected Rozen's suggestion: "The assertion is as false as it is offensive. Whoever said it has no idea what they are talking about. Dennis Ross's many decades of service speak volumes about his commitment to this country and to our vital interests, and he is a critical part of the president's team."[56]

That Denis felt the need to respond indicated not just that there was concern about the internal debate getting out of hand but also that there needed to be limits on how the disagreement was aired. It also seemed to mark an upturn in the U.S.-Israel relationship.

Coming to Israel's Rescue on the Flotilla and Netanyahu's July Trip to Washington

On Memorial Day, May 31, 2010, Israeli navy commandos intercepted a Turkish flotilla of six ships intending to disrupt Israel's blockade of Gaza, one of which, the *Mavi Marmara*, had armed people on it who resisted the Israelis commandeering the vessel. Nine people, all Turkish citizens, were killed. Turkish prime minister Recep Tayyip Erdogan, outraged over the deaths, demanded an immediate meeting of the UN Security Council. Prime Minister Netanyahu was visiting Canada at the time, and he recognized he had a disaster on his hands. He looked to us to protect the Israelis from a UN effort to condemn and sanction Israel. Working through the day and with the president coordinating our actions closely with Netanyahu in two phone calls, we succeeded in containing the UN's response.

Netanyahu came to the White House in early July and thanked President Obama for what he had done on the flotilla. He then told the president that if we could launch direct negotiations with the Palestinians, he would be prepared from the outset to seriously address their needs on territory, if they addressed Israeli security needs at the same time. For him to move on territory, he needed to know that the United States was prepared to meet Israel's security requirements in the context of a peace deal. After the meeting, the president, for the first time, said, "I believe that Bibi is serious . . . I want to move on this."

He told Tom Donilon to have James "Hoss" Cartwright, the vice chair of the JCS, lead a team to review Israel's requirements and find the best way to meet them, and he asked me to go with Cartwright to be sure this got handled in a way that addressed Netanyahu's concerns.

Cartwright and I left a few days later for Israel and would take several more trips during the remainder of the summer to meet Netanyahu, Barak, and members of the Israeli military.[57] By August, Mitchell found that Abu Mazen, who had let nearly nine months of the ten-month moratorium go by, was also now ready to resume direct talks.

With Netanyahu looking serious and Abu Mazen now prepared to go to direct talks, there was only one problem: Abu Mazen said the moratorium must not end on September 26. As part of the deal in getting cabinet acceptance of the moratorium, Netanyahu had promised it would not be extended. In late August, Secretary Clinton asked me to raise the issue of a possible extension with Netanyahu, believing it made more sense for me, rather than George Mitchell, to do so. I raised it with Molcho first, who said he thought it would be very hard for Netanyahu, given his earlier commitment. When I asked the prime minister about an extension, he said there was no way. Even if he was getting something of strategic value for doing so? I asked. Being coy, he asked me what I had in mind. I said he knew what was of value to him. He would get compensation for an extension. Again, he wanted me to offer him something. I demurred at this point, saying I did not know what could be on offer to him, but presumably it would be something he could use to justify an extension and a change in his position.

I reported to Secretary Clinton that Netanyahu's response suggested that, although it might be hard and the price tag high, he was willing to do a deal on this. She followed up, and her conversation with him went much like mine. The problem would, of course, have been more manageable if, in his discussions with Abu Mazen, Netanyahu was putting enough of real substance on the table to build our leverage on the Palestinians not to walk away from the negotiating table.

However, even though the talks that began on September 1–2 in Washington were initially good, Netanyahu was not prepared to say much about the scope of withdrawal without evidence that the Palestinians were serious about security. Abu Mazen spoke only in generalities about Israeli security needs. He said these issues had been settled by a plan General Jones had proposed in the last year of the Bush administration.* But there was no Jones plan, something that General Jones, now the national security adviser, acknowledged. Even though he would not offer more concrete assurances on security, Abu Mazen still wanted to know when the IDF would be out of the West Bank entirely. Full withdrawal, for him, spelled the end of Israeli occupation, and he envisioned three or four years for this. Netanyahu's time line was very different. He saw an extended Israeli military presence, even if small, in the Jordan Valley for decades. At one point in their discussions, in front of Secretary Clinton and George Mitchell, when Abu Mazen pressed Netanyahu, he spoke of an Israeli presence for forty years. Abu Mazen's response was, "Then you can keep the territory."

Once again, Abu Mazen was refusing to continue the negotiations if the moratorium was ended. Netanyahu was saying he could not extend it, especially since Abu Mazen had refused to negotiate directly for the first nine months of the moratorium, and now after a few weeks of direct talks was insisting on its extension.

The president, who had found Netanyahu serious in July, now was again suspicious. He felt the prime minister had promised to put a real proposal on territory on the table and he was not doing it, proving again that he talked a good game but never acted on his words.

In this setting, the president met Abu Mazen in Washington before both headed to New York for the UN General Assembly. When he was asked about the moratorium in a press conference, Obama surprised me by saying

---

* Condoleezza Rice had appointed Jones as envoy on security issues. She asked him to assess what Israel and the Palestinians would need if there was a peace agreement, and Jones put together teams to evaluate what would be necessary if the Israelis withdrew. At one point, Jones told Abu Mazen that NATO forces could replace the IDF. But his work was not completed by the end of the Bush administration. General Cartwright and I would evaluate the work of Jones's teams and build on it. Secretary Kerry would then have John Allen take our work and develop the ideas much further.

that he thought it best to extend it for a short period, even though he understood the political difficulties in Israel.

Not surprisingly, with the president publicly supporting the extension of the moratorium, Abu Mazen was unwilling to budge on his position: he would not stay at the table if the moratorium on new housing starts lapsed. We made an effort to reach an understanding on building restraint with the Israelis, and initially did so, but Abu Mazen was not interested. For him, it was all or nothing. He would not accept a limitation on what might be built now.[58]

We were stuck. Negotiations had begun on September 1, and with the September 26 deadline just days away, they were going to collapse. I again raised the idea of a compensation package for Israel, asking Ehud Barak and Yitzhak Molcho, who were in New York, whether this would allow Netanyahu to justify an extension. Barak raised a series of political and military payoffs, including support at the UN and additional F-35 stealth aircraft; Secretary Clinton was prepared to consider them. Molcho reported that the only thing that could make it politically palatable for Netanyahu was for us to release Jonathan Pollard. That was an achievement the right would endorse. For me, it was déjà vu—I was taken back to Wye River and Bill Clinton. Secretary Clinton raised it with President Obama and, though hesitant, he allowed us to take a few soundings of departmental reactions. Once again, the intelligence community was dead set against it, and in the end, no decision was made and Netanyahu ended the moratorium.

However, not long afterward, when new building began, Netanyahu came back to the secretary and offered to impose a halt on new construction within thirty days in return for a compensation package.[59] This set in motion a complicated negotiation over the coming month, involving what units would be grandfathered, how long the moratorium would continue, as well as what we would provide Israel. On November 1, Secretary Clinton met with Netanyahu for eight hours in New York and reached an agreement in principle, and subsequently we drafted a letter spelling out the package of assurances and the military hardware we were committing to Israel. But it all came to naught when Netanyahu informed us he could not gain cabinet approval for a new moratorium on building in the West Bank without announcing twelve hundred new units in Jerusalem at the same time. Abu Mazen would never agree to that quid pro quo, and we would be buying nothing with our package.

Though the president had allowed the secretary and me to pursue these talks, it was clear he was relieved when we pulled the plug. He did not feel we were getting enough for this. For such compensation, he wanted to know what Netanyahu would actually present on borders. Obama made clear he was still willing to offer compensation, but only if Netanyahu would move on withdrawal—which he doubted. Though Abu Mazen had shown little flexibility and squandered the moratorium, President Obama, seeing the Israelis as the stronger party and the Palestinians as the weaker one, put the onus on Israel.

Discussions on the Substance, Vetoing the Settlements Resolution, and the May Speeches

Secretary Clinton had invested in the direct talks in September and worked hard to sustain them. When we had to abandon our efforts to revive the talks, she discussed with Mitchell and me the need to focus on the substance of borders and security.[60] She decided—and the president accepted—that we would shift our effort back to a parallel discussion on the core issues, only now she would do more of it directly and separately with the leaders.[61]

The secretary then launched her own version of parallel talks with the leaders, and it replicated past peace efforts. Just like Kissinger's conversations with Eban and Rabin, Carter's at Camp David, President Clinton's (and mine) with Barak, Condoleezza Rice's with Olmert, Hillary Clinton asked Netanyahu in two long, secure calls what he could do. Echoing her predecessors, Secretary Clinton said, "We are your only friends. Why can't you share this just with us? I am not going to tell the Palestinians. I need to have a sense of what you can do, and what might be possible in light of that." Netanyahu answered in generalities about Israeli security needs—what settlement blocs were required to be secure, the importance of the Jordan Valley—and finally, after repeated prodding, he said that Israel could withdraw from most of the territory. He did not want to give percentages, but he understood what the Palestinians wanted, and if the Israeli security needs were accepted by us and met, he could be *generally* responsive.

Secretary Clinton marveled at how tough it had been to extract even this. And I told her it was not unique to Netanyahu. Israeli prime ministers see it as a slippery slope: whatever they offer, they are convinced will be an opening for us to ask for more when it proves insufficient to the Palestinians. Moreover, they believe that territory is their sole leverage with the Palestinians; therefore, they are determined to hold on to it until they know what they will get in return.

Conversely, although Abu Mazen's style was less grudging than Netanyahu's, he gave very little. Oftentimes he reverted to saying, "We Palestinians have given our concessions already—accepting June 4, 1967, meant agreeing that Israel would be getting 78 percent of historic Palestine." Of course, this left out security—which mattered most to Israel—refugees, and Jerusalem, not to mention the fact that the June 4 border without adjustment was acceptable to no Israeli leader.

Secretary Clinton's conversations convinced her that the best thing we could offer, at some point, would be a variation on the Clinton Parameters and present it as a basis for negotiations. She raised this with President Obama in January, and this might well have become the focal point for our internal discussions at that time had it not been for the eruption of the Arab Awakening.

Although the Arab Awakening consumed all the policy-making oxygen for the next few months, the Israeli-Palestinian issue did not go away. Abu Mazen began to press the "internationalization" button. This was his plan B, his alternative to negotiations. Going to the UN was a way for Palestinians to put pressure on Israel by isolating it internationally. In 2011, the Palestinians sought a resolution condemning Israeli settlement activity, calling it illegal and setting the stage for what could be sanctions later on.

On the settlements, the quandary was clear: if the United States vetoed the resolution, it would be the first veto in the UN Security Council of the Obama presidency—and it would have been on something the Obama administration fervently opposed. And yet, if we failed to veto, we would be countenancing a shift away from negotiations and to international forums, where Israel was isolated and the deck was stacked against it.[62] Our efforts to dissuade our European allies from going down this path got nowhere thanks largely to their sympathy for the Palestinians and their opposition to settlements, which they saw through the lens of their own benighted colonial pasts.

The internal debate on what to do about the resolution involved two meetings. In the first one, Secretary Clinton brought Jeff Feltman, her assistant secretary for Near Eastern affairs. She asked him to describe his concerns that a U.S. veto of a settlements resolution would suddenly make us a target in the demonstrations on the Arab street. According to Feltman, until this point, no one was making the United States an issue in the squares in Tunis or Cairo or Sana or elsewhere, but he feared they would now.[63] Robert Gates chimed in, endorsing Feltman's concerns and saying it would be a grave mistake to veto the resolution. Susan Rice was even more adamant, claiming a veto would undo all the good we had accomplished at the UN through the first two years of the administration and vitiate our ability to get anything done in the future—not to mention the "grave damage" it would do to us with the Arabs.

I could barely contain myself. I interjected that everything I had just heard reflected a set of assumptions about a region that were simply incorrect: "No one in Tahrir Square or elsewhere in the region is thinking about settlements or Palestinians. No one is paying attention to this. They are thinking about self-determination for themselves, justice for themselves. They are preoccupied with defining the relationship between ruler and ruled. I am not saying they are indifferent to the Palestinians, but they are completely absorbed by what they see as an internal revolution—it is a moment of release and loss of fear. We should veto this resolution because we told the Palestinians not to do it. And we can veto this resolution because the people in the region are consumed by upheaval that has nothing to do with the Palestinians or Israelis."

Vice President Biden agreed with me, and I could see that I had also affected Secretary Clinton, who was nodding approvingly. The president kept his own counsel at this point, saying he would decide later what to do on the resolution. For now, he said, let's see if we can head off the resolution.

After consulting with the Europeans, we put together a package designed to give the Palestinians a payoff for walking back the resolution. Among other things, we were prepared to formally accept 1967 with mutually agreed swaps as the basis for the final borders between Israel and a Palestinian state.[64] With the UNSC getting ready to move on the resolution, the president took one last stab at Abu Mazen, calling him and asking directly whether he could accept what we were offering in return for dropping the resolution. I was alone in the Oval Office with the president for the call, and when Abu Mazen said he needed to consult with his colleagues, I wrote a note to the president saying, "This is his way of saying no." President Obama nodded, and after he ended the call, he said to me, "When we veto this, it is not going to produce any response in the area, is it?" I repeated what I had said in the Situation Room: "No one in the region is paying attention to this." And, in fact, when we vetoed it, there was no reaction in the region.

But the Europeans retained their focus on the Palestinians. They remained preoccupied with this conflict. As I said in the opening of the book, Cameron, Merkel, and Sarkozy felt that the Arab Spring would be radicalized if we could not move on the Palestinians. In their eyes, Netanyahu would be responsible for turning the Arab Spring into an Arab

Winter. Exactly how this was the case was never explained but simply taken as a given. And in every conversation Tom Donilon held with his counterparts, they were insistent that the United States must present parameters spelling out the political horizon for resolving borders, security, refugees, and Jerusalem. Hillary Clinton was hearing this repeatedly. The Europeans were saying if we did not do so, they would. In fact, at one point the British, French, and Germans put out a set of principles that were specific on borders and Jerusalem and general on security and refugees—leaning, not surprisingly, closely to the Palestinian positions.

Prime Minister Netanyahu, understanding that doing nothing was only feeding the European pressure on us and their own impulse to do something, visited Germany in February 2011 and told Chancellor Merkel that he would come out with an initiative. But Netanyahu rarely moved quickly and, in any case, wanted U.S. support for whatever the Israelis would offer. He sent Molcho to see me in March and April, and we tried to reach an agreement on the content of an Israeli initiative. Molcho acknowledged up front that Israel must present something that would be credible to the world, and as a result he was much more forward-leaning than Netanyahu had been with Secretary Clinton, particularly on borders. However, to go as far as he was prepared to go on territory, he needed the United States to support Israeli demands on security and refugees, and to defer any discussion on Jerusalem.

Although wanting to encourage him, given his more flexible position on borders, I was honest, telling him the administration would see the initiative as unbalanced. Palestinians would be conceding on Israeli needs on security and refugees and Israel only on territory and not on Jerusalem. If Jerusalem was left out, Palestinians would not have a capital for their state even as they were conceding that refugees could return to their state but not to Israel. While Molcho told me he could not touch Jerusalem at this juncture, we both saw great promise in our discussions and wanted to continue them.

But I was instructed to put them on hold. The internal debate on the settlements resolution at the UN had rekindled the discussion of whether we should offer our own initiative in which we would present U.S. parameters for ending the conflict. I had briefed both Tom Donilon and Hillary Clinton on the Molcho discussions, and I felt that if I continued the conversation with Molcho, we could actually present a parameters proposal the Israelis could accept. I mistakenly raised the idea of sharing in advance with the Israelis what the president might say in a speech, suggesting that this would give Netanyahu a stake in cooperating with us and being responsive on any initiative. But Denis McDonough and Susan Rice vehemently objected, insisting that "we can't let them tell us what to say. We cannot trust them, they will go to the Congress and try to screw us." With partisan politics in high gear and Speaker of the House John Boehner having already invited Netanyahu to address a joint session of the Congress in May, their arguments trumped mine with the president—and we would not share anything with the Israelis.

Before Mitchell left his post in April 2011, he favored laying out our positions on all the issues. He and I were in agreement that we needed to lean toward the Palestinians on territory and toward the Israelis on security. We disagreed, however, about outlining positions on refugees and Jerusalem. He wanted to present our positions on all four of the core issues; I felt that would guarantee only that we would get two nos. Abu Mazen would not be prepared to concede on refugees—the animating myth of the Palestinian national movement—and Netanyahu was clearly not prepared to concede on Jerusalem by accepting two capitals for two states. If neither was willing to move on the narrative issues, we would surely get two rejections—and gain nothing. On this issue, my arguments prevailed, and the president decided we would do parameters only on borders and security.

The internal debate over the speech soon spilled over into the public— once again with my role erroneously portrayed—when, on May 11, the lead story in *The New York Times* quoted unnamed officials saying President Obama and Secretary Clinton were both in favor of giving the speech and only I was against it. Ultimately, President Obama gave the speech at the State Department on May 19, the day prior to Netanyahu's arrival in Washington. Netanyahu, convinced that the president was trying to "jam him," decried the speech, focusing only on the part that called for the border to be based on 1967 and mutually agreed swaps, and declaring that Israel would not be forced to an indefensible border. Another lead article appeared in *The New York Times* two days after the speech and a day after what appeared to be a contentious meeting between Obama and Netanyahu in the Oval Office. The article focused—inaccurately—on my putative opposition to the speech and raised the question of "how much of a split the president is willing to make not only with the Israeli leader, but with his own hand-picked Middle East advisor."[65]

This was Saturday morning, May 21, 2011. The president was still smarting over the previous day's meeting with Netanyahu—but not because of the content of the meeting, which much like in March 2010 had actually gone well. Just as Netanyahu then felt he had been made to look bad, now it was Obama's turn to feel that way. During their private meeting, the president asked the prime minister why he was so upset over the speech, and Netanyahu said because no one had coordinated with him in advance: "If you had worked with us and not just confronted me with this speech, I would have reacted differently." When I entered the Oval Office after their one-on-one meeting, Obama walked over to me and said that I had been right to suggest that we coordinate with the Israelis on the speech. Then, in front of White House chief of staff Bill Daley, Donilon, McDonough, Rhodes, and Shapiro, he said the meeting had been good. The prime minister explained why he was upset, and the president said, "I explained the timing on the speech and my need to go to Europe having framed the issue and seized the initiative" so the United States and Israel would not be confronted by an ill-considered European approach driven by Sarkozy at the G-8. This, in fact, was why the president felt he had to give the speech before he left for the G-8 the next day, and when he explained this to Netanyahu, he "got it," just as Obama now appreciated why the speech had set the PM off.

What happened next changed the mood dramatically. The two leaders had not met the press before their meeting. Following the meeting, Netanyahu huddled with his team, and after fifteen minutes the men talked to the media. Had they met the press before seeing their respective teams, I am convinced things would have been different. President Obama did his part, welcoming the prime minister and saying they had had a very constructive discussion—putting a good spin on the meeting. No doubt because Netanyahu's team insisted he needed to maintain his strong public line for his political base, the prime minister proceeded to lecture Obama in front of the press, as if the president had called for Israel to roll its borders back to the 1967 lines.[66] As Netanyahu was talking, Bill Daley was standing next to me muttering, "Outrageous, outrageous, how can he do this in the president's office." As soon as the meeting with the press was over, with Obama not in bad spirits, but with Daley and others suddenly decrying what Netanyahu had done to him, the president's attitude changed.

Obama was scheduled to give another speech, this one at AIPAC on Sunday, May 22, before he left for Europe. I came to the Oval Office with Ben Rhodes, Denis McDonough, and Tom Donilon on Saturday morning to see him. With the front-page *New York Times* article essentially portraying me as opposed to him, the president glared at me as I entered, and said, "I am not giving a red-meat speech; I am not backing off what I said on Thursday." And I responded, "I am not asking you to do that." And with that we got into a thoughtful discussion about what should be in the speech. The president described what he wanted to say, and I made a number of suggestions. Ben wrote it beautifully, and President Obama worked carefully to fine-tune it. The one thing he wanted to confront was the disingenuous point that he had called for Israel to go back to the 1967 lines—he had not. The border would be adjusted by having settlement blocs and swaps—that is what mutually agreed swaps meant.[67]

In the speech, the president said:

> Since my position has been misrepresented several times, let me reaffirm what "1967 and mutually agreed swaps" means. By definition, it means that the parties themselves—Israelis and Palestinians—will negotiate a border that is different than the one that existed on June 4, 1967 . . . It is a well-known formula to all who have worked on the issue for a generation. It allows the parties themselves to account for the changes that have taken place over the last 44 years.

He went on to say, "If there is a controversy, then, it's not based on substance. What I did on Thursday was to say publicly what has long been acknowledged privately. I've done so because we can't afford to wait another decade, or another two decades or another three decades to achieve peace."[68]

Obama achieved his dual aim of not backing off while defusing a seeming crisis with Israel. Molcho thanked me immediately after the speech; no one could now create a default position that the border had to be that of June 4, 1967, he said, because the president was clear that the border had to be adjusted. Netanyahu welcomed the president's speech—even though, in fact, its meaning had not changed. We would spend much of the summer trying to take President Obama's two speeches, three days apart, and make them the basis for a Quartet document, one issued by the United States, the EU, the Russians, and the UN.

After much work with Netanyahu, Tony Blair, and Lady Catherine Ashton, we forged a paper that we all agreed on.[69] Abu Mazen, however, rejected it because it described as an outcome of the talks, not a principle for them, that there would be two states for two peoples: Israel the state of the Jewish people and Palestine the state of the Palestinian people. He would not accept anything that suggested Palestinian recognition of Israel as the state of the Jewish people. Was this a tactic, because Netanyahu had made it a public issue and he wanted to get something for it? Or was it strategic and he was not willing to acknowledge Israel this way? The answer in 2011 was not clear—and it would be no clearer after John Kerry's efforts in 2014.

The Kerry Effort and the Obama Approach to Israel

In the second term, John Kerry made Israeli-Palestinian peace a priority. Despite earlier failed efforts, the president gave his secretary of state a license to do so. Kerry's efforts were high profile and largely unimpeded by the White House, until he sought to present an American framework of principles to guide the negotiations on permanent status; this was ambitious, designed to be something like the Clinton Parameters. Though not a bridging proposal, the principles were meant to encapsulate the basic guidelines for how to resolve each of the core issues, and the two parties would accept them as a basis for negotiating their differences.

The basis for what Kerry would discuss with the parties was a document that emerged from discussions I had in a back channel with Yitzhak Molcho and Hussein Agha. Molcho, of course, was Netanyahu's negotiator and most trusted adviser, even though he had never formally been a member of the government. Agha was a British academic who was born in Iraq and grew up in Lebanon. He joined Fatah as a young man in the late 1960s. He was trusted by Abu Mazen but was completely deniable.* Agha ran an informal "track two" set of discussions with a number of Israelis, including Dore Gold, and it was through Gold that Molcho had first met him. Agha and Molcho began to meet privately and developed a relationship. They separately informed me of their discussions and asked if I could join them. I quickly saw the value of the three-way discussions and suggested that I could try to shape a framework out of this dialogue—a true brainstorming discussion that obligated neither side and neither leader, but that offered a way to forge possible points of agreement that could be formalized at some point. Starting in late 2011, when I was still in the Obama administration, we began to meet regularly, usually in London. Both Agha and Molcho

---

* Agha became close to Arafat and all those around Arafat, including Abu Mazen, at that time. He negotiated the Beilin–Abu Mazen document—an understanding finalized on November 1, 1995, three days before Rabin's assassination. Because of the assassination, the agreement was never formally adopted, but it did cover all the final status issues. Abu Mazen would seek to open a back channel in 1999 after Barak became prime minister, employing Agha, and we got to know each other at that time.

understood that I would keep Secretary Clinton and Tom Donilon in the picture and show them drafts that I was developing. This process continued after I left the administration.

While the initial focus was on forging a framework of principles for how to resolve each of the core issues of final status issues—borders, security, refugees, and Jerusalem—we agreed to make our product a U.S. proposal to the two sides, with the understanding that the United States would not present the proposal until after Agha and Molcho had gone to Abu Mazen and Netanyahu separately to see if they would accept our draft as the basis for talks. Each leader would be able to say he had reservations about the framework and would be able to raise those reservations over the course of the negotiations. Clinton and Donilon were enthusiastic, particularly when they began to see drafts that indicated an agreement might well be possible. In the wake of the recent failure to produce a Quartet document and restart a formal peace process, they were optimistic about the potential for more discreet back-channel discussions to move the process forward.

In 2013, when John Kerry became secretary of state, our meetings accelerated. Kerry felt the need to show that something was happening, believing correctly that a public process was required, both to restore hope among Israelis and Palestinians and to prevent unhelpful international initiatives from being propounded. While our discussions produced progress in what we were drafting, our ideas did not alter either leader's mutual distrust of the other, and that was a key failing of our efforts. Either because Kerry understood this or because he believed that there would be inevitable confusion between front and back channels since Yitzhak Molcho, the key Israeli negotiator, participated in both, Kerry pressed us to reach agreement before he succeeded in launching a formal nine-month negotiating process in July 2013.*

We were not able to conclude our work prior to that time. Our back channel, which was expanded to include the retired Israeli general Mike Herzog, could not produce results at the pace that Secretary Kerry wanted. We worked very deliberately: we talked through the needs of each side, reached understandings, and only then put our ideas in writing. But once our ideas were in writing, each side felt the need to revise what was written after having had time to think about it and to consider whether they

---

* President Obama spoke to both leaders about this channel when he visited Jerusalem and Ramallah in March 2013. He expressed the hope that we would finish our efforts in six to eight weeks.

thought they could sell the proposals in the draft—and that applied to me as well.

Having made unprecedented progress, in December 2013 we concluded our efforts on all the issues except that of Jerusalem, on which we outlined five different options. Because the formal negotiations had yielded only very general positions on each side, Kerry was prepared to suggest adopting our draft with some adjustments, including modifying our approach to security. He did face opposition. Senior U.S. officials told me that Susan Rice felt our document was "imbalanced" and required basic redrafting.[70] Kerry resisted, but accepted some additional modifications. Since every line in our draft had emerged from painstaking discussions over two years, Kerry would spend a great deal of time negotiating these changes with the Israelis. He spent far less time going over the text with the Palestinians, though he shaped the proposal President Obama presented to Mahmoud Abbas in March 2014. That proposal went beyond what had been agreed with the Israelis, particularly on Jerusalem. This U.S.-proposed framework of principles for resolving the conflict covered all the core issues, but Abbas never responded to it.[71]

At this point, with the nine-month limit on negotiations in danger of expiring, Kerry sought to keep the negotiations going by offering a package of items for each side. His package included releasing Jonathan Pollard in exchange for Israel's releasing Palestinian prisoners and limiting settlement activity, and for Abu Mazen's extending the negotiations and forgoing moves in international forums. Again Kerry faced opposition from the White House. According to what both U.S. and Israeli officials told me, Kerry could not provide answers to the Israelis because Rice was micromanaging every detail from the White House.[72] Though I was not directly involved in these talks, it got so bad that one senior Israeli official asked me: "Are we supposed to negotiate with Kerry and then again with Rice?"

Whether extending the negotiations would have made a difference is unclear. In reality, the differences between Kerry and Rice were probably not decisive, but they added to Israel's concerns that the White House was tilted against them on this issue.

These concerns became more pronounced during the Gaza conflict in 2014, especially as the Israelis felt the White House was quick to criticize IDF attacks that killed civilians before hearing Israel's explanation of the target and what had happened.[73]

Interestingly, tough criticism from the White House about Israeli targeting contrasted sharply with our uniformed military's views of Israel's actions in Gaza. General Martin Dempsey, the chairman of the Joint Chiefs of Staff, later spoke of how much the United States had to learn from the Israeli effort to limit civilian casualties during the Gaza conflict:

> I actually do think that Israel went to extraordinary lengths to limit collateral damage and civilian casualties. In fact, about three months ago we sent . . . a team of senior officers and noncommissioned officers over to work with the IDF to get the lessons from that particular operation in Gaza . . . They did some extraordinary things to try to limit civilian casualties to include calling out, you know, making it known that they were going to destroy a particular structure.[74]

The tone from the White House was obviously much more critical. In fact, in the second term, the White House posture was clearly tougher toward Israel, reflecting in no small part the new attitude that Susan Rice brought to the national security adviser position.

By the fall of 2014, tensions rose to new levels, with Israeli finance minister Yair Lapid speaking of a "crisis" in the relationship,[75] and an unnamed senior White House official privately calling Prime Minister Netanyahu a "chicken shit."[76] The combination of Rice's approach, provocative Israeli announcements of new settlement activity, and Netanyahu's vehement opposition to a possible comprehensive nuclear deal with Iran accounted for the venom.

Attempts to tamp down the rhetoric worked for a time, but there was a new eruption in January 2015. John Boehner, going behind the backs of his Democratic counterparts and the president, invited Netanyahu to address a joint session of Congress on the subject of Iran. The image of an Israeli prime minister seeking and getting a public platform before the Congress to criticize the president's policy was too much for the White House, particularly since President Obama, in a phone call with Netanyahu a short time earlier, had asked him not to meddle in internal U.S. politics during the three months the president felt he needed to see if an agreement was possible. But the outrage extended beyond the White House.* Boehner's invitation, which had been worked out privately with Israel's ambassador to the United States, Ron Dermer, triggered a firestorm of criticism outside the adminis-

---

* Thomas L. Friedman described the act as "churlish, reckless," and a danger "for the future of the Israeli-American relations." And a delegation of Democratic representatives known for their support of Israel protested to the Israeli ambassador, asking him to have the prime minister cancel his appearance.

tration. It was not just the impropriety of the act but its overtly partisan nature—effectively pitting Republicans against Democrats on Israel.[77] The White House announced that the president, the vice president, and the secretary of state would not see the prime minister during his visit, citing the proximity of the visit to the Israeli election two weeks later.

Relations soured further in the immediate aftermath of the election. Netanyahu, fearing he might lose, tacked to the right. He declared on the eve of the election that there would be no Palestinian state as long as he was prime minister, and on election day he played on fears of Israeli Arabs voting "in droves" to get his voters to the polls. Netanyahu succeeded in winning the election, but President Obama clearly had had enough. He had his press secretary, Josh Earnest, say that the United States would now have to "reevaluate" its options at the UN and elsewhere, given Israeli opposition to two states. Even Netanyahu's efforts to walk back his statements had no effect, with the president suggesting the prime minister had revealed his true position. Obama added in an interview that Netanyahu's rhetoric on the Arabs "was contrary to what is the best of Israel's traditions—that although Israel was founded based on the historic Jewish homeland . . . Israeli democracy has been premised on everybody in the country being treated fairly and equally."[78] For at least several days, Obama was willing to have a very public feud with Netanyahu. One would have to go back to the worst days of the Israeli siege of Beirut and the Sabra and Shatila massacres in August and September of 1982 to find a lower point in the U.S.-Israel relationship.

At this point, there appeared to be little dissonance within the administration. Obama, Rice, and Kerry were all on the same page. Equally important, those around them in the White House and the State Department were also in agreement. In Obama's second term, that was not typically the case when it came to the Middle East.

Gaps between the White House and the State Department on Israel are certainly not unusual, though in the Obama administration the historical pattern tended to be reversed, with the White House often being tougher than State. The differences in views typically reflected a long-standing split between those who saw working closely with the Israelis as the key to affecting Israeli behavior favorably, and those who did not. That gap was not unique to the Obama administration. One saw it in the Truman, Kennedy, Nixon, and both Bush administrations. In the Eisenhower and Carter administrations, this tension did not exist because there was little serious advocacy for working closely with the Israelis. And, for Clinton, working closely with the Israelis was the norm.

President Obama was comfortable working closely with Israel on security, but he tilted against it on the peace issue—not because he was anti-
Israeli or lacked sympathy for Israel's position but because he genuinely
believed that the onus for acting boldly was more on Israel. Israel, in his
eyes, had the power and the means to shape the future—much more so than
the Palestinians. He expressed his views on this asymmetry very clearly in
an interview with Jeff Goldberg on the eve of Netanyahu's visit in March 2014.
He made the point that time was running out for a peace settlement and
that Abu Mazen's presence created a unique opportunity. But he said nothing about what Abu Mazen had to do; the responsibility for acting was
exclusively Netanyahu's. Indeed, he went so far as to say that Netanyahu
needed to act if Israel was to preserve itself:

> What I've said to him privately is the same thing that I say publicly,
> which is the situation will not improve or resolve itself. This is not a sit-
> uation where you wait and the problem goes away. There are going to be
> more Palestinians, not fewer Palestinians, as time goes on. There are
> going to be more Arab-Israelis, not fewer Arab-Israelis, as time goes on.
> And for Bibi to seize the moment in a way that perhaps only he can,
> precisely because of the political tradition that he comes out of and the
> credibility he has with the right inside of Israel, for him to seize this mo-
> ment is perhaps the greatest gift he could give to future generations of
> Israelis. But it's hard. And as somebody who occupies a fairly tough
> job himself, I'm always sympathetic to somebody else's politics.[79]

Neither in this interview nor in any subsequent public comments did
President Obama suggest that there was a moment for Abu Mazen to seize.
Even when Abu Mazen visited the president later in March and Obama presented to him principles that went far toward meeting Palestinian needs on
all the permanent status issues—including on Jerusalem, where a position,
not coordinated with the Israelis, called for two capitals for two states—the
Palestinian president still would not respond. And yet the administration
offered no criticism of him. On the contrary, it gave him a pass by effectively
blaming his "shutdown" on Israeli settlement policy.[80]

For the president, Abu Mazen was too weak to criticize. At one point he
said Netanyahu was too strong and Abbas too weak to make peace—and
Israel did not seem aware of where its policies were leading it.[81] In his interview with Goldberg, he said:

I have not yet heard, however, a persuasive vision of how Israel survives as a democracy and a Jewish state at peace with its neighbors in the absence of a peace deal with the Palestinians and a two-state solution. . . . There comes a point where you can't manage this anymore, and then you start having to make very difficult choices. Do you resign yourself to what amounts to a permanent occupation of the West Bank? Is that the character of Israel as a state for a long period of time?[82]

Here was a president who genuinely worried about Israel and our ability to prevent its isolation internationally. He also saw the convergence of Israeli and Sunni Arab interests, which became even more pronounced at the time of the Gaza conflict and the struggle with ISIS, but "because of the Palestinian issue," the president believed, those converging interests could not be translated into actual cooperation.[83]

President Obama was a friend of Israel. He always responded to Israel's security needs. When, during the Gaza conflict in the summer of 2014, Tony Blinken, the deputy national security adviser, told him Israel was making an urgent request for funds for more Iron Dome defensive missiles, the president gave immediate approval. There was no impulse to withhold this as leverage on Israel's behavior in the conflict, even though Obama was concerned about the casualties among Palestinian civilians that Israel was inflicting.

Moreover, even when Obama was prepared to speak of reevaluating our approach to Israel after the 2015 Israeli elections, he went out of his way to emphasize that our reevaluation was "not in reference to our commitment to Israel's military edge in the region, Israel's security, our intelligence co operation, our military cooperation. That continues unabated. And I will continue to do whatever I need to do to make sure that our friends in Israel are safe."[84]

As he also explained: "Regardless of disagreements we have on policy," our security cooperation would not be altered because it helped keep "the Israeli people safe" and that "cooperation also helps the American people stay safe."[85] Even at this moment of real tension and genuine anger toward Netanyahu, Obama was offering a reminder about the depth of the relationship, particularly on security. He would speak even more poignantly after the conclusion of the framework understanding with the Iranians on their nuclear program: "I would consider it a failure on my part, a fundamental failure of my presidency, if on my watch, or as a consequence of work that I had done, Israel was rendered more vulnerable."[86]

But Israel's security was one thing, and peace was another. Obama believed Israel was capable of doing more on peace. And it could help change the regional realities—and our place in the region—if it would only move on the Palestinians. But what if the Palestinians were not prepared to move? What if they were not capable of moving—regardless of Israeli actions? He never seemed to ask that question.

Obama came into office believing that we needed to distance ourselves from Israel. He evolved. He defended Israel in international forums. He worried about the delegitimization movement if Israel did not take the initiative toward the Palestinians to arrest this development. He realized that the United States' distancing from Israel was not the answer. But for President Barack Obama, an uncritical embrace would also never be the hallmark of his policy toward the Jewish state. His instinct to see the Palestinians as the victims in the conflict remained too strong, and in the last years of his presidency, if that meant having the Israelis see that there were consequences for their policies, so be it.

12

LESSONS FROM THE PAST AND
IMPLICATIONS FOR THE FUTURE

In his book on American foreign policy since the Truman administration, Stephen Sestanovich points out that "almost every new occupant of the Oval Office thought the world had changed in some fundamental way that his predecessor either totally misunderstood or failed to manage effectively."[1] Small wonder, then, that every president since Truman has felt the need to change our course on foreign policy. As we have seen, our policy toward Israel and the Middle East was no exception.

Yet notwithstanding the impulse to chart a new direction, there have been a number of interrelated assumptions about Israel and the region that embedded themselves in at least part of the national security apparatus—and frequently informed presidents. From Truman to Obama, these assumptions endured and formed a set of understandings about how to approach the region and Israel's place in it. Three stand out: the need to distance from Israel to gain Arab responsiveness, concern about the high costs of cooperating with the Israelis, and the belief that resolving the Palestinian problem is the key to improving the U.S. position in the region. Not surprisingly, all three of these assumptions informed those who saw Israel through a competitive, not cooperative lens.

History shows that these assumptions were fundamentally flawed. Take the belief that we must distance ourselves from Israel. Eisenhower, Nixon,

Carter, Bush 41, and Obama consciously pulled away from Israel, thinking we would gain with the Arabs. Not only was there never a benefit, in many cases our relations with Arab states worsened. That was certainly true in the Eisenhower, Nixon, and Obama administrations. Recall that distancing began at the very outset of the Eisenhower administration and reached its zenith during the Suez War and its aftermath when the president threatened Israel with force and sanctions. What happened to our position in the region? It weakened dramatically. So much so that after Suez, we could not even convince the king of Saudi Arabia to visit the United States, much less contemplate opposing Nasser. Nixon's efforts similarly yielded a worse situation. By seeking to appeal to the Arabs with the Rogers Plan and the suspension of F-4 Phantoms to Israel, we actually signaled to the Egyptians and Soviets that there was no cost in ramping up the Soviet military presence in Egypt to unprecedented levels. For his part, Obama was stunned when he met King Abdullah after very deliberate distancing from Israel and found that the author of the Arab Peace Initiative in 2002, who had promised diplomatic relations with Israel if it withdrew from the occupied territories, was in June 2009 a leader who "would be the last to make peace with Israel." Every administration that distanced from Israel succeeded only in building expectations of what more we might do to accommodate Arab interests, not what Arab leaders might do in response to our distancing. Yet when there was no response from the Arabs, no one seemed to question the underlying assumption.

Similarly, the decisions to cooperate with Israel did not produce the expected negative fallout with our Arab friends, though the anticipation of dire consequences was very high, at least up to the Reagan administration. Ibn Saud's views played a major role in coloring the perceptions of our leading national security officials in having them oppose first partition of Palestine and then recognition of Israel. Yet after Truman recognized the State of Israel, the king of Saudi Arabia, within a short time, expanded the Saudi relationship with the United States, including increasing the American role in Aramco and the production of Saudi oil. Similarly, during the Kennedy administration, Dean Rusk strongly opposed our first real arms sale to Israel, the Hawk antiaircraft missile, fearing it would set a precedent and destroy our relations with the Arabs. But the same day Rusk was seeing the Saudi crown prince in New York, the news of the Hawk sale became public. Faisal never even raised the issue—he was focused on Yemen and Nasser. Fear of Arab reaction to holding a strategic dialogue with Israel mandated secrecy during the Carter administration; not only did it leak in 1980 without producing a reaction, but when the Reagan administration openly adopted it, there was no meaningful reaction or fallout among our Arab friends. No one sought to cooperate less with the United States. Indeed, as the scope of U.S. strategic and military cooperation with Israel has grown to unprecedented levels, the U.S. presence in a number of Arab Gulf states has also dramatically increased.*

What of the centrality of the Palestinian issue to America's regional posture? No assumption has been more enduring or accepted at face value. To be fair, American officials—from presidents on down—have been told repeatedly by Arab leaders that the Palestinian issue costs the United States in the region. We are identified with an injustice that to them is fundamental—and this is surely a perception that Arab leaders, both friends of the United States and foes, have sought to cultivate. Lacking legitimacy, Arab leaders do not want to look like they are on the wrong side of an issue that speaks to Arab dignity and the sense of a historic wrong. But raising it with American officials is also useful for trying to put us on the defensive and in a position where we are supposed to do more for them and not the reverse.

The Palestinian issue has indeed been a centerpiece for Arab leaders—but more to use as leverage against us or against each other. Rarely has any Arab leader done much for the Palestinians. I can find only one example, where Crown Prince Abdullah threatened to "reevaluate" Saudi Arabia's relationship with the United States if we did not act on the Palestinian issue. This took place discreetly, in August 2001, in a letter to President Bush. The Saudis had expressed growing frustration with the administration for having walked away from any peacemaking efforts at a time when the second

---

* One could argue that our massive airlift of military material to Israel during the 1973 Yom Kippur War led to the oil embargo in which the United States was singled out more than any other country. There is certainly something to that argument. But several points also mitigate it. First, the Saudis had economic interests in changing market share and wresting control of pricing and production decisions from the Western oil companies, and the decision to cut back on production ostensibly because of the conflict served these broader objectives. Second, there has not been an embargo in more than forty years. The Saudis were not prepared to use oil as part of the conflict with the Israelis, in no small part because the Saudis have emphasized that they don't want to politicize their oil production decisions. Third, that did not prevent them from increasing production in 2011 to make up for the European embargo on purchasing Iranian oil. True, this helped to stabilize the price, a traditional Saudi interest, but it also had the political effect of increasing the pressure on Iran. At the same time, the Saudis told the Chinese that if they cut back on oil purchases from Iran, Saudi Arabia would make up the difference. In other words, the Saudis are prepared to make decisions on oil that are guided not only by narrow economic motivations.

intifada was producing Palestinian bombs in Israel and very tough Israeli responses against Palestinians that largely throttled life in the territories. Abdullah's letter produced a panicky response from the White House, which included President Bush writing to the Saudi leader and promising to support self-determination for the Palestinians. Even though there was little practical follow-up by the administration, the Saudis were satisfied and made no further threats. It was as if the Saudis wanted to see what they could get the administration to commit to, and having won this commitment, even if unfulfilled, they were satisfied.

True, the 9/11 attacks occurred a few weeks later, changing our preoccupation and no doubt scaring the Saudis about our possible reaction, given the fact that fifteen of the nineteen hijackers were Saudi citizens. The Saudis did not press the issue again until April 2002, when the crown prince felt acute embarrassment at meeting with the president of the United States when Israel had Arafat under siege. Yet he went ahead with the visit, and the president's promise to do what he could to end the siege was sufficient.

The point is not that the Palestinians don't matter. They do. But the hard truth is that they are not a priority for Arab leaders. And it is the priorities of Arab leaders that drive their behavior toward the United States. The belief that we would produce a strategic realignment that serves our interests or develop a larger American military presence in key Arab states—the essence of General Mattis's statement that he felt the impact of the Palestinian issue every day on our military-security posture—misses the reality of Arab behavior. If their priorities and needs match ours, then they will respond to us. But that is rarely, if ever, going to be completely the case, and that should come as no surprise to us.

The priorities of Arab leaders revolve around survival and security. Domestic stability comes first. Protection from regional rivals relates both to internal security and threats from the outside. To the extent that regional rivals can exploit the Palestinian issue to stir up domestic discontent, Arab leaders will be sensitive to it. It is, however, an issue they use and would like to see addressed, but it is not one they are prepared to run risks to resolve. Yes, they want us to make it go away—provided we ask little of them.[2]

Again, the historical record demonstrates that Arab relations with the United States are guided by their priorities, not ours. Eisenhower found this out when he tried to organize an alliance in the region against the Soviets. This strategy was our priority, not the Arabs', and it went nowhere—except with Iraq before the coup in 1958, and only because the Iraqi leadership thought they could exploit it in their military competition with Egypt. Ironically, Nasser used outreach to the Soviets to build his appeal on the Arab street by showing he was prepared to defy the colonial powers that had humiliated the Arabs for so long. Nasser's aim was to strengthen his leverage in the region and dominate it at the expense of other Arab leaders, triggering what Malcolm Kerr called the "Arab Cold War." It was the regional rivalry among Arabs that shaped this period and defined their priorities. So much so that even while the Saudis had little to say about the Hawks for Israel, Crown Prince (and later King) Faisal forcefully argued with President Kennedy that our economic assistance to Egypt was making it easier for Nasser to use his military to threaten the monarchies. Our outreach to Egypt during the Kennedy administration was interpreted by the Saudis as coming at their expense and was seen as a threat—and they pleaded for us to stop it. That was their preoccupation, not U.S. arms to Israel.[3]

Once again we see echoes in today's Middle East and perceptions of the Obama administration. Only today, the Saudis see the Obama outreach to Iran as coming at their expense. They consider Iran their main rival, with whom they are locked in a struggle over the balance of power in the region. Just as King Faisal saw Nasser's Egypt representing a threat to the future of the al-Saud monarchy and did not understand the United States' effort at outreach, so, too, does the Saudi leadership today see Iran in such existential terms. What compounds the problem is that the Obama administration is also seen as insufficiently worried about the danger of the Muslim Brotherhood, the other threat to the monarchies in Saudi eyes. It is for this reason that the Saudis are angry that President Obama withheld weapons assistance to the Egyptian military in its life-and-death struggle with the Brotherhood.

It is American credibility that matters to those Arab states that depend on the United States to counter the threats they see in the region. They may not expect us to provide for their internal security, though they do look to us for counterterror and intelligence support. But Arab leaders want the United States to provide a defensive shield for them that dissuades their regional adversaries from making more overt threats. They want us to stand with them and resist changes in the regional balance of power.

Recall Kissinger's description of the messages the White House was receiving from the Saudis and our other leading Arab friends in the fall of 1969 after the coup that brought Qaddafi to power in Libya. All of them reflected the fear of the region going the way of the radical nationalists. They feared that the balance of power was shifting against America's friends, and that the United States was doing nothing about it. The messages were both a plea and a signal that our friends would have to make their own adjustments if we were not going to do something about the shifting balance in the area. These are the same messages the Obama administration is hearing from the Saudis, Emirates, and Egyptians today. During the Nixon administration, it took a display of American resolve and effectiveness in response to the Syrian threat to Jordan in September 1970 to begin to shift the perception of the United States. Doing something similar today—to successfully set ISIS back in Iraq, Syria, and elsewhere while also credibly building the Syrian opposition to Assad—will probably be required to shift the current impressions of President Obama.

My point is not to argue for such a shift in American policy per se, though I do believe some demonstrations of effective American power are needed in the Middle East and elsewhere. Rather, the historical record reveals that U.S. credibility and reliability are far more important than anything else in shaping Arab leaders' responsiveness to us. Would it be good if we could resolve the Palestinian conflict? Certainly—and that could in fact be a measure of our effectiveness. However, even if we are seen as much more reliable, Arab priorities will determine the scope of their cooperation with us. Of course, there will always be limits. The political culture in the region will always require that no Arab government appear to be surrendering its sovereignty or independence.

It was not our relationship with Israel that made it difficult for Saudi Arabia to accept U.S. forces in large numbers on their territory after the Iraqi invasion of Kuwait in 1990. It was the effect on internal Saudi dynamics and claims to the legitimacy of the House of Saud—and the need not to appear to be inviting a foreign occupation. President George H. W. Bush instinctively understood this, and he personally promised that we would withdraw our forces once the Iraqi threat was ended.

That is why Mattis's point so dramatically misses the mark. If tomorrow there were no Palestinian conflict, there would still be limits on the extent of U.S. military presence that would be acceptable in Saudi Arabia and the Emirates. Of course, if the threat they face is extreme and survival is at stake, the concerns about our presence will be trumped by the more immediate danger. That is what happened in 1990 in Saudi Arabia.

The lesson here is that with key Arab friends of the United States, there will be a floor below which they will not allow the relationship to go, and a ceiling above which it cannot rise. Our policy is conducted within those boundaries. Obviously, we want to move the relationship in political, diplomatic, economic, and security terms closer to the ceiling, and the challenge for our policy is to effectuate such an outcome. Resolving the Israeli-Palestinian conflict would help in this regard. Good statecraft, in which we are seen as being credible and reliable, is almost certainly more important.

One might argue that with the Arab Awakening of 2011, Arab regimes will need to be more attentive to their publics and the populist instincts on issues like Israel that they are certain to express. Perhaps, if the awakenings had been more successful in yielding a sustained revolutionary change in the power of Arab publics, this argument would have more meaning. It is, unfortunately, the authoritarian regimes that have reimposed themselves. To be sure, regimes that lack legitimacy—or depend on ruling on the basis of fear of the alternative—are unlikely to take risks for peace with Israel or expose themselves by cooperating overtly with the Israelis. Similarly, their need to keep security cooperation with us within certain bounds will be as strong as ever.

Assumptions About Israel and Implications for Policy

To this point, I have focused on those assumptions that have endured and shaped U.S. foreign policy: mistakenly putting the Palestinian issue as the fulcrum of regional politics and wrongly predicting high costs to us of too close an identification with Israel. But there are other assumptions more geared toward the Israelis that have also endured over time—some of which have been shared by those inclined to cooperate with the Israelis as well as by those who are not so inclined. Two stand out. First is Israel's reluctance to share its bottom lines with different administrations on how far it is willing to go on peace. From Nixon to Carter to Clinton to Bush 43 and to Obama, we have seen Israeli leaders holding back on what they reveal. Second, many of those who were convinced that our association with Israel was costly for the United States also believed that Israel never took our interests into account. Robert Gates, for one, articulated this position in the three administrations where he held a senior policy-making position—Bush 41, Bush 43, and Obama.

There is some validity to each of these assumptions. In the first instance, it is true that the Israelis are disinclined to reveal bottom lines to us. Although there may have been times, notably during Golda Meir's tenure, when the Israelis had actually not thought through what they were prepared to live with, the hesitancy more typically was driven by the fear that whatever they told us would never be enough. To be fair, there was more to it than that. The Israelis would hold back, wanting us to draw something out of their putative Arab partner, not wanting us to ask that Israel always reveal its positions first. This was especially true with the Palestinians, whom the Israelis always saw adopting only maximal positions. They wanted to hold back until such time as the Palestinians revealed some readiness to compromise. They wanted to see signs that we were pressing the Palestinians and not only them.

On our side, it was not just the Obama administration that felt the Israelis were the stronger party and could therefore afford to reveal their positions to us. Condoleezza Rice, too, believed this. She felt we needed a move from the Israelis to gain leverage on the Palestinians. The problem, of course, is that this convinced the Israelis, during Rice and Obama's times, that any move made by them would simply result in the Palestinians pocketing whatever was offered and demanding more—and our going along with it. A senior Israeli official told me about Prime Minister Netanyahu's conversation with President Obama in their March 2014 meeting. Netanyahu asked, "How do I know that if I move farther that will be it, that when the Palestinians say no you won't once again come back and pressure me for more? When does this stop?"[4] True, there was a tactical element for the Israelis. But there was also a strategic dynamic at work here. Israeli leaders saw the United States putting them on a slippery slope of ever-larger concessions.

How might we change this traditional pattern? By acknowledging their fear, by leveling with them and offering assurances about what we will and won't ask of them. In concrete terms, this means being prepared to recognize their redlines, while also making clear up front what we think will and won't work with the Palestinians. If the Israelis can't go as far as we think necessary, they should know at the outset that we won't make the effort to mobilize pressure on the Palestinians to accept it. If, however, the Israelis are prepared to go as far as we consider necessary—for example, on the key issues of borders, security, refugees, and Jerusalem—and the Palestinians reject their offers, we must assure the Israelis in advance that we will not ask them for more—and then stick to it and publicly hold the Palestinians responsible.

On peace, it has been a question of Israeli trust—or lack of it—in the United States. On the issue of Israel not taking account of U.S. interests, that reflects American distrust of Israel. The Reagan administration in its first two years was constantly surprised by the Israelis. As a result, when it was trying to establish strategic cooperation, the focus was on getting Israel's leaders to commit to not surprising us, to not taking unilateral acts that would be harmful to our interests. President George H. W. Bush in his first meeting with Prime Minister Yitzhak Shamir put as much emphasis on this issue as he did on the question of settlements. It has been a preoccupation of President Obama from early in his presidency. Much like on the peace issue, there is no perfect answer, because the Israelis must balance their relationship with us with what they see as existential threats. That was the case when the Israelis bombed the Osirak and al-Kibar reactors—and, of course, it could be the case if the Israelis were to strike Iran's nuclear facilities. In the past, there was a perception of an existential danger to the state and a belief that the United States was not going to deal with it effectively—and so Israel acted according to its perceived interests.

Perhaps the best approach is one that tries to distinguish with the Israelis between those issues that actually do pose existential threats and those that do not. The Israelis often have not drawn such a distinction. During the Reagan administration, striking the Osirak reactor was one thing, but bombing the PLO headquarters in Beirut in the summer of 1981—just as President Reagan was about to lift the suspension on aircraft deliveries to Israel—was quite another. The PLO's presence there was not an existential threat, but Israel was sending a message without regard to the effect on us. It was the readiness to take such actions that fed the view in much of the bureaucracy that Israel frequently acted to spoil our relations with the Arabs or to gain whatever advantage it could in the region. During the Kennedy administration, it was not only the U.S. bureaucracy that felt this; the president did as well. Recall that Kennedy worried deeply about Israeli actions; he particularly feared an impulse to exploit regional turmoil to seize the West Bank from Jordan. In 1961 and again in 1963, President Kennedy sent blunt messages to Prime Minister Ben-Gurion warning him not to do anything in response to the upheaval related first to the breakup of the UAR and, two years later, to the failed unity talks among Egypt, Syria, and Iraq.

Again, if there is a lesson from the past, it is be clear with Israel about what matters to us, while also demonstrating an awareness of what matters to them. Having in-depth and regular strategic discussions at a senior level is important, and they need to involve the closest aides of the president and the prime minister. Such discussions permit both sides to put their concerns on the table. They allow for distinctions to be drawn between important issues on the one hand and existential ones on the other. One model that worked in the Obama administration was the strategic dialogue between the White House and the prime minister's office on Iran. Yaakov Amidror, who served as Prime Minister Netanyahu's national security adviser until the end of 2013, told me that while the Israelis did not agree with everything they heard in this dialogue, "It showed that the Americans were very serious about their approach on Iran. We might not have the same views, but we understood each other's position very well and also understood that our differences were the result of different circumstances. We also understood the importance of not surprising the administration, because America's interests were also at stake."[5]

It may seem an obvious point, but this kind of a dialogue always works better when it is led by those who very much believe in the U.S.-Israel relationship. The Donilon-Amidror-led dialogue was an effective mechanism because of the personal commitments of the two national security advisers. Lacking such a commitment, its successor, led by Susan Rice and Yossi Cohen, has not worked. Because the Israelis need the United States' friendship more than nearly anything else, and will always feel a basic insecurity, presidents would be well advised to have someone sympathetic to their predicament lead such dialogues.

Having witnessed this over the years, and having had plenty of discussions with Israeli leaders and their closest aides, I can say that they are more responsive to those they perceive truly understand their concerns. Donilon was able to speak frankly to Prime Minister Netanyahu and General Amidror, and they took his concerns very much into account as a result. I had much the same experience with Netanyahu and his predecessors whom I worked closely with—Rabin, Peres, Barak, and Sharon.[6] Not surprisingly, I didn't hesitate to challenge Israeli positions or point out where they were counterproductive, because my basic approach was not informed by a desire to please the Arabs at Israel's expense—a position that has often led Israeli leaders to resist what they were being asked to do by American officials.

Not surprisingly, the Israelis are well aware of the assumptions that drive U.S. policy in the region, and they often read U.S. requests through the prism of this knowledge. It makes them less responsive, less trusting of our demands, and more inclined to take the very unilateral steps that feed the perception that Israel costs us regionally and internationally. This cycle can be broken by intensive discussions led by those who empathize with Israel and demonstrate that they understand the nature of Israel's concerns. The irony is that those officials are the ones most capable of asking more of Israel.[7]

To be sure, the U.S.-Israel relationship cannot be rooted on solid footing if it consists only of the United States being responsive to Israel and not the reverse—or, for that matter, if Israel is doing little to help itself diplomatically. We are the stronger actor in this relationship, and that puts a heavier burden on us. But it does not relieve the Israelis of the need to be mindful of what concerns us. Nor should it put them in a position where they come to us first for help with others before they are prepared to do anything on their own. That, too, can wear on the relationship.

When I was in the White House, I spent an enormous amount of time responding to Israeli pleas to help them fend off what they perceived as harmful or threatening initiatives internationally. Oftentimes it was resolutions in the Human Rights Council or at the UN or even in the European Union. It was natural for the Israelis to come to us because of our international influence and the reality that we have been Israel's one true friend. Still, when I often asked my Israeli counterparts what they had done to try to affect the issue they were calling me about, I frequently discovered that they had done very little.

Israeli leaders need to accept more responsibility in this regard. I often felt that they believed the deck was so stacked against them that it was futile to make any effort. But the reality is that there is much the Israelis can do. With the Europeans in particular—especially with the British, the French, and the Germans—they need to create the same kind of channels they have sought for so long with the White House. Specifically, the prime minister should create a direct channel with the British prime minister, the French president, and the German chancellor—and his or her closest adviser must have private channels with their lead advisers. The Israelis should brief them frequently on what they are doing with regard to the Palestinians and other issues—and be prepared at times to take some of the Europeans' advice. That will give each of these leaders more of a stake in what the Israelis are doing and will temper the areas where they are inclined to be critical of Israel. Prime Minister Netanyahu, particularly when Ehud Barak was his defense minister, did a good job of this on Iran, but he did considerably less on the Palestinians. True, gaps in outlook were far greater on the Palestinians; nonetheless, the more the Israelis explain their position and the initiatives they might take in advance of doing so on the peace issue, the more they can affect the Europeans, particularly if they are prepared to accept some suggestions from the British, French, or Germans.

Obviously, this cannot be just procedural. It actually requires the Israelis to take initiatives or alter their policy in some respects. I am not suggesting that Israel concede what it feels it cannot or should not. For example, Israel will not compromise on security. But the Israeli policy on settlements is the emblem of what the Europeans most reject and take as proof that Israel will never withdraw from the territories. This is the embodiment of Israeli occupation, and seems to belie Prime Minister Netanyahu's public commitment to two states. Why, for example, if his government is committed to two states, would he build in what would be the Palestinian state? This question was frequently posed to me by Europeans and Palestinians.

It matters little that Netanyahu may be building primarily in the "blocs" or in existing Jewish neighborhoods in East Jerusalem, areas that from the time of Clinton's Camp David we have understood would become part of Israel in return for territorial swaps. To preserve his governing coalition, the prime minister has not admitted that the building is limited to these areas. On the contrary, the impression is that the Israelis are building everywhere in the occupied territories and literally gobbling up the land, meaning that Israel not only gets no credit for limiting where it builds but also feeds the skepticism about Israeli intentions.

To help improve its position with the Europeans, and to lessen the political burden of always defending Israeli actions, Israel needs to adjust its approach to settlement building. It should make its settlement policy consistent with its two-state policy by declaring that until it can reach agreement with the Palestinians on the border, it will build only in what it considers to be Israel—and that it will no longer build in what it thinks should be part of the Palestinian state. True, this will cost the prime minister politically, but it will undoubtedly serve Israel's strategic interest.[8]

At a time of increasing efforts to delegitimize Israel internationally, few steps could be more important. It will surely help with us. Even those in the Obama administration who view Israel through the competitive-cost lens will see Israel taking a difficult step. At a time when the Netanyahu government's opposition to the framework understanding on the Iranian nuclear program continues to be intense, it is especially important for Israel not to be out of step with the international community on the Palestinian issue. Indeed, even if the nuclear deal with Iran proves difficult to finalize, Prime Minister Netanyahu's determination to push the U.S. Congress to oppose it may well sour relations further with the Obama administration and inevitably isolate Israel if it fails to take an initiative on the Palestinian issue.[9]

Concluding Thoughts

From Truman to Obama, the U.S.-Israel relationship has come a long way. David Ben-Gurion, Israel's first prime minister, desperately sought an alliance with the United States, certain that Israel needed the support of a major power. Today, he would be amazed by the nature of the relationship and the character of American commitments to Israel. Truman, facing a phalanx of national security advisers who were convinced that a close relationship with Israel would doom America's position in the Middle East, would also be surprised by the depth of the relationship. And yet it has happened.

Politics may have helped this process, but politics did not produce it. Ronald Reagan launched strategic cooperation with Israel because he saw Israel helping in the competition with the Soviets and Soviet client states. Succeeding presidents built on the foundation laid by the Reagan administration. Bush 41 and Obama sustained it—not for political reasons, but because they felt they had inherited a commitment and they believed it could enhance Israel's readiness to take risks for peace. Clinton and Bush 43 shared these views but also more readily saw Israel as a strategic partner—and as the only democracy in the Middle East.

That said, every president since Truman has also been prepared to adopt positions that the Israeli government—and its friends in Congress—opposed, if they felt our interests dictated such postures. Eisenhower, Carter, Bush 41, and Obama took positions critical of Israel. Similarly, whether on arms sales to the Arabs or on approaches to Iran, when administrations felt it was in our interests to take a decision regardless of Israel's attitudes and the position of AIPAC, they would prevail. Carter succeeded on selling F-15s; Reagan did the same with AWACS. Bush blocked loan guarantees to Israel; and Obama prevented new congressional sanctions against Iran.

This is not to say that congressional support or the role of AIPAC is not significant. Both are profoundly important for sustaining support for Israel in every sense—materially, politically, and publicly. But here again, the basis of support is driven by the perception of Israel as a country that shares America's values. It is a democracy in a region where democracy does not exist. There continues to be strong instinctive support for Israel throughout America, even in areas where the Jewish community is very small. Could this change over time as the United States becomes a country where minorities—Hispanics, Asians, African Americans—who have little connection to Israel come to constitute the majority? The short answer is yes. Consider the polling during the Gaza war in 2014: there was decidedly less support for Israel in the minority communities. Beyond minority attitudes, there are other disturbing trends with a segment of public opinion: among eighteen- to twenty-nine-year-olds, in the public at large, there was a nearly even split on the question of who was to blame in the 2014 war between Israel and Hamas.[10]

Similarly, Jewish Americans in the same cohort were and are much more prone to question Israeli policies toward the Palestinians.[11] While there remains a strong favorable view of Israel in the public at large, these trends should nonetheless set off alarm bells for those who care about the U.S.-Israel relationship—and they need to be addressed.

With that in mind, Israel's supporters in this country and Israeli decision makers should consider several actions. First, develop a serious approach to outreach and education in the minority communities about Israel and realities in the Middle East. Second, counter any impression that Israel is a partisan issue. The contrived Boehner invitation to Netanyahu to speak at a joint session of the Congress on Iran fooled no one and was a mistake. With demographics in this country changing, ties to Israel must remain an American interest—not a Republican or Democratic one. Third, elevate Israeli democratic values and stop right-wing efforts to get the Knesset to adopt restrictive legislation on issues like nationality or NGOs or the independent power of the Israeli Supreme Court. The last thing Israel needs now is to have its basic democratic character called into question. Finally, take an initiative on peace not necessarily because the Palestinians will respond but to undercut the delegitimization movement. Indeed, just as an initiative on limiting settlement activity to the blocs—the areas that are likely to remain a part of Israel—might be useful in Europe, it might be of value here as well.[12]

Of course, any credible peace initiative would be well received from a policy—and not just a public—standpoint. However, with the narrow-based rightist coalition that emerged from the March 2015 election, it is hard to imagine Israel's government adopting any such initiative. If Prime Minister Netanyahu does not broaden the government and make a different approach possible, Israel will find it difficult to blunt the delegitimization movement. In this event, it is not clear whether the Obama administration would be able to forestall international actions against Israel, even if it had the inclination to do so. On the contrary, Obama's readiness to "reevaluate" our policy may well indicate our readiness to change our posture in the UN and be less protective of Israel. The administration might even support a UN Security Council resolution on parameters for settling the conflict.

Obviously, the legacy from the Obama administration could affect the next administration's approach to Israel. If Obama's foreign policy in general is being questioned, there will be an impulse to dissociate from it—and one can anticipate that improving relations with Israel would be high on the agenda. This should not be taken as a given, but whether or not it comes to pass, there are some clear dos and don'ts for each side to keep in mind for the future of the U.S.-Israel relationship. What is the starting point?

Being honest with each other is crucial. Avoiding surprises is essential. Direct and regular communication between the president and the prime minister is important, but it needs to be buttressed by a trusted back channel of close advisers. Misunderstandings must be corrected quickly, and this is where the trusted advisers play a role. Disagreements will happen, but they should be managed. High-level dialogue should focus not just on the immediate challenges in the region but also offer comparative assessments of potential emerging problems or threats, particularly because the Middle East is going to be characterized by upheaval for at least the coming decade.

The reality of regional strife and conflict between radical Islamists and non-Islamists is likely to keep our relationship with Israel in perspective, regardless of the tensions of the moment with this government or future Israeli governments. Turmoil is going to define the Middle East for the foreseeable future. Egypt will remain embroiled in conflict between the military and the Muslim Brotherhood for years to come, and the outcome is uncertain. The emergence of ISIS and the war in Syria will continue to spread misery there and in the surrounding states, threatening to deepen the conflict in Iraq, making Lebanon increasingly less capable of sorting out its problems, and posing more dangers for stability in Jordan—not to mention the struggle it will continue to provoke over the very identity of Islam. The Gulf states already feel threatened by ISIS, even as Iran pushes to alter the regional balance of power in its favor—a factor that has led the Saudis to draw the line in Yemen and engage in the conflict there. If a deal on the nuclear issue is reached, the Gulf states are likely to be even more fearful of an Iran freed from the burden of sanctions. A peace deal between the Israelis and Palestinians—now looking increasingly less likely—would have little effect on any of these issues even if it were to materialize. Of course, removing the Palestinian conflict as a moral issue for Israel and as a source of additional instability would be a good thing, but it would not stop one barrel bomb from being dropped in Syria, the reemergence of the sectarian conflict in Iraq, or the internal battle with the Islamists in Egypt. In other words, it would *not* be a game changer in the region.

Turmoil and uncertainty will be the hallmark of the Middle East in the coming years. Whatever its problems, Israel will remain the one country in the region that is basically stable. For now and the foreseeable future, it will remain the only country in the Middle East governed by the rule of law, separation of powers, an independent judiciary, regularly scheduled elections where the loser accepts the outcome, freedom of speech and assembly, a vibrant and open media, respect for women's rights and for gay rights, artistic freedom, active civil society groups—and an innovative, dynamic economy.

Israel will have to deal with its secular-religious divide and its demographic issues—including its Arab minority—but it has shown a capacity to cope with its problems, unlike the other countries in the region that are still searching for answers related to the questions of basic identity. Tribe, clan, sect, Islamist vs. secular identity remain to be sorted out in the rest of the Middle East, and none of these will be settled soon. Israel's problems pale by comparison, and its capacity to respond to its problems appears far greater.

Since its humble beginnings, Israel has come a long way—and so has the U.S.-Israel relationship. Those in the early years of the Truman and Eisenhower administrations who saw in the emergence of Israel only doom and gloom for the United States were wrong. With all its tensions and problems, the relationship has flourished. Its success was far from assured, but it has taken on a life of its own. With the right kind of continuing management and commitment on both sides, it will remain certain, if not doomed, to succeed.

NOTES

1. The Evolution of U.S. Policy Toward Israel

1. To the extent that there was a very limited improvement during the Kennedy and Reagan administrations, it was driven by what we did bilaterally with these leaders and had nothing to do with Israel.

2. *Foreign Relations of the United States (FRUS)*, "The Secretary of State to the Minister in Egypt (Kirk)," March 15, 1994, vol. 5. pp. 590–91, vol. 5: http://digicoll.library .wisc.edu/cgi bin/FRUS/FRUS idx?type=turn&entity=FRUS.FRUS1994v05.p0602 &id=FRUS.FRUS1994v05.

3. *The Diaries of Edward R. Stettinius, Jr., 1943–46*, ed. Thomas M. Campbell and George C. Herring (New York: New Viewpoints, 1975), p. 211.

4. Dennis Ross and David Makovsky, *Myths, Illusions, and Peace: Finding a New Direction in the Middle East* (New York: Penguin, 2009), p. 33; Charles E. Bohlen, *Witness to History* (New York: Norton, 1973), pp. 211–12.

5. Loy W. Henderson to Secretary of State James F. Byrnes, August 20, 1945. State Department Papers. NLT-691, National Archives, College Park, MD, quoted in Allis Radosh and Ronald Radosh, *A Safe Haven: Harry S. Truman and the Founding of Israel* (New York: HarperCollins, 2009), p. 90.

6. "Report of President Roosevelt in Person to the Congress on the Crimea Conference," *The New York Times*, March 2, 1945, http://timesmachine.nytimes.com /timesmachine/1945/03/02/issue.html.

7. Radosh and Radosh, *A Safe Haven*, p. 34.

8. Ibid., p. 33.

9. Ibid., p. 34.

10. Alfred Steinberg, *The Man from Missouri* (New York: Putnam, 1962), p. 304, quoted in Peter Grose, *Israel in the Mind of America* (New York: Knopf, 1983), p. 113; and Ross and Makovsky, *Myths, Illusions, and Peace*, p. 33.

11. Harrison to Truman, n.d., 1945, in David Niles Papers, box 29, Harry S. Truman Presidential Library; *Memoirs of Harry S. Truman,* vol. 2: *Years of Trial and Hope, 1946–1952* (Garden City, NY: Doubleday, 1956), p. 137.

12. Truman, *Years of Trial and Hope,* pp. 135–36.

13. Churchill himself had vocally opposed the White Paper of 1939 in the House of Commons for betraying the commitments the United Kingdom had made to the Jews in the Balfour Declaration of 1917.

14. Truman, *Years of Trial and Hope,* p. 142; *FRUS* 1945, vol. 8: pp. 785–86.

15. "The Secretary of State to the British Ambassador (Halifax)," October 24, 1945, http://digicoll.library.wisc.edu/cgi-bin/FRUS/FRUS-idx?type=turn&entity=FRUS .FRUS1945v08.p.0797&id=FRUS.FRUS1945v08.

16. "Anglo-American Committee of Inquiry—Chapter I," Avalon Project, http://avalon .law.yale.edu/20th_century/angch01.asp, and *FRUS* 1946, vol. 7, pp. 585–86; "The Acting Secretary of State to Certain American Diplomatic and Consular Officers," *FRUS,* April 25, 1946, http://digicoll.library.wisc.edu/cgi-bin/FRUS/FRUS-idx?type =goto&id=FRUS.FRUS1946v07&isize=M&submit=Go+to+page&page=585.

17. Dean Acheson, *Present at the Creation: My Years in the State Department* (New York: Norton, 1969), p. 172; Herbert Druks, *The Uncertain Friendship: The U.S. and Israel from Roosevelt to Kennedy* (Westport, CT: Greenwood, 2001), p. 87. Acheson would become Truman's secretary of state, but at this point, he was the under secretary. At the time, the British were insisting that Jewish forces in Palestine, including the Haganah—the forerunner of the Israel Defense Forces—and the underground groups, the Irgun and the Stern Gang, be disbanded.

18. Acheson, *Present at the Creation,* pp. 174–75.

19. Michael B. Oren, *Power, Faith, and Fantasy: America in the Middle East: 1776 to the Present* (New York: Norton, 2007), pp. 487–88.

20. James G. McDonald interview with Harry S. Truman, July 27, 1946, Benjamin Akzin Files, American Zionist Emergency Council Papers, Zionist Archives, New York, quoted in Druks, *The Uncertain Friendship,* p. 89. See James McDonald, *My Mission in Israel, 1948–1951* (New York: Simon & Schuster, 1951), pp. 3–9. Later Truman would send McDonald to Israel as America's first ambassador over the opposition of the State Department.

21. Nahum Goldmann, *Memories: The Autobiography of Nahum Goldmann,* trans. Helen Sebba (London: Weidenfeld and Nicolson, 1970), p. 235. Radosh and Radosh, *Safe Haven,* pp. 180–82.

22. Ibid.

23. Harry S. Truman, "Statement by the President Following the Adjournment of the Palestine Conference in London," October 4, 1946, *Public Papers of the Presidents, Harry S. Truman,* 1946, no. 227, pp. 442–44 online at American Presidency Project, www.presidency.ucsb.edu/ws/?pid=12520.

24. Benny Morris, *One State, Two States: Resolving the Israel/Palestine Conflict* (New Haven, CT: Yale University Press, 2009), pp. 89–98.

25. Eddie Jacobson, Truman's friend and former business partner, interceded with the president, arranging the meeting with Chaim Weizmann. After his presidency, Truman planned to visit Israel with Jacobson, but Jacobson died before they could take the trip.

26. *FRUS* 1948, vol. 5, part 2, no. 838, p. 1704, "The Acting Secretary of State to the Special Representative of the United States in Israel (McDonald)," December 30, 1948, *Asia, and Africa,* vol. 5, part 2, http://historystate.gov/historicaldocuments /frus1948v05p2/d838.

27. "Memorandum by the Acting Secretary of State," *FRUS* 1949, vol. 6, no. 735, p. 1109, June 10, 1949, http://history.state.gov/historicaldocuments/frus1949v06/d735.
28. Harry S. Truman, "The President's News Conference," *Public Papers of the Presidents*, American Presidency Project, August 16, 1945, Harry S. Truman, 1945, no. 106, pp. 224–29, online at www.presidency.ucsb.edu/ws/?pid=12389.
29. Truman, *Years of Trial and Hope*, p. 137.
30. Eliahu Elath, *Harry S. Truman—The Man and the Statesman* (Jerusalem: Hebrew University, 1977), p. 30.
31. Blaustein notes, September 29, 1945, Blaustein Papers, quoted in Zvi Ganin, *Truman, American Jewry, and Israel, 1945–1948* (New York: Holmes and Meier, 1979), pp. 40n40, 197.
32. Henry A. Wallace, *The Price of Vision: The Diary of Henry A. Wallace, 1942–1946* (Boston: Houghton Mifflin, 1973), p. 607.
33. Truman, *Years of Trial and Hope*, p. 169; *FRUS* 1948, vol. 5, part 2, no. 776, "President Truman to the President of the Provisional Government of Israel (Weizmann)," November 29, 1948, http://history.state.gov/historicaldocuments/frus1948v05p2/d776.
34. "President Chaim Weizmann of the Provisional Government of Israel to President Truman," *FRUS* 1949, *The Near East, South Asia, and Africa*, vol. 6, p. 600, http://digicoll.library.wisc.edu/cgi-bin/FRUS/FRUS-idx?type=goto&id=FRUS.FRUS1949v06&isize=M&submit=Go+to+page&page=600.
35. Steven L. Spiegel, *The Other Arab-Israeli Conflict: Making America's Middle East Policy, from Truman to Reagan*, p. 46; "The Acting Secretary of State to the Embassy in Israel," *FRUS* 1949, vol. 6, no. 700, pp. 1012–1074, May 28, 1949, http://history.state.gov/historicaldocuments/fros1949v06/d700.
36. This is contrary to the argument made by John B. Judis in *Genesis: Truman, American Jews, and the Origins of the Arab/Israeli Conflict* (New York: Farrar, Straus and Giroux, 2014), pp. 271ff.
37. Clark M. Clifford, "Recognizing Israel: The Behind-the-Scenes Struggle in 1948 Between the President and the State Department," *American Heritage* 28, no. 3 (April 1977): p. 4.
38. "Memorandum of Conversation, by the Acting Secretary of State," July 30, 1946, *FRUS* 1946, vol. 7, pp. 673–74, *The Near East and Africa*, http://digicoll.library.wisc.edu/cgi-bin/FRUS/FRUS-idx?type=goto&id=FRUS.FRUS1946v07&isize=M&submit=Go+to+page&page=673.
39. Acheson, *Present at the Creation*, p. 169.
40. Clark M. Clifford, Eugene V. Rostow, and Barbara Tuchman, *The Palestine Question in American History* (New York: Arno, 1978), p. 39.
41. Clark Clifford, *Counsel to the President: A Memoir* pp. 11–12; with Richard Holbrooke (New York: Random House, 1991), "Memorandum of Conversations, by the Under Secretary of State (Lovett)," *FRUS* 1948, vol. 5, part 2, no. 246, pp. 972–76, http://digicoll.library.wisc.edu/cgi-bin/FRUS/FRUS-idx?type=goto&id=FRUS.FRUS1948v05p2&isize=M&submit=Go+to+page&page=1005.
42. In fact, this was a preoccupation of British intelligence and the Colonial Office that illegal Jewish immigrants to Palestine would include enemy agents, first Nazis and later Soviets. See Fritz Liebreich, *Britain's Naval and Political Reaction to the Illegal Immigration of Jews to Palestine, 1945–1948* (New York: Routledge, 2005), pp. 41–44.
43. Clifford, *Counsel to the President*, pp. 12–23.
44. Clifford, *Counsel to the President*, pp. 13–23; *FRUS* 1948, vol. 5, part 2, no. 276, pp. 1005–1007, "Memorandum of Conversations, by the Under Secretary of State

(Lovett)," May 17, 1948, http://history.state.gov/historicaldocuments/frus1948v05p2 /d276.

45. Chester Bowles to Clark Clifford, September 23, 1948, folder 1, box 12, Clifford Papers, Harry S. Truman Presidential Library, quoted in Michael J. Cohen, *Truman and Israel* (Berkeley, CA: University of California Press, 1990), p. 244.

46. Radosh and Radosh, *Safe Haven*, p. 351.

47. Acheson, *Present at the Creation*, p. 169.

48. Walter Isaacson and Evan Thomas, *The Wise Men: Six Friends and the World They Made* (New York: Simon & Schuster, 1986), p. 451.

49. *FRUS* 1945, vol. 8, p. 687, "The Minister in Saudi Arabia (Eddy) to the Secretary of State," February 1, 1945, http://digicoll.library.wisc.edu/cgi-bin/FRUS/FRUS-idx ?type=turn&entity=FRUS.FRUS1945v08.p.0699&id=FRUS.FRUS1945v08.

50. See the State Department memorandum prepared for Truman before Potsdam, *FRUS*, "Palestine: Jewish Immigration, *Briefing Book Paper*" (1945), vol. 1, no. 646, pp. 972–74, June 22, 1945, http://images.library.wisc.edu/FRUS/EFacs/1945Berlinv01 /reference/frus.frus1945berlinv01.i0024.pdf.

51. Khayr al-Din Al-Zirkili, a Syrian and Saudi national, became director of the Saudi Foreign Ministry in 1946. His four-volume work in Arabic, *Shibh al-jazyrah fy 'ahd al-malik 'Abdal 'azyz* (The Arabian Peninsula During the Period of King Abdulaziz), relies on original Saudi documents and letters between him and the king.

52. My friend Efraim Halevy, former head of Mossad, brought this to my attention. He drew on the recently published book by Michael Kahanov, *Saudi Arabia and the Conflict in Palestine. 'Arav ha-Sa'udit yeha-sikhsukh be-Falastin* (Jerusalem: Carmel, 2012). Kahanov's book, published in Hebrew in 2012, draws on al-Zirkili's four-volume work.

53. Martin Gilbert, *Churchill and the Jews: A Lifelong Friendship* (New York: Holt, 2008), p. 235.

54. Spiegel, *The Other Arab-Israeli Conflict*, p. 17.

55. Clifford, "Recognizing Israel," p. 6.

56. Central Intelligence Agency, "The Consequences of the Partition of Palestine" (ORE 55), November 28, 1947, p. 1, www.foia.cia.gov/sites/default/files/document _conversions/89801/DOC_0000256628.pdf.

57. *FRUS* 1946, vol. 7, pp. 631–33, "Memorandum by the Joint Chiefs of Staff to the State-War-Navy Coordinating Committee," *FRUS*, June 21, 1946, http://digicoll.library .wisc.edu/cgi-bin/FRUS/FRUS-idx?type=turn&entity=FRUS.FRUS1946v07.p0643 &id=FRUS.FRUS1946v07.

58. Isaacson and Thomas, *The Wise Men*, p. 452.

59. James Forrestal, *The Forrestal Diaries* (New York: Viking, 1951), p. 357.

60. *FRUS* 1948, vol. 5, part 2, no. 10, pp. 545–54, "Memorandum by the Director of the Policy Planning Staff (Kennan) to the Secretary of State" [and attached report], January 20, 1948, http://history.state.gov/historicaldocuments/frus1948v05p2/d10, pp. 545–54.

61. *FRUS* 1948, vol. 5, part 2, no. 77. pp. 690–96, "Memorandum by the President's Special Counsel (Clifford) to President Truman," ibid., March 8, 1948, history.state .gov/historicaldocuments/frus1948v05p2/d77.

62. Clark M. Clifford, "Memo Supporting a Statement by Truman Recognizing Israel," May 9, 1948, Clark Clifford Papers, Harry S. Truman Presidential Library, www .trumanlibrary.org/whistlestop/study_collections/israel/large/documents/index .php?documentdate=1948-05-09&documentid=3-14&collectionid=ROI&page number=1.

63. Truman, *Years of Trial and Hope*, p. 165.
64. Clifford, *Counsel to the President*, p. 25; Dan Kurzman, *Ben-Gurion: Prophet of Fire* (New York: Simon & Schuster, 1983), p. 416.
65. Clifford, "Recognizing Israel," p. 5.

2. The Eisenhower Administration and the Pursuit of Arab Allies

1. Ray Takeyh provides an excellent overview of American cold war priorities in the Middle East during the Eisenhower administration in *The Origins of the Eisenhower Doctrine: The US, Britain and Nasser's Egypt, 1953–57* (New York: St. Martin's Press, 2000), pp. 1–25.
2. The members of the Baghdad Pact—Turkey, Iran, Pakistan, Britain, and Iraq— seemed more interested in acquiring arms and their regional rivalries than in joining us to counter the Soviets. With the anti-Western coup in July 1958 brutally ending the Hashemite monarchy in Baghdad in 1959, Iraq dropped out, and the Baghdad Pact became the Central Treaty Organization (CENTO).
3. *FRUS* 1952–54, vol. 9, part 1, no. 27, pp. 77–78, "Memorandum of Conversation, by the Second Secretary of Embassy in Lebanon (Meyer)," May 17, 1953, http://history .state.gov/historicaldocuments/frus1952-54v09p1/d27; *FRUS* 1952–54 vol. 9, part 1, no. 25, p. 70, "Memorandum of Conversation, by the Second Secretary of Embassy in Lebanon (Meyer)," May 16, 1953, http://history.state.gov/historicaldocuments /frus1952-54v09p1/d5.
4. *FRUS* 1952–54, vol. 9, no. 5, p. 20, "Memorandum of Conversation, Prepared in the Embassy in Cairo," May 12, 1953, http://history.state.gov/historicaldocuments /frus1952-54v09p1/d5.
5. *FRUS* 1952–54, vol. 9, part 1, p. 14, "Memorandum of Conversation, Prepared in the Embassy in Cairo," May 11, 1953, http://history.state.gov/historicaldocuments/frus 1952–54v09p1/d4. Dulles repeated the offer when he met with the four military commanders of the RCC, telling them that Egypt was "one of the countries we would like to help with military supplies and equipment." *FRUS* 1952–54, vol. 9, part 1, no. 5, p. 20, "Memorandum of Conversation, Prepared in the Embassy in Cairo," May 12, 1953, http://history.state.gov/historicaldocuments/frus1952-54v09p1/d5.
6. *FRUS* 1952–54, vol. 9, part 1, no. 13, p. 37, "Memorandum of Conversation, Prepared in the Embassy of Israel," May 14, 1953, http://history.state.gov/historicaldocuments /frus1952–54v09p1/d13; *FRUS* 1952–54, vol. 9, part 1, no. 25, p. 70; May 16, 1953, http://history.state.gov/historicaldocuments/frus1952-54v09p1/d25.
7. Jeremy M. Sharp, "U.S. Foreign Aid to Israel," Congressional Research Service, April 11, 2014, Appendix B, p. 27.
8. Indeed, I would draw on some of its principles more than forty years later in our negotiations with the Israelis, Palestinians, and Syrians.
9. Wilbur Crane Eveland, *Ropes of Sand: America's Failure in the Middle East* (New York: Norton, 1980), pp. 155–56.
10. Spiegel, *The Other Arab-Israeli Conflict*, p. 67; Eveland, *Ropes of Sand*, pp. 157–59.
11. Miles Copeland, *The Game of Nations: The Amorality of Power Politics* (New York: Simon & Schuster, 1970), pp. 145–59; Takeyh, *The Origins of the Eisenhower Doctrine*, p. 8: Eveland, *Ropes of Sand*, pp. 101–102 and 135–38.
12. Copeland, *Game of Nations*, pp. 145–59; and Efraim Halevy, "Diplomacy and Intelligence in the Middle East: How and Why Are the Two Inexorably Intertwined?" Seventh Annual Isaiah Berlin Lecture, November 8, 2009.
13. "Transcript of Secretary Dulles' News Conference," October 4, 1955, *Department of State Bulletin* 33, no. 851 (October 17, 1955): 604, as quoted in Spiegel, *The Other*

Arab-Israeli Conflict, p. 66. Kermit Roosevelt was sent to see Nasser after Eisenhower became aware of the deal but before it was announced. Whereas Dulles thought it was possible to dissuade Nasser from going through with the deal, Roosevelt thought otherwise. Instead, he convinced Nasser to say that the arms made Egypt's borders secure enough for him now to pursue peace. Nasser was not prepared to make any gestures, but he told Roosevelt he could privately convey that he would not dismiss efforts to defuse Arab-Israeli tensions—and Dulles seemed to have taken this seriously enough to publicly rationalize the deal. See Hugh Wilford, *America's Great Game: The CIA's Secret Arabists and the Shaping of the Modern Middle East* (New York: Basic Books, 2013), pp. 196–97.

14. "Security Council Adopts Resolution Condemning Israel for Gaza," Jewish Telegraphic Agency, March 30, 1955, www.jta.org/1955/03/30/archive/security-council-adopts -resolution-condemning-israel-for-gaza.

15. Dwight D. Eisenhower, *The White House Years, vol. 2: Waging Peace, 1956–1961* (New York: Doubleday, 1965), p. 26.

16. *FRUS 1955–57*, vol. 15, no. 164, pp. 302–307, "Message from Robert B. Anderson to the Secretary of State, at Karachi," March 6, 1956, http://history.state.gov/historical documents/frus1955–57v15/d164.

17. *FRUS 1955–57*, vol. 15, no. 187, pp. 342–43," Diary Entry by the President," March 13, 1956, http://history.state.gov/historicaldocuments/frus1955–57v15/d187.

18. Ibid.

19. *FRUS 1955–1957*, vol. 15, no. 103, pp. 185–87, "Letter from Prime Minister Ben-Gurion to President Eisenhower [attachment]," February 14, 1956, http://history.state .gov/frus1955–57v15/d103.

20. David Ben-Gurion, *Israel: A Personal History* (New York: Funk & Wagnalls, 1971), pp. 474–75.

21. Steven A. Cook, *The Struggle for Egypt: From Nasser to Tahrir Square* (New York: Oxford University Press, 2012), pp. 66–67.

22. Eisenhower, *Waging Peace*, p. 35.

23. Ibid., p. 36.

24. Ibid., p. 38.

25. Ibid., pp. 39–41.

26. Ibid., p. 73.

27. Ibid., p. 76.

28. Ibid., p. 73.

29. Ibid., p. 74.

30. John Foster Dulles, "Statement by Secretary Dulles in the General Assembly, November 1," *Department of State Bulletin*, November 12, 1956, p. 754.

31. Ben-Gurion, *Personal History*, p. 509.

32. Eisenhower, *Waging Peace*, p. 83.

33. Ibid., pp. 187–88.

34. Ibid., p. 94.

35. Cablegram, Eisenhower to Dulles, December 12, 1956, p. 2, quoted in Spiegel, *The Other Arab-Israeli Conflict*, p. 84.

36. Eisenhower, *Waging Peace*, pp. 96–97.

37. Ibid., p. 178.

38. Ibid., pp. 684–85; Appendix J.

39. Ibid., p. 185.

40. Ibid., pp. 187–88.

41. Ibid., p. 189.
42. Eveland, *Ropes of Sand*, pp. 114–255. Wilbur Eveland describes at great length his efforts on behalf of Allen Dulles and the CIA to plan, organize, and carry out such a coup.
43. Ibid.
44. Eisenhower, *Waging Peace*, p. 202; Eveland, *Ropes of Sand*, p. 257.
45. Eisenhower, *Waging Peace*, pp. 265–67.
46. Ibid., pp. 269–70.
47. *FRUS* 1958–60, vol. 13, no. 35, pp. 82–83, "Memorandum of a Conversation," August 3, 1958, http://history.state.gov/historicaldocuments/frus1958–60v13/d36.
48. *FRUS* 1958–60, vol. 13, no. 36, pp. 85–87, "Letter from Prime Minister Ben-Gurion to Secretary of State Dulles [attachment]," August 5, 1958, http://history.state.gov/historicaldocuments/frus1958–60v13/d36.
49. Eisenhower, *Waging Peace*, p. 288.
50. *FRUS* 1958–60, vol. 12, no. 51, pp. 187–99, "NSC 582011: U.S. Policy Toward the Near East," November 4, 1958, http://history.state.gov/historicaldocuments/frus1958–60v12/d51.
51. Herbert Druks, *The Uncertain Friendship: The U.S. and Israel from Roosevelt to Kennedy* (Westport, CT: Greenwood, 2001), p. 203.
52. *FRUS* 1958–60, vol. 13, no. 131, pp. 280–88, "Memorandum of a Conversation, White House, Washington," March 10, 1960, http://history.state.gov/historicaldocuments/frus1958-60v13/d131.
53. Druks, *The Uncertain Friendship*, p. 206.
54. Ibid., p. 209.
55. Hal Lehrman, "American Policy and Arab-Israeli Peace: Our Course in the Light of Near East Realities," *Commentary*, June 1, 1954, p. 550, www.commentarymagazine.com/article/american-policy-and-arab-israeli-peaceour-course-in-the-light-of-near-east-realities/.
56. Letter, Eisenhower to Winston Churchill, March 29, 1956, p. 2, quoted in Spiegel, *The Other Arab-Israeli Conflict*, p. 56.
57. *FRUS* 1952–54, vol. 9, part 1, no. 13, p. 39, "Memorandum of Conversation, Prepared in the Embassy in Israel," May 14, 1953, http://history.state.gov/historicaldocuments/frus1952–54v09p1/d13.
58. Donald Neff, *Warriors at Suez: Eisenhower Takes America into the Middle East* (New York: Simon & Schuster, 1981), p. 107.
59. Ibid., p. 433.
60. Eisenhower, *Waging Peace*, p. 74.
61. *FRUS* 1958–60, vol. 13, no. 264, pp. 600–607, "Memorandum of a Conversation," September 26, 1960, http://history.state.gov/frus1958–60v13/d264.
62. FRUS 1955–57, vol. 15, no. 232, p. 439, "Memorandum of a Conversation," April 1, 1956, http://history.state.gov/historicaldocuments/frus1955–57v15/d232.
63. White House Memorandum of Conference with the President, July 23, 1958, 3:00 p.m., pp. 1–2, quoted in Spiegel, *The Other Arab-Israeli Conflict*, p. 92.
64. Foreign Office Notation on U.S. Official Views, November 1953, Israel Foreign Office Papers, 2472/7, Israel State Archives, Jerusalem, quoted in Druks, *The Uncertain Friendship*, p. 166.
65. Yossi Melman and Dan Raviv, *Friends in Deed: Inside the U.S.-Israeli Alliance* (New York: Hyperion, 1994), p. 61.
66. Efraim Halevy, discussion with the author, December 2013.

67. "The President's News Conference," April 29, 1954, *Public Papers of the Presidents, Dwight D. Eisenhower, 1954*, p. 436, online at www.presidency.ucsb.edu/ws/index.php?pid=10223. &st=&st=.
68. Dwight D. Eisenhower Papers, White House Central Files, Eisenhower Library, File OCB, Records 1953–54, quoted in Isaac Alteras, *Eisenhower and Israel: U.S.-Israeli Relations, 1953–1960* (Gainesville: University Press of Florida, 1993), p. 102.
69. Undated Israel Foreign Office Papers, A.H. 00/107/6, Israel State Archives, Jerusalem, as quoted in Druks, *The Uncertain Friendship*, p. 155.
70. *FRUS* 1955–57, vol. 15, no. 14, p. 21, "Memorandum of a Conversation," January 11, 1956, http://history.state.gov/historicaldocuments/frus1955–57v15/d14.
71. Abba Eban–John F. Dulles conversation, October 8, 1954, Israel Foreign Office Papers, 2480/5, Israel State Archives, quoted in Druks, *The Uncertain Friendship*, p. 163.
72. Nadav Safran, *Israel: The Embattled Ally* (Cambridge, MA: Harvard University Press, 1981), p. 352.
73. Eveland, *Ropes of Sand*, p. 193.
74. *FRUS* 1955–57, vol. 15, no. 226, p. 425, "Diary Entry by the President," *FRUS*, March 28, 1956, http://history.state.gov/historicaldocuments/frus1955–57v15/d226.
75. "Memorandum of Conversation, Prepared in the Embassy, in Cairo," May 11, 1953, *FRUS* 1952–54, vol. 9, part 1, no. 4, pp. 12 and 18, http://history.state.gov/historical documents/frus1952–54v09p1/d4.
76. Eisenhower, *Waging Peace*, p. 201.
77. Ibid., p. 290.
78. Ibid., p. 106.
79. Warren Bass, *Support Any Friend: Kennedy's Middle East and the Making of the U.S.-Israel Alliance* (New York: Oxford University Press, 2003), p. 63.

3. The Kennedy Administration: Breaking Taboos and Pursuing a New Balance

1. Myer Feldman, interview by John F. Stewart, December 11, 1966, pp. 458–460, John F. Kennedy Presidential Library, http://archive2.jfklibrary.org/JFKOH /Feldman,%20Myer/JFKOH-MF-10/JFKOH-MF-10-TR.pdf.
2. Bass, *Support Any Friend*, pp. 73–74.
3. *FRUS* 1961–63, vol. 17, no. 9, pp. 18–20, "Telegram from the Department of State to the Embassy in the United Arab Republic," February 8, 1961, http://history.state .gov/historicaldocuments/frus1961–63v17/d9.
4. Robert Komer, interview by Elizabeth Farmer, January 30, 1970, p. 49, John F. Kennedy Library, http://web2.millercenter.org/lbj/oralhistory/komer_robert_1970_0130 .pdf.
5. *FRUS* 1961–63, vol. 17, no. 57, pp. 134–41, "Memorandum of a Conversation," May 30, 1961, http://history.state.gov/historicaldocuments/frus1961–63v17/d57.
6. Ibid.
7. *FRUS* 1961–63, vol. 17, no. 68, pp. 164–66, "National Intelligence Estimate," June 27, 1961, http://history.state.gov/historicaldocuments/frus1961–63v17/d68.
8. *FRUS* 1961–63, vol. 17, no. 74, p. 173, "Memorandum from Robert W. Komer of the National Security Council Staff to the President's Deputy Special Assistant for National Security Affairs (Rostow)," June 30, 1961, http://history.state.gov/historical documents/frus1961–63v17/d74.
9. *FRUS* 1961–63, vol. 17, no. 17, no. 111, pp. 262–64, "Telegram from the Department of State to the Embassy in Jordan," September 28, 1961, http://history.state.gov /historicaldocuments/frus1961–63v17/d111.

10. *FRUS* 1961–63, vol. 17, no. 116, p. 274 n3, "Telegram from the Embassy in Jordan to the Department of State," October 1, 1961, http://history.state.gov/historicaldocuments/frus1961-63v17/d116.
11. *FRUS* 1961–63, vol. 17, no. 119, p. 281, "Telegram from the Department of State to the Embassy in the United Arab Republic," October 3, 1961, http://history.state.gov/historicaldocuments/frus1961-63v17/d119.
12. Nina J. Noring and Glenn W. LaFantasie, eds., "National Security Action Memorandum No. 105," ibid., no. 128, http://history.state.gov/historicaldocuments/frus1961-63v17/d128.
13. Bowles telegram to State, February 21, 1962, POF, box 127, UAR Security, 1962, JFKL, quoted in Bass, *Support Any Friend*, p. 89.
14. *FRUS* 1961–63, vol. 17, no. 191, p. 471, "Memorandum of Conversation," February 13, 1962, http://history.state.gov/historicaldocuments/frus1961-63v17/d191.
15. Chester Bowles, "A Look at the Middle East Today, April 12, 1962," *Department of State Bulletin*, May 7, 1962, pp. 765–66.
16. John F. Kennedy, "Remarks of Senator John F. Kennedy, National Conference of Christians and Jews, Cleveland, Ohio," February 24, 1957, JFKL, www.jfklibrary.org/Research/Research-Aids/JFK-Speeches/Cleveland-OH_19570224.aspx.
17. Myer Feldman, interview by John F. Stewart, JFKL, August 20, 1966, pp. 405–407, http://archive2.jfklibrary.org/JFKOH/Feldman,%20Myer/JFKOH-MF-09/JFKOH-MF-09-TR.pdf.
18. Ibid., p. 408.
19. Ibid., p. 409.
20. Ibid.
21. Ibid., p. 411.
22. Ibid., pp. 411–17.
23. Ibid., pp. 418–19.
24. Ibid.
25. Badeau telegram to JFK, Rusk, and Grant, August 24, 1962, NSF, box 427, Komer Papers, Israel, 1961–63, JFKL, quoted in Bass, *Support Any Friend*, p. 173.
26. Feldman interview, August 20, 1966, pp. 421–27.
27. Komer handwritten note, June 18, 1962, NSF, box 428, Komer Papers, Israel, Security (Missile), Development Sale of Hawks, JFKL, quoted in Bass, *Support Any Friend*, p. 154.
28. Bundy letter to Talbot, April 3, 1962, DoD files, Records of the Secretary of Defense, Office of Assistant Secretary of Defense, Israel State Archives, box 89, Israel 1962, NA, quoted in Bass, *Support Any Friend*, p. 158.
29. Bass, *Support Any Friend*, pp. 159–161; Bundy memorandum to Talbot, May 23, 1962, DoD files, OASD-ISA, box 89, Israel 1962, NA, quoted in Bass, *Support Any Friend*, pp. 160–61.
30. Myer Feldman interview by John Stewart, JFKL, July 29, 1967, p. 540, http://archive2.jfklibrary.org/JFK/Feldman,%20Myer/JFKOH-MF-11-TR.pdf.
31. *FRUS* 1961–63, vol. 17, no. 288, pp. 706–707, "Memorandum from the Department of State Executive Secretary (Brubeck) to the President's Special Assistant for National Security Affairs (Bundy)," June 4, 1962, http://history.state.gov/historicaldocuments/frus1961-63v17/d288.
32. Feldman interview, July 29, 1967, pp. 503–505.
33. *FRUS* 1961–63, vol. 18, no. 100, pp. 228–229, "Telegram from the Department of State to the Embassy in Jordan," November 16, 1962, http://history.state.gov/historicaldocuments/frus1961-63v18/d100.

34. *FRUS* 1961–63, vol. 18, no. 178, p. 397, "Memorandum from Robert W. Komer of the National Security Council Staff to the President's Special Assistant for National Security Affairs (Bundy)," March 6, 1963, http://history.state.gov/historicaldocuments/frus1961-63v18/d178.

35. JFK letter to Nasser, April 18, 1963, POF, box 127, UAR Security 1963 File, JFKL, as quoted in Bass, *Support Any Friend*, p. 117.

36. Feldman interview, July 29, 1967, p. 508.

37. Ibid., p. 509.

38. *FRUS* 1961–63, vol. 18, no. 220, pp. 481–82, "Memorandum from the Department of State Executive Secretary (Brubeck) to the President's Special Assistant for National Security Affairs (Bundy)," April 27, 1963, http://history.state.gov/historical documents/frus1961-63v18/d220.

39. Feldman interview, December 11, 1966, pp. 478–80. At a different point in his series of interviews, Feldman says that in sending the 6th Fleet, the president did not make the decision on whether it would "help or hinder Israel" (July 29, 1967, p. 522). http://archive2.jfklibrary.org/JFKOH/Feldman,%20Myer/JFKOH-MF-11/JFKOH -MF-11-TR.pdf.

40. *FRUS* 1961–63, vol. 18, no. 228, pp. 496–99, "Memorandum of Telephone Conversation Between the President's Special Assistant for National Security Affairs (Bundy) and Acting Secretary of State Ball," April 29, 1963, https://history.state.gov /historicaldocuments/frus1961-63v18/d228.

41. Feldman interview, July 29, 1967, p. 535.

42. *FRUS* 1961–63, vol. 18, no. 121, pp. 276–83, "Memorandum of Conversation," http://history.state.gov/historicaldocuments/frus1961-63v18/d121.

43. Ibid.

44. CIA Board of National Estimate Chairman Sherman Kent memo to DCI McCone, March 6, 1963, NSF, Box 119, Israel, General, JFKL, as quoted in Bass, *Support Any Friend*, pp. 208–209.

45. JFK letter to Ben-Gurion, May 18, 1963, POF, Box 119a, Israel, Security, JFKL, quoted in Bass, *Support Any Friend*, p. 216.

46. Feldman interview, John Stewart, August 26, 1967, pp. 556–57, http://archive1 .jfklibrary.org/JFKOH/Feldman,%20Myer/JFKOH-MF-12/JFKOH-MF-12-TR.pdf.

47. Feldman interview, July 29, 1967, pp. 544–46.

48. The State Department and AID had been prepared to offer only $10 million for Israel but were forced to increase the amount to $45 million. See Feldman interview, August 26, 1967, pp. 573–78.

49. The Syrians had a presence in the northeast corner of the Kinneret (Sea of Galilee) and would fire at Israeli boats that came too close to the eastern shore. In a March 26, 2000, meeting with President Clinton and me, Assad claimed that as a youth, he would swim in the lake.

50. "Speech by Senator John F. Kennedy, Zionists of America Convention, Statler Hilton Hotel, New York, NY," August 26, 1960, American Presidency Project, www .presidency.ucsb.edu/ws/?pid=74217.

51. "Z.O.A. Convention Opens; Kennedy Lauds 'Experience of Zionism,'" Jewish Telegraphic Agency, June 29, 1962, www.jta.org/1962/06/29/archive/z-o-a-convention -opens-kennedy-lauds-experience-of-zionism.

52. Richard Reeves, *President Kennedy: Profile of Power* (New York: Simon & Schuster, 1993), p. 144.

53. Feldman interview, July 29, 1966, pp. 540–42.

54. "Address of Senator John F. Kennedy Accepting the Democratic Party Nomination for the Presidency of the United States," July 15, 1960, American Presidency Project, www.presidency.uesb.edu/ws/?pid=25966.
55. Feldman interview, December 11, 1966, pp. 464–66 and 447–50.
56. *FRUS 1961–63*, vol. 18, no. 19, pp. 56–57, "Notes of Conference," August 14, 1962, http://history.state.gov/historicaldocuments/frus1961-63v18/d19.
57. Bass, *Support Any Friend*, p. 58.
58. Feldman interview, December 11, 1966, pp. 475–76.
59. Bass, *Support Any Friend*, p. 165.
60. *FRUS 1961–63*, vol. 17, no. 296, pp. 728–730, "Telegram from the Embassy of Greece to the Department of State," June 15, 1962, http://history.state.gov/historical documents/frus1961–63v17/d296.
61. Feldman interview, July 29, 1967, pp. 539–40.
62. *FRUS 1961–63*, vol. 18, no. 250, pp. 540–41, "Memorandum from Robert W. Komer of the National Security Council Staff to President Kennedy," May 16, 1963, https://history.state.gov/historicaldocuments/frus1961-63v18/d250.
63. *FRUS 1961–63*, vol. 18, no. 109, p. 255, "Memorandum from Robert W. Komer of the National Security Council Staff to President Kennedy," December 5, 1962, https://history.state.gov/historicaldocuments/frus1961-63v18/d109.
64. *FRUS 1961–63*, vol. 18, no. 368, pp. 798–99, "Memorandum for the Record," November 21, 1963, http://history.state.gov/historicaldocuments/frus1961–63v18/d368.
65. Some of our ambassadors to the conservative monarchies, reflecting their ties to the Saudis and the Jordanians, raised questions not about Israel but about the relationship with Nasser. Kermit Roosevelt, who became the head of Gulf Oil and was therefore close to the Saudis, very much echoed their fears about Nasser. As for the CIA, apart from McCone's position cited above, two days before Kennedy took office, the agency provided an assessment of Israel's nuclear program in which it is hard to escape the embedded anti-Semitism: "With reference to the recent revelation of the existence of a nuclear reactor in Beersheba [sic], the fact that Israel is working in this field should have come as no surprise inasmuch as almost every nuclear scientist who has contributed to the development of nuclear weapons in the US has been a Jew and a great number of prominent nuclear scientists have come to Israel." CIA Information Report, January 18, 1961, POF, box 119A, Israel, Security, David Ben-Gurion, JFKL, quoted in Bass, *Support Any Friend* p. 195.
66. Bass, *Support Any Friend*, p. 122. The Joint Chiefs of Staff had not, echoing CIA views on most issues, and going so far as to say that a nuclear Israel might lead Nasser and the Arabs to cut off oil to the West. See *FRUS 1961–63*, vol. 17, no. 95, pp. 216–21, "Paper Prepared by the Joint Chiefs of Staff," n.d., http://history.state.gov/historicaldocuments/frus1961-63v17/d95.
67. Bass, *Support Any Friend*, p. 122.
68. JFK letter to Eshkol, October 2, 1963, MH 3377/10, Israel State Archives, Jerusalem, as quoted in Bass, *Support Any Friend*, p. 236.

4. Lyndon Baines Johnson: Emotional Ties but Constrained by Vietnam

1. Robert Komer interview, Joe B. Frantz, Lyndon B. Johnson Presidential Library, January 30, 1970, p. 49, http://web2.millercenter.org/lbj/oralhistory/komer_robert _1970_0130.pdf.
2. *FRUS 1964–68*, vol. 18, no. 35, pp. 80–81, "Memorandum for the Record," April 2, 1964, http://history.state.gov/historicaldocuments/frus1964–68v18/d35.

3. When Ambassador Lucius Battle suggested to Nasser that he apologize for these incidents and moderate his posture lest he lose access to American wheat aid—which at this point provided 53 percent of Egypt's bread supply—Nasser let loose with a rhetorical fusillade: "The American Ambassador says that our behavior is not acceptable. Well, let us tell them that those who do not accept our behavior can go and drink from the sea . . . We will cut the tongues of anybody who talks badly about us . . . We are not going to accept gangsterism by cowboys." See Michael B. Oren, *Six Days of War: June 1967 and the Making of the Modern Middle East* (New York: Oxford University Press, 2002), p. 21; William J. Burns, *Economic Aid and the American Policy Toward Egypt, 1955–1981* (Albany: State University of New York Press, 1985), pp. 159–60.

4. *FRUS 1964–67*, vol. 18, no. 108, p. 240, "National Security Action Memorandum No. 319," November 20, 1964, http://history.state.gov/historicaldocuments/frus 1964-68v18/d108.

5. *FRUS 1964–68*, vol. 18, no. 78, pp. 182–84. "Information Memorandum from the Assistant Secretary of State for Near Eastern and South Asian Affairs (Talbot) to Secretary of State Rusk," July 22, 1964, http://history.state.gov/historicaldocuments /frus1964-68v18/d78.

6. *FRUS 1964–68*, vol. 18, no. 7, pp. 11–15, "Memorandum for Record," ibid., January 10, 1964, http://history.state.gov/historicaldocuments/frus1964-68v18/d7.

7. *FRUS 1964–68*, vol. 18, no. 42, pp. 101–102, "Special National Intelligence Estimate," April 15, 1964, http://history.state.gov/historicaldocuments/frus1964-68v18/d42.

8. Ibid.

9. *FRUS 1964–68*, vol. 18, no. 29, pp. 68–72, "Memorandum from the President's Special Assistant for National Security Affairs (Bundy) to President Johnson," March 13, 1964, http://history.state.gov/historicaldocuments/frus1964-68v18/d29.

10. *FRUS 1964–68*, vol. 18, no. 33, pp. 76–78, "Memorandum from Robert W. Komer of the National Security Council Staff to the President's Deputy Special Counsel (Feldman)," March 23, 1964, http://history.state.gov/historicaldocuments/frus1964 -68v18/d33.

11. Komer memorandum of conversation with Harriman, February 25, 1954, State Department doc. 4878, p. 3, as quoted in Spiegel, *The Other Arab-Israeli Conflict*, p. 133.

12. Ibid., pp. 2–3.

13. Komer interview, pp. 49–50.

14. Ibid., p. 50.

15. Oren, *Six Days*, p. 54.

16. Ibid., p. 9.

17. Asher Susser, *On Both Banks of the Jordan: A Political Biography of Wasfi Al-Tall* (Portland, OR: Frank Cass, 1994), pp. 119–29, and Public Record Office, FCO 17/231, Jordan-UAR relations: Amman to Foreign Office, January 9, 1967, as quoted in Oren, *Six Days*, p. 37.

18. Oren, *Six Days*, p. 55.

19. LBJ, National Security Files, History of the Middle East Crisis, box 17: Saunders to Rostow, May 15, 1967; and Memos to the President (W. Rostow), box 16: Saunders to Rostow, May 16, 1967; Middle East, Israel boxes 140, 141: W. Rostow to the President, May 15, 1967, quoted in Oren, *Six Days*, pp. 103–104.

20. Ibid., p. 73.

21. Ibid., p. 79.

22. William B. Quandt, *Decade of Decisions: American Policy Toward the Arab-Israeli Conflict, 1967–1976* (Berkeley: University of California Press, 1977), p. 41.

23. Oren, *Six Days*, p. 72.
24. Arthur J. Goldberg, interview by Ted Gittinger, March 23, 1983, p. 15, Lyndon B. Johnson Presidential Library, http://web2.millercenter.org/lbj/oralhistory/goldberg _arthur_1983_0323.pdf.
25. Ibid.
26. Lyndon B. Johnson, *The Vantage Point: Perspectives of the Presidency, 1963–1969* (New York: Holt, 1971), p. 290.
27. Quandt, *Decade of Decisions*, pp. 41–42.
28. *FRUS 1964–68*, vol. 19, no. 8, pp. 10–11, "Telegram from the State Department to the Embassy of Israel," May 17, 1967, http://history.state.gov/historicaldocuments/ frus1964–68v19/d8.
29. Lyndon B. Johnson, *The Vantage Point*, 290–91; Quandt, *Decade of Decisions*, pp. 40–43; Moshe A. Gilboa, *Shesh shanim, shisa yamim (Six Years, Six Days)* (Tel Aviv: Am Oved, 1968), p. 145; David Dishon, ed., *Middle East Record III, 1967* (Jerusalem: Keter Publishing, 1971), pp. 194–96.
30. Arthur J. Goldberg interview, p. 12.
31. Johnson, *Vantage Point*, p. 291.
32. Ibid.
33. Ibid.
34. Dean Rusk, interview by Paige E. Mulhollan, Lyndon B. Johnson Presidential Library, March 8, 1970, p. 3, http://web2.millercenter.org/lbj/oralhistory/rusk_dean _1970_0308.pdf.
35. LBJ, National Security File, Memos to the President (W. Rostow), box 16: Overall Arab and Israeli Military Capabilities, as quoted in Oren, *Six Days*, p. 104.
36. Gideon Rafael, *Destination Peace: Three Decades of Israeli Foreign Policy; A Personal Memoir* (New York: Stein & Day, 1981), pp. 143–45, quoted in Oren, *Six Days*, p. 108.
37. Robert S. McNamara, interview by Robert Dallek, Lyndon B. Johnson Presidential Library, March 26, 1993, p. 14, http://web2.millercenter.org/lbj/oralhistory/mcna mara_robert_1993_0326.pdf.
38. *FRUS 1964–68*, vol. 19, no. 72, pp. 127–36, "Memorandum for the Record," May 26, 1967, http://history.state.gov/historicaldocuments/frus1964–68v19/d72.
39. Johnson, *Vantage Point*, p. 293.
40. Oren, *Six Days*, p. 114.
41. Johnson, *Vantage Point*, pp. 293–94.
42. Quoted in Quandt, *Decade of Decisions*, pp. 53–54 (emphasis added).
43. Goldberg interview, p. 13.
44. LBJ, National Security File, National Security Council History, Middle East Crisis 2, box 17: Johnson to Eshkol, May 27, 1967; Johnson to Barbour, May 27, 1967, quoted in Oren, *Six Days*, p. 123; Foreign Ministry Sources quoted in Michael Brecher, *Decisions in Israel's Foreign Policy* (New Haven, CT: Yale University Press, 1975), p. 400.
45. With regard to his message to Eban, Goldberg said that "the Israelis could determine what was required for their own security. I didn't want them fooled." See Goldberg interview, pp. 13–14.
46. Oren, *Six Days*, p. 139.
47. Menahem Mansoor, *Political and Diplomatic History of the Arab World, 1900–1967*, entry for May 16, quoted in Oren, *Six Days*, p. 63.
48. Gamal Abdel Nasser, "Statement by President Nasser to Members of the Egyptian National Assembly," Israeli Ministry of Foreign Affairs, May 29, 1967, www.mfa

.gov.il/mfa/foreignpolicy/mfadocuments/yearbook1/pages/8%20statement%20
by%20president%20nasser%20to%20members%20of%20the.aspx.

49. BBC, *Daily Report, Middle East, Africa, and Western Europe*, No. 1, quoted in
Oren, *Six Days*, p. 164.

50. As noted in *Foreign Relations of the United States, Arab Israeli Crisis and War:
1964–1968*, "Walt Rostow sent a copy to the President, at 2:10 p.m., with a memorandum calling it the 'full flavor and feeling of one of our Arabist Ambassadors.' Rostow
also attached a copy of telegram 8313 from Cairo, June 1, which reported the Bel-
gian Ambassador's view that Nasser 'would not budge an inch on Aqaba' and that
Israeli military action would be preferable to action by the Western powers. Rostow's memorandum states he wanted the President to have before him as wide a
range of perspectives as possible." *FRUS* 1964–68, vol. 19, no. 117, p. 314*n1*, "Telegram from the Embassy in Syria to the Department of State," June 1, 1967, https://
history.state.gov/historicaldocuments/frus1964-68v19/d117.

51. Oren, *Six Days*, pp. 140–41.

52. Ibid., p. 147.

53. Ibid.

54. *FRUS* 1964–68, vol. 19, no. 72, pp. 127–36, "Memorandum for the Record," May 26,
1967, http://history.state.gov/historicaldocuments/frus1964-68v19/d72.

55. LBJ, National Security Files, NSC Histories, Middle East Crisis, box 17: Reflections
Pre-Eban (Saunders), May 25, 1967; box 18: Arab-Israel: Where We Are and Where
We're Going (Saunders), May 31, 1967, as quoted in Oren, *Six Days*, p. 165.

56. Johnson, *Vantage Point*, p. 298.

57. There are differing accounts on whether it was done deliberately by Israel or was an
accident caused by the fog of war—Rusk and Helms were convinced it was the former, McNamara and Johnson, the latter.

58. Johnson, *Vantage Point*, pp. 300–303.

59. *FRUS* 1964–68, vol. 19, no. 178, p. 329*n2*, "Telegram from the Embassy in the
United Arab Republic to the Department of State," June 6, 1967, https://history
.state.gov/historicaldocuments/frus1964-68v19/d178.

60. Johnson, *Vantage Point*, p. 303.

61. Ibid., p. 304.

62. Earle G. Wheeler letter to Steven Spiegel, May 29, 1975, quoted in Spiegel, *The Other
Arab-Israeli Conflict*, p. 161.

63. Lyndon B. Johnson, "Remarks at the 125th Anniversary Meeting of B'nai B'rith,"
September 10, 1968, *Public Papers of the Presidents*, Lyndon B. Johnson, 1968,
pp. 944–50, online at the American Presidency Project, www.presidency.vesb.edu
/ws/?pid=29109.

64. Lyndon B. Johnson, "Toasts of the President and President Zalman Shazar of Israel," *Public Papers of the Presidents*, American Presidency Project, August 2, 1966,
Lyndon B. Johnson, 1966, no. 3.65, pp. 796–97, online at www.presidency.ucsb.edu
/ws/?pid=27754.

65. Harry McPherson, interview by T. H. Baker, January 16, 1969, p. 27, Oral History,
Lyndon B. Johnson Presidential Library, http://web1.millercenter.org/poh/transcripts
/mcpherson_harry_1969_0116.pdf.

66. Robert Dallek, *Flawed Giant: Lyndon Johnson and His Times, 1961–1973* (New
York: Oxford University Press, 1998), pp. 428–29.

67. Israeli State Archives, 3977/20, Foreign Ministry Files, Relations with the United
States, December 12, 1966, as quoted in Oren, *Six Days*, p. 34.

68. Rusk memo of conversation with Talbot, State Department memorandum 1080, April 20, 1965, pp. 2–3, as quoted in Spiegel, *The Other Arab-Israeli Conflict*, p. 134.
69. Dean Rusk interview, p. 8.
70. Ibid., p. 4.
71. Quandt, *Decade of Decisions*, p. 67.
72. Spiegel, *The Other Arab-Israeli Conflict*, p. 158.
73. LBJ National Security File, History of the Middle East Conflict, box 18: Text of Cable from Mr. Yost, June 1, 1967, as quoted in Oren, *Six Days*, p. 144.
74. Johnson, *Vantage Point*, p. 304.
75. Eugene Rostow, interview by Paige E. Mulhollan, Lyndon B. Johnson Presidential Library, December 2, 1968, p. 35, http://web2.millercenter.org/lbj/oralhistory/rostow_eugene_1968_1202.pdf (emphasis added).
76. U.S. Department of Defense, *Military Assistance Facts*, May 1966, p. 21; *Military Assistance and Foreign Military Sales Facts*, May 1973, p. 19, as quoted in Spiegel, *The Other Arab-Israeli Conflict*, p. 135.
77. Efraim Halevy, in discussion with the author, December 2013.

5. Nixon and Ford: Dysfunction, War, and Interim Agreements

1. Richard M. Nixon, *RN: The Memoirs of Richard Nixon* (New York: Grosset and Dunlap, 1978), p. 477.
2. Ibid.
3. Henry Kissinger, *White House Years* (Boston: Little, Brown, 1979), p. 351.
4. Ibid., p. 559.
5. Ibid., p. 351.
6. Richard Nixon, "President's News Conference of January 27," *Department of State Bulletin*, February 17, 1969, pp. 142–43.
7. Kissinger, *White House Years*, p. 559.
8. Yitzhak Rabin, *The Rabin Memoirs* (Boston: Little, Brown, 1979), p. 147.
9. Kissinger, *White House Years*, p. 358.
10. Spiegel, *The Other Arab-Israeli Conflict*, p. 183.
11. Kissinger, *White House Years*, pp. 368–69.
12. At the time, the war of attrition threatened to escalate as Israel responded to Egyptian artillery attacks against its positions; fedayeen attacks out of Jordan produced Israeli retaliation; and terror and hijacking of planes bound for Israel also produced Israeli retaliatory actions against Lebanon, which led to the Lebanese government declaring a state of emergency. See Kissinger, *White House Years*, pp. 363–64.
13. Ibid., p. 373.
14. Ibid., p. 371.
15. Ibid.
16. Ibid., p. 371; Rabin, *Memoirs*, p. 154.
17. Kissinger, *White House Years*, p. 371; Rabin, *Memoirs*, pp. 154–55.
18. Rabin, *Memoirs*, p. 158.
19. Kissinger, *White House Years*, pp. 374–75.
20. Ibid., p. 373.
21. On the secret Israeli-Jordanian talks, see Moshe Shemesh, "On Two Parallel Tracks—The Secret Jordanian-Israeli Talks (July 1967–September 1973)," *Israel Studies* 15, no. 3 (2010): 87–120.
22. Rabin, *Memoirs*, p. 159.

23. Kissinger, *White House Years*, p. 373.
24. Nixon, *RN*, p. 479.
25. Kissinger, *White House Years*, p. 378.
26. Ibid., p. 563.
27. Ibid.
28. Ibid.
29. Nixon, *RN*, p. 480.
30. Nixon note to Kissinger, cited in Kissinger, *White House Years*, p. 564.
31. Ibid., p. 572.
32. Rabin, *Memoirs*, p. 171.
33. Ibid., p. 172.
34. Ibid., p. 175.
35. Kissinger, *White House Years*, pp. 576–78.
36. Rabin, *Memoirs*, p. 177.
37. Kissinger, *White House Years*, pp. 581–82.
38. Spiegel, *The Other Arab-Israeli Conflict*, p. 193; Richard M. Nixon, "A Conversation with the President About Foreign Policy," July 1, 1970, *Public Papers of the Presidents*, Richard M. Nixon, 1970, no. 208, pp. 543–59, online at American Presidency Project, www.presidency.ucsb.edu/ws/index.php?pid=2567.
39. Kissinger, *White House Years*, pp. 579–80.
40. Rabin, *Memoirs*, pp. 178–79.
41. Kissinger, *White House Years*, p. 584.
42. Hedrick Smith, "Charges of Egyptian Truce Violations Straining American-Israeli Relations," *The New York Times*, August 18, 1970, http://timesmachine.nytimes.com/timesmachine/1970/08/18/78802619.html?pageNumber=2.
43. Rabin, *Memoirs*, p. 185.
44. Nixon, *RN*, p. 482.
45. Kissinger, *White House Years*, p. 596.
46. Nixon, *RN*, p. 483.
47. Negotiations over the release of the passengers would proceed over the following days, with the hostages released in exchange for four Palestinian prisoners, and the plane in Cairo being blown up in anticipation of a counterattack.
48. While Hussein had joined Nasser in 1967 and his forces fought with the fedayeen against the IDF in the battle at Karameh in 1968, he also was quietly cooperating with the Israelis, so they did not see him as a threat. If he were to be replaced by radical forces, the threat to Israel would grow dramatically.
49. Kissinger, *White House Years*, p. 602.
50. Ibid., p. 612.
51. Ibid., p. 626.
52. Ibid., p. 631.
53. *FRUS 1967–72*, vol. 24, no. 327, pp. 914–15, "Memorandum from the President's Assistant for National Security Affairs (Kissinger) to President Nixon," September 25, 1970, https://history.state.gov/historicaldocuments/frus1969-76v24/d327.
54. Rabin, *Memoirs*, p. 189.
55. Ibid.
56. Nixon, *RN*, p. 481.
57. Kissinger, *White House Years*, p. 1277.
58. Ibid., p. 1277.
59. Ibid., p. 1279.

60. Rabin, *Memoirs*, p. 194.
61. Ibid., p. 195.
62. Ibid.
63. Ibid., pp. 196–97.
64. Kissinger, *White House Years*, p. 1282.
65. To make matters worse, in the follow-up to Rogers's trip, our lead representative in Egypt, Donald Bergus, provided comments to an Egyptian position paper on their negotiating position on reopening the canal. At the time, the White House was unaware of the Bergus draft, which Kissinger would later say "bore a striking resemblance to the formal Egyptian proposal that was ultimately submitted to us by Sadat." When the draft was leaked, the Israelis were enraged, seeing us as urging the Egyptians to put forward terms that they could never accept. Egypt, too, was angered by the outcome, for when the Bergus draft leaked, the State Department felt obliged to say it did not represent a formal U.S. position. Ibid., p. 1284.
66. Ibid., pp. 1284–1285.
67. Ibid. p. 1285.
68. Ibid., pp. 1295–1297. The Soviets did, in fact, provide additional weapons, making possible the Egyptian-Syrian attack that caught Israel and the United States by surprise on October 6, 1973.
69. Nixon, *RN*, p. 787.
70. Richard Nixon, "The President's News Conference," September 5, 1973, *Public Papers of the Presidents*, Richard M. Nixon, no. 246, pp. 732–43, online at American Presidency Project, http://www.presidency.ucsb.edu/ws/?pid=3948.
71. *FRUS* 1969–76, vol. 15, no. 132, pp. 538–42, "Memorandum for the President's File by the President's Assistant for National Security Affairs (Kissinger)," June 23, 1973, http://history.state.gov/historicaldocuments/frus1969-76v15/d132.
72. Nixon, *RN*, p. 920.
73. *FRUS*, 1969–76, vol. 25, no. 115, pp. 340–42, "Memorandum of Conversation Between Henry Kissinger and Israeli Chargé Mordechai Shalev," October 7, 1973, http://history.state.gov/historicaldocuments/FRUS1969-76v25/d115.
74. Ibid.
75. *FRUS* 1969–76, vol. 25, no. 117, pp. 345–46, "Transcript of Telephone Conversation Between President Nixon and Secretary of State Kissinger," October 7, 1973, http://history.state.gov/historicaldocuments/frus1969-76v25/d117.
76. *FRUS* 1969–76, vol. 25, no. 143, pp. 419–23, "Memorandum of Conversation," October 10, 1973, http://history.state.gov/historicaldocuments/frus1969-76v25/d143.
77. Nixon, *RN*, p. 921, quoted in Ross and Makovsky, *Myths, Illusions, and Peace*, p. 63.
78. *FRUS* 1969–76, vol. 25, no. 173, pp. 482–86, "Memorandum of Conversation," October 13, 1973, http://history.state.gov/historicaldocuments/frus1969-76v25/d173.
79. Quandt, *Decade of Decisions*, p. 182.
80. Henry Kissinger, *Crisis: The Anatomy of Two Major Foreign Policy Crises* (New York: Simon & Schuster, 2003), p. 147.
81. *FRUS* 1969–76, vol. 25, no. 135, p. 397, "Memorandum of Conversation," October 9, 1973, http://history.state.gov/historicaldocuments/frus/1969–76v25/d135.
82. *FRUS* 1969–76, vol. 25, no. 165, pp. 455–57 "Transcript of Telephone Conversation Between Secretary of State Kissinger and the British Ambassador (Cromer)," October 12, 1973, http://history.state.gov/historicaldocuments/frus1969-76v25/d165.

83. *FRUS* 1969–76, vol. 25, no. 250, pp. 689–700, "Minutes of the Secretary of State's Staff Meeting," October 23, 1973, http://history.state.gov/historicaldocuments/frus1969-76v25/d250. For a full discussion of U.S. decision making on withholding resupply to Israel, see Ross and Makovsky, *Myths, Illusions, and Peace*, pp. 57–68.

84. *FRUS* 1969–76, vol. 25, no. 167, p. 467, "Transcript of Conversation Between Secretary of State Kissinger and Secretary of Defense Schlesinger," October 13, 1973, http://history.state.gov/historicaldocuments/frus1969-76v25/d167.

85. *FRUS* 1969–76, vol. 25, no. 181, pp. 500–17, "Memorandum of Conversation," October 14, 1973, http://history.state.gov/historicaldocuments/frus1969-76v25/d181.

86. Nixon, *RN*, p. 927.

87. *FRUS* 1969–76, vol. 25, no. 195, p. 567, "Memorandum of Conversation," October 17, 1973, http://history.state.gov/historicaldocuments/frus1969-76v25/d195.

88. Ibid., pp. 568–69.

89. *FRUS* 1969–76, vol. 25, no. 218, pp. 627–29, "Telegram from the President's Deputy Assistant for National Security Affairs (Scowcroft) to Secretary of State Kissinger," October 20, 1973, http://history.state.gov/historicaldocuments/frus1969-76v25/d218.

90. *FRUS* 1969–76, vol. 25, no. 267, pp. 734–35, "Message from Soviet General Secretary Brezhnev to President Nixon," n.d., http://history.state.gov/historicaldocuments/frus1969-76v25/d267.

91. "Excerpts from Second Segment of Frost's Television Interview with Richard Nixon," *The New York Times*, May 13, 1977, quoted in Spiegel, *The Other Arab-Israeli Conflict*, p. 265.

92. Zeev Schiff, *A History of the Israeli Army: 1874 to the Present* (New York: Macmillan, 1985), pp. 225–28.

93. *FRUS* 1969–76, vol. 25, no. 305, pp. 816, "Memorandum of Conversation," November 1, 1973, http://history.state.gov/historicaldocuments/frus1969-76v25/d305.

94. Ibid., p. 833.

95. Ibid., p. 809.

96. *FRUS* 1969–76, vol. 25, no. 306, pp. 831. "Memorandum of Conversation," November 1, 1973, http://history.state.gov/historicaldocuments/frus1969-76v25/d306.

97. Ibid., p. 833.

98. The Saudis adopted this posture after the administration's request for $2.2 billion for Israel had gone to the Hill on October 19.

99. *FRUS* 1969–76, vol. 25, no. 259, p. 715, "Minutes of the Washington Special Actions Group Meeting," October 23, 1973, http://history.state.gov/historicaldocuments/frus1969-76v25/d259.

100. Thomas O'Toole and Lou Cannon, "Jobs, Oil Put Ahead of Environment, Israel," *The Washington Post*, December 22, 1973, as quoted in Alan Dowty, *Middle East Crisis: U.S. Decision-making in 1958, 1970, and 1973* (Berkeley: University of California Press, 1984), p. 284.

101. Spiegel, *The Other Arab-Israeli Conflict*, pp. 271–72; Nixon, *RN*, p. 986.

102. Richard Nixon, "Question-and-Answer Session at the Annual Convention of the National Association of Broadcasters, Houston, Texas," March 19, 1974, *Public Papers of the Presidents*, Richard M. Nixon, 1974, no. 83, pp. 282–98, American Presidency Project, www.presidency.ucsb.edu/ws/?pid=4391.

103. In the Sinai I agreement, the Israelis agreed to withdraw from west of the Suez Canal and to pull back their forces east of the canal a short distance. Egypt agreed to thin out its forces to the east of the canal, actually reducing them from fifty thousand to seven thousand. While Egypt would not accept Israel's demand for

nonbelligerency, Sadat made a commitment to Kissinger in private that the Egyptians would reopen the canal and rebuild the Egyptian cities along it. This meant that Egypt would have little stake in resuming the fighting. Though the terms were not very different from what might have been possible in 1971, Sadat needed to show that Egypt had made gains in the war, and that required Israeli withdrawal from west of the canal—a presence that did not exist prior to the 1973 war. Israel, for its part, needed to reduce the mobilization of its forces, which was difficult for it to sustain economically and yet was required given their extended forward presence.

104. Matti Golan, *The Secret Conversations of Henry Kissinger* (New York: Quadrangle, 1976), p. 195.
105. Edward Sheehan, *The Arabs, Israelis, and Kissinger: A Secret History of American Diplomacy in the Middle East* (New York: Reader's Digest Press, 1976), pp. 122, 124.
106. Nixon, *RN*, p. 1008.
107. Gerald R. Ford, *A Time to Heal: The Autobiography of Gerald R. Ford* (New York: Harper, 1979), p. 245.
108. Sheehan, *The Arabs, Israelis, and Kissinger*, p. 161.
109. Rabin, *Memoirs*, p. 255.
110. Ibid., p. 265.
111. Ibid.
112. Spiegel, *The Other Arab-Israeli Conflict*, p. 294.
113. Ford, *A Time to Heal*, p. 247.
114. Rabin, *Memoirs*, pp. 262–68.
115. *FRUS 1969–76*, vol. 26, no. 227, pp. 828–32, "Memorandum of Agreement," September 1, 1975, http://history.state.gov/historicaldocuments/frus1969-76v26/d227; "Letter from President Ford to Prime Minister Rabin, September 11, 1975," quoted in Quandt, *Peace Process*, Appendix C, available online at www.brookings.edu/~/media/Press/Books/2005/peaceprocess3/Appendix-C.pdf?1a=en.
116. Hearings, the Palestinian Issue in the Middle East Peace Efforts, Special Subcommittee on Investigations of the Committee on International Relations, House of Representatives, 94th Congress, 1st session, pp. 178–80.
117. William W. Scranton, "Statement of March 23," *Department of State Bulletin*, April 19, 1976, p. 528.
118. Labor saw settlements in security terms, not in terms designed to preclude territorial withdrawal and a compromise. Likud's ideology was different, believing that the West Bank, or its biblical name Judea and Samaria, was part of the land of Israel and should not be surrendered.
119. Nixon, *RN*, pp. 481–82.
120. Kissinger, *White House Years*, pp. 372–73.
121. Nixon, *RN*, p. 1008.
122. Kissinger, *White House Years*, pp. 558–59.
123. Ibid., p. 599.
124. Most CIA specialists, along with the U.S. ambassador to Jordan, doubted that King Hussein could survive. Since the PLO factions were, in the words of Hume Horan, then the political counselor of our embassy in Amman, "the darling of Arab intellectuals and the Arab street," this was a real issue. Only Jack O'Connell, the CIA's station chief in Jordan, was convinced of King Hussein's staying power. Kai Bird, *The Good Spy: The Life and Death of Robert Ames* (New York: Crown, 2014), pp. 95–96.
125. Spiegel, *The Other Arab-Israeli Conflict*, p. 221.

6. The Carter Presidency: The Pursuit of Peace and Constant Tension with Israel
 1. Jimmy Carter, *Keeping Faith: Memoirs of a President* (New York: Bantam Books, 1982), p. 273.
 2. Ibid., p. 289.
 3. Indeed, it is striking that in Carter's diary, the peace issue captures his interest, passion, and sense of strategic stakes, while his commentary in the period leading up to the fall of the shah—late October 1978 to January 1979—is not only limited by comparison but also largely devoid of any discussion of the strategic consequences.
 4. James Schlesinger, interview by James Sterling Young et al., July 19–20, 1984, p. 54, Presidential Oral History Program, Miller Center of Public Affairs, University of Virginia, http://web1.millercenter.org/poh/transcripts/ohp_1984_0719_schlesinger .pdf.
 5. Ibid.
 6. Zbigniew Brzezinski, *Power and Principle: Memoirs of the National Security Adviser, 1977–1981* (New York: Farrar, Straus and Giroux, 1985), p. 515.
 7. "Visit of Crown Prince Fahd of Saudi Arabia: Toasts of the President and the Crown Prince at a Dinner Honoring His Royal Highness," May 24, 1977, *Public Papers of the Presidents*, Jimmy Carter, 1977, Book I, pp. 1006–1008, online at American Presidency Project, www.presidency.ucsb.edu/ws/index.php?pid=7581.
 8. Brzezinski, *Power and Principle*, p. 89.
 9. Ibid., p. 238; Cyrus Vance, *Hard Choices: Four Critical Years in Managing America's Foreign Policy* (New York: Simon & Schuster, 1983), p. 165.
10. Brzezinski, *Power and Principle*, pp. 92–93.
11. Ibid., p. 83.
12. Carter, *Keeping Faith*, p. 278.
13. Vance, *Hard Choices*, p. 164.
14. In April 2012, I would moderate a panel discussion at the National Archives with Sam Lewis, Richard Murphy, William Quandt, and Harold Saunders to commemorate the Nixon administration's approach to the Middle East. Quandt and Saunders both made the point that incremental process had played itself out and even Kissinger understood this at the end of the Ford administration. See "Nixon Administration Middle East Policy," C-SPAN video, April 23, 2012, www.c-span.org /video/?305617-1/nixon-administration-middle-east-policy; Vance, *Hard Choices*, p. 163; *Toward Peace in the Middle East: Report of a Study Group* (Washington, DC: Brookings Institution, 1975).
15. Vance, *Hard Choices*, p. 167.
16. Ibid., p. 171.
17. Ibid., pp. 172–73.
18. Jimmy Carter, *White House Diary* (New York: Farrar, Straus and Giroux, 2010), p. 31.
19. Jimmy Carter, "The President's News Conference," March 9, 1977, *Public Papers of the Presidents*, Jimmy Carter, 1977, Book I, pp. 340–48, online at American Presidency Project, www.presidency.ucsb.edu/ws/index.php?pid=7139.
20. Quoted in Brzezinski, *Power and Principle*, p. 91.
21. William B. Quandt, *Peace Process: American Diplomacy and the Arab-Israeli Conflict Since 1967* (Washington, DC: Brookings Institution, 2005), p. 182.
22. Brzezinski, *Power and Principle*, p. 91.
23. Vance, *Hard Choices*, p. 174.
24. Carter, *Keeping Faith*, pp. 283–84.
25. Vance, *Hard Choices*, p. 176.

26. Carter, *White House Diary*, p. 44.
27. Carter, *Keeping Faith*, p. 285.
28. Carter later in his memoir qualified his positive comments by noting that Assad sabotaged the efforts to get to Geneva by not being willing "to attend under any reasonable circumstances." But this was neither his private impression at the time nor the image that he projected publicly. Ibid., p. 286.
29. "Meeting with President Assad of Syria: Toasts of the President and President Assad at a Dinner Hosted by President Carter," May 9, 1977, *Public Papers of the Presidents*, Jimmy Carter, 1977, Book I, pp. 844–47, online at American Presidency Project, www.presidency.ucsb.edu/ws/?pid=7490.
30. Carter, *Keeping Faith*, p. 288.
31. Ibid.
32. Quandt, *Peace Process*, p. 182.
33. Brzezinski, *Power and Principle*, p. 96.
34. Carter, *Keeping Faith*, p. 288.
35. Ibid., p. 290.
36. Moshe Dayan, *Breakthrough: A Personal Account of the Egypt-Israel Peace Negotiations* (New York: Random House, 1981), pp. 19 20.
37. UNSCR 242 did not refer to the Palestinians by name but instead made a reference only to settling the refugee problem.
38. Spiegel, *The Other Arab-Israeli Conflict*, p. 340.
39. Dayan, *Breakthrough*, pp. 50–52.
40. Ibid., p. 60.
41. Ibid., p. 59.
42. Ibid., pp. 60–61.
43. Spiegel, *The Other Arab-Israeli Conflict*, p. 338.
44. Brzezinski, *Power and Principle*, pp. 108–109.
45. Carter, *White House Diary*, pp. 112–13 (emphasis added).
46. Brzezinski, *Power and Principle*, pp. 109–10.
47. Ibid., p. 110; Quandt, *Peace Process*, p. 192.
48. Quandt, *Peace Process*, pp. 191–92.
49. Brzezinski, *Power and Principle*, p. 112.
50. Carter, *Keeping Faith*, pp. 297–98.
51. Dayan, *Breakthrough*, p. 91.
52. While in Israel, most of Sadat's time was, understandably, devoted to public meetings and statements to maximize their psychological impact. In the remaining time for private discussions, Sadat and Begin agreed to three general principles: no more wars between the two countries; formal restoration of Egyptian sovereignty over the Sinai; and demilitarization over most of the Sinai, with limited deployment areas along the Suez Canal and the Gidi and Mitla passes.
53. Carter, *White House Diary*, p. 150; Vance, *Hard Choices*, pp. 195–97.
54. At this point, Begin was not asking us to make his ideas American proposals, something that both Ehud Barak and Benjamin Netanyahu would later seek.
55. Carter, *White House Diary*, pp. 150–51.
56. Ibid., p. 161.
57. Ibid.
58. Carter, *Keeping Faith*, p. 303.
59. Vance, *Hard Choices*, p. 202.
60. Ibid.
61. Carter, *White House Diary*, pp. 165–68.

62. Ibid. pp. 169–70.
63. Brzezinski, *Power and Principle*, pp. 243–44.
64. Quandt, *Peace Process*, p. 196.
65. Ibid.
66. Vance, *Hard Choices*, p. 206.
67. Jimmy Carter, "Terrorist Attack in Israel: Statement by the President," March 11, 1978, *Public Papers of the Presidents*, Jimmy Carter, 1977, Book I, p. 505, online at American Presidency Project, www.presidency.ucsb.edu/ws/index.php?pid=30483.
68. Carter, *White House Diary*, pp. 178, 179.
69. Ibid., p. 176.
70. Vance, *Hard Choices*, p. 210.
71. Ibid.
72. Brzezinski, *Power and Principle*, p. 247.
73. Carter, *Keeping Faith*, p. 313.
74. Ibid., pp. 315–16.
75. Brzezinski, *Power and Principle*, p. 249.
76. Vance, *Hard Choices*, pp. 215–16.
77. Carter, *White House Diary*, p. 207.
78. Carter, *Keeping Faith*, p. 315.
79. Carter, *White House Diary*, p. 210.
80. Carter, *Keeping Faith*, pp. 316–18.
81. Ibid., p. 333.
82. Ibid., pp. 348–49.
83. Ibid.
84. Vance, *Hard Choices*, pp. 220–22.
85. Ibid., p. 223.
86. Ibid., pp. 222–24; Carter, *Keeping Faith*, pp. 392–93.
87. Vance, *Hard Choices*, p. 225; Carter, *Keeping Faith*, p. 397.
88. Spiegel, *The Other Arab-Israeli Conflict*, p. 362.
89. Carter, *Keeping Faith*, p. 397.
90. Stuart Eizenstat, in conversation with the author, August 2, 2013.
91. Ibid.
92. Carter, *White House Diary*, p. 245.
93. Ibid., pp. 246–47.
94. Ibid., p. 247.
95. Ibid., p. 256.
96. Vance, *Hard Choices*, p. 251.
97. Spiegel, *The Other Arab-Israeli Conflict*, pp. 372–75.
98. Brzezinski, *Power and Principle*, p. 360.
99. Ibid., p. 358.
100. Ibid.
101. See Carter, *White House Diary*, pp. 255–58; Brzezinski, *Power and Principle*, p. 362.
102. Carter, *White House Diary*, p. 259.
103. Carter, *Keeping Faith*, pp. 411–12.
104. Ibid., p. 412.
105. Brzezinski, *Power and Principle*, p. 444.
106. Ibid., p. 445.
107. Ibid., pp. 449–54.
108. Ibid.

109. James Schlesinger interview, p. 100.
110. Stuart Eizenstat conversation with the author, August 2, 2013.
111. Carter, *Keeping Faith*, p. 277.
112. Carter, *White House Diary*, p. 245 (emphasis added).
113. Jimmy Carter, interview by James Sterling Young et al., November 29, 1982, pp. 35–36. Presidential Oral History Program, Miller Center of Public Affairs, University of Virginia, http://web1.millercenter.org/poh/transcripts/ohp_1982_1129 _Carter.pdf.
114. Quoted in Brzezinski, *Power and Principle*, pp. 277–78.
115. Spiegel, *The Other Arab-Israeli Conflict*, p. 380.

7. The Reagan Administration and the Policy of Duality

1. Ronald Reagan, "Recognizing the Israeli Asset," *The Washington Post*, August 15, 1979, p. 25.
2. George Shultz, in conversation with the author, October 30, 2013.
3. Ronald Reagan, *An American Life: The Autobiography* (New York: Simon & Schuster, 1990), p. 410.
4. Nixon did so as part of his outreach to the Arabs, not in response to Israeli behavior.
5. Shultz conversation with the author. Perhaps because of the climate he created in the Pentagon, the staff of the JCS even drafted a paper that raised the possibility of joint U.S.-Soviet action against Israeli "aggression" in Lebanon, a position that went too far for Weinberger. *Middle East Policy Survey* 51 (March 12, 1982): 1, as quoted in Spiegel, *The Other Arab-Israeli Conflict*, p. 425.
6. Alexander M. Haig, Jr., *Caveat: Realism, Reagan, and Foreign Policy* (New York: Macmillan, 1984), pp. 169–70.
7. Caspar Weinberger, interview by Stephen Knott, November 19, 2002, p. 24, Presidential Oral History Program, Miller Center of Public Affairs, http://web1.miller center.org/poh/transcripts/ohp_2002_1119_weinberger.pdf.
8. Caspar W. Weinberger, *Fighting for Peace: Seven Critical Years in the Pentagon* (New York: Warner, 1990), p. 143n2.
9. Reagan, *American Life*, p. 410.
10. Ibid., p. 411.
11. Ibid.
12. Haig, *Caveat*, p. 180.
13. Reagan, *American Life*, p. 412.
14. Ibid., p. 411.
15. Ronald Reagan, "The President's News Conference," October 1, 1981, *Public Papers of the Presidents, Ronald Reagan, 1981*, p. 867, online at American Presidency Project, www.presidency.ucsb.edu/ws/index.php?pid=44327.
16. Reagan, *American Life*, p. 415.
17. Haig, *Caveat*, p. 187.
18. Falwell was a well-known evangelist and supporter of Israel who had significant support among the right wing of the Republican Party—the beginnings of Christian evangelical support for Israel and connections to the Republican Party.
19. Haig, *Caveat*, p. 187.
20. Since 1976, when Syrian forces had initially gone into Lebanon to defend the Christian forces, the Israelis and Syrians had respected certain redlines. At that time, it was Rabin who had tacitly communicated that so long as the Syrians did not operate aircraft over Lebanon or move their forces into the southern part of the country, Israel would not react to their presence. Hafez al Assad understood,

and the redlines held. In April 1981, the Syrians had switched sides in the ongoing Lebanese civil war and were now supporting the Muslim forces against the Christian Phalange militia, which was backed by the Israelis. When the Syrians not only sided with the Muslim militias fighting the Phalange but also landed airborne forces to dislodge the Christian troops from the strategically important positions they were holding in the Sannin mountains—and were using helicopters to support their forces—the Israelis shot down the helicopters.

21. Haig, *Caveat*, p. 183.
22. Ibid., p. 184.
23. Reagan, *American Life*, p. 413.
24. Melman and Raviv, *Friends in Deed*, p. 197.
25. In another diary entry, Reagan noted, "There was never a mention of this to us by the outgoing administration. Ambassador Lewis cabled word to us after the Israeli attack and now we find there was a stack of cables and memos tucked away in State Department files." Ronald Reagan, *The Reagan Diaries*, ed., Douglas Brinkley (New York: Harper, 2009), p. 25.
26. Reagan, *American Life*, p. 413.
27. Caspar Weinberger interview, p. 25.
28. Ibid.
29. Howard Teicher and Gayle Radley Teicher, *Twin Pillars to Desert Storm: America's Flawed Vision in the Middle East from Nixon to Bush* (New York: William Morrow, 1993), p. 143.
30. Ibid., p. 155.
31. Ibid., p. 143.
32. Ibid., p. 150.
33. The Israelis' June 7 raid on the Osirak reactor took place three days after Begin had met with Sadat, creating the impression that the Egyptian president either colluded with the Israelis in the bombing or was at least informed of it. The July 17 bombing of the PLO office in Beirut, which killed a number of noncombatants, took place two days after Bud McFarlane had gone to see Begin in Israel with the express purpose of trying to remove the tension caused by the Osirak bombing and resume the F-16 supplies. Worse for Reagan, it occurred while he was en route to a G-7 summit in Canada—one certain to be affected by the Israeli attack, which would likely put pressure on the United States at a time when the president had a very different agenda for this economic meeting.
34. Melman and Raviv, *Friends in Deed*, p. 200.
35. "Transcript of Prime Minister Begin's Statement to the U.S. Envoy to Israel," *The New York Times*, December 21, 1981, www.nytimes.com/1981/12/21/world/transcript-of -prime-minister-begin-s-statement-to-the-us-envoy-to-israel.html.
36. Yehuda Avner, "When Washington Bridled and Begin Fumed," *The Jerusalem Post*, October 6, 2008, www.jpost.com/Opinion/Op-Ed-Contributors/When-Washington -bridled-and-Begin-fumed.
37. Reagan, *American Life*, p. 419.
38. Melman and Raviv, *Friends in Deed*, pp. 216–17.
39. Haig, *Caveat*, p. 326.
40. Reagan, *American Life*, p. 419.
41. Haig, *Caveat*, p. 318.
42. Ibid.
43. Spiegel, *The Other Arab-Israeli Conflict*, pp. 415, 419.
44. Haig, *Caveat*, p. 343.

45. Ibid.
46. Laurence T. Barrett, *Gambling with History: Reagan in the White House* (New York: Doubleday, 1983), p. 271.
47. Reagan, *American Life*, p. 423.
48. Haig remained until July 5, when Shultz conveyed to him that Reagan felt it was time for him to go—more than a week before Shultz's confirmation.
49. George P. Shultz, *Turmoil and Triumph: My Years as Secretary of State* (New York: Scribner, 1993) p. 54.
50. George Shultz conversation with the author.
51. Reagan, *American Life*, pp. 425–26.
52. Ibid., pp. 427–28.
53. Ibid., p. 428.
54. Ze'ev Schiff and Ehud Ya'ari, *Israel's Lebanon War*, trans. Ina Friedman (New York: Simon & Schuster, 1984), pp. 109–10.
55. Reagan, *American Life*, p. 430.
56. The group consisted of Bud McFarlane, deputy national security adviser; Larry Eagleburger, under secretary of state for political affairs; Nicholas Veliotes, assistant secretary of state for Near Eastern affairs; Bob Ames, the CIA's lead Middle East specialist; Paul Wolfowitz, director of the Policy Planning Staff; Charlie Hill, Shultz's special assistant; Bill Kirby, deputy to Veliotes for Middle East peace; and Alan Kreczko from the office of the legal adviser. I had moved to the S/P for the first twenty months of the Reagan administration. Wolfowitz was my boss, and while he would not tell me the specifics of the discussions, he asked me to prepare answers to key questions before the meetings, including whether the June 4, 1967, lines were defensible, the consequences of Palestinian statehood, and the viability of a Jordanian-Palestinian "federation."
57. Shultz, *Turmoil and Triumph*, p. 86.
58. Ibid., p. 90.
59. Ibid., pp. 91–92.
60. Ibid., p. 92.
61. Ibid., p. 93.
62. Bird, *The Good Spy*, p. 274; Shultz, *Turmoil and Triumph*, p. 93.
63. Shultz, *Turmoil and Triumph*, p. 95.
64. Reagan, *American Life*, p. 434.
65. Shultz, *Turmoil and Triumph*, pp. 103–104.
66. Anita Shapira, *Israel: A History* (Waltham, MA: Brandeis University Press, 2012), pp. 384–85.
67. Both tasks were made more difficult after Sharon essentially forced Gemayel to accept an agreement that Shultz described as dictated by the Israelis: "Sharon had gone too far in pressing, and Gemayel had given in too easily . . . The result was worthless and the process had wasted valuable time." Shultz, *Turmoil and Triumph*, p. 112.
68. Ibid.
69. Ibid.
70. Ibid., p. 440.
71. The commission found that the relevant Israeli officials, knowing the violent history of the Phalange, should never have allowed its forces into the camps in the emotionally laden period after the assassination of Bashir Gemayel, and, having done so, should have intervened immediately on getting the first reports of the killings in the camps.
72. Shultz, *Turmoil and Triumph*, p. 221.

73. McFarlane remained in this position for only a few months and then became Reagan's national security adviser, replacing Donald Rumsfeld, who became the Middle East envoy in McFarlane's place.

74. Jumblatt told the story that when he would visit Hafez al Assad, the Syrian president would remind him that he was sitting in the chair his father, Kamal Jumblatt, used to sit in—an unsubtle reminder that the fate that befell his father, reportedly killed by the Syrians, could be his as well.

75. Shultz, *Turmoil and Triumph*, p. 227.

76. Reagan, *American Life*, p. 462.

77. Ibid., p. 464.

78. Shultz, *Turmoil and Triumph*, p. 437.

79. Melman and Raviv, *Friends in Deed*, p. 232.

80. Ibid.

81. Ronald Reagan, "Remarks of the President and Prime Minister Yitzhak Shamir of Israel Following Their Meetings," November 29, 1983, *Public Papers of the Presidents*, Ronald Reagan, 1983, Book II, pp. 1631–1633, online at American Presidency Project, www.presidency.ucsb.edu/ws/index.php?pid=40815&st=Shamir&st1=.

82. Teicher and Teicher, *Twin Pillars*, p. 274.

83. In this connection, Shultz told me he was very much affected by a comment Shamir had made to Prime Minister Margaret Thatcher: "The United Kingdom and the United States can afford to make mistakes. Israel cannot." For Shultz, this meant that while he felt a responsibility to let Israeli leaders know his views, he also believed that he could not impose those views on them if they felt "their security would be threatened." All this led him to say that when it came to Israel, "President Reagan and I were on the same wavelength." George Shultz conversation with the author.

84. Shultz, *Turmoil and Triumph*, p. 432.

85. Ibid., p. 939.

86. Specifically, the agreement called for an international meeting to be convened at the invitation of the UN secretary-general. It would include the five permanent members of the Security Council and all the parties to the Middle East conflict, be based on Resolutions 242 and 338 and the renunciation of violence, have as its aim comprehensive peace in the area and security for all states, address the legitimate rights of the Palestinians, and set up bilateral committees for negotiations. A joint Jordanian-Palestinian delegation would negotiate the Palestinian issue with Israel, and Israel and Jordan would deal separately with each other on issues of mutual interest. And, finally, the UN could neither veto any agreement reached bilaterally nor impose any solution.

87. Shultz was trying to produce quick changes on the ground to empower Palestinians, while also showing that the interim arrangements would not be the end of the road. The Israelis might go along with more rapid changes given the need to end the intifada, but the Palestinians and the Arabs had to see that these were not disconnected from the need for an agreement on the core issues of the conflict.

88. During the transition, I became the key point of contact for Baker and the incoming team with Shultz. Shultz had me work with Charlie Hill, who kept me abreast of what was happening with the Swedes. Hill briefed me as well on the indirect contacts we had with Mohammad Fadlallah, the leader of Hezbollah, in an effort to get our hostages out of Lebanon. We were offering no payment of any kind for their release, but through an American journalist of Lebanese descent we were conducting a conversation with Fadlallah, and I would pick it up in the Bush administration.

89. Reagan's explanation in his memoirs reflects all these key justifications. *American Life*, p. 505.
90. For a detailed account, see Shultz, *Turmoil and Triumph*, chapter 42.
91. Reagan, *American Life*, p. 506.
92. Shultz, *Turmoil and Triumph*, p. 793.
93. Mitch Ginsberg, "When Rouhani Unwittingly Told an Israeli Agent How to Deal with Iran," *The Times of Israel*, September 30, 2013, www.timesofisrael.com/when -rouhani-told-an-undercover-israeli-envoy-how-to-deal-with-iran/.
94. Shultz's description of Joseph Levy demonstrates the impact his student had on his views: "All the students were smart. But Levy was different. He was gifted; he was a very special human being. When the 1967 war had broken out, Levy returned to fight, and I learned he had been killed. And I asked myself, What kind of a country can command the loyalty of such a person? And I looked at that country and its situation and its living under constant threat, and it affected me." George Shultz conversation with the author.
95. Reagan, *American Life*, p. 463.

8. George H. W. Bush and Israel: Discord and Responsiveness

1. Memorandum of Conversation, "One-on-One Meeting with Prime Minister Shamir of Israel," April 6, 1989, p. 1, George Bush Presidential Library, available at http://bush41library.edu/files/memcons.telcons/1989-04-06-shamir.pdf.
2. George H. W. Bush, "The President's News Conference," September 12, 1991, *Public Papers of the Presidents*, George H. W. Bush, 1991, Book II, p. 1142, online at American Presidency Project, www.presidency.ucsb.edu/ws/index.php?pid=19969.
3. James A. Baker III, *The Politics of Diplomacy: Revolution, War and Peace, 1989–1992* (New York: Putnam, 1995), p. 116.
4. Craig Fuller, Fred Khedouri, and Robert Teeter called on me often and were largely responsible for arranging time on the vice president's schedule for me to discuss foreign policy issues with him.
5. Baker, *Politics of Diplomacy*, p. 373.
6. MemCon, "Meeting with Shamir," April 6, 1989.
7. Baker, *Politics of Diplomacy*, p. 123.
8. Ibid., p. 122.
9. Memorandum of Conversation, "Meeting with Foreign Minister Arens of Israel," March 13, 1989, p. 3, George Bush Presidential Library, http://bushlibrary.tamu .edu/files/memcons-telcons/1989-03-13–Arens.pdf.
10. MemCon, "Meeting with Shamir," April 6, 1989.
11. Baker, *Politics of Diplomacy*, p. 123.
12. I would soon hear about this directly and see the effect on the president's view of Shamir. As a result, I went to Eli Rubenstein, Shamir's close aide, and said, "You need to have the prime minister set the record straight. Have him write a letter and say he was sorry if he had left the president with a misimpression; he had no intent to be misleading, he valued the relationship too much to ever do that." Unfortunately, it would take months for such a letter to be produced, and when it finally came, most of it was a justification for the Israeli approach to settlements and very little of it took the form of an apology. Predictably, rather than improving the situation, it made it worse.
13. Robert M. Gates, interview by Timothy J. Naftali et al., July 23–24, 2000, p. 88, George H. W. Bush Oral History Project, Miller Center of Public Affairs, http:// web1.millercenter.org/poh/transcripts/ohp_2000_0723_gates.pdf.

14. Baker, *Politics of Diplomacy*, pp. 540–41.
15. Thomas L. Friedman, "Baker, in a Middle East Blueprint, Asks Israel to Reach Out to Arabs," *The New York Times*, May 23, 1989, www.nytimes.com/1989/05/23/world /baker-in-a-middle-east-blueprint-asks-israel-to-reach-out-to-arabs.html.
16. Shortly after the speech, as I was flying on Air Force One to Europe with Baker and Bush, John Sununu, the White House chief of staff, remarked that Baker's speech to AIPAC had generated many supportive letters. Interestingly, the president seemed less impressed with that and more that Baker had done the right thing: telling people there what they needed to hear, not what they wanted to hear. Here again was the Bush personal code manifesting itself: one should not pander. Other statements by both Baker and the president reinforced this image. At a congressional hearing in June 1990, Baker responded memorably to a comment by Congressman Mel Levine on our efforts to launch an Israeli-Palestinian dialogue. Levine lauded Baker's efforts but blamed our failure to produce the dialogue on the president's ill-timed statement against Israeli settlement building in Jerusalem. Baker said that it was not the president who was at fault, but the parties. Baker was never one to allow a wedge to be opened between himself and the president. He put the principal blame on the Israelis, declaring, "When you're serious about peace, call us." To punctuate his point, he gave the White House switchboard number: 456-1414. See John M. Goshko, "U.S. Faults Israel on Territories," *The Washington Post*, May 23, 1989.
17. When I asked Baker about this, he responded, "You know me, and I would not say something like that."
18. George H. W. Bush, "The President's News Conference," September 12, 1991, American Presidency Project, www.presidency.ucsb.edu/ws/?pid=19969.
19. Melman and Raviv, *Friends in Deed*, p. 438.
20. J. J. Goldberg, *Jewish Power: Inside The American Jewish Establishment* (Reading, MA: Addison-Wesley, 1996), p. 31.
21. Baker, *Politics of Diplomacy*, p. 117.
22. Ibid., p. 125.
23. Ibid.
24. Rabin had secretly approached me very early in the Bush administration to use our channel in Tunis for him to send messages to Abu Iyad, the nom de guerre of Salah Khalaf, the number two in the PLO. Rabin did not trust Arafat but felt that Abu Iyad was serious and wanted to see what was possible. Abu Iyad was assassinated by Abu Nidal in Tunis on January 14, 1991, just before the Gulf War started.
25. Our formula was actually a question: "As regards the participants in the Israeli-Palestinian dialogue, would the government of Israel be ready to consider on a name-by-name basis any Palestinian who was a resident in the territories?" Using the words "resident in the territories" allowed for a deportee who was back and anyone who did not have a Jerusalem identity card—meaning any dual addressee with a residence outside Jerusalem—to fit that description.
26. Gates interview, July 23, 2000, p. 45.
27. Ibid., p. 46.
28. Baker, *Politics of Diplomacy*, p. 263
29. George H. W. Bush, "Remarks and an Exchange with Reporters on the Iraqi Invasion of Kuwait," August 5, 1990, *Public Papers of the Presidents*, George H. W. Bush, 1990, Book II, p. 1102, American Presidency Project, www.presidency.ucsb.edu/ws /?pid=18741.
30. George Bush and Brent Scowcroft, *A World Transformed* (New York: Knopf, 1998), p. 329.

31. Richard B. Cheney, interview by Richard Betts, May 16–17, 2000, p. 88, George H. W. Bush Oral History Project, Miller Center of Public Affairs, http://web1.millercenter.org/poh/transcripts/ohp_2000_0316_cheney.pdf. Bush, in his initial phone call, had told the king, "When we work out a plan, once we are there, we will stay until we are asked to leave. You have my solemn word on this." Bush and Scowcroft, *World Transformed*, p. 330.

32. Baker, *Politics of Diplomacy*, p. 292.

33. Ibid., p. 293.

34. Ibid.

35. Ibid., p. 296.

36. Ibid.

37. Melman and Raviv, *Friends in Deed*, p. 382.

38. Ibid., p. 384.

39. We would fly to Saudi Arabia from Geneva and, as usual, I would ride with Bandar from the airport to the palace. This time he greeted me saying, "You almost gave me a heart attack. Jimmy Baker meeting for six and a half hours [with Tariq Aziz], I was scared to death he would do a deal and let Saddam escape. Now is the time to finish him."

40. Melman and Raviv, *Friends in Deed*, p. 384. Wolfowitz confirmed this in several discussions we had in 2014.

41. Ibid., p. 385; Paul Wolfowitz, in conversation with the author, March 2013.

42. Melman and Raviv, *Friends in Deed*, p. 385.

43. Ibid.

44. King Hussein refused to join the coalition against Saddam, perhaps because he feared that Iraq could foment instability among his sizable Palestinian population. He did, however, maintain secret contacts with Israel throughout this period and warned Shamir that he would have no choice but to resist any Israeli use of Jordanian airspace to attack Iraq—helping to explain why Arens was asking for a corridor through Saudi Arabia.

45. Baker, *Politics of Diplomacy*, p. 387.

46. Ibid., pp. 387–88.

47. These other items included an electronic downlink with our intelligence satellites to provide continuous information on Iraqi deployments, and putting an Israeli general in Central Command headquarters.

48. Bush and Scowcroft, *World Transformed*, p. 456.

49. Bandar bin Sultan, in conversation with the author, March 1991.

50. The regional peace conference was designed to be a bridge between the Arab desire for an umbrella for the talks and the Israeli fear that an international conference would preempt bilateral negotiations.

51. The two had been close colleagues since their days working for Kissinger.

52. Baker would outline examples of what we wanted each to consider doing. The Arab states should be willing to consider covert exchanges with the Israelis on intelligence, prenotification of military exercises, meetings with nonofficial Israelis (journalists, scholars, etc.), and dropping the secondary boycott of those doing business with Israel. The Israelis should be willing to consider easing conditions on the Palestinians in the territories, ending the practice of Palestinian deportations, and declaring a willingness to withdraw from its security zone in south Lebanon after six to twelve months of tranquility.

53. Baker, *Politics of Diplomacy*, p. 452. I was with him at the small dinner with Faisal and am quoting directly from that meeting.

54. Baker writes in his memoirs that he lowered his voice when saying this so the Syrians could not hear him. At the time I was certain they could. I wrote Baker's night notes to the president and used that mechanism to explain the costs of forgoing the multilateral, knowing that Baker would read the notes before sending them.
55. Mark Tolts, "Post-Soviet Aliyah and Jewish Demographic Transformation," 2009, Berman Jewish Policy Archive, p. 3, www.bjpa.org/Publications/details.cfm?PublicationID=11924.
56. In the intervening time, Shamir had heard from AIPAC and Yoram Ettinger, who was serving in the Israeli embassy, that they had the votes and there was no need to delay. This would turn out to be a bad miscalculation.
57. Dan Ephron, "Mahmoud Abbas: A President Speaks Out," *The Daily Beast*, April 24, 2011, www.thedailybeast.com/articles/2011/04/24/palestinian-president-mahmoud-abbas-speaks-out-about-obamas-betrayal-and-more.html.

9. The Clinton Administration and Israel: Strategic Partners for Peace

1. Martin Indyk, *Innocent Abroad: An Intimate Account of American Peace Diplomacy in the Middle East* (New York: Simon & Schuster, 2009), p. 16.
2. Ibid., p. 28.
3. Though I had not wanted to leave the State Department and got Baker to agree that I would return right after the election, win or lose, he wanted to have his close circle of advisers around him at the White House. So Bob Zoellick, Margaret Tutwiler, Janet Mullins, and I went with him. Bush, who tended to categorize people as professional or political, told Baker he understood why he was bringing Bob, Margaret, and Janet, but asked why he was bringing me. "He is a professional."
4. Interestingly, Baker, who was not enthusiastic about leaving his position as secretary of state, tried one last gambit that he hoped would give him a diplomatic undertaking so important that the president would not ask him to move to the White House. He would privately say that Assad was willing to attend a White House summit with Rabin; Baker had convinced Assad that it would help Bush in the presidential election. Assad agreed to consider the idea initially, only to reject it a short time later. Rabin was impressed that Baker was willing to try this and felt that Assad's readiness even to consider it was testimony to the credibility that Baker and Bush had with the Syrian leader.
5. Given the centrality of the issue in the collective mind-set, the Arab-Israeli conflict was the crown jewel of the Bureau of Near Eastern Affairs at the State Department. Making me the envoy would deny the assistant secretary, Ed Djerejian, his main responsibility. As I told Tom Donilon, if I were in Ed's shoes, I would strongly oppose having the job taken away from the bureau and given to me, and added, "The secretary does not need the trouble."
6. Indyk, *Innocent Abroad*, p. 18.
7. Those monitors were part of the Multinational Force and Observers, and the U.S. contingent from the outset had numbered fewer than a thousand.
8. Indyk, *Innocent Abroad*, pp. 18–19.
9. Ibid., p. 29.
10. When Martin Indyk saw him shortly after the private meeting and asked the president how we had done, Clinton answered, "We did well." Ibid.
11. Christopher had been sensitive to how he might be seen by the Jewish community given his role in the Carter administration, so Senator Joe Lieberman set up a meeting for him with Jewish leaders during the transition. Unlike Baker, Christopher kept much more of an open-door policy to the Jewish community during his tenure.

12. He wanted us to share this only with President Clinton. I told Itamar Rabinovich that Martin Indyk would have to know, along with Tony Lake, but assured him we would not widen the circle beyond them.

13. The Declaration of Principles laid out a broad understanding in which the Israelis would gradually get out of the business of running Palestinian lives, with a timetable for the creation of a Palestinian authority, first in Gaza and Jericho and then in the cities of the West Bank. There was a three-month timetable for the first agreement and a nine-month timetable for the interim agreement to follow. The core issues of the conflict—security, borders, settlements, refugees, Jerusalem, and relations with neighboring states—would be dealt with in permanent status talks that would begin after the first two years. These talks were to conclude by the end of the five-year interim period. Once the permanent status was resolved and implemented, the two sides agreed that UN Resolutions 242 and 338 would be fulfilled.

14. With our having conveyed Rabin's commitment to us on full withdrawal, I saw little likelihood that Assad would want to put that at risk. I also assumed that Rabin would not walk away from what he had put in our pocket. But in fact, he would have second thoughts.

15. William H. Clinton, "Remarks on the Israeli-Palestinian Declaration of Principles and an Exchange with Reporters," September 10, 1993, *Public Papers of the Presidents*, Bill Clinton, 1993, Book II, p. 464, American Presidency Project, www .presidency.vcsb.edu/ws/index.php?pid=47057.

16. Bill Clinton, *My Life* (New York: Knopf, 2004), pp. 541–42.

17. Clinton would give both Christopher and me the same ties to commemorate the event. See Clinton, *My Life*, p. 542.

18. Ibid., pp. 544–45.

19. Ibid.

20. He could connect with any leader and relate to his or her problems. In briefing Clinton before the meeting, I had mentioned that Assad thought Western leaders felt only Israel had public opinion—but he had it, too, particularly as someone who saw himself as the standard-bearer of Arab nationalism. At one point, Clinton spoke of the political problems that Assad would inevitably face when he had to sell peace to those in the region who felt Israel had no place in their midst. At the end of this first Geneva meeting with Assad, the Syrian president came up to me and said, "You know I liked Bush and Baker, but President Clinton, he is a real person!"

21. What were the key differences? In 1948, the Syrian forces had penetrated to the west of the international border, known as the 1923 line, in three areas. As part of the 1949 Armistice Agreements, the Syrians withdrew from those areas behind the international border. Three demilitarized zones, whose final status was to be resolved once there was a peace agreement, were created. The Israelis sought to cultivate the DMZs, believing they were their territories; the Syrians attacked the Israelis in the zones, and each side's forces came to occupy different parts of the DMZs until the Six-Day War. The Israelis on the ground controlled two-thirds of the DMZs by that time, while the Syrians controlled the rest. But that also meant that the Syrians were on the waterline of the Sea of Galilee, in the northwest quarter, and on the Jordan River that fed into the sea from the north.

22. Both requests were nearly impossible: a formal peace agreement was a prerequisite for F-16s, and a newly passed law mandated an equal allocation of dollars to cover the cost of debt forgiveness, which was not feasible. Following Bush's decision to cancel Egypt's debt at the time of the Gulf War, Congress passed a law saying that any such debt forgiveness in the future would require the allocation of money equal

to the debt to be provided to the U.S. Treasury. This was done because U.S. farmers owed a mountain of debt and they wanted to be treated the same as Egypt.

23. The agreement would have several noteworthy elements: Israeli provision of water to meet Jordanian needs, swaps of territories, and lease arrangements that permitted continued Israeli use of certain lands. These set precedents that could all be useful in an Israeli-Palestinian permanent status accord.

24. In the A areas, the Palestinians would have civil and security responsibility; in the B areas, the Palestinians would have civil responsibility and responsibility for law and order, but not for dealing with terror; and in the C areas, Israel would retain all civil and security responsibilities. When these were finally shown to Arafat on a map in September in Taba, it caused a crisis when he realized that the A areas involved only the Palestinian cities, accounting for 2.3 percent of the territory. Uri Savir and Arafat's aide, Nabil Abu Rudeina, called me to speak together to Arafat to prevent him from walking out.

25. Following the signing of the Declaration of Principles at the White House, Congress adopted legislation that allowed us to provide assistance to the PLO and let it have an office so long as it lived up to its obligations on violence and terror. The law waived previous legislation that precluded any ties with the PLO and required the administration to report every six months on PLO activity and whether it was fulfilling its obligations. I told Arafat that without the Interim Agreement, Congress was unlikely to authorize a new waiver and we would have to close the office—the symbol of his ties to the only global superpower.

26. Clinton, *My Life*, p. 672.

27. Ibid., p. 679.

28. Ibid., p. 80.

29. He performed brilliantly at the Summit of Peacemakers in Sharm el-Sheikh, which would produce follow-on mechanisms and working groups on fighting terror. He told Arafat in uncharacteristically blunt terms that there would be no U.S.-Palestinian relationship if he did not now go after Hamas and Islamic Jihad. And for the next several months, Arafat indeed went after their infrastructure, including in the mosques in Gaza. Clinton announced in Israel the formation of new U.S.-Israel cooperation on terror and the provision of additional U.S. assistance to bolster the antiterror efforts. He also delivered an extraordinary speech, most of which departed from the prepared script, to several thousand Israeli youth in Tel Aviv the day after the Sharm summit. When he was planeside, about to depart Israel, and he saw Uri with me, he came up to Uri and asked, "Did this help?" Uri said, "More than you can imagine."

30. Only Hussein, Arafat, and Netanyahu attended the summit. Mubarak stayed away, not wanting to be associated with it. At the White House, Netanyahu resisted making any concessions on the tunnel and was excoriated by Hussein at the lunch in our presence and that of the Palestinians. But Netanyahu agreed to resume negotiations on redeployment from Hebron, something that the Interim Agreement had required and Peres had postponed until after the election because of the controversy and complications bound up with the one Palestinian city where there was also an Israeli presence. I would end up carrying out two extended shuttles that led to an agreement five days before Clinton's inauguration for a second term.

31. In fact, I discovered later that his help for Peres was not limited to the overt steps of which I was aware. Unbeknownst to me, he had opened a discreet channel to the Peres campaign, using democratic consultants Doug Schoen and Zeev Furst, to provide advice. Interestingly, Clinton's inability to help Peres win in 1996—an elec-

tion that Peres barely lost—did not prevent him from sending his team of key political operatives, James Carville, Stanley Greenberg, and Robert Shrum, to help Ehud Barak defeat Netanyahu in 1999. The circumstances were different, but the president's commitment to fulfilling the Rabin legacy was undiminished.

32. Clinton, *My Life*, p. 714.
33. Later, in 1998, he would use Ronald Lauder, a wealthy American Jewish leader who had struck up an acquaintance with Walid Muallem, as a go-between with Assad to see if something could be done. Lauder's efforts stopped at the point where Assad required a map of Israel.
34. Clinton, *My Life*, p. 747.
35. Ibid.
36. He could and would express his frustration with Netanyahu. At one point in 1998, he chose not to see him, which was an embarrassment for Netanyahu in Israel, particularly since the two were in Los Angeles at the same time and their planes were parked side by side at the airport.
37. Mossad poisoned Meshaal. Jordanian police witnessed the assault and captured the Israeli operatives: Hussein insisted that the Israelis provide the antidote for the poison and its formula to save Meshaal. If they did not, Jordan would break off relations within twenty-four hours. There were, in addition, no guarantees that the Jordanians would release the captured Israeli agents. Netanyahu eventually had the antidote sent.
38. The October 11, 1997, issue of *The Economist* labeled Netanyahu "Israel's serial bungler," www.economist.com/node/102018.
39. In May 1996, prior to the Israeli election, the PNC voted to annul the articles in the charter that rejected Israel—and the words had actually been negotiated with the Peres government.
40. George Tenet, the head of the CIA, who had spent the week at Wye working on the security issues, told the president that he would resign if Pollard were released as part of the deal—and that settled the issue for Clinton.
41. This is described in Dennis Ross, *The Missing Peace: The Inside Story of the Fight for Middle East Peace* (New York: Farrar, Straus and Giroux, 2004), pp. 511–30. Barak was misled by Lauder's explanation of a paper he had produced by going between Netanyahu and Assad. Barak was led to believe that the paper represented an agreement on the core issues between the two. As I explain, Assad never accepted the points that Lauder had initially shown Barak.
42. Natan Sharansky told Clinton as much, which Clinton conveys in his memoir. Clinton, *My Life*, p. 883.
43. Clinton, *My Life*, p. 886.
44. Ibid., p. 916.
45. Ibid.
46. We would broker an agreement, creating a U.S.-led fact-finding group with international members, whose purpose was to identify the sources of the violence and learn lessons from what had happened. It would be cochaired by George Mitchell and Warren Rudman, and would issue a report in May 2001 that would become known as the Mitchell Report.
47. We met alone, and I asked if a deal was possible. He said yes because both sides were serious. When I probed on the specifics, he was vague until I outlined what I thought the Israelis could do on each issue and whether he could accept that—and he said yes.
48. Barak had called early elections, feeling this allowed what was now a minority government to still make big decisions and a deal. The elections would be a referendum on the deal.

49. Ross, *Missing Peace*, p. 938.
50. Ibid., p. 943.
51. Ibid., p. 944.

10. Bush 43: Terror, Partnership, and Bureaucratic Divisions

1. Condoleezza Rice, "Promoting the National Interest," *Foreign Affairs*, January/February 2000, www.foreignaffairs.com/articles/55630/condoleezza-rice/campaign-2000-promoting-the-national-interest.
2. George W. Bush, *Decision Points* (New York: Crown, 2010), p. 400.
3. Condoleezza Rice, *No Higher Honor: A Memoir of My Years in Washington* (New York: Crown, 2011), p. 55.
4. Robert Danin, in conversation with the author, February 28, 2014.
5. Dick Cheney, *In My Time: A Personal and Political Memoir*, with Liz Cheney (New York: Threshold, 2011), p. 380.
6. George W. Bush, "Prepared Text of Bush's Knesset Speech," *The Wall Street Journal*, May 15, 2008, www.wsj.com/articles/SB121083798995894943.
7. I worked for Powell during the Reagan and Bush administrations. At times during the latter I served as a channel between him and James Baker.
8. Robert Danin conversation with the author.
9. Ron Suskind, *The Price of Loyalty: George W. Bush, the White House, and the Education of Paul O'Neill* (New York: Simon & Schuster, 2004), p. 71.
10. Ibid., pp. 72–74; Ron Suskind, "Faith, Certainty and the Presidency of George W. Bush," *The New York Times Magazine*, October 17, 2004, www.nytimes.com/2004/10/17/magazine/17BUSH.html.
11. Aaron David Miller, "Israel's Lawyer," *The Washington Post*, May 23, 2005, www.washingtonpost.com/wp-dyn/content/article/2005/05/22/AR2005052200883.html.
12. Ross and Makovsky, *Myths, Illusions, and Peace*, p. 92; Elliott Abrams, *Tested by Zion: The Bush Administration and the Israeli-Palestinian Conflict* (New York: Cambridge University Press, 2013), p. 6.
13. Former senior State Department official, quoted in Abrams, *Tested by Zion*, p. 6.
14. Cheney, *In My Time*, p. 380.
15. Elisabeth Bumiller, "Bush Aide Attacks Clinton on the Mideast, Then Retracts Remark," *The New York Times*, March 1, 2001, www.nytimes.com/2002/03/01/world/bush-aide-attacks-clinton-on-mideast-then-retracts-remark.html.
16. Abrams, *Tested by Zion*, p. 7.
17. Colin L. Powell, "Remarks with Israeli Prime Minister Ariel Sharon," press availability following meeting, Jerusalem, June 28, 2001, http://2001-2009.state.gov/secretary/former/powell/remarks/2001/3829.htm.
18. "The Tenet Plan: Israeli-Palestinian Ceasefire and Security Plan," Avalon Project, proposed by CIA Director George Tenet, June 13, 2001, http://avalon.law.yale.edu/21st_century/mid023.asp
19. "Remarks Prior to Discussions with Prime Minister Ariel Sharon of Israel and an Exchange with Reporters," March 20, 2001, *Public Papers of the Presidents*, George W. Bush, Book I, p. 266, American Presidency Project, www.presidency.ucsb.edu/ws/index.php?pid=45787, quoted in Abrams, *Tested by Zion*, p. 8.
20. In his 1992 campaign for reelection, George H. W. Bush's support from Jewish voters "dropped from 35 to 11 percent, an unprecedented decline." To contextualize, Republican candidates had averaged 17.5 percent of the Jewish vote between 1992 and 2005. Jay P. Lefkowitz, "The Election and the Jewish Vote," *Commentary*, February 1, 2005, www.commentarymagazine.com/article/the-election-and-the-jewish-vote/.

21. Itamar Rabinovich, *The Lingering Conflict: Israel, the Arabs, and the Middle East, 1948–2011* (Washington, DC: Brookings Institution Press, 2011), p. 131.

22. Abrams, *Tested by Zion*, pp. 14–15.

23. Jane Perlez, "Bush Senior, on His Son's Behalf, Reassures Saudi Leader," *The New York Times*, July 15, 2001, www.nytimes.com/2001/07/15/world/bush-senior-on -his-son-s-behalf-reassures-saudi-leader.html.

24. Robert G. Kaiser and David B. Ottaway, "Saudi Leader's Anger Revealed Shaky Ties; Bush's Response Eased a Deep Rift on Mideast Policy; Then Came Sep. 11," *The Washington Post*, February 10, 2002; Abrams, *Tested by Zion*, pp. 14–15; Senior Bush administration official, in conversation with the author, March 10, 2014.

25. Bob Woodward, *State of Denial: Bush at War, Part III* (New York: Simon & Schuster, 2006), p. 76.

26. Clinton was explicit in saying the "parameters" represented his ideas, not American policy, and would expire when he left office if they were not accepted.

27. Eric Edelman, in conversation with the author, March 10, 2014.

28. Jane Perlez, "U.S. Says Killings by Israel Inflame Mideast Conflict," *The New York Times*, August 28, 2001, www.nytimes.com/2001/08/28/world/us-says-killings-by -israel-inflame-mideast-conflict.html. It is noteworthy that the State Department had been opposed to Israeli targeted killings even earlier, protesting when Cheney had offered a mild acknowledgment that Israel might be justified in carrying out some preemptive strikes to prevent suicide bombings. Note his words in an August 3 interview in response to a question: "In Israel, what they've done, of course, over the years, occasionally, in an effort to preempt terrorist activities, is to go after the terrorists. And in some cases, I suppose, by their lights it is justified. If you've got an organization that has plotted or is plotting some kind of suicide bomber attack, for example, and they have hard evidence of who it is and where they're located, I think there's some justification in their trying to protect themselves by preempting." "Cheney Discusses Patients' Rights, ANWR, and Kyoto," Fox News, August 3, 2001, www.foxnews.com/story/2001/08/03/cheney-discusses-patients-rights-anwr-and -kyoto/.

29. Perlez, "U.S. Says Killings."

30. Bush, *Decision Points*, pp. 396–97.

31. Christopher M. Blanchard, "Al Qaeda: Statements and Evolving Ideology," *Congressional Research Service*, July 9, 2007, http://fas.org/sgp/crs/terror/RL32759.pdf.

32. Abrams, *Tested by Zion*, p. 20.

33. Ibid., p. 19. Douglas J. Feith quotes Powell telling Bush in a September 13 meeting of the National Security Council that as part of mobilizing others to join us in fighting terror, we needed to get Palestinian-Israeli diplomacy going "so we can show we are engaged." Douglas J. Feith, *War and Decision: Inside the Pentagon at the Dawn of the War on Terrorism* (New York: Harper, 2008), p. 13.

34. Daniel Kurtzer et al., *The Peace Puzzle: America's Quest for Arab-Israeli Peace, 1989–2011* (New York: Cornell University Press, 2013), pp. 161–62.

35. Abrams, *Tested by Zion*, p. 20.

36. Stephen Hadley, in conversation with the author, March 10, 2014.

37. Kurtzer et al., *Peace Puzzle*, p. 162.

38. "Statement by Israeli Prime Minister Ariel Sharon," October 4, 2001, http://mfa.gov .il/MFA/PressRoom/2001/Pages/Statement%20by%20Israeli%20PM%20Ariel%20 Sharon%20-%204-Oct-2001.aspx.

39. "Press Briefing by Ari Fleischer," October 5, 2001, American Presidency Project, www.presidency.ucsb.edu/ws/?pid=47576.

40. I had gotten to know Genger when I was our negotiator and he reached out to me to open a channel to Sharon. I found him to be authoritative about Sharon's views. If I wanted to get a message to Sharon—or see him on a visit with no visibility—I would contact Genger. I also found that he was willing to try to persuade Sharon on particular issues if he was also convinced.

41. Abrams, *Tested by Zion*, p. 22.

42. Rice, *No Higher Honor*, p. 133.

43. Eric Edelman conversation with the author.

44. Rice, *No Higher Honor*, p. 135.

45. Colin L. Powell, "United States Position on Terrorists and Peace in the Middle East," Remarks at the McConnell Center for Political Leadership, University of Louisville, November 19, 2001, http://2001-2009.state.gov/secretary/former/powell/remarks/2001/6219.htm.

46. Rice, *No Higher Honor*, p. 135.

47. Bush, *Decision Points*, p. 401.

48. Eric Edelman and Senior Bush administration official, in conversation with the author, March 10, 2014.

49. On February 17, 2002, in an interview with Thomas L. Friedman of *The New York Times*, the crown prince offered diplomatic relations with Israel in return for withdrawal to the June 4, 1967, lines. It was a far-reaching move for the Saudis. But the plan would be adopted in Beirut on March 28, the day after the Park Hotel bombing in Israel in which 30 Israelis were killed and 140 wounded at a Passover seder. Not a single delegate or official at the Arab League summit condemned the bombing or offered condolences—a message that had far more resonance in Israel than the adoption of the resolution.

50. The security fence around Gaza prevented suicide bombers coming out of the strip into Israel.

51. Fifty-two Palestinians were killed in Jenin, nearly all of them gunmen, and twenty-three members of the IDF died in the fighting.

52. Rice, *No Higher Honor*, p. 138.

53. Ibid., p. 139.

54. Abrams, *Tested by Zion*, p. 32.

55. Kurtzer et al., *Peace Puzzle*, pp. 168–69.

56. Cheney, *In My Time*, p. 380.

57. Rice, *No Higher Honor*, p. 140.

58. Cheney, *In My Time*, p. 381.

59. Abrams, *Tested by Zion*, p. 31.

60. Rice, *No Higher Honor*, p. 140.

61. Abrams, *Tested by Zion*, p. 34.

62. Ibid., p. 35.

63. Rice, *No Higher Honor*, p. 140.

64. Ibid.

65. Stephen Hadley conversation with the author.

66. Bush, *Decision Points*, p. 402; Rice, *No Higher Honor*, p. 141.

67. Bush, *Decision Points*, p. 403.

68. Gamal Helal, in conversation with the author.

69. Rice, *No Higher Honor*, p. 141.

70. Bush, *Decision Points*, p. 404.

71. Ibid., p. 403.

72. Ibid., p. 404.

73. Rice, *No Higher Honor*, p. 143.
74. Robert Danin conversation with the author, February, 28, 2014.
75. Stephen Hadley, in conversation with the author, March 10, 2014.
76. Rice, *No Higher Honor*, p. 144.
77. George W. Bush, "President Bush Calls for New Palestinian Leadership," June 24, 2002, http://georgewbush-whitehouse.archives.gov/news/releases/2002/06/20020624 -3.html.
78. Bush, *Decision Points*, p. 404.
79. Rice, *No Higher Honor*, p. 145.
80. Ibid., p. 333.
81. Abrams, *Tested by Zion*, p. 49.
82. William J. Burns, in conversation with the author.
83. We saw it as the basis for war if the Iraqis did not comply; they saw it as a basis to return to the Security Council to determine if there had been noncompliance and, if so, to decide on the consequences.
84. Tony Blair, *A Journey: My Political Life* (New York: Knopf, 2010), p. 400.
85. See Ross and Makovsky, *Myths, Illusions, and Peace*, p. 85.
86. Senior Bush administration official in conversation with the author, March 16, 2014.
87. There was unhappiness about the Roadmap among Sharon's advisers. I had meetings in Israel in late October 2002 and was told about its problems, both procedural and substantive, but also that Sharon felt his relationship with the president would allow him to manage it. Its formal title was "A Performance-Based Roadmap to a Permanent Two-State Solution to the Israeli-Palestinian Conflict"; it called for three phases to be completed by 2005. In the first phase, the Palestinians were to reform internally, including the reorganization of their security forces, and to fulfill their security responsibilities. The Israelis were to withdraw their forces to where they had been on September 28, 2000, and freeze all settlement activity including natural growth. The second phase would include elections on the Palestinian side, and negotiations should produce a state with provisional borders. The third phase would then deal with the issues of permanent status—borders, security, settlements, refugees, and Jerusalem. Each phase was to commence only when the obligations from the preceding phase had been fulfilled.
88. Abrams, *Tested by Zion*, p. 58.
89. Robert Danin, in conversation with the author, February 28, 2014.
90. Abrams, *Tested by Zion*, p. 75.
91. Ibid.
92. George W. Bush, "President Bush Troubled with Israeli Helicopter Gunship Attacks," June 10, 2003, http://georgewbush-whitehouse.archives.gov/news/releases/2003/06 /20030610-13.html.
93. Rice, *No Higher Honor*, p. 219.
94. I would hear his views privately when I met Sharon shortly before his first speech on disengagement, in December 2003 at the Herzliya Conference. The most memorable point he made to me was that he was going to act because the generation after him was driven by "politics and not Israel's strategic needs."
95. Stephen Hadley, in conversation with the author, March 10, 2014.
96. Ibid. In addition, Bush believed that Sharon's "bold move achieved two important goals: It extricated Israel from the costly occupation of Gaza. And by returning territory to Palestinian control, it served as a down payment on a future state." Bush, *Decision Points*, p. 406.
97. Rice, *No Higher Honor*, p. 281.

98. It is worth noting that Bush also put the refugee issue in the context of securing Israel as a Jewish state. "Ariel Sharon and George W. Bush's Letters in Full," *Haaretz*, June 6, 2009, http://www.haaretz.com/news/ariel-sharon-and-george-w-bush-letters -in-full-1.277418.

99. Rice, *No Higher Honor*, p. 283. Sharon's response to Bush would commit to the Roadmap, limiting settlement growth, removing unauthorized settler outposts, and assuring that the security fence would be for security and not a "political barrier" and would be "temporary rather than permanent, and therefore will not prejudice any final status issues including final borders." "Sharon and Bush's Letters."

100. Rice, *No Higher Honor*, p. 283.

101. Bush, *Decision Points*, p. 90.

102. Bob Woodward, *State of Denial*, p. 365.

103. Ibid., p. 329.

104. Dennis Ross, *Statecraft: And How to Restore America's Standing in the World* (New York: Farrar, Straus and Giroux, 2007), pp. 10–11.

105. Senior Bush administration official, in conversation with the author, March 10, 2014.

106. Rice requested only one commitment from Bush when he asked her to become secretary of state and that was on Palestinian statehood: "'Mr. President,' I said, 'we need to get an agreement and establish a Palestinian state.'" Bush would re-count this to Abbas in their May 2005 meeting. Rice, *No Higher Honor*, p. 293, and Abrams, *Tested by Zion*, p. 133.

107. Rice, *No Higher Honor*, p. 293.

108. Abrams, *Tested by Zion*, p. 131.

109. The Bush administration did not take advantage of the Interim Agreement signed by Clinton, which created criteria for who could be candidates in the elections for the Palestinian Legislative Council. For Palestinian election results, see Ben Fishman, "Hamas, Fatah, and Palestinian Politics after January 25," in *Hamas Tri-umphant: Implications for Security, Politics, Economy, and Strategy*, ed. Robert Sat-loff, Washington Institute for Near East Policy, February 2006, www.washington institute.org/uploads/Documents/pubs/PolicyFocus53.pdf.

110. Abrams, *Tested by Zion*, p. 169.

111. Ibid., p. 175.

112. Bush, *Decision Points*, p. 413.

113. Rice, *No Higher Honor*, pp. 477–78.

114. Ibid., p. 480.

115. Ibid., pp. 480–81.

116. Abrams, *Tested by Zion*, p. 181.

117. Steven Gutkin, "Olmert: Only World Force Would End Clash," Associated Press, August 2, 2006, www.washingtonpost.com/wp-dyn/content/article/2006/08/02 /AR2006080200281.html.

118. Abrams, *Tested by Zion*, p. 181.

119. Rice, *No Higher Honor*, p. 488.

120. Bush, *Decision Points*, p. 414.

121. Ibid.

122. Ibid.

123. Rice, *No Higher Honor*, p. 491.

124. While the deployment of a more robust UNIFIL and the Lebanese army to the border in place of any visible Hezbollah presence certainly made the border more secure, no one doubted that Hezbollah remained the real force in the area and from

time to time would detain UNIFIL forces. The failure to prevent the rearmament of Hezbollah was a function of the Lebanese government's fear of a resolution that would control the border with Syria, believing this might trigger a civil war with Hezbollah, which by 2008 would impose its will in fighting in Beirut.

125. Rice, *No Higher Honor*, p. 493.
126. Philip Zelikow, "Building Security in the Broader Middle East," Washington Institute for Near East Policy, September 15, 2006, www.washingtoninstitute.org/html /pdf/Zelikow091506.pdf.
127. Abrams, *Tested by Zion*, p. 198.
128. Philip Zelikow, e-mail message to the author, March 3, 2014.
129. Abrams, *Tested by Zion*, p. 198.
130. Ibid.
131. Like Kissinger, Baker after the Gulf War saw an opportunity for an initiative. This was, of course, a war in which we had worked mightily to keep Israel from involving itself.
132. Abrams, *Tested by Zion*, p. 200.
133. Rice, *No Higher Honor*, p. 549.
134. Ibid., p. 550.
135. Rice had asked to see me privately in December 2006, and she told me then she wanted to push for a comprehensive deal and asked whether I thought it was possible and what the trade-offs would be. I told her the key was to satisfy the Israelis on security and refugees (to ensure the Jewish character of the state) and to meet the Palestinian needs on territory and a capital in Jerusalem. I also said I thought that after the Lebanon war, Olmert lacked the political credibility to deliver, and Abbas seemed too weak vis-à-vis Hamas. She disagreed, maintaining that their weakness increased our leverage. I said I preferred to build from the ground up to create a better context for peacemaking. But she felt this was not the time to play "small ball."
136. Abrams, *Tested by Zion*, p. 222.
137. Ibid, pp. 199–202.
138. Cheney, *In My Time*, pp. 465–68.
139. Ibid., p. 468.
140. Robert Gates, *Duty: Memoirs of a Secretary at War* (New York: Knopf, 2012), p. 175.
141. See David Makovsky, "The Silent Strike: How Israel Bombed a Syrian Nuclear Installation and Kept It Secret," *The New Yorker*, September 17, 2012, www.newyorker .com/magazine/2012/09/17/the-silent-strike; Abrams, *Tested by Zion*, p. 247.
142. Abrams, *Tested by Zion*, p. 247.
143. Gates, *Duty*, pp. 175–76.
144. Ibid.; Abrams, *Tested by Zion*, p. 247.
145. Gates, *Duty*, p. 177.
146. Ibid., pp. 190–91.
147. Ibid. p. 191
148. Ibid., pp. 191–92.
149. Ibid.
150. Stephen Hadley, in conversation with the author, March 10, 2014.
151. Eric Edelman, in conversation with the author, March 10, 2014.
152. Gates, *Duty*, p. 183.
153. It was, perhaps, not an accident that Congress would pass a law during the Bush years that required the State Department to report on the status of U.S. efforts to preserve Israel's qualitative military edge in the region.

154. According to Abrams, Rice held up the announcement of the MOU so it would not take place while Olmert was in Washington but would come only in August; after Lebanon, Abrams felt that Rice had a testy relationship with Olmert.
155. R. Nicholas Burns, in conversation with the author, September 2013.
156. Abbas asked for the proposal in writing and for a formal map, and Olmert was prepared to offer it more formally only if Abbas accepted his proposal, or at least offered a counterproposal. He did neither, feeding the perception that he wanted to treat Olmert's offer as a point of departure for future discussions, not as an end point.
157. Rice, *No Higher Honor*, p. 473.
158. Abrams, *Tested by Zion*, p. 297.
159. Ibid., pp. 301–302.
160. Bush, "Knesset Speech."
161. Rice, *No Higher Honor*, p. 655.
162. Ibid., p. 56.
163. Abrams, *Tested by Zion*, p. 245.
164. Rice, *No Higher Honor*, p. 616.
165. Ibid.
166. Ibid., p. 147.
167. Ibid., pp. 134–35.

11. Obama and Israel: Support for Security, Little Chemistry, and Constant Challenges

1. The NSS was the traditional National Security Council staff, renamed because there was going to be a parallel structure on homeland security and terror. The Central Region office would encompass four senior directorates, involving the region from Morocco through India, and have responsibility for the areas where we were fighting two wars.
2. He began to use the term "indispensable nation" only in his second term in his speech at West Point, a speech designed to counter the impression that his policy was one of retreating from our responsibilities internationally. Barack Obama, "Remarks by the President at the United States Military Academy Commencement Ceremony," May 28, 2014, www.whitehouse.gov/the-press-office/2014/05/28 /remarks-president-united-states-military-academy-commencement-ceremony.
3. Jeffrey Goldberg, "Obama to Israel—Time Is Running Out," *Bloomberg View*, March 2, 2014, www.bloombergview.com/articles/2014-03-02/obama-to-israel-time -is-running-out.
4. James Mann, *The Obamians: The Struggle Inside the White House to Redefine American Power* (New York: Viking, 2012), p. 342. The deputies meetings examined literally every issue and developed the options to be considered for the "principals" and the president.
5. David Remnick, "Going the Distance: On and Off the Road with Barack Obama," *The New Yorker*, January 27, 2014, www.newyorker.com/magazine/2014/01/27 /going-the-distance-2.
6. McDonough and Rhodes had been with Obama throughout the presidential campaign and were very close to him. McDonough would play multiple roles at the NSS, starting by managing media relations, becoming the chief of staff, and then the senior deputy when Donilon became the national security adviser. Later, in the second term, McDonough became chief of staff at the White House. Rhodes began

as the main speechwriter on national security issues and later became a deputy national security adviser in charge of dealing with the media and messaging.

7. Barack Obama, "Remarks by the President on a New Beginning," June 4, 2009, www.whitehouse.gov/the-press-office/remarks-president-cairo-university-6-04-09.

8. From Reagan onward, every administration had treated the settlement issue as a political problem, saying it was an obstacle to peace. This terminology was different; it said settlements were illegitimate.

9. Scott Wilson, "Obama Searches for Middle East Peace," *The Washington Post*, July 14, 2012, www.washingtonpost.com/politics/obama-searches-for-middle-east-peace/2012/07/14/gJQAQQiKlW_story.html.

10. This view also did not take into account that the Bush 43 administration's effort at Annapolis had actually produced from Olmert an unprecedented offer to Abu Mazen, which had gone unanswered by the Palestinian president.

11. Wilson, "Obama Searches for Middle East Peace."

12. Rahm left the administration shortly after the Wye River summit. He accompanied the president to it, and Netanyahu's effort to get Jonathan Pollard pardoned at the end colored his view of the Israeli prime minister and how to deal with him.

13. David Petraeus, "Statement Before the Senate Armed Services Committee," Washington, DC, March 16, 2010; Rabinovich, *Lingering Conflict*, p. 187.

14. Goldberg, "Obama to Israel—Time Is Running Out."

15. Presidential candidate Barack Obama, in a meeting of his assembled national security advisers in Richmond, Virginia, October 22, 2008.

16. Gates, *Duty*, p. 388.

17. Much has been written by David Sanger and others on joint U.S.-Israeli efforts to set back the Iranian nuclear program. See David E. Sanger, *Confront and Conceal: Obama's Secret Wars and Surprising Use of American Power* (New York: Crown, 2012), pp. 190–220.

18. Wilson, "Obama Searches for Middle East Peace." Rahm Emanuel also felt it was possible to go after the settlements politically because doing so did not affect Israeli security.

19. Barack Obama, "Remarks by the President on a New Beginning," June 4, 2009, www.whitehouse.gov/the_press_office/Remarks-by-the-President-at-Cairo-University-6-04-09.

20. Barack Obama, "Remarks by the President on the Situation in Egypt," February 1, 2011, www.whitehouse.gov/the-press-office/2011/02/01/remarks-president-situation-egypt; "Press Briefing by Press Secretary Robert Gibbs," February 2, 2011, www.whitehouse.gov/the-press-office/2011/02/02/press-briefing-press-secretary-robert-gibbs-222011.

21. Both claimed to own the same religious truth as the Saudis, and both declared monarchies to be incompatible with Islam.

22. Later, after Mohammad Morsi had been elected president and allowed his intelligence channel to the Israelis to help broker a cease-fire to stop the fighting in Gaza between Hamas and Israel, the administration would restrain its criticism of Morsi's decree that he would not be bound by judicial oversight, a move that did much to discredit him in Egypt, though apparently not with us. Indeed, the administration's public response to Morsi's decision to ignore the judiciary was to say, "This is an Egyptian political process." That very posture led to a consensus in much of the region that the Obama administration was supporting the Brotherhood. Hillary Clinton was aware of this and asked me at one point what we could do to counter

this impression that seemed so widespread across the region. See Mark C. Toner, Daily Press Briefing, December 7, 2012, www.state.gov/r/pa/prs/dpb/2012/12/201670 .htm.

23. Sisi moved when there was seemingly a popular counterrevolution against Morsi. Cooperation with the Israelis would manifest itself most clearly during the Israeli-Hamas conflict in the summer of 2014. Sisi, who had been elected president, would propose cease-fire terms developed to show that Hamas had not gained from the conflict. Hamas is the Palestinian wing of the Muslim Brotherhood, and Sisi saw the Brotherhood and jihadis as one and the same—enemies of Egypt.

24. With Secretary of Defense Leon Panetta having already conveyed to Tantawi what was at stake, the field marshal was "unavailable" when Obama called. At the time, I was on the phone with Yitzhak Molcho, who was being relayed the minute-by-minute situation within the embassy offices as the mob moved closer to the outer doors of the top two floors, where the remaining Israelis were located. The president placed the call after Panetta's intervention amid signs that the Egyptian security forces still had not intervened. I speculated then that the reason Tantawi did not take the president's call was that he did not want it to appear that he acted only under Obama's pressure. The military eventually arrived to protect the embassy, but not until after some offices were ransacked.

25. Elizabeth Flock, "Saudi King Abdullah to Syria: 'Stop the Killing Machine,'" *The Washington Post*, August 8, 2011, www.washingtonpost.com/blogs/worldviews /post/saudi-king-abdullah-to-syria-stop-the-killing-machine/2011/08/08 /gIQASy3n2I_blog.html.

26. In 2014, he accused those pressing for more action in Syria of having forgotten the lessons of Iraq: "The point is that for some reason many who were proponents of what I consider to be a disastrous decision to go into Iraq haven't really learned the lesson of the last decade, and they keep on just playing the same note over and over again. Why? I don't know. But my job as Commander-in-Chief is to look at what is going to advance our security interests over the long term, and keep our military in reserve for where we absolutely need it. There are going to be times where there are disasters and difficulties and challenges all around the world, and not all of those are going to be immediately solvable by us." Barack Obama, "Remarks by President Obama and President Benigno Aquino III of the Philippines in Joint Press Conference," April 28, 2014, www.whitehouse.gov/the-press-office/2014 /04/28/remarks-president-obama-and-president-benigno-aquino-iii -philippines-joi.

27. Barack Obama, "Remarks by President Obama in Address to the United Nations General Assembly," September 24, 2013, www.whitehouse.gov/the-press-office/2013 /09/24/remarks-president-obama-address-united-nations-general-assembly.

28. Barack Obama, "Remarks by the President to the White House Press Corps," August 20, 2012, www.whitehouse.gov/the-press-office/2012/08/20/remarks-president -white-house-press-corps.

29. Even after this statement, it took the administration a few months before lethal assistance actually began to reach any member of the Syrian opposition forces, and the amounts were very small.

30. Barack Obama, "Remarks by the President at the Acceptance of the Nobel Peace Prize," December 10, 2009, www.whitehouse.gov/the-press-office/remarks-president -acceptance-nobel-peace-prize.

31. I remained in regular contact with the most senior Israeli officials, seeing them often in Washington when they came and in Israel when I visited, which I continued

to do frequently after leaving the government. As long as Donilon remained national security adviser, I was often used to convey messages in both directions even after I left the administration.

32. Ben Hubbard, "Slow, Grinding Strategy of Inflicting Syria Misery," *The New York Times*, April 26, 2014, www.nytimes.com/2014/04/27/world/middleeast/slow-grinding -strategy-of-inflicting-syria-misery.html?_r=0.

33. No military strikes would have been able to attack and destroy all of the CW sites, many of which were unknown to us or were in populated areas we would have been reluctant to attack from the air.

34. Mohammed bin Nawaf bin Abdul Aziz Al Saud, "Saudi Arabia Will Go It Alone," *The New York Times*, December 17, 2013, www.nytimes.com/2013/12/18/opinion /saudi-arabia-will-go-it-alone.html.http://www.nytimes.com/2013/12/18 /opinion/saudi-arabia-will-go-it-alone.html.

35. Goldberg, "Obama to Israel—Time Is Running Out."

36. Obama asked Gates to remain secretary of defense—a sign of bipartisanship that unfortunately did not buy the president very much from the Republicans. But with us winding down the war in Iraq and still being deeply engaged in Afghanistan, it was a smart decision.

37. Gates, *Duty*, p. 192.

38. James Mattis, interview by Wolf Blitzer, "Turmoil in the Mideast and Southwest Asia and Its Implications for American Security," July 20, 2013, Aspen Institute, www.youtube.com/watch?v=l5Un0NUmGRk&feature=c4-overview&list =UUoiTVuiMdqBRMSBGMEcmxCw; Jeffrey Goldberg, "An American General Warns the Israeli Right," *Bloomberg View*, July 25, 2013, www.bloombergview.com /articles/2013-07-25/an-american-general-warns-the-israeli-right-.

39. John Kerry had gotten the Palestinians to agree to the resumption of talks and to forgo for the life of these talks—nine months—any initiative to raise their status in international organizations. Netanyahu had also agreed to resume a negotiating process with the Palestinians as a result of Kerry's efforts. In addition, Netanyahu agreed to release long-serving Palestinian prisoners, the so-called pre-Oslo prisoners, in four tranches. None of his predecessors had been prepared to release these prisoners, all of whom had Israeli blood on their hands.

40. This was an agreement among the permanent five members of the Security Council plus Germany, the P5+1, with Iran on their nuclear program. It involved what I would describe in articles as a "cap for a cap"—a cap on the Iranian nuclear program in return for a cap on our sanctions. It would be reached on November 24, 2013.

41. Former State Department official, in conversation with the author, November 12, 2014.

42. Benjamin Netanyahu, "Excerpts from PM Netanyahu's Remarks at the Start of the Weekly Cabinet Meeting," communicated by the Prime Minister Media Adviser, November 24, 2013, https://likud.org.il/en/members-of-the-knesset/benjamin -netanyahu/benjamin-netanyahu-articles/1186-excerpts-from-pm-netanyahu-s -remarks-at-the-start-of-the-weekly-cabinet-meeting.

43. See the White House statement on the call, September 11, 2012, www.whitehouse .gov/the-press-office/2012/09/11/readout-president-s-call-israeli-prime-minister -netanyahu.

44. Abe Foxman, in conversation with the author.

45. Gates, *Duty*, p. 392.

46. Paul Richter, "Gates Warns Against Israeli Strike on Iran's Nuclear Facilities," *Los Angeles Times*, April 16, 2009, http://articles.latimes.com/2009/apr/16/world/fg-us

-iran16; Laura Rozen, "Mullen: Strikes Would Delay Iran, His 'Last Option,'" *Politico*, April 18, 2010, www.politico.com/blogs/laurarozen/0410/Mullen_Strikes_would _delay_Iran_his_last_option.html; Mike Mullen, interview by John Dickerson, *Face the Nation*, CBS, July 5, 2009, www.cbsnews.com/video/watch/?id=5134361n &tag=api.

47. Goldberg, "Obama to Israel—Time Is Running Out."
48. Barack Obama, "Remarks by President Obama and Prime Minister Netanyahu of Israel in Joint Press Conference," March 20, 2013, www.whitehouse.gov/the-press -office/2013/03/20/remarks-president-obama-and-prime-minister-netanyahu -israel-joint-press-.
49. I initiated the discussions with the Omanis in 2009 that eventually led to the back channel.
50. Senior administration officials told me that they were eager for Israeli input on what would be needed on verification in an agreement as well as for Israeli views on building a fire wall between the Iranian civil capability and possible military applications.
51. I challenged this after I got to the White House, saying every administration has respected presidential commitments made to Israel and to others. How can we not accept that commitment? I was told the president would not retreat from this guidance—guidance that reflected the anti-Bush sentiment, the attitude toward settlements, and the lack of real debate on Israeli-related issues at the time.
52. State Department spokesman P. J. Crowley's public readout of the call included the harm that had been done "to the bilateral relationship" and that we now expected Israel to take "specific actions" to show it was "committed to this relationship and to the peace process." See Mark Landler, "Clinton Rebukes Israel on Housing An- nouncement," *The New York Times*, March 12, 2010, www.nytimes.com/2010/03/13 /world/middleeast/13diplo.html.
53. Rahm had been angry at Netanyahu's speech earlier in the day at AIPAC, in which he declared that Jerusalem was Israel's capital, not a settlement—a seemingly defi- ant response to the U.S. reaction to the Ramat Shlomo incident. In response, Rahm directed that this was a private meeting and thus no photo would be released.
54. The unannounced hold on tenders and building, which would last for five months, was what Abu Mazen had asked Mitchell to produce. We would, in fact, produce it, but Abu Mazen would not take advantage of it.
55. Laura Rozen, "Fierce Debate on Israel Underway Inside Obama Administration," *Politico*, March 28, 2010, www.politico.com/blogs/laurarozen/0310/Fierce_debate _on_Israel_underway_inside_Obama_administration.html.
56. Ibid.
57. Cartwright put together teams to go over all of the Israeli requirements, including border security, early warning, airspace protection, naval and sea security, electro- magnetic spectrum functions and needs, strategic and missile defense require- ments, and counterterror and infrastructure protection. The Israelis had counterpart teams in each of these areas. The work went on until early 2011, and General John Allen, who participated in this effort, took the lead in an even more ambitious approach to developing a layered strategy for Israeli defense needs in 2013–2014.
58. With neither side yielding on the moratorium, we tried a new tack. We told the Israelis that if they could not extend the moratorium, the only chance we had of getting Abu Mazen to stay in the negotiations was to offer him a new American position on the substance: we would promise him that our position would now be that the border should be based on 1967 lines and mutually agreed swaps. They did

not like it, but still did not budge. Abu Mazen treated this move as if it was nothing and turned us down. Mitchell and David Hale, his well-respected deputy, were convinced that offering this position on the substance would be a big gain for the Palestinians and Abu Mazen would be able to trumpet it. But he blew off Hale.

59. Netanyahu seemed to be motivated by a desire to reconcile two conflicting needs: he did not want everything stuck with the Palestinians and yet he wanted to manage his political base, highly sympathetic to the settler movement.

60. I told her we had made some headway on the security discussions with the Israelis, though the Israeli military was hesitating, reluctant to look like they were making political recommendations on the border.

61. The secretary gave a speech at the Brookings Institution in December in which she described this approach, making the point that we would ask direct, tough questions on all the core issues and expect "substantive answers" from both sides. And we would offer our ideas "and bridging proposals at the appropriate time." Hillary Rodham Clinton, "Remarks at the Brookings Institution's Saban Center for Middle East Policy Seventh Annual Forum," December 10, 2010, www.state.gov/secretary /20092013clinton/rm/2010/12/152664.htm.

62. More resolutions were adopted against Israel than any other country. The serial abusers of human rights that sat on the UN Human Rights Council made Israel the target. For a discussion of this issue, see Rosa Freedman, "The United Nations Human Rights Council: More of the Same?," *Wisconsin International Law Journal* 31, no. 2 (2013), http://hosted.law.wisc.edu/wordpress/wilj/files/2014/01/Freedman_final_v2.pdf.

63. Feltman explained his concerns: we would have to beef up security at U.S. embassies, and the UAE foreign minister said he hoped we would veto because it would shift the focus from anger at Mubarak to us.

64. The package also included a readiness to support a UN fact-finding visit to the territories as a way of providing for some UN involvement, showing how much the administration wanted to avoid a veto.

65. Helene Cooper and Mark Landler, "Obama's Peace Tack Contrasts with Key Aide, Friend of Israel," *The New York Times*, May 11, 2011, www.nytimes.com/2011/05/21 /world/middleeast/21ross.html?pagewanted=all.

66. It is noteworthy that on two occasions over the previous eight months, Netanyahu had been advised that we were about to adopt this position on 1967 and mutually agreed swaps—first to try to keep the talks going in September, and then in February to head off the settlements resolution at the UN.

67. This had been the position of Barak at Camp David, and effectively what Sharon got in the Bush letter in 2004; it also was the Olmert and Livni position in 2008. It was true that Netanyahu had not adopted it, but that was more for tactical than strategic reasons.

68. Barack Obama, "Remarks by the President at the AIPAC Policy Conference 2011," May 22, 2011, www.whitehouse.gov/the-press-office/2011/05/22/remarks-president -aipac-policy-conference-2011.

69. Blair was the Quartet's Middle East envoy. Lady Ashton was the European Union's high representative for foreign affairs and security policy.

70. She actually said this to a leading Israeli political figure who visited her in March 2014.

71. U.S. and Israeli officials briefed me on this.

72. Senior Israeli officials told me that at key moments they could not get answers from Kerry. Members of Kerry's team confirmed that Rice was dragging everything out and limiting their flexibility.

73. The White House was reacting to the attacks on UN schools where Palestinian families had taken refuge, and Israel was facing attacks from or very near those sites.

74. Martin Dempsey, interview by Jeff McCausland, "Ethics and the Profession of Arms," Carnegie Council for Ethics, New York, November 6, 2014, www.youtube .com/watch?v=YRkdt7r-qUs.

75. Itamar Sharon, "Lapid: We Must Fix 'Crisis' in Ties with Washington," *The Times of Israel*, October 25, 2014, www.timesofisrael.com/lapid-we-must-repair-relations -with-washington/.

76. Jeffrey Goldberg, "The Crisis in U.S.-Israel Relations Is Officially Here," *The Atlantic*, October 28, 2014, www.theatlantic.com/international/archive/2014/10/the -crisis-in-us-israel-relations-is-officially-here/382031/.

77. A senior White House official told me this.

78. Barack Obama, interviewed by Sam Stein, "Obama Details His Disappointment With Netanyahu In First Post-Election Comments," *Huffington Post*, March 20, 2015. http://www.huffingtonpost.com/2015/03/21/obama-huffpost-interview-trans cript_n_6905450.html?1426972456.

79. Goldberg, "Obama to Israel—Time Is Running Out."

80. Martin Indyk, the American envoy to the negotiations, publicly acknowledged that Abu Mazen had "shut down," even as Netanyahu had moved, in Indyk's words, to "the zone of a possible agreement." But Indyk also said that the Israeli settlement activity had been the reason for Abu Mazen shutting down—effectively justifying it, even though what the United States was prepared to present dealt with all the core issues of the conflict, including Jerusalem. Indyk was widely reported to have been the unnamed American official who had given an interview to the Israeli press after the breakdown of the talks that also blamed settlement activity for sabotaging the talks—and this interview was apparently authorized and reflected Obama's views. Martin Indyk, "The Pursuit of Middle East Peace: A Status Report," Washington Institute for Near East Policy, May 8, 2014, www.washingtoninstitute.org /uploads/Documents/other/IndykKeynote20140508.pdf; Mark Landler, "Mideast Peace Effort Pauses to Let Failure Sink In," *The New York Times*, May 15, 2014, www .nytimes.com/2014/05/16/world/mideast-peace-effort-pauses-to-let-failure-sink-in .html.

81. Interview with Barack Obama by Thomas L. Friedman, "Obama and the World: President Obama Talks to Thomas L. Friedman About Iraq, Putin and Israel," *The New York Times*, August 8, 2014, www.nytimes.com/2014/08/09/opinion/president -obama-thomas-l-friedman-iraq-and-world-affairs.html?hp&action=click &pgtype=Homepage&version=LargeMediaHeadlineSum&module=b-lede -package-region&region=lede-package&WT.nav=lede-package&_r=1.

82. Goldberg, "Obama to Israel—Time Is Running Out."

83. Ibid.

84. Barack Obama, "Remarks by President Obama and President Ghani of Afghanistan in Joint Press Conference," March 24, 2015. http://www.whitehouse.gov/the -press-office/2015/03/24/remarks-president-obama-and-president-ghani -afghanistan-joint-press-conf.

85. Obama, interviewed by Sam Stein, *The Huffington Post*. Josh Earnest, "Press Briefing by Press Secretary Josh Earnest," March 20, 2015. https://www.whitehouse.gov /the-press-office/2015/03/20/press-briefing-press-secretary-josh-earnest-3202015.

86. Barack Obama, interviewed by Thomas L. Friedman, "Iran and the Obama Doctrine," *The New York Times*, April 5, 2015, http://www.nytimes.com/2015/04/06

/opinion/thomas-friedman-the-obama-doctrine-and-iran-interview.html?hp
&action=click&pgtype=Homepage&module=c-column-top-span-region&region
=c-column-top-span-region&WT.nav=c-column-top-span-region&_r=0.

12. Lessons from the Past and Implications for the Future
 1. Stephen Sestanovich, *Maximalist: America in the World from Truman to Obama* (New York: Knopf, 2014), p. 7.
 2. In the 1950s and 1960s, Nasser sought to use the conflict with Israel as a club against his Arab rivals, particularly the Arab monarchies. They, in turn, accused him of hiding behind the skirts of the United Nations Emergency Force in the Sinai desert to avoid having to fight Israel. Saddam Hussein seized the mantle of rejectionists on the Palestinian's behalf after Sadat's trip to Jerusalem—and notwithstanding Carter's efforts with the Saudis and his belief that if they would respond to him, they would fall in line with the Saddam-led Arab consensus to isolate Egypt after Camp David rather than respond to us. The Iranians have sought to champion the issue to build their following and undermine our friends, but with the emerging Shia-Sunni divide playing out, principally in Syria, they have had little resonance in the region.
 3. Not only did Faisal not mention the sale with Rusk when news of it came out the same day as their meeting, but a week later, when he saw Kennedy, it was our support for Egypt—not Israel—that he discussed with the president.
 4. Senior Israeli official, in conversation with the author, March 2014.
 5. Yaakov Amidror, in conversation with the author, October 2013.
 6. In Sharon's case, I dealt with him in an official capacity when he held positions other than prime minister. When he became prime minister, and I was no longer in the government, I still saw him nearly every time I went to Israel for private discussions.
 7. I was once asked by Javier Solana, the European Union's high representative for foreign affairs and security policy, why the Israelis did not listen to him. I told him it was because he came to his meetings with a list of things Israel must do to respond to the Palestinians. I said, "By the second item on your list, they have tuned you out. They see you as indifferent to their needs and focused only on the Palestinians. Why not," I went on, "start your next meeting by asking them, 'What concerns you? What can I do to help? Where should I push the Palestinians?' After you have done that, then you can say that it would help you to move the Palestinians if you could tell them they would do X or Y." Marc Otte, Solana's deputy, was the one EU official who operated this way—and naturally, the Israelis were more responsive to him.
 8. Because the two sides have different views of the scope of the Palestinian state, the Israelis should declare that they will negotiate on borders with the Palestinians, but until it is agreed upon, they will build only in those areas that they think will be part of Israel: to the west of the security barrier and the existing Jewish neighborhoods in Jerusalem.
 9. John Kerry stated to Congress in April 2014 that Iran was two months away from being able to produce weapons-grade fissile material.
 10. Lydia Saad, "Americans' Sympathies for Israel Match All-Time High," Gallup, March 15, 2013, www.gallup.com/poll/161387/americans-sympathies-israel-match-time-high.aspx; Michael Lipka, "Strong Support for Israel in U.S. Cuts Across Religious Lines," Pew Research Center, February 27, 2014, www.pewresearch.org/fact-tank/2014/02/27/strong-support-for-israel-in-u-s-cuts-across-religious-lines/.

11. "Connection with and Attitudes Toward Israel," Pew Research Center, October 1, 2013, www.pewforum.org/2013/10/01/chapter-5-connection-with-and-attitudes-towards-israel/.

12. This could also help with signs that more Republicans than Democrats support Israel.

ACKNOWLEDGMENTS

The late Harvey Sicherman was a man of rare wit and insight. He was my colleague and friend and served on the State Department's Policy Planning Staff when I was its director during the Bush 41 administration. Harvey's keen sense of irony, always accompanied by his gentle laugh, often led him to speak about how on a number of issues we were "doomed to succeed." What he meant was that our basic interests and needs would lead us to overcome our missteps and find the right path. Not infrequently, he was talking about our relationship with Israel. As I thought about both the evolution and the trajectory of our relations with Israel, Harvey came to mind and I owe the title of this book to him.

Many others have helped as I crafted *Doomed to Succeed*. I am lucky to be based at the Washington Institute for Near East Policy. There is no better place to write a book than the institute. Robert Satloff, its executive director, leads the institute brilliantly. He has fostered a dynamic intellectual environment that is at once collegial and intellectually vibrant. I want to thank Rob for his friendship and support. I also want to thank Howard Berkowitz, emeritus chairman of the board; Marty Gross, chairman of the board; and Richard Abramson, president of the institute. All have been strong believers in this project and great supporters of my work. I also want to thank the William Davidson Foundation. I became the William Davidson Distinguished Fellow at the institute in 2013, and am deeply appreciative of the foundation's generous support.

At the institute, I have benefitted from the tireless work of two extremely talented younger scholars, Cory Felder and Harry Reis. Both served as my all-purpose assistants, Cory from the time I returned to the institute at the end of 2011 until May 2014 when he began his graduate work, and Harry since that time. Their research efforts, including bibliographic help and tracking down of archival and source materials, have been extraordinary. They also both brought a critical eye to the text and were wonderful sounding boards. It is no exaggeration to say that this book could not have been published without them, and I am very much in their debt.

Gilad Wenig, who is at the Washington Institute but will shortly be off to Cambridge University, and Henry Shuller, who is at Harvard, both provided invaluable help with fact-checking and finalizing the notes, and I want to thank them both for their painstaking work.

I also very much benefited from Eric Chinski's guidance, and am most appreciative of all the help he gave me. As editor in chief at FSG, he has multiple responsibilities and many manuscripts to review. Even after becoming a new father, he was always available, and his edits and comments have made the text sharper and more readable. Peng Shepard, Eric's former assistant, was extremely helpful in managing the process of transforming the manuscript into a book and did a wonderful job of keeping everything on track. Her replacement, Laird Gallagher, picked right up where she left off, and I want to thank them both for their efforts.

Esther Newberg, my agent, has been a deep believer in the importance of the U.S.-Israel relationship and was enthusiastic about this project from the moment we first spoke about it. I am lucky to have her as both my agent and my friend—and, always, to have her in my corner.

I also want to thank those who were willing to be interviewed for this book. Robert Danin, Tom Donilon, Eric Edelman, Stuart Eizenstat, Steve Hadley, John Hannah, Efraim Halevy, Gamal Helal, George Shultz, and Paul Wolfowitz all gave generously of their time and offered insights on people, events, and developments over different administrations and periods.

Two other special people deserve special thanks. My colleague David Makovsky, with whom I share a passion for the subject of this book and other subjects, gave me detailed comments on a number of different chapters. I value his insights and friendship, and the book is definitely better because of his input. The same is true for my son, Gabriel, whose substantive comments were very helpful and led me to clarify a number of points in the chapter about the Obama administration. I am grateful to him for this and so much more.

Finally, I want to thank my wife, Debbie. She continues not just to tolerate what I do but to support it as well. And for that I owe her more than I can ever tell her.

INDEX

PERMISSIONS ACKNOWLEDGMENTS

A NOTE ABOUT THE AUTHOR

Dennis Ross is a counselor and the William Davidson Distinguished Fellow at the Washington Institute for Near East Policy. He is also a Distinguished Professor in the Practice of Diplomacy at Georgetown University. He was the director of policy planning in the State Department under George H. W. Bush, was Bill Clinton's Middle East peace envoy, and served as a special assistant to President Barack Obama.